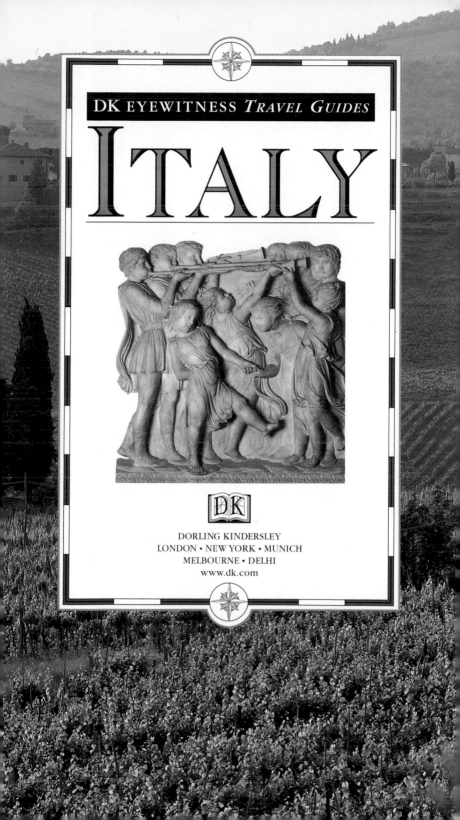

DK EYEWITNESS *TRAVEL GUIDES*

ITALY

DORLING KINDERSLEY
LONDON • NEW YORK • MUNICH
MELBOURNE • DELHI
www.dk.com

A DORLING KINDERSLEY BOOK

www.dk.com

PROJECT EDITOR Fiona Wild
ART EDITORS Vanessa Courtier, Annette Jacobs
EDITORS Francesca Machiavelli, Sophie Martin,
Helen Townsend, Nicky Tyrrell
DESIGNERS Jo Doran, Anthea Forlee,
Paul Jackson, Marisa Renzullo

MAIN CONTRIBUTORS
Ros Belford, Susie Boulton, Christopher Catling,
Sam Cole, Paul Duncan, Olivia Ercoli, Andrew Gumbel,
Tim Jepson, Ferdie McDonald, Jane Shaw

MAPS
Lovell Johns Ltd,
Dorling Kindersley Cartography

PHOTOGRAPHER
John Heseltine

ILLUSTRATORS
Stephen Conlin, Donati Giudici Associati srl, Stephen Gyapay,
Roger Hutchins, Maltings Partnership, Simon Roulstone,
Paul Weston, John Woodcock

Reproduced by Colourscan (Singapore)
Printed and bound by South China Printing Co. Ltd., China

First published in Great Britain in 1996
by Dorling Kindersley Limited
80 Strand, London WC2R 0RL
Reprinted with revisions 1997, 1999, 2000, 2001, 2002

Copyright 1996, 2002 © Dorling Kindersley Limited, London
A Penguin Company

A CIP CATALOGUE RECORD IS AVAILABLE FROM THE BRITISH LIBRARY.
ISBN 0-7513-4691-8

**The information in every DK Eyewitness Travel Guide is
checked regularly.**

Every effort has been made to ensure that this book is as up-to-date
as possible at the time of going to press. Some details, however,
such as telephone numbers, opening hours, prices, gallery hanging
arrangements and travel information are liable to change. The
publishers cannot accept responsibility for any consequences
arising from the use of this book, nor for any material on third
party websites, and cannot guarantee that any website address
in this book will be a suitable source of travel information.

We value the views and suggestions of our readers very highly.
Please write to: Senior Publishing Manager, DK Eyewitness
Travel Guides, Dorling Kindersley, 80 Strand, London WC2R 0RL.

◁ **Fertile wine-growing region around Panzano in Chianti, Tuscany**

CONTENTS

David **by Bernini, Rome**

INTRODUCING ITALY

NORTHEAST ITALY

NORTHWEST ITALY

Gondolas weaving through the maze of canals in Venice

Basilica of San Francesco in Assisi, started in 1228

How to Use this Guide

THIS GUIDE helps you get the most from your visit to Italy, providing expert recommendations as well as detailed practical information. *Introducing Italy* maps the whole country and sets it in its historical and cultural context. The 15 regional chapters, plus *Rome*, *Florence* and *Venice*, describe important sights with the help of maps and images. Each section is introduced with features on regional architecture and food specialities. *Travellers' Needs* gives details of hotels and restaurants and the *Survival Guide* contains practical information on everything from transport to personal safety.

ROME

The centre of Rome has been divided into five sightseeing areas. Each area has its own chapter, which opens with a list of the sights described. All the sights are numbered and plotted on an *Area Map*. The detailed information for each sight is presented in numerical order, making it easy to locate within the chapter.

Sights at a Glance lists the chapter's sights by category: Churches, Museums and Galleries, Historic Buildings, Streets and Piazzas.

All pages relating to Rome have red thumb tabs.

A locator map shows where you are in relation to other areas of the city centre.

1 Area Map
For easy reference, the sights are numbered and located on a map. The sights are also shown on the Street Finder on pages 433–41.

2 Street-by-Street Map
This gives a bird's-eye view of the heart of each sightseeing area.

A suggested route for a walk is shown in red.

Stars indicate the sights that no visitor should miss.

3 Detailed information
All the sights in Rome are described individually. Addresses and practical information are provided. The key to the symbols used in the information block is shown on the back flap.

SICILY

On a crossroads in the Mediterranean, part of Europe and Africa, yet belonging to neither, Sicily was tramped across by half the ancient civilized world...

Exploring Sicily

SIGHTS AT A GLANCE

GETTING AROUND

1 Introduction
The landscape, history and character of each region is described here, showing how the area has developed over the centuries and what it offers to the visitor today.

ITALY AREA BY AREA

Apart from Rome, Florence and Venice, Italy has been divided into 15 areas, each of which has a separate chapter. The most interesting towns and places to visit have been numbered on a *Pictorial Map*.

Each area of Italy can be identified quickly by its colour coding, shown on the inside front cover.

2 Pictorial Map
This shows the main road network and gives an illustrated overview of the whole region. All entries are numbered and there are also useful tips on getting around the region by car and train.

Mount Etna

Catania

FOOD AND DRINK ON TRADITIONAL SICILIAN CUISINE

3 Detailed information
All the important towns and other places to visit are described individually. They are listed in order, following the numbering given on the Pictorial Map. Within each entry, information is given on the most important sights. The name of the provincial capital is given for smaller towns at the top of each entry.

Tindari

Messina

Taormina

Monreale

Story boxes explore specific subjects further.

For all the top sights, a Visitors' Checklist provides the practical information you need to plan your visit.

4 Italy's top sights
These are given two or more full pages. Historic buildings are dissected to reveal their interiors; museums and galleries have colour-coded floorplans to help you locate the most interesting exhibits.

INTRODUCING
ITALY

Putting Italy on the Map

Italy sits at the heart of the Mediterranean, shielded from the rest of Europe by the vast sweep of the Alps. The Po, its longest river, arcs across the industrial north, while the Apennine mountains split the boot-shaped peninsula down its length. Italy, with a population of 57.5 million governed from Rome, covers 301,268 sq km (116,320 sq miles) and includes Sicily and Sardinia.

Aerial view of Venice, showing the Grand Canal

◁ View over Florence of the richly decorated 15th-century Duomo and Campanile

Satellite photograph of southern Europe and the Mediterranean

KEY

▬▬▬	Motorway
▬▬▬	Major road
- - - -	Ferry service
—·—·—	International boundary

0 kilometres   200

0 miles   100

Northern Italy

AIRLINE CONNECTIONS link the rest of Europe with
Milan, Turin, Bologna, Pisa, Florence, Verona
and Venice. Major roads and railways also provide
excellent links to cities all over Europe. Transport
services are very efficient, with motorways and
railways along both coasts, and across the area's
main east-to-west axis at the foot of the Alps. Milan,
Verona and Bologna are the key transport hubs, while
Florence forms the focus of links to the south.

Florence by Road
*Good fast roads link Florence to Pisa
to the west, Rome and Siena to the
south, and Bologna to the north.*

FLORENCE AND ENVIRONS

KEY

Ferry port

Airport

FS Main railway station

International boundary

Regional boundary

Motorway

Main road

Railway line

VENICE

Marco Polo

Mestre

FS

N14

Canale Osellino

V e n e t a

N11

L a g u n a

Turkey-Egypt-
Greece-Ancona

FS Santa Lucia

San Marco

0 kilometres   4

0 miles   2

Venice by Road
*Venice is joined to
the mainland by a
causeway. This pro-
vides easy access to
motorway links with
Verona and Padua.*

AUSTRIA

N50

nico

Cortina d'Ampezzo

N52

Tolmezzo

lluno

N13

Udine

Cividale del Friuli

tre

N56

A4

Pordenone

Gorizia

solo

Treviso

A13

Aquileia

Mestre

Grado Trieste

VENICE

Po
Delta

anean
ills

lua

SLOVENIA

Greece
Turkey
Egypt

Valli di
omacchio

Ravenna

A14

enza

Rimini

SAN MARINO

Pèsaro
Fano

San Leo

Urbino

Greece

sepolcro

Urbania

Ionian Islands

Ancona

Cyprus

eso

Arezzo

Sibillini

Jesi

Conero
Peninsula

Turkey

Cortona

Gubbio

Grotte di
Frasassi

Loreto

N71

Perugia

Lago
Trasimeno

Assisi

si

Spello

N3

Ascoli Piceno

Orvieto

Montefalco

Norcia

Todi

Spoleto

A24

Pescara

terbo

N2

A1

L'Aquila

SS17

Lanciano

SS5

SS17

Sulmona

Isole Tremiti

Scanno

San Severo

SS17

ROME
VATICAN CITY

A1

N82

Lucera

Foggia

Sermoneta

Troia

N89

Sperlonga

Brindisi

Terracina

Formia

Benevento

0 kilometres   100

Gaeta

Caserta

0 miles   50

Taranto

NAPLES

Monte
Vesuvio

Reggio di
Calabria

KEY TO COLOUR-CODING

Northeast Italy

Venice

The Veneto and Friuli

Trentino-Alto Adige

Northwest Italy

Lombardy

Valle d'Aosta and Piedmont

Liguria

Central Italy

Emilia-Romagna

Florence

Tuscany

Umbria

Le Marche

Southern Italy

INTERNATIONAL AIRLINE services operate
to Rome, Naples and Palermo in
southern Italy. Transport links within
the region are generally slower than
in the north, particularly inland and
on the islands of Sicily and Sardinia.
Coastal road and rail links are
good, however, especially those
linking Rome and Naples, the
region's main transport hubs.
Two trans-Apennine motor-
ways offer the quickest
cross-country routes.

Sicily and Sardinia

*Ferries operate to Sicily
from Naples, Villa San
Giovanni and Reggio
di Calabria. Onward
connections include
boats to Malta and
Tunisia. Ferries run to
Sardinia from several
mainland ports, notably
from Genoa and Livorno.*

KEY

⛴	Ferry port
✈	Airport
- - -	International boundary
– – –	Regional boundary
▬▬	Motorway
▬▬	Main road
——	Railway line

Rome by Road
*Motorway links approach
Rome from Naples,
Pescara and Florence.
All feed into the city's
ring road, the Grande
Raccordo Anulare.*

ROME AND ENVIRONS

0 kilometres   10

0 miles   5

VIA CASSIA
VIA FLAMINIA
VIA SALARIA
VIA NOMENTANA
A1
GRANDE RACCORDO ANULARE (GRA)
VIA TIBURTINA
A24
VATICAN CITY
FS
VIA AURELIA
VIA CASILINA
A2
VIA APPIA NUOVA
VIA CRISTOFORO COLOMBO
A12
Leonardo
da Vinci
(Fiumicino)
Tevere
(Tiber)
Ciampino

Vasto
Termoli
Isole Tremiti
Rodi
Garganico
Vieste
Gargano
Peninsula
San Severo
Manfredonia
Lucera
Foggia
Troia
Trani
Bari
Albania
Greece
Egypt
Beneventó
aserta
Castel del
Monte
Ruvo di
Puglia
Melfi
Venosa
Alberobello
Greece
Lagopesole
Brindisi
Monte
Vesuvio
Matera
mpei
Salerno
Taranto
Lecce
Amalfi
Sorrento
Metaponto
Greece
ori
Paestum
Galatina
Otranto
Cilento
Maratea
Rossano
Cosenza
Sant'Eufemia Lamezia
Isole Eolie
Tropea
Stilo
Gerace
Naples
Milazzo
Messina
Tindari
Villa San Giovanni
Reggio di Calabria
Naples
Malta
Enna
Taormina
A20
A19
Catania
Naples
iazza
Armerina
Pantalica
Siracusa
Malta
Noto

0 kilometres   100

0 miles   50

KEY TO COLOUR-CODING

Rome and Lazio

Rome

Lazio

Southern Italy

Naples and Campania

Abruzzo, Molise and Puglia

Basilicata and Calabria

Sicily

Sardinia

A PORTRAIT OF ITALY

I TALY HAS DRAWN PEOPLE *in search of culture and romance for many centuries. Few countries can compete with its Classical origins, its art, architecture, musical and literary traditions, its scenery or food and wine. The ambiguity of its modern image is also fascinating: since World War II Italy has climbed into the top ten world economies, yet at its heart it retains many of the customs, traditions and regional allegiances of its agricultural heritage.*

Italy has no single cultural identity. From the northern snow-capped peaks of the Alps, to the rugged southern shores of

Wedding Ferrari in typical Italian style

Sicily, lies a plethora of distinctive regions and peoples. Politically, Italy is a young country: it did not exist as a unified nation state until 1861, and its 21 regions have maintained their cultural individuality. Visitors to Italy are often pleasantly surprised by the diversity of its dialects, cuisines and architecture. There is also a larger regional division. People speak of two distinct Italies: the rich industrial north and the poorer agricultural south, known as *Il Mezzogiorno* or Land of the Midday Sun. The frontier separating the two is indeterminate, lying somewhere between Rome and Naples.

The north is directly responsible for Italy's place among the world's top industrial nations. It has been the powerhouse behind the Italian economic miracle, its success achieved by internationally renowned names such as Fiat, Prada, Ferragamo, Pirelli, Olivetti, Zanussi, Alessi and Armani. The south, in contrast, has high unemployment, is in the grip of organized crime, and some of its

A secluded villa surrounded by cypress trees on a Tuscan hilltop

◁ Three sundials covering the façade of Palazzo del Governatore, on Piazza Garibaldi, Parma areas rank among the most depressed in Europe. However, many southern towns have benefited from an injection of Millennium funds.

A conversation in the open air

The historic divide between north and south is a powerful factor in contemporary politics. The federalist party, the Northern League, owes its popularity to this split. Those in favour of separation complain that the south is a drain on resources: Milan is seen as efficient and rich, while Naples is viewed as chaotic, dirty and corrupt.

History and geography have both contributed to the division. The north is closer in both location and spirit to Germany and France while the south has suffered a succession of invasions from foreign powers: Carthaginians and Greeks in ancient times, Saracens and Normans in the Middle Ages and until the middle of the last century, the Bourbons from Spain held sway.

TRADITION

Distinctive variations in Italy's regions have much to do with the mountainous landscape and inaccessible valleys. Tuscan and Ligurian hill-towns, for instance, have quite different silhouettes, and the farmhouses in Puglia, the famous *trulli*, are unlike those found in the landscape of Emilia-Romagna.

For many travellers, the Italian journey comes to an end in Campania, in southern Italy. Further south the landscape, architecture, dialects, food, and even the appearance of the people, have closer affinities with the Eastern Mediterranean and North Africa than with Europe. In the far south, study of the local dialects has revealed traces of ancient Greek and old Albanian, preserved in tightly knit communities isolated by the rugged geography. Christianity and pagan ritual are closely linked; sometimes the Virgin is portrayed as a thinly disguised Demeter, the Earth goddess.

Throughout Italy, ancient techniques of husbandry endure and many livelihoods are closely connected to the land and the seasons. Main crops include sugar beet, maize, wheat, olives and grapes; colourful Easter celebrations *(see p62)* pay tribute to the bounty of the soil. Although some of the north's postwar economic prosperity can be attributed to industry (especially car production in and around Turin), much of it has grown from the expansion of family-owned artisan businesses and the export of hand-made goods abroad. This is recognized as a distinct sector of the economy. The internationally successful retail clothes chain Prada is a recent example. The "Made

Café-goers relaxing in Marina di Pisa, Tuscany

Medieval skyscrapers emerging from the Tuscan landscape of San Gimignano

in Italy" label, found on goods such as clothes, shoes and leather bags, guarantees a high standard.

CULTURE AND ARTS

Sophia Loren

The arts in Italy have had a long and glorious history and Italians are very proud of this. Given the fact that Italy has more than 100,000 monuments (archaeological sites, cathedrals, churches, houses and statues), all of which have major historical significance, it is not surprising that there is a shortage of funds to keep them in good repair. Many museums in Italy, particularly those in the south, are closed, or partially closed. You may find churches in Venice hidden behind permanent scaffolding or those in Naples shut due to recent earthquake damage. However, with tourism now accounting for around 3 per cent of Italy's Gross Domestic Product, efforts are being made to put as many buildings and collections on show as possible. The Jubilee 2000 helped matters by allocating large amounts of money for the restoration of buildings and sites belonging to the Catholic Church.

The performing arts are also underfunded, yet there are some spectacular cultural festivals. Almost every town of any size has its own opera house and La Scala opera house in Milan shows world-class productions.

Cinema is another flourishing art form in Italy and has been so since its invention. The sets at Cinecittà, on the

Bernini's 17th-century Fontana del Tritone, Rome

Roadside stall near Positano, Campania

outskirts of Rome, have been used by many famous directors such as Fellini, Pasolini, de Sica, Visconti and many others. Italian films such as *La Vita è Bella* and *The Son's Room* have found critical acclaim and box-office success both in Italy and abroad. In Italy the arts belong to everyone: opera is attended by people from all backgrounds, regardless of social status, as are cinemas and galleries.

SOCIAL CUSTOMS AND POLITICS

Italian society is still highly traditional, and Italians can be very formal. Between the generations degrees of familiarity exist: reserve *ciao* (hello or goodbye)

Italian chic, Armani style

for friends your age or younger, and greet older people with *piacere* (pleased to meet you), *buon giorno* (good day) or *buona sera* (good evening) and on parting, say *arrivederci* (goodbye). Strangers are met with a handshake, but family and friends receive a kiss.

Italian chic decrees that the clothes you wear should give the impression of wealth. If Italians wear similar outfits, it is because they are conformists in fashion as in other aspects of daily life.

Italian politics, in contrast, are not so well regulated. Governments in the postwar era have consistently been short-lived coalitions, dominated by the Christian Democrats. In 1993 Italy experienced a political crisis when an organized network of corruption was exposed, disgracing a huge number of politicians and businessmen. However, the investigations failed to eradicate corruption and led to the formation of two large coalitions, centre-left and centre-right. Silvio Berlusconi, leader of the Forza Italia party, became prime minister in 1994 but lasted only a short while as he, too, was accused of corruption. In 1998 Massimo D'Alema became Italy's first left-wing Prime Minister. In 2001 the centre-left coalition, led by Francesco Rutelli, the former mayor of Rome, lost the election to Berlusconi's centre-right coalition.

MODERN LIFE

Food and football are the great constants; Italians live for both. Much time is spent on preparing food and eating.

Statue of Emperor Domitian in the Vatican Gardens

The solution to heavy traffic in Rome: motorbikes and scooters

The Italian diet, particularly in the south, is among the healthiest in the world. Football is a national passion and inspires massive public interest and media attention, not least as a way of expressing regional loyalties.

As far as religion is concerned, the number of practising Catholics has been in decline for some years. Although Rome lies at the centre of world Catholicism, today many Italians are uninterested in religion, but still attend mass in number on saints' days or feast days. As a consequence of immigration, other religions are now on the increase.

Strolling through one of Bologna's many porticoes

The emphasis on conformity and a commitment to the institution of the family remain key factors in Italian society despite the country's low, and falling, birth rate. Grandparents, children and grandchildren still live in family units, although this is becoming less common. All children are pampered but the most cherished ones are, usually, male. Women's Liberation fought a powerful campaign in the 1970s and did much to change attitudes to women in the workplace, particularly in metropolitan areas. However, the idea that men should help with housework and the care of the children is still a fairly foreign notion among the older generation.

With the miracle of its postwar economic recovery, where industry and technology were united with design, Italy has become a success story. Although the economy has been dented by the worldwide recession of the early 1990s, the exposure of corruption in many walks of public life and political upheaval, Italy appears unchanged to foreign visitors. Its ability to keep its regional identities and traditional values allows it to ride out any changes virtually unscathed.

Medieval and Early Renaissance Art

THE STORY OF early Italian art, from the 13th century until the late 15th century, illuminates one of the richest periods in European art history. For the first time since Classical antiquity, painters and sculptors created a convincing pictorial space in which figures, modelled "in the round", were given life. Ethereal buildings were replaced by those firmly rooted in the real world, reproducing what artists actually saw. This revolution in art included the reintroduction of the fresco technique, giving artists huge surfaces for telling pictorial stories.

1235 Bonaventura Berlinghieri, *St Francis Altarpiece* (San Francesco, Pescia)

c.1305 Giotto di Bondone, *The Meeting at the Golden Gate* (Cappella degli Scrovegni, Padua) Giotto broke away from the ornate Byzantine style to visualize naturalness and human emotions. His way of working would later be dubbed the Florentine style.

1285 Duccio di Buoninsegna, *Rucellai Madonna*, panel (Uffizi, Florence). Duccio dominated the Sienese painting style which combined bold linear movements with a new human intimacy.

1339 Ambrogio Lorenzetti, *Good Government Enthroned* (Sala dei Nove, Palazzo Pubblico, Siena)

1220	1240	1260	1280	1300	1320	1

MIDDLE AGES   **FORERUNNERS TO RENAISSANCE**

1220	1240	1260	1280	1300	1320	1

c.1259 Nicola Pisano, Pulpit (Baptistry, Pisa cathedral)

c.1316–18 Simone Martini, *Vision of St Martin* (Lower Church of San Francesco, Assisi)

c.1265 Coppo di Marcovaldo, *Madonna and Child* (Santa Monica dei Servi, Orvieto)

c.1297 Giovanni Pisano, Pulpit (Sant'Andrea, Pistoia)

c.1280 Cimabue, *Madonna Enthroned with Angels and Prophets*, also known as *Santa Trinità Madonna* (Uffizi, Florence)

c.1336 Andrea Pisano, *Baptism of St John the Baptist*, panel on the South Doors (Baptistry, Florence cathedral)

c.1291 Pietro Cavallini, *Last Judgment*, detail (Santa Cecilia, Trastevere, Rome)

c.1425–52 Lorenzo Ghiberti, *Gates of Paradise*, panel on the East Doors. (Baptistry, Florence cathedral). These elaborate doors mark a transition from the Gothic style to the Early Renaissance style, in Florence.

c.1435 Donatello, *David* (Museo del Bargello, Florence)

1357 Andrea Orcagna, *Enthroned Christ with Madonna and Saints* (Strozzi Altarpiece, Santa Maria Novella, Florence)

c.1452–65 Piero della Francesca, detail of *The Dream of Constantine* (San Francesco, Arezzo)

c.1456 Paolo Uccello, *Battle of San Romano* (Uffizi, Florence)

c.1410 Nanni di Banco, *Four Crowned Martyrs* (Orsanmichele, Florence)

| 1360 | 1380 | 1400 | 1420 | 1440 | 1460 |

EARLY RENAISSANCE

| 1360 | 1380 | 1400 | 1420 | 1440 | 1460 |

1423 Gentile da Fabriano, *Adoration of the Magi* (Uffizi, Florence)

c.1440 Fra Angelico, *Annunciation* (San Marco, Florence)

c.1350 Francesco Traini, *Triumph of Death* (Campo Santo, Pisa)

c.1463 Piero della Francesca, *Resurrection* (Pinacoteca, Sansepolcro)

c.1465 Fra Filippo Lippi, *Madonna with Child and Angels* (Uffizi, Florence)

c.1465–74 Andrea Mantegna, *Arrival of Cardinal Francesco Gonzaga* (Palazzo Ducale, Mantova)

c.1425–8 Masaccio, *The Tribute Money* (Cappella Brancacci, Florence)

c.1470 Andrea del Verrocchio, *David* (Bargello, Florence)

FRESCO TECHNIQUE

Fresco, meaning "fresh", refers to the technique of painting onto a thin layer of damp, freshly laid plaster. Pigments are drawn into the plaster by surface tension and the colour becomes fixed as the plaster dries. The pigments react with the lime in the plaster to produce strong, rich colours, such as those in Masaccio's *The Tribute Money*.

***The Tribute Money* by Masaccio (Cappella Brancacci, Florence)**

High Renaissance Art

THE HIGH RENAISSANCE in the late 15th century was marked by an increasing sense of realism in many religious works, and the technical mastery of such renowned artists as Michelangelo, Leonardo da Vinci and Raphael. The different schools of Renaissance painting, while drawing on Classical models, produced varying styles: Florentine painting was noted for its cool clarity, while sensuous colour and warm light characterized many Venetian works. By the mid-16th century, however, these styles shifted to the fanciful, contorted imagery of Mannerism.

c.1480 Andrea Mantegna, *Dead Christ* (Brera, Milan)

1481–2 Sistine Chapel wall frescoes painted by various artists.

c.1481–2 Pietro Perugino, *Christ Delivering the Keys of the Kingdom to St Peter*, wall fresco (Sistine Chapel, Rome)

c.1483–88 Andrea del Verrocchio, completed by Alessandro Leopardi, *Equestrian Monument of Bartolomeo Colleoni* (Campo dei Santi Giovanni e Paolo, Venice)

c.1487 Giovanni Bellini, *San Giobbe Altarpiece* (Accademia, Venice)

c.1503–1505 Leonardo da Vinci, *Mona Lisa* (Louvre, Paris)

c.1495 Leonardo da Vinci, *Last Supper* (Santa Maria delle Grazie, Milan)

1505 Raphael, *Madonna of the Goldfinch* (Uffizi, Florence)

1519–26 Titian, *Madonna of the Pesaro Family* (Santa Maria Gloriosa dei Frari, Venice)

1508–12 Michelangelo, *Sistine Chapel ceiling* (The Vatican, Rome). Over 200 preliminary drawings were made for this incredible vision of God's power and humanity's spiritual awakening.

1480	1500	1520

HIGH RENAISSANCE

1480	1500	1520

1485 Leonardo da Vinci, *Virgin of the Rocks* (Louvre, Paris)

1499–1504 Luca Signorelli, *Damned Consigned to Hell* (Cappella Nuova, Orvieto cathedral)

1501–1504 Michelangelo, *David* (Galleria dell'Accademia, Florence)

1505 Giovanni Bellini, *Madonna and Child with Four Saints* (San Zaccaria altarpiece, Accademia, Venice)

c.1485 Sandro Botticelli, *Birth of Venus* (Uffizi, Florence)

c.1486 Leonardo da Vinci, *Uomo Vitruviano* (Accademia, Venice)

c.1508 Giorgione, *Tempesta* (Accademia, Venice)

1509 Raphael, *School of Athens* (Stanza della Segnatura, The Vatican, Rome). The scale, magnificence and harmony of this fresco represent the ideals of the High Renaissance. These ideals sought to express superhuman rather than human values.

1517 Sodoma, *Marriage of Alexander and Roxana* (Villa Farnesina, Rome)

1516 Michelangelo, *Dying Slave* (Louvre, Paris)

1512–14 Raphael, *Angel Delivering St Peter from Prison*, detail from the *Liberation of St Peter from Prison* (Stanza di Eliodoro, The Vatican, Rome)

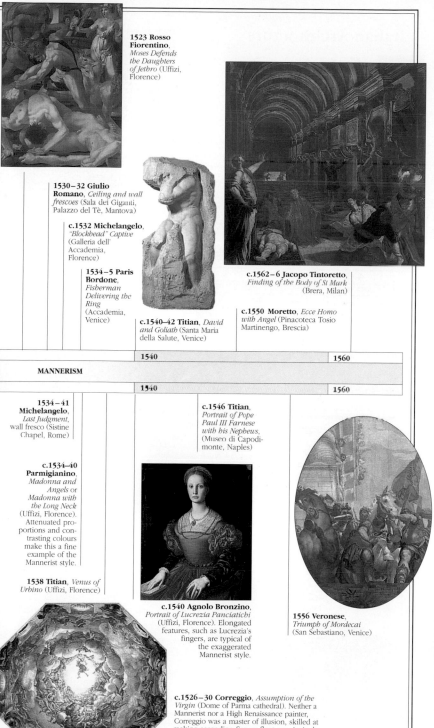

1523 Rosso Fiorentino, *Moses Defends the Daughters of Jethro* (Uffizi, Florence)

1530–32 Giulio Romano, *Ceiling and wall frescoes* (Sala dei Giganti, Palazzo del Tè, Mantova)

c.1532 Michelangelo, *"Blockhead" Captive* (Galleria dell' Accademia, Florence)

1534–5 Paris Bordone, *Fisherman Delivering the Ring* (Accademia, Venice)

c.1540–42 Titian, *David and Goliath* (Santa Maria della Salute, Venice)

c.1562–6 Jacopo Tintoretto, *Finding of the Body of St Mark* (Brera, Milan)

c.1550 Moretto, *Ecce Homo with Angel* (Pinacoteca Tosio Martinengo, Brescia)

1540   1560

MANNERISM

1540   1560

1534–41 Michelangelo, *Last Judgment*, wall fresco (Sistine Chapel, Rome)

c.1534–40 Parmigianino, *Madonna and Angels* or *Madonna with the Long Neck* (Uffizi, Florence). Attenuated proportions and contrasting colours make this a fine example of the Mannerist style.

1538 Titian, *Venus of Urbino* (Uffizi, Florence)

c.1546 Titian, *Portrait of Pope Paul III Farnese with his Nephews*, (Museo di Capodimonte, Naples)

c.1540 Agnolo Bronzino, *Portrait of Lucrezia Panciatichi* (Uffizi, Florence). Elongated features, such as Lucrezia's fingers, are typical of the exaggerated Mannerist style.

1556 Veronese, *Triumph of Mordecai* (San Sebastiano, Venice)

c.1526–30 Correggio, *Assumption of the Virgin* (Dome of Parma cathedral). Neither a Mannerist nor a High Renaissance painter, Correggio was a master of illusion, skilled at making ascending figures float convincingly, as seen in the fresco above.

Italian Architecture

THE BUILDINGS OF ITALY span almost 3,000 years, drawing influences from a wide variety of sources. Etruscan and Roman buildings borrowed heavily from ancient Greece, while in later centuries Norman, Arabic and Byzantine styles coloured Italy's Romanesque and Gothic architecture. Classical ideals infused the country's Renaissance buildings, later giving way to the inspired innovations of the Baroque period.

Corinthian capital

Orvieto's Duomo displays the ornate and intricate decoration, notably sculpture, common to many Gothic cathedrals. Building stretched from the 13th to the early 17th centuries.

The Basilica di San Marco

The Basilica di San Marco (AD 832–1094) in Venice combines Classical, Romanesque and Gothic architecture, but its key inspiration was Byzantine (see pp106–9).

200	400	600	800	1000
CLASSICAL		**BYZANTINE**		**ROMANESQUE**
200	400	600	800	1000

Triumphal arches such as Rome's Arch of Constantine (AD 313) were a uniquely Roman invention. Built to celebrate military victories, they were adorned with reliefs depicting episodes from successful campaigns (see p370).

The round-arched Romanesque style emerged from the Dark Ages in structures such as the Duomo in Modena. The churches usually had simple interiors that derived from Roman basilicas.

The building of domes over square or rectangular spaces was a major development of the Byzantine era.

ETRUSCAN ARCHITECTURE

Virtually the only architectural memorials to the Etruscans are their necropolises (c.6th century BC), found primarily in Tuscany, Lazio and Umbria. Little else survives, probably because most day-to-day buildings were made from wood. The Etruscans' close cultural and trading ties with Greece, however, suggest their architecture would have borrowed heavily from Greek models. Rome, in turn, looked to Etruscan architecture for inspiration, and most early Roman public buildings were probably Etruscan in style.

Model of Etruscan temple with Classical Greek portico

The cathedral of Monreale in Sicily, built in the 12th century, contains Norman elements blended with exotic Arabic and Byzantine decoration (see pp514–15).

Bramante's *Tempietto at San Pietro in Montorio, Rome (built 1502–10) was a Renaissance tribute to the precise, Classical temples of ancient Rome (see p370).*

Baroque façades, *such as this one added to Syracuse's Duomo between 1728 and 1754, were often grafted onto older churches.*

Industrial innovations *in glass and metal were applied in new buildings, like Mengoni's imposing Galleria Vittorio Emanuele II (1865) in Milan (see p188).*

The Classical ideals of Rome and ancient Greece were reintroduced into Italian architecture during the Renaissance.

Papal patronage and the vigour of the Counter-Reformation fuelled the Baroque, a period of architectural splendour, invention and exuberance.

The Mole Antonelliana (1863–89), in Turin, topped by a soaring granite spire, was for a time the tallest building in the world *(p216)*.

Torre Velasca's 26-floor tower in Milan (1950s) pioneered the use of reinforced concrete.

	1400	1600	1800	2000
	RENAISSANCE	BAROQUE	19th CENTURY	20th CENTURY
	1400	1600	1800	2000

Siena's Duomo (1136–1382), an imposing Romanesque-Gothic cathedral, went through 200 years of architectural transformation *(see pp332–3)*.

Santa Maria Novella in Florence has a Renaissance façade (1456–70) by Alberti and a Gothic interior.

Gian Lorenzo Bernini (1598–1680), architect of St Peter's Square, was a dominant figure in Roman Baroque.

Andrea Palladio (1508–80) built Neo-Classical villas and palazzi. His style was imitated in Europe for over two centuries *(see p76)*.

Lantern

Inner shell

Outer skin of dome, supported by 24 ribs

Brunelleschi's dome *for the Duomo in Florence, completed in 1436, was a masterpiece of Renaissance design and ingenious engineering (see p245).*

The Gesù *in Rome was designed for the Jesuits by Vignola in 1568. With its powerful façade and lavish decoration it was the prototype for countless other Baroque churches (see p371).*

The Pirelli building *in Milan, designed by Ponti and Nervi (late 1950s), is a great example of modern Italian architecture (see p179).*

Saints and Symbols in Italian Art

SAINTS AND SYMBOLS are especially important in Italian art. They form part of an established visual language used by artists to narrate stories of the Bible and the Catholic church to church-goers. Paintings of the saints were the focus for prayer and each offered assistance in a particular aspect of daily life. Patron saints protected specific cities, or trades, and individuals who bore their name. Saints' days and religious festivals still play an important part in Italian life.

THE EVANGELISTS

The four evangelists, Matthew, Mark, Luke and John are each represented by a winged creature, standing for a divine mission.

Eagle (St John)

St John carries a book of the Gospel bearing his name.

St Thomas Aquinas is usually shown with a star, barely visible in this painting on his Dominican habit.

St Dominic is usually portrayed wearing the habit of his order. The lily is another of his attributes.

St Cosmas and St Damian are always shown together, dressed in physicians' clothing.

St Mark the Evangelist often holds his book of the Gospels.

St Lawrence carries a palm leaf as well as the gridiron on which he was roasted.

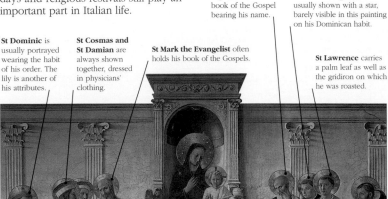

Virgin Enthroned with the Child and Saints (c.1450) was painted on dry plaster by the Dominican friar, Fra Angelico. It is on display at the Museo di San Marco, Florence (see p268).

The Virgin, usually shown in blue robes, is depicted as Mater Amabilis – the "Mother Worthy of Love".

St Peter Martyr, here with a palm leaf, is sometimes depicted with a head wound, carrying a sword.

SYMBOLS

In order to identify different saints or martyrs they were given "attributes" or symbols – particular objects to carry, or clothing to wear. These were items that played a particular role in their life story. Martyrs were known by their instruments of torture or death. Symbolism also appears in the sky, animals, flowers, colours and numbers.

The lamb symbolizes Christ, the Lamb of God, or in early Christian art, the sinner.

The skull is a "memento mori" to remind us of death and impermanence.

**Winged man
(St Matthew)**

**Winged lion
(St Mark)**

**Winged ox
(St Luke)**

Giovanni Bellini's painting of
***Madonna and Child with Four
Saints*** (see p115)

St Peter the Apostle, the
"rock" on which the Christian
church was founded, carries
the keys to heaven.

The Madonna, with the Christ
Child, is an emblem of perfect
motherly love.

St Catherine of Alexandria
is shown here with a piece
of the wheel on which she
was martyred.

St Jerome is always portrayed as an old man, often a
hermit, whose life was
devoted to scholarship.

Detail from **Madonna and Child
with Four Saints**, *by Giovanni Bellini.
The painting was produced for an
altarpiece at San Zaccaria, Venice
in 1505, where it is still on display.*

The angel, a messenger
of God to man, is por-
trayed in this scene as a
musician of Heaven.

St Lucy is depicted here holding
her own eyes in a dish. She
became the patron saint of the
blind and symbolizes light.

The lily, *flower of the Virgin,
is the symbol of purity, resurrection, peace and chastity.*

The cockle shell *most often
represents pilgrimage. It is a
particular attribute of St Roch.*

The palm *represents, in
Christian art, a martyr's
triumph over death.*

Writers, Poets and Dramatists

ITALY HAS PRODUCED many writers (in Latin and Italian) who have won worldwide acclaim. Each of them provides an illuminating insight into the country's turbulent past: the classical poets Virgil, Horace and Ovid give vivid accounts of the concerns and values of ancient Rome; medieval Florence and Tuscany are brought to life in the poetry of Dante and Petrarch and the salacious tales of Boccaccio. In less than a century these three great writers created a new literary language to rank with any in Europe. Italy's modern literature still commands international attention – Umberto Eco has to his credit one of the most widely read books of the 20th century.

Primo Levi *(1919–87) gave an astonishing account of his survival of the Jewish Holocaust and World War II's aftermath in* The Truce *and* If This Is A Man.

Trentino-Alto Adige

Valle d'Aosta and Piedmont

Lombardy

Liguria

Emilia-Romagna

Tuscany

Umberto Eco *(born 1932), a professor at the University of Bologna, wrote the novel* The Name Of The Rose, *which explored his passion for the Middle Ages. The book was made into a film (above) in 1986.*

Dario Fo (born 1926) won the Nobel prize for Literature in 1997.

Giovanni Boccaccio *(1313–75) is notable for providing a fascinating social record of his era.* The Decameron, *his captivating collection of 100 short stories, is set in the plague-stricken Florence of 1348.*

Pinocchio, *written by Carlo Collodi (1826–90) in 1911, is one of the world's best known children's stories. "Collodi" was Carlo Lorenzini's pseudonym, taken after his mother's birthplace in Tuscany.*

Dante's *(1265–1321)* Divine Comedy *(c.1321), is a journey through Hell, Purgatory and Paradise. It includes horrific accounts of the torments suffered by the damned.*

Venetian author Carlo Goldoni (1707–93) *reacted against the satirical tradition of* La Commedia dell'Arte, *preferring to write more forgiving plays on contemporary Venice society.*

CLASSICAL ROMAN WRITERS

Texts in Latin by Classical Roman philosophers, poets, dramatists and politicians are part of the bedrock of Western culture. Today the names Virgil *(The Aeneid)*, Ovid *(Metamorphoses)* and Pliny *(Historia Naturalis)* are literary legends. Fascinating histories such as Livy's *Early History of Rome*, Caesar's *Gallic Wars*, Tacitus's *Annals* and Suetonius's *The Twelve Caesars*, give us an invaluable window on the distant Roman past, as do the caustic *Satires* of Juvenal. Many Latin works owe their survival to the teams of medieval monks who diligently copied and illustrated them. In the Renaissance the stories of Ovid's *Metamorphoses* were plundered by many writers and the works of Cicero had a profound influence on prose style; Seneca was seen as a master of tragedy and Plautus's *Pot of Gold* served as a model for comedies.

Detail from medieval copy of Pliny's *Historia Naturalis*

Petrarch (1304–74), *one of the earliest and greatest lyric poets, produced works which showed the first indications of Humanism.*

St Francis of Assisi (1182–1226) *was the first author to write in Italian instead of formal Latin. As well as letters and sermons, he wrote poems and songs, including the popular Canticle of the Sun.*

Roman writer Alberto Moravia (1907–90) is usually labelled a "Neo-Realist". His novels and short stories focus on the corrupt values of contemporary society. Among his best known works are *Gli Indifferenti* and *Agostino*.

*he Veneto
nd Friuli*

Le Marche

mbria

Lazio

Abruzzo, Molise and Puglia

Campania

Basilicata and Calabria

Sicily

The Sicilian *Nobel Prize-winner, Luigi Pirandello (1867–1936), was preoccupied with the theme of multiple personality.* Six Characters In Search Of An Author *is his most famous work.*

| 0 kilometres | 200 |
| 0 miles | 100 |

Music and Opera in Italy

BEFORE ITALY'S UNIFICATION, particularly during the 17th and 18th centuries, each major city had its own traditions of music-making. Rome, as the papal city, had musical traditions less hedonistic than elsewhere, and avoided opera. Florence had its day at the turn of the 16th century, with its celebrated *camerata* (groups set on reviving the traditions of Ancient Greek spectacle). Venice fostered church music on a grand scale, and Naples, during the 18th century, was renowned for comic opera. In the 19th century, Milan became the undisputed centre of Italian opera, centred on La Scala.

Stradivarius violin

THE MEDIEVAL AND RENAISSANCE PERIODS

THROUGH BOCCACCIO *(see p30)*, among others, it is known that singing, dancing and poetry often went hand in hand in medieval and Renaissance Italy. Italy concentrated on music as part of a spectacle rather than as a pure art form.

Important contributors to the music of these periods include Guido d'Arezzo (c.995–1050), a monk who perfected musical notation, and Francesco Landini (1325–97), one of the first known composers whose songs displayed a distinct concern for lyricism. The next

150 years were to be characterized by the *Ars Perfecta* style, culminating with composer Giovanni Palestrina (1525–94). His vocal style subjected dissonance to strict control, and it was employed for most church music. Madrigals (vocal settings of poems by Petrarch and other poets) were also popular.

The early 17th century saw Italian composers such as Carlo Gesualdo (c.1561–1613) and Claudio Monteverdi challenge these traditions by introducing more declamation and more of the unexpected.

La Pietà, Venice, where Vivaldi performed

THE BAROQUE ERA

CLAUDIO MONTEVERDI'S music straddled the transition from the Renaissance period to 17th-century Baroque. The word "baroque" means highly ornamented, even bizarre, and embellishment was rife. Monteverdi's madrigals began as standard pieces for four voices but ended up as mini-operas. This was due to the popularity of an individual instrumental style and the development of the *basso continuo* (a supporting organ, harpsichord or lute that unleashed the possibility for solos and duets). At this point, the beginnings of the string orchestra were in place.

A new fashion for declamation meant that various emotional states were being represented with sighs and sobs rather than just description. Monteverdi's *Vespers* followed others' in exploiting the stereophonic possibilities of San Marco in Venice by contrasting different forces

MAJOR ITALIAN COMPOSERS THROUGH THE AGES

Claudio Monteverdi *(1567–1643) was best known for his Vespers of 1610. Both his madrigals and operas are considered major landmarks in the development of music.*

Antonio Vivaldi *(1678–1741) wrote over 600 concertos, many of which are for the violin. The Four Seasons, a set of concertos, is among the best-selling classical music of all time.*

Gioachino Rossini *(1792–1868) was most famous for his comic operas, like The Barber of Seville. The romantic, expressive side of his more serious works was often overlooked.*

Luciano Pavarotti performing in the most modern surroundings

in different parts of the building. In the 1680s, Arcangelo Corelli (1653–1713) turned to classicism. Corelli was famous for the *Concerto Grosso*, a style that contrasted the solo string group with the full ensemble. He was followed by Antonio Vivaldi (1678–1741), who concentrated his efforts on developing the solo form of the *Concerto Grosso*. He used wind and plucked instruments as well as violins.

THE EMERGENCE OF OPERA

OPERA FIRST emerged during the wedding celebrations of Italy's wealthy 16th-century families. Monteverdi was the first composer to establish

Giuseppe Verdi (1813–1901), whose first works were for La Scala, was the most important opera composer of the 19th century. His most celebrated works include Rigoletto *and* Aida.

his work firmly in the opera repertoire. During the 17th century, Alessandro Scarlatti (1660–1725) formulated a model which consisted of an orchestral overture followed by a sequence of narrative, set as *recitative*, and interrupted by *da capo* (three-part) arias. Themes for the weightier *opera seria* were largely drawn from mythology, while the lighter *opera buffa* had stock scenes that sometimes owed a large debt to the traditions of Commedia dell'Arte. Famous for his comic operas, such as *The Barber of Seville*, was the composer Gioachino Rossini. Among other contributors, Vincenzo Bellini (1801–35) and Gaetano Donizetti (1797–1848) developed *bel canto* singing, a style stressing fine tone and ornamentation.

The two most prominent opera composers of the latter half of the 19th century were Giuseppe Verdi and Giacomo Puccini (1858–1924). Verdi often turned to the works of Shakespeare as well as to more recent subjects in order to form a basis for his work, while many composers, like Puccini, turned to the new trend of *verismo* (slices of contemporary realism) – *La Bohème* is one of the most refined examples of this style.

Puccini's *Tosca*, first staged in 1900

THE 20TH CENTURY

IN THE EARLY 20th century, Puccini's *La Fanciulla del West* (The Girl of the West) brought cowboys into opera, *Turandot* looked towards the Orient and *Tosca* brought torture and murder. Some composers have attempted to emulate French and German music, and only a few Italian pieces, such as those by Ottorino Respighi (1879–1936), have been regularly performed. The most important name in Italian music today is Luciano Berio (born 1925), who developed Music Theatre, a relatively new art form lying somewhere between drama and opera. Recently, however, Berio has continued the tradition of Grand Opera with his elaborate production of *Un Re in Ascolto*. But it is perhaps Luciano Pavarotti who must be credited with renewing an international interest in opera. In the 1990s, his often televised performances with "Three Tenors" stars José Carreras and Placido Domingo secured a massive world audience for opera. Another star of opera and classical music is internationally renowned conductor Riccardo Muti, director of La Scala.

The illuminated interior of Rome's Teatro dell'Opera

Italian Design

ITALY HAS HAD PHENOMENAL success evolving stylish, desirable forms for everyday objects. Its 20th-century achievements can be credited to a handful of forward-thinking industrial giants, such as Olivetti, willing to entrust important product decisions to a group of inspired designers, like Ettore Sottsass. The design genius was to rethink the function of consumer objects, apply new technology, and then make the result look seductive.

The streamlined aesthetic of Italian design extends even to pasta; this Marille version was created by car designer Giorgio Giugiaro for Voiello in 1983.

Sleek, sculptural Alessi cutlery (1988), designed by Ettore Sottsass, combines maximum utility with elegance and aesthetic integrity.

The Alessi kettle (1985), designed by Michael Graves, achieved such popularity in its first year of production that over 100,000 were sold.

One of the best known coffeemakers is Bialetti's Moka Express. Although designed in 1930, it is still enormously popular today.

Christophe Pilet's chair, designed for Giulio Cappellini's collection of contemporary furniture, expresses the idea of the living style of the 1990s.

The folding Cumano table, designed by Achille Castiglione for Zanotta in 1979, is still revered as a "designer object".

The Patty Difusa chair, with unusual wooden arms that curve into legs, was designed by William Sawaya for Sawaya & Moroni in Milan.

Pininfarina's streamlined form for the Ferrari Testarossa (1986) pushes car design almost into the realms of sculpture.

Light in weight, and compact in shape, Olivetti's Valentine typewriter revolutionized the role of the desk typewriter. Designed by Ettore Sottsass in 1969, its portability allowed the user to work anywhere.

Italian printer Giambattista Bodoni (1740–1813) designed the sophisticated typeface that bears his name and is still popular 200 years after its creation.

Milan's Giorgio Armani is best known for his updating of classic items such as the jacket, creating a flattering, smart and comfortable, "deconstructed" look.

Prada, the Milan-based fashion house headed by Miuccia Prada, features minimalist, cutting-edge designs and the use of innovative fabrics.

Florence has a long reputation as a producer of high quality crafts, particularly fashion accessories such as handbags, shoes, belts, jewellery and briefcases.

Gucci's classic items, including bags and shoes, are a revered totem for the fashion-conscious.

The Artemide company is renowned for combining metal and glass in many of their designs, especially lamps and lighting fixtures.

Piaggio's innovative Vespa scooter (1946), by Corradino d'Ascanio, provided cheap, fast and reliable transport at a time when few could afford the expense of a car. Hugely successful, the Vespa is still a common sight on Italy's streets.

The Fiat 500 (1957), like the Vespa, became a symbol of mobility and democratization, an expression of Italy's rapid postwar recovery.

Scientists, Inventors and Explorers

ITALY HAS fostered a long tradition of important scientific thought and discovery, fuelled in the Renaissance by such men as Galileo, who searched for a new understanding of the universe. Meanwhile, explorers such as Columbus had set off to find new worlds, a move heralded in the 13th century by Marco Polo. The spirit of scientific enquiry continued up to the 20th century, with the invention of radio and pioneering work in the field of nuclear physics.

Guglielmo Marconi invented the first practical system for sending radio signals. In 1901, he succeeded in picking up a signal that had been sent to England from Newfoundland.

Trentino-Alto Adige

Lombardy

Valle d'Aosta and Piedmont

The Veneto and Friuli

After deducing *that an electric current made frogs' legs move, Alessandro Volta invented the electric battery, a "pile" of metal discs in contact with acid. He demonstrated it to Napoleon in 1801.*

Liguria

Tuscany

Genoese-born *Christopher Columbus sailed west from Spain in 1492. He reached the Indies in three months, navigating with such aids as an astrolabe.*

The explorer *Amerigo Vespucci established that the New World was a separate land mass. A pamphlet wrongly described him as its discoverer, and so, in 1507, America acquired its name.*

Leonardo da Vinci *was the ultimate Renaissance man, accomplished in both arts and sciences. He conceived his first design for a flying machine in c.1488, more than 400 years before the first aeroplane took off. This model is based on one of his technical drawings.*

The telescope *enabled astronomers to produce accurate lunar maps. Domenico Cassini, astronomy professor at Bologna University, refined the instrument. In 1665 he traced the meridian line in the church of San Petronio.*

```
0 kilometres          200

0 miles          100
```

Padua University, founded in 1222, was a centre of scientific learning in the Renaissance. Galileo, inventor of the telescope, taught physics here, and the lectern he used is still on view.

The Venetian Marco Polo set off for the east as a youth in 1271. He stayed at the court of the Mongol emperor, Kublai Khan, for nearly two decades before returning home. He is seen here arriving at Hormuz in the Persian Gulf from India.

Galileo Galilei proved that the earth revolved around the sun, over-turning Church doctrine. He was convicted of heresy in 1633. Here he shows the rings of Saturn to Venetian senators.

Emilia-omagna

Le Marche

Umbria

Lazio

Abruzzo, Molise and Puglia

Winner of the Nobel Prize for Physics in 1938, Enrico Fermi directed the first controlled nuclear chain reaction. He built the world's first nuclear reactor for producing power at the University of Chicago, US.

Campania

Basilicata and Calabria

Pliny the Elder wrote his catalogue of human knowledge, *Natural History*, in AD 77. He died when Vesuvius erupted two years later, but his book retained its authority for 1,500 years.

Spectacles were invented in Italy in the 13th century. They are first recorded in Venice, still an important centre for glasswork today.

Sicily

The mathematician Archimedes was born in c.287 BC in Syracuse, Sicily, then a Greek colony. Legend has it that he discovered the principle of specific gravity while in the bath.

TEMPLA DOMVM EXPOSITIS:VICOS:FORA:MOENIA PONTES:
VIRGINEAM TRIVII QVOD REPARARIS AQVAM:
PRISCA LICET NAVTIS STATVAS DARE COMMODA PORTVS:
ET VATICANVM CINGERE SIXTE IVGVM:
PLVS TAMEN VRBS DEBET: NAM QVAE SQVALORE LATEBAT:
CERNITVR IN CELEBRI BIBLIOTHECA LOCO.

THE HISTORY OF ITALY

THE CONCEPT of Italy as a geographic entity goes back to the time of the Etruscans, but Italy's history is one of discord and division. Prior to the 19th century, the only time the peninsula was united was under the Romans, who by the 2nd century BC had subdued the other Italian tribes. Rome became the capital of a huge empire, introducing its language, laws and calendar to most of Europe before succumbing to Germanic invaders in the 5th century AD.

Julius Caesar

Another important legacy of the Roman empire was Christianity and the position of the pope as head of the Catholic church. The medieval papacy summoned the Franks to drive out the Lombards and, in AD 800, crowned the Frankish king Charlemagne Holy Roman Emperor. Unfortunately, what seemed to be the dawn of a new age turned out to be anything but. For five centuries popes and emperors fought to decide which of them should be in charge of their nebulous empire.

Meanwhile, a succession of foreign invaders – Normans, Angevins and Aragonese – took advantage of the situation to conquer Sicily and the south.

The north, in contrast, saw a growth of independent city states, the most powerful being Venice, fabulously wealthy through trade with the East. Other cities, such as Genoa, Florence, Milan, Pisa and Siena, also had their days of glory. Northern Italy became the most prosperous and cultured region in western Europe and it was the artists and scholars of 15th-century Florence who inspired the Renaissance. Small, fragmented states, however, could not compete with great powers. In the 16th century Italy's petty kingdoms fell prey to a foreign invader, this time to Spain, and the north subsequently came under the control of Austria.

One small kingdom that remained independent was Piedmont, but during a war between Austria and France it fell to Napoleon in 1796. In the 19th century, however, it was Piedmont that became the focus for a movement towards a united Italy, a goal that was achieved in 1870, thanks largely to the heroic military exploits of Garibaldi. In the 1920s, the Fascists seized power and, in 1946, the monarchy was abandoned for today's republic.

16th-century map of Italy, of the kind used by Venetian and Genoese sailors

◁ Fresco by Melozzo da Forlì of the court of Sixtus IV (1471–84), a powerful and worldly Renaissance pope

The Age of the Etruscans

THE ETRUSCANS were Italy's first major civilization. The frescoes, jewellery and pottery found in their tombs are evidence of a highly artistic, cultured people. Their origin is a mystery, as is their language, but from the 9th century BC they spread through central Italy, their chief rivals being the Greeks in the south. Etruria was never a unified state, just a loose confederation of cities. In the 6th century Etruscan kings ruled Rome, the city that would ultimately eclipse them.

ITALY IN 650 BC

▨	*Etruscan kingdoms*
☐	*Greek colonies*

The double flute was a speciality of the Etruscans. The instrument was played at festivals and funerals alike.

Terracotta Winged Horses
This beautiful relief of yoked horses (4th century BC) decorated the façade of the Ara della Regina temple at Tarquinia.

Bronze Sheep's Liver
The inscriptions served as a guide for telling the future from animals' entrails.

Terracotta Cremation Urn
The lid of the urn shows the deceased holding a writing tablet. The Etruscans introduced the alphabet to Italy.

TOMB OF THE LEOPARDS
Feasts and revelry are common themes in the frescoes that decorate Etruscan tombs. These musicians are from a tomb fresco (c.500 BC) at Tarquinia *(see p450).*

TIMELINE

900 BC	800 BC	700 BC	
9th century BC Pre-urban communities established along river valleys in Etruria	**753 BC** Legendary date of foundation of Rome by Romulus	**c.700 BC** Growth of cities in Etruria; earliest Etruscan inscriptions	**616 BC** Etruscans become rulers of Rome under Tarquino the Older
c.900 BC First traces of Iron Age in Italy; Villanovan period	**c.800 BC** Greeks settle in Sicily and south of Italy	**715–673 BC** Reign of the wise Numa Pompilius, second king of Rome	*Etruscan gold earrings*

A Boxing Match
Athletic competitions were held at funerals. This vase, which dates from about 500 BC, was made in Etruria, but imitates the Greek black-figure style of pottery.

The musicians and the dancer in the tomb painting are painted with a realism that indicates the influence of Greek art.

The lyre was made from a tortoise shell and played with a plectrum.

Where to See Etruscan Italy

Rock tombs *like these at Sovana (p336) are common in the volcanic tufa of central Italy.*

Tuscany, Lazio and Umbria are rich in Etruscan remains, especially tombs. There are huge necropolises in Lazio at Cerveteri and Tarquinia (p450). The latter also has an important museum. Other museums with major collections of Etruscan art and artifacts include Villa Giulia (p430) and the Vatican's Museo Gregoriano (p412) in Rome, the Museo Archeologico in Florence (p269), the Museo Nazionale in Chiusi (p322) and the Museo Guarnacci in Volterra (p324).

Apollo of Veii
This magnificent statue of Apollo (c.500 BC) shows the stylized facial features characteristic of Etruscan art.

Bronze Mirror
Wealthy Etruscans lived in great luxury. The women used polished bronze mirrors with engraved backs. This one shows Helen of Troy and the goddess Aphrodite.

Temple of Neptune
This fine temple at Paestum (5th century BC) is a legacy of Greek colonization of the south.

Mixing bowl, imported from Greece

509 BC Last Etruscan king, Tarquinius Superbus, expelled from Rome; establishment of Roman Republic

450 BC Roman law codified in the Twelve Tables

390 BC Gauls sack Rome; Capitol saved thanks to alarm sounded by cackling geese

600 BC

500 BC

400 BC

499 BC Battle of Lake Regillus; Romans defeat alliance of Latins and Etruscans

396 BC Veii, a major Etruscan city in present-day Lazio, falls to Rome

474 BC Etruscan fleet defeated by Greeks off Cumae; blow to Etruscan naval power

c.400 BC Gauls start to settle along valley of the Po

Relief of Capitoline geese, found in the Roman Forum

From Republic to Empire

FROM THE SCORES of tribes inhabiting ancient Italy, one people, the Romans, emerged to conquer the peninsula and impose their language, customs and laws on the rest.

Roman mask and helmet (1st century BC)

Rome's success was due to superb skill in military and civil organization. The state was a republic ruled by two consuls, elected each year, but as the extent of Rome's conquests grew, power passed to generals such as Julius Caesar. The Republic became unworkable and Caesar's heirs became the first Roman emperors.

Cisalpine Gaul was annexed in 202–191 BC.

Etruria was in Roman hands by 265 BC.

Julius Caesar
The great general, conqueror of Gaul, returned to Italy in 49 BC to defeat Pompey. His rise to absolute power marked the end of the Republic.

Oscan Inscription
The languages of the peoples conquered by Rome lived on for centuries before being replaced by Latin. The Oscans lived in what is now Campania.

War Elephant
In 218 BC the great Carthaginian general Hannibal brought 37 elephants across the Alps – to spread alarm in the Roman ranks.

Roman Aqueduct
The Romans' talent for engineering found its most spectacular expression in huge aqueducts. These could be up to 80 km (50 miles) long, though for most of that distance the water ran underground.

High ground

Cleaning vent

Reservoir   **Underground water channel**   **Arches carrying water across low ground**

Map labels: AQUILEIA, VIA POSTUMIA, VERONA, Padus, PLACENTIA Piacenza, GENUA Genoa, VIA AEMILIA, BONONIA Bologna, FLORENTIA Florence, ARIMINUM Rimini, FANUM FORTUN Fano, PISAE Pisa, Arnus, ARRETIUM Arezzo, POPULONIA, CLUSIUM Chiusi, ALBA FUCENS, ROMA, TIBUR Tivoli, PANORMUS Palermo

TIMELINE

312 BC Building of Via Appia and Aqua Appia aqueduct	**275 BC** Greek King Pyrrhus defeated by Romans at Beneventum	**218 BC** Second Punic War; Hannibal crosses the Alps
308 BC Etruscan city of Tarquinii falls to Rome	**264–241 BC** First Punic War (between Rome and Carthage)	**216 BC** Roman defeat at Battle of Cannae
300 BC	**250 BC**	**200 BC**

Via Appia

265 BC Romans capture last Etruscan city

237 BC Romans occupy Corsica and Sardinia

Hannibal, Carthaginian leader in the Second Punic War

191 BC Gaulish territory south of the Alps falls to Rome

287–212 BC Life of Archimedes, the great Greek mathematician of Syracuse

Cicero Addresses the Senate
State business was debated in the Senate. The great orator Cicero (106–43 BC) argued for the Republic and against tyranny.

Roman Legionary
This bronze shows a legionary in standard kit of helmet, breastplate, leather kilt with iron plates, greaves on his shins, and sandals.

RFINIUM
ERIA

The Via Appia
was extended from Capua to Brindisi in 190 BC.

CAPUA
VIA APPIA
BRUNDISIUM
Brindisi
TARENTUM
Taranto

Sicily
became the first Roman province in 241 BC.

RHEGIUM
Reggio di Calabria

WHERE TO SEE ITALY FROM THE REPUBLICAN ERA

Republican structures are very rare, most having been rebuilt under the Empire. In Rome itself, two notable exceptions are the 2nd-century BC Temples of the Forum Boarium (p423). However, the legacy of the age to modern Italy is not hard to appreciate. Countless roads, such as the Via Appia Antica (p431), and towns were planned originally by Roman engineers. Two striking examples of towns with original Roman street plans are Lucca (pp310–11) and Como (p185).

***These huge basalt blocks** at Tharros in Sardinia (p535) were part of a Roman road.*

ROMAN ROADS

After conquering other tribes, the Romans imposed their authority by building roads along which legions could march rapidly to deal with any trouble. They also built towns. Many, such as Ariminum (Rimini), were "colonies", settlements for Roman citizens – often veteran legionaries.

Aerial View of Bologna
Roman street plans are still visible in city centres today. The route of the old Via Aemilia cuts straight through the centre of Bologna.

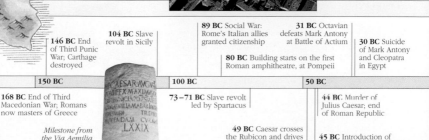

146 BC End of Third Punic War; Carthage destroyed	**104 BC** Slave revolt in Sicily	**89 BC** Social War: Rome's Italian allies granted citizenship	**31 BC** Octavian defeats Mark Antony at Battle of Actium
		80 BC Building starts on the first Roman amphitheatre, at Pompeii	**30 BC** Suicide of Mark Antony and Cleopatra in Egypt
150 BC		**100 BC**	**50 BC**
168 BC End of Third Macedonian War; Romans now masters of Greece		**73–71 BC** Slave revolt led by Spartacus	**44 BC** Murder of Julius Caesar; end of Roman Republic
Milestone from the Via Aemilia		**49 BC** Caesar crosses the Rubicon and drives Pompey from Rome	**45 BC** Introduction of 12-month Julian calendar

The Golden Age of Rome

FROM THE AGE of Augustus to the reign of Trajan, Rome's power grew until her empire stretched from Britain to the Red Sea. Despite the extravagance of emperors such as Nero, taxes and booty from military campaigns continually refilled the Imperial coffers. Under the wiser rule of Trajan, Hadrian and Marcus Aurelius in the 2nd century AD, Roman citizens enjoyed wealth and comfort, with most of the work performed by slaves. Entertainment included visits to the baths, the theatre and the games. The town of Pompeii, buried when Vesuvius erupted in AD 79, preserves many fascinating details of everyday life.

ROMAN EMPIRE IN AD 117

Maximum extent of the Empire

Mosaic of Gladiators
Bloodthirsty gladiatorial combats were very popular. The gladiators were mostly slaves captured in war.

Frescoes of festoons and medallions

Trajan's Column
The carvings record Trajan's successful campaigns in Dacia (present-day Romania) in the first decade of the 2nd century AD.

The triclinium
(main dining room) had a beautiful frieze of cupids.

Roman Shops
Buildings in towns were lined with small shops open to the street, like this pharmacy. The front was closed with wooden panels and locked at night.

HOUSE OF THE VETTII

This reconstruction shows one of Pompeii's finest houses *(see pp478–9)*. The Vettii were not aristocrats, but freedmen, former slaves, who had made a fortune through trade. The rooms were richly decorated with frescoes and sculptures.

TIMELINE

50 BC		AD 1		AD 50	
	9 BC Dedication of Ara Pacis *(see p400)* in Rome to celebrate peace after wars in Gaul and Spain	**AD 17** Tiberius fixes boundary of Empire along the Rhine and Danube	*Bronze cooking pots from kitchen at Pompeii*		**AD 79** Eruption of Vesuvius destroys Pompeii and Herculaneum
	27 BC Augustus takes title Princeps, in effect becoming the first Roman emperor	**AD 37–41** Reign of Caligula	**AD 67** Traditional date for martyrdom of St Peter and St Paul in Rome		
		AD 43 Roman conquest of Britain in reign of Claudius		**AD 80** Inaugural games in Colosseum	
		AD 68 Deposition and suicide of Nero			

Augustus
The adopted son of Julius Caesar became the first emperor, reducing the Roman Senate to impotence and ruling by decree.

The atrium had a skylight in the roof with a pool that collected rainwater below.

Front entrance

WHERE TO SEE IMPERIAL ROME

The best places to discover how people lived are Pompeii (*pp478–9*) and Herculaneum. Artifacts and works of art from these sites are held at the Museo Archeologico in Naples (*pp474–5*), while local museums all over Italy contain statues and other remains. Famous sights in Rome include the Pantheon (*p394*) and the Colosseum (*p383*). Hadrian's Villa, at Tivoli (*p452*), and Ostia (*p451*) are also fascinating to visit, but the whole country preserves traces of Rome's glory – from the Arch of Augustus in Aosta (*p207*) to Villa del Casale (*p521*) in Sicily.

The Forum (pp380–81), with its temples and law courts, was the centre of daily life in ancient Rome.

Reception room

Mosaic of a Banquet
The Romans ate reclining on low couches. A popular accompaniment for many dishes was garum, a salty sauce made of dried fish.

Peristyle or colonnade

The internal garden was a feature borrowed by the Romans from the Greeks.

Household Shrine
Religious rites were practised both in public and in private. This shrine from the House of the Vettii was dedicated to the lares, *the household gods.*

AD 97 Roman Empire reaches largest extent in reign of Trajan

AD 161–180 Reign of Marcus Aurelius

AD 193–211 Reign of Septimius Severus

AD 212 Roman citizenship extended to include people from all parts of the Empire

AD 100   **AD 150**   **AD 200**

Late 1st century AD Amphitheatre of Verona built

AD 134 Hadrian's Villa at Tivoli completed

AD 125 Pantheon rebuilt by Hadrian

Emperor Septimius Severus

AD 216 Baths of Caracalla completed in Rome

The Splitting of the Empire

Glass flask with Christian symbol (4th century AD)

A DECISIVE TURNING POINT in the history of the Roman Empire came with Emperor Constantine's conversion to Christianity in AD 312 and his decision to build a new capital at Constantinople (Byzantium). By the 5th century the Empire was split into two. Rome and the Western Empire could not stem the tide of Germanic invaders migrating southwards and Italy fell first to the Goths and later to the Lombards. The Eastern Empire retained nominal control over parts of Italy from its stronghold at Ravenna, which became the richest, most powerful city of the age, while the great palaces and arenas of Rome were reduced to ruins.

ITALY IN AD 600

- Byzantine territories
- Lombard territories

The Donation of Constantine
A medieval legend, encouraged by the papacy, tells how Constantine granted Pope Sylvester temporal power over Rome.

Belisarius
(500–565) was a general who won much of Italy back from the Goths.

Justinian reigned from 527 to 565. He was a great lawgiver and one of the most powerful Byzantine emperors.

Theodolinda of the Lombards
The 6th-century queen converted her people to orthodox Catholicism. Here, gold is melted for the church she built at Monza (see p193).

TIMELINE

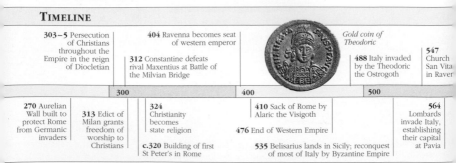

303–5 Persecution of Christians throughout the Empire in the reign of Diocletian

312 Constantine defeats rival Maxentius at Battle of the Milvian Bridge

404 Ravenna becomes seat of western emperor

Gold coin of Theodoric

488 Italy invaded by the Theodoric the Ostrogoth

547 Church San Vita in Raver

270 Aurelian Wall built to protect Rome from Germanic invaders

313 Edict of Milan grants freedom of worship to Christians

324 Christianity becomes state religion

c.320 Building of first St Peter's in Rome

410 Sack of Rome by Alaric the Visigoth

476 End of Western Empire

535 Belisarius lands in Sicily; reconquest of most of Italy by Byzantine Empire

564 Lombards invade Italy, establishing their capital at Pavia

| 300 | 400 | 500 |

Charlemagne
The King of the Franks was invited by the pope to crush the Lombards. In return, he was crowned Holy Roman Emperor in AD 800.

Saracens Besieging Messina *(843)*
In the 9th century Sicily was conquered by Muslims from Africa. Saracen raiders even reached Rome, where Pope Leo IV built a new wall to defend the Vatican.

The emperor holds a large gold paten, the dish in which the bread is placed for Mass.

Maximian, Archbishop of Ravenna

WHERE TO SEE EARLY CHRISTIAN AND BYZANTINE ITALY

Though the fall of the Roman Empire led to war, famine and depopulation, the continuity of the Christian religion has preserved many monuments of the late Empire and Byzantine period. Rome has the catacombs *(p432)* and great basilicas, such as Santa Maria Maggiore *(p403)*. In Ravenna, the administrative capital of the Byzantine Empire, are the churches of San Vitale and Sant'Apollinare *(pp260–61)* with their magnificent mosaics. Sicily and the south also preserve many Byzantine churches, while the finest example of late Byzantine architecture is San Marco in Venice *(pp106–9)*.

Stilo in Calabria has a beautiful Byzantine church, the Cattolica (p504), *dating from the 10th century.*

Priests

THE COURT OF JUSTINIAN

Byzantine churches were decorated with glorious mosaics of coloured glass and gold leaf. This one from the apse of the church of San Vitale in Ravenna *(see p260)*, completed in 547, depicts members of the Imperial court.

Santa Costanza in Rome (p431) *was built in the 4th century as the mausoleum of Constantine's daughter. Late Roman mosaics decorate the vaults.*

.595 Lombards control two thirds of Italy

752 Lombard King Aistulf takes Byzantine stronghold of Ravenna

774 Charlemagne conquers Italy and takes Lombard crown

800 Charlemagne crowned Holy Roman Emperor in St Peter's

878 Saracens capture city of Syracuse from Byzantine Empire and gain control of Sicily

600	700	800	900

Gregory the Great (reigned 590–604)

599 Pope Gregory negotiates peace between the Lombards and the Byzantine Empire

754 Pope appeals to Franks for help; King Pepin invades Italy and defeats Lombards

6th-century Lombard gold helmet in the Bargello museum, Florence (see p275)

The Rise of Venice

MEDIEVAL ITALY saw waves of foreign invaders joining in the struggle for power between popes and emperors. In the confusion, many northern cities asserted their independence from feudal overlords. The most powerful was Venice, governed by its doge and Great Council, which grew rich through trade with the East and by shipping Crusaders to fight the Saracens in the Holy Land. Its maritime rivals on the west coast were Genoa and Pisa.

Enrico Dandolo, Doge of Venice (c.1120–1205)

THE MEDITERRANEAN (1250)
— *Genoese trade routes*
— *Venetian trade routes*

Matilda of Tuscany
Matilda, Countess of Tuscany (1046–1115) supported the radical Pope Gregory VII against the Emperor Henry IV. When she died, she left her lands to the church.

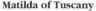

Basilica San Marco   **Doge's Palace**

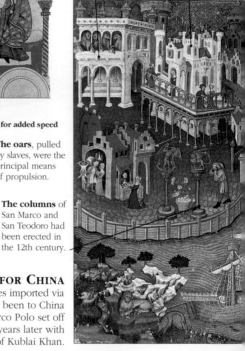

Canopy over the half-deck

Sails – for added speed

The oars, pulled by slaves, were the principal means of propulsion.

Venetian Galley
The galleys used by Venice, both as warships and for carrying cargo, were similar to ancient Greek vessels.

The columns of San Marco and San Teodoro had been erected in the 12th century.

MARCO POLO'S DEPARTURE FOR CHINA
Venice traded in Chinese silks and spices imported via the Middle East, but no Venetian had been to China before Marco Polo's father Nicolò. Marco Polo set off with his father in 1271, returning 25 years later with fantastic tales of his time at the court of Kublai Khan.

TIMELINE

1000 Doge of Venice, Pietro Orseolo II, defeats Dalmatian pirates in Adriatic

11th century School of Law at Bologna develops into Europe's first university

Medieval students

1139 Naples incorporated into Kingdom of Sicily

1000	1050	1100

1030 Norman knight Rainulf granted county of Aversa by Duke of Naples

1061 Normans Robert Guiscard and Roger de Hauteville capture Messina from the Arabs

1063 San Marco in Venice rebuilt

1084 Normans sack Rome

1076 Salerno, last Lombard city, falls to Normans

1073–85 Pope Gregory VII reforms church and papacy

1130 Rog[er] II crown[ed] king of Sicily

1115 Death of Countess Matilda

St Francis of Assisi
(1181–1226)
In The Dream of
Pope Innocent III
*by Giotto, painted
around 1290–1295,
St Francis holds up
the tottering edifice
of the Roman church.
The Franciscans' rule
of poverty brought
about a religious
revival in reaction
to the wealth of
the church.*

Monastery of
Sant'Apollonia

Today's Riva degli
Schiavoni

WHERE TO SEE EARLY MEDIEVAL ITALY

Of the many churches built in this period, especially fine examples are Venice's San Marco (p106), Sant'Antonio (p152) in Padua and the Duomo in Pisa (p314). The Leaning Tower (p316) also dates back to the 12th century. Medieval castles include Frederick II's Castel del Monte in Puglia (p493) and Castello dell'Imperatore in Prato.

Castello dell' Imperatore, Prato, was built about 1240.

Nicolò Polo, his brother Maffeo and son Marco prepare to embark. They sailed first to Acre in the Levant.

Fourth Crusade
Discord between the leaders of the crusade and Pope Innocent III culminated in the sacking of Constantinople in 1204.

Frederick II
(1194–1250)
The emperor kept a court of poets and scholars in Sicily. He won Jerusalem from the Arabs by diplomacy, but was constantly at war with the pope and the cities of Lombardy.

1155 Frederick Barbarossa crowned Holy Roman Emperor
1198 Frederick II becomes king of Sicily
1204 Sacking of Constantinople
1209 Franciscan Order founded
1216 Dominican Order founded
1250 Death of Frederick II
1260 Urban IV invites Charles of Anjou to rule Naples and Sicily
1265 Birth of Dante

1150 | 1200 | 1250

Frederick Barbarossa dressed as a Crusader
1220 Frederick II crowned Holy Roman Emperor
1228 Gregory IX excommunicates Frederick II; struggle between Guelphs (the papal party) and Ghibellines (supporters of the emperor)
1237 Lombard League defeat Frederick at Battle of Cortenuova
1271 Marco Polo sets off on journey to China

The Late Middle Ages

OLD FEUDS BETWEEN pope and emperor thrived throughout the 14th century, kept alive by two warring factions – the Guelphs, who backed the papacy, and the Ghibellines, who favoured Imperial power. The cities of Lombardy and Tuscany used the political confusion to grow in strength. It was against this turbulent backdrop that a great new age in painting was inspired by artists such as Duccio and Giotto. Also at this time the Florentine poets Dante and Petrarch laid the foundations of Italian literature.

Sienese bishop's staff

ITALY IN 1350

- ▨ *Papal States*
- ☐ *Holy Roman Empire*
- ▨ *Angevin Kingdom of Naples*

MEDIEVAL TOWN SQUARE

Throughout central Italy, the town square was an expression of civic pride and independence. Towns, such as Perugia *(see pp342–3)*, tried to overshadow their rivals in the splendour of their town halls. The centre of Perugia has changed little since the 14th century when the town's main rival was Siena.

The campanile or bell tower

A griffin, symbol of Perugia

Condottieri
Cities paid condottieri, *leaders of bands of mercenaries, to fight their wars. Siena hired Guidoriccio da Fogliano, seen here in a fresco by Simone Martini (1330).*

The main chamber of the town hall, the Sala dei Notari, is decorated with the coats of arms of Perugia's mayors.

Dante's Inferno
One of the harshest punishments in Dante's vision of hell is reserved for corrupt popes, such as Boniface VIII (reigned 1294–1303), who are placed upside down in fiery pits.

The Fontana Maggiore was begun in 1275 and includes panels by Nicola Pisano. Prominently placed, it is an emblem of the town's wealth.

TIMELINE

The poet and scholar Petrarch

1275		1300		1325

- **1282** Sicilian Vespers; uprising against French rule in Palermo; 2,000 French soldiers killed
- **1298** Marco Polo returns from China to Venice
- **1296** Work begins on the Duomo in Florence
- **1309–43** Reign of Robert the Wise of Naples
- **1310** Work begins on Palazzo Ducale in Venice
- **1313** Birth of Boccaccio

- **1282** Peter of Aragon lands at Trapani, conquers Sicily and is crowned king in Palermo
- **1304** Birth of Petrarch
- **1309** Clement V moves papacy to Avignon
- **1321** Dante completes *La Divina Commedia* and dies the same year
- **1337** Death of Giotto

The Black Death
Bubonic plague reached Italy in 1347, carried on Genoese ships from the Black Sea. It killed over a third of the population, reducing the remainder to a state of superstitious terror.

WHERE TO SEE LATE MEDIEVAL ITALY

Many central Italian cities and towns have public buildings from the 13th and 14th centuries; among the most impressive are Palazzo Vecchio (*p283*) in Florence and Siena's Palazzo Pubblico (*p330*). Smaller towns that preserve much of their medieval character include Volterra (*p324*) and the walled Monteriggioni (*p324*) in Tuscany, Gubbio (*p342*) and Todi (*p349*) in Umbria and Viterbo (*pp448–9*) in Lazio. The Duomo in Orvieto (*pp348–9*) is a fine example of a late 13th-century Gothic cathedral.

Piazza dei Priori *in Volterra (p324) is one of the most beautiful medieval squares in Italy.*

The cathedral was started in 1350 and used to include an outside pulpit in the square.

Construction of Alessandria
Almost all towns were ringed with strong walls. This fresco (1407) by Spinello Aretino is a valuable record of medieval building techniques.

Return of Pope Gregory XI to Rome *(1378)*
For 70 years the popes had lived in Avignon, protected by the French kings, while nobles and republicans fought for control of Rome.

1339 Simon Boccanegra becomes first doge of Genoa; Giovanna I Queen of Naples

Medieval doctor

1347–9 Black Death

1378–1415 Period of Schism, with rival popes and antipopes in Rome and Avignon

1380 Genoese fleet surrenders to Venetians at Chioggia

1350	1375	1400

1354 Cola di Rienzo killed in Rome

1385 Gian Galeazzo Visconti becomes ruler of Milan

1406 Pisa annexed by Florence

1347 Cola di Rienzo tries to re-establish Roman Republic

1378 Gregory XI returns from Avignon to Rome

The Renaissance

Leonardo da Vinci (1452–1519)

Fifteenth-century Italy saw a flowering of the arts and scholarship unmatched in Europe since the days of Greece and Rome. Architects turned from the Gothic to Classical models for inspiration, while painting, with its new understanding of perspective and anatomy, produced a generation of artists that included such giants as Leonardo da Vinci, Raphael and Michelangelo. The patronage for this cultural "rebirth" came from the wealthy families that ruled the city states of the north, led by the Medici of Florence. In spite of intense rivalry, they oversaw a period of uneasy stability out of which the Renaissance grew.

ITALY IN 1492
- Republic of Florence
- Papal States
- Aragonese possessions

Handing over the Keys of St Peter
Perugino's fresco in the Sistine Chapel (see p416) links the authority of the pope to the New Testament and, through the Classical buildings in the background, to ancient Rome.

Galeazzo Maria Sforza was the son of Milan's ruler.

Piero de' Medici, Lorenzo's father, was given the nickname "the Gouty".

Self-portrait of the artist

Execution of Savonarola (1498)
Having assumed the leadership of Florence in 1494, the fanatical monk was hanged, then burned for heresy in Piazza della Signoria.

TIMELINE

1420 Martin V re-establishes papacy in Rome

1435 Publication of *On Painting* by Alberti, which contains the first system for the use of linear perspective

1436 Brunelleschi completes dome of Florence cathedral

1458–64 War between Houses of Aragon and Anjou over Kingdom of Naples

1469 Lorenzo the Magnificent becomes ruler of Florence

1425

1450

1434 Cosimo de' Medici comes to power in Florence

1442 Naples captured by Alfonso of Aragon

1452 Birth of Leonardo da Vinci

Cosimo de' Medici

1444 Federico da Montefeltro becomes Duke of Urbino

1453 Fall of Constantinople

Filippo Brunelleschi

The Battle of Pavia (*1525*)
The French King Francis I was captured at this battle against the army of the Habsburg Emperor Charles V, who won control of Italy.

THE PROCESSION OF THE MAGI

Benozzo Gozzoli's fresco (1459) in the Palazzo Medici-Riccardi, Florence, depicts members of the Medici family and other contemporary notables. It contains many references to a great church council held in Florence in 1439

WHERE TO SEE RENAISSANCE ITALY

Many cities were flourishing centres of the arts in the 15th century. None can rival Florence (*pp262–303*) with its great palazzi and the Uffizi gallery (*pp278–81*), but Venice (*pp80–131*), Urbino (*pp360–61*) and Mantova (*p199*) all preserve great treasures. In Rome, do not miss the Vatican's Sistine Chapel and Raphael Rooms (*pp414–17*).

The **Spedale degli Innocenti** *by Brunelleschi in Florence (p269) shows the Classical symmetry and restraint of Renaissance architecture.*

Humanism
Carpaccio's painting of St Augustine is thought to show Cardinal Bessarion (c.1395–1472), one of the scholars who revived interest in Classical philosophy, especially Plato.

Lorenzo de' Medici (the Magnificent) was depicted as one of the three kings travelling to Bethlehem.

Pope Julius II
During his reign (1503–13), the worldly Julius made the papacy a major power in European politics. Raphael's portrait shows him as a shrewd old statesman.

1487 Birth of Titian

1483 Sixtus IV consecrates Sistine Chapel

1494 Italy invaded by Charles VIII of France

1503 Giuliano della Rovere elected Pope Julius II; he proves the most powerful of the Renaissance popes

Niccolò Machiavelli

1527 Rome sacked by Imperial troops

1475

1500

1475 Birth of Michelangelo

1483 Birth of Raphael

Raphael

1512 Michelangelo completes Sistine Chapel ceiling

1525 Francis I of France captured at Battle of Pavia

1513 Giovanni de' Medici crowned Pope Leo X

1498 Savonarola executed; Machiavelli secretary to ruling Council in Florence

1532 Machiavelli's book *The Prince* is published, five years after his death

The Counter-Reformation

Gian Lorenzo Bernini

AFTER THE SACK OF ROME in 1527, Italy was at the mercy of Charles V, Holy Roman Emperor and King of Spain. Pope Clement VII, who had opposed Charles, crowned him emperor in Bologna. In response to the growing threat from Protestantism, a series of reforms, known as the Counter-Reformation and backed by the Inquisition, imposed rigid orthodoxy. New religious orders, such as the Jesuits, were set up to take the battle for men's souls far overseas. The missionary spirit of the age inspired the dramatic forms of the Baroque.

ITALY IN 1550

▨ *Spanish possessions*

☐ *States allied with Spain*

Emperor Charles V and Pope Clement VII
The two former enemies settled their differences and the future destiny of Italy in the Treaty of Barcelona (1529).

The Virgin Mary
intervenes on the side of the Christians.

BAROQUE STUCCO DECORATION

This stucco relief by Giacomo Serpotta (c.1690) in the Oratory of Santa Zita in Palermo is a magnificent example of Late Baroque exuberance. The subject is a favourite of the period, the Battle of Lepanto, a great naval triumph for the combined forces of Christendom against the Turks (1571).

The centre of the ingenious creation is, in effect, a framed painting in perspective.

Baroque Architecture
Guarino Guarini's decoration of the dome of the Chapel of the Holy Shroud in Turin (see p213) was completed in 1694.

The young boy
rests his hand on a helmet, symbol of the victorious Christians.

TIMELINE

1530–37 Alessandro de' Medici ruler of Florence	**1542** Inquisition established in Rome	*Andrea Palladio*		**1580** Death of architect Palladio	**1600** Philosopher Giordano Bruno burned for heresy in Rome
	1545–63 Council of Trent sets out agenda of Counter-Reformation			**1589** Palestrina publishes setting of the Latin Hymnal	

1550		**1575**	

1540 Founding of Jesuit Order	**1541** Michelangelo completes *Last Judgment* in Sistine Chapel		**1571** Victory over Turkish fleet at Battle of Lepanto	
			1564 Birth of Galileo	
1529 Charles V crowned Holy Roman Emperor in San Petronio, Bologna		**1560** San Carlo Borromeo appointed Bishop of Milan	*Giovanni Pierluigi da Palestrina*	

Trial of Galileo
The great astronomer was often in trouble with the Inquisition. He was summoned to Rome in 1633 and forced to deny that the Earth and planets moved round the sun.

Lepanto was the last major sea battle in which Venetian galleys played an important role.

Cherubs, a favourite motif in Baroque decoration

St Ignatius Loyola
The Spanish saint was the founder of the Jesuits – sanctioned by the pope in Rome in 1540.

The turban, symbol of the defeated Turks

Revolt of Masaniello *(1647) High taxes made Spanish rule in Naples unpopular. A proposed tax on fruit sparked off this failed revolt.*

WHERE TO SEE BAROQUE ITALY

The Ecstasy of St Teresa *by Bernini (p402) has the dynamic theatricality characteristic of the best Baroque sculpture*

The Baroque is strongly associated with Rome and in particular with its great public spaces such as Piazza Navona *(pp388–9)* and the many churches by Borromini and Bernini. Other cities and towns with striking Baroque architecture include Lecce *(pp496–7)* in Puglia, Palermo *(pp510–13)*, Noto *(p527)* and Syracuse *(pp526–7)* in Sicily, and Turin *(pp212–17)*.

The Grand Tour

The Romantic poet Shelley, visitor to Italy

THE TREATY of Aix-la-Chapelle in 1748 marked the start of 50 years of peace. It was about this time that Italy, with its great art treasures and Classical ruins, including the newly excavated Pompeii, became Europe's first great tourist destination. Young English "milords" visited Rome, Florence and Venice as part of a new type of pilgrimage, the Grand Tour; while artists and poets sought inspiration in Rome's glorious past. In 1800, Napoleon, who conquered and briefly united Italy, threatened to destroy the old order, but in 1815 the status quo was restored.

Charles III's Fleet at Naples *(1753)*
Ruler of Naples from 1734 to 1759, when he became King of Spain, Charles attempted genuine political reforms.

Goethe in the Roman Campagna
Goethe toured Italy in the 1780s. Great poets who followed his example included the Romantics Keats, Shelley and Byron.

Farnese Hercules
(see p475)

Venetian Carnival
The colourful folklore of Carnival attracted many tourists, but Venice's days of greatness were over. In 1797, the proud maritime republic was ceded to Austria by Napoleon.

The Dying Galatian
(see p376)

GALLERY OF VIEWS OF ANCIENT ROME BY PANNINI
Giovanni Pannini (1691–1765) painted views of Roman ruins for foreigners. This painting is a *capriccio,* an imaginary scene incorporating many well-known views and Classical statues.

TIMELINE

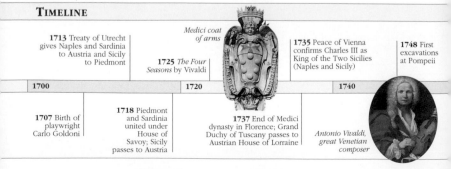

1713 Treaty of Utrecht gives Naples and Sardinia to Austria and Sicily to Piedmont

Medici coat of arms

1725 *The Four Seasons* by Vivaldi

1735 Peace of Vienna confirms Charles III as King of the Two Sicilies (Naples and Sicily)

1748 First excavations at Pompeii

1700   **1720**   **1740**

1707 Birth of playwright Carlo Goldoni

1718 Piedmont and Sardinia united under House of Savoy; Sicily passes to Austria

1737 End of Medici dynasty in Florence; Grand Duchy of Tuscany passes to Austrian House of Lorraine

Antonio Vivaldi, great Venetian composer

View of the Roman Forum by Piranesi
The popular series of etchings Vedute di Roma (Views of Rome) *by Giovanni Battista Piranesi (1720–78) inspired a new interest in excavating the ruins of ancient Rome.*

The Colosseum was as popular a subject in the 18th century as it is on today's picture postcards.

The Laocoön
(see p407)

View of the Pantheon
(see p394)

(see p407)
(see p394)

WHERE TO SEE 18TH-CENTURY ITALY

The 18th century produced two of Rome's best-loved tourist attractions: the Spanish Steps *(p399)* and the Trevi Fountain *(p400)*. It was also the age of the first purpose-built museums, including the Vatican's Museo Pio-Clementino *(p411)*. The Neo-Classical sculpture of Antonio Canova (1757–1822) was immensely popular during this period. His tomb is in Santa Maria Gloriosa dei Frari in Venice *(pp94–5)*. Of Neo-Classical buildings, the most imposing is a vast monument to enlightened despotism: the Palazzo Reale at Caserta *(p480)*.

***Pauline Borghese**, Napoleon's sister, was the model for Antonio Canova's* Venus *(1805) in the Villa Borghese collection in Rome (p429).*

Napoleon
When Napoleon conquered Italy in 1800, he was seen by many as a liberator. The enchantment wore off as he took priceless works of art back to Paris.

Congress of Vienna *(1815)*
The conference decided that Austria should keep Lombardy and Venice, thereby sowing the seeds of the Italian unification movement.

	La Scala Opera House, Milan (see p187)	**1797** Venice given to Austria by Treaty of Campo Formio; France controls rest of northern Italy	**1800–1801** Napoleon conquers Italy
	1778 La Scala opened in Milan		**1808** Murat becomes King of Naples / **1809** Pope Pius VII exiled from Rome
1760	**1780**		**1800**
1773 Pope dissolves Jesuit Order	**1780** Joseph II succeeds to Austrian throne; minor reforms in Lombardy		**1806** Joseph Bonaparte becomes King of Naples
1768 Corsica sold by Genoa to France			
1765–90 Reign of Leopold Grand Duke of Tuscany, who introduces enlightened reforms	**1796–7** Napoleon's first campaign in northern Italy		**1815** Congress of Vienna restores status quo in Italy, though Austria keeps Venice

The Risorgimento

THE WORD "RISORGIMENTO" (resurgence) describes the five decades of struggle for liberation from foreign rule, culminating in the unification of Italy in 1870. In 1848, patriots rose up against the Austrians in Milan and Venice, the Bourbons in Sicily and the pope in Rome, where a republic was declared. Garibaldi valiantly defended the republic, but all the uprisings were too localized. By 1859, the movement was better organized with Vittorio Emanuele II at its head. Two years saw the conquest of all but Venice and Rome, both of which fell within a decade.

Vittorio Emanuele

ITALY IN 1861

▢ *Kingdom of Italy*

The guns were rusty, old converted flintlocks.

Giuseppe Mazzini
(1805–72)
An exile for much of his life, Mazzini fought alongside Garibaldi to unite Italy as a republic, rather than a kingdom.

The red shirt was the badge of the Garibaldini.

Italian Railways
The short railway line from Naples to Portici was opened in 1839. Politically fragmented, Italy was slow to create an effective rail network.

Revolt of Messina
When, in 1848, Messina revolted, Ferdinand II subjected the town to a savage bombardment, earning himself the nickname King Bomba.

TIMELINE

1831 Insurrection in Romagna and Le Marche against papal rule

1840 First major railway links established

1849 Accession of Vittorio Emanuele II as ruler of Piedmont

1820	1830	1840	1850

1820s Carbonari secret society active in Papal States

1831 Mazzini founds *Giovine Italia* (Young Italy) movement

Daniele Manin, hero of the Venetian uprising of 1848

1847 Economic crisis

1848 Revolutions throughout Italy

1852 Cavour becomes prime minister of Piedmont

1849 Republic of Rome crushed by French troops

Battle of Solferino *(1859)*
With the help of a French army led by Napoleon III, the Piedmontese won Milan and Lombardy from the Austrians.

WHERE TO SEE RISORGIMENTO ITALY

Almost every town in Italy honours the heroes of the Risorgimento with a Via Garibaldi, a Via Cavour, a Piazza Vittorio, a Via Mazzini and a Via XX Settembre (the date of the fall of Rome in 1870). Many cities also have Risorgimento museums. One of the best is in Turin *(p215).*

The Victor Emmanuel Monument *(p374) is a prominent, but largely unloved, Roman landmark.*

Two old paddle steamers brought the Thousand from Quarto near Genoa.

Count Camillo di Cavour *(1810–61)*
Cavour's diplomacy as prime minister of Piedmont ensured that the House of Savoy became rulers of the new Italy. He also coined the word "Risorgimento".

The skiffs were lent by other ships moored in Marsala harbour.

Giuseppe Verdi
(1813–1901)
Composers such as Verdi, Donizetti and Rossini made the 19th century the great era of Italian opera. Verdi's early operas inspired the Risorgimento.

GARIBALDI AND THE THOUSAND

Giuseppe Garibaldi (1807–82) was a leader of courage and genius. In 1860, he landed at Marsala with 1,000 volunteers. The garrison at Palermo surrendered, Sicily fell and he went on to conquer Naples, thus presenting Vittorio Emanuele with half a kingdom.

1859 Battles of Magenta and Solferino; Piedmont acquires Lombardy from Austria and duchies of Parma, Modena and Tuscany

1861 Kingdom of Italy proclaimed with capital at Turin

Pope Pius IX, who remained a virtual prisoner in the Vatican when Rome became capital of Italy

1882 Deaths of Garibaldi and Pope Pius IX

1893 Troops sent to suppress insurrection in Sicily

1860 | **1870** | **1880** | **1890**

1866 Italy wins Venice from Austria

1878 Death of Vittorio Emanuele; accession of King Umberto I

1870 Rome falls to royalist troops and is made capital of new kingdom; Vatican announces doctrine of papal infallibility

1860 Garibaldi and the Thousand capture Kingdom of the Two Sicilies

1890 Italian colony of Eritrea established by royal decree

Twentieth-Century Italy

Fascism under Mussolini (1922–43) promised the Italians greatness, but delivered only humiliation. In spite of this, Italy has become one of Europe's leading economies with a standard of living undreamt of at the turn of the century. This has been achieved in the face of great obstacles. Since 1946, the Republic has passed through many crises: a series of unstable coalitions, the terrorist outrages in the 1970s and, recently, corruption scandals involving numerous government ministers and officials.

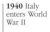

1936 Fiat produces first "Topolino" car

1922 Fascists march on Rome; Mussolini invited to form government

1918 Austrian advance halted at the river Piave, just north of Venice

1940 Italy enters World War II

1943 Allies land in Sicily; Italy signs armistice and new Badoglio government declares war on Germany

1900 Assassination of King Umberto I

1915 Italy enters World War I

1911–12 Italy conquers Libya

1900	1920	1940

1900	1920	1940

1908 Earthquake destroys many towns and villages in Calabria and eastern Sicily; Messina almost completely razed to the ground; over 150,000 die

1936 Italy conquers Abyssinia; pact with Germany, forming anti-Communist "Axis"

1920s Postwar years see continued emigration to the United States. Here, emigrants cheer as they reach New York aboard the *Giulio Cesare*

1943 Mussolini imprisoned, then freed by Germans

1946 Referendum in which Italy votes to become a republic; Christian Democrat party forms first of a long series of coalition governments

1917 Defeat at Caporetto on Italy's northeastern border; Italian troops, such as these Alpini, retreat to defensive positions

1909 In his *Futurist Manifesto*, Filippo Marinetti condemns all traditional art as too static. His idea of a new dynamic art is expressed in works such as Umberto Boccioni's bronze *Unique Forms of Continuity in Space*

1960 *La Dolce Vita*, Federico Fellini's film satire on Rome's decadent café society, is released

1978 Prime Minister Aldo Moro kidnapped and assassinated by the Red Brigades

1994 TV magnate Silvio Berlusconi becomes prime minister after forming political party "Forza Italia". Alleged financial irregularities force him to resign later that year

1996 Fire destroys La Fenice theatre in Venice

1996 Earthquake in Assisi seriously damages the Basilica di San Francesco, destroying Giotto's frescoes

1992 Judge Giovanni Falcone killed by Mafia in Sicily

1992 Scandals expose widespread corruption in the postwar political system

1966 River Arno bursts its banks, flooding Florence and damaging many priceless works of art

1990 World Cup staged in Italy

2000 Rome enters the 21st century with millions of pilgrims celebrating the Holy Year known as the Jubilee

| 1960 | 1980 | 2000 |

| 1960 | 1980 | 2000 |

1960 Olympic Games held in Rome

1978 Election of Pope John Paul II

1983 Bettino Craxi, Italy's first Socialist prime minister, forms government

1999 Roberto Benigni wins 3 Oscars for his film *La Vita e Bella*, including best actor and best foreign language film

1969 Bomb outrage in Milan at Piazza Fontana; 13 killed and many injured

1982 Italian football team wins World Cup in Spain

1997 Dario Fo wins the Nobel prize for literature

1999 Italy joins the EU common currency

1957 Treaty of Rome; Italy one of the six founder members of the European Economic Community

ITALIAN CINEMA SINCE WORLD WAR II

The social problems of late 1940s Italy inspired a wave of cinema known as Neo-Realism. Leading exponents included Roberto Rossellini, who made *Roma Città Aperta* (1945), Vittorio de Sica, the director of *Bicycle Thieves* (1948), Pierpaolo Pasolini and Luchino Visconti. Since that time, the major Italian directors have cultivated their own personal styles.

Vittorio de Sica (1901–74)

Visconti's later films, such as *Death in Venice* (1971), show formal beauty and decadence, while Federico Fellini's *La Dolce Vita* (1960) and *Roma* (1972) depict life as a grotesque carnival. Italy has also produced some commercially successful films, such as Sergio Leone's late 1960s westerns and the Oscar-winning *Cinema Paradiso* and *La Vita è Bella*.

ITALY THROUGH THE YEAR

THROUGHOUT ITALY, the variety of local character and colour is astonishing. This is mainly due to the survival of regionalism, particularly in the southern parts of the country. Old traditions, customs and lifestyles are still greatly respected and there is a deep attachment to the land, which is reflected in a healthy interest in the food and produce, as well as a perseverance of seasonal religious and secular events. Annual festivals, whether in rural or urban areas, range from wine-tasting and gastronomic celebrations to elaborate commemorations of every patron saint imaginable.

SPRING

THE ITALIAN SPRING begins early, particularly in the south. City streets and main sights are rarely overcrowded (except at Easter in Rome). The weather, however, can be unpredictable and wet in the central and northern parts of the country. Spring specialities, such as asparagus, spinach and artichokes, begin to feature on restaurant menus. This is a season of great celebration; festivals and fairs abound, especially in Sicily, and the Easter papal address always draws massive crowds to St Peter's.

Tuscan asparagus

MARCH

Mostra Vini Spumanti, *(mid-Mar)*, Madonna di Campiglio, Trentino-Alto Adige. Fair celebrating sparkling wine.
Sa Sartiglia, Oristano, Sardinia. Three-day carnival ending on Shrove Tuesday.

Procession of the Grieving Madonna on the isle of Procida

Su e zo per i ponti *(Sun, varies)*, Venice. A lively race through the city's streets, up and down the bridges.

APRIL

Procession of the Grieving Madonna *(Good Friday)*, Procida, Campania. A colourful religious procession throughout the island.
Holy Week *(Easter Week)*. Numerous Easter celebrations from Palm Sunday to Easter Sunday, throughout the country.
Papal Address *(Easter Sunday)*, Rome. The pope makes his Easter address from the Vatican.
Dance of the Devils and Death *(Easter Sunday)*, Prizzi, Sicily. Dance recital symbolizing the attempts of evil to vanquish the forces of God.
Scoppio del Carro *(Easter Sunday)*, Florence. Firework display is lit by a mechanical dove in front of the Duomo.
Festa della Madonna che Scappa in Piazza *(Easter Sunday)*, Sulmona, Abruzzo. Re-enactment of a meeting between the Virgin and the Risen Christ.
Festa degli Aquiloni *(first Sun after Easter)*, San Miniato, Tuscany. Kite lovers perform aerial acrobatics at this festival.
Festa di San Marco *(25 Apr)*, Venice. St Mark, the patron saint of Venice, is commemorated by a gondola race across St Mark's Basin.
Mostra Mercato Internazionale dell'Artigianato *(last week)*, Florence. An important European exhibition of arts and crafts.

Spring strawberries

Scoppio del Carro (Explosion of the Carriage) festival in Florence

Sagra Musicale Lucchese *(Apr–Jul)*, Lucca, Tuscany. Festival of sacred music held in Romanesque churches.

MAY

Festa di Sant'Efisio *(1 May)*, Cagliari, Sardinia. Paraders in traditional Sardinian costume.
Festa di San Nicola *(7–9 May)*, Bari, Puglia. A statue of St Nicholas is taken to the sea.
Festa dei Ceri *(15 May)*, Gubbio, Umbria. Festival, including a race with four teams carrying large candles.
Festa di San Domenico Abate *(first Thu)*, Cocullo, Abruzzo. Includes a procession with a statue of St Dominic covered with live snakes.
Festa della Mela *(late May)*, Ora (Auer), Trentino-Alto Adige. An annual "Festival of the Apple".
Greek Drama in Theatre *(May–Jun)*, Syracuse, Sicily. Festival of Greek drama.
Maggio Musicale *(May–Jun)*, Florence. This is the city's biggest arts festival, including music, drama and dance.

Street carpeted with flowers for the Infiorata in Genzano

SUMMER

SUMMER brings the crowds to Italy, particularly the cities. Italians, however, flee and head for the coast, usually in August. The queues for tourist attractions can be long and hotels are often fully booked. Festivals vary; religious events are interspersed with those of the arts and local folklore.

JUNE

Festa della Fragola
(1 Jun), Borgo San Martino, Piedmont. Musical and folkloric performances in celebration of the strawberry.
Biennale *(Jun – Sep)*, Venice. The world's biggest exhibition of contemporary art takes place during odd-numbered years only.
Infiorata *(Corpus Christi day)*, Genzano, Lazio. A procession through streets carpeted with flowers.
Festa di San Giovanni *(mid-Jun – mid-Jul)*, Turin, Piedmont. Festival in honour of the city's patron saint, John.
Calcio Storico *(24 Jun and two other days in Jun)*, Florence. Football in 16th-century costumes; fireworks.
Festa di Sant'Andrea *(27 Jun)*, Amalfi, Campania.

Fireworks and processions.
Festival dei Due Mondi *(late Jun – early Jul)*, Spoleto, Umbria. International festival of drama, music and dance.
Gioco del Ponte *(last Sun)*, Pisa. "The Bridge Parade" of marchers in antique armour.
Tevere Expo *(end Jun)*, on the Tiber, Rome. Arts and crafts, food and wine stalls, folk music and fireworks.

JULY

Corsa del Palio *(2 Jul)*, Siena. Tuscany's most famous event *(see p331)* presents a medieval flag-waving exhibition and horse race.
Festa della Madonna della Bruna *(first Sun)*, Matera, Basilicata. A lively procession of clergymen and knights in costume.

Festa dei Noiantri *(last two weeks of Jul)*, Rome. A colourful race of the city's horse-drawn carriages.
Festa della Santa Maria del Carmine *(16 Jul)*, Naples. Featuring the illumination of the city's bell tower.
Umbria Jazz *(Jul)*, Perugia. World-famous jazz artists perform.

Musician from Florence's Calcio

International Film Festival *(Jul–Aug)*, Taormina, Sicily.

The Sienese Palio in action

Opera Festival *(Jul–Aug)*, Verona, Veneto. Renowned opera festival *(see p137)* overlapping with the **Shakespeare Festival**, providing music, drama, opera and dance.

AUGUST

Medieval Palio *(first weekend Aug)* Feltre, Veneto. Parades and archery competitions, medieval-style.
Festa del Mare *(15 Aug)*, Diano Marina, Liguria. This "Festival of the Sea" boasts a spectacular firework display.
Festa dei Candelieri *(14 Aug)*, Sassari, Sardinia. "Festival of the Candle", dating from the 16th century.
Corsa del Palio *(16 Aug)*, Siena, Tuscany. See July entry.
Venice Film Festival *(late Aug – early Sep)*. International festival on the Lido.
Rossini Festival *(Aug – Sep)*, Pesaro, Le Marche. A celebration of the composer's work, in his birthplace.
Settimane Musicali di Stresa *(late Aug – end Sep)*, Stresa, Lombardy. Four weeks of concerts and recitals.

Sun, sand and sea – essential ingredients of a Tuscan beach holiday

AUTUMN

AUTUMN IS A SLOW, gentle season in Italy but that doesn't mean there are fewer festivals and fairs. In addition to the various religious events at this time of year, gastronomic festivals are especially popular, commemorating such delectables as chestnuts, local cheeses, sausages and mushrooms. Autumn is the season of the *vendemmia*, the grape harvest, which is often used as an excuse for village festivities at which the latest local wines flow freely.

The climate *(see pp68–9)* in late autumn is often cold and wet in the north. The south, however, can be quite warm right through October.

Advertisement for the September Palio in Asti, Piedmont

SEPTEMBER

Sagra dell'Uva *(early Sep)*, Rome. Harvest festival with grapes at bargain prices and lots of folk entertainment.
Neapolitan Song Contest *(7 Sep)*, Piazza di Piedigrotta, Naples. Usually entered by couples; the singer often plays a mandolin, while their partner plays the castanets.
Festa di San Sebastiano e Santa Lucia *(1–3 Sep)*, Sassari, Sardinia. Includes a contest where competitors improvise short poems.
Procession of the Macchina di Santa Rosa *(3 Sep)*, Viterbo, Lazio. Commemoration of the saint's body being transported to the Church of Santa Rosa in 1258.

The widely cultivated olive tree

Giostra del Saracino *(first Sun)*, Arezzo, Umbria. Joust of the Saracen and knights, dating from the 13th century.
Regata Storica *(first Sun)*, Venice. A procession of historic boats followed by a colourful gondola race.
Human chess game *(second week)*, Marostica, near Vicenza. A popular costumed game held in the main square every even year.
Rassegna del Chianti Classico *(second week)*, Chianti, Tuscany. Celebration of the local wines.
The Miracle of San Gennaro *(19 Sep)*, Naples. Re-enactment of the liquefaction of the saint's blood, in a lively mass at the Duomo.
Palio *(third Sun)*, Asti, Piedmont. Includes a costumed medieval procession and bareback horse racing.

OCTOBER

Amici della Musica *(Oct–Apr)*, Florence, Tuscany. The "Friends of Music" concert season begins.
Fiera del Tartufo *(first Sun)*, Alba, Piedmont. A variety of events centred around the locally grown white truffle.
Festa di San Francesco *(4 Oct)*, Assisi, Umbria. Feast in honour of the saint.
Wine festivals *(first week)*, Castelli Romani, Lazio.
Sagra del Tordo *(last Sun)* Montalcino, Tuscany. Celebration of the thrush; costumed archery contests.
Festa dell'Uva *(dates vary)*, Bolzano, Trentino-Alto Adige. Grape festival with live music and a costumed procession featuring allegoric carts.

A roast chestnut stall in autumn

NOVEMBER

Festa dei Popoli *(Nov–Dec)*, Florence, Tuscany. Film festival showing films in their original languages with Italian sub-titles.
Festa della Salute *(21 Nov)*, Venice. Cherished by Venetian locals, this feast gives thanks to the Virgin Mary in memory of a 1630 plague.

The human chess game in the town square of Marostica

WINTER

THERE ARE FAIRS, markets and religious events up and down the country at this time of year. Neapolitan Christmas cribs are famous and nearly every church has one. The Christmas holiday itself is low key; more is made of other religious events such as the liquefaction of San Gennaro's blood in Naples and the Carnevale in Venice.

Rome during one of its rare snowfalls

DECEMBER

Festa di Sant'Ambrogio
(early Dec), Milan. The official opening of La Scala Opera season *(see p187).*
Festa della Madonna di Loreto *(10 Dec)*, Loreto, Le Marche. Celebration of the Virgin's Holy House.
Mercato della Befana *(mid-Dec–mid-Jan)*, Rome. Well-known Christmas fair held in Piazza Navona.
The Miracle of San Gennaro *(19 Dec)*, Naples. See September.
Christmas fair *(mid Dec)*, Naples. Fair selling crib figures and decorations.
Fiaccole di Natale *(Christmas Eve)*, Abbadia di San Salvatore, Tuscany. Features carols and processions in memory of the first shepherds.
Midnight Mass *(24 Dec)*, at churches all over the country.
Christmas Day *(25 Dec)*, St Peter's Square, Rome. Public blessing by the pope.

La Befana at Piazza Navona, Rome

JANUARY

Capodanno *(1 Jan)*, all over the country. New Year's Day is celebrated with fireworks

and volleys from hunters firing into the air to scare off ghosts and spirits of the old year and welcome in the new.
La Befana *(6 Jan)*, throughout Italy. Children's holiday with presents and sweets.
Pitti Immagine Uomo, Pitti Immagine Donna, Pitti Immagine Bimbo, Fortezza da Basso, Florence. Month of international fashion shows for women, men and children.
Festa di San Sebastiano *(20 Jan)*, Dolceacqua, Liguria. A laurel tree covered with colourful communion hosts is carried through town.
Festa d'o' Cippo di Sant'-Antonio *(17 Jan)*, Naples. A procession for St Anthony, protector of animals.
Carnevale *(a month-long event finishing Shrove Tue)*, Viareggio, Tuscany. A carnival famous for its lively, topically themed floats.
Fair of St Orsa *(30–31 Jan)*, Aosta, Valle d'Aosta. Exhibition of traditional arts and crafts.

Carnevale, Viareggio

FEBRUARY

Carnevale *(last ten days before Lent, finishing Shrove Tuesday)*, Venice. Pre-Lent festival meaning "farewell to meat". Events are

organized, but anyone can buy a mask and watch the array of gorgeous costumes on show.
Sagra delle Mandorle in Fiore *(first or second week)*, Agrigento, Sicily. Annual almond blossom celebration.
Bacanal del Gnoco *(11 Feb)*, Verona. Traditional masked procession with both international and local allegorical floats. Masked balls are held in the town's squares.
Carnevale *(dates vary)*, Mamoiada, Sardinia. Processions include *mamuthones* wearing sinister black masks.

Carnevale revellers in Venice

PUBLIC HOLIDAYS

New Year's Day (1 Jan)
Epiphany (6 Jan)
Easter Sunday and Monday
Liberation Day (25 Apr)
Labour Day (1 May)
Ferragosto (15 Aug)
All Saints' Day (1 Nov)
Immaculate Conception (8 Dec)
Christmas Day (25 Dec)
Santo Stefano (26 Dec)

The Sporting Year

FOOTBALL IS BY FAR the most important sport in Italy, uniting the country when the national team *(Azzurri)* plays. Other sports throughout the year also attract a large following, so fans are never at a loss for varied activities. For most big sporting events, tickets can be obtained for cash at club outlets such as the venue itself. Agencies provide hard-to-get tickets at often higher prices. Beware of the inevitable touts at popular events as their expensive tickets may not be valid.

World Cup mania

Calcio Fiorentino, one of Italy's few indigenous sports, is said to be the medieval precursor of modern football.

The professional water polo season takes place from March through to July. The Canottieri Napoli team play consistently well through the championship.

Coppa Italia football final

Memorial d'Aloia rowing competition, held in Umbria

Italian Tennis Open, Rome

Giro d'Italia is one of the world's most prestigious cycling races. Marco Pantani, left, won both the Giro and the Tour de France in 1998.

January	February	March	April	May	June

Indoor Athletics Championships

Swimming is a popular competitive water sport and the Indoor Championships are held in February. Olympic medallist Luca Sacchi is one of Italy's top swimmers.

International Showjumping, Rome

The Italian leg of the Circuito Mondiale in Mugello. Luca Cadalora was champion in 1991.

Although the San Marino Grand Prix is not technically an Italian motor race, it is held each May at Imola, near the home of Ferrari (see p252).

The Italian Outdoor Swimming Championships *are held each year in July. Top swimmer Giorgio Lamberti and his team mates, pictured above, celebrate a relay team victory.*

Italy has some of the best ski resorts in Europe, and in 2006 Turin will host the Winter Olympics. Above is Alberto Tomba, winner of the 94–95 Cup.

The Italian Grand Prix, *held annually at Monza, is Italy's round of the international Formula One World Championship. Giancarlo Fisichella is one of Italy's best up-and-coming young drivers.*

Trofeo dei Templi rowing competition, Sicily

The San Remo Car Rally, *held each year in October, was made famous by driver Micky Biason and the Lancia Delta Integrale.*

	August	September	October	November	December

Roberto Baggio, below right, in action at the 1994 World Cup

Siena Palio (*see p331*), held on 2 July and 16 August

The Italian football *season runs from September through to June. It culminates with the Coppa Italia final, which is equivalent to the British FA Cup. Italy's football obsession, however, reaches fever pitch when the World Cup takes place every four years.*

The Outdoor Athletics Championship *has become very popular in recent years, especially the steeplechase, where Francesco Panetta made his name.*

KEY TO SPORTING SEASONS

	Football
	Water polo
	Rugby
	Basketball
	Volleyball
	Skiing

The Climate of Italy

THE ITALIAN PENINSULA has a varied climate falling into three distinct geographical regions. Cold Alpine winters and warm, wet summers characterize the northern regions. In the extensive Po Valley, arid summers contrast with freezing, damp winters. The rest of Italy has a pleasant climate with long, hot summers and mild winters. Cooler weather along the backbone of the Apennines can bring snow during the winter months.

TRENTINO-ALTO ADIGE

°C				
	16	28	17	
	4	17	5	5
				-5
☼	6 hrs	8 hrs	4 hrs	2 hrs
☂	67 mm	100 mm	83 mm	20 mm
month	Apr	Jul	Oct	Jan

Average monthly maximum temperature

Average monthly minimum temperature

Average daily hours of sunshine

Average monthly rainfall

LOMBARDY

°C				
	18	28	17	
	8	18	10	6
				-1
☼	5 hrs	9 hrs	5 hrs	3 hrs
☂	74 mm	78 mm	89 mm	64 mm
month	Apr	Jul	Oct	Jan

VALLE D'AOSTA AND PIEDMONT

°C				
	17	26	17	
	6	15	7	7
				-2.5
☼	5 hrs	9 hrs	4 hrs	3 hrs
☂	95 mm	87 mm	85 mm	45 mm
month	Apr	Jul	Oct	Jan

LIGURIA

°C				
	18	28	21	
	11.5	20	14	12
				6.5
☼	7 hrs	9 hrs	8 hrs	4 hrs
☂	66 mm	30 mm	74 mm	69 mm
month	Apr	Jul	Oct	Jan

TUSCANY

°C				
	17	29	20	
	8	16	15	10
				2
☼	8 hrs	11 hrs	6 hrs	5 hrs
☂	72 mm	30 mm	90 mm	65 mm
month	Apr	Jul	Oct	Jan

SARDINIA

°C				
	19	29	22	
	10	20	14	14
				7
☼	8 hrs	11 hrs	6 hrs	4 hrs
☂	31 mm	7 mm	48 mm	50 mm
month	Apr	Jul	Oct	Jan

EMILIA-ROMAGNA

°C				
	17	30	16	
	8.5	19	10	4
				-1
☼	6 hrs	11 hrs	5 hrs	3 hrs
☂	58 mm	39 mm	81 mm	46 mm
month	Apr	Jul	Oct	Jan

Trento

Aosta · Milano · Brescia · Verona · Padov

· Torino

Parma · Modena · Bologn

Genova R

FIREN

· Livorno

Olbia ·

· Sassari

Cagliari

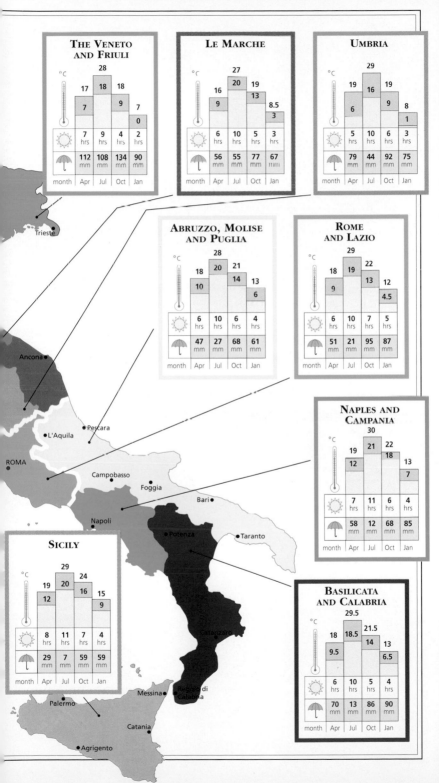

THE VENETO AND FRIULI

°C

month	Apr	Jul	Oct	Jan
	17	28	18	
	7	18	9	7
				0
☀	7 hrs	9 hrs	4 hrs	2 hrs
☂	112 mm	108 mm	134 mm	90 mm

LE MARCHE

°C

month	Apr	Jul	Oct	Jan
	16	27	19	
	9	20	13	8.5
				3
☀	6 hrs	10 hrs	5 hrs	3 hrs
☂	56 mm	55 mm	77 mm	67 mm

UMBRIA

°C

month	Apr	Jul	Oct	Jan
	19	29	19	
	6	16	9	8
				1
☀	5 hrs	10 hrs	6 hrs	3 hrs
☂	79 mm	44 mm	92 mm	75 mm

ABRUZZO, MOLISE AND PUGLIA

°C

month	Apr	Jul	Oct	Jan
	18	28	21	
	10	20	14	13
				6
☀	6 hrs	10 hrs	6 hrs	4 hrs
☂	47 mm	27 mm	68 mm	61 mm

ROME AND LAZIO

°C

month	Apr	Jul	Oct	Jan
	18	29	22	
	9	19	13	12
				4.5
☀	6 hrs	10 hrs	7 hrs	5 hrs
☂	51 mm	21 mm	95 mm	87 mm

NAPLES AND CAMPANIA

°C

month	Apr	Jul	Oct	Jan
	19	30	22	
	12	21	18	13
				7
☀	7 hrs	11 hrs	6 hrs	4 hrs
☂	58 mm	12 mm	68 mm	85 mm

SICILY

°C

month	Apr	Jul	Oct	Jan
	19	29	24	
	12	20	16	15
				9
☀	8 hrs	11 hrs	7 hrs	4 hrs
☂	29 mm	7 mm	59 mm	59 mm

BASILICATA AND CALABRIA

°C

month	Apr	Jul	Oct	Jan
	18	29.5	21.5	
	9.5	18.5	14	13
				6.5
☀	6 hrs	10 hrs	5 hrs	4 hrs
☂	70 mm	13 mm	86 mm	90 mm

Trieste
Ancona
L'Aquila
Pescara
ROMA
Campobasso
Foggia
Bari
Napoli
Potenza
Taranto
Catanzaro
Messina
Reggio di Calabria
Palermo
Catania
Agrigento

NORTHEAST ITALY

Northeast Italy at a Glance

THE SHEER VARIETY TO BE FOUND in northeast Italy makes it a fascinating area to explore. The majestic Dolomites dominate the north, straddling Trentino-Alto Adige and the Veneto, and are dotted with medieval castles and modern skiing resorts. On the plain, the cities of Verona, Vicenza and Padua are all noted for outstanding architecture and museums, while the rural hinterland boasts beautiful villas. The incomparable and spectacular city of Venice, with its magnificent monuments, rises from the lagoon. Further east, in Friuli, there are important Roman remains. This map pinpoints some of the highlights.

*Castel Tirolo,
Merano*

TRENTINO-ALTO ADIGE
(See pp160–69)

*Palazzo Pretorio,
Trento*

The Veneto

Alto Adige *is a dramatic region of snow-covered mountain valleys scattered with forbidding castles and onion-domed churches in the Tyrolean style* (see pp164–5).

The Dolomites (see pp78–9) *form the spectacular backdrop to many towns in northeast Italy, among them Trento, the region's capital* (see pp168–9).

*La Rotonda,
Vicenza*

*Ponte Scaligero,
Verona*

0 kilometres   40

0 miles   20

Verona *is one of the loveliest cities in the Veneto, boasting the Castelvecchio and a Roman arena now used for performances of opera* (see pp136–41).

Vicenza, *a model Renaissance city, is dominated by the buildings of Palladio, such as the Palazzo della Ragione and La Rotonda* (see pp144–7).

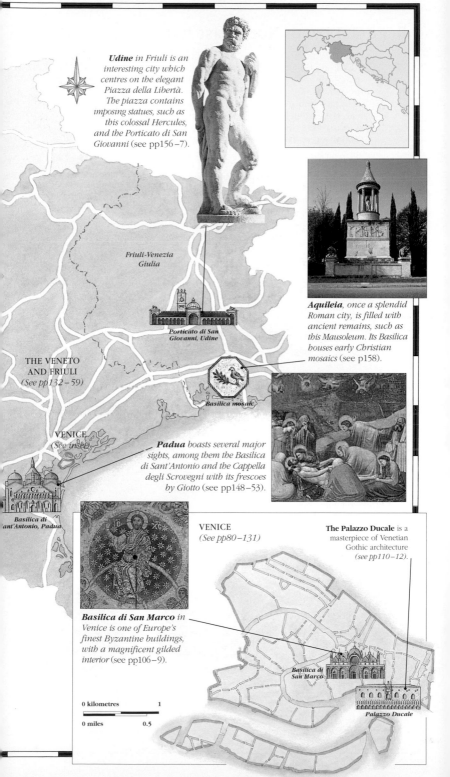

Udine in Friuli is an interesting city which centres on the elegant Piazza della Libertà. The piazza contains imposing statues, such as this colossal Hercules, and the Porticato di San Giovanni (see pp156–7).

Friuli-Venezia Giulia

Porticato di San Giovanni, Udine

Aquileia, once a splendid Roman city, is filled with ancient remains, such as this Mausoleum. Its Basilica houses early Christian mosaics (see p158).

THE VENETO AND FRIULI
(See pp132–59)

Basilica mosaic

VENICE
(See inset)

Padua boasts several major sights, among them the Basilica di Sant'Antonio and the Cappella degli Scrovegni with its frescoes by Giotto (see pp148–53).

Basilica di ant'Antonio, Padua

VENICE
(See pp80–131)

The Palazzo Ducale is a masterpiece of Venetian Gothic architecture (see pp110–12).

Basilica di San Marco in Venice is one of Europe's finest Byzantine buildings, with a magnificent gilded interior (see pp106–9).

Basilica di San Marco

Palazzo Ducale

0 kilometres   1

0 miles   0.5

Regional Food: Northeast Italy

Mᴀɴʏ ᴛʀᴀᴅɪᴛɪᴏɴᴀʟ sᴘᴇᴄɪᴀʟɪᴛɪᴇs of the Veneto are dominated, not surprisingly, by fresh fish and seafood from Lake Garda and the Adriatic. This is complemented by seasonal produce – peas, courgettes, asparagus from Bassano del Grappa, radicchio from Treviso – and meat and cheese from the mainland. Pasta is eaten throughout the northeast, but more typical is polenta, made from maize flour, and also the many types of risotto. The influences from neighbouring countries and trading partners may be tasted in the sweet and sour, spicy or pickled dishes found throughout the region, from the mountains in the north to the beaches of the south.

Gelati

Radicchio alla Griglia *is a dish of slightly bitter red endive leaves from Treviso which are grilled lightly over a hot fire.*

Crab
Mussels
Bream
Squid
Prawns
Scallops
Red mullet

Antipasto di Frutti di Mare *is a mixed seafood platter, dressed with a little olive oil and lemon juice. It is a particular favourite in Venice, where the seafood comes fresh from the Adriatic.*

Fiori di Zucchini, *a seasonal delight, are courgette flowers stuffed with delicate fish mousse then fried in a light batter.*

Brodo di Pesce, *or fish soup, is typically Venetian and served all along the coast. It usually contains a mixture of fish, and is sometimes flavoured with saffron from Friuli.*

Risotto alle Seppie *contains cuttlefish ink, which colours the rice a dramatic black in this traditional risotto.*

Risi e Bisi, *a soft and liquid risotto – almost a thick soup – is made of rice with fresh peas and small pieces of bacon.*

Carpaccio, *wafer-thin slices of raw beef sprinkled with oil, is here served with rocket leaves and slivers of Parmesan cheese.*

Zuppa di Cozze *is a classic way of cooking mussels, with a delicious sauce of white wine, garlic and parsley.*

Spaghetti alle Vongole *often appears on coastal menus: it is spaghetti with fresh clams in a piquant, chilli-pepper sauce.*

Polenta*, like pasta, is a filling staple of the Italian diet. Made from maize, it is often grilled and served with a tasty sauce.*

Sarde in Saor *is a traditional Venetian dish of fried fresh sardines marinated in a sweet and sour sauce.*

Anguille in Umido *are eels, gently stewed in an aromatic tomato sauce flavoured with white wine and garlic.*

Fegato alla Veneziana *is a traditional Venetian speciality of tender calf's liver, lightly cooked on a bed of onions.*

Tiramisù*, Italy's most famous dessert, is a wonderfully rich blend of coffee-soaked sponge cake and mascarpone cheese.*

THE WINES OF THE NORTHEAST

The Veneto produces large quantities of everyday wines – red, white and rosé *(chiaretto)*. When choosing an unknown white, you might select a Bianco di Custoza rather than an anonymous Soave. But do not rule out Soave; there are some fine examples, notably by Pieropan and Anselmi. The best whites from the northeast come from Friuli, where winemakers Puiatti, Schiopetto, Jermann and Gravner excel in their craft. Trentino-Alto Adige, too, produces some crisp whites. Much light and fruity red wine is produced near Bardolino and Valpolicella, with some outstanding bottles coming from Allegrini and Masi. Recioto della Valpolicella is a rich, sweet dessert wine, while Recioto Amarone is less sweet, but stronger still.

Recioto Amarone *is a rich and full-bodied red wine, full of fruit and very high in alcohol.*

Bianco di Custoza *is a dry white "super Soave" from the eastern shores of Lake Garda. Good white wine producers in the Veneto region include Pieropan, Anselmi, Maculan, Tedeschi, Allegrini and Cavalchina.*

Pieropan *produces some of Soave's finest quality wine. The single-vineyard wines from this renowned estate are excellent.*

Prosecco *is the Veneto's own sparkling wine, and a delightful aperitivo. It may be secco (dry) or amabile (medium-sweet).*

Bianco di Custoza

Collio Pinot Bianco

Collio Pinot Bianco *is a superb, fragrant white wine made in the Collio hills next to the Slovenian border. Puiatti is a top producer.*

Understanding Architecture in Venice and the Veneto

TRADE CONTACT WITH THE EAST led medieval Venice to develop its own exotic style – known as Venetian Gothic – blending Byzantine domes and Islamic minarets with European Gothic pointed arches and quatrefoils. In the 16th century, Palladio introduced his interpretations of Classical architecture through a series of churches, public buildings and rural villas in Venice and the Veneto. The 17th century brought the Baroque style, though its exuberance was tempered by Palladio-influenced restraint.

**Andrea Palladio
(1508 – 80)**

THE ARCHITECTURE OF VENICE: BYZANTINE TO BAROQUE

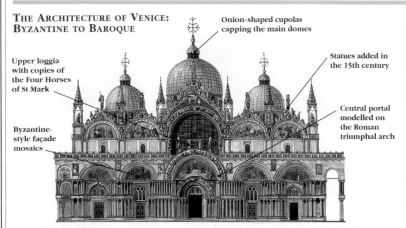

Onion-shaped cupolas capping the main domes

Upper loggia with copies of the Four Horses of St Mark

Statues added in the 15th century

Byzantine-style façade mosaics

Central portal modelled on the Roman triumphal arch

The Basilica di San Marco, western Europe's finest Byzantine church (completed 11th century), was given lavish treatment to make it a dazzling shrine for the relics of St Mark, the Evangelist, and a fitting symbol of Venetian aspirations (see pp106–9).

THE GENIUS OF PALLADIO

Doric columns supporting the ground floor, Ionic above

Shaded loggias for escaping the heat

Palazzo Chiericati is a huge mansion of 1550, its simple style borrowed from the ancient Romans. It was once surrounded by water to reflect the statues of Classical deities along its roof (see p146).

Symmetrical façade

Arcades linking the wings to the central block

Villa Barbaro at Masèr was one of the villas designed by Palladio from the 1550s when it became fashionable for rich Venetians to acquire rural estates. This villa is typical, combining a working farm, housed in the side wings, with the elegant buildings of a country house (see p143).

WHERE TO SEE THE ARCHITECTURE

A vaporetto trip along the Grand Canal in Venice *(see pp84–7)* is a splendid way of getting an overview of Venetian architecture. Ca' d'Oro, Ca' Rezzonico and Ca' Pesaro may also be visited as they contain museums and a visit to the Basilica di San Marco

Typical Venetian Gothic window

and the Palazzo Ducale is a must. There are numerous examples of Palladio's architecture in the Veneto, but the star is the Villa Barbaro *(see p143)*. Several of his villas line the Brenta Canal *(see p154)*, and the town of Vicenza *(see pp144–7)* is full of his buildings, including La Rotonda, his famous villa.

Arcading influenced by the Palazzo Ducale

Florid tracery inlaid with azure

Finials once covered in gold leaf

***Ca d'Oro**, the 15th-century "House of Gold", reveals Moorish influence in its roof finials and sinuous pointed arches (see p90).*

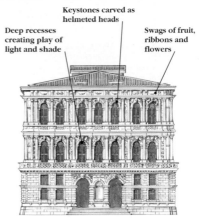

Keystones carved as helmeted heads

Deep recesses creating play of light and shade

Swags of fruit, ribbons and flowers

***The 17th-century Ca' Pesaro** typifies the Venetian Baroque style – Classical columns and rich, but subtle ornamentation (see p85).*

Giant composite columns

Istrian marble, chosen to catch the changing light of the lagoon

Statues and memorials to patrons of the church

***San Giorgio Maggiore**, built in 1559–80, is marvellously sited at the entrance to the Venetian inner harbour. It broke from the prevailing Gothic style, introducing the clean simplicity and harmonious proportions of Classical architecture to Venice, and more resembles an ancient Roman temple than a Christian church (see pp116–17).*

Pediment with coat of arms

Sundials at each end

The Dolomites

THE DOLOMITES ARE THE MOST DISTINCTIVE and beautiful mountains in Italy. They were formed of mineralized coral which was laid down beneath the sea during the Triassic era, and uplifted when the European and African continental plates dramatically collided 60 million years ago. Unlike the glacier-eroded saddles and ridges of the main body of the Alps, the pale rocks here have been carved by the corrosive effects of ice, sun and rain, sculpting the cliffs, spires and "organ pipes" that we see today. The eastern and western ranges of the Dolomites have slightly different characteristics; the eastern section is the more awe-inspiring, especially the Catinaccio (or Rosengarten) range which is particularly beautiful, turning rose pink in the dawn sunlight.

Onion dome, a
common local feature

STRADA DELLE DOLOMITI

One of the most spectacular routes through the Dolomites links Bolzano *(see p166)* with Cortina d'Ampezzo *(see p155)*. It follows the lie of the land, passing some of the greatest peaks, and the most majestic landscape.

DISTINCTIVE PEAKS OF THE DOLOMITES

The peaks of the Dolomites include several with distinctive shapes and some of the highest mountains in the range. Many are easily identifiable and have been individually named.

Marmolada 3,343 m (10,968 ft)

Sasso Lungo 3,179 m (10,430 ft)

Cinque Torri 2,366 m (7,762 ft)

The Cinque Torri *or Five Towers rise from a single base between Canazei and Cortina d'Ampezzo.*

Sasso Lungo *is a tall peak easily recognized by its distinctive scar. It is joined to the Sasso Piatto.*

Marmolada *is the highest peak in the Dolomite chain. A cable-car ascends to 3,000 m above the glacier.*

Lago di Misurina is a large and beautiful lake lying beside the resort of Misurina. The crystal clear waters reflect the surrounding mountains, mirroring various peaks such as the distinctive and dramatic Sorapiss, in shimmering colours.

Outdoor activities in this area of dramatic landscapes include skiing in winter, and walking and rambling along the footpaths, and to picnic sites, in summer. Chair-lifts from the main resorts provide easy access up into the mountains themselves, transporting you into some breathtaking scenery.

Torri del Vaiolet 2,243 m (7,375 ft)	Tre Cime di Lavaredo 2,999 m (9,839 ft)

The Torri del Vaiolet is part of the beautiful Catinaccio range, known for its colour.

Tre Cime di Lavaredo or Drei Zinnen dominate the valleys north of the Lago di Misurina.

NATURE IN THE DOLOMITES

Forests and meadows support a breathtaking richness of wildlife in the region. Alpine plants, which flower between June and September, have evolved their miniature form to survive the harsh winds.

The Flora

Gentian roots are used to make a bitter local liqueur.

The orange mountain lily thrives on sun-baked slopes.

The pretty burser's saxifrage grows in clusters on rocks.

Devil's claw has distinctive pink flower heads.

The Fauna

The ptarmigan changes its plumage from mottled brown in summer to snow white in winter for effective camouflage. It feeds on mountain berries and young plant shoots.

The chamois, a shy mountain antelope prized for its soft skin, is protected in the national parks, where hunting is forbidden.

Roe deer are very common as their natural predators – wolves and lynx – have now died out. Their keen appetite for tree saplings causes problems for foresters.

VENICE

LYING IN THE *extreme northeast of Italy, Venice, gateway to the Orient, became an independent Byzantine province in the 10th century. Exclusive trading links with the East and victory in the Crusade of 1204 brought wealth and power, which were only gradually eroded by European and Turkish rivals. Today, Venice's ties are with the local Veneto region which stretches from the flat river plains to the Dolomites.*

Venice is one of the few cities in the world that can be truly described as unique. It survives against all the odds, built on a series of low mud banks amid the tidal waters of the Adriatic, and regularly subject to floods. During the Middle Ages, under the leadership of successive doges, Venice expanded its power and influence throughout the Mediterranean to Constantinople (modern Istanbul). The immense wealth of the city was celebrated in art and architecture throughout the city.

The riches of St Mark's alone bear witness to Venice's position as a world power from the 12th to 14th centuries. After slowly losing ground to the new states of Europe, however, it fell to Napoleon in 1797. Finally, Venice joined the Kingdom of Italy in 1866, so bringing unity to the country for the first time in its history. Today, Venice has found a new role. Her palazzi have become museums, shops, hotels and apartments and her convents have been turned into centres for art restoration. Yet little of the essential fabric of Venice has altered in 200 years. The city's sounds are still those of footsteps and the cries of boatmen. The only engines are those of barges delivering supplies or waterbuses ferrying passengers between stops. The same well-worn streets are still trodden. More than 12 million visitors a year succumb to the magic of this improbable place whose "streets are full of water" and where the glories of the past are evident at every turn.

A busy street on the island of Burano, with its distinctive, brightly painted houses

◁ Gondola prows, with their characteristic *ferri*, and Santa Maria della Salute in the background

Exploring Venice

VENICE IS DIVIDED into six ancient administrative districts or *sestieri*: Cannaregio, Castello, San Marco, Dorsoduro, San Polo and Santa Croce. Visitors usually start at Piazza San Marco, heading for the magnificent Basilica and the Palazzo Ducale, probably the busiest part of the city. You can walk to most places in Venice itself, and take a ride on a waterbus to any of the islands.

SIGHTS AT A GLANCE

Churches

Basilica di San Marco pp106–9 18
Madonna dell'Orto 1
San Giacomo dell'Orio 6
San Giovanni Grisostomo 3
San Giovanni in Bragora 29
Santi Giovanni e Paolo 24
Santa Maria Formosa 26
Santa Maria Gloriosa dei Frari pp94–5 8
Santa Maria dei Miracoli 4
Santa Maria della Salute 17
San Nicolò dei Mendicoli 13
San Pantalon 11
San Polo 7
San Rocco 10
San Sebastiano 14
Santo Stefano 23
San Zaccaria 27

Buildings and Monuments

Arsenale 30
Campanile 21

Palazzo Ducale pp110–12 19
Rialto 5
Scuola di San Giorgio degli Schiavoni 28
Statue of Colleoni 25
Torre dell'Orologio 20

Museums and Galleries

Accademia pp102–3 15
Ca' d'Oro 2
Ca' Rezzonico 12
Museo Correr 22
Peggy Guggenheim Collection 16
Scuola Grande di San Rocco pp96–7 9

Lagoon

Burano 33
Murano 32
Torcello pp118–9 34

```
0 metres          500
0 yards           500
```

KEY

Street-by-Street: San Polo *pp92–3*

Street-by-Street: Dorsoduro *pp98–9*

Street-by-Street: Piazza San Marco *pp104–5*

✈ International airport

FS Railway station

⛴ Ferry boarding point

⬛ *Vaporetto* boarding point

Traghetto crossing (see p636)

Gondola mooring

ℹ Tourist information

Santa Maria della Salute, at the mouth of the Grand Canal

SEE ALSO
- *Street Finder* pp120–29
- *Where to Stay* pp542–4
- *Where to Eat* pp578–9

LOCATOR MAP

Verona
Padua
VENICE

THE LAGOON

Marco Polo

Mestre

Venezia

GETTING AROUND

The only road into Venice is the N11 from Mestre, which carries you over the causeway to the Tronchetto and Piazzale Roma where there are car parks and bus stops. Rail travellers arrive at Santa Lucia station on the Grand Canal. In the city, public transport is by *vaporetto*, or waterbus – the No.1 is best for sightseeing as it travels the length of the Grand Canal (*see pp130–31*).

The Grand Canal: Santa Lucia to the Rialto

THE BEST WAY to view the Grand Canal as it winds through the heart of the city is from a *vaporetto*, or waterbus. Several lines travel the length of the canal *(see p636)*. The palaces lining the waterway were built over a span of five centuries and present a panoramic survey of the city's history, almost all bearing the name of some once-great Venetian family.

San Marcuola
The church was rebuilt in the 18th century, but the planned new façade overlooking the canal was never completed.

San Geremia houses the relics of St Lucy, once kept in the church of Santa Lucia where the railway station now stands.

Palazzo Labia
Between 1745–50, Giambattista Tiepolo decorated the ballroom with scenes from the life of Cleopatra.

Canale di Cannaregio

Palazzo Corner-Contarini

San Marcuola

Ferrovia

Ponte degli Scalzi

Fondaco dei Turchi
A warehouse for Turkish traders in the 17th–19th centuries, this is now the Natural History Museum.

San Simeone Piccolo
This 18th-century domed church is based on the Pantheon in Rome.

THE GONDOLAS OF VENICE

The gondola has been a part of Venice since the 11th century. With its slim hull and flat underside, the craft is perfectly adapted to negotiating narrow, shallow canals. There is a slight leftward curve to the prow, which counteracts the force of the oar, preventing the gondola from going round in circles.

In 1562 it was decreed that all gondolas should be black to stop people making an ostentatious show of their wealth. For special occasions they are decorated with flowers. Today, gondola rides are expensive and usually taken by tourists *(see p637)*. However, *traghetti* (gondola ferries) are a cheap, convenient way of crossing the Grand Canal.

Gondolas tied up by steps

Ca' d'Oro
The delicate Gothic tracery of the façade makes this a striking landmark. Its art collection (see p90) includes Bernini's model for a fountain (c.1648).

See Venice Street Finder maps 1, 2, 3

LOCATOR MAP

Palazzo Vendramin Calergi
This is one of the finest early Renaissance palaces in Venice. The German composer Richard Wagner (left) died here in 1883.

The Pescheria has been the site of a busy fish market for six centuries.

Palazzo Sagredo
Graceful Veneto-Byzantine and Gothic arches are both featured on the waterfront façade.

Palazzo Michiel dalle Colonne takes its name from its distinctive colonnade.

The Rialto Bridge *(see p93)* spans the canal in the commercial heart of the city.

Ca' d'Oro

San Stae
The façade of this Baroque church is richly adorned with statues. It is a popular concert venue.

San Stae

Ca' Pesaro
The huge, stately Baroque palace today houses a gallery of modern art and the Oriental Museum.

Rialto

The Grand Canal: the Rialto to San Marco

AFTER PASSING the Rialto, the canal doubles back on itself along a stretch known as La Volta (the bend). It then widens out and the views become more spectacular approaching San Marco. Façades may have faded and foundations frayed with the tides, yet the canal remains, in the words of the French ambassador in 1495, "the most beautiful street in the world".

Palazzo Mocenigo
Lord Byron stayed in this huge 18th-century palace in 1818.

Sant' Angelo

San Tomà

Palazzo Garzoni
is a renovated Gothic palace, now part of the university.

Ca' Rezzonico
Now a museum of 18th-century Venice (see p99), the palace was the last home of the poet Robert Browning, seen here with his son Pen.

San Samuele

Ca' Rezzonico

Palazzo Grassi
The elegant palazzo dates from the 1730s. Bought by Fiat in 1984, it is now used for art exhibitions.

Ponte dell'Accademia

Accademia

Palazzo Capello Malipiero
The palace was rebuilt in 1622. Beside it stands the 12th-century campanile of San Samuele.

Accademia
The world's greatest collection of Venetian paintings is housed here in the former Scuola della Carità (see pp102–3), which has a Baroque façade by Giorgio Massari.

Palazzo Barbaro
Novelist Henry James wrote The Aspern Papers *here in 1888.*

Rialto

San Silvestro

The Riva del Vin is the quay where wine *(vin)* used to be unloaded. It is one of the few spots where you can sit and relax on the banks of the Grand Canal.

LOCATOR MAP

See Venice Street Finder maps 6, 7

Palazzo Barzizza, rebuilt in the 17th century, preserves its early 13th-century façade.

Peggy Guggenheim Collection
A one-storey palazzo houses Guggenheim's great modern art collection (see pp100–1).

Santa Maria della Salute
The vast weight of this Baroque church is supported by over one million timber piles (see p101).

Palazzo Gritti-Pisani
The former home of the Gritti family is now the luxury Gritti Palace Hotel (see p544).

Santa Maria del Giglio

Salute

San Marco Vallaresso

Harry's Bar, founded in 1931 by Giuseppe Cipriani, is famous for its cocktails.

Palazzo Dario
Beautiful coloured marbles give the 1487 palace a highly individual façade. Legend has it the building is cursed.

The Dogana di Mare (customs house), built in the 17th century, is crowned by two bronze Atlases supporting a golden globe topped by a weathervane.

Travelling slowly along the Grand Canal by gondola ▷

Madonna dell'Orto, with 15th-century façade statues of St Christopher and the Apostles

Madonna dell'Orto **1**

Campo Madonna dell'Orto. **Map** 2 F2.
041 275 04 62. *Madonna dell'Orto.* 10am–5pm Mon–Sat, 1–5pm Sun.

THIS LOVELY Gothic church, founded in the mid-14th century, was dedicated to St Christopher, patron saint of travellers, to protect the boatmen who ferried passengers to the islands in the northern lagoon. A 15th-century statue of the saint, recently restored by the Venice in Peril fund, still stands above the main portal. The dedication was changed and the church reconstructed in the early 15th century, following the strange discovery, in a nearby vegetable garden *(orto),* of a statue of the Virgin Mary said to have miraculous powers.

The interior, faced almost entirely in brick, is large and uncluttered. On the right is a magnificent painting by Cima da Conegliano, *St John the Baptist and Other Saints* (c.1493). The vacant space in the chapel opposite belongs to Giovanni Bellini's *Madonna with Child* (c.1478), stolen in 1993 for the third time.

The church's greatest remaining treasures are the works of art by Tintoretto, who was a parishioner of the church. His tomb, which is marked with a plaque, lies with that of his children, in the chapel to the right of the chancel. The most

dramatic of his works are the towering masterpieces that decorate the chancel (1562–4). On the right wall is the *Last Judgment,* whose turbulent content caused John Ruskin's wife, Effie, to flee the church in horror. In *The Adoration of the Golden Calf* on the left wall, the figure carrying the calf, fourth from the left, is believed to be a portrait of the artist. Inside the chapel of San Mauro, off the end of the right nave, stands a statue of the Madonna by Giovanni de' Santi. It was restored by the Venice in Peril fund, and inspired the rededication of the church.

Ca' d'Oro **2**

Calle Ca' d'Oro. **Map** 3 A4.
041 523 87 90. *Ca' d'Oro.* 8:15am–6:45pm daily (1:30pm Mon).

IN 1420 Marino Contarini, a wealthy patrician, commissioned the construction of what he hoped would be the city's most magnificent palace *(see p77).* The building's intricate carving was entrusted to a team of Venetian and Lombard craftsmen, while the façade was beautifully adorned with the most elaborate and expensive decorative finishes of the day, including gold leaf, vermilion and ultramarine.

Tullio Lombardo's *Double Portrait*

The magnificent Gothic façade of the Ca' d'Oro, or House of Gold

Over the years the palace was extensively remodelled, and by the 18th century was in a state of semi-dereliction. In 1846 it was bought by the Russian Prince Troubetzkoy for the famous ballerina Maria Taglioni. Under her direction the palace suffered barbaric restoration, losing, among other things, its staircase and much of its original stonework. It was finally rescued by Baron Giorgio Franchetti, a wealthy patron of the arts, who bequeathed both the building and his private art collection to the state in 1915.

Pride of place on the first of the gallery's two floors goes to Andrea Mantegna's *St Sebastian* (1506), the artist's last work, which occupies a special alcove of its own. Elsewhere, the floor's main exhibits are ranged around the *portego* (gallery). This is largely dominated by the vivid 15th-century *Double Portrait* (c.1493) by the sculptor Tullio Lombardo; Sansovino's lunette of the *Madonna and Child* (c.1530); and several bronze reliefs by the Paduan Andrea Briosco, "Il Riccio" (1470–1532). Rooms leading off the *portego* to the right contain numerous bronzes and medallions, with some examples by Pisanello and Gentile Bellini. Paintings here also include the famous *Madonna of the Beautiful Eyes,* attributed to Giovanni Bellini, a *Madonna and Child,* attributed to Alvise Vivarini (both late 15th century), and Carpaccio's *Annunciation* and *Death of the Virgin* (both c.1504). A room to the left of the *portego* contains non-Venetian paintings, notably a *Flagellation* by Luca Signorelli (c.1480). A lovely staircase leads to the second floor, which opens with a room hung with tapestries. It has bronzes by Alessandro Vittoria and paintings by

Titian and Van Dyck. The *portego* displays frescoes (c.1532) by Pordenone from the cloister of Santo Stefano, while an anteroom contains damaged frescoes by Titian and Giorgione taken from the Fondaco dei Tedeschi.

Giovanni Bellini's 1513 altarpiece in San Giovanni Grisostomo

San Giovanni Grisostomo ❸

Campo San Giovanni Grisostomo. **Map** 3 B5. [041 522 71 55. 🚊 *Rialto.* 🕓 *4–5:30pm daily.*

THIS PRETTY little terracotta-coloured church lies in a bustling quarter close to the Rialto. Built between 1479 and 1504, it is a lovely Renaissance design, the last work of Mauro Coducci.

The interior is built on a Greek-cross plan. The light meter illuminates Giovanni Bellini's *St Jerome with Saints Christopher and Augustine* (1513) above the first altar on the right. This was most probably Bellini's last painting, executed when he was in his eighties.

Over the high altar hangs Sebastiano del Piombo's *St John Chrysostom and Six Saints* (1509–11).

Santa Maria dei Miracoli ❹

Campo dei Miracoli. **Map** 3 B5. [041 275 04 62. 🚊 *Rialto, Fondamente Nuove.* 🕓 *10am–5pm Mon–Sat, 1–5pm Sun & public hols.* 🔖🔒

AN EXQUISITE masterpiece of early Renaissance architecture, the Miracoli is the church where many Venetians like to get married. Tucked away in a maze of alleys and waterways in eastern Cannaregio, it is small and somewhat elusive.

Santa Maria dei Miracoli is decorated in various shades of marble, with some fine bas reliefs and sculpture. It was built in 1481–9 by the architect Pietro Lombardo and his sons to enshrine *The Virgin and Child* (1408), a painting believed to have miraculous powers. The picture, by Nicolò di Pietro, can still be seen above the altar.

The interior of the church is embellished by pink, white and grey marble, at its best when lit up by rays of pale sunshine. It is crowned by

Decorative column from inside Santa Maria dei Miracoli

a barrel-vaulted ceiling (1528) which has 50 portraits of saints and prophets. The balustrade, between the nave and the chancel, is decorated by Tullio Lombardo's carved figures of St Francis, Archangel Gabriel, the Virgin and St Clare.

The screen around the high altar and the medallions of the Evangelists in the cupola spandrels are also Lombardo's work. Above the main door, the choir gallery was used by the nuns from the neighbouring convent, who entered the church through an overhead gallery. Santa Maria dei Miracoli has recently undergone a major restoration programme, which was funded by the American Save Venice organization.

SANTA MARIA DEI MIRACOLI
This beautifully proportioned façade is composed of decorated panels and multicoloured polished marble.

Carving of saint

The semi-circular crowning lunette emphasizes the church's jewel-box appearance.

A false loggia is formed of Ionic arches, inset with windows. The marble used was reportedly left over from the building of San Marco.

***Virgin and Child* by Giorgio Lascaris**

The marble panels are fixed to the bricks by metal hooks. This method prevents the build-up of damp and salt water behind the panels, and dates from the Renaissance.

Street-by-Street: San Polo

THE RIALTO BRIDGE and markets make this area a magnet for visitors. Traditionally the city's commercial quarter, it was here that bankers, brokers and merchants conducted their affairs. Streets are no longer lined with stalls selling spices and fine fabrics, but the food markets and pasta shops are unmissable. Away from the bridge, streets quickly become less crowded, leading to tiny piazzas and quiet churches.

The Rialto Markets have existed for centuries, and are renowned for their produce. The Pescheria sells fresh fish and seafood.

The 17th-century church of San Cassiano houses a carved altar (1696) and a *Crucifixion* by Tintoretto (1568).

Sant'Aponal has a façade decorated with worn Gothic reliefs. The church was founded in the 11th century, but is now deconsecrated.

The Frari

San Silvestro

San Giovanni Elemosinario is an inconspicuous church that was rebuilt in the early 16th century, although its campanile dates from the end of the 14th century. Inside it are interesting frescoes by Pordenone.

KEY

– – – Suggested route

0 metres   75

0 yards   75

STAR SIGHT

★ **Rialto**

LOCATOR MAP
*See Venice Street Finder
maps 2, 3, 6, 7*

The lively Erberia, selling fresh fruit and vegetables

Rialto **❺**

Ponte di Rialto. **Map** 7 A1. 🚤 *Rialto*.

San Giacomo di Rialto's clock face (1410), which has sadly been a poor time-keeper over the years, adorns one of Venice's oldest churches.

Market entrance

THE RIALTO takes its name from *rivo alto* (high bank) and was one of the first areas of Venice to be inhabited. A banking and then market district, it remains one of the city's busiest and most bustling areas. Locals and visitors alike jostle among the colourful stalls of the Erberia (fruit and vegetable market) and Pescheria (fish market).

Stone bridges were built in Venice as early as the 12th century, but it was not until 1588, after the collapse, decay or sabotage of earlier wooden structures, that a solid stone bridge was designed for the Rialto. Completed in 1591, the new bridge remained the only means of crossing the Grand Canal until 1854, when the Accademia bridge was built.

Few visitors leave Venice without crossing the famous bridge. It is a wonderful place to watch and photograph the constant activity of boats on the Grand Canal below.

San Giacomo dell'Orio **❻**

Campo San Giacomo dell'Orio.
Map 2 E5. [041 275 04 62.
🚤 *Riva di Biasio or San Stae*.
🕐 *10am–5pm Mon–Sat, 1–5pm Sun & public hols.* 🏛 🏛

★ Rialto
*One of Venice's most
famous sights, the bridge
offers fine views of the
Grand Canal, and marks
the heart of the city* **❺**

THIS CHURCH is a focal point of a quiet quarter of Santa Croce. The name "dell'Orio" (locally dall'Orio) may derive from a laurel tree *(alloro)* that once stood near the church. San Giacomo was founded in the 9th century,

rebuilt in 1225 and thereafter repeatedly modified, resulting in a mixture of styles. The campanile, basilica ground plan and Byzantine columns survive from the 13th century. The ship's keel roof and the columns are Gothic, and the apses are Renaissance.

The new sacristy contains a beautiful ceiling by Veronese and some interesting altar paintings.

San Polo **❼**

Campo San Polo. **Map** 6 F1,
[041 275 04 62. 🚤 *San Silvestro*.
🕐 *10am–5pm Mon–Sat, 1–5pm Sun
& public hols.* 🏛 🏛

FOUNDED IN THE 9th century, rebuilt in the 15th and revamped in the early 19th in Neo-Classical style, the church of San Polo is worth visiting for the lovely Gothic portal and the Romanesque lions at the foot of the 14th-century campanile – one holds a serpent between its paws, the other a human head.

Inside, follow the signs for the *Via Crucis del Tiepolo* – 14 pictures of the Stations of the Cross (1749) by the painter Giandomenico Tiepolo: many include vivid portraits of Venetian life. The church also has paintings by Veronese, Palma il Giovane (the Younger) and a dramatic *Last Supper* by Tintoretto.

A Romanesque lion at the base of San Polo's 14th-century campanile

Santa Maria Gloriosa dei Frari ➑

MORE COMMONLY KNOWN as the Frari (a corruption of Frati, meaning brothers), this vast Gothic church dwarfs the eastern area of San Polo. The first church on the site was built by Franciscan friars in 1250–1338, but was replaced by a larger building completed in the mid-15th century. The airy interior is striking for its sheer size and for the quality of its works of art, including masterpieces by Titian and Giovanni Bellini, a statue by Donatello and several grandiose tombs.

Foscari Monument
Doge Foscari died in 1457, after a long and eventful 34-year reign.

The campanile
is 83 m (262 ft) high, the tallest in the city after that of San Marco.

★ **Assumption of the Virgin**
Titian's glowing and spectacular work (1518) draws the eye through the monk's choir, to the altar, and heavenwards.

Rood Screen
(1475)
Pietro Lombardo and Bartolomeo Bon carved the rood screen and its decorative marble figures.

Entrance

The *Madonna di Ca' Pesaro* (1526) shows Titian's mastery of light and colour.

★ **Monks' Choir**
This consists of three-tiered stalls (1468), carved with bas-reliefs of saints and Venetian city scenes.

FLOORPLAN

The Frari's imposing cruciform interior, which is 90 m (295 ft) long, holds 12 sights that should not be missed.

KEY TO FLOORPLAN

1 Tomb of Canova
2 Monument to Titian
3 *Madonna di Ca' Pesaro* by Titian
4 Choir stalls
5 Corner Chapel
6 Tomb of Monteverdi
7 Tomb of Doge Nicolò Tron
8 High altar with *Assumption of the Virgin* (1518) by Titian
9 Tomb of Doge Francesco Foscari
10 *John the Baptist* (c.1450) by Donatello
11 B Vivarini's altar painting (1474), Bernardo Chapel
12 *Madonna and Child with Saints* (1488) by Bellini

VISITORS' CHECKLIST

Campo dei Frari. Map 6 D1.
041 275 04 62. San Tomà. 9am–6pm Mon–Sat, 1–6pm Sun & religious hols. except for those attending mass. frequent.

★ Madonna and Child
The sacristy's altarpiece (1488) by Bellini, with its sublime use of colour, is one of Venice's most beautiful Renaissance paintings.

The former monastery, which houses the State Archives, has two cloisters, one in the style of Sansovino, another designed by Palladio.

Tomb of Canova
Canova designed, but never constructed, a Neo-Classical marble pyramid like this as a monument for Titian. After Canova's death in 1822, the sculptor's pupils used a similar design for their master's tomb.

STAR FEATURES

★ **Assumption of the Virgin** by Titian

★ **Madonna and Child** by Bellini

★ **Monks' Choir**

Scuola Grande di San Rocco 9

Restored main entrance to the Scuola di San Rocco

FOUNDED IN HONOUR of San Rocco (St Roch), a saint who dedicated his life to helping the sick, the Scuola started out as a charitable confraternity. Construction began in 1515 under Bartolomeo Bon and was continued by Scarpagnino until his death in 1549. The work was financed by donations from Venetians keen to invoke San Rocco's protection and the Scuola quickly became one of the wealthiest in Venice. In 1564 its members decided to commission Tintoretto to decorate its walls and ceilings. His earliest paintings, the first of over 50 works he eventually left in the Scuola, fill the small Sala dell'Albergo off the Upper Hall. His later paintings occupy the Ground Floor Hall, immediately within the entrance.

Tintoretto's magnificent *Crucifixion*, painted in 1565 for the Sala dell'Albergo in the Scuola di San Rocco

GROUND FLOOR HALL

THE GROUND FLOOR cycle was executed in 1583–7, when Tintoretto was in his sixties, and consists of eight paintings illustrating the life of Mary. The series starts with an *Annunciation* and ends with an *Assumption*, which was restored some years ago.

The tranquil scenes of *The Flight into Egypt*, *St Mary Magdalene* and *St Mary of Egypt* are remarkable for their serenity. This is portrayed most

Detail from *The Flight into Egypt* (1582–7) by Tintoretto

lucidly by the Virgin's isolated spiritual contemplation in the *St Mary of Egypt*. In all three paintings, the landscapes are rendered with rapid strokes, and are an important part of the composition.

UPPER HALL AND SALA DELL'ALBERGO

SCARPAGNINO'S great staircase (1544–6), with its upper flight decorated with two vast paintings commemorating the plague of 1630, leads to the Upper Hall. Here, biblical subjects decorate the ceiling and walls, painted by Tintoretto from 1575–81.

The ceiling paintings portray scenes from the Old Testament. The three large and dynamic square paintings in the centre show episodes from the Book of Exodus: *Moses Strikes Water from the Rock*, *The Miracle of the Bronze Serpent* and *The Fall of Manna in the Desert*. These all allude to the charitable

aims of the Scuola in alleviating thirst, sickness and hunger respectively. All three paintings are crowded compositions displaying much violent movement.

The vast wall paintings in the hall feature episodes from the New Testament, linking with the ceiling paintings. Two of the most striking paintings are *The Temptation of Christ*, which shows a handsome young Satan offering Christ two loaves of bread, and *The Adoration of the Shepherds*. Like *The Temptation of Christ*, *The Adoration* is composed in two halves, with a female figure, shepherds and ox below, and the Holy Family and onlookers above.

The beautiful carvings below the paintings were added in the 17th century by sculptor Francesco Pianta. The figures are allegorical and include (near the altar) a caricature of Tintoretto with his palette and brushes, representing Painting.

The easel painting *Christ Carrying the Cross*, also in the

Detail from *The Temptation of Christ* (1578–81) by Tintoretto

Upper Hall, was once attributed to Giorgione, though many believe it to be by Titian.

Near the entrance to the Sala dell'Albergo, you can see the *Annunciation* by Titian. The Sala dell'Albergo itself holds the most breathtaking of his works – the *Crucifixion*

(1565). Henry James remarked of this painting: "no single picture contains more of human life; there is everything in it, including the most exquisite beauty." Tintoretto began the cycle of paintings in this room in 1564, when he won the commission with the ceiling painting *San Rocco in Glory.* On the wall opposite the *Crucifixion* are paintings of episodes from the Passion: *Christ before Pilate, The Crowning with Thorns* and *The Ascent to Calvary.*

San Rocco ❿

Campo San Rocco. **Map** 6 D1. �831 *San Tomà.* ⏰ *Apr–Oct: 8am–12:30pm, 3–5pm daily; Nov–Mar: 8am–12:30pm Mon–Fri; 2–4pm Sat, Sun, public hols.*

SHARING THE LITTLE square with the celebrated Scuola Grande di San Rocco is the church of the same name. Designed by Bartolomeo Bon in 1489 and largely rebuilt in 1725, the exterior suffers from a mixture of styles. The façade, similar in concept to the Scuola, was added in 1765–71. Inside, the chancel is decorated with a series of paintings by Tintoretto depicting scenes from the life of San Rocco.

San Pantalon ⓫

Campo San Pantalon.
Map 6 D2. 📞 *041 270 24 64.*
�831 *San Tomà.* ⏰ *4–6pm Sun–Fri.*

Fumiani's epic ceiling painting (1680–1740) in San Pantalon

KEY TO PAINTINGS

◻ GROUND FLOOR HALL **1** The Annunciation; **2** The Adoration of the Three Kings; **3** The Flight into Egypt; **4** The Massacre of the Innocents; **5** St Mary Magdalene; **6** St Mary of Egypt; **7** The Presentation in the Temple; **8** The Assumption.

◻ UPPER HALL WALLS **9** San Rocco; **10** St Sebastian; **11** The Adoration of the Shepherds; **12** The Baptism of Christ; **13** The Resurrection; **14** The Agony in the Garden; **15** The Last Supper; **16** The Vision of San Rocco; **17** The Miracle of the Loaves and Fishes; **18** The Resurrection of Lazarus; **19** The Ascension; **20** Christ Heals the Paralytic; **21** The Temptation of Christ.

◻ UPPER HALL CEILING **22** Moses Saved from the Waters; **23** The Pillar of Fire; **24** Samuel and Saul; **25** Jacob's Ladder; **26** Elijah on a Chariot of Fire; **27** Elijah Fed by the Angels; **28** Daniel Saved by the Angels; **29** The Passover; **30** The Fall of Manna; **31** The Sacrifice of Isaac; **32** The Miracle of the Bronze Serpent; **33** Jonah Emerges from the Whale; **34** Moses Strikes Water from the Rock; **35** Adam and Eve; **36** Three Children in the Furnace; **37** God Appears to Moses; **38** Samson Brings out Water from the Jawbone of an Ass; **39** The Vision of the Prophet Ezekiel; **40** The Vision of Jeremiah; **41** Elisha Distributes Bread; **42** Abraham and Melchizedeck.

THE OVERWHELMING feature of this late 17th-century church is its vast painted ceiling, dark, awe-inspiring and remarkable for its illusionistic effect of height. The ceiling comprises a total of 40 scenes, and admirers claim that this is the world's largest work of art on canvas.

The scenes show the martyrdom and apotheosis of the physician St Pantalon. The artist, Gian Antonio Fumiani, took 24 years (1680–1704) to achieve the masterpiece, before allegedly falling to his death from the scaffolding.

Ground Floor Hall

Upper Hall

Street-by-Street: Dorsoduro

Santa Margherita

THE SESTIERE OF DORSODURO was built up on a stratum of solid subsoil – the name means "hard backbone". It has as its focal point the lively Campo Santa Margherita, the largest open space in this part of Venice. The square bustles with activity, particularly in the morning when the market stalls are open, and in the evening when it is the haunt of students from nearby Ca' Foscari, now part of Venice university. The surrounding streets contain some architectural stunners, notably Ca' Rezzonico and the Scuola Grande dei Carmini, which has decorations by Tiepolo. Of the area's waterways, the delightful Rio San Barnaba is best appreciated from the Ponte dei Pugni, near the barge selling fruit and vegetables – itself a time-honoured Venetian sight. Alongside the Rio Terrà Canal there are some lively cafés and a fascinating shop selling masks for Carnevale.

Campo Santa Margherita is an ideal place for relaxing in a café.

Palazzo Zenobio, built at the end of the 17th century, has been an Armenian college since 1850. With permission, visitors can see the fine 18th-century ballroom.

Scuola Grande dei Carmini contains nine ceiling panels (1739–44) in the hall on the upper floor, painted by Tiepolo for the Carmelite confraternity.

Santa Maria dei Carmini has a Gothic side porch carved with Byzantine reliefs.

Fondamenta Gherardini runs beside the Rio San Barnaba, one of the prettiest canals in the *sestiere*.

KEY

- – – Suggested route

0 metres   50
0 yards   50

★ Ca' Rezzonico
The ballroom covers the width of the palazzo once owned by Browning **12**

Palazzo Giustinian was home to Wagner in 1858.

Ca' Foscari was completed in 1437 for Doge Francesco Foscari.

LOCATOR MAP
See Venice Street Finder maps 5, 6

Tiepolo's *New World* fresco, part of a series in Ca' Rezzonico

Ca' Rezzonico **12**

Fondamenta Rezzonico 3136.
Map 6 E3. 041 241 01 00.
Ca' Rezzonico. Times vary – phone in advance to check.
1 Jan, 1 May, 25 Dec.

THIS PALAZZO HOUSES the museum of 18th-century Venice, its rooms furnished with frescoes, paintings and period pieces taken from other palaces or museums. Building began with Longhena (architect of La Salute, *see p101*) in 1667, but the funds of the Bon family, who commissioned it, ran dry before the second floor was started. In 1712 the unfinished palace was bought by the Rezzonico family of Genoa. A large portion of their fortune was spent on the completion of the palace.

The Rezzonico family sold it on, in 1888, to the famous poet Robert Browning and his son, Pen. The outstanding attraction in the palace today is Giorgio Massari's ballroom, which occupies the entire breadth of the building. It is adorned with gilded chandeliers, carved furniture by Andrea Brustolon and a ceiling with *trompe l'oeil* frescoes. Other rooms have frescoes by Giambattista Tiepolo, including his lively *Nuptial Allegory* (1758), and one by his son, Giandomenico, originally in his villa at Zianigo. There are paintings by Longhi, Guardi, and – rare in Venice – Canaletto. On the top floor is a reconstructed 18th-century apothecary's shop and a puppet theatre.

Ponte dei Pugni was a traditional scene of fist fights between rival factions. They were finally banned in 1705 for being too violent.

San Barnaba is a thriving community, with its own floating barge stall crammed with fresh fruit and vegetables. It is a focal point for tourists and locals alike.

STAR SIGHT

★ Ca' Rezzonico

Nave of San Nicolò dei Mendicoli, one of the oldest churches in Venice

San Sebastiano ⓮

Campo San Sebastiano. **Map** 5 C3.
📞 041 275 04 62. 🚇 San Basilio.
🕐 10am–5pm Mon–Sat. ⬤ Sun &
public hols. 📷 ♿

THIS CHURCH HAS one of the
most homogeneous inter-
iors in the whole of Venice.
The splendour was created by
Veronese who, from 1555 to
1560 and again in the 1570s,
was commissioned to decorate
the sacristy ceiling, the nave
ceiling, the frieze, the east
end of the choir, the high
altar, the doors of the organ
panels and the chancel.

The paintings are typical of
the artist and feature radiant
colours and rich costumes.
Those on the sacristy ceiling
depict the *Coronation of the
Virgin* and the *Four Evangelists*.

Of the other paintings, the
finest are the three which tell
the story of Esther, Queen of
Xerxes I of Persia, famous for
securing the deliverance of
the Jewish people.

Appropriately, the artist is
buried in the church. His
tomb is situated in front of
the beautifully paved chapel
to the left of the chancel.

San Nicolò dei Mendicoli ⓭

Campo San Nicolò. **Map** 5 A3.
📞 041 270 24 64. 🚇 San Basilio.
🕐 10am–noon Mon–Sat.

CONTRASTING WITH the
remote and rundown
area which surrounds it, this
church still remains one of
the most charming in Venice.
Founded in the 7th century,
it has been rebuilt extensively
over the years. The little
porch on the north flank
is 15th century and once
sheltered the beggars, or
mendicanti, who gave the
church its name.

Thanks to the Venice in
Peril fund, in the 1970s the
church underwent one of the
most comprehensive restoration programmes since the
floods of 1966. Flooding had
become such a problem that
the priest often ferried himself
around the church in a small
wicker boat. The floor, which
was 30 cm (1 ft) below the

level of the canals, was
rebuilt and raised slightly to
prevent further flood damage.
The roofs and lower walls
were reconstructed, and
paintings and statues restored.

The interior is delightfully
embellished, particularly the
nave with its 16th-century
gilded wooden statues. These
include the figure of San
Nicolò himself. On the upper
walls is a series of paintings
of the life of Christ (c.1553)
by Alvise dal Friso and other
pupils of Veronese.

Outside, a small column
supports a stone lion, in a
humbler echo of the Column
of San Marco in the Piazzetta.

Accademia ⓯

See pp102–3.

Peggy Guggenheim Collection ⓰

Palazzo Venier dei Leoni. **Map** 6 F4.
📞 041 520 62 88. 🚇 Accademia.
🕐 10am–6pm Wed–Mon (to 10pm
Sat). ⬤ 25 Dec. 📷 ♿ ▨ 🛍 🏛

INTENDED AS A four-storey
palace, the 18th-century
Palazzo Venier dei Leoni in fact
never rose beyond the ground
floor – hence its nickname,

The truncated palazzo housing the Peggy Guggenheim Collection

Il Palazzo Nonfinito (The Unfinished Palace). In 1949 the building was bought as a home by the American millionairess Peggy Guggenheim (1898–1979), a collector, dealer and patron of the arts.

A perspicacious and high-spirited woman, she initially befriended, and then furthered the careers of, many innovative abstract and Surrealist artists. One was Max Ernst, who became her second husband. The collection consists of 200 fine paintings and sculptures, each representing the 20th century's most influential modern art movements. The dining room has notable Cubist works of art, including *The Poet* by Pablo Picasso, and an entire room is devoted to Jackson Pollock, who was "discovered" by Guggenheim.

Bird in Space by Constantin Brancusi

Other artists represented are Braque, Chagall, de Chirico, Dalí, Duchamp, Léger, Kandinsky, Klee, Mondrian, Miró, Malevich, Rothko, Bacon and Magritte, whose Surreal *Empire of Light* (1953–4) shows a night scene of a darkened house in a wooded setting with a bright day sky above. The sculpture collection, which includes Constantin Brancusi's elegant *Bird in Space* (c.1923), is laid out in the house and garden.

Perhaps the most provocative piece is Marino Marini's *Angelo della Città* (Angel of the Citadel, 1948), located on the terrace overlooking the Grand Canal. This shows a prominently displayed man sitting on a horse, erect in all respects. Embarrassed onlookers avert their gaze to enjoy views of the Grand Canal.

The Guggenheim is one of the most visited sights of Venice, and the best place in the city to see modern art. Light-filled rooms and the large modern canvases provide a striking contrast to the Renaissance paintings which usually form the highlights in most Venetian churches and museums. A bonus for English speakers is the team of assistants, who are often visiting arts graduates from Britain.

The garden has been paved and features an array of sculptures. Peggy Guggenheim's ashes are also preserved here, near the place where her pet dogs were buried. A shop and restaurant are housed in buildings off the garden. Call for information on temporary exhibits.

The Baroque church of Santa Maria della Salute, at the mouth of the Grand Canal

Santa Maria della Salute ⑰

Campo della Salute. **Map** 7 A4.
☎ 041 523 79 51. 🚤 *Salute.*
⏰ 9am–noon, 3–5pm daily (to 6:30pm Jun–Sep). 🎫 to sacristy.

THE GREAT BAROQUE church of Santa Maria della Salute, standing at the entrance of the Grand Canal, is one of the most imposing architectural landmarks of Venice. Henry James likened it to "some great lady on the threshold of her salon".

The church was built in thanksgiving for the city's deliverance from the plague epidemic of 1630, hence the name *Salute*, which means health and salvation.

Each November, in celebration, worshippers light candles and approach across a bridge of boats spanning the mouth of the Grand Canal for the occasion.

Baldassare Longhena started the church in 1630 at the age of 32, and worked on it for the rest of his life. It was not completed until 1687, five years after his death.

The interior is comparatively sober. It consists of a large octagonal space below the cupola and six chapels radiating from the ambulatory. The large domed chancel and grandiose high altar dominate the view from the main door.

The altar's sculptural group by Giusto Le Corte represents the Virgin and Child giving protection to Venice from the plague. The best of the paintings are in the sacristy to the left of the altar: Titian's early altarpiece of *St Mark Enthroned with Saints Cosmas, Damian, Roch and Sebastian* (1511–12) and his dramatic ceiling paintings of *Cain and Abel, The Sacrifice of Abraham and Isaac* and *David and Goliath* (1540–9). *The Wedding at Cana* (1551) on the wall opposite the entrance is a major work by Jacopo Tintoretto.

Interior of the Salute with the octagonal space at its core

Accademia ⑮

Sᴘᴀɴɴɪɴɢ ꜰɪᴠᴇ ᴄᴇɴᴛᴜʀɪᴇꜱ, the matchless collection of paintings in the Accademia provides a complete spectrum of the Venetian school, from the medieval Byzantine period through the Renaissance to the Baroque and later. The basis of the collection was the Accademia di Belle Arti founded in 1750 by the painter Giovanni Battista Piazzetta. In 1807 Napoleon moved the collection to these premises, and enriched it with works of art removed from churches and monasteries.

The Tempest
In this enigmatic landscape (c.1507), Giorgione was probably creating a fantasy rather than portraying any specific subject.

KEY TO FLOORPLAN

- ☐ Byzantine and International Gothic
- ☐ Renaissance
- ☐ Baroque, Genre and Landscape
- ☐ Ceremonial Painting
- ☐ Temporary exhibitions
- ☐ Non-exhibition space

The courtyard (1561) designed by Palladio

The former church of Santa Maria della Carità

Feast in the House of Levi (1573) by Paolo Veronese

Bookshop

Entrance

Madonna and Child between St John the Baptist and a Saint
In this beautiful painting (c.1504), Giovanni Bellini places the figures in a spacious landscape, so marking a new phase in his development.

Coronation of the Virgin
Paolo Veneziano's polyptych (1325) has a central image of the Virgin surrounded by a panoply of religious scenes. This detail shows episodes from the Life of St Francis.

Healing of the Madman (c.1496) by Vittore Carpaccio

VISITORS' CHECKLIST

Campo della Carità. **Map** 6 E3.
(041 522 22 47.
Accademia. 9am–7pm
Tue–Sun (later Apr–Oct),
9am–2pm Mon (last adm: 30
mins before closing). 1 Jan,
1 May, 25 Dec.

BYZANTINE AND INTERNATIONAL GOTHIC

ROOM 1 SHOWS the influence of Byzantine art on the early Venetian painters. In Paolo Veneziano's glowing *Coronation of the Virgin* (1325), the linear rhythms are unmistakably Gothic, but the gold background and central panel are distinctly Byzantine.

In contrast, *The Coronation of the Virgin* (1448) by Michele Giambono reveals a delicate naturalism, typical of the International Gothic style.

RENAISSANCE

THE RENAISSANCE came late to Venice, but by the second quarter of the 15th century it had transformed the city into a thriving art centre rivalling Florence and Rome. Central to Venetian art in the 15th century was the *Sacra Conversazione*, in which the Madonna is portrayed with various saints in a harmonious composition. Giovanni Bellini's altarpiece for San Giobbe (c.1487) in room 2 is one of the finest examples of this subject.

In contrast, the High Renaissance exuberance of Paolo Veronese is exemplified in the monumental *Feast in the House of Levi* (1573). The painting occupies a whole wall in room 10. Tintoretto's huge masterpiece *The Miracle of St Mark Freeing a Slave* (1548) is also on display here.

BAROQUE, GENRE AND LANDSCAPE

VENICE LACKED native Baroque painters, but a few non-Venetians kept the Venetian school alive in the 17th century. The most notable was the Genoese Bernardo Strozzi (1581–1644). The artist was a great admirer of the work of Veronese, as can be seen in his *Feast at the House of Simon* (1629) in room 11. Also represented in this room is Giambattista Tiepolo, the greatest Venetian painter of the 18th century.

The long corridor (12) and the rooms that lead from it are largely devoted to light-hearted landscape and genre paintings from the 18th century. Among them are pastoral scenes by Francesco Zuccarelli, works by Marco Ricci, scenes of Venetian society by Pietro Longhi and a view of Venice by Canaletto (1763). This is a fine example of his sense of perspective.

CEREMONIAL PAINTING

ROOMS 20 and 21 return to the Renaissance, featuring two great cycles of paintings from the late 16th century. The detail in these large-scale anecdotal canvases provides a fascinating glimpse of the life, customs and appearance of Venice at the time.

Room 20 houses *The Stories of the Cross* by Venice's leading artists. In room 21, minutely detailed *Scenes from the Legend of St Ursula* (1490s) by Carpaccio mix reality and imagination by linking episodes from the life of the saint to the settings and costumes of 15th-century Venice.

Feast in the House of Levi (1573) by Paolo Veronese

Street-by-Street: Piazza San Marco

THROUGHOUT ITS LONG history Piazza San Marco has witnessed pageants, processions, political activities and countless Carnival festivities. Visitors flock here in their thousands for two of the city's most important historic sights – the Basilica and the Palazzo Ducale. These magnificent buildings complement lesser sights, such as the Campanile, Museo Correr and Torre dell'Orologio, not to mention the gardens of the Giardinetti Reali, open-air orchestras, elegant cafés – notably Quadri and Florian's – and numerous smart shops.

Lion of St Mark

Torre dell'Orologio
The clock tower, with hidden clockwork figures, dates from the Renaissance 🄩

Gondolas are moored in the Bacino Orseolo, named after Doge Pietro Orseolo who established a hospice for pilgrims here in 977.

The Piazza was described by Napoleon as the "most elegant drawing room in Europe".

MERCERIE

PROCURATIE VECCHIE

PIAZZA SAN MARCO

PROCURATIE NUOVE

Museo Correr
Giovanni Bellini's Pietà *(1455–60) is one of many masterpieces hanging in the galleries of the Correr* 🄩

Harry's Bar has attracted American visitors since Giuseppe Cipriani and his friend Harry set it up in 1931. Shown here is Ernest Hemingway, one of the bar's many famous patrons.

San Marco Vallaresso

The Campanile
The present Campanile replaced one that collapsed in 1902 **㉑**

★ **Basilica di San Marco**
This 13th-century façade mosaic shows the body of St Mark being carried into the basilica **⑱**

LOCATOR MAP
See Venice Street Finder map /

The Bridge of Sighs (1600) was built as a passageway between the Palazzo Ducale and the prison. It reputedly took its name from the sighs of prisoners being led to trial.

Ponte della Paglia

★ **Palazzo Ducale**
Once home to Venice's rulers, and to the offices of State, the Doges' Palace is a triumph of Gothic architecture **⑲**

The vaulting of the stairway in the magnificent Libreria Sansoviniana (1588) is decorated with frescoes and gilded stucco. The national library of St Mark is housed here.

San Marco Giardinetti

The Zecca, designed by Sansovino and started in 1537, was the city mint until 1870, and gave its name to the *zecchino* or Venetian ducat.

0 metres	75
0 yards	75

STAR SIGHTS

★ **Basilica di San Marco**

★ **Palazzo Ducale**

Basilica di San Marco ⑱

VENICE'S FAMOUS BASILICA blends the architectural and decorative styles of East and West to create one of the greatest buildings in Europe. The exterior owes its almost Oriental splendour to countless treasures from the Republic's overseas empire. Among these are copies of the famous bronze horses, brought from Constantinople in 1204, and a wealth of columns, bas-reliefs and coloured marbles studded across the main façade. Mosaics from different epochs adorn the five doorways, while the main portal is framed by some of Italy's loveliest Romanesque carving (1240–65).

The Pentecost Dome, showing the Descent of the Holy Ghost as a dove, was probably the first dome to be decorated with mosaics.

St Mark and Angels
The statues crowning the central arch are additions from the early 15th century.

The elegant arches echo those of the lower floor, forming a repeat pattern.

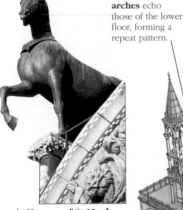

★ Horses of St Mark
The four horses are replicas of the gilded bronze originals, now protected inside the Basilica's museum.

STAR FEATURES

★ Façade Mosaics

★ Horses of St Mark

Romanesque carvings adorn the arches of the main portal.

Entrance

★ Façade Mosaics
A 17th-century mosaic shows the body of St Mark being taken from Alexandria, reputedly smuggled past Muslim guards under slices of pork.

Ciborium
The fine alabaster columns of the altar canopy, or baldacchino, are adorned with scenes from the New Testament.

The Ascension Dome
features a magnificent 13th-century mosaic of Christ surrounded by angels, the 12 Apostles and the Virgin Mary.

St Mark's body, believed lost in the fire of AD 976, supposedly reappeared when the new church was consecrated in 1094. The remains are housed in the altar.

St Mark's Treasury

The Mosaic Pavement shows beautiful pictures of birds and beasts, some of which are allegorical.

The Tetrarchs
This charming sculptured group in porphyry (4th-century Egyptian) is thought to represent Diocletian, Maximian, Valerian and Constantine. Collectively they were the Tetrarchs, appointed by Diocletian to help rule the Roman Empire.

THE BUILDING OF ST MARK'S

Built on a Greek cross plan and crowned with five huge domes, this is the third church to stand on the site. The first, which enshrined the body of St Mark in the 9th century, was destroyed by fire. The second was pulled down in favour of a church reflecting Venice's growing power. The present design was inspired by the Church of the Apostles in Constantinople and was completed and decorated over the centuries. From 1075, all ships returning from abroad had, by law, to bring back a precious gift to adorn "the House of St Mark". The mosaics inside are mostly 12th–13th century and cover 4,240 sq m (45,622 sq ft). Some were later replaced by such artists as Titian and Tintoretto. Until 1807 St Mark's was the doge's private chapel, used for ceremonies of State, after which it succeeded San Pietro di Castello as the cathedral of Venice.

13th-century carving of a grape harvester on the main portal

Exploring the Basilica

S⊤ MARK'S MAGNIFICENT INTERIOR is clad with dazzling
mosaics, which begin in the *narthex*, or atrium of
the Basilica, and culminate in the glittering panels of
the Pentecost and Ascension domes. The Genesis
Cupola in the atrium has a stunning Creation of the
World described in concentric circles. The *pavimento*
or floor is also patterned with mosaics in marble and
glass. Steps from the atrium lead to the Museo Marciano,
home to the Basilica's famous horses. Other treasures
include the jewel-encrusted Pala d'Oro, behind the high
altar, the Nicopeia icon and the
precious hoards of silver, gold
and glassware in the Treasury.

Madonna di Nicopeia
*This Byzantine icon,
looted in 1204, is one of
Venice's most revered images.*

The **Porta dei
Fiori** or Gate
of Flowers is
decorated with
13th-century
reliefs.

**Cappella
dei Mascoli**

**North
side aisle**

★ Pentecost Dome
*Showing the Apostles
touched by tongues of
flame, the Pentecost Dome
was lavishly decorated
in the 12th century.*

Atrium

**Steps to
Museo Marciano**

**Cappella
Zen**

Baptistry

★ Ascension Dome
*A mosaic of Christ in Glory decorates the
enormous central dome. This masterpiece
was created by 13th-century Venetian
craftsmen, who were strongly influenced
by the art and architecture of Byzantium.*

★ Treasury
*A repository
for precious
artifacts from
both Italy and
Constantinople,
the treasury
houses objects
such as this
11th-century
silver-gilt coffer.*

★ **Pala d'Oro**
*The altar-
piece, created
in the 10th
century by
medieval
goldsmiths,
is made up
of 250 panels
such as this one.*

The sacristy door
has fine bronze
panels by
Sansovino which
include portraits
of himself with
Titian and Aretino.

**The Altar of the
Sacrament** is
decorated with
mosaics of the
parables and miracles
of Christ dating from
the late 12th or early
13th century.

The columns of the
inner façade are
thought to be fragments
of the first basilica.

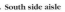
South side aisle

STAR FEATURES

★ Pala d'Oro

★ Treasury

★ Ascension and
Pentecost Domes

MOSAICS

CLOTHING THE DOMES, walls and floor of the Basilica are over 4,000 sq m (43,000 sq ft) of gleaming golden mosaics. The earliest, dating from the 12th century, were the work of mosaicists from the East. Their delicate techniques were soon adopted by Venetian craftsmen, who gradually took over the Basilica's decoration, combining Byzantine inspiration with Western influences. During the 16th century, many sketches by Tintoretto, Titian, Veronese, and other leading artists were reproduced in mosaic.

Among the most dazzling mosaics – many of which have been heavily restored – are those in the 13th-century central Ascension Dome and the 12th-century Pentecost Dome over the nave.

PALA D'ORO

BEYOND THE CAPPELLA di San Clemente lies the entrance to the most valuable treasure of San Marco: the Pala d'Oro. This jewel-spangled altar-piece, situated behind the high altar, consists of 250 enamel paintings on gold foil, enclosed within a gilded silver Gothic frame. Originally commissioned in Byzantium in AD 976, the altarpiece was further embellished over the

centuries. Napoleon stole some of the precious stones in 1797, but the screen still gleams with pearls, rubies, sapphires and amethysts.

MUSEO MARCIANO

STEPS FROM the atrium, signposted Loggia dei Cavalli, take you up to the church museum, where the gallery offers a splendid view into the basilica. The gilded bronze horses, housed in a room at the far end of the museum, were stolen from the top of the Hippodrome (ancient racecourse) in Constantinople (modern Istanbul) in 1204 but their origin, either Roman or Hellenistic, remains a mystery. Also on show are mosaics, medieval manu-scripts and antique tapestries.

BAPTISTRY AND CHAPELS

THE BAPTISTRY (closed to the public) was added by Doge Andrea Dandolo (1343–54), who is buried here, with Sansovino, who designed the font. The adjoining Cappella Zen (also closed to the public) became a funeral chapel for Cardinal Zen in 1504 in return for a bequest to the State. The left transept of the Cappella dei Mascoli is decorated with scenes from the life of Mary, while the third chapel in the same transept houses the icon of the Madonna of Nicopeia. Looted in 1204, it was once carried into battle at the head of the Byzantine army.

Noah and the Flood, atrium mosaics from the 13th century

Palazzo Ducale ⑲

THE PALAZZO DUCALE (Doges' Palace) was the official residence of each Venetian ruler (doge) and was founded in the 9th century. The present palace owes its external appearance to the building work of the 14th and early 15th centuries. To create their airy Gothic masterpiece, the Venetians broke with tradition by perching the bulk of the palace (built in pink Veronese marble) on top of an apparent fretwork of loggias and arcades (built from white Istrian stone).

Mars by Sansovino

★ **Giants' Staircase**
This 15th-century staircase is crowned by Sansovino's statues of Mars and Neptune, symbols of Venice's power.

Sala del Senato

Sala del Collegio

Anticollegio

The Arco Foscari
has copies of Antonio Rizzo's 15th-century Adam and Eve.

★ **Porta della Carta**
This 15th-century Gothic gate is the principal entrance to the palace. From it, a vaulted passageway leads to the Arco Foscari and the internal courtyard.

Courtyard

★ **Sala del Maggior Consiglio**
This vast hall was used as a meeting place for members of Venice's Great Council. Tintoretto's huge Paradise *(1590) fills the end wall.*

Sala dello Scudo

The walls of this room, once part of the doge's private apartments, are covered with maps of the world. In the centre of the room are two giant 18th-century globes.

Sala delle
Quattro Porte

Sala del Consiglio
dei Dieci

Sala della
Bussola

Torture Chamber

Interrogations took place in the Torture Chamber. Suspects were hung by their wrists from a cord in the centre of the room.

Drunkenness of Noah

This early 15th-century sculpture, symbolic of the frailty of man, is set on the corner of the palace.

The Bridge
of Sighs

The Ponte della Paglia, built of Istrian stone, has a pretty balustrade of columns and sculpted pine cones.

Main
entrance

The Loggia

Each arch of the ground level portico supports two arches of the loggia, which commands fine views of the lagoon.

STAR FEATURES

★ Giants' Staircase

★ Porta della Carta

★ Sala del Maggior Consiglio

Exploring the Palazzo Ducale

A TOUR OF THE PALAZZO DUCALE takes you through a succession of richly decorated chambers and halls, arranged over three floors, culminating with the Bridge of Sighs which links the palace to the prisons. Casanova was once imprisoned here and made a daring escape from the Palazzo through a hole in the roof.

Jacopo and Domenico Tintoretto's *Paradise*, one of the world's largest paintings, in the Sala del Maggior Consiglio

SCALA D'ORO AND COURTYARD

A PASSAGE from the Porta del Frumento opens into the palace courtyard. The ticket office and palace entrance are to the left. At the top of Antonio Rizzo's 15th-century Giants' Staircase, the new doge would be crowned with the *zogia* or dogal cap. The Scala d'Oro (golden staircase), designed by Jacopo Sansovino, leads to the palace's upper floors. It takes its name, however, from the elaborate gilt stucco vault created by Alessandro Vittoria (1554–8).

SALA DELLE QUATTRO PORTE TO THE SALA DEL SENATO

THE SECOND FLIGHT of the Scala d'Oro leads to the Sala delle Quattro Porte, with a ceiling designed by Palladio and frescoed by Tintoretto. The end walls of the next room, the Anticollegio, are decorated with mythological scenes by Tintoretto, while Veronese's masterly *Rape of Europa* (1580), opposite the window, is one of the palace's most dramatic works. The

adjoining Sala del Collegio was where the doge and his counsellors met to receive ambassadors and discuss matters of State. Embellishing the magnificent ceiling are 11 paintings by Veronese. In the next room, the Sala del Senato, the doge and some 200 senators discussed foreign affairs. The paintings are by Tintoretto and pupils.

A bocca di leone for denunciations

SALA DEL CONSIGLIO DEI DIECI TO THE ARMERIA

THE Sala del Consiglio dei Dieci was the meeting room of the powerful Council of Ten, founded in 1310 to protect State security. Two fine works by Veronese adorn the ceiling: *Age and Youth* and *Juno Offering the Ducal Crown to Venice* (both

Dialectic (c.1577) by Veronese in the Palazzo Ducale's Sala del Collegio

1553–4). In the Sala della Bussola, offenders awaited their fate in front of the Council of Ten. The room's *bocca di leone* (lion's mouth), was used to post secret denunciations and was just one of several in the palace. The wooden door here leads to the State Inquisitors' Room and thence to the torture chamber and prisons. The Armoury – one of the finest such collections anywhere in Europe – occupies the following rooms.

SALA DEL MAGGIOR CONSIGLIO

THE SCALA DEI CENSORI takes you to the second floor and past the Sala del Guariento and Antonio Rizzo's statues of Adam and Eve (1480s) to the magnificent Sala del Maggior Consiglio. A vast chamber, it was used as a meeting place for the Great Council and for grand State banquets. By the mid-16th century the Great Council had around 2,000 members. Any Venetian of high birth over 25 was entitled to a seat unless he married a commoner. Tintoretto's huge *Paradise* (1587–90) occupies the eastern wall. Measuring 7.45 by 24.65 m (25 by 81 ft), it is one of the largest paintings in the world. The itinerary then continues in more sombre vein, crossing the Bridge of Sighs to enter the dank world of the prisons.

Torre dell'Orologio 20

Piazza San Marco. **Map** 7 B2. 🚤 *San Marco.* ⬤ *for restoration.*

THIS RICHLY decorated clock tower on the north side of the piazza was built in the late 15th century. Mauro Coducci is thought to have worked on the design. With its display of the phases of the moon and the signs of the zodiac, the gilt and blue enamel clock face was designed with

The clock face of the Torre dell'Orologio

seafarers in mind. According to a gruesome local legend, once the clock was completed, the two inventors of the complex mechanism had their eyes gouged out to prevent them from ever creating a replica.

On the upper level, the winged lion of St Mark stands against a star-spangled blue backdrop. At the very top the two huge bronze figures, known as the *Mori*, or Moors, because of their dark patina, strike the bell on the hour.

Campanile 21

Piazza San Marco. **Map** 7 B2. 🎧 *041 522 40 64.* 🚤 *San Marco.* ⬤ *May–Sep: 9am–9pm; Oct–Dec, Feb–Apr: 9:30am–3:45pm daily.* ⬤ *Jan.* 📷

FROM THE TOP of St Mark's campanile, high above the piazza, visitors can enjoy views of the city, the lagoon and, visibility permitting, the peaks of the Alps. It was from this viewpoint that Galileo demonstrated his telescope to Doge Leonardo Donà in 1609. To do so he would have climbed the internal ramp. Access is achieved far less strenuously these days, via a lift.

The first tower, completed in 1173, was built as a lighthouse to assist navigators in the lagoon. It took on a less benevolent role in the Middle Ages, when offenders were imprisoned – and in some cases left to die – in a cage

hung near its summit. With the exception of several 16th-century renovations, the tower survived unharmed until 14 July 1902 when, with little warning, its foundations gave way and it suddenly collapsed. The only casualties were the Loggetta at the foot of the tower and the custodian's cat. Donations for reconstruction came flooding in and the following year the foundation stone was laid for a campanile *"dov' era e com'era"* ("where it was and as it was"). The new tower was finally opened on 25 April (the Feast of St Mark) 1912.

Museo Correr 22

Procuratie Nuove. Entrance in Ala Napoleonica. **Map** 7 B2. 🎧 *041 522 56 25.* 🚤 *San Marco.* ⬤ *Apr–Oct: 9am–7pm; Nov–Mar: 9am–5pm.* ⬤ *1 Jan, 25 Dec.* 📷

TEODORO CORRER bequeathed his extensive collection of works of art to Venice in 1830, thus forming the core of the city's fine civic museum. Its first rooms form a suitably Neo-Classical backdrop for early statues by Antonio Canova (1757–1822). The rest of the floor covers the history of the Venetian Republic, with maps, coins, armour and a host of doge-related exhibits.

***Young Man in a Red Hat* (c.1490) by Carpaccio in the Museo Correr**

The second floor contains the picture gallery, whose collection is second only to that of the Accademia.

The paintings are hung chronologically, enabling you to trace the evolution of Venetian painting, and to see the influence that Ferrarese, Paduan and Flemish artists had on the Venetian school. The gallery's most famous works are by Carpaccio: *Portrait of a Young Man in a Red Hat* (c.1490), and *Two Venetian Ladies* (c.1507). The latter is traditionally, but probably incorrectly, known as *The Courtesans* because of the ladies' low-cut dresses. The Museo del Risorgimento on the same floor looks at the history of Venice until unification with Italy in 1866.

The ceiling of Santo Stefano, built in the form of a ship's keel

Santo Stefano 23

Campo Santo Stefano. **Map** 6 F2. 🎧 *041 275 04 62.* 🚤 *Accademia or Sant'Angelo.* ⬤ *10am–5pm Mon–Sat, 1–5pm Sun.* 📷 🔔

DECONSECRATED six times on account of the blood spilled within its walls, Santo Stefano – one of Venice's most beautiful churches – is now remarkably serene. Built in the 14th century, and altered in the 15th, the church has a carved portal by Bartolomeo Bon, and a campanile with a typical Venetian tilt. The interior has a splendid ship's keel ceiling, carved tie-beams, and the sacristy crammed with valuable paintings.

Santi Giovanni e Paolo ㉔

KNOWN MORE COLLOQUIALLY as San Zanipolo, Santi Giovanni e Paolo vies with the Frari *(see pp94–5)* as the city's greatest Gothic church. Built by the Dominicans in the 14th century, it is striking for its vast scale and architectural austerity. Known as the Pantheon of Venice, it houses monuments to no fewer than 25 doges. Among these are several fine works of art, executed by the Lombardi family and other leading sculptors.

The bronze statue is a monument to Doge Sebastiano Venier, who was Commander of the Fleet at Lepanto.

The Nave
The cross-vaulted interior is tied by wooden beams and supported by stone columns.

★ Tomb of Nicolò Marcello
This magnificent Renaissance monument to Doge Nicolò Marcello (died 1474) was sculpted by Pietro Lombardo.

The doorway, which is decorated with Byzantine reliefs and carvings by Bartolomeo Bon, is one of Venice's earliest Renaissance architectural works.

Entrance

★ Tomb of Pietro Mocenigo
Pietro Lombardo's superb tomb (1481) commemorates the doge's military pursuits when he was Grand Captain of the Venetian forces.

★ Polyptych by Bellini
This painting (c.1465) shows St Vincent Ferrer, a Spanish cleric, flanked by St Sebastian and St Christopher.

**The Baroque high
altar**, begun in
1619, is attributed
to Baldassare
Longhena.

**16th-century
altar statues
by Vittoria**

**16th-century
frescoes
attributed to
Palma il Giovane**

★ **Tomb of Andrea
Vendramin**
*Lombardo's masterpiece
(1476–8) takes the form of
a Roman triumphal arch.*

STAR FEATURES

★ **Doges' Tombs**

★ **Polyptych by Bellini**

Statue of Colleoni ㉕

Campo Santi Giovanni e Paolo.
Map 3 C5. 🚤 *Ospedale Civile.*

BARTOLOMEO COLLEONI, the
famous *condottiere* or
commander of mercenaries,
left his fortune to the
Republic on condition that
his statue was placed in front
of San Marco. A prominent
statue in the piazza would
have broken with precedent,
so the Senate cunningly had
Colleoni raised before the
Scuola di San Marco instead of
the basilica. A touchstone of
early Renaissance sculpture,
the equestrian statue of the
proud warrior (1481–8) is
by the Florentine Andrea
Verrocchio, but was cast in
bronze after his death by
Alessandro Leopardi. The
statue has a strong sense of
power and movement which
arguably ranks it alongside
the works of Donatello.

Santa Maria Formosa ㉖

Campo Santa Maria Formosa.
Map 7 C1. **(** *041 275 04 62.*
🚤 *Rialto.* ⭕ *10am–5pm Mon–Sat,
1–5pm Sun.* 📷 🔲

DESIGNED BY Mauro Coducci
in 1492, this church is
most unusual in having two
main façades – one which
overlooks the *campo*, the
other overlooks the canal.
The bell tower or campanile,
added in 1688, is noted for
the grotesque face at its base.
Two paintings stand out in
the interior: a triptych (1473)
by Bartolomeo Vivarini
and Palma il Vecchio's
St Barbara (c.1510).

San Zaccaria ㉗

Campo San Zaccaria. **Map** 8 D2.
(*041 522 12 57.* 🚤 *San Zaccaria.*
⭕ *10am–noon, 4–6pm Mon–Sat.*
📷 *(chapel).*

SET IN A QUIET square just a
stone's throw from the Riva
degli Schiavoni, the church of
San Zaccaria is a successful
blend of flamboyant Gothic

Palma il Vecchio's *St Barbara*
(c.1510) in Santa Maria Formosa

and Classical Renaissance
styles. Founded in the 9th
century, its façade was later
rebuilt by Antonio Gambello
in Gothic style. When
Gambello died in 1481,
Mauro Coducci completed the
upper section, adding many
of its Renaissance panels.
The interior's artistic
highlight is Giovanni Bellini's
serene and sumptuously
coloured *Madonna and Child
with Saints* (1505) in the
north aisle. A door off the
right nave leads to the Chapel
of St Athanasius which in turn
leads to the Chapel of San
Tarasio. The chapel contains
vault frescoes (1442) by the
Florentine Andrea del
Castagno, and polyptychs
(1443–4) by Antonio Vivarini
and Giovanni d'Alemagna.

A Renaissance panel by Coducci
on the façade of San Zaccaria

Scuola di San Giorgio degli Schiavoni ㉘

Calle Furlani. **Map** 8 E1. **C** *041 522 88 28.* San Zaccaria. Apr–Oct: 9:30am–12:30pm, 3:30–6:30pm Tue–Sat (Sun am only); Nov–Mar: 10am–12:30pm, 3–6pm Tue–Sat (Sun am only). 1 Jan, 1 May, 25 Dec and other religious hols.

18th-century engraving of the Arsenale

WITHIN THIS small gem are some of the finest paintings of Vittore Carpaccio. They were commissioned by the Schiavoni, or Dalmatian Slav community in Venice.

The Scuola was established in 1451 and rebuilt in 1551. It has changed very little since. The exquisite frieze, executed between 1502 and 1508, shows scenes from the lives of patron saints: St George, St Tryphone and St Jerome. Each episode of the narrative cycle is remarkable for its vivid colouring, minutely observed detail and historic record of Venetian life. Outstanding among them are *St George Slaying the Dragon* and *St Jerome Leading the Tamed Lion to the Monastery*.

San Giovanni in Bragora ㉙

Campo Bandiera e Moro. **Map** 8 E2. **C** *041 270 24 64.* Arsenale. 3:30–5:30pm Mon–Sat.

THE EXISTING church is essentially Gothic (1475–9) and the interior contains major works of art that demonstrate the transition from Gothic to early Renaissance. Bartolomeo Vivarini's altarpiece *Madonna and Child with Saints* (1478) is unmistakably Gothic. Contrasting with this is Cima da Conegliano's large-scale *Baptism of Christ* (1492–5), which adorns the main altar.

Arsenale ㉚

Map 8 F1. Arsenale. **Museo Storico Navale** Campo San Biagio. **Map** 8 F3. **C** *041 520 02 76.* 8:45am–1:30pm Mon–Fri; 8:45am–1pm Sat. public hols.

THE ARSENALE was founded in the 12th century and by the 16th had become the greatest naval shipyard in the world, capable of constructing a whole galley in 24 hours, using an assembly-line system. Surrounded by crenellated walls, it was like a city within a city. Today the site is largely disused. Its impressive 15th-century gateway, twin towers and guardian lions can be viewed from the *campo* or bridge outside. The gateway was built by Antonio Gambello and is often cited as Venice's first Renaissance construction.

Around the corner, in Campo San Biagio, the **Museo Storico Navale** charts Venetian naval history from the heyday of the Arsenale to the present. Exhibits include friezes from famous galleys of the past and a replica of the *Bucintoro*, the Doge's ceremonial barge.

San Giorgio Maggiore ㉛

Map 8 D4. **C** *041 522 78 27.* San Giorgio. 9:30am–12:30pm, 2:30–5pm daily (7pm May–Sep). **Fondazione Cini** **C** *041 528 99 00.* Mon–Fri by appt.

APPEARING LIKE a stage set across the water from the Piazzetta is the little island of

St George Slaying the Dragon (1502–8) by Carpaccio, in the Scuola di San Giorgio degli Schiavoni

San Giorgio Maggiore. The church and monastery, constructed between 1559–80, are among Andrea Palladio's greatest architectural achievements. The church's temple front and the spacious interior with its perfect proportions and cool beauty are typically Palladian *(see pp76–7)*. These qualities are echoed by the church of Il Redentore on the nearby island of Giudecca, built by Palladio in 1577–92.

On the chancel walls of San Giorgio Maggiore, are two fine paintings by Tintoretto: *The Last Supper* and *Gathering of the Manna* (both 1594). In the Chapel of the Dead is his last work, *The Deposition* (1592–4), finished by his son Domenico.

The top of the campanile affords superb views of the city and lagoon. You can see the monastery cloisters below, now part of the **Fondazione Cini**, a cultural centre that is used to host international exhibitions.

Palladio's San Giorgio Maggiore

Murano ❷

🚤 *41, 42 from San Zaccaria; "Dir" from Ferrovia and Piazza Roma.*

LIKE THE CITY of Venice, Murano comprises a cluster of small islands, connected by bridges. It has been the centre of the glassmaking industry since 1291, when the furnaces and craftsmen were moved here from the city because of the risk of fire and the disagreeable effects of smoke. Some of the houses on the water date from this period.

The colonnaded exterior of Murano's Basilica dei Santi Maria e Donato

🏛 Museo Vetrario
Palazzo Giustinian, Fondamenta Giustinian. [041 73 95 86. ○ 10am–5pm (Nov–Mar: 4pm) Thu–Tue. ● 1 Jan, 1 May, 25 Dec. ◪ ▯

In the 15th and 16th centuries Murano was the principal glass-producing centre in Europe and today, most tourists visit for glass alone. The Museo Vetrario in the Palazzo Giustinian houses a fine collection of antique pieces. The prize exhibit is the dark blue Barovier wedding cup (1470–80), with enamel work by Angelo Barovier.

🏛 Basilica dei Santi Maria e Donato
Fondamenta Giustinian. [041 73 90 56. ○ 9am–noon, 3:30–7pm daily.

The architectural highlight of the island is the Basilica dei Santi Maria e Donato, with its lovely colonnaded apse. Despite some heavy-handed restoration undertaken in the 19th century, this 12th-century church still retains much of its original beauty. Visitors should note the Gothic ship's keel roof, the apse with its mosaic Madonna and the beautiful medieval mosaic floor, which dates from 1140.

Burano ❸

🚤 *12 from Fondamente Nuove; 14 from San Zaccaria.*

BURANO IS THE MOST colourful of the lagoon islands and can be distinguished from a distance by the tilting tower of its church. In contrast with the haunting Torcello, the island is densely populated, its waterways fringed with brightly painted houses, such as the Casa Bepi.

The main thoroughfare is Via Baldassare Galuppi, named after the Burano-born composer. It features traditional lace and linen stalls and open-air trattorias serving fresh fish.

🏛 Scuola dei Merletti
Piazza Baldassare Galuppi. [041 73 00 34. ○ 10am–5pm (4pm Nov–Mar) Wed–Mon. ● public hols. ◪

Venetian glass goblet

The people of Burano are fishermen and lacemakers by tradition. You can still see fishermen scraping their boats or mending nets, but today lacemakers are rare. In the 16th century the local lace was the most sought-after in Europe – it was so delicate it became known as *punto in aria* ("points in the air"). After a slump in the 18th century, the industry revived and a lace-making school, or Scuola dei Merletti, was set up in 1872. Although authentic Burano lace is hard to find today, you can watch it being made by Burano women at the school. There is also a museum which displays fine examples of antique lace.

The multicoloured Casa Bepi on the island of Burano

Torcello ⊛

ESTABLISHED BETWEEN the 5th and 6th centuries, the island of Torcello boasts the oldest building in the lagoon – the cathedral of Santa Maria dell'Assunta. Founded in AD 639, it contains some splendid ancient mosaics. The adjoining church of Santa Fosca, of pure Byzantine design, is another mark of Torcello's former glory – before being eclipsed by Venice it had a population of 20,000.

★ Apse Mosaic
The 13th-century Madonna, set against a gold background, is one of the most beautiful mosaics in Venice.

★ Doomsday Mosaics
The highly decorative 12th-century mosaic of the Last Judgment covers the west wall.

Pulpit
The present basilica dates from 1008, but includes earlier features. The pulpit contains 7th-century fragments.

The Roman sarcophagus
below the altar is said to contain the relics of St Heliodorus.

★ Iconostasis
The exquisite Byzantine marble panels of the rood screen are carved with peacocks, lions and flowers.

Nave Columns
Two rows of slender marble columns, 18 in all, separate the three naves. Their finely carved capitals date from the 11th century.

Torcello's Last Canals
Silted canals and malaria hastened Torcello's decline. One of the remaining waterways runs from the vaporetto *stop to the basilica.*

The altar
was rebuilt in 1939 and stands below a 15th-century wood relief of *Santa Fosca Sleeping.*

The central dome
and cross sections are supported by columns of Greek marble with Corinthian capitals.

Santa Fosca
Built in the 11th and 12th centuries on a Greek-cross plan, the church has a serene Byzantine interior with a central pentagonal apse.

The Portico of Santa Fosca, with its elegant stilted arches, is built on three sides of the church, and probably dates from the 12th century.

Vaporetto **boarding point**

The Museo dell'Estuario
houses many old church treasures.

STAR FEATURES

★ Apse Mosaic

★ Doomsday Mosaics

★ Iconostasis

Attila's Throne
It was said that the 5th-century king of the Huns used this marble seat as his throne.

VENICE STREET FINDER

ALL THE MAP REFERENCES given for sights, hotels and restaurants in Venice refer to this section of the book. The key map below shows which areas of the city are covered by the Street Finder. The first figure of the map reference indicates which map to turn to, and the letter and number which follow are for the grid reference. Standard Italian spelling has been used on all the maps in this book,

but when exploring Venice you will find that the names on many street signs are written in Venetian dialect. Mostly this means only a slight variation in spelling (as in the word Sotoportico/Sotoportego below), but some names look totally different. For example, the church of Santi Giovanni e Paolo *(see map 3)*, is frequently signposted as "San Zanipolo". A further map showing the vaporetto routes follows the street maps.

RECOGNIZING STREET NAMES

The signs for street *(calle)*, canal *(rio)* and square *(campo)* will soon become familiar, but the Venetians have a colourful vocabulary for the maze of alleys which makes up the city. When exploring, the following may help.

FONDAMENTA S. SEVERO	RIO TERRA GESUATI
Fondamenta is a street that runs alongside a canal, often named after the canal it follows.	**Rio Terrà** is a filled-in canal. Similar to a *rio terrà* is a *piscina*, which often forms a square.

SOTOPORTEGO E PONTE S. CRISTOFORO

Sotoportico or Sotoportego means a covered passageway.

SALIZADA PIO X	RIVA DEI PARTIGIANI
Salizzada is a main street (formerly a paved street).	**Riva** is a wide *fondamenta*, often facing the lagoon.

RUGAGIUFFA	CORTE DEI DO POZZI
Ruga is a street lined with shops.	**Corte** means a courtyard.

RIO MENUO O DE LA VERONA

Many streets and canals in Venice often have more than one name: *o* means "or".

```
0 metres          500
0 yards           500
```

MURANO
(Inset on maps 3–4)

KEY TO STREET FINDER

	Major sight
	Place of interest
	Railway station
	Ferry boarding point
	Vaporetto boarding point
	Traghetto crossing
	Gondola mooring
	Bus terminus
	Tourist information
	Hospital with casualty unit
	Parking
	Police station
	Church
	Synagogue
	Post office
=	Railway line

SCALE OF MAP PAGES

0 metres	200
0 yards	200

SCALE OF MURANO INSET

0 metres	500
0 yards	500

MURANO

CAMPO SPORTIVO

CALLE DEL CONVENTO

CALLE VOLPI

COM D CIMITERO

CALLE DELL'ARTIGIANO

FONDAMENTA STRADA

FONDAMENTA SEBA

CALLE SAN BERNARDO

CALLE BRUSSA

RAMO VENIER

CALLE DEL CRISTO

Venier

Canale

CAMPO SAN BERNARDO

CAMPO SAN SALVADOR

CALLE CONTERIE

CALLE DEL MISTRO

Canale di San Donato

FONDAMENTA SANTI SEBASTIANO

FMTA SAN LORENZO

SS Maria e Donato

FONDAMENTA LORENZO RADI

Ponte San Donato

FONDAMENTA GIUSTINIAN

Canale Serenella

CALLE VIVARINI

STRADA VIA VENIER

degli Angeli

FMTA DA MULA

RAMO DA MULA

FONDAMENTA

CAVOUR

Museo dell'Arte Vetraria

FONDAMENTA ANDREA NAVAGERO

Museo

Canal Grande

Ponte Vivarini

Palazzo da Mula

FMTA ANTONIO COLLEONI

CALLE S GIACOMO

CALLE S GIACOMO

Serenella

STRADA VICINALE ORTI

CALLE SAN CIPRIANO

San Pietro Martire

C BERTOLINI

CALLE BERTOLINI

LIPU STO STEFANO

VETRAI

CPLO MANTIN

CPLO TURELLA

CPLO BIGAGLIA

FMTA SAN GIOVANNI DEI BATTUTI

Navagero

C PARADISO

2

Canale Ondello

FONDAMENTA SERENELLA

FONDAMENTA

CALLE MOTTA

CALLE DELL'OLIO

VIALE GARIBALDI

VIA BRIATI

FMTA PIAVE

Faro

Faro

3

Colonna

Canale dei Marani

4

Canale delle Fondamente Nuove

aletto

NDAMENTE NUOVE

CALLE DELLE CAPPUCCINE

Ospedale Civile

CALLE DI SANTA GIUSTINA

Rio di Santa Giustina

FONDAMENTA DI SANTA GIUSTINA

MOSCHETTE

DELLE TOLE

C.D. CAFFETTIER

CALLE SAN FRANCESCO

Celestia

CALLE DEGLI ORTI

FMTA CASE NUOVE

C SAGREDO

San Francesco della Vigna

5

Venice Vaporetto Routes

ROUTES AROUND THE LAGOON

- Torcello 🚏⑫
- Mazzorbo 🚏⑫
- Burano 🚏⑫
- Treporti 🚏⑫⑬
- Sant' Erasmo 🚏⑬
- Vignole 🚏⑬
- Punta Sabbioni 🚏⑫⑭⑯
- San Nicolò 🚏⑯
- Santa Maria Elisabetta (Lido) 🚏①⑥⑭⑯⑯②⑧②Ⓝ
- Casino 🚏⑯

See main map

Laguna Veneta

MARE ADRIATICO

The Vaporetto Routes

The ACTV network runs regular services around the city and out to most of the islands. Some services are circular; others extend their routes during the high season. More details of the different types of vaporetti and how to use them are given on pages 636–7.

Canale delle Sacch

- Sant'Alvise 🚏㊶㊷㊿㊾   41, 42,
- Ponte dei Tre Archi 🚏㊶㊷㊿㊾

41, 42, 51, 52, 71, 72

CANNAREGIO

- Ponte delle Gug 🚏㊶㊷㊿㊾
- San M 🚏①
- Ferrovia 🚏①㊶㊷㊿㊾㊿⑥②Ⓝ㊾ FS   1, 41, 42, 51-   52, 82, N-G
- Riva di Biasio 🚏①
- S Su

SANTA CROCE

- Tronchetto B 🚏㊷⑧②Ⓝ㊾   72, 82, N, 71, G2

P

- Piazzale Roma 🚏①㊶㊷㊿㊿⑥②Ⓝ㊾
  P

SAN POLO

- San Tomà 🚏①⑧②Ⓝ
- San San 🚏⑧②Ⓝ   An
- Ca' Rezzonico 🚏①
- Accademia 🚏①⑧②Ⓝ
- S

Bacino della Stazione Marittima   41, 42, 51, 52, 61, 62,

- Santa Marta 🚏㊶㊷㊿㊿⑥㊾

82, N, G2

- San Basilio 🚏⑧②Ⓝ
- Zattere 🚏㊿⑥②Ⓝ㊾
- Fusina ←

41, 42, 51, 52, 61, 62, 82, N, G1, G2

Canale della Giudec

- Sacca Fisola 🚏㊶㊷⑧②

Canale di Fusina

- Sant'Eufemia 🚏㊶㊷⑧②

GIUDECCA

- Palanca 🚏⑧②Ⓝ

| 0 metres | 500 |
| 0 yards | 500 |

KEY

12	*Vaporetto* route
	Ferry boarding point
	Vaporetto boarding point
FS	Railway station
P	Parking

ROUTES

① Piazzale Roma – Lido

⑥ San Zaccaria – Lido

⑫ F. Nuove – Burano – Punta Sabbioni

⑬ F. Nuove – Sant'Erasmo – Treporti

⑭ San Zaccaria – Punta Sabbioni

⑳ San Zaccaria – San Lazzaro

㊶ Circular (via Murano) – anticlockwise

㊷ Circular (via Murano) – clockwise

� Circular (via Lido) – anticlockwise

㊿ Circular (via Lido) – clockwise

� Lido – Zattere – Piazzale Roma

⑦①⑦② Summer line only
San Zaccaria – Tronchetto

㊵ San Zaccaria – Piazzale Roma – Lido

Ⓝ Lido – Tronchetto – San Zaccaria
(night service)

Ⓖ① Punta Sabbioni – Fusina

Ⓖ② Circular (Via San Marco)

Ⓖ③ San Giustina – Tessera airport

THE VENETO AND FRIULI

THE VENETO IS A REGION OF TREMENDOUS CONTRASTS, *encompassing the breathtaking natural beauty of the Dolomites, Lake Garda (Italy's largest lake) and the rolling Euganean Hills, and the man-made delights of magnificent ancient cities such as Verona, Vicenza and Padua. Neighbouring Friuli-Venezia Giulia lines the border with Slovenia to the east, taking in the Carnic Hills in the north, the Roman town of Aquileia and the bustling Adriatic port of Trieste.*

The Romans built frontier posts on this fertile land of silt deposits, and these survive today as the cities of Vicenza, Padua, Verona and Treviso. Strategically placed at the hub of the empire's road network, the cities prospered under Roman rule, but suffered in the wave of Germanic invasions of the 5th century AD.

The region's fortunes revived under the benign rule of the Venetian empire. The medieval cities of the Veneto lay on important trade routes such as the Serenissima, the road connecting the flourishing port cities of Venice and Genoa, and the Brenner Pass, used by commercial travellers crossing the Alps from northern Europe. Wealth from agriculture, commerce and the spoils of war paid for the beautification of these cities through the building of Renaissance palaces and public buildings, many designed by the Veneto's great architect, Andrea Palladio. His palazzi and villas are telling symbols of the leisured existence once enjoyed by the area's aristocrats.

Today the Veneto is a thriving wine exporter, textile producer and agricultural centre, and Friuli is a focus for new technology, while remaining largely agricultural. Both regions are popular tourist destinations, despite lying a little in the shadow of Venice, and boast an abundant and enchanting variety of attractions.

A leisurely *passeggiata* in one of Verona's ancient streets

◁ The Renaissance bridge by Palladio at Bassano del Grappa in the Veneto

Exploring the Veneto and Friuli

T HE FLAT LANDSCAPE of the Veneto plain is dramatically off-
set by the spectacular Dolomite mountains which form
the northwestern border to the Veneto. Friuli, Italy's most
northeasterly region, lies tucked up against Austria to the
north and Slovenia to the east. Both the Veneto and Friuli
are bordered to the south by the Adriatic, with its beaches
and ports, which provide a contrast with the area's gently
rolling countryside, the vast stretch of Lake Garda and
the many attractive resorts and ancient towns.

View of Verona from the Teatro Romano

CORTINA
D'AMPEZZO

PIEVE DI
CADORE

PARCO NAZIONALE DELLE
DOLOMITI BELLUNESI

BELLUNO

VITTORIO
VENETO

CONEGLIANO

Innsbruck

Trento

FELTRE

RIVA DEL
GARDA

ASIAGO

ASOLO

TREVISO

Bolzano
Trento

RECOARO
TERME

BASSANO
DEL GRAPPA

CASTELFRANCO
VENETO

THIENE

MAROSTICA

LAKE GARDA

GARDA

VICENZA

PESCHIERA
DEL GARDA

VERONA

VENICE

Brescia

SOAVE

LONIGO

PADUA

BRENTA
CANAL

VILLAFRANCA
DI VERONA

ABANO TERME

Adige

EUGANEAN HILLS

CHIOGGIA

Mantova

MONSELICE

Baccchiglione

N10

ROVIGO

Adige

Po di Vene

Po

Ravenna

Ferrara
Bologna

KEY

═══ Motorway

▬▬▬ Major road

▭▭▭ Minor road

▬▬▬ Scenic route

〜〜 River

☀ Viewpoint

0 kilometres   25

0 miles   20

SEE ALSO

- *Where to Stay* pp544–7
- *Where to Eat* pp580–82

GETTING AROUND

An extensive rail network and good bus services make this region easy to explore by public transport, though only buses operate around Lake Garda. Motorways and main roads provide good links between the main cities. The Venice Simplon-Orient-Express train, which operates from London to Venice, offers a novel approach to the area.

The bridge at Cividale del Friuli

A mountain chalet in Cortina d'Ampezzo

SIGHTS AT A GLANCE

Verona ❶

VERONA IS A VIBRANT trading centre, the second biggest city in the Veneto region (after Venice) and one of the most prosperous in northern Italy. Its ancient centre boasts many magnificent Roman ruins, second only to those of Rome itself, and fine palazzi built of *rosso di Verona*, the local pink-tinged limestone, by the city's medieval rulers. Verona has two main focal points: the massive 1st-century AD Arena, which is still the setting for major events, and Piazza Erbe with its colourful market.

Scaligeri statue in Castelvecchio

One of the main attractions, however, is the church of San Zeno Maggiore *(see pp140–41)*, which boasts unusual medieval bronze door panels: they are carved with extraordinary scenes, some biblical, others on the life of San Zeno.

View of Verona from the
Museo Archeologico

Verona's Rulers

In 1263 the Scaligeri began their 124-year rule of Verona. They used ruthless tactics in their rise to power, but once established, the Scaligeri family brought peace to a city racked by civil strife and inter-family rivalry. They proved to be relatively just and cultured rulers – the poet Dante was welcomed to their court in 1301, and dedicated the final part of his epic *Divine Comedy* to the ruling Cangrande I. Today their legacy remains in their ornate tombs and in Castelvecchio.

In 1387 Verona fell to the Visconti of Milan, and a succession of outsiders – Venice, France and Austria – then ruled the city until the Veneto was united with Italy in 1866.

Verona's enormous Roman Arena seen from Piazza Brà

KEY

FS	Railway station
	Bus terminus
P	Parking
	Tourist information
	Church

Ponte Scaligero, part of the old defence system of Castelvecchio

VISITORS' CHECKLIST

🏛 254,700. ✈ Villafranca 14
km (9 miles) SW. 🚉 Porta Nuova,
Piazza XXV Aprile. 🚌 Piazza
Cittadella. 🛈 Via degli Alpini 9
(045 806 86 80). 🖰 daily.
🎟 Tickets valid for churches.
🎭 Apr: VinItaly wine fair; Jun–
Aug: Estate Teatrale Veronese;
Jul–Sep: Opera Festival.

♣ Castelvecchio

Corso Castelvecchio 2. 📞 045 801
54 35. 🕐 Tue–Sun. 🎟 📷 📹
This impressive castle, built by
Cangrande II between 1355
and 1375, now houses one
of the finest art galleries
in the Veneto outside
Venice. It is arranged to
give striking views of the
castle itself as well as the
exhibits displayed within.

The first section contains
a wealth of late Roman
and early Christian material –
silver plate, 5th century
brooches, glass painted with a
portrait of Christ the Shepherd
in gold, and the carved marble
sarcophagus of Saints Sergius
and Bacchus (1179).

The section on medieval and
early Renaissance art vividly
demonstrates the influence of
northern art on local painters:
the emphasis is on brutal
realism as opposed to serene
idealism. The late Renaissance
works include a fine collection
of 15th-century Madonnas.

Jewellery, suits of armour,
swords and shield bosses,
Veronese's *Deposition* (1565)
and a portrait painting attributed to either Titian or to
Lorenzo Lotto are on display
in further sections.

Outside, a walkway offers
views of the river Adige and
the medieval **Ponte Scaligero**
crossing it, and of the 14th-
century equestrian statue of
Cangrande I which once
graced his tomb (*see p138*).

♪ Arena

Piazza Brà. 📞 045 800 32 04. 🕐
Tue–Sun. ⬤ 25–26 Dec, 1 Jan. 🎟 📷
Verona's Roman amphitheatre,
completed in AD 30, is the
third largest in the world, after
Rome's Colosseum and the
amphitheatre at Santa Maria
Capua Vetere, near Naples.

The interior, still virtually intact,
could hold almost the entire
population of Roman Verona,
and visitors came from across
the Veneto to watch gladiatorial
combats and mock battles.
Since then, the Arena has
seen executions, fairs,
bullfights, and theatre and
opera productions.

⛪ San Fermo Maggiore

Via San Fermo. 📞 045 59 28 13.
🕐 Tue–Sun. 🎟 📷
San Fermo Maggiore is not one
but two churches: this is most
clearly seen from the outside,
where the apse has pointed
Gothic elements rising above a
sturdy Romanesque base. The
lower church, begun in 1065
by Benedictine monks on the
site of an earlier sanctuary, has
frescoes on the simple arcades.

The more impressive upper
church dates from 1313 and is
covered with a splendid ship's
keel roof. The interior also
boasts much medieval fresco
work including a 14th-century
section by Stefano da Zevio
depicting Musician Angels.
Nearby is the Brenzoni mausoleum (c.1440) by Giovanni di
Bartolo, and above it a 1426
fresco of the *Annunciation*
by Pisanello (1377–1455).

The 11th-century apse of the lower church of San Fermo Maggiore

Exploring Verona

Since the days of the Roman empire, Piazza Erbe – built on the site of the ancient Roman forum – has been the centre of Verona. Many of the city's fine palazzi, churches and monuments are nearly as ancient, several dating from the medieval period.

The fountain, erected in the 14th century at the centre of Piazza Erbe

⚜ Piazza Erbe

Piazza Erbe is named after the city's old herb market. Today's stalls, shaded by umbrellas, sell everything from herb-flavoured roast suckling pig in bread rolls to succulent fresh-picked fruit and delicious wild mushrooms.

At the northern end of Piazza Erbe stands the Baroque **Palazzo Maffei** (1668), surmounted by statues. In front of it rises a column supporting the **Venetian lion**, which marks Verona's absorption, in 1405, into the Venetian empire. On the west side is the **Casa dei Mercanti**, a largely 17th-century building which dates originally from 1301. Opposite, coloured wall frescoes are still visible above the cafés.

The **fountain** in the middle of the piazza is often overshadowed by the market stalls, though the statue at its centre dates from Roman times. It serves as a reminder that this piazza has been used as a market-place for 2,000 years.

⚜ Piazza dei Signori

Torre dei Lamberti 📞 045 803 27 26. ⏱ Tue–Sun. 🎫
In the centre of the square stands an elegant 19th-century **statue of Dante**, whose gaze seems fixed on the forbidding **Palazzo del Capitano**, once the home of Verona's military commanders. Beside it is the

equally intimidating **Palazzo della Ragione**, the palace of Reason, or law court; both were built in the 14th century. The courtyard of the law court has a handsome external stone staircase, added in 1446–50. Stunning views of the Alps can be enjoyed by those prepared to climb the 84-m (275-ft) **Torre dei Lamberti**, which rises from the western side of the courtyard.

Behind the statue of Dante is the **Loggia del Consiglio** (1493), the council chamber topped by statues of Roman worthies born in Verona: they include Pliny the Elder, the natural historian, and Vitruvius, the architectural theorist.

The square is linked to Piazza Erbe by the Arco della Costa, or the Arch of the Rib, named after the whale rib long ago hung beneath it.

The frescoed Renaissance façade of the Loggia del Consiglio on Piazza dei Signori

🔒 Tombs of the Scaligeri

Via Arche Scaligeri.
Beside the entrance to the tiny Romanesque church of **Santa Maria Antica**, once the parish church of the powerful Scaligeri family, lie a profusion of bizarre tombs of the one-time rulers of Verona.

Over the entrance to the church is the impressive tomb of Cangrande I (died 1329), surmounted by an equestrian statue of the ruler, a copy of the original which is now in Castelvecchio (see p137).

The other Scaligeri tombs are next to the church, behind a wrought-iron fence which incorporates the ladder emblem of the family's original name (della Scala, meaning "of the steps"). Towering above the fence are the tombs of Mastino II (died 1351) and Cansignorio (died 1375), splendidly decorated with a profusion of tiny Gothic spires. Other members of the Scaligeri family lie within a series of plainer tombs which stand nearer the church wall.

14th-century Scaligeri tomb

🔒 Sant'Anastasia

Piazza Sant'Anastasia. 📞 045 59 28 13. ⏱ Tue–Sun. 🎫
The huge and lofty church of Sant'Anastasia was begun in 1290. Faded 15th-century frescoes and carved scenes from the life of St Peter Martyr adorn its Gothic portal.

Inside, there are two notable holy water stoups, supported on figures of beggars, known locally as i gobbi (the hunchbacks). These figures were carved a century apart: the earlier one (on the left) dates from 1495.

The sacristy, off the north aisle, is home to the fine but unfortunately damaged fresco of St George and the Princess (1433–8) by Pisanello.

ROMEO AND JULIET

The tragic story of Romeo and Juliet, two young lovers from rival families (the Capulets and the Montagues in Shakespeare's play), was written by Luigi da Porto of Vicenza in the 1520s and has inspired countless poems, films, ballets and dramas.

At the **Casa di Giulietta** (Juliet's house), No. 27 Via Cappello, Romeo is said to have climbed to Juliet's balcony; in reality this is a restored 13th-century inn. Crowds throng to see the simple façade, and stand on the small marble balcony. The run-down house dubbed the **Casa di Romeo** stands a few streets away in Via Arche Scaligeri, east of Piazza dei Signori.

The so-called **Tomba di Giulietta** is displayed in a crypt below the cloister of San Francesco al Corso on Via del Pontiere. The stone sarcophagus lies in an extremely atmospheric setting.

The so-called Casa di Giulietta

🏠 Duomo
Piazza Duomo. 📞 045 59 28 13.
🕐 Tue–Sun. 🎟️ 🚻

Verona's cathedral was begun in 1139 and is fronted by a magnificent Romanesque portal carved by Nicolò, one of the two master masons responsible for the façade of San Zeno (*see pp140–41*). Here he sculpted the sword-bearing figures of Oliver and Roland, two of Charlemagne's knights, whose exploits were much celebrated in medieval poetry. Alongside them stand evangelists and saints with wide eyes and flowing beards. To the south there is a second Romanesque portal carved with Jonah and the Whale and with comically grotesque caryatids.

The highlight of the interior is Titian's lovely *Assumption* (1535–40), and outside there is a Romanesque cloister in which the excavated ruins of earlier churches are visible. The 8th-century baptistry, or San Giovanni in Fonte (St John of the Spring), was built from Roman masonry; the marble font was carved in 1200.

🎭 Teatro Romano
Rigaste Redentore 2. 📞 045 800 03 60. 🕐 Tue–Sun. 🎟️

This theatre was built in the 1st century BC; little now survives of the original stage area, but the semicircular seating area remains largely intact. It offers entrancing views over the city: in the foreground is the only one of three Roman bridges to have survived, though it was rebuilt after World War II.

🏛️ Museo Archeologico
Rigaste Redentore 2. 📞 045 800 03 60. 🕐 8am–6:30pm Tue–Sun. 🎟️

A lift carries visitors from the Teatro Romano up the cliffs to the monastery above, now an archaeological museum.

The exhibits around the tiny cloister and in the old monks' cells include mosaics, pottery, glass and tombstones. There is also a fine bronze bust of the ambitious first Roman emperor, Augustus (63 BC–AD 14), who succeeded in overcoming his opponents, including Mark Antony and Cleopatra, to become the sole ruler of the Roman world in 31 BC.

Statuary and formal hedges in the Renaissance Giardino Giusti

🌳 Giardino Giusti
Via Giardino Giusti 2. 📞 045 803 40 29. 🕐 daily. ⬤ 25 Dec. 🎟️ 🚻

This is one of Italy's finest Renaissance gardens. It was laid out in 1580 and, as with other gardens of the period, there is a deliberate juxtaposition of nature and artifice: the formal lower garden of clipped box hedges, gravel walks and potted plants contrasts with wilder, natural woods above.

John Evelyn, an English author and diarist who visited Verona in 1661, thought this the finest garden in Europe.

🏠 San Giorgio in Braida
Lungadige San Giorgio. 📞 045 834 02 32. 🕐 daily.

This lovely domed Renaissance church was begun in about 1530 by Michele Sanmicheli. The altar includes the famous *Martyrdom of St George* (1566) by Veronese, and above the west door is the *Baptism of Christ*, usually attributed to Tintoretto (1518–94).

The imposing façade of Verona's Duomo, Santa Maria Matricolare

Verona: San Zeno Maggiore

Detail from San Zeno's façade

SAN ZENO, built in 1123–35 to house the shrine of Verona's patron saint, is the most ornate Romanesque church in northern Italy. The façade is adorned with an impressive rose window, marble reliefs, and a graceful porch canopy. The highlight, however, is the fascinating 11th- and 12th-century bronze door panels. A squat tower just north of San Zeno is said to cover the tomb of King Pepin of Italy (777–810).

Nave Ceiling
The nave has a magnificent example of a ship's keel ceiling, so called because it resembles the inside of an upturned boat. This ceiling was constructed in 1386 when the apse was rebuilt.

The bell tower, started in 1045, reached its present height of 72 m (236 ft) in 1178.

Altarpiece by Mantegna
The Madonna's halo in Andrea Mantegna's altarpiece of the Virgin and Child with saints (1457–59) echoes the shape of the church's rose window.

Former washroom

★ Cloister (1123)
The arches are rounded Romanesque on one side, pointed Gothic on another.

Crypt
The vaulted crypt contains the tomb of San Zeno, appointed first bishop of Verona in AD 362, who died in AD 380.

Nave and Main Altar
The plan of the church is modelled on an ancient Roman basilica, the Hall of Justice. The main altar is situated in the raised sanctuary where the judge's throne would have stood.

Striped brickwork is typical of Romanesque buildings in Verona. Courses of local pink brick are alternated with ivory-coloured tufa.

BRONZE DOOR PANELS

The 48 bronze panels of the west doors are primitive but forceful in their depiction of biblical stories and scenes from the life of San Zeno. Those on the left date from 1030 and survive from an earlier church on the site; those on the right were made after the earthquake in 1137. The panels are the work of three separate craftsmen, and are linked with masks. Huge staring eyes and Ottoman-style hats, armour and architecture feature prominently. Among the scenes, some of which are unclear, are Adam and Eve, Salome dancing for the head of John the Baptist, and a startling Descent into Limbo.

Descent into limbo   Christ in Glory   Human head

The rose window, dating from the early 12th century, symbolizes the Wheel of Fortune: figures on the rim show the rise and fall of human luck.

The Romanesque porch is one of the finest examples of the style in northern Italy. Since 1138 it has shielded biblical bas-reliefs, above the west doors, from the elements.

Marble side panels, which were carved in 1140, depict events from the Life of Christ (to the left of the doors) and scenes from the Book of Genesis (to the right).

★ West Doors
Each of the wooden doors has 24 bronze plates nailed on to make the doors look like solid metal. A multi-coloured bas-relief above them depicts San Zeno, flanked by the people of Verona, vanquishing the devil.

STAR FEATURES

★ West Doors

★ Cloister

Lake Garda ②

GARDA, THE LARGEST AND EASTERNMOST of the Italian
lakes, borders three regions: Trentino to the north,
Lombardy to the west and south, and the Veneto to the
south and east. The low-lying countryside around the
southern stretches becomes increasingly dramatic further
north, until impressive rocky cliffs, sometimes swathed
in pines, hug the shoreline of the northern tip. The
numerous sporting facilities, many sights, and splendid
scenery of snow-capped mountains help make the lake
a favourite summer
playground.

Eastern tip of Sirmione Peninsula
*Beyond the town is a path which
follows the rim of the peninsula,
passing boiling sulphur springs.*

Riva's waterfront is dominated by an old fortress
of the Scaligeri. Wind-
surfers favour this
resort because of
the consistent off-
shore winds.

Gardone is noted for its exotically-planted
park and for the Villa il Vittoriale, the Art
Deco home of the poet Gabriele d'Annunzio,
which is filled with curiosities.

The Republic of Salò was
established here by Mussolini
in 1943. The cathedral in this
elegant and attractive town of
pastel-painted houses contains
an altarpiece by Veneziano.

The streets
of Malcesine
cluster below an
imposing medieval
castle. A cable car
climbs to the summit
of Monte Baldo (1,745
m/5,725 ft), offering
far-reaching views.

0 kilometres   5

0 miles   5

The lake is named after
this long-established town.

Bardolino gave its name to
the well-known red wine.

The hydrofoils,
*catamarans and
steamers which ply
the lake offer glimpses
of villas and gardens
which cannot be seen
from the coastal road.*

Peschiera's attractive enclosed
harbour and fortress were built by
the Austrians in the 1860s, during
the Italian Wars of Independence.

KEY

••• Steamer route
••• Car ferry
🔼 Sailing club or centre
i Tourist information
🌿 Viewpoint

Sirmione
*A fascinating medieval castle,
the Rocca Scaligera, dominates
the town of Sirmione. At the tip
of the peninsula lie Roman ruins.*

Map labels: Riva del Garda, Torbole, Limone sul Garda, Tremosine, Malcesine, Campione del Garda, Assenza, Tignale, Brenzone, Gargnano, Castelletto, Bogliaco, Maderno, Gardone Riviera, Torri del Benaco, Portese, San Felice del Bonaco, Garda, Manerba, Moniga, Bardolino, Padenghe sul Garda, Sirmione, Lazise, Desenzano, Peschiera

The 16th-century wooden bridge by Palladio at Bassano del Grappa

Bassano del Grappa ❸

Vicenza. 🏠 39,000. 🇫🇸 🚌
ℹ️ *Largo Corona d'Italia 35 (0424 52 43 51).* 🛒 *Thu & Sat am.*

THIS PEACEFUL TOWN lies at the foot of Monte Grappa. The river Brenta is straddled by the graceful Ponte degli Alpini, which was designed in 1569 by Palladio. It is built of timber to allow it to flex when lit by the spring meltwaters. Bassano is well known for its majolica products (decorated and glazed earthenware), some of which are on display in the **Palazzo Sturm**. The town is also synonymous with the popular Italian after-dinner drink, the clear spirit known as *grappa*. It is produced from the lees *(graspa)* left over from wine production, information about the process is given in the **Museo degli Alpini**.

🏛 **Palazzo Sturm**
Via Ferracina. (0424 52 49 33.
◻ Apr–Oct: Tue–Sun; Nov–Mar: Fri–Sun. 🎟

🏛 **Museo degli Alpini**
Via Anagarano 2. (0424 50 36 62.
◻ Tue–Sun. ● 6–16 Jan.

Asolo ❹

Treviso. 🏠 2,000. 🚌 ℹ️ *Piazza d'Annunzio 3 (0423 52 90 46).* 🛒 Sat.

ASOLO IS beautifully sited among the cypress-clad foothills of the Dolomites. This tiny walled town was once ruled by Queen Caterina Cornaro (1454–1510), the Venetian wife of the King of Cyprus, who poisoned her husband so that Venice would gain Cyprus. Cardinal Pietro Bembo, a poet, coined the verb *asolare* to describe the bittersweet life of enforced idleness she endured in exile here. Among others who have fallen in love with the narrow streets and grand houses was poet Robert Browning, who named a volume of poems *Asolanda* (1889) after Asolo.

ENVIRONS: At Masèr, 10 km (6 miles) east of the town, stands the magnificent **Villa Barbaro** *(see pp76–7).* It was designed by Palladio in about 1555, in conjunction with the artist Veronese, and perfectly blends symmetry and light, airy rooms with sumptuous *trompe l'oeil* frescoes.

🏠 **Villa Barbaro**
Masèr. (0423 92 30 04.
◻ Mar–Oct: Tue, Sat, Sun & hols pm; Nov–Feb: Sat, Sun & hols pm. ● 24 Dec–6 Jan, Easter Sun. 🎟

Castelfranco Veneto ❺

Treviso. 🏠 30,000. 🇫🇸 🚌
ℹ️ *Via Francesco M Preti 39 (0423 49 50 00).* 🛒 *Tue am & Fri am.*

FORTIFIED IN 1199 by rulers of Treviso as a defence against the neighbouring Paduans, the historic core of this town lies within well-preserved walls. In the **Casa di Giorgione**, said to be the birthplace of the painter Giorgione (1478–1511), about whom little is known, there is a museum devoted to his life. Giorgione innovatively used landscape to create mood, adding figures to intensify the atmosphere – for instance in his broodingly mysterious but evocative most famous work, *The Tempest (see p102).* Another of his few directly attributable works hangs here in the **Duomo**: the *Madonna and Child with Saints Liberal and Francis* (1504).

ENVIRONS: About 8 km (5 miles) northeast of the town, at the village of Fanzolo, lies the **Villa Emo** (c.1555). Designed by Palladio, it is a typical example of his work: a cube flanked by two symmetrical wings. Inside there are lavish frescoes by Zelotti.

🏠 **Casa di Giorgione**
Piazzetta del Duomo. (0423 49 12 40. ◻ Tue–Sun. ● public hols. 🎟
🏠 **Villa Emo**
Fanzolo di Vedelago. (0423 47 64 14. ◻ Apr–Oct: Mon–Sat am, Sun pm; Nov–Mar: Sat & Sun pm. ● 15 Dec–15 Jan. 🎟 📷

Fresco (c.1561) by Veronese adorning the Villa Barbaro near Asolo

Street-by-Street: Vicenza ➏

Face at No. 21 Contrà Porti

VICENZA IS KNOWN as the adoptive city of Andrea Palladio (1508–80), who started out as a stonemason and became the most influential architect of his time. The evolution of his distinctive style is visible all around the city. In the centre is the monumental basilica he adapted to serve as the town hall, nearby is the Teatro Olimpico, and all around are the palaces he built for Vicenza's wealthy citizens.

Contrà Porti
is bordered by some of the most elegant palazzi in Vicenza.

Loggia del Capitaniato
This covered arcade was designed by Palladio in 1571.

Palazzo Valmarana Braga
Palladio's impressive building of 1566 is decorated with giant pilasters and sculpted scenes. It was not completed until 1680, 100 years after the architect's death.

San Lorenzo

Piazza Stazione

Duomo
Vicenza's cathedral was rebuilt after bomb damage during World War II left only the façade and choir entirely intact.

Andrea Palladio
This memorial to Vicenza's most famous citizen is usually surrounded by market stalls.

CORSO ANDREA PALLADIO
CONTRÀ CAVOUR
VIA BATTISTI
CONTRÀ P. LAMPÈRTICO
CONTRÀ GARIBALDI
C. MUSCHERIA
CONTRÀ PESCHERIE VECC
CONTRÀ SAN ANTONIO
PIAZZA DEL DUOMO

0 kilometres   2

0 miles   1

KEY

– – – Suggested route

STAR SIGHT

★ **Piazza dei Signori**

A large hall is all that remains of the 15th-century Palazzo della Ragione.

Torre di Piazza, built in the 12th century, is an impressive 82 m (269 ft) high.

Santa Corona

Teatro Olimpico Museo Civico

CONTRÀ S BARBARA
PIAZZA DELLE BIADE
CONTRÀ CATENA
C GAZZOLE
CONTRÀ PIANCOLI
CONTRÀ SAN PAOLO
CONTRÀ PONTE SAN MICHELE
ERBE
PESCARIA
RETRONE

La Rotonda
Monte Berico
Villa Valmarana
ai Nani

VISITORS' CHECKLIST

🏛 116,000. 🚊 🚌 *Piazza Stazione*. 🛈 *Piazza Matteotti 12 (0444 32 08 54).* 🚌 *Tue & Thu.* 🎭 *May–Jun & Sep–Oct: Theatre season; Jul: Son et Lumière.*

★ **Piazza dei Signori**
Palladio's elegant buildings flank the Piazza dei Signori, including the majestic two-tier colonnades of the 16th-century "Basilica", built around the old Palazzo della Ragione.

The Quartiere delle Barche contains numerous attractive palaces built in the 14th-century Venetian Gothic style.

Ponte San Michele
This elegant stone bridge, built in 1620, provides lovely views of the surrounding town.

Piazza delle Erbe, the city's market square, is overlooked by a 13th-century prison tower.

Casa Pigafetta
This striking 15th-century house was the birthplace of Antonio Pigafetta, who in 1519 set sail round the world with Magellan.

The lion of St Mark gazing down on Piazza dei Signori

🏛 **Piazza dei Signori**
Basilica 📞 *0444 32 36 81.*
🕐 *Tue–Sun.* 🎟

This square at the heart of Vicenza is dominated by the Palazzo della Ragione, often referred to as the **Basilica**. Its green, copper-clad roof is shaped like an upturned boat with a balustrade bristling with the statues of Greek and Roman gods. The colonnades were designed by Palladio in 1549 as a facing to support the city's 15th-century town hall, which had begun to subside. This was Palladio's first public commission, and a great success. Beside it stands the 12th-century Torre di Piazza.

The **Loggia del Capitaniato**, to the northwest, was built by Palladio in 1571: the Loggia's upper rooms contain the city's council chamber.

🏛 **Contrà Porti**
Contrà (an abbreviation of *contrada*, or district) is the Vicenza dialect word for street. On one side of the Contrà is a series of pretty Gothic buildings with painted windows and ornate balconies, reminiscent of Venice and a reminder that Vicenza was once part of the Venetian empire.

Several elegant Palladian palazzi stand on this street. Palazzo Porto Barbarano (No. 11), Palazzo Thiene (No. 12) and Palazzo Iseppo da Porto (No. 21) illustrate the sheer variety of Palladio's style – all share Classical elements but each is unique. An intriguing detail is that Palazzo Thiene appears to be of stone, though it is in fact built of cheap, lightweight brick, cleverly rendered to look like masonry.

Exploring Vicenza

VICENZA, THE GREAT PALLADIAN CITY and one of the wealthiest cities in the Veneto, is celebrated the world over for its splendid and varied architecture; it also offers the visitor elegant shops and cafés to visit.

Brusazorzi's ceiling fresco in the large entrance hall of the Museo Civico

🏛 Museo Civico
Piazza Matteotti. 📞 0444 32 13 48.
🕐 Tue–Sun. 🏷 ♿

The excellent Museo Civico is housed in **Palazzo Chiericati** (*see p76*) by Palladio, built in 1550. Inside is a fresco by Domenico Brusazorzi of a naked charioteer, representing the Sun, who appears to fly over the entrance hall. The upstairs rooms hold many excellent pictures. Among the Gothic altarpieces from churches in Vicenza is Hans Memling's *Crucifixion* (1468–70), the central panel from a triptych whose side panels are now located in New York.

Other rooms contain works by the local artist Bartolomeo Montagna (c.1450–1523).

🔒 Santa Corona
Contrà Santa Corona. 📞 0444 32 36 44. 🕐 daily.

This great Gothic church was built in 1261 to house a thorn donated by Louis IX of France and said to be from Christ's Crown of Thorns. The Cappella Porto houses the tomb of Luigi da Porto (died 1529), author of the novel *Giulietta e Romeo*, on which Shakespeare based his famous play. Notable paintings include Giovanni Bellini's *Baptism of Christ* (c.1500) and the *Adoration of the Magi* (1573) by Paolo Veronese.

🎭 TEATRO OLIMPICO
Piazza Matteotti. 📞 0444 32 37 81.
🕐 Tue–Sun. 🏷 ♿ 📷

Europe's oldest surviving indoor theatre is a fine and remarkable structure, largely made of wood and plaster, and painted to look like marble. Palladio began work on the design in 1579, but he died the following year. His pupil, Vincenzo Scamozzi, took over the project, completing the theatre in time for its opening performance of Sophocles' tragic drama, *Oedipus Rex*, on 3 March 1585.

Odeon Frescoes
The gods of Mount Olympus, after which the theatre is named, decorate the Odeon, a room used for music recitals.

The Anteodeon contains frescoes depicting the theatre's opening performance, and oil lamps from the original stage set.

Main ticket office

Stage Set
Scamozzi's scenery represents the Greek city of Thebes. The streets are cleverly painted in perspective and rise at a steep angle to give the illusion of great length.

The Auditorium
was designed by Palladio to resemble the outdoor theatres of ancient Greece and Rome, such as the Arena at Verona (*see p137*), with a semi-circle of "stone" benches and a ceiling painted to portray the sky.

🔓 San Lorenzo

Piazza San Lorenzo. ◯ *daily.*

The portal of this church is a magnificent example of Gothic stone carving, richly decorated with the figures of the Virgin and Child, and St Francis and St Clare. Inside there are fine tombs, and damaged frescoes. The lovely cloister, north of the church, is an attractive, flower-filled haven of calm.

🔓 Monte Berico

Basilica di Monte Berico. 📞 *0444 32 09 99.* ◯ *daily.*

Monte Berico is the green, cypress-clad hill to the south of Vicenza to which wealthy residents once escaped, in the heat of summer, to enjoy the cooler air and pastoral charms of their country estates. Today, shady *portici*, or colonnades, adorned with shrines, line the wide avenue linking central Vicenza to the basilica on top of the hill. The domed basili-

La Rotonda (1550–52), most famous of all Palladio's works

ca itself, built in the 15th century and enlarged in the 18th, is dedicated to the Virgin who appeared here during the 1426–8 plague to announce that Vicenza would be spared.

The ornate interior contains a moving *Pietà* fresco (1500) by Bartolomeo Montagna, a fossil collection in the cloister, and Veronese's fine painting, *The Supper of St Gregory the Great* (1572), in the refectory.

The Baroque hilltop church, the Basilica di Monte Berico

🏛 Villa Valmarana ai Nani

Via dei Nani 12. 📞 *0444 54 39 76.* ◯ *mid-Mar–5 Nov: Tue–Sun.* 🎫

The wall alongside the Villa Valmarana, built in 1688 by Antonio Muttoni, is topped by figures of dwarfs (*nani*) which give the building its name.

Inside, the walls are covered with frescoes by Tiepolo, in which the gods of Mount Olympus float about on clouds watching scenes from the epics of Homer and Virgil. In the separate Foresteria

(guest house), the 18th-century frescoes depicting peasant life and the seasons, painted by Tiepolo's son Giandomenico, are equally decorative but are imbued with an earthy realism.

The villa can be reached by an enjoyable, ten-minute walk from the basilica on Monte Berico. Head downhill along Via Massimo d'Azeglio to the high-walled convent on the right where the road ends, then take Via San Bastiano.

🏛 La Rotonda

Via Rotonda 25. 📞 *0444 32 17 93.* **Villa** ◯ *mid-Mar–4 Nov: Wed.* 🎫 **Garden** ◯ *Mar–Oct: Tue–Thu.* 🎫

With its perfectly regular, symmetrical forms, this villa, also known as the Villa Capra Valmarana, is the epitome of Palladio's architecture *(see pp76–7)* of which there are several fine examples throughout the Veneto. The design, consisting of a dome rising above a cube, received immediate acclaim for the way it blends perfectly with its surroundings. A pleasant contrast exists between the terracotta roof tiles, the white walls and the green lawns.

The villa, built in 1550–52, has inspired many copies in cities as far away as London, St Petersburg and Delhi. Fans of *Don Giovanni* will enjoy spotting locations used in Joseph Losey's 1979 film.

La Rotonda can be reached by bus from town, or on foot, following the path that passes beside the Villa Valmarana ai Nani.

The façade statues of stately toga-clad figures are portraits of sponsors who paid for the theatre's construction.

The courtyard giving access to the Teatro is decorated with ancient sculptures. These were donated by members of the Olympic Academy, the learned body that built the theatre.

Main entrance

Street-by-Street: Padua **7**

Padua (Padova) is an old university town with
an illustrious academic history. Rich in art and
architecture, it has two particularly outstanding
sights. The magnificent Cappella degli Scrovegni
(see pp150–51), north of the city centre, is
famous for Giotto's lyrical frescoes.
Close to the railway station, it forms
part of the complex incorporating the
Eremitani church and museums. The
Basilica di Sant'Antonio, which forms
the focal point in the southern part of
the city, is one of the most popular
pilgrimage destinations in Italy.

Palazzo del Capitanio
*Built between 1599 and
1605 for the head of the
city's militia, the tower incorporates an astronomical
clock made
in 1344.*

**Piazza dei
Signori** is
bordered by
attractive arcades
which house
small speciality
shops, cafés and old-
fashioned wine bars.

Corte Capitaniato, a 14th-
century arts faculty (open for
concerts), contains frescoes
which include a rare portrait
of the poet Petrarch.

Loggia della Gran Guardia
*This fine Renaissance build-
ing dating from 1523 once
housed the Council of
Nobles. It is now used as
a conference centre.*

**Ufficio di
Turismo**

PIAZZA
CAPITANIATO

VIA SAN CLEMENTE

PIAZZA
DEI
SIGNORI

VIA MONTE DI PIETA

VIA MANIN

PIAZZA
DEL
DUOMO

V GRITTI

VIA VANDELLI

VIA SONCIN

**★ Duomo
and Baptistry**
*The 12th-century baptistry
of the Duomo contains one
of the most complete
medieval fresco cycles to
survive in Italy, painted by
Giusto de' Menabuoi in 1378.*

**The Palazzo del
Monte di Pietà** has
16th-century arcades
and statues enclosing
a medieval building.

KEY

– – – – Suggested route

0 metres	75
0 yards	75

STAR SIGHT

★ Duomo and
Baptistry

Caffè Pedrocchi
Built like a Classical temple, the Caffè Pedrocchi has been a famous meeting place for students and intellectuals since it opened in 1831.

A bronze statue of a woman (1973) by Emilio Greco stands at the centre of this largely pedestrianized square.

Stazione
Chiesa degli Eremitani
Cappella degli Scrovegni
Museo Civico

Palazzo della Ragione, the medieval court of justice, contains magnificent frescoes.

Padua University
Founded in 1222, this is Italy's second oldest university. Elena Piscopia was the first woman graduate, in 1678.

Basilica di Sant'Antonio
Orto Botanico

Piazza delle Erbe
There are some excellent views to be had over the market place from the 15th-century loggia which runs alongside the 13th-century Palazzo della Ragione.

Duomo and Baptistry
Piazza Duomo.
Baptistry 049 66 28 14. daily.

The Duomo was built in 1552 to plans partly by Michelangelo, on the site of an earlier, 14th-century cathedral. Beside it stands a domed baptistry (c.1200). The interior is entirely decorated with vibrant frescoes painted by Giusto de' Menabuoi, dating from around 1378. The frescoes depict episodes from the Bible, including scenes of the Creation, the Miracles, the Passion, the Crucifixion and the Resurrection of Christ.

Palazzo della Ragione
Piazza delle Erbe. 049 820 50 06. Tue–Sun. 1 Jan, 25 Dec.

The "Palace of Reason", which is also known as the Salone, was built in 1218 to serve as Padua's law court and council chamber. The vast main hall was originally decorated with frescoes by Giotto, but fire destroyed his work in 1420. The Salone is breathtaking in its sheer size. It is the largest undivided medieval hall in Europe, 80 m (260 ft) long, 27 m (90 ft) wide and 27 m (90 ft) high. Frescoes painted in 1420–25 by Nicola Miretto cover its walls: the fascinating panels – 333 of them – depict the months of the year, with appropriate gods, signs of the zodiac and seasonal activities. A 1466 copy of the huge Gattamelata statue *(see p152)* by Donatello stands at one end of the hall.

Caffè Pedrocchi
Via VIII Febbraio 15. 049 878 12 31. daily.
Caffè Pedrocchi opened in 1831, and became famous throughout Italy as the café that never closed its doors. Today people come as much to talk, play cards or watch the world go by as to eat or drink. The upstairs rooms, decorated in florid Moorish, Egyptian, medieval, Greek and other styles, are used for concerts and lectures.

Padua: Cappella degli Scrovegni

ENRICO SCROVEGNI built this chapel in 1303, hoping thereby to spare his dead father, a usurer, from the eternal damnation in hell described by the poet Dante in his *Inferno*. The interior of the chapel is entirely covered with beautiful frescoes of scenes from the life of Christ, painted by Giotto between 1303 and 1305. As works of great narrative force, they exerted a powerful influence on the development of European art.

The Nativity
The naturalism of the Virgin's pose marks a departure from Byzantine stylization, as does the use of natural blue for the sky, in place of celestial gold.

Expulsion of the Merchants
Christ's physical rage, the cowering merchant and the child hiding his face show an animation that is characteristic of Giotto's style.

The Coretti
Giotto painted the two panels known as the Coretti as an exercise in perspective, creating the illusion of an arch with a room beyond.

View towards altar

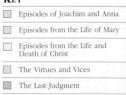

West entrance · North side · Altar · South side · West entrance

GALLERY GUIDE
The scenes, which are depicted in sequence, are fully explained on a small board, printed in several languages with a basic numbered key, which you will be offered on entry to the chapel. Owing to the small size of the chapel, the number of visitors at any one time is limited, which results in long queues. Visitors are requested to spend 15 minutes in a decontamination chamber and the duration of the visit itself is also restricted to 15 minutes. Booking is compulsory.

KEY
- Episodes of Joachim and Anna
- Episodes from the Life of Mary
- Episodes from the Life and Death of Christ
- The Virtues and Vices
- The Last Judgment

The Last Judgment
This scene fills the entire west wall of the chapel. Its formal composition is closer to Byzantine tradition than some of the other frescoes, with parts probably painted by assistants. A model of the chapel is shown (centre left, at the bottom) being offered to the Virgin by Scrovegni.

VISITORS' CHECKLIST

Piazza Eremitani. 049 820 45 50. to Piazzale Boschetti. Feb–Oct: 9am–7pm daily; Nov–Jan: 9am–6pm daily. public hols. Adv booking necessary.

Mary is Presented at the Temple
Giotto sets many scenes against an architectural background, using the laws of perspective to give a sense of three dimensions.

View towards entrance

Injustice
The Vices and Virtues are painted in monochrome. Here Injustice is symbolized by scenes of war, murder and robbery.

Lament over the Dead Christ
Giotto's figures express their grief in different ways: some huddle together, another gestures wildly.

GIOTTO

The great Florentine artist Giotto (1266–1337) is regarded as the father of Western art. His work, with its sense of pictorial space, naturalism and narrative drama, marks a decisive break with the Byzantine tradition of the preceding 1,000 years. He is the first Italian master whose name has passed into posterity, and although he was regarded in his lifetime as a great artist, few of the works attributed to him are fully documented. Some may have been painted by others, but his authorship of the frescoes in the Scrovegni Chapel need not be doubted.

Exploring Padua

PADUA IS A CITY OF MANY ATTRACTIONS, with a rich history: this is reflected in the major museum complex which occupies a group of 14th-century monastic buildings attached to the church of the Eremitani, a reclusive Augustinian order. The admission ticket includes entry to the Cappella degli Scrovegni (see pp150–51), which stands on the same site. Padua is, in addition, the setting for one of Italy's most important churches – the splendid Basilica di Sant'Antonio – and for one of the earliest universities to be founded in Italy.

🏛 Chiesa degli Eremitani and Museo Civico Eremitani

Piazza Eremitani. ☎ 049 820 45 50.
Museum ⬚ Tue–Sun. 🌐
Chapel ⬚ daily.

The Eremitani church, built from 1276 to 1306, contains magnificent roof and wall tombs. Among them is that of Marco Benavides (1489–1582), a professor of law at the city university, whose Renaissance tomb was the work of Florentine architect Ammannati (1511–92). Celebrated frescoes (1454–7) by Mantegna, portraying scenes from the lives of St James and St Christopher, were destroyed during a bombing raid in 1944. Two scenes from this magnificent series survive in the Cappella Ovetari, south of the sanctuary: *The Martyrdom of St James* and *The Martyrdom of St Christopher*.

The Museo Civico Eremitani comprises a coin collection (which includes rare Roman medallions and an almost complete set of Venetian coinage), an archaeological section and an art gallery.

The rich archaeological collection contains interesting Roman tombs, fine mosaics and impressive life-size statues. Renaissance bronzes include the comical *Drinking Satyr* by Il Riccio (1470–1532).

The beautiful 14th-century Crucifix from the Cappella degli Scrovegni is in the Quadreria Emo Capodilista, as well as works by Giotto, and 15th- to 18th-century paintings from the Venetian and Flemish schools.

A 1st-century AD tomb in the archaeological collection

15th-century *Angels in Armour* by Guariento, Museo Civico Eremitani

🔒 Basilica di Sant'Antonio

Piazza del Santo.

This exotic church, with its minaret-like spires and Byzantine domes, is also known as Il Santo. It was built from 1232 to house the remains of St Anthony of Padua, a preacher who modelled himself on St Francis of Assisi. Although he was a simple man who rejected worldly wealth, the citizens of Padua built one of the most lavish churches in Christendom to serve as his shrine.

The influence of Byzantine architecture is clearly visible in the basilica's outline: a cone-shaped central dome rises above seven encircling domes; the façade combines Gothic and Romanesque elements.

Inside, the high altar features Donatello's magnificent reliefs (1444–5) on the miracles of St Anthony, and his statues of the Crucifixion, the Virgin and Paduan saints. The tomb of St Anthony, hung with offerings, lies in the north transept; large marble reliefs depicting the saint's life, carved in 1505–77 by various artists, adorn the walls around it. A lively fresco scene of the Crucifixion by Altichiero da Zevio (1380s) adorns the south transept.

🏇 Statue of Gattamelata

Beside the entrance to the basilica stands one of the great works of the Renaissance: a statue of the mercenary soldier Gattamelata. This gritty portrait was created in 1443–52, in honour of a man who during his life did great service to the Venetian Republic. The artist Donatello won fame for the monument, the first equestrian statue made on such a large scale since Roman times.

The Basilica di Sant'Antonio, and Donatello's statue of Gattamelata

⛪ Scuola del Santo and Oratorio di San Giorgio

Piazza del Santo. 【 049 875 52 35.
Scuola del Santo ◯ daily. ● 1 Jan,
25 Dec. ✎ **Oratorio di San Giorgio**
◯ daily. ● 1 Jan, 25 Dec. ✎

Five excellent frescoes, including the earliest documented paintings by Titian, are to be found in these two buildings. The Scuola del Santo contains two scenes from the life of St Anthony, which were painted by Titian in 1511. The works in the San Giorgio oratory were executed by Altichicro da Zevio and Jacopo Avenzo, who painted them in 1378–84.

❧ Orto Botanico

Via Orto Botanico 15. 【 049 827 21
19. ◯ daily (Nov–Mar: Mon–Sat am).
✎ ♿

Padua's botanical garden, the oldest in Europe (1545), still retains much of its original appearance. The gardens and hothouses were used to cultivate the first lilac trees (1568), sunflowers (1568) and potatoes (1590) to be grown in Italy.

⛪ Palazzo del Bo

Via VIII Febbraio 2. 【 049 820 97
73. ◯ for guided tours only. ✎ Tue,
Thu, Sat am, Mon, Wed, Fri pm ✎

The historic main university building originally housed the medical faculty, renowned throughout Europe. Among its famous teachers and students was Gabriele Fallopio (1523–62), after whom the Fallopian tubes are named.

Guided tours include the pulpit Galileo used when he taught physics here from 1592 until 1610 and the wooden anatomy theatre, built in 1594 and now the oldest surviving medical lecture theatre in the world.

The 16th-century anatomy theatre in the old medical faculty of the university's Palazzo del Bo, Padua

The Euganean Hills, formed by ancient volcanic activity

Euganean Hills ❽

FS ⛙ to Terme Euganee, Montegrotto
Terme. ℹ Viale Stazione 60,
Montegrotto Terme (049 79 33 84).

THE CONICAL Euganean Hills, remnants of long-extinct volcanoes, rise abruptly out of the surrounding plain. Hot water springs bubble up out of the ground at Abano Terme and Montegrotto Terme where scores of establishments offer thermal treatments, ranging from mud baths to immersion in the hot sulphurated waters. Spa cures originated in Roman times; remains of the original baths and theatre are still visible at Montegrotto Terme.

⛪ Abbazia di Praglia

Via Abbazia di Praglia, Bresseo di
Teolo. 【 049 990 00 10. ◯ Tue–
Sun pm. ● Jan. ✎

The Benedictine monastery at Praglia, 6 km (4 miles) west of Abano Terme, is a peaceful haven in the tree-clad hills where the monks grow herbs and restore manuscripts. They lead guided tours of parts of the abbey and the church (1490–1548), which is noted for its beautiful cloister. There are also richly carved stalls in both the choir and the refectory, and paintings and frescoes by Zelotti, a 16th-century painter from Verona, in the dome of the church and the refectory.

🏛 Casa di Petrarca

Via Valleselle 4, Arquà Petrarca.
【 0429 71 82 94. ◯ Tue–Sun. ✎

The picturesque town of Arquà Petrarca, on the southern edge of the Euganean Hills, is named in honour of Francesco Petrarca, the medieval poet known in English as Petrarch (1304–74). Petrarch spent the last few years of his life here, living in a house frescoed with scenes from his lyrical poems, overlooking a landscape of olive groves and vineyards. He lies buried in a simple sarcophagus in front of the church.

The Casa di Petrarca (part 14th century) in Arquà Petrarca

⛪ Villa Barbarigo

Valsanzibio. 【 049 913 00 42.
◯ Mar–Nov. ✎

To the north of Arquà is the 18th-century Villa Barbarigo at Valsanzibio, which boasts one of the finest Baroque gardens in the Veneto. These were planned by Antonio Barbarigo in 1669, and are a grandiose mix of statuary, fountains, a maze, formal parterres, lakes and avenues of cypress trees.

The 16th-century Villa Foscari at Malcontenta, beside the Brenta Canal

Brenta Canal ❾

Padua and Venezia. **FS** *Venezia Mestre, Dolo, Mira.* 🚌 *to Mira, Dolo and Strà.* **ℹ** *Via Nazionale 420, Mira (041 42 49 73).* **Canal trips on *Il Burchiello:*** Via Orlandini 3, Padua. **☎** *049 877 47 12.* 🖥️

OVER THE CENTURIES, in order to prevent the Venetian lagoon silting up, the rivers flowing into it were diverted. The river Brenta was canalized in two sections: the older branch, between Padua and Fusina (just west of Venice), dates back to the 1500s and flows for 36 km (22 miles). Its potential as a transport route was quickly realized and fine villas were built along its length. Many of these elegant buildings can still be admired today – the N11 road runs alongside most of the canal's length – and three of them are open to the public. The 18th-century **Villa Nazionale** at Strà has an extravagant frescoed ceiling by Tiepolo. The **Villa Widmann-Foscari** at Mira (a pretty village) was built in 1719 and contains an interior decorated in French Rococo style. In the village of Malcontenta is **Villa Foscari**, or Villa Malcontenta, one of Palladio's loveliest villas *(see pp76–7)*. It was built in 1560 and the interior decorated with magnificent frescoes by Zelotti.

These villas may also be visited as part of an indulgent 8.5-hour guided tour from Padua, travelling to Venice (or, on alternate days, from Venice to Padua) along the river in a leisurely fashion on board the *Burchiello* motor launch – the cost for the one-way journey, however, is fairly prohibitive.

🏛️ **Villa Nazionale**
Via Pisani, Strà. **☎** *049 50 20 74.* ⬜ *Tue–Sun.* ⬛ *1 Jan, 1 May, 25 Dec.* 🖥️ 🖥️

🏛️ **Villa Widmann-Foscari**
Via Nazionale 420, Mira Porte. **☎** *041 42 41 56.* ⬜ *Apr–Oct: Tue–Sun; Nov–Mar: Sat & Sun.* 🖥️ 🖥️

🏛️ **Villa Foscari**
Via dei Turisti, Malcontenta. **☎** *041 547 00 12.* ⬜ *Tue & Sat am.* ⬛ *Nov–Apr.* 🖥️

Treviso ❿

🏘️ *81,700.* 🚆 **FS** **ℹ** *Piazzetta Monte di Pietà 8 (0422 54 76 32).* 🗓️ *Tue & Sat am.*

DESPITE COMPARISONS with Venice, the lovely fortified city of Treviso has its own very distinctive character.

A good place to start a tour of the streets, some lined with attractive balconied houses beside willow-fringed canals, is **Calmaggiore**. The street links the Duomo with the Palazzo dei Trecento, the rebuilt 13th-century town hall.

The **Duomo** was founded in the 12th century but rebuilt several times. Inside, Titian's *Annunciation* (1570) vies for attention with the striking *Adoration of the Magi* fresco (1520) by Titian's arch-rival, Il Pordenone. More paintings by Titian and other artists of the Renaissance may be seen in the **Museo Civico**.

The fish market, which dates from medieval times, is held on an island in the middle of Treviso's river Sile; this allows the remains of the day's trading to be flushed away.

The bulky Dominican church of **San Nicolò**, nestling by the 16th-century city wall, contains interesting tombs and frescoes, including, on a wall of the chapter house, the first-ever depiction of spectacles in art. A magnificent tomb (1500) by Antonio Rizzo is framed by a fresco of pageboys (c.1500) by Lorenzo Lotto.

🏛️ **Museo Civico**
Borgo Cavour 24. **☎** *0422 59 13 37.* ⬜ *Tue–Sun.* ⬛ *25 Dec.* 🖥️

The houses of the medieval town of Treviso overlooking ancient canals

The façade and entrance to the Renaissance Palazzo dei Rettori in Belluno

Conegliano ⓫

Treviso. 🚶 35,000. 🚈 🚌 ℹ️ *Via XX Settembre 61 (0438 212 30).* 🏪 *Fri.*

CONEGLIANO lies among Prosecco-producing vineyards, and winemakers from all over Italy learn their craft at Conegliano's renowned wine school. Via XX Settembre, the winding and arcaded main street, is lined with fine 15th- to 18th-century palazzi, many in the Venetian Gothic style or decorated with fading frescoes. The **Duomo** contains the town's one great work of art, an altarpiece painted by local artist Cima da Conegliano (1460–1518) depicting the *Virgin and Child with Saints* (1493).

A mythical statue on Conegliano's theatre

Reproductions of Cima's most famous works are on show in the **Casa di Cima**, the artist's birthplace. The detailed landscapes in the background of his paintings were based on the hills around the town; the same views can still be seen from the gardens surrounding the Castelvecchio (old castle).

🏛 Casa di Cima
Via Cima. 📞 *0438 216 60 (phone to arrange visit).* 🕐 *Sat & Sun pm.* 🖼

Belluno ⓬

🚶 36,000. 🚈 🚌 ℹ️ *Piazza dei Martiri 8 (0437 94 00 83).* 🏪 *Sat.*

PICTURESQUE BELLUNO, capital of Belluno province, serves as a bridge between the two different parts of the Veneto, with the flat plains to the south and the Dolomite peaks to the north. Both are encapsulated in the views to be seen from the 12th-century **Porta Rugo** at the southern end of Via Mezzaterra, the main street of the old town. More spectacular still are the views from the bell tower of the 16th-century **Duomo** (subsequently rebuilt). The nearby baptistry houses a font cover with the figure of John the Baptist carved by Andrea Brustolon (1662–1732). Brustolon's works also grace the churches of San Pietro (on Via San Pietro) and Santo Stefano (Piazza Santo Stefano). North of Piazza del Duomo stands the city's most elegant building, the **Palazzo dei Rettori** (1491) – once home to the town's Venetian rulers – and the 12th-century **Torre Civica**, all that now survives of a medieval castle.

The **Museo Civico** contains paintings by Bartolomeo Montagna (1450–1523) and Sebastiano Ricci (1659–1734), and a notable archaeological section. North of the museum is Belluno's finest square, the **Piazza del Mercato**, with its arcaded Renaissance palaces and its fountain of 1410.

South of the town are the ski resorts of the Alpe del Nevegal; in the summer a chair lift operates from Faverghera up the flank of the mountain to a height of 1,600 m (5,250 ft) offering extensive views.

🏛 Museo Civico
Piazza Duomo 16. 📞 *0437 94 48 36.* 🕐 *mid-Apr–Sep: Tue–Sun; Oct–mid-Apr: Mon–Sat.* 🖼 🎥 🔲

Cortina d'Ampezzo ⓭

Belluno. 🚶 6,800. 🚌 ℹ️ *Piazzetta San Francesco 8 (0436 32 31).* 🏪 *Tue & Fri.*

ITALY'S TOP SKI RESORT, much favoured by the smart set from Turin and Milan, is well supplied with restaurants and bars. Cortina is set amid the extremely dramatic scenery of the Dolomites *(see pp78–9)*, which explains part of the resort's attraction: all around, crags and spires thrust their distinctive weather-beaten shapes above the trees.

Cortina benefits from better than average sports facilities, thanks to hosting the 1956 Winter Olympics. In addition to downhill and cross-country skiing, there is also a ski jump and a bobsleigh run for those who favour something more adventurous than usual, as well as an Olympic ice stadium, several swimming pools, tennis courts and riding facilities.

During the summer months, Cortina becomes an excellent base for walkers. Useful information on trails and guided walks is available from the tourist office or, during the summer, from the Guides' office opposite.

Corso Italia in Cortina d'Ampezzo, Italy's most important ski resort

Traditional copper pans on display in the Museo Carnico in Tolmezzo

Tolmezzo ⓮

🏛 *10,000.* 🚌 ℹ️ *Piazza XX Settembre (0433 448 98).*
🛒 *Mon.*

Tolmezzo is the capital of the Carnia region, named after the Celtic tribe that inhabited the area around the 4th century BC. The town is surrounded by the high peaks of the Carnic Alps, including the pyramidal Monte Amariana (1,906 m – 6,253 ft) to the east. The best place to begin a tour of the region is the **Museo delle Arti Popolari**, which has displays of local costumes, crafts, textiles and agriculture.

Southwest of the town, a scenic road climbs 14 km (8.5 miles) to the ski resort of **Sella Chianzutan**, a good base for walking in the summer. More resorts line the road, west of Tolmezzo, to **Ampezzo**, at which point a minor road heads north through the gorge of the River Lumiei. Following this road to the Ponte di Buso bridge and the **Lago di Sauris** is an excellent introduction to the majestic Carnic Alps.

Above this point the road is often impassable in winter, but in summer there are flower-filled meadows all along the road up to Sella di Razzo, and then back along the **Pesarina Valley**, via Comeglians and Ravascletto. Returning south, **Zuglio** was once the Roman town of Forum Iulii Carnicum, guarding the road over the pass. Today it is worth a detour for the remains of its Roman basilica, baths and forum.

🏛 Museo delle Arti Popolari
Via della Vittoria 2.
☎ *0433 432 33.* 🕐 *Tue–Sun.*
🔴 *1 Jan, Easter, 25 Dec.* 📷

Pordenone ⓯

🏛 *49,000.* 🚆 🚌 ℹ️ *Corso Vittorio Emanuele II 38 (0434 219 12).*
🛒 *Sat am & Wed.*

Old Pordenone consists of one long street, the **Corso Vittorio Emanuele**, lined with pretty arcaded houses of pink brick, some with the faded traces of decorative frescoes on their façades. The 13th-century **Palazzo Comunale** forms a striking conclusion to the street with its eccentrically shaped roofline of curves and minaret-like side towers, and its 16th-century clocktower. Opposite is the **Museo Civico**, housed in the 17th-century Palazzo Ricchieri, where works by the local artist Il Pordenone (1484–1539) are on display.

Around the corner stands the **Duomo**, which contains the lovely altar painting of the *Madonna della Misericordia* (1515) by Il Pordenone. The bell tower beside the Duomo is a fine example of Romanesque decorative brickwork.

🏛 Museo Civico
Corso Vittorio Emanuele 51. ☎ *0434 39 23 11.* 🕐 *Tue–Fri.* 🔴 *public hols.* 📷 ♿

Udine ⓰

🏛 *99,000.* 🚆 🚌 ℹ️ *Piazza I Maggio 7 (0432 29 59 72).* 🛒 *Sat.*

Udine is a city of varied and surprising architecture. In the centre lies **Piazza della Libertà**, where the Loggia del Lionello (1448–56), built of pink stone in Venetian Gothic style, stands beside the Art Deco Caffè Contarena. Opposite, the Renaissance symmetry of the Porticato di San Giovanni is interrupted by the Torre dell'Orologio (Clock Tower, 1527) crowned by two bronze Moors who strike the hours. Note also the fountain of 1542, the two 18th-century statues, and the column supporting the Lion of St Mark.

Beyond the **Arco Bollani**, a gateway designed by Palladio in 1556, steps lead up to a 26-m (85-ft) hill which offers sweeping views over the city. On the hill is the 16th-century castle, now the **Musei Civici e Galleria di Storia e Arte Antica**, which houses fine art and archaeology collections.

Southeast of Piazza Matteotti, where a small market is held, at the end of Via Savorgnana, stands the **Oratorio della Purità**, and the **Duomo** with its octagonal bell tower. Both contain important paintings and frescoes by Giambattista Tiepolo (1696–1770). More of Tiepolo's work can be seen in the **Palazzo Arcivescovile**, which the artist decorated with frescoes.

Lago di Sauris, an artificial lake lying in the Carnic Alps above Tolmezzo

The arcaded Porticato di San Giovanni on Piazza della Libertà, Udine

ENVIRONS: Outside Codroipo, 24 km (15 miles) west, rises the imposing **Villa Manin**. A road passes through the villa's grounds, so its massive size can be seen even when the house – once the retreat of Ludovico Manin, the last doge of Venice (1725–1802) – and its magnificent gardens are closed to the public.

🏛 Musei Civici e Galleria di Storia e Arte Antica
Castello di Udine. 【 0432 50 28 72. ◯ Tue–Sat (Sun am). ● 1 Jan, Easter, 1 May, 25 Dec. 🎦 ৬

🏯 Palazzo Arcivescovile
Piazza Patriarcato 1. 【 0432 250 03. ◯ Wed–Sun. ● 1 Jan, Easter, 25 Dec. 🎦 ৬

🏯 Villa Manin
Passariano. 【 0432 90 66 57. ◯ Tue–Sun. ● 1 Jan, 25 & 31 Dec. **Gardens** ◯ Easter–Oct: Tue–Sun. ৬

Cividale del Friuli ⓱

🏯 11,000. ⏚ ▭ ℹ Corso Paolino d' Aquileia 10 (0432 73 14 61). ▣ Sat.

A GATE IN THE medieval walls of Cividale leads down the main street and straight to the dramatic ravine of the River Natisone, which is spanned by the arch of the **Ponte del Diavolo** (Devil's Bridge).

Above the river's north bank stands the **Tempietto Longobardo** (Lombardic Chapel), a very rare example of an 8th-century church decorated with reliefs of saints, modelled in stucco. The town's history is traced in the excellent **Museo Archeologico Nazionale**,

which contains the excavated remains of buildings from a Roman town, and a collection of Lombardic items including jewellery, ivory and weapons.

Next door is the **Duomo**, rebuilt in 1453 after a fire, with its beautiful silver altarpiece (13th century). The **Museo Cristiano**, off the south aisle, contains sculptures from the original church: of particular interest is the altar donated by Ratchis, the Lombardic Duke of Friuli and later King of Italy (737–44), which is finely carved with scenes from the Life of Christ, including a charming Nativity. There is in addition the unusual baptismal font of Patriarch Callisto (737–56): this octagonal structure, with a roof supported by pillars, is decorated with symbols of the Evangelists.

🏠 Tempietto Longobardo
Piazzetta San Biagio. ◯ daily. 🎦

Interior view of the Tempietto Longobardo in Cividale del Friuli

🏛 Museo Archeologico Nazionale
Palazzo dei Provveditori Veneti, Piazza del Duomo 1. 【 0432 70 07 00. ◯ daily. ● 1 Jan, Easter, 1 May, 25 Dec. 🎦 ৬

🏛 Museo Cristiano
Piazza del Duomo. 【 0432 73 11 44. ◯ daily. ৬

Gorizia ⓲

🏯 37,000. ⏚ ▭ ℹ Palazzo della Regione, Via Roma 5 (0481 38 62 25). ▣ Thu, Fri.

G ORIZIA WAS AT the centre of fierce fighting during both world wars and was split in two by the 1947 Treaty of Paris, leaving part in Italy, part in Yugoslavia (now Slovenia).

The town's arcaded streets and pastel-painted houses have been carefully restored following substantial damage during World War II. A visit to the modern Museo Provinciale della Grande Guerra (Museum of the Great War), housed in the basement of the **Museo Provinciale**, provides a fascinating introduction to the realities of war. The museum uses videos, photographs, and life size mock-ups of trenches, latrines and gun emplacements to show the waste, squalor and heroism of war.

The Lion of Venice above the entrance to Gorizia's castle

Rooms on the upper floor of the museum house temporary exhibitions and items from the town's art collection, which includes works by local artists.

On a mound nearby rises the castle, encircled by 16th-century fortifications. From here there are extensive views stretching over the town to the mountains beyond.

ENVIRONS: To the southwest of Gorizia, scenic country roads pass through the foothills of the **Carso**, a limestone plateau stretching down to Trieste. The plateau is dotted with fields enclosed by drystone walls, and gouged with tunnels, caves and underground rivers.

🏛 Museo Provinciale
Borgo Castello 13. 【 0481 53 39 26. ◯ Tue–Sun. ● 1 Jan, 25 Dec. 🎦

The attractive harbourside at Grado, along the coast south of Aquileia

Aquileia ⑲

🏛 3,300. 🚌 🛈 Piazza Capitolo 4 (0431 91 94 91). 🚌 Tue.

AQUILEIA, now little more than a village but encircled by the ruins of palatial villas, baths, temples and market buildings, provides a poignant reminder of the lost splendour of the Roman Empire.

It was here that Emperor Augustus received Herod the Great, King of Judea, in 10 BC, and it was here too, in AD 381, that the early Christian church held a major council attended by the learned saints Ambrose and Jerome to settle doctrinal issues. In the 5th century, however, the town was abandoned following several sackings. Fortunately, substantial parts of the early Christian basilica have survived, which contain the town's particular treasure: ornate floor mosaics.

⛪ Basilica

Piazza Capitolo. 📞 0431 910 67. 🕐 daily. **Crypt** 🎫

The basilica was founded in about AD 313 and much of the original structure still survives, including the magnificent floor mosaics of the nave and **Cripta degli Scavi** below. The designs are a mixture of geometric patterns, biblical stories and scenes from everyday life in ancient Aquileia. There is a lively portrayal of the tale of Jonah, who was swallowed by an extraordinary sea monster: the fishing boats are also surrounded by a rich array of creatures from the deep, including wide-eyed dolphins and squid.

🏛 Museo Archeologico Nazionale

Via Roma 1. 📞 0431 910 16. 🕐 daily. 🌑 1 Jan, 1 May, 25 Dec. 🎫 ♿

The mosaics in the basilica demonstrate a tradition of craftsmanship that flourished in the city from the 2nd century AD. Additional examples of mosaics and stone carvings from the Classical era (1st to 3rd centuries) are on display in this museum, together with glass, amber, and a collection of flies, beautifully worked in gold, that formed the adornment of a Roman matron's veil.

🏛 Museo Paleocristiano

Località Monastero. 📞 0431 911 31. 🕐 daily. 🌑 1 Jan, 1 May, 25 Dec.

This museum, which stands not far from Aquileia's ancient harbour beside the once-navigable River Natissa, focuses on the development of art during the early Christian era.

ENVIRONS: South of Udine, **Palmanova** is worth a visit for its remarkable octagonal layout and intact walls. The town was built in 1593 by the Venetians to commemorate the Battle of Lepanto.

Grado sits on a group of low islands in the middle of the Adriatic lagoon, attached to the mainland by a narrow causeway. The town grew into a port for Aquileia in the 2nd century and was used as a haven by Aquileia's citizens during the barbarian invasions. Today, Grado is a popular seaside resort. At the centre of the old town stands the **Duomo**, which contains 6th-century frescoes in the apse, similar to those covering the vaults of San Marco in Venice (see pp106–9). Nearby, in the little church of **Santa Maria delle Grazie**, there are yet more 6th-century mosaics.

SYMBOLISM IN EARLY CHRISTIAN ART

Christians were persecuted until their religion was granted official status by Constantine the Great in AD 313. Prior to this they had developed a language of secret symbols to express their beliefs, many of which can be seen in the mosaics and marble tomb chests of Aquileia. Many of these and other symbols later found their way into popular bestiaries and folk art.

Part of the 4th-century floor mosaic in the basilica at Aquileia

The Winged figure of Victory holding a laurel wreath was a Classical symbol of triumph, and holiness. Later, it came to represent Christ's resurrection, and more generally, victory over death.

Trieste ⑳

🏙 *218,000.* ✈ 🚉 🚌 ℹ *Riva III Novembre 9 (040 347 83 12).* 🗓 *Tue–Sat.*

TRIESTE IS AN atmospheric city, tucked up next to Slovenia, with a long, bustling harbour lined with handsome buildings and lapped by the waves of the Adriatic Sea.

🏛 Acquario Marino
Molo Pescheria 2. 📞 *040 30 62 01.* 🕐 *Tue–Sun (Nov–Mar: am only).* ⬤ *public hols.* 🎫 ⅙
The city's aquarium is one of the most popular attractions in Trieste. It contains examples of the fascinating marine life in the Adriatic.

♦ Castello di San Giusto
Piazza Cattedrale 3.
📞 *040 30 93 62.* 🕐 *daily.*
⬤ *1 & 6 Jan, 25 & 26 Dec.* 🎫
Up above the harbour stands a hilltop castle – built by the city's Venetian governors from 1368 – set on a terrace from which there are sweeping views over the Gulf of Trieste. The castle houses a museum containing 19th-century prints of Trieste, and a collection of weapons and armour.

⛪ Basilica Paleocristiana
Via Madonna del Mare 11. 📞 *040 436 31.* 🕐 *10–noon Wed.*
Beside the castle lie the substantial ruins of the Roman basilica or law court built around AD 100. Note the stone magistrates' bench and throne.

⛪ Duomo
Piazza Cattedrale. 📞 *040 30 96 66.* 🕐 *daily.* ⅙
In the church of **San Giusto**, the city's Duomo, magistrates' bench and throne of the Roman basilica were reinterpreted to become the seat of the bishop and clergy. Because the building was formed in the 14th century by linking two 5th-century churches that stood side by side, there are two thrones and benches here. The two apses are decorated with very fine 13th-century mosaics in the Venetian style.

🏛 Museo di Storia ed Arte ed Orto Lapidario
Via della Cattedrale 15. 📞 *040 31 05 00.* 🕐 *Tue–Sun.* ⬤ *public hols.* 🎫
The important archaeological collection held here provides fascinating evidence of Trieste's extensive trade links with the ancient Greek world.

13th-century mosaics in the apse of San Giusto, Trieste's Duomo

ENVIRONS: From **Villa Opicina**, just north of Trieste, sweeping views may be had over the city, its bay and south down the coast of Slovenia. A little beyond, at Borgo Grotta Gigante, lies the **Grotta del Gigante**, a huge cavern filled with stunning "organ pipe" formations and tall columns of stalagmites.

At Grignano, 8 km (5 miles) northwest of the city, stands the **Castello di Miramare**, a white castle set in lush green gardens beside the sparkling blue Adriatic. It was built by the Habsburg Archduke Maximilian in 1856–60 as his summer retreat, a few years before he was assassinated in Mexico. It is still furnished in contemporary style.

⛰ Grotta del Gigante
Borgo Grotta Gigante.
📞 *040 32 73 12.*
🕐 *Tue–Sun (Jul & Aug: daily).* 🎫 📷
♦ Castello di Miramare
Miramare, Grignano.
📞 *040 22 41 43.* 🕐 *daily.* ⅙

The Castello del Miramare on the bay of Trieste

The Tortoise *biding in his shell represented darkness and ignorance, while the cockerel, who crows at dawn, signified light and enlightenment.*

ICHTHUS, or fish, *was an acronym for* Iesous CHristos THeou Uios Soter *– Jesus Christ, Son of God, Saviour, in ancient Greek.*

Colourful birds, *such as peacocks, symbolized immortality and the glorious transformation of the soul when it arrives in Heaven.*

TRENTINO-ALTO ADIGE

THE ITALIAN-SPEAKING *Trentino – named after Trento, the regional capital – and the German-speaking Alto Adige or Südtirol (South Tyrol, the region bordering the upper reaches of the River Adige) differ dramatically in culture. However, they do share one feature in common: the majestic Dolomites that form the backdrop to every town and village, covered in snow for three months of every year and carpeted with exquisite Alpine plants for another three.*

The region's mountains have been cut by glaciers into a series of deep, broad valleys. Many of these face south, so it remains unusually warm and sunny, even in winter. Travellers have passed up and down these valleys for generations – as confirmed by the extraordinary discovery, in 1991, of a 5,000-year-old man's body found emerging from the surface of a melting glacier in Alto Adige. The frozen corpse wore leather boots, stuffed with hay for warmth, and was armed with a copper ice pick.

The paths that Neolithic man once trod became major road networks under the Romans, when many of the region's cities were founded. By the Middle Ages, Alto Adige had established its very own distinctive culture under the Counts of Tyrol, whose land (later appropriated by the Habsburgs) straddled both sides of today's Italian/Austrian border. The Tyrolean nobility built the castles that still line the valleys and the mountain passes, in order to protect travellers from brigands.

Another ancient legacy is the tradition of hospitality to be found in the numerous guesthouses along the valleys. Many of these are built in the distinctive Tyrolean style, with beautiful timber balconies for making the most of the winter sun, and overhanging roof eaves to keep snow at a distance. Cosy in winter, with log fires and warming food, and offering marvellous views, they make the ideal base for enjoying the region's mountain footpaths and ski slopes.

Skiers enjoying the slopes around Monte Spinale, near Madonna di Campiglio, in Trentino

◁ A typical view of the Dolomites between Bressanone and Ortisei, in Alto Adige

Exploring Trentino-Alto Adige

TRENTINO-ALTO ADIGE is a region where unspoiled nature is complemented by a wealth of sporting opportunities. The tributary valleys feeding into the Adige valley contain lakes, rivers and streams, and also woodland, vineyards and Alpine pasture full of butterflies, birds and flowers. Southeast of the region rise the distinctive limestone peaks of the Dolomites, while further north the area becomes more mountainous still, enclosed finally by the splendid heights of the Alps.

Via Ponte Aquila in Bressanone

SIGHTS AT A GLANCE

KEY

▬	Motorway
▬	Major road
▬	Minor road
▬	Scenic route
〰	River
✲	Viewpoint

0 kilometres   25

0 miles   10

Castel Tirolo above the town of Merano

View of the Dolomites from Madonna di Campiglio

GETTING AROUND

The region's main artery is the Brenner Pass road: it runs from Austria in the north, following the River Adige from Bolzano to Trento, and southwards on to Verona. Both the motorway and the main road beside it are among the busiest in Europe, and the valley roads can also be congested during the ski season. Winter driving can be hazardous, requiring special tyres and snow chains. Trains and coaches also serve the main towns, but car transport is more effective.

SEE ALSO

- **Where to Stay** pp547–9

- **Where to Eat** pp582–4

Abbazia di Monte Maria, founded in the 12th century, near Malles Venosta

Malles Venosta ❶
MALS IM VINSCHGAU

🏠 4,600. 🚌 ℹ️ *Via San Benedetto 1 (0473 83 11 90).* 🛒 *Wed.*

Malles Venosta sits in high border country, close to Switzerland and Austria, and was a customs point during the Middle Ages. The town has several Gothic churches, whose spires and towers give an appealing skyline, mirroring the jagged peaks that rise all around. The oldest is the tiny church of **San Benedetto**, a 9th-century Carolingian building on Via San Benedetto, with frescoes of its patrons.

ENVIRONS: The medieval **Castel Coira** (Churburg) rises at Sluderno (Schluderns), 4 km (2.5 miles) southeast of Malles. It now contains an excellent collection of weapons and armour.

Clinging to the mountainside 5 km (3 miles) north of Malles, just above the town of Burgusio (Burgeis), is the Benedictine **Abbazia di Monte Maria** (Marienberg), founded in the 12th century but enlarged in the 18th and 19th. The church's crypt shelters an outstanding series of 12th-century frescoes.

The glorious medieval town of **Glorenza** lies just 2 km (1.25 miles) south of Malles.

♟ Castel Coira
Churburg, Sluderno. 📞 *0473 61 52 41.* 🕐 *20 Mar–Nov: Tue–Sun by guided tour only.* 🎫

🏛 Abbazia di Monte Maria
📞 *0473 83 13 06.* 🕐 *Apr–Oct: Mon–Sat; Nov–Mar: groups by appt only.* ● *public hols.* 🎫 🎫

Merano ❷
MERAN

🏠 35,000. 🚆 🚌 ℹ️ *Corso della Libertà 45 (0473 23 52 23).* 🛒 *Tue & Fri.*

Merano is an attractive spa town to which Austrians, Germans and Italians come to drink the waters, take therapeutic baths and stroll through the riverside gardens – before taking coffee and pastries in one of the Belle Epoque cafés. On Corso Libertà, a street of smart shops and hotels, stands the **Kurhaus** or Spa Hall built in 1914, now a concert venue. The 15th-century **Castello Principesco** was home to the Habsburg Archduke Sigismund

The Art Nouveau façade of the Kurhaus in Merano

and is still furnished in period style. Inviting gardens line the River Passirio, which winds its way through the town. The Passeggiata Lungo Passirio d'Inverno (Winter Walk) lines the north bank to the Roman bridge, Ponte Romano; the Passeggiata d'Estate (Summer Walk) on the south bank leads to the medieval Ponte Passirio.

ENVIRONS: The romantic 12th-century **Castel Tirolo**, home of the Counts of Tyrol who gave their name to the Tyrol region, lies 4 km (2.5 miles) to the north. It now houses a museum of Tyrolean history.

♟ Castello Principesco
Via Galilei. 📞 *0473 25 03 29.* 🕐 *Tue–Sun.* ● *Jan–Feb.* 🎫

♟ Castel Tirolo
Via Castello 24, Tirolo. 📞 *0473 22 02 21.* 🕐 *May–Oct: Tue–Sun.* ● *Nov–Apr.* 🎫 🎫

Vipiteno ❸
STERZING

🏠 5,600. 🚆 🚌 ℹ️ *Piazza Città 3 (0472 76 53 25).* 🛒 *days vary each month.*

Vipiteno, surrounded by mineral-rich valleys, is very Tyrolean in feel. On Via Città Nuova, lined with fine mansions, rise the Gothic **Palazzo Comunale**, containing Renaissance sculpture and paintings, and the Torre dei Dodici, the symbol of the town. Wood carvings in

Wrought-iron sign Vipiteno

the **Museo Multscher** are by Hans Multscher; the Bavarian sculptor came to Vipiteno in 1456–8 to carve the altar for the parish **church**, which lies just south of the town.

To the west, the charming **Val di Racines** includes waterfalls and a natural rock bridge.

🏛 Palazzo Comunale
Via Città Nuova 21. 📞 *0472 76 51 08.* 🕐 *Mon–Fri.* ● *public hols.*

🏛 Museo Multscher
Via della Commenda. 📞 *0472 76 58 79.* 🕐 *Apr–Oct: Tue–Sat.* ● *public hols.* 🎫

The medieval castle dominating the town of Brunico

Brunico ❹
BRUNECK

🏛 13,000. **FS** 🚌 **ℹ** Via Europa 26 (0474 55 57 22). 🛒 Wed.

THE ATTRACTIVE TOWN of Brunico, overlooked by the imposing form of its medieval **castle**, retains 14th-century fortifications and a network of narrow streets that can only be explored on foot. The church of **St Ursula**, to the north-west of St Ursula's Gate, contains a series of outstanding mid-15th-century altar reliefs of the Nativity. In the **Museo Etnografico di Teodone**, the town's folklore museum, there are displays of traditional agricultural life and local costumes; it also provides visitors with an ideal opportunity to visit a 16th century farmhouse and barn.

St Ursula's Gate sundial, Brunico

🏛 **Museo Etnografico di Teodone**
Via Duca Diet 24, Teodone. 📞 0474 55 20 87. 🕐 mid-Apr–Oct: Tue – Sat, Sun pm. 🈳 ♿ 🚻

Bressanone ❺
BRIXEN

🏛 18,000. **FS** 🚌
ℹ Viale Stazione 9 (0472 83 64 01). 🛒 Mon.

THE NARROW MEDIEVAL alleys of Bressanone cluster around the cathedral and the palace of the prince-bishops who ruled the town for much of its history. The **Duomo**, on Piazza del Duomo, was rebuilt in the 18th century but retains its 12th-century cloister, decorated with superb 15th-century frescoes. The lavish interiors of Palazzo Vescovile, the bishops' Renaissance palace, house the **Museo Diocesano**. It contains precious items from the Middle Ages, as well as the **Museo dei Presepi**, with its collection of wooden crib figures that are carved locally.

ENVIRONS: At Velturno (Feldthurns), just 8 km (5 miles) southwest, stands the Renaissance **Castello di Velturno**, the summer retreat of the rulers of Bressanone noted for its frescoed rooms. A little over 3 km (2 miles) north of Bressanone lies the

Abbazia di Novacella, a picturesque group of fortified monastic buildings with an outstanding series of cloister frescoes. Further north up the valley, at **Rio di Pusteria** (Mühlbach), the remains of a 16th-century fortified barrier can be seen to the east of the town. The barrier funnelled ancient travellers through the customs post that divided Tyrol from the Görz district.

High above Rio di Pusteria, to the southeast, looms the massive outline of the **Castello di Rodengo** (Rodeneck). The castle contains wonderful 13th-century frescoes showing battle scenes, the Last Judgment and courtly episodes from the *Iwein* romance by Hartmann von Aue, the medieval poet.

🏛 **Museo Diocesano**
Palazzo Vescovile, Piazza Palazzo Vescovile 2. 📞 0472 83 05 05. 🕐 mid-Mar–Oct: Tue–Sun. 🈳

🏛 **Museo dei Presepi**
Palazzo Vescovile, Piazza Palazzo Vescovile 2. 📞 0472 83 05 05. 🕐 mid-Mar–Oct: Tue–Sun; Dec & Jan: daily. 🔒 24 & 25 Dec. 🈳

🏯 **Castello di Velturno**
Velturno. 📞 0472 85 55 25.

🏛 **Abbazia di Novacella**
Varna. 📞 0472 83 61 89. 🕐 Mon–Sat. 🔒 public hols. 🈳🈳

🏯 **Castello di Rodengo**
Rodengo. 📞 0472 45 40 56. 🕐 May–mid-Oct: Tue–Sun. 🈳 🈳

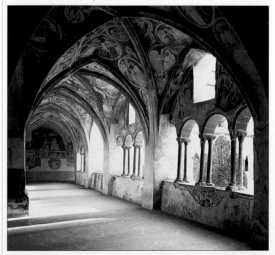

The cloisters of Bressanone Duomo with their 15th-century frescoes

The Baroque interior of the church of St Ulrich in Ortisei

Bolzano ❻

BOZEN

🏠 98,000. **FS** 🚌 **ℹ** *Piazza Walther 8 (0471 30 70 00).* 🛒 *Sat.*

BOLZANO, THE CAPITAL of the Alto Adige, is the gateway between the Italian-speaking Trentino region and the German-speaking Alto Adige or Südtirol, and has a marked Tyrolean atmosphere. The old centre, **Piazza Walther**, is dominated by the 15th-century Gothic **Duomo**, with its multicoloured mosaic-patterned roof and elaborate spire. The "wine door" inside the Duomo is carved with figures at work among vines and reflects the importance of wine to the local economy. In the middle of Piazza Walther is a statue of Walther von der Vogelweide, the 13th-century troubadour – born, according to legend, in this area. North of the square, the streets are lined with houses adorned with intricate gables, balconies and oriel windows. The outdoor market, starting at Piazza Grano, forms an inviting array of local produce that continues along the arcaded Via dei Portici. This street continues to the **Museo Civico**, where South Tyrolean history is introduced through domestic interiors, wood carvings and costumes, while the new **Museo Archeologico**

The Duomo spire, Bolzano

houses the famous 5,000-year-old "Iceman". The **Chiesa dei Domenicani** (Dominican church), on Piazza Domenicani, has 14th-century *Triumph of Death* frescoes and a frescoed cloister.

🏛 **Museo Civico**
Via Cassa di Risparmio 14.
☎ *0471 97 46 25.* ◗ *Tue–Sat.*
● *1 Jan, 1 May, 25 & 26 Dec.* 📷
🏛 **Museo Archeologico**
Via Museo 43. **☎** *0471 98 20 98.*
◗ *Tue–Sat.* ● *1 Jan, 1 May, 25 Dec.*
📷 📷 📷

Ortisei ❼

SANKT ULRICH

🏠 4,500. 🚌 **ℹ** *Via Rezia 1 (0471 79 63 28).* 🛒 *Fri.*

ORTISEI IS THE prosperous main resort for the pretty Val Gardena and Alpe di Siusi region, and a major centre for

woodcarving; good examples of local craftsmanship may be seen in local shops, in the **Museo della Val Gardena** (which also focuses on local archaeology), and in the church of **St Ulrich**.

To the south is the **Alpe di Siusi** (Seiser Alm) region, noted for its Alpine meadows, balconied farmsteads and onion-domed churches. The best way to explore this beautiful area is by cableway from Ortisei: to the northeast another cablecar runs to 2,518-m (8,260-ft) high Monte Seceda, and walks from here lead into the Odle Dolomites.

🏛 **Museo della Val Gardena**
Via Rezia 83. **☎** *0471 79 75 54.*
◗ *Feb, Mar: Tue, Fri; Jun, Sep, Oct: Tue–Fri pm; Jul, Aug: Tue–Sun.* 📷

Canazei ❽

🏠 1,800. 🚌 **ℹ** *Via Roma 34 (0462 60 11 13).* 🛒 *Sat.*

LOCATED AT THE BASE of some of the highest and most awe-inspiring groups of peaks, Canazei is a good base for exploring the Dolomites. In summer, chair-lifts climb to viewpoints where the beauty of the encircling mountains can be appreciated to the full. The most popular viewpoints are Pecol and Col dei Rossi, reached by the Belvedere cableway from Via Pareda in Canazei: the cliffs of the Sella group are visible to the north,

Skiers enjoying views of the Dolomites above Canazei

with Sasso Lungo to the west and Marmolada, the highest of the Dolomites at 3,343 m (10,965 ft), to the south.

ENVIRONS: At **Vigo di Fassa**, 13 km (8 miles) southwest, the **Museo Ladino** focuses on the Ladin-speaking people of some of the valleys. Ladin – a Rhaeto-Romance language – is taught in local schools and the ancient traditions, costumes and music still thrive.

🏛 **Museo Ladino**
Via Milano 5, Pozzo di Fassa. [
0462 76 42 67. ◯ phone to check.

Cavalese ❾

🏠 3,600. 🚌 🚻 Via Fratelli Bronzetti 60 (0462 24 11 11).
🗓 last Tue of month (not Jul).

The frescoed façade of the Palazzo della Magnifica Comunità

CAVALESE IS THE chief town in the Val di Fiemme, a pretty region of flower-filled aromatic pastures, delightful wooded valleys and Tyrolean architecture. At the centre of the town stands the **Palazzo della Magnifica Comunità**. Originally built in the 13th century, this was the seat of the medieval governing council which ruled the area as a semi-autonomous region. Today the panelled interiors contain medieval paintings by local artists, and an archaeology collection. Most visitors come for the excellent summer and winter resort facilities, and to climb, by cable car, to the 2,229 m (7,311 ft) top of **Alpe Cermis**, the mountain that rises to the south of the town.

ENVIRONS: The church in **Tesero**, the next village east, bears a 15th-century fresco by an unknown painter depicting

Vines growing on the terraced slopes of the Cembra valley

Sabbath-breakers. The church itself, dating back to 1450, has a flurry of Gothic vaulting, and a modern representation of the Crucifixion painted against a background of the village.

At **Predazzo**, about 13 km (8 miles) east, the **Museo Geologico e Mineralogico** explains the local geology.

🏛 **Palazzo della Magnifica Comunità**
Piazza Cesare Battisti 2.
[0462 34 03 65. ◯ Jul–Aug & 27 Dec–7 Jan: Mon–Sat pm
● 15 Aug. 🗓
🏛 **Museo Geologico e Mineralogico**
Piazza Santi Filippo e Giacomo 1.
[0462 50 23 92.
● for long-term restoration.

San Martino di Castrozza ❿

🏠 4/0. 🚌 🚻 Via Passo Rolle 165 (0439 76 88 67).

THE RESORT OF San Martino occupies one of the most scenic and accessible valleys in the southern Dolomites, making it very popular with walkers and skiers. Cable cars rise to the peak of **Alpe Tognola** (2,163 m, 7,095 ft), southwest of the town, and up the **Cima della Rosetta** (2,609 m, 8,557 ft) to the east. Both offer magnificent views of the Pale di San Martino Dolomitic peaks, a stirring sight as the massive rock peaks, split by

Piramidi di Segonzano, near Cembra

glaciers, rise above a sea of green meadows and woodland. San Martino is almost entirely surrounded by forest, which once supplied the Venetian Republic with timber for ships. The forest is now protected, and as a result it is possible to see Alpine flowers, mushrooms, birds and other wildlife with relative ease.

Cembra ⓫

🏠 2,500. 🚌 🚻 Piazza Toniolli 2 (0461 68 31 10). 🗓 Wed.

THE WINE-PRODUCING town of Cembra nestles on the terraced slopes of a scenic valley of flower-filled villages. Some 6 km (4 miles) east of Cembra stand the **Piramidi di Segonzano**, a rare series of erosion pillars, some over 30 m (100 ft) high, each topped by a rock. The footpath to the pillars is well signposted, with informative noticeboards along the way explaining the formation of the bizarre columns, which are similar in appearance to giant termites' nests. Their setting amid bird-filled woodland makes the steep climb up to the site well worthwhile. A further reward is the fine view, from the top of the hill, along the Cembra valley and westwards as far as the Brenta group of Dolomites.

🎋 **Piramidi di Segonzano**
Strada Statale 612 to Cavalese.
[0461 68 31 10. ◯ daily.

The impressive falls of the Cascate di Nardis, Madonna di Campiglio

Madonna di Campiglio ⑫

🏔 1,300. 🚌 ℹ️ Via Pradalago 4 (0465 44 20 00).
🏛 Jun–Sep: Tue & Thu.

MADONNA DI CAMPIGLIO is the chief resort in the Val Meledrio. Nestling between the Brenta and Adamello groups of peaks, it makes the perfect base for walking or skiing amid the magnificent mountain terrain. Cableways radiate out from the town in every direction, giving easy access to the peaks.

ENVIRONS: The church at **Pinzolo**, 14 km (9 miles) south, has a well-preserved fresco depicting a *Dance of Death* (1539). The inevitable march of the figures, both rich and poor, is underlined by a text written in local dialect.

North of Pinzolo, the road west from Carisolo leads to the verdant and popular, yet unspoilt, **Val Genova**. About 4 km (2 miles) along the valley is the spectacular **Cascate di Nardis**, a waterfall that plunges down 90 m (300 ft). The two masses of rock at the bottom are said to be the forms of petrified demons.

Trento ⑬

🏔 105,000. FS 🚌 ℹ️ Via Manci 2 (0461 98 38 80). 🏛 Thu.

TRENTO, THE CAPITAL of the region to which it gave its name, is also the most attractive town in Trentino: it has a fine Romanesque cathedral and a richly decorated castle, and streets lined with handsome Renaissance mansions. Trento is noted as the venue for the **Council of Trent** (1545–63), set up by the Catholic Church to consider reforms that might encourage breakaway groups, in particular the German Protestants, to return to the fold. The reforms, which ushered in the period of the Counter-Reformation, were only partly successful.

The **Duomo**, site of some of the Council meetings, was built in robust Romanesque style from the 13th century. It was three centuries before it was completed, in 1515, but the builders maintained architectural harmony by ignoring Gothic and Renaissance styles entirely. The result is a church of unusual integrity, noble and assured. The Duomo stands on **Piazza Duomo**, the city's main square, which was first laid out by the Romans as their central market place or forum. Trento's Roman name, Tridentum, is commemorated in the figure of Neptune who stands holding his trident at the top of the 18th-century fountain, which stands in the middle of the main square.

🏛 Museo Diocesano Tridentino
Piazza Duomo 18. ℃ 0461 23 44 19.
🕐 Mon–Sat. ● 1 Jan & public hols.
This museum is housed in the **Palazzo Pretorio**, an imposing medieval building that stands on the eastern side of Piazza Duomo. Its contents include early ivory reliquaries, Flemish tapestries and paintings depicting the Council of Trent.

⚜ Castello del Buonconsiglio
Via Bernardo Clesio 5.
℃ 0461 23 37 70. 🕐 Tue–Sun.
● 1 Jan, 1 Nov, 25 Dec.
This large castle, built in the 13th century and later enlarged with additional buildings, is part of the defences of the town. Trento was an important frontier on the main road linking Italy to northern Europe, and thick walls still encircle the town.

Inner courtyard of the Magno Palazzo

The southern section of the castle consists of the magnificent **Magno Palazzo** (1530), built for the ruling prince-bishops of Trento, who were given extensive powers by the Holy Roman Emperor in order to foster loyalty and discourage defection to the pope. The lavish decoration (which includes frescoes of virile satyrs and nymphs by Gerolamo Romanino, 1531–2) speaks of massive wealth and a luxurious lifestyle. The fine rooms, now the setting for the **Museo Provinciale**, contain paintings, ceramics and 15th-century wood carvings, and prehistoric, Etruscan and Roman items. The **Torre dell'Aquila** (Eagle Tower) nearby contains frescoes painted around

Palazzo Pretorio and the Duomo in Trento's main square

The commanding form of the Ossario del Castel Dante in Rovereto

1400. They depict the Months of the Year in charming detail: the month of January, for instance, has some delightful snowballing scenes.

ENVIRONS: Immediately to the west of Trento a scenic round-trip along a winding road leads up the north flank of **Monte Bondone** and back, via **Vezzano**, down the western slopes. The views along the route are magnificent, in particular from Vaneze and Vason. East of Trento, Pergine marks the start of the **Val Sugana**, a broad valley with attractive and popular lakes. In the hills north of Lake Levico lies the spa town of **Levico Terme**, distinguished by elegant Neo-Classical buildings set amid beautifully wooded parkland.

Rovereto ⓮

🏠 33,000. FS 🚌 🅸 Piazza Rosmini (0464 43 03 63). 🅐 Tue.

ROVERETO WAS at the centre of fierce fighting during World War I, after which the Venetian castle (built in 1416) that dominates the town was transformed into the **Museo Storico della Guerra**, a war museum. The displays feature several highlights, including sections devoted to wartime humour, spying and propaganda. Contemporary photographs tell the story of the 20th century's two world wars in harrowing detail. Near the entrance to the museum, stairs lead out onto the castle roof for a view of the imposing **Ossario del Castel Dante**.

Some distance away is the **Campana dei Caduti** (Bell of the Fallen), one of the largest bells in Italy, which was cast from melted-down cannons at the end of World War II and mounted in an imposing building above the town; it is rung daily at sunset. From the memorial there are extensive views over the valley. Below the war museum stands the **Museo Civico**, housing collections on archaeology, art, natural history and folklore.

ENVIRONS: A little over 8 km (5 miles) north of Rovereto is the prominent landmark of **Castel Beseno**, rising on a hill to the east. This enormous castle, by far the largest in the region, was built and rebuilt from the 12th century to the 18th to guard the junction of the three valleys. The ruins are undergoing restoration: 16th-century frescoes may be seen.

To the south of Rovereto, the main road passes through a valley littered with massive house-sized boulders created by landslips: these are known as the **Ruina Dantesca**, because they are mentioned in Dante's *Inferno* (XII, 4–9).

Five kilometres (3 miles) to the south, at Lavini di Marco, fossilized dinosaur footprints have recently been discovered.

🏛 **Museo Storico della Guerra**
Via Castelbarco 7. 📞 0464 43 81 00. 🕐 mid-Mar–Nov: Tue–Sun. 🔲
🏛 **Museo Civico**
Borgo Santa Caterina 41.
📞 0464 43 90 55. 🕐 Tue–Sun. 🔵 public hols. 🔲 🔲
🏰 **Castel Beseno**
Besenello. 📞 0464 83 46 00. 🕐 Mar–Nov: Tue–Sun. 🔲

Castello di Avio in its lush setting

Castello di Avio ⓯

Via Castello, Sabbionara d'Avio.
📞 0464 68 44 53. 🚌 FS to Vo, then 3 km (2 mile) walk. 🕐 Feb–mid-Dec: 10am–1pm, 2–5pm Tue–Sun. 🔲

CASTLES LINE THE Adige valley all the way to the Brenner Pass, but few are as accessible as the Castello di Avio, southwest of Ala. It was founded in the 11th century, considerably extended in the 13th, and today offers visitors far-reaching views. Among the numerous frescoes with secular themes is a rare series in the Casa delle Guardie (the Sentry House) depicting 13th-century battle scenes.

The extensive walls enclosing Castel Beseno above Rovereto

NORTHWEST ITALY

Northwest Italy at a Glance

THE NORTHWEST OF ITALY is made up of three very different geological characteristics: the jagged Alps, the flat plain, and the undulating shoreline of the Mediterranean. Within this varied landscape, some of it still wild and unspoilt, lie extremely rich and diverse vestiges of the area's substantial cultural heritage. The major sights, in the regions of Valle d'Aosta and Piedmont, Liguria and Lombardy, are shown on this map.

Valle d'Aosta

Parco Nazionale del Gran Paradiso

Basilica di Sant'Andrea, Vercelli

The Parco Nazionale del Gran Paradiso *is a beautiful wilderness, and the habitat of rare Alpine fauna and flora (see pp208–9).*

Mole Antonelliana, Turin

VALLE D'AOSTA AND PIEDMONT
(See pp202–21)

Piedmont

LIGURIA
(See pp222–35)

The capital of Piedmont *is Turin, an elegant and bustling city of splendid Baroque architecture. Its skyline is dramatically dominated by the Mole Antonelliana (see p216).*

San Remo *is a typical Riviera resort, with palm trees and a casino. The onion-domed outline of the Russian church adds an exotic flavour to the town (see p226).*

The casino, San Remo

The Basilica di Sant'Andrea *in Vercelli is an important Romanesque building, one of the earliest to use Gothic elements (see p220).*

◁ Typical shuttered Ligurian façades in Santa Margherita Ligure

LOMBARDY
(See pp180–201)

ella, Lake
ggiore

Duomo, Milan

Certosa di
Pavia

Portofino

***Isola Bella** is an
enchanting island on
romantic Lake Maggiore.
Nearby lies beautiful Lake
Como (see pp184–5).*

***Milan's Duomo**, with its dis-
tinctive bristling spires, is one of
the many architectural gems in
this stylish city (see p187).*

***Portofino** is
one of Italy's most
exclusive resorts.
Nestling in a creek,
its pretty pastel-
coloured houses
surround a yacht-
filled harbour
(see p232).*

***The Certosa di Pavia**, a charming Carthusian
monastery, includes a richly decorated Gothic
church with a magnificent Renaissance façade,
and a series of attractive cloisters (see pp196–7).*

0 kilometres   50

0 miles   25

Regional Food: Northwest Italy

R ICHNESS AND HEARTINESS characterize the food of northwest Italy, an area dominated by the presence of the Alps. Here, unlike in the rest of Italy, butter is used in cooking as much as oil. The area is the home of rice growing in Italy, and risotto naturally features prominently on local menus, complementing the ubiquitous pasta dishes. Cheeses are also a speciality, as are truffles – which grow in the clay soil of Piedmont – and nuts of all types. Garlic, saffron, basil and wine are other favourite ingredients in the aromatic sauces. Grissini, the crisp breadsticks found on every restaurant table, originate in Turin.

Grissini

Onion and Herb Focaccia is made from dough enriched with olive oil; it may also be baked plain, or with olives or tomato.

Green peppers

Orange peppers

Red peppers

Bagna Caôda

Spring onions

Celery

Yellow peppers

Bresaola, *wafer-thin slices of cured raw beef, is served as an antipasto with olive oil and a squeeze of lemon.*

Farinata *is a flat bread made of oil and chickpea flour. It is relatively thin, similar to a pancake and eaten as a snack.*

Bagna Caôda *is an anchovy-based dip flavoured with garlic, olive oil, butter and sometimes truffles. It is served hot, fondue-style, and eaten with sliced raw vegetables which are dipped into it. It is a speciality of Piedmont.*

Risotto alla milanese *is a rich and delicious Milanese dish of rice, white wine, onion, saffron and grated Parmesan cheese.*

Trenette al pesto, *a Genoese speciality, consists of noodles with a sauce of basil, garlic, pine nuts, Parmesan and oil.*

Pansôti with Walnut Sauce *is Ligurian, spinach- and egg-filled pasta, with a sauce of nuts, garlic, herbs, ricotta cheese and olive oil.*

Manzo brasato al Barolo *is a Piedmont dish of lean beef marinated in red wine and garlic, then stewed gently until tender.*

Cacciucco, *found on Livorno menus, is a rich stew of mixed fish and seafood cooked with wine, garlic and herbs.*

Costolette alla milanese *are veal cutlets dipped in egg and breadcrumbs, fried in butter and served with lemon.*

Ossobuco *is shin of veal with marrow bone in a tomato and wine sauce, with a hint of garlic, anchovy and lemon.*

Fagiano tartufato *– stuffed pheasant – is filled with white truffles and pork fat; it is then wrapped in bacon and roasted.*

Spezzatino di pollo *is a chicken quarter cooked with tomato sauce containing wine and, sometimes, truffles.*

CHEESE

The lush Alpine meadows in the northwest help to produce some of the finest cheeses in Italy. They include the blue-veined yet mild Gorgonzola; the delicate Mascarpone, a cream cheese much used in desserts; and Taleggio, a soft, creamy cheese to be eaten young, all from Lombardy. Fontina, a semi-hard cheese made in the Valle d'Aosta, has a nutty, slightly sweet taste.

Fontina   Taleggio

Gorgonzola

Spinaci alla Piemontese, *a side order, is a blend of spinach, anchovies, butter and garlic, with croutons.*

Amaretti *are light and delicious macaroon-type biscuits, usually taken with coffee, made from almonds and egg whites. They are often wrapped in pretty coloured paper.*

Torta di nocciole, *a Piedmontese nut tart, includes hazelnuts, eggs and butter among its ingredients.*

Zabaione *is a frothy concoction of egg, sugar and Marsala wine, accompanied by sponge fingers. It is served hot or cold.*

Panettone *from Milan is a light yeast cake which contains candied fruit. It is traditionally eaten at Christmas.*

The Wines of Northwest Italy

G RAPES ARE GROWN throughout the northwest – from the cliffs of Liguria to the steep mountainsides of Valle d'Aosta. The best wines, however, come from Piedmont, in particular the Langhe hills southwest of Turin, source of two of Italy's finest reds: the rich, powerful, long-lived Barolo and Barbaresco. Both of these are now showing the benefits of modern techniques and a renewed interest in high-quality wine making. Lighter,

Medieval illustration of a grape crusher

everyday red wines that go well with the local cuisine include Dolcetto and the popular Barbera. Another Piedmont speciality is sparkling *spumante*, Italians' instinctive choice whenever there is something around to celebrate.

Castiglione Falletto in the heart of Piedmont

Turin

Chieri

PIEDMONT

MONFERRATO

Barbera d'Alba comes from the adaptable Barbera grape, which can grow on almost any slope. Its ubiquitous nature means that the wines it yields can be light and full of fruit, as well as dense, strong and full-flavoured. Good producers include Aldo Conterno, Voerzio, Pio Cesare, Altare, Gaja, Vaira and Vietti.

Canale

Barba

Alb

Bra

Saluzzo

Barolo • Castig Fallet

Dolcetto is grown in seven different areas. Dolcetto d'Alba has a delicious perfume and deep purple colour. Best drunk within one or two years, it ranges in flavour from fresh and fruity to the rich, concentrated plumminess of some of the top wines, such as those produced by Giuseppe Mascarello.

Dogliani

Mondovi

LANG

Cuneo

KEY

☐	Barolo
☐	Barbaresco
☐	Other vineyard areas

0 kilometres	25
0 miles	15

Barolo, prized the world over for its complex array of flavours and firm tannins, is made from the Nebbiolo grape and may take up to 20 years to mature. Vigna Colonnello is a top Barolo from Aldo Conterno, made only in the best years like 1993, 1990 and 1989.

The white truffle of Alba is an autumn speciality from the Langhe hills. Highly prized for its earthy scent, it is excellent with Barolo.

Moscato d'Asti is an excellent aperitivo *or light dessert wine made from the aromatic, fruity Moscato grape. It is light in alcohol with a gently sweet finish and may have a slight sparkle. Ideal for refreshing the palate after a hearty Piedmontese meal, Araldica's versatile Moscato is delicious when served well chilled.*

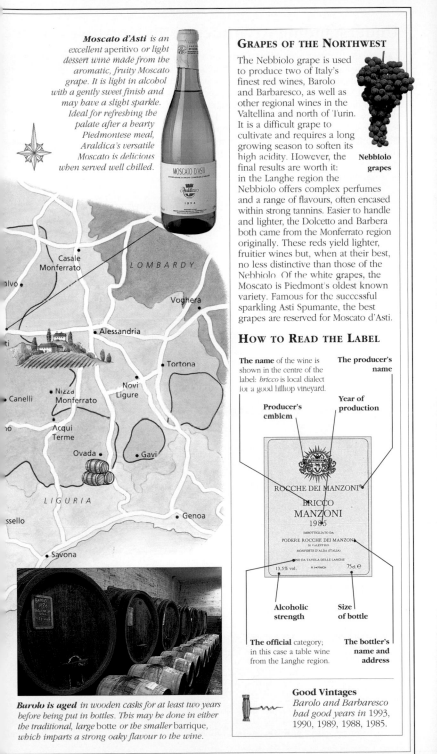

GRAPES OF THE NORTHWEST

The Nebbiolo grape is used to produce two of Italy's finest red wines, Barolo and Barbaresco, as well as other regional wines in the Valtellina and north of Turin. It is a difficult grape to cultivate and requires a long growing season to soften its high acidity. However, the final results are worth it: in the Langhe region the Nebbiolo offers complex perfumes and a range of flavours, often encased within strong tannins. Easier to handle and lighter, the Dolcetto and Barbera both came from the Monferrato region originally. These reds yield lighter, fruitier wines but, when at their best, no less distinctive than those of the Nebbiolo. Of the white grapes, the Moscato is Piedmont's oldest known variety. Famous for the successful sparkling Asti Spumante, the best grapes are reserved for Moscato d'Asti.

Nebbiolo grapes

HOW TO READ THE LABEL

The name of the wine is shown in the centre of the label: *bricco* is local dialect for a good hilltop vineyard.

The producer's name

Producer's emblem

Year of production

ROCCHE DEI MANZONI

BRICCO
MANZONI
1985

IMBOTTIGLIATO DA
PODERE ROCCHE DEI MANZONI
IN VALENTINO
MONFORTE D'ALBA (ITALIA)

VINO DA TAVOLA DELLE LANGHE

13,5% vol.　　R 1-477M/CN　　75cl ℮

Alcoholic strength

Size of bottle

The official category; in this case a table wine from the Langhe region.

The bottler's name and address

Good Vintages
Barolo and Barbaresco had good years in 1993, 1990, 1989, 1988, 1985.

Map showing places including Casale Monferrato, LOMBARDY, Voghera, Alessandria, Tortona, Novi Ligure, Nizza Monferrato, Canelli, Acqui Terme, Ovada, Gavi, LIGURIA, Genoa, Savona, ssello, alvo.

Barolo is aged in wooden casks for at least two years before being put in bottles. This may be done in either the traditional, large botte *or the smaller* barrique, *which imparts a strong oaky flavour to the wine.*

Understanding Architecture in Northwest Italy

ALTHOUGH THE BUILDINGS of the northwest tend to be solid and imposing – a result partly of the more severe climate – there is no distinctive architectural stamp as there is around Venice, Florence or even in Rome. Instead, a variety of buildings in different styles, many borrowed or reinterpreted from elsewhere, are dotted across the area: enchanting medieval castles, outstanding Romanesque and Gothic buildings, unusual Baroque structures. The northwest is also rich in modern architecture – in terms of both design and materials – influenced by the region's industrial developments and its strong flair for innovative design, which also often draws its inspiration from earlier architectural styles.

Castello Sforzesco, 1451–66 *(see p186)*

CHARACTERISTICS OF NORTHWEST ITALIAN ARCHITECTURE

Double row of defensive walls

Wooden balcony

Few windows

Massive square tower

Pointed turret

Battlements

***Castello di Fénis**, one of the finest castles in the Valle d'Aosta, is a 14th-century fortress with asymmetrical towers, turrets and crenellated walls. Frescoes adorn the interior (see p207).*

Alternating bands of marble

Rose window

Lions support columns and porch above

Elaborate carving

***Cappella Colleoni**, Bergamo (1476), mixes rich, decorative elements in this early Renaissance masterpiece (see p193).*

Rose window

Octagonal drum influenced by the Duomo in Florence

Highly ornate façade

Patterned marble design

***Monza's Duomo** (1390s) typifies the Lombard style of Romanesque architecture with its marble stripes and ornate carving (see p193).*

Massive scale

Ornate window surrounds

Rotunda

Balcony

Curved brickwork

***Palazzo Carignano** is perhaps the finest product of Turin's idiosyncratic Baroque school. Guarini's masterpiece (1679) boasts an extraordinary undulating brick façade and a fine rotunda (see p215).*

WHERE TO SEE THE ARCHITECTURE

The road to Aosta is flanked by numerous medieval castles *(see p206)* while inspirational Romanesque and Gothic churches are found in Lombardy – at Monza *(p193)*, Pavia *(p195)*, Milan *(pp186–193)*, and Como *(pp184–5)*. The 15th-century Certosa di Pavia *(pp196–7)* is a must, as well as the charming city of Mantova *(p199)*. Turin *(pp212–16)* is famous for its unique Baroque school, and Bergamo for its exuberance. Architecture from the last two centuries is best represented in Milan and Turin, and in Genoa some exciting new redevelopment projects are taking place.

Renzo Piano's mast structure (1992) in Genoa's redeveloped port

19TH–20TH CENTURY ARCHITECTURE

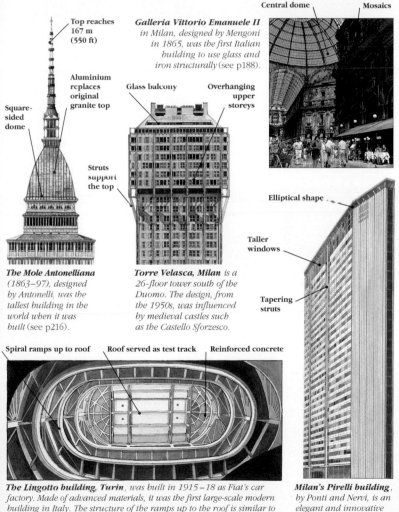

Top reaches 167 m (550 ft)

Aluminium replaces original granite top

Squared-sided dome

Struts support the top

The Mole Antonelliana *(1863–97), designed by Antonelli, was the tallest building in the world when it was built (see p216).*

Glass balcony

Overhanging upper storeys

Torre Velasca, Milan *is a 26-floor tower south of the Duomo. The design, from the 1950s, was influenced by medieval castles such as the Castello Sforzesco.*

Galleria Vittorio Emanuele II in Milan, designed by Mengoni in 1865, was the first Italian building to use glass and iron structurally (see p188).

Central dome

Mosaics

Elliptical shape

Taller windows

Tapering struts

Spiral ramps up to roof   Roof served as test track   Reinforced concrete

The Lingotto building, Turin, *was built in 1915–18 as Fiat's car factory. Made of advanced materials, it was the first large-scale modern building in Italy. The structure of the ramps up to the roof is similar to the interior of Guarini's Baroque dome for San Lorenzo in Turin.*

Milan's Pirelli building, *by Ponti and Nervi, is an elegant and innovative skyscraper built in 1959.*

LOMBARDY

THE REGION OF LOMBARDY *stretches from the Alps, on the border with Switzerland, down through the romantic lakes of Como and Maggiore to the broad, flat plain of the River Po. It is an area of lakeside villas with azalea-filled gardens, of wealthy towns with imposing palazzi and highly decorated churches, and of efficient, modern industry and large-scale agriculture, the financial heart of Italy. At its centre stands Milan, the style-conscious capital of Lombardy.*

The region was named after the Lombards or Longobards, a barbarian tribe that invaded Italy in the 6th century AD. During the Middle Ages, Lombardy was part of the Holy Roman Empire, but not always loyal to its German emperors. The Lombards, who had a talent for banking and commerce, resented any outside interference with their prosperity.

The 12th century saw the rise of the Lega Lombarda, or Lombard League, a band of forceful separatists founded to counter the brutal imperialism of Frederick Barbarossa (their most modern incarnation was the Lega Nord political party). Power was seized by the region's great families, most notably the Visconti and the Sforza of Milan, from the 14th to the early 16th century. These dynasties also became great patrons of the arts, commissioning exquisite palaces, churches and artworks, many of which can still be seen. Bergamo, Mantova and Cremona – not to mention Milan itself – contain a remarkably rich array of art treasures. Here are such pinnacles of European civilization as the charterhouse at Pavia, Leonardo da Vinci's *Last Supper* and the magnificent paintings of the Pinacoteca di Brera in Milan.

Lombardy – famous as the birthplace of Virgil, Monteverdi, Stradivarius and Donizetti – today offers visitors the contrasting pleasures of lyrical lakeside landscapes (resorts on lakes Como and Maggiore have attracted poets, aristocrats and gamblers for centuries) and beautiful, bustling cities.

Strolling through Milan's enormous Galleria Vittorio Emanuele II

◁ The peaceful shores of the beautiful Lake Como, southwest of Bellagio

Exploring Lombardy

THE ENORMOUS PLAIN of the River Po runs through much of Lombardy, providing a landscape that is flat and perfectly suited to the consequent expansion of industry in the region. This is, however, also a region of great contrasts. To the north, in a still unspoilt setting in the foothills of the mountains, lie the lakes Como and Maggiore, as well as the dramatic valleys and peaks of the Parco Nazionale dello Stelvio around Bormio, Sondrio and Val Camonica. Further south, busy industrialized areas give way to huge tracts of agriculture dotted with towns of great beauty such as Cremona, Mantova and Pavia, which offer a rich and splendid array of artistic pleasures.

SIGHTS AT A GLANCE

Bergamo **5**
Brescia **9**
*Certosa di Pavia
  pp196–7* **12**
Cremona **13**
Lago d'Iseo **8**
Lake Como **1**
Lake Maggiore **2**
Lodi **10**
Mantova **15**
*Milan (Milano)
  pp186–93* **3**
Monza **4**
Parco Nazionale dello
  Stelvio **6**
Pavia **11**
Sabbioneta **14**
Val Camonica **7**

SEE ALSO

- *Where to Stay* pp549–51
- *Where to Eat* pp584–6

**Passo di Gavia in the Parco Nazionale dello
Stelvio on the eastern fringes of Lombardy**

0 kilometres   25

0 miles   20

A view of Isola Bella on Lake Maggiore

The colourful façade of the Cappella Colleoni in Bergamo

KEY

- ▬ Motorway
- ▬ Major road
- ▬ Minor road
- ▬ Scenic route
- ▬ River
- ✵ Viewpoint

GETTING AROUND

Milan has two international airports, which are obvious gateways into northern Italy, and the vast and flat Lombard plain has its advantages when it comes to transport: roads and railway lines criss-cross it and make trips between the larger towns very easy. The lakes, however, are better visited by car, as only two main towns are served by trains, though there are bus and boat services around the shores. The Parco Nazionale dello Stelvio and the mountains are more remote still, but offer good tourist facilities.

Lake Como ❶

Set in an idyllic landscape of mountains and rugged hillsides, Lake Como has for centuries attracted visitors who come here to go boating, for walks in the hills, or for relaxation and inspiration. The northern stretches, in particular, are shrouded in an almost eerie calm. The long and narrow lake, crafted into a wishbone shape by glacial erosion, offers fine views up to the Alps and down to the towns of Como and Lecco.

View of the lake near Como

The northern stretches are wilder and less populated than the southern part, offering visitors great tranquillity.

Menaggio is one of a string of popular resorts lining the west bank.

Varenna, a ferry port, is overlooked by a ruined 11th-century castle. At Fiumelatte, just south, there is a foaming stream, the "river of milk".

Villa Carlotta nestles among lush gardens with lovely views.

Cernobbio was a favourite resort of the exiled Queen Caroline of England in the early 19th century.

Bellagio
This delightful resort on the cusp of the lake's two arms has elegant lakeside promenades and cafés.

The southeastern arm of the lake is also called the Lago di Lecco.

Lecco, home to the 19th-century novelist, Manzoni.

The scenic route just south of Bellagio climbs a hill to offer far-reaching lake views.

0 kilometres   15

0 miles   10

Como
The town, which gave its name to the lake, boasts a fine Duomo in mixed Gothic and Renaissance styles, with carvings on its façade.

KEY

⋯	Car ferry route
•••	Ferry route
🔷	Sailing and boating centre
ℹ	Tourist information
▬	Motorway
▬	Major road
═	Minor road
☀	Viewpoint

Tadoline's copy (1834) of Canova's
Cupid and Psyche in Villa Carlotta

Exploring Lake Como

In the heart of **Como** lies the elegant Piazza Cavour. Nearby rises the beautiful 14th-century **Duomo**, with its 15th- and 16th-century reliefs and paintings, and fine tombs. The 18th-century dome is by Turin's famous Baroque architect, Juvarra. Next to the Duomo stand the 13th-century Broletto (town hall), charmingly striped in white, pink and grey, and the tall Torre del Comune. **Villa Carlotta** is an elegant 18th-century summerhouse, known for its gardens. In springtime, rhododendrons, camellias and azaleas burst into colour in this pretty setting. Inside, the villa houses a collection of sculptures.

Lecco, a small industrial town lying to the south of the lake's eastern arm, was the birthplace of the writer Alessandro Manzoni (1785–1873). The author's childhood home, the **Casa Natale di Manzoni** is devoted to memorabilia of his life and works. In Piazza Manzoni, a monument depicts scenes from his most famous novel, *I Promessi Sposi (The Betrothed)* – set partly in 17th-century Lecco as well as Milan.

🏛 **Villa Carlotta**
Tremezzo, Como. 📞 0344 404 05.
🕐 daily. ⬤ Nov–mid-Mar. 🎟
🏛 **Casa Natale di Manzoni**
Via Guanella 1, Lecco. 📞 0341 48
12 47. 🕐 Tue–Sun am. ⬤ 1 Jan,
Easter, 1 May, 15 Aug, 25 Dec. 🎟

Lake Maggiore ❷

L AKE MAGGIORE, the second largest Italian lake after Lake Garda, is a long expanse of water nestling right against the mountains and stretching into Alpine Switzerland; it is warmer in atmosphere and more romantic than Lake Como. The gently sloping shores are dotted with camellias, azaleas and verbena vegetation – from which the ancient lake derived its Roman name, Verbanus.

A huge copper statue of Cardinal Carlo Borromeo, the chief patron of the lake, stands in **Arona**, the town where he was born in 1538. It is possible to climb up and look out over the lake through his eyes and ears. Arona also boasts a ruined castle and a chapel, Santa Maria, dedicated to the Borromeo family.

Further up the western coast of the lake is **Stresa**, the chief resort and main jumping-off point for visits to the islands; the town is full of villas and verdant gardens, where many visitors take a stroll. Behind Stresa, a cable car ride away, rises Monte Mottarone, a snow-capped peak offering spectacular panoramic views of the

The statue of Carlo
Borromeo in Arona

surrounding mountains, including Monte Rosa.

The **Borromean islands**, at the centre of the lake near Stresa, are small jewels of natural beauty augmented by artificial grottoes, architectural follies and landscaped parks. The **Isola Bella** is home to the 17th-century **Palazzo Borromeo** and its splendid garden of landscaped terraces, fountains, peacocks, statues and grottoes. Isola Madre is largely given over to a botanical garden. San Giovanni is the most exclusive and smallest of the isles, with a villa which once belonged to the conductor Arturo Toscanini (1867–1957).

The lake becomes quieter towards the Swiss border, but continues to be lined with attractive villas. The **Villa Taranto**, on the outskirts of Verbania, houses one of the best exotic botanical collections.

About 3 km (2 miles) west of **Cannobio**, a market town near Switzerland, is the dramatic gorge and tumbling waterfall of the Orrido di Sant'Anna, which can be reached by boat.

🏛 **Palazzo Borromeo**
Isola Bella. 🛥 from Stresa. 📞 0323
305 56. 🕐 Apr–Oct: daily. 🎟
🏛 **Villa Taranto**
Via Vittorio Veneto III, Verbania,
Palanza. 📞 0323 55 66 67.
🕐 Apr–Oct: daily. 🎟 🔖

Isola Bella's 17th-century Palazzo Borromeo and garden on Lake Maggiore

Milan ❸

CENTRE OF FASHION, business and finance, Milan has a bustling, businesslike feel about it. It is smart rather than attractive – a city of wealth as opposed to imagination and the heartland of the Italian economy. To the Goths, who took it over from the Romans, it was called "Mailand", the land of May, a place of warmth and inspiration. It has long been an important trading centre at the junction of transalpine routes, and a prize for powerful dynasties. Today, it is the best place to see Italy at its most cosmopolitan and stylish.

Detail from the Duomo

Portrait of a Young Woman by Pollaiuolo, Museo Poldi-Pezzoli

♠ Castello Sforzesco

Piazza Castello. 📞 *02 88 46 37 03.*
⭘ *Tue–Sun.* ⬤ *public hols.* 👤
The first castle on this site was built by the Visconti family, but demolished when their reign ended in the mid-15th century. Milan's new ruler, Francesco Sforza, built in its place this Renaissance palace, which combines a forbidding exterior with a delightful interior. The castle is based on a series of courtyards, the most beautiful of which, the Cortile della Rocchetta, is a graceful arcaded square designed by Bramante and Filarete. The palace now contains, together with sections on Applied Arts, Archaeology and Coins, the **Civiche Raccolte d'Arte Antica**. This fine collection of furniture, antiquities and paintings includes Michelangelo's unfinished sculpture, known as the

Michelangelo's *Rondanini Pietà* (c.1564) in the Castello Sforzesco

Rondanini Pietà. The canvases in the picture collection, dating from the Renaissance to the 18th century, are particularly impressive. The Cappella Ducale contains Gothic frescoes by an unknown artist.

🏛 Museo Poldi-Pezzoli

Via Alessandro Manzoni 12.
📞 *02 79 48 89.* ⭘ *Tue–Sun.* 🈂
Giacomo Poldi-Pezzoli was a wealthy nobleman who, on his death in 1879, bequeathed his magnificent art collection to the state. Its most famous painting is the 15th-century Renaissance *Portrait of a Young Woman* by Antonio Pollaiuolo, though there are also works by Piero della Francesca, Botticelli and Mantegna, among others. The applied arts section is richly endowed with fascinating items ranging from rugs and lace to glass, enamels and porcelain, as well as sculpture, jewellery and sundials, displayed in fine settings.

SIGHTS AT A GLANCE

0 metres 500
0 yards 500

KEY

🅼 Metro station

🚍 Bus terminus

🅿 Parking

ℹ Tourist information

✝ Church

🎭 Teatro alla Scala

Piazza della Scala. 📞 02 72 00 37 44.
🔵 **Box Office** 📞 02 860 775.
Museo Teatrale 📞 02 8879 473.
⬜ daily. ⚫ Sun in winter, public
hols. 🔳 🔳 W www.lascala.milano.it
This Neo-Classical theatre,
known as La Scala, opened
in 1778 and is one of the
most prestigious opera houses
in the world. It has one of the
largest stages in Europe and
hosts sumptuous productions.

**The façade of the world-famous
Teatro alla Scala**

⛪ Duomo

Piazza del Duomo. 📞 02 86 46 34 56.
📷 for roof. ♿
Situated at the very heart of
Milan is its giant cathedral, one
of the largest Gothic churches
in the world at 157 m (514 ft)
long and, at its widest point,
92 m (301 ft) across. It was
begun in the 14th century
under Prince Gian Galeazzo
Visconti but not completed
until more than 500 years later.

The building's most startling
feature is the extraordinary
roof, with its 135 spires and
innumerable statues and
gargoyles, and from which,
on a clear day, there are far-
reaching views to the Alps.

Below, the façade incor-
porates a dazzling assortment
of styles from Gothic through
to Renaissance and Neo-
Classical. The bronze doors are
faced with bas-reliefs recount-
ing episodes from the life of
the Virgin, the life of Sant'
Ambrogio, and scenes retelling
the history of Milan. Note,
around the apse, the delicate
Gothic tracery of the windows.

Inside, the aisles are divided
by 52 giant pillars and lit from
all sides by remarkable stained
glass. Look out for the Visconti
family symbol – a
serpent swallowing
a man – in the fine
tracery of the apse
windows. Among
the many tombs
and statues is a
depiction of San
Bartolomeo Flayed,
carrying his skin.

The treasury,
lying beneath the
main altar, contains
much medieval
gold and silver-
work. In addition,
excavations have
revealed remains of
the original 4th-
century baptistry.

An extra
200 standing
tickets are put on
sale half an hour before each
performance. In the adjoining
Museo Teatrale you can
admire sets and costumes of
past productions, portraits of
conductors and theatrical items
dating back to Roman times.
There is also a good view of
the auditorium, with its gilded
box galleries, *trompe l'oeil*
effects and huge chandelier.

The Gothic Duomo, crowned with spires

Exploring Milan

IN ADDITION TO THE GREAT MONUMENTS in Milan, such as
the cathedral and the castle, there is a host of varied
and interesting museums, churches and civic buildings
which provide an enthralling mix of old and new. This
chic and busy metropolis offers plenty of opportunities
for cultural activities, gastronomic adventures, designer-
fashion shopping or just strolling about, Milan-style.

The glass ceiling and dome covering the Galleria Vittorio Emanuele II

🎪 Galleria Vittorio Emanuele II

Main entrances on Piazza del Duomo
and Piazza della Scala.

This ornate shopping arcade,
known as *il Salotto di Milano*
(Milan's drawing room), was
designed by the architect
Giuseppe Mengoni in 1865.
The galleria had a tragic start,
however, as Mengoni fell to his
death from the scaffolding not
long before its inauguration
in 1877 (a year before the
arcade was actually finished).
Tourists are nevertheless
attracted to its stylish shops,
cafés and restaurants, which
include Il Salotto, said to serve
the finest coffee in all Milan.

The galleria itself has a floor
plan in the shape of a Latin
cross, with an octagonal centre
adorned with mosaics
representing four continents
(Europe, America, Africa and
Asia), together with others
representing Art, Agriculture,
Science and Industry. Its finest
feature is its metal and
glass roof, crowned with a
magnificent central dome.
The roof was the first
structure in Italy to use metal
and glass in a structural way,
rather than just decoratively.
The floors are decorated with
mosaics of the signs of the
zodiac; tourists may be seen

stepping on the genitals of
Taurus the Bull, in order to
bring good luck.

🏛 Museo del Duomo

Palazzo Reale, Piazza del Duomo 14.
[02 86 03 58. **◯** *Tue – Sun.*
◉ *public hols.* 🖾

The museum is in the Palazzo
Reale (Royal Palace), for centuries home to the Visconti and
other rulers of Milan. It charts
the history of the Duomo from
its 14th-century origins (and
the pre-existing church on its
site) until the 1886 competition held to redesign its façade.

Among the exhibits there are
16th- and 17th-century wooden
models of the cathedral, and
many of the original medieval
sculptures – including figures
thought to be Gian Galeazzo
Visconti and Galeazzo Maria
Sforza. There are also stained-
glass windows, paintings,
tapestries and a pair of very
elaborately carved choir stalls.
Another section focuses on
some of the 20th-century
amendments to the cathedral.

🏛 Civico Museo d'Arte Contemporanea

Palazzo Reale, Piazza del Duomo 12.
[02 62 08 32 19.
◉ *for restoration.* 🖾

The Museum of Contemporary
Art (or CIMAC), on the second
floor of the Palazzo Reale,
is a refreshingly up-to-date
gallery. Opened in 1984, it is
still expanding, but the emphasis is heavily on Italian works:
from the 19th century to pieces
by members of the Futurist
movement (Umberto Boccioni
in particular), from abstract art
to the more diverse productions of the present day. Look
out for works by Carlo Carrà
(1881–1966), Filippo De Pisis
(1896–1956), Giorgio Morandi
(1890–1964)
and Tancredi, as well as those
by more familiar artists such
as Modigliani (1884–1920) and
De Chirico (1888–1978).
Among the non-Italian artists
are Post-Impressionists (Van
Gogh, Cézanne, Gauguin),
Picasso – a bequest of 30
etchings – and Matisse, Klee,
Mondrian and Kandinsky.

Still Life (1920) by Giorgio Morandi in the Museo d'Arte Contemporanea

While CIMAC is being restored, about 100 of its most famous paintings are on display at the Museo del Novecento, in the Palazzo della Permanente (Via Turati 34, Tel: 02 655 14 45).

🏛 Pinacoteca Ambrosiana

Piazza Pio XI 2. **[** 02 80 69 21. **◯** Tue–Sun. ⌨

The recently renovated Ambrosiana is home to the magnificent library of Cardinal Federico Borromeo, whose 30,000 manuscripts, including a 5th-century illustrated *Iliad*, early editions of Dante's *Divine Comedy* (1353) and Leonardo's *Atlantic Codex* (15th century), survive to this day.

The building also houses an interesting art gallery, originally bequeathed by Borromeo on his death in 1618. The collection of paintings and sculpture attests to the cardinal's broadranging if slightly quirky taste, and now ranges from 14th-century pieces to works of the early 19th century. Among the canvases are the *Portrait of a Musician* by Leonardo da Vinci (1452–1519) and the *Portrait of a Young Woman*, attributed to his pupil, Ambrogio da Predis. Other masterpieces include the *Madonna of the Canopy* by Botticelli (15th century), a cartoon version of Raphael's Vatican fresco, *The*

Fruit Basket (c. 1596) by Caravaggio in the Pinacoteca Ambrosiana

School of Athens (16th century), and Caravaggio's *Fruit Basket* (the first painting in Italy to have a still life as its subject). There is also a strong collection of Venetian art, with paintings by Tiepolo, Titian, Giorgione and Bassano, and panel paintings by the late 15th-century Lombard painter, Bergognone.

🔒 San Satiro

Via Torino. **◯** daily.

This unassuming church, its full title Santa Maria presso San Satiro, is one of the most beautiful Renaissance buildings in Milan. It stands on the site of a 9th-century sanctuary,

little of which remains apart from the Cappella della Pietà (off the left aisle), beside an 11th-century bell tower.

The interior appears to be in the shape of a Greek cross. This, however, is an illusion created by various *trompe l'oeil* effects in stucco, as space restrictions led Bramante (who became entrusted with its construction in the late 15th century) to choose a T-shaped plan. Above the altar is a 13th-century fresco. An octagonal baptistry containing terracottas lies off the right aisle. The church's façade was finished only in the 19th century.

DESIGNER FASHION IN MILAN

Italians are famous for the attention they pay to their self-image, and here in Milan, Italian chic can be seen in the cluster of top-name shops which occupy the Quadrilatero, the parallelogram of streets delineated by Via Montenapoleone, Via Sant'Andrea, Via della Spiga and Borgospesso. Unlike the Paris fashion scene, which concentrates on flamboyant, often outrageous new designs for women, Milan is more understated in its stylishness: well-cut suits, elegant accessories, chic but wearable shoes. In a sense, the Quadrilatero merely reflects an up-market version of the fashions seen in the streets of any town in Italy: the values of style and comfort are the same; only the astronomical prices serve as a reminder that this is the shopping terrain of the glamorous and very well-heeled.

Dress by Prada

Via Montenapoleone, focus of Milan's smartest shops

Milan: Pinacoteca di Brera

MILAN'S FINEST art collection is held in an imposing 17th-century building, the Palazzo di Brera. This is where, in the 18th century, the Accademia di Belle Arti was founded; the picture collection developed along-side the academy. Inside the Brera hang some of the finest examples of Italian Renaissance and Baroque painting, including works by Piero della Francesca, Mantegna, Canaletto, Bellini, Raphael, Tintoretto, Veronese and Caravaggio. The collection also includes 20th-century works by some of Italy's most famous modern artists.

Mother and Son *(1917)*
The metaphysical paint-ings of Carlo Carrà show a dream world full of strange and obscure symbols.

Portrait of Moisè Kisling
Modigliani's angular portrait of 1915 reflects his interest in African sculpture.

Twin staircases lead up to the first-floor entrance of the Pinacoteca.

The Kiss *(1859)*
Francesco Hayez's painting is one of the most reproduced works of Italian 19th-century art. Patriotic and sentimental, it became a symbol of the optimism surrounding the unification of Italy.

The bronze statue (1809) by Canova de-picts Napoleon as a demi-god with Victory wings in his hand.

KEY TO FLOORPLAN

☐ 15th- to 16th-century Italian painting

☐ 16th- to 17th-century Dutch and Flemish painting

☐ 17th-century Italian painting

☐ 18th- to 19th-century Italian painting

☐ 20th-century Italian painting and sculpture

☐ Non-exhibition space

Works by Rubens and Van Dyck represent some of the non-Italian artists on show.

VISITORS' CHECKLIST

Via Brera 28. 📞 02 72 26 31.
Ⓜ Lanza, Montenapoleone &
Duomo. 🚌 60, 61. 🕐 9am–
6pm Tue–Sat; 9am–8pm Sun &
public hols (last adm: 1 hr before
closing). 🔴 1 Jan, 1 May, 25 Dec.
🚫 📷 🚻 Ⓦ www.beniculturali.it

★ **Dead Christ by Mantegna**
*The subtle lighting and dramatic
perspective of this lamentation by
Mantegna (1430–1506) make it
one of his greatest masterpieces.*

GALLERY GUIDE
*The collection is displayed in 38 rooms,
and was first built up by paintings from
churches, later from acquisitions. Not
all of it is permanently on view – this is
due to restoration work and research.*

Twinned columns
support the arcades
in the courtyard.

The stone façade
presents a regular
and slightly austere
appearance.

**Madonna della
Candeletta** *(c.1490)
This painting by Carlo
Crivelli was the central
part of a polyptych. It is
richly detailed with
much distinctive
ornamentation.*

**Main entrance
from Via Brera**

★ **Marriage
of the Virgin
by Raphael**
*This graceful
altarpiece was
painted in
1504. The cir-
cular temple is
signed with
the artist's
name.*

STAR PAINTINGS

★ **Dead Christ
by Mantegna**

★ **Marriage of the
Virgin by Raphael**

Milan: Southwest of the Centre

SOME OF MILAN'S FINEST TREASURES are to be found in its religious buildings: the ancient monasteries and churches make up some very fine architectural ensembles in themselves, as well as incorporating important ruins and relics dating back to Roman times. It is also in Milan that one of the most famous images in the world is to be found: Leonardo's evocative masterpiece, the *Last Supper*.

San Lorenzo Maggiore viewed from the northeast

The entrance to Sant'Ambrogio, flanked by unequal bell towers

Sant'Ambrogio

Piazza Sant'Ambrogio 15. **[** 02 86 45 08 95. **[** daily. **[**
Sant'Ambrogio, or St Ambrose, is the patron saint of Milan, a man who was so eloquent that bees were said to fly into his mouth, attracted by his honey tongue. As bishop of Milan in the 4th century, he worked hard to avoid a schism in the church. This is the basilica that he began building in AD 379, though most of it today is 10th-century Romanesque. A medieval gateway leads to the bronze doors of the entrance, flanked by two bell towers. Inside, note the fine rib vaulting and the beautiful pulpit, and the striking 9th-century altar decorated with gold, silver and precious gems, crowned by a canopy. In a chapel off the south aisle, fine mosaics line a stunning cupola. Down in the crypt lies the tomb of Sant'Ambrogio himself.

Up above the portico, a small museum contains architectural fragments, tapestries and paintings relating to the church.

San Lorenzo Maggiore

Corso di Porta Ticinese. **[** 02 89 40 41 29. **[** daily. **[** for the Cappella.
This church contains the most important collection of Roman and early Christian remains in Milan. The octagonal basilica was built in the 4th century, above what was probably a Roman amphitheatre, and subsequently rebuilt in the 12th and 16th centuries.

In front of the church stands a row of 16 Roman columns and, in commemoration of his Edict, a statue of the Emperor Constantine. Fine 4th-century mosaics adorn the Cappella di Sant'Aquilino, a Romanesque chapel, which also contains two early Christian sarcophagi. Other Roman architectural elements, which were incorporated into the building of this church, may be seen in a chamber below the chapel.

Santa Maria delle Grazie

Piazza Santa Maria delle Grazie 2.
[02 498 75 88. **Cenacolo [** 02 89 42 11 46 (booking compulsory – up to 60 days in advance). **[** Tue – Sun. **[** public hols. **[** **[**
This beautiful 15th-century Renaissance convent, its lovely apse and calm small cloister designed by Bramante, contains one of the key images of western civilization: the *Cenacolo (Last Supper)* by Leonardo da Vinci. The image captures the moment at which Christ tells His disciples that one of them will betray Him. The Christ figure is unfinished: Leonardo did not consider himself to be worthy enough to complete it.

The artist also spurned the standard fresco technique of painting on wet plaster, applying tempera to the dry wall instead. The result is full of subtlety but has deteriorated badly: the paint is flaking off, and restoration has proved difficult. The painting is now protected by a filtering system.

Leonardo da Vinci's *Last Supper* (1495–7) adorning the refectory wall of Santa Maria delle Grazie

THE EDICT OF MILAN

Milan was colonised by the Romans in 222 BC, and quickly grew to be an important city at the junction of various trading routes. As the Roman Empire grew and then split into two, emperors began to neglect Rome for the better-placed Mediolanum (literally, city in the middle of the plain). It was here that Emperor Constantine declared his edict of AD 313, in which Christianity was officially recognized, thus effectively making it the religion of the empire. The emperor is said to have been converted following a vision, but by the 4th century adopting Christianity was the only way to unite the now disparate empire.

Emperor Constantine

Constantine: it is prized for the iron strip, said to have been one of the nails from the cross of Christ. More local treasures may be found in the Duomo's **Museo Serpero**, including a silver hen standing over seven tiny chicks – which symbolize Lombardy and the seven provinces it ruled – and a relic said to be John the Baptist's tooth.

🏎 **Autodromo**
Parco di Monza. [039 248 21.
○ daily. ● public hols. 🅿 ♿
🛈 **Duomo**
Piazza Duomo. [039 32 34 04.
Museo Serpero ○ Tue–Sun.
🅿

Monza ❹

Milano. 🏛 125,000. FS 🚌
🛈 Palazzo Comunale, Piazza Carducci (039 32 32 22). 🗓 Thu & Sat.

THESE DAYS MONZA is merely a satellite of Milan, famous for its international Formula One **Autodromo**, which lies inside a vast and beautiful park on the edge of Monza. The park also includes an elegant Rococo hunting lodge called the Villa Reale, and a large golf course. At one time, however, Monza was one of the most important towns in Lombardy: Theodolinda, the 6th-century Lombard queen, built its first cathedral and bequeathed her treasure to the town.

At the heart of the town centre is the present **Duomo**, with its notable green and white 14th-century façade and beautiful 15th-century frescoes portraying Theodolinda's life. Behind the high altar is the small Iron Crown, believed to have belonged to Emperor

Leonello d'Este (c.1440) by Pisanello in the Accademia Carrara, Bergamo

Bergamo ❺

🏛 150,000. FS 🚌 🛈 Piazzale Marconi 106 (035 24 22 26).
🗓 Mon.

BERGAMO IS A DELIGHTFUL hilltop town that owes much of its artistic inspiration and architectural splendour to the influence of Venice, which ruled it from the 15th to the late 18th century. The town is divided into two distinct parts: Bergamo Alta crowning the hill, with its cluster of attractive medieval and Renaissance buildings, and the more modern and airy Bergamo Bassa lying below.

The jewel of the upper town is **Piazza Vecchia**, containing one of the most appealing architectural ensembles in the region. Its buildings include the 12th-century Torre del Comune with its fine clock and curfew bell that rings every night at 10pm, the late 16th-century Biblioteca Civica and the attractive 12th-century Palazzo della Ragione, or law courts, adorned with a statue of the lion of Venice.

The arcades of the Palazzo della Ragione lead to Piazza del Duomo, the square of the Neo-Classical Duomo, which is dominated by the façade of the **Cappella Colleoni**

Detail from the Cappella Colleoni

(see p178). The chapel was built in 1476 to house the tomb of Bergamo's famous political leader, Bartolomeo Colleoni. The chapel is flanked by two 14th-century buildings: an octagonal baptistry and the porch leading to the Romanesque basilica of Santa Maria Maggiore. The basilica's austere exterior contrasts with its Baroque interior, which contains the tomb of Gaetano Donizetti (1797–1848), the operatic composer who was born in Bergamo.

The **Galleria dell'Accademia Carrara** is the highlight of Bergamo Bassa, a major picture gallery with a fine collection of works by Venetian masters and local artists, as well as masterpieces from the rest of Italy: 15th-century works by Pisanello, Crivelli, Mantegna, Giovanni Bellini and Botticelli; 16th-century paintings by Titian, Raphael and Perugino; 18th-century canvases by Tiepolo, Guardi and Canaletto. Major artists represented from the rest of Europe include Holbein, Dürer, Brueghel and Velázquez.

🏛 **Galleria dell'Accademia Carrara**
Piazza dell'Accademia. [035 39 96 43. ○ Wed–Mon. ● public hols. 🅿

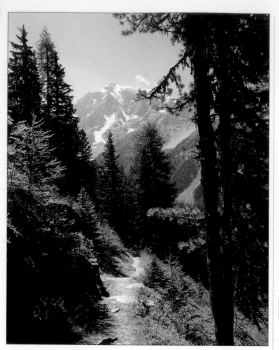

A leafy pathway through the Parco Nazionale dello Stelvio

Parco Nazionale dello Stelvio **❻**

Trento, Bolzano, Sondrio & Brescia.
🚌 from Bormio to Santa Caterina & Madonna dei Monti. 🚹 Via Roma 131b (0342 90 33 00).

THE STELVIO, Italy's largest national park, is the gateway from Lombardy to the glacier-strewn Dolomite mountains stretching into Trentino-Alto Adige. The glaciers are dotted with more than 50 lakes, and dominated by craggy peaks such as Gran Zebrù, Cevedale and Ortles – the tallest mountain here at 3,905 m (12,811 ft). The dramatic, winding roads of the Stelvio are the dread of cyclists in the annual Giro d'Italia, Italy's answer to the Tour de France. For walkers, the area provides virtually unlimited hiking, and access to remote areas populated by ibexes, marmots, chamois and eagles. The only real population centre in the Lombardy part of the park is at **Bormio**, which boasts plenty of winter and summer sports facilities, and is a good base from which to explore the area. The town's **Giardino Botanico** displays some of the species of mountain plants found in the region.

🌿 Giardino Botanico Alpino Retia
Località Rovinaccia, Bormio.
🕐 May–Sep: daily. 🈺

Val Camonica **❼**

Brescia. 🚉 🚌 Capo di Ponte.
🚹 Via Briscioli, Capo di Ponte (0364 420 80).

THIS ATTRACTIVE BROAD valley formed by a glacier is the setting for an extraordinary series of prehistoric carvings on rock. These form an astonishing outdoor mural from the Lago d'Iseo to Capo di Ponte and beyond, and the entire valley has been declared a cultural protection zone by UNESCO. More than 180,000 engravings from the Neolithic era until early Roman times have been discovered, some as recently as the 1970s; the best are in the **Parco Nazionale delle Incisioni Rupestri** around Capo di Ponte. Do not miss the Naquane rock which is carved with nearly 1,000 figures from the last Ice Age. The **Centro Camuno** focuses on, among other things, the Roman settlement in the valley.

🏛 Centro Camuno in Studi Preistorici
Via Mancini 7, Capo di Monte.
📞 0364 420 91.
🕐 Tue–Sun am. ♿

Lago d'Iseo **❽**

Bergamo & Brescia. 🚉 🚌 🚢 Iseo.
🚹 Lungolago Marconi 2, Iseo (030 98 02 09).

THIS GLACIATED LAKE lying in wine-producing country is not only surrounded by tall mountains and waterfalls, but also boasts a mini-mountain of its own, in the form of the island of Monte Isola. Along the shores of the lake are a clutch of fishing villages such as Sale Marasino and Iseo itself. From Marone, on the east bank of the lake, a road leads to the village of **Cislano**, about 5 km (3 miles) away. Here, extraordinary spire-like rock formations rise from the ground, each spire topped by

Prehistoric engraving of a mounted hunter and stag in the Val Camonica

The partly Renaissance Ponte Coperto, straddling the River Ticino at Pavia

a boulder. These distinctive erosion pillars, one of the strangest and most beautiful natural wonders in Lombardy, are known locally as the "Fairies of the Forest".

Brescia 9

🏠 190,000. 🚉 🚌 🛈 Corso Zanardelli 38 (030 434 18). 🔵 Sat.

LOMBARDY'S SECOND city after Milan boasts a rich artistic heritage, ranging from Roman temples to the triumphalist Mussolini-era architecture of its main square, Piazza Vittoriale. The major sights include the Roman ruins around Piazza del Foro, consisting of the **Tempio Capitolino** – a three-part Capitoline temple, now incorporating a museum – and a theatre; the **Pinacoteca Civica Tosio Martinengo**, containing works by Raphael, Lorenzo Lotto and local artists; and the **Duomo** on Piazza Paolo VI, with its 11th-century core and white 17th-century exterior. One of the relics in the Duomo is the banner from the *Carroccio*, or sacred ox cart, which served as a symbol for the medieval Lega Lombarda. **Piazza della Loggia**, where the market is held, is named after the Renaissance loggia, built partly by Palladio. The 18th-century church of San Nazaro e San Celso on Via Bronzoni contains an altarpiece by Titian.

🛐 **Tempio Capitolino**
Via Musei 57a. 📞 030 460 31. 🔵 Tue–Sun. 🔴 1 Jan, 1 May, 1 Nov, 25 Dec. 🖼
🏛 **Pinacoteca Civica Tosio Martinengo**
Via Martinengo da Barco. 📞 030 377 49 99. 🔵 Tue–Sun. 🔴 1 Jan, 1 May, 1 Nov, 25 Dec. 🖼 ♿

Lodi 10

Milano. 🏠 40,000. 🚉 🚌
🛈 Piazza Broletto 4 (0371 42 13 91). 🔵 Wed, Thu, Sat & Sun.

THIS IS A CHARMING medieval town of pastel-coloured houses with wrought-iron gateways, pretty courtyards and gardens. Just off Piazza della Vittoria, the arcaded square on which the 12th-century Duomo stands, is the fine Renaissance church of the **Incoronata**. The magnificent octagonal interior is entirely decorated with wall paintings and gilding, and crowned with a dome. One of the chapels has 15th-century works by Bergognone.

Pavia 11

🏠 81,000. 🚉 🚌 🛈 Via Fabio Filzi 2 (0382 221 56). 🔵 Wed & Sat.

DURING PAVIA'S golden age, the city was the Lombards' capital, and later witnessed coronations of Charlemagne and Frederick Barbarossa. Even after it lost its status to Milan in 1359, Pavia

The Roman Tempio Capitolino in Brescia

remained an important city, and great Romanesque churches, tall towers and other monuments still reflect this.

As well as the Charterhouse *(see pp196–7)* just north of Pavia, there is the sandstone **Basilica di San Michele** off Corso Garibaldi. The building was founded in the 7th century but largely rebuilt in the 12th after being struck by lightning. Its façade is decorated with symbols and friezes of fantastic animals, and inside there are intricate carvings on the columns; a chapel to the right of the main altar contains a 7th-century silver crucifix.

In the centre of the town, around Piazza della Vittoria, stand several ancient monuments. These include the medieval **Broletto** (town hall) with its 16th-century façade and the recently renovated **Duomo**, originally begun in 1488 and worked on in turn by Amadeo, Leonardo da Vinci and Bramante. The dome was added in the 1880s. The 11th-century Torre Civica, which stood next to it, collapsed suddenly in 1989. Crossing the river is the **Ponte Coperto**, a Renaissance covered bridge with a consecrated church halfway along it. The bridge was rebuilt after World War II.

Pavia is also the site of one of Europe's oldest (1361) and most respected universities, now residing around a series of Neo-Classical courtyards off Strada Nuova. This road continues northwards to the 14th-century castle, now home to the **Museo Civico**.

Northwest of Piazza Castello is the 12th-century church, **San Pietro in Ciel d'Oro**. It no longer boasts the fine gilded ceiling from which it derives its name, but does still contain a magnificent shrine to St Augustine, whose bones were allegedly brought to Pavia from Carthage in the 8th century. The body of Boëthius (c.480–524), an important philosopher, is buried down in the crypt.

🏛 **Museo Civico**
Castello Visconteo, Piazza Castello. 📞 0382 338 53. 🔵 Tue–Fri am & Sat. 🔴 public hols. 🖼

Certosa di Pavia ⑫

THE CHARTERHOUSE 8 km (5 miles) north of Pavia is the pinnacle of Renaissance architecture in Lombardy, a gloriously decorated Carthusian monastery built over 200 years. Conceived as a monument to Gian Galeazzo Visconti, the Milanese ruler who founded the complex in 1396, this shrine was created by the great 15th-century craftsman Giovanni Antonio Amadeo, among others, who used innovative techniques of relief work and multicoloured decoration. The Certosa is still home to Carthusian monks, who are under a strict vow of silence.

The choir stalls (15th century) are deeply carved and inlaid with intricate marquetry.

The tomb of Gian Galeazzo Visconti (1351–1402) in the south transept.

Pietra Dura Altar
Several of the 17th-century altars in the chapels have lavish designs worked in semi-precious stones ("pietra dura").

The grilles date from c.1660.

The side chapels are richly decorated with marble, *trompe l'oeil* frescoes and ornate altars and altarpieces.

The interior of the church is largely Gothic.

★ Frescoes by Bergognone (c.1488–93)
This striking portrait of Christ is one of several frescoes by Bergognone in the transept and chapels, together with an altar painting of Sant'Ambrogio.

Tomb of Ludovico il Moro and Beatrice d'Este
This realistic marble portrait of Ludovico and his child bride was begun by Cristoforo Solari in 1497, some 11 years before Ludovico's death.

Great Cloister
This huge cloister is reached through the Small Cloister. It is framed on three sides by the two-storey monks' cells, each backed by a small garden. A hatch beside the door permits food to be delivered without any communication.

Monk's cell

The New Sacristy is painted with colourful ceiling frescoes.

This delightful, arcaded Small Cloister, with fine terracotta ornamentation, contains a small garden, planted in formal designs.

★ Renaissance Façade
The 15th-century lower part of the façade is profusely decorated with statues and carvings of Roman emperors, saints (here St Peter), apostles and prophets. The upper part dates from 1500.

Main entrance to the Certosa

★ Altarpiece by Perugino
The six-panel altarpiece was painted in 1496 but now only one panel – that depicting God the Father – is original; it is flanked by two paintings by Bergognone.

STAR FEATURES

★ Renaissance Façade

★ Altarpiece by Perugino

★ Frescoes by Bergognone

The Duomo on Piazza del Comune, Cremona

Cremona ⑬

👥 76,000. 🚆 🚌 ℹ️ *Piazza del Comune 5 (0372 232 33).* 🚢 *Wed & Sat.* 🔲 *www.cremonaturismo.it*

CREMONA, A MAJOR agricultural market, is most famous for music, thanks to native sons such as the composer Claudio Monteverdi (1567–1643) and the violin-maker Stradivarius (1644–1737). The town itself is dominated by the beautiful Piazza del Comune, bordered by outstanding buildings.

The main attraction is the exuberant part-Romanesque **Duomo**, and its bell tower – said to be the tallest medieval tower in Italy – known as the **Torrazzo**; the two are linked by a Renaissance loggia. The wonderful façade is dominated by the large 13th-century rose window and by a number of intricate touches, including a small portico with statues of the Virgin and saints. Inside, the Duomo is sumptuously decorated with magnificent early 16th-century frescoes and Flemish tapestries, as well as paintings in the side chapels. The top of the Torrazzo offers sweeping views. Outside the Duomo, note the pulpit where itinerant preachers, including San Bernardino of Siena, used to speak to onlookers.

Next to the Duomo stands an octagonal 12th-century baptistry, while on the other side of the piazza rise the arcades of the late 13th-century **Loggia dei Militi** where the town's lords once met, now a war memorial.

The **Palazzo del Comune** is the other major building on the square. It was rebuilt in the 13th century (the windows are more recent) and now contains four rare violins: one each by Guarnieri del Gesù, Andrea and Niccolò Amati, and Stradivarius. The **Museo Stradivariano** displays drawings, models and violins that were made by the master craftsman. The **Museo Civico**, housed in a 16th-century palazzo, contains paintings, wood carvings, the cathedral's treasure, ceramics and a section on archaeology.

On the eastern outskirts of the town, on the road to Casalmaggiore, lies the Renaissance church of **San Sigismondo**. It was here that Francesco Sforza married Bianca Visconti in 1441, and the church was subsequently rebuilt (from 1463) in honour of the event. The interior is richly decorated with 16th-century paintings, altarpieces and frescoes by artists of the Cremona school (Campi family, Gatti and Boccaccino).

🏛 **Torrazzo**
Piazza del Comune. ⏱ *Easter–1 Nov: daily.* 📷
🏛 **Palazzo del Comune**
Piazza del Comune. 📞 *0372 221 38.* ⏱ *Tue–Sun.* ⚫ *public hols.* 📷 ♿
🏛 **Museo Stradivariano**
Via Palestro 17. 📞 *0372 46 18 86.* ⏱ *Tue–Sun.* ⚫ *public hols.* 📷
🏛 **Museo Civico**
Via Ugolani Dati 4. 📞 *0372 46 18 85.* ⏱ *Tue–Sun.* ⚫ *public hols.* 📷 ♿

Sabbioneta ⑭

Mantova. 👥 *4,600.* 🚌 *from Mantova.* ℹ️ *Piazza d'Armi (0375 22 10 44).* 🚢 *Wed am.* 📷 *apply to the tourist information centre.* 📷

SABBIONETA is the result of a delightful experiment in the theory of Renaissance architecture. It was built by Vespasiano Gonzaga Colonna (1531–91) as an ideal city, and within its hexagonal walls is a perfect gridwork arrangement of streets and buildings designed on a human scale. The finest buildings include the splendid Teatro All'Antica designed by Scamozzi, the Palazzo Ducale and the frescoed Palazzo del Giardino, which may be visited as part of a tour of the town.

ANTONIO STRADIVARI AND HIS VIOLINS

Cremona is where the violin was developed. The instrument-maker Andrea Amati made the first ones in the 1530s, and they soon became popular with the royal courts throughout Europe because of their superior tone to the medieval fiddle.

It was Antonio Stradivari, known as Stradivarius (1644–1737) – the pupil of Andrea Amati's grandson

19th-century engraving of Antonio Stradivari

Niccolò – who raised the level of craftsmanship to genius. He used to go walking in the forests of the Dolomites in search of the perfect wood for his instruments. Stradivarius produced more than 1,100 violins in his workshop, of which more than 400 exist to this day and remain unrivalled by modern techniques or equipment. The main stopping-off points on a Stradivarius tour of Cremona are the Museo Stradivariano, the violin room in the Palazzo del Comune, and the great man's tombstone on Piazza Roma.

The ceiling of the Camera degli Sposi, by Mantegna, in the Palazzo Ducale

Mantova ⓯

🏛 55,000. 🚉 🚌 🛈 *Piazza Andrea Mantegna 6 (0376 32 82 53).* 🛒 *Thu.*

Mantova is a striking if stern-looking place of fine squares and aristocratic architecture, bordered on three sides by lakes formed by the swollen banks of the River Mincio. The climate can be humid as a result, but Mantova (Mantua) more than makes up for it with a keen sense of cultural history: it was the birthplace of the poet Virgil and playground for three centuries of the Gonzaga dukes. It was also the refuge where Shakespeare sent Romeo into exile from Verona, and the setting for Verdi's opera *Rigoletto*. These links are all celebrated in street names, signposts and monuments around the town. The theatrical connections are enhanced by the 18th-century **Teatro Scientifico Bibiena**, on Via Accademia, which Mozart's father thought was the finest he had ever seen.

Mantova is focused on three attractive main squares: Piazza dell'Erbe, Piazza del Broletto, named after the 13th-century building adorned with a statue of the poet Virgil, and the cobbled Piazza Sordello. On one side of Piazza Sordello is the **Duomo**, with an 18th-century façade and fine interior stuccoes by Giulio Romano (c.1492–1546); on another side, the forbidding façade of the Palazzo Bonacolsi, with its tall prison tower. Piazza dell'Erbe is dominated by the **Basilica**

di Sant'Andrea (15th century), designed largely by Alberti, the early Renaissance architect and theorist, and now flanked by an arcade of shops. The square is also notable for the appealing 11th-century Rotonda di San Lorenzo, and the part-13th-century Palazzo della Ragione with its 15th-century clock tower.

Detail from the 15th-century clock tower on Piazza dell'Erbe

🏛 Palazzo Ducale

Piazza Sordello. **0376 32 02 83.** 🕐 *Tue–Sun.* 🔴 *1 Jan, 1 May, 25 Dec.* 📷 *available upon request from the Tourist Office (0376 32 82 53).* 📷

The highlight of Mantova is the Palazzo Ducale, the vast home of the Gonzaga family which covers the northeastern corner of the town and incorporates Castello San Giorgio (a 14th-century fortress), a basilica, and the palace proper. With around 500 rooms, it used to be Europe's largest palace. The many impressive works of art include an unfinished series of 15th-century frescoes by Pisanello, retelling episodes from the Arthurian legends; a large portrait by Rubens (17th century) of the ducal family in the Salone degli Arcieri; and – most absorbing of all – the frescoes by Mantegna in the **Camera degli Sposi** (1465–74). These portray Lodovico Gonzaga and members of his family and court in all their magnificence *(pp200–201)*. The entire room is decorated with images of people, animals and fantastic landscapes, and completed by a light-hearted *trompe l'oeil* ceiling of figures, putti and a blue sky.

🏛 Palazzo Tè

Viale Tè. **0376 32 32 66.** 🕐 *Mon pm, Tue–Sun.* 🔴 *1 Jan, 1 May, 25 Dec.* 📷 📷

At the other end of town stands the early 16th-century Palazzo Tè, built by Giulio Romano for the Gonzaga family as a base from which they could go horse riding. Here the artworks conspire with the architecture to produce striking effects: in the **Sala dei Giganti**, for instance, the frescoed Titans seem to be tearing down the very pillars of the room. Also remarkable is the **Sala di Amore e Psiche**, decorated with erotic scenes from Apuleius' *Golden Ass* and said to celebrate Federico II's love for his mistress. Other rooms are lavishly painted with horses and Zodiac signs.

The 13th-century façade of Palazzo Ducale overlooking Piazza Sordello

15th-century fresco, by Mantegna, from the Camera degli Sposi in the Palazzo Ducale

VALLE D'AOSTA AND PIEDMONT

PIEDMONT AND THE NEIGHBOURING VALLE D'AOSTA *are – apart from Turin and its cultural splendours – essentially countryside. To the north lie the Alps, with ski resorts such as Courmayeur, and the wild stretches of the Parco Nazionale del Gran Paradiso. To the south lie the vineyard-clad hills around Barolo, and seemingly endless fields of grain and rice, used in the local dish, risotto.*

The northwest is also rich in culture. From the 11th century to the 18th, both the verdant Valle d'Aosta and Piedmont were part of the French-speaking principality of Savoy and enjoyed the influences of both sides of the Alpine divide. Even today, French and dialectal variants are still spoken in the remote valleys of Piedmont and in much of the Valle d'Aosta. It was only under Duke Emanuele Filiberto in the 16th century that the region was brought definitively into the Italian sphere of influence; and later it was to play the key role in the Risorgimento *(see pp58–9)*, the ambitious movement that united Italy under a king from Piedmont. The vestiges of this history are to be found in the medieval castles of the Valle d'Aosta and the extraordinary clusters of chapels known as *sacri monti* dotted around the foothills of the Alps. Piedmont also spawned a school of painting, which is in evidence in the small parish churches and excellent fine art collections in the region. The most impressive architecture in the northwest, however, is undoubtedly to be found in Turin, a much underrated and surprisingly elegant Baroque city which boasts, among other things, one of the best Egyptian museums in the world. Piedmont is also known for its industry – Fiat in Turin, Olivetti in Ivrea, Ferrero in Alba – but it has not forgotten its agricultural roots, and food and drink play an important role in the life of the region: the hills of southern Piedmont produce many of the great Italian red wines.

Taking vermouth in one of Turin's cafés

◁ The 13th-century Châtelard castle in the Valle d'Aosta

Exploring Valle d'Aosta and Piedmont

THE VAST FLAT PLAIN of the Po, covered with the watery expanse
of rice fields around Vercelli and Novara, eventually gives way,
in the west, to the majestic heights of the Alps. Turin, the largest city
in the area and the capital of Piedmont, stands at the edge of the
plain, nestling almost in the shadow of the mountains. Further northwest, attractive Alpine valleys headed by dramatic peaks provide
the setting for the traditional villages,
ancient towns and castles around
Aosta. The Parco Nazionale del
Gran Paradiso is an unspoilt
tract of breathtaking scenery.

Rice fields around Vercelli

SIGHTS AT A GLANCE

DOMODOSSOLA

17

Bellinzona

**RISERVA NATURALE
VALGRANDE E
MONTE MOTTAC**

VERBANIA
*Lake
Maggiore*

STRESA

18

VARALLO

19

LAKE ORTA

ARONA

Varese

**UARIO
OPA**

ILA

**PARCO REGIONALE
DELLA VALLE
DEL TICINO**

Milano

20

NOVARA

Ticino

21

VERCELLI

**CASALE
MONFERRATO**

Milano

Po

Piacenza

ALESSANDRIA

22

ASTI

Tanaro

TORTONA

NOVI LIGURE

ACQUI TERME

Genova

**PARCO NATURALE
DELLE CAPANNE
DI MARCAROLO**

avona

SSIO

Turin, the capital of Piedmont, in the valley of the Po

GETTING AROUND

The Fréjus Pass links France with northwest
Italy (the Mont Blanc Tunnel is due to reopen
in 2002), while the tunnel under the Simplon
or Sempione Pass provides a direct rail route
from Switzerland. From the rest of Italy there
are excellent motorway connections across the
plain to Turin and up to Aosta. The region is
well served with rail links, and buses connect
the main towns and outlying resorts. Getting
around the mountains is more difficult, making
the car the best method of transport.

St Pierre castle in the Valle d'Aosta

SEE ALSO

• **Where to Stay** pp551–4

• **Where to Eat** pp586–8

0 kilometres   25

0 miles   20

KEY

▭▭▭ Motorway

▬▬ Major road

▬▬ Minor road

▭▭▭ Scenic route

〰 River

☆ Viewpoint

Monte Bianco ①

Aosta. **FS** *Pré-St-Didier.*
🚌 *Courmayeur.* **ℹ** *Piazzale Monte Bianco 13, Courmayeur (0165 84 20 60).*

MONTE BIANCO – Mont Blanc as it is also known – the tallest mountain in the Alps at 4,810 m (15,780 ft), dominates the western Aosta valley and its attractive all-year resort, **Courmayeur**. A series of cable car rides from Entrèves, 5 km (3 miles) further north, leads to Chamonix. Passing its highest point (3,842 m, 12,606 ft) at Aiguille du Midi, it offers one of the most spectacular views in the Alps. From Pré-St-Didier, below Courmayeur, the **Little St Bernard Pass** with its small glaciers, forests and ravines can be explored.

Colle del Gran San Bernardo ②

Aosta. **FS** 🚌 *Aosta.* **ℹ** *Strada Statale Gran San Bernardo 13, Etroubles (0165 785 59).* ⊙ *daily.*

THE GREAT ST BERNARD pass is synonymous with the hardy mountain rescue dogs that have been trained locally by Catholic monks since the 11th century. The **Monks' Hospice**, founded around 1050 by St Bernard of Aosta, lies just over the Swiss border (bring your passport), on the shores of a lovely lake; the dogs are still being trained here.

A St Bernard dog

The pretty Great St Bernard valley itself includes the town of Etroubles, set in a forest of conifers, the hamlet of St-Oyen with its pretty parish church, and the resort of St-Rhémy-en-Bosses.

♜ Monks' Hospice
Colle San Bernardo, Switzerland.
℡ *00 41 277 87 12 36.* ⊙ *daily.*

Monte Cervino ③

Aosta. **FS** 🚌 *Breuil-Cervinia.* **ℹ** *Via Carrel 29, Breuil-Cervinia (0166 94 91 36).*

THE DISTINCTIVE triangular peak of Monte Cervino (the Matterhorn) rises to 4,478 m (14,691 ft) and is easily recognizable. Below the mountain lies a scattering of attractive villages like Antey-St-André, Valtournanche (which gave its name to the valley) and the resort of **Breuil-Cervinia**. From Breuil a cable car rises to the Plateau Rosa (3,480 m, 11,418 ft) offering dramatic views of the surrounding mountains. This entire area is a paradise for both skiers and walkers.

Monte Rosa ④

Aosta. **FS** *Verrès.* 🚌 *St-Jacques.* **ℹ** *Route Varasc, Champoluc (0125 30 71 13).*

MONTE ROSA, Italy's second highest mountain, overlooks the picturesque Ayas and Gressoney valleys. The rolling lower Ayas valley is dominated by the ruins of the 11th-century **Castello di Graines**, perched on a large rock. Higher up, the resort of Champoluc has a cable car connection with the striking **Testa Grigia** (3,315 m/ 10,877 ft). The Gressoney valley is home to the Walser people, who speak an obscure German dialect. At the bottom of the valley, north of Pont-St-Martin with its Roman bridge, lies **Issime**: the 16th-century church here has a fresco of the Last Judgment on its façade.

♜ Castello di Graines
Graines, Strada Statale 506. ⊙ *daily.*

MEDIEVAL CASTLES AND FORTS IN THE VALLE D'AOSTA

The mountains alone provided insufficient protection to the fragmented kingdoms that covered the Valle d'Aosta in the Middle Ages. The medieval lords, who ruled ruthlessly over their small domains, built castles to enforce their often fragile power. Of the many built, 70 castles survive in some form to this day. You will pass a number of them if you drive into Italy by the Mont Blanc tunnel; they stretch from Aosta to Pont-St-Martin.

Originally Aosta castles were designed to be defensive and threatening, such as the looming tower of **Montmayer**, perched high on a huge rock by the Valgrisenche valley. Nearby, the equally forbidding dark tower of **Ussel** throws a melancholy, brooding watchfulness over the valley.

Fénis and **Verrès** represent an important shift in the function of the feudal castle. Both Fénis, a splendid 14th-century showpiece *(see p178)*, and Verrès were not just important military outposts but also examples of palatial opulence and good living. **Issogne** too furthered this luxurious trend with its elaborate frescoes, loggias and fountains.

Decoration was also important to Vittorio Emanuele II, owner of **Sarre**, who turned the halls of his fortress into a plush hunting lodge. The owners of **Châtelard**, set in some of the highest vineyards in Europe, placed fine wine production alongside military aims.

The strategically sited 14th-century castle at Verrès

The 12th-century cloister, with 40 carved columns of darkened marble, in Sant'Orso

Aosta ❺

🏠 37,000. ⓕ�s ➡ 🚉 Piazza Chanoux 8 (0165 23 66 27). 🔄 Tue.

LYING ON A PLAIN surrounded by dramatic mountains, the town of Aosta provides a remarkable mixture of ancient culture and spectacular, rich scenery. The Romans captured it from Salassian Gauls in 25 BC, and Aosta is still dotted with fine Roman architecture built in honour of Emperor Augustus – indeed the town was once called *Augusta Praetoria*, and its name only evolved into Aosta over the centuries. The medieval town was later fortified by the Challant family and then by the Dukes of Aosta, who added towers to the old Roman walls.

Modern Aosta is a bustling place with rambling suburbs, a crossroads for local industries and tourists on their way to the mountains. The centre, how-ever, still consists of a delightful grid of large squares and sur-prising architectural treasures, which justify Aosta's nickname of "Rome of the Alps".

🏛 Roman Ruins

Roman Theatre, Via Baillage. 🔾 *daily.*
Amphitheatre, Convento di San Giuseppe, Via dell'Anfiteatro. 📞 0165 26 21 49. 🔾 *daily, phone con-vent ahead.* 🎟 🕭 **Roman Forum**, Piazza Giovanni XXIII. 🔾 *daily.*
During Roman times, entry to Aosta was over the **bridge** to the east of the town (beyond the modern bridge) and through the **Arch of Augustus**. This triumphal arch is today marred only by a roof added in the 18th century. Ahead stands the **Porta Pretoria**, its

double row of stone arches flanked by a medieval tower; the gateway originally stood about 2.5 m (8 ft) higher than at present. Equally well preserved is the town's **Roman Theatre**, with a section of its 20-m (65-ft) high façade. The elliptical **Amphitheatre**, a little to the north, is reached through the convent of San Giuseppe. In the old town, next to the cathedral, lies the **Roman Forum**, or market place, with its huge cryptoporticus: the function of this impressive underground gallery, with its massive arches, remains the object of speculation.

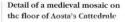

Detail of a medieval mosaic on the floor of Aosta's Cattedrale

🏛 Cattedrale

Piazza Giovanni XXIII. 🔾 *daily.* **Museo del Tesoro** 🔾 *Jun–Sep: daily; Oct–May: Sun & public hols pm.* 🎟
This relatively modest shrine to St John the Baptist was first built in the 12th century, but has been altered many times since. The interior is Gothic, with finely carved 15th-century

choir stalls, and floor mosaics depicting sacred and pagan scenes. Next door, the **Museo del Tesoro** contains a rich collection of statuettes and reliquaries, and a number of impressive medieval tombs.

🏛 Sant'Orso

Via Sant'Orso. 📞 0165 26 20 26. 🔾 *daily.* 🕭
East of the town walls is the architectural highlight of Aosta: a medieval complex of church buildings. Sant'Orso itself has a simple and unusual Gothic façade characterized by a thin, very tall portal. The interior has 11th-century frescoes, a crypt of the same date holding the tomb of St Orso, patron saint of Aosta, and a beautiful **cloister** with columns and capitals carved into highly detailed figures and animals.

ENVIRONS: The castle at **Fénis** *(see p206)*, 12 km (8 miles) east, is one of the few castles in the Aosta valley with a well-preserved interior, including beautiful frescoes and wooden galleries. **Issogne**, 38 km (23 miles) southeast, is the setting for another highly decorated castle, remodelled around 1490. It is filled with frescoes and decorative motifs, including a wrought-iron fountain in the shape of a pomegranate tree.

♣ Castello di Fénis

Fénis. 📞 0165 76 42 63. 🔾 *daily.* ● 1 Jan, 25 Dec. 🎟
♣ Castello di Issogne

Issogne. 📞 0125 92 93 73. 🔾 *daily.* ● 1 Jan, 25 Dec. 🎟

Some of the impressive ruins standing in the Roman Forum in Aosta

Parco Nazionale del Gran Paradiso ❻

A BREATHTAKING WILDERNESS of dramatic mountains and lush meadows, the Gran Paradiso is Italy's foremost national park, created in 1922 from part of a former royal hunting reserve of the House of Savoy. It is mainly a summer resort for walkers due to its unspoiled scenery, rare wildlife and unusual Alpine flowers, though there is also cross-country skiing during the winter months. The king of the park is the ibex, a relative of the goat family all but extinct in the rest of Europe. The park is also prized by naturalists for its chamois, ptarmigan, golden eagles, rare butterflies and marmots.

Castello di Aymavilles
The 18th-century core of this castle is framed by medieval corner towers.

Goletta Waterfall
is an impressive cascade near the Lago di Goletta.

Male Ibex
The ibex lives largely above the tree line. Groups are often seen around Col Lauson at dawn and dusk, and also around Pont in June.

Val di Rhêmes-Notre-Dame
This peaceful and broad valley offers magnificent scenery with waterfalls and fast-flowing streams running from the glacier at its head.

Cascata di Lillaz
This tall, dramatic waterfall, situated a little to the east of the rustic village of Lillaz, is best observed after the spring snow melt.

Cogne is the main resort and a good base from which to explore the park. Maps of the park's routes and footpaths are available here.

VISITORS' CHECKLIST

Piemonte and Valle d'Aosta. ℹ️ Segreteria Turistica, Via Umberto I 1, Noasca (0124 90 10 70). Other information offices at Ceresole Reale & Cogne. ◯ Jul, Aug & public hols. 🚉 Aosta & Pont Canavese. 🚌 from Aosta or Pont Canavese to the different valleys. 🎫 **Paradisia Alpine Garden**, Valnontey, Cogne. 📞 0165 740 40. ◯ mid-Jun–mid-Sep: daily. 🅿️ ♿ 📷 🌐 www.parks.it

Lillaz is sedate and off the beaten track, while Valnontey and Cogne are two of the busiest resorts.

★ Paradisia Alpine Garden
The botanic garden contains a collection of Alpine plants, including the delicate "twinflower".

STAR SIGHTS

★ **Paradisia Alpine Garden**

★ **Valnontey**

0 kilometres 5
0 miles 5

★ Valnontey
This lovely valley, after which the resort is named, provides dramatic views of glaciers and easy access to various footpaths.

KEY

ℹ️ Tourist information

🚃 Main road

🔆 Viewpoint

The small resort of Ceresole Reale under winter snow

Lake Ceresole Reale ❼

Torino. 🚌 to Ceresole Reale. ℹ Corso Vercelli 1, Ivrea (0125 61 81 31); Comune di Ceresole (0124 95 31 21).

O N THE SOUTHERN, Piedmont side of the extensive Parco Nazionale del Gran Paradiso (see pp208–9) lies the small resort of Ceresole Reale, on the shores of a spectacular mountain lake. The route from Cuorgnè goes through the rolling countryside of the Canavese and follows the N460 along a narrow gorge with a cascading stream. At **Noasca**, a spectacular waterfall may be seen high above the houses.

Ceresole Reale lies in a basin surrounded by meadows and forests of larch, and framed by mountains – the Gran Paradiso range to the north, Levanna to the southwest – which are reflected in the clear waters of the lake. The lake itself is actually a dammed reservoir, providing energy to supply Turin with electricity. This nevertheless unspoiled corner is a good base for walking, climbing and hiking, and also offers facilities for skiing during the winter.

Via Lattea ❽

Torino. 🚊 Oulx. 🚌 to Sauze d'Oulx. ℹ Via Louset, Sestriere (0122 75 54 44).

T HE CLOSEST RING of mountain resorts to Turin, and as a consequence popular for weekend excursions, is known colloquially as the Via Lattea or "milky way". Villages like **Bardonecchia** and **Sauze d'Oulx** preserve traditional old stone and wood buildings that have been a feature of the region for centuries. The small church in Bardonecchia has, in addition, a fine 15th-century carved choir. In contrast, the super-modern complex at **Sestriere** has been purpose-built to accommodate skiers in winter and hikers in summer.

From Bardonecchia a chair-lift operates some of the way up **Punta Colomion**, which rises immediately to the south of the resort. The summit, at 2,054 m (6,738 ft), offers fine views, and numerous hiking and walking possibilities.

Susa ❾

Torino. 🏛 7,000. 🚊 🚌 ℹ Corso Inghilterra 39 (0122 62 24 70). 🛒 Tue.

T HIS ATTRACTIVE mountain town flourished in Roman times: the **Arch of Augustus**, built in 8 BC and still standing, commemorates the alliance between the local Gaulish

The impressive part-Roman gateway, Porta Savoia, in Susa

chieftain and the Emperor Augustus. Other relics from the Roman period include two arches of an aqueduct, sections of an amphitheatre and traces of the old town walls. **Porta Savoia**, an imposing Roman gateway dating from the 4th century, was remodelled in the Middle Ages.

Most of the historic centre of the town is medieval, including the castle of Countess Adelaide and the **Duomo**, both originally 11th century. The Duomo, much altered since then, houses a polyptych (c.1500) attributed to Bergognone, and a precious 14th-century Flemish triptych portraying the Virgin and Saints. South of the town lies the Gothic church of **San Francesco**, surrounded by an area of early medieval houses.

A street in the traditional village of Bardonecchia, on the Via Lattea

Carved capitals on the Porta dello Zodiaco at the Sacra di San Michele

Sacra di San Michele ⑩

Strada Sacra San Michele. 🄲 *011 93 91 30.* 🚍 *Jul–Aug from Avigliana & Turin.* ⏲ *9:30am–12:30pm, 3–6pm Tue–Sun (Nov–Mar: to 5pm). Phone to arrange group visits.*

THIS SOMEWHAT forbidding abbey complex is perched on a ridge halfway up Monte Pirchiriano, at 962 m (3,156 ft). Its monastic community was founded around the year 1000, possibly on the site of a previous sanctuary, though the exterior looks every bit as much a fortress as the spiritual refuge that it was for 600 years.

During its prime, the abbey attracted pilgrims on their way to Rome, and as a result it grew enormously wealthy and powerful, controlling over 100 other abbeys in Italy, France and Spain. It was also subsequently attacked and looted several times, despite being fortified, before falling into decline and eventually being suppressed in 1662.

The sanctuary is reached by climbing 154 steep steps hewn out of the rock, which offer wonderful views over the surrounding countryside and up to the Alps. At the very top of this stairway, known as the Scalone dei Morti (Stairway of the Dead), is the Romanesque Porta dello Zodiaco, a doorway carved with creatures and symbols relating to the signs of the Zodiac. Beyond the doorway a few more steps lead into the church itself, which dates from the 12th–13th centuries and incorporates traces of an earlier building. The interior houses 15th- and 16th-century paintings and frescoes, and a 16th-century triptych by the Piedmontese artist Defendente Ferrari. The crypt holds the tombs of the early dukes and princes of the House of Savoy-Carignano.

Avigliana ⑪

Torino. 🏠 *9,500.* 🚆 🚍 ℹ️ *Piazza del Popolo 2a (011 932 86 50).* 🔵 *Thu.*

ON A FINE DAY, this small town perched beside two glacier-fed lakes and encircled by tall mountains looks breathtakingly beautiful. Avigliana is overlooked by a castle, first erected in the mid-10th century but now in ruins, which was once the home of the Counts of Savoy. Until the early 15th century the town was one of their favourite bases.

The medieval houses here are largely unspoiled, particularly in the two main *piazzas*, Santa Maria and Conte Rosso. Other buildings of note are the Casa della Porta Ferrata and the 15th-century Casa dei Savoia, both on Via XX Settembre.

The church of San Giovanni (13th–14th century) contains early 16th-century paintings by Defendente Ferrari.

Pinerolo ⑫

Torino. 🏠 *36,000.* 🚆 🚍 ℹ️ *Viale Giolitti 7–9 (0121 79 55 89).* 🔵 *Wed & Sat.*

PINEROLO LIES in an attractive setting beside hills at the confluence of the Lemina and Chisone valleys. The town was the capital of the Acaia family, a branch of the House of Savoy, and in the 14th and 15th centuries it was known for the cultural atmosphere that prevailed here under the family's patronage. However, the town enjoyed none of the stability of Turin: it was occupied by the French five times between the 15th and 18th centuries. During the 17th century the French demolished many of the town's ancient buildings in order to make Pinerolo a defensive stronghold; among the political prisoners allegedly held here was the notorious "Man in the Iron Mask". Today the town is a busy centre of commerce.

A number of monumental buildings do remain, however. The **Duomo**, at the centre of the town, was remodelled in Gothic style in the 15th–16th centuries and has a fine portal and an impressive bell tower. Via Principi d'Acaia climbs up to the 14th-century palace of the Princes of Acaia, and to the 15th-century church of **San Maurizio**, where the Acaia princes are buried; beside it rises a 14th-century bell tower.

The medieval arcades surrounding Piazza Conte Rosso in Avigliana

Turin ⓭

MENTION TURIN (Torino) and most people will think of industry and prosperity. It is certainly an economic powerhouse but it is also a town of grace and charm, with superb Baroque architecture and excellent museums, set against the dramatic scenery of the foothills of the Alps. Turin is also, of course, home to the famous Turin Shroud, the Fiat car company, and the Juventus football team. The 2006 Winter Olympics will be held here.

Statue of Emperor Augustus in front of the Roman Porta Palatina

Exploring Turin

Though settled by the Romans (**Porta Palatina** is an impressive 1st-century AD relic), and the seat of a university since the Middle Ages, Turin came into its own only after 1563, when Emanuele Filiberto of Savoy moved his capital here. Three centuries of steady prosperity ensued. Turin then became the power base for Italy's unification movement and, from 1861 to 1865, the capital of the newly united country. Subsequently its main power was economic. The car company **Fiat** (Fabbrica Italiana Automobili Torino), was established here in 1899 and grew to be one of the biggest firms in Europe. After World War II, Turin attracted thousands of poor Italians from the south who came to work in its factories. Though there have been social conflicts and labour disputes as a result, managers and workers do unite over football: the Juventus team is owned by the much-revered Fiat boss, Gianni Agnelli.

F I A T

The Fiat car factory logo

🏛 Duomo

Piazza San Giovanni. ⭕ *daily.* ♿
The cathedral, built in 1497–8 and dedicated to St John the Baptist, is the only example of Renaissance architecture in Turin. The sober square bell

TURIN TOWN CENTRE

Armeria Reale ⑤
Duomo ②
Mole Antonelliana ⑨
Museo Egizio and
  Galleria Sabauda ⑦
Palazzo Carignano ⑧
Palazzo Madama ⑥
Palazzo Reale ④
Porta Palatina ①
San Lorenzo ③

0 metres   500
0 yards   500

KEY

FS   Parking
P   Tourist information
🛈   Church
🚉   Railway station

The 15th-century Duomo, with the Cappella della Sacra Sindone beyond

tower, which predates the rest of the church by 30 years, stands in refreshing contrast to Turin's sumptuous Baroque buildings; its top was designed by Filippo Juvarra in 1720. Inside, the Duomo is heavy with statuary and paintings. Through a black marble arch on the right side of the church is the **Cappella della Sacra Sindone** (Chapel of the Holy Shroud), which is actually incorporated into the Palazzo Reale (see p216). The chapel is a remarkable feat, designed by Guarino Guarini (1624–83), with an extraordinary mesh-like cupola; the exterior view is equally eccentric. On top of the altar is the urn containing the famous Shroud itself.

🚩 Palazzo Madama

Piazza Castello. ⬤ for restoration (due to reopen mid 2002).

Turin's main square once contained a medieval castle which incorporated elements of the original Roman city walls. The castle was later enlarged and remodelled, and a new façade by Juvarra was added, at the request of a royal widow, in the 18th century. The Palazzo Madama – as it was subsequently renamed – now sits in the centre of the square with a stately, balustraded façade.

The interior, with its grand staircase and first floor, both designed by Juvarra,

is home to the **Museo Civico d'Arte Antica**. This extensive collection contains treasures which range in date from the Graeco-Roman era to the 19th century. The display includes the famous and mysterious *Portrait of an Unknown Man* by Antonello da Messina (15th century) among the paintings and sculptures, and reproductions of the Duc de Berry's beautiful *Book of Hours* from c.1420. Other sections contain displays of jewellery, majolica and glass, complementing the textiles and furniture.

The façade of the Palazzo Madama, designed by Filippo Juvarra in 1718–21

THE TURIN SHROUD

Detail of the mysterious 12th-century Turin Shroud

The most famous – and most dubious – holy relic of them all is kept in Turin's Duomo. The shroud, said to be the winding-sheet in which the body of Christ was wrapped after His crucifixion, owes its fame to the fact that the shroud bears the imprint of a crucified man with a wound in his side, and bruises from what might have been a crown of thorns.

The shroud is one of the most famous medieval relics. Its early history is unclear, but the House of Savoy was in possession of it around 1450, and had it displayed in Guarini's chapel from 1694. The "original" shroud – which sits in a silver casket inside an iron box within a marble coffer inside the urn on the chapel altar – is not on view, though a replica is, together with a welter of scientific explanations as to the shroud's possible origins. In 1988, however, the myth of the shroud was exploded: a carbon-dating test showed that it dates back no further than the 12th century. The shroud nevertheless remains an object of religious veneration.

Exploring Turin

THE CITY OF TURIN IS BLESSED with numerous interesting museums, which are housed in splendid palazzi and civic buildings. The centre itself is relatively small, with broad, straight streets, often bordered with historic cafés and shops, which are pleasant places to stroll along. The city is also famous for its innovative cuisine and boasts some of the country's finest restaurants.

Granite statue of Ramses II (13th century BC) in the Museo Egizio

🏛 Museo Egizio

Via Accademia delle Scienze 6.
📞 011 561 77 76. ⭕ Tue–Sun.
⬤ 1 Jan, 1 May, 25 Dec. 📷 ♿

Turin owes its magnificent Egyptian Museum – one of the most important in the world – largely to the Piedmont-born Bernardo Drovetti, who was stationed in Egypt as French Consul General at the time of the Napoleonic Wars. It was the booty he brought back that formed the basis of this very fine collection of Egyptian artifacts. On the ground floor, the items on display include monumental sculptures and reconstructed temples; upstairs, there are collections of papyrus and everyday objects. Among the most impressive sculptures are a black granite Ramses II (13th century BC, or 19th dynasty), the slightly earlier Amenophis II, and the basalt figure of Gemenef-Har-Bak, a vizier from the 26th dynasty. The Sala della Nubia contains a breathtaking reconstruction of the 15th-century BC **Rock Temple of Ellessiya**.

Extraordinary wall and tomb paintings are displayed on the upper floor, together with items of daily use such as the tools used for measuring, weaving, fishing and hunting. The 14th-century BC Tomb of Kha and Merit, complete with the food, tools and ornaments buried with them for the afterlife, is particularly fascinating. The papyrus collection is beautiful and of enormous interest to scholars: these documents have been vital to modern understanding of Egyptian language, customs and history – one document, the *Papiro dei Re* (Royal Papyrus), crucially lists all the pharaohs up to the 17th dynasty, with their dates.

G Ferrari's *St Peter and a Donor* (16th century), Galleria Sabauda

🏛 Galleria Sabauda

Via Accademia delle Scienze 6.
📞 011 54 74 40. ⭕ Tue–Sun.
📷 ♿

The Palazzo dell'Accademia delle Scienze, the building by Guarini in which the Egyptian Museum is housed, is also home to the House of Savoy's main painting collection. The top two floors are the setting for a stunning array of works by Italian, French, Flemish and Dutch masters.

The collection was originally begun in the second half of the 15th century, and has been expanded over the centuries since. It is grouped in regional schools and contains a section on Piedmontese painting, which is not often represented in other galleries: this includes masterpieces by Gaudenzio Ferrari (c.1480–1546) and two early 16th-century paintings by Defendente Ferrari. Among works of particular interest from other Italian schools are Antonio and Piero Pollaiuolo's 15th-century *Tobias and the*

Detail from an 18th-dynasty papyrus Book of the Dead, Museo Egizio

Archangel Raphael, and the *Ritratto di Gentiluomo* (portrait of a nobleman) by Bronzino. Bellini, Mantegna, and Veronese are among other Italian artists represented.

The section on Dutch and Flemish art includes works such as Jan Van Eyck's *St Francis* (15th century) and Rembrandt's *Old Man Sleeping* (17th century), as well as portraits by Van Dyck, which include a study of Charles I's children, and his *Principe Tommaso di Savoia-Carignano* (1634). Among the French works on display are 17th-century landscape paintings by Claude Lorrain and Poussin.

Spacious arcades on Turin's Via Roma

🏛 Palazzo Carignano

Via Accademia delle Scienze 5. **011 562 11 47.** Tue–Sun. 1 Jan, 25 Dec.

The main façade of Palazzo Carignano by Guarini

This Baroque palazzo is not only Guarini's masterpiece, it is arguably the finest building in Turin, with its magnificent brick façade and ornate rotunda. It was built in 1679 for the Carignano family – an offshoot of the main House of Savoy and ancestors of the Italian kings – but came into its own in the 19th century when the first king of Italy, Vittorio Emanuele II was born here in 1829. After Italy was unified in 1861 by a series of referenda, the former royal residence was used as the first national parliament building.

The palazzo is now home to the **Museo Nazionale del Risorgimento**, which through paintings and a collection of artifacts (housed in the rooms where history was made), tells the story of unification. It introduces Mazzini, Cavour and Garibaldi – key figures in the Risorgimento (*see pp58–9*).

🏛 Via Roma

Via Roma is Turin's main street, running through the heart of the historic centre. It leads from Piazza Castello at its northern end down through Piazza San Carlo to the distinctive arched façade of Stazione Porta Nuova, which forms a focal point at the southern end. The station was built in 1868 and looks out over the green and pleasant gardens of the 19th-century Piazza Carlo Felice. The square is framed by shops and cafés and provides an excellent vista up Via Roma from a calm vantage point. Via Roma itself is a magnificent concourse lined with stylish fashion shops and shaded arcades, interrupted only by cobbled squares, crisscrossed by tramlines. A grid pattern of side streets branch off either side of Via Roma, revealing additional shopping arcades.

🏛 Piazza San Carlo

This square halfway along Via Roma comprises an ensemble of Baroque architecture so sophisticated as to earn it the nickname of "Turin's drawing room". At the southern end rise the twin churches of Santa Cristina and San Carlo; both were built in the 1630s though **Santa Cristina** has a Baroque façade, crowned with statues, which was designed by Juvarra in the early 18th century.

At the centre of the square stands a 19th-century statue of Emanuele Filiberto resheathing his sword. The work, by Carlo Marocchetti, has become an emblem of the city. At the corners of the square, frescoes depict the Holy Shroud. The **Galleria San Federico**, in the square's northwestern corner, is a stylish shopping arcade.

Piazza San Carlo is known for its society cafés. In one such establishment, in 1786, Antonio Benedetto Carpano invented the drink known as vermouth, which is still very popular in Turin today.

🌿 Parco del Valentino

Corso Massimo D'Azeglio. daily. **Borgo Medioevale** **011 669 93 72.** daily. **Orto Botanico** Jun–Sep: Sat & Sun
This park beside the river contains the **Borgo Medioevale**, a complex of buildings resembling a medieval village and castle, which was built for an exhibition in the late 1880s. The buildings show different types of design and construction, based on traditional houses and castles which can be found scattered throughout Piedmont and in the Valle d'Aosta.

The **Orto Botanico**, beside the medieval complex, is an impressive botanical garden in a pleasant setting.

Looking south across the elegant Piazza San Carlo, "Turin's drawing room"

Turin: Symbols of the City

T URIN'S ARCHITECTURE MIRRORS the city's transition from monarchic power to industrial power. Witness the ostentation of the Baroque apartments of the Savoy royal family; and contrast them with the futuristic Mole Antonelliana, a tall structure which heralded the dawn of the modern industrial age. Much of Turin's history in the 20th century has been dominated by the motor car: Fiat made Turin its home and, despite some industrial unrest, the city's workers replied by rewarding it with success. For the curious, Turin's motor museum is worth a visit, as it maps out the history of Italian car design.

The 19th-century tower, Mole Antonelliana, dominating Turin

Mole Antonelliana
Via Montebello 20. 011 817 20 80.
Museo del Cinema 011 812 56 58. Tue–Sun.

This eccentric building is the Turin equivalent of the Eiffel Tower in Paris: an unmissably tall landmark that serves no clear purpose except perhaps to act as a signature for the city as a whole. It looks similar to a glorified lightning conductor: indeed an electric storm struck down the top 47 m (155 ft) in 1954, which was subsequently replaced. The 167-m (550-ft) Mole, by Alessandro Antonelli (1798–1888), was originally planned to be a synagogue, but the city finished it in 1897 and used it to house the Risorgimento museum. The Mole ("massive structure") – for a time the tallest building in the world – became a symbol of Italian

Inside the dome of San Lorenzo

unity. The building houses the Cinema Museum, designed with the help of British director Peter Greenaway.

Palazzo Reale
Piazzetta Reale. 011 436 14 55.
Tue–Sun. 1 Jan, 1 May, 25 Dec.

The Palazzo Reale was the seat of the Savoy royal family from 1660 until the unification of Italy in 1861. Behind the austere façade, designed by Amedeo di Castellamonte, lie richly decorated state apartments; the ceilings were painted by Morello, Miel and Seyter in the 17th century. The many splendid furnishings, tapestries and ornaments date from the 17th to the 19th centuries; they include the elaborate Chinese Cabinet, the Alcove Room, the lavishly decorated Throne Room, and the innovative Scala delle Forbici, or Scissor Stairs, created by Juvarra in 1720. Behind the palace are extensive gardens, which extend northwards.

To the left of the main entrance to the palace is **San Lorenzo**. This fine Baroque building, begun in 1634, is by architect Guarino Guarini, its ornate interior boasting another of his extraordinary, geometric domes.

Armeria Reale
Piazza Castello 191. 011 54 38 89.
Tue–Sun. 1 Jan, 1 May, 15 Aug, 25 Dec.

One wing of the Palazzo Reale, on the northern side of the main square, provides the splendid setting for one of the most extensive and breathtaking collections of arms and armoury in the world.

The armoury originally belonged to the House of Savoy, and was opened to the public in 1837. The fine rooms, such as the splendid Galleria Beaumont, designed by Juvarra in 1733, hold treasures ranging in date from Roman and Etruscan times to the 19th century. The collection has some particularly magnificent medieval and Renaissance items from some of the greatest armourers and gunsmiths in the world, including a pistol of Charles V. One section is devoted largely to Oriental arms and armour.

The adjoining but separate Royal Library contains a collection of drawings and manuscripts, including a self-portrait by Leonardo da Vinci.

ENVIRONS: About 3 km (2 miles) out of the city centre lies a colossal hall built in the 1960s for the famous **Museo dell'Automobile**. Founded by two motoring pioneers in 1933, it now houses over 150 veteran, vintage and classic cars. The collection includes

A lavishly decorated gallery in the 17th-century Palazzo Reale, a royal home until unification

glorious Bugattis, Maseratis, Lancias, Fiats and also a number of fine foreign cars. The first petrol-driven car made in Italy (1896) is kept here, as well as the first Fiat (1899) and the 1929 Isotta Fraschini *coupé de ville* that was used to transport Gloria Swanson in the Hollywood film *Sunset Boulevard*. Note also that a large number of the sports cars from the 1950s have the steering wheel on the right – ie British – side: this brief trend was in deference to the great British car makers such as Aston Martin.

There is also a library and a documentation centre which are both open to the public.

Designs from 1949 for the Ferrari 166 MM

🏛 **Museo dell'Automobile**
Corso Unità d'Italia 40. 📞 011 67 76 66. ⏰ Tue–Sun. ⬤ 1 Jan, 25 Dec. 📷♿

Stupinigi ⓮

Piazza Principe Amedeo 7, Stupinigi. 📞 011 358 12 20. 🚌 63 to Piazza Caio Mario & then 41. ⏰ Tue–Sun. 📷♿

An interior view of the 18th-century Palazzina di Caccia di Stupinigi

I N 1729–30 THE ARCHITECT Filippo Juvarra (1676–1736) designed the magnificent hunting lodge of Stupinigi – known as the Palazzina di Caccia di Stupinigi – at a beautiful location 9 km (5 miles) southwest of Turin. It was created for Vittorio

Amedeo II and is one of the very finest hunting lodges, built on an impressive scale, reminiscent of the palace of Versailles in France.

The dynamic and complex plan incorporates semicircles and an octagon, with the main block consisting of a dome rising above a circular building from which wings jut out, not unlike the arms of a windmill.

The mass of the central section is lightened by balustrading topped with urns and figures, while the dome is crowned with an 18th-century bronze figure of a stag.

The huge interior includes rooms sumptuously decorated with *trompe l'oeil* paintings and frescoes on a hunting theme – the 18th-century *Triumph of Diana*, for instance, in the main *salone*. About 40 of those rooms house the interesting **Museo d'Arte e di Ammobiliamento**, a museum specializing in 17th- and 18th-century furniture and furnishings. Many of the ornate items on display in these rooms were originally kept in other former royal residences.

Outside there are extensive grounds, which feature an elegant combination of spectacular broad avenues, parkland and colourful formal parterres.

Basilica di Superga ⓯

Strada Basilica di Superga 73, Comune di Torino. 📞 011 898 00 83. 🚋 Sassi. 🚌 79 fr Sassi. ⏰ May–Sep: 9am–noon, 3–6pm; Oct–Apr: 10am–noon, 3–5pm. ⬤ 8 Sep. **Tombs** ⬤ Fri, public hols. **Donation**.

O N A HILL to the east of Turin, reachable by car or by railway, stands the superb Baroque basilica of Superga, built by Juvarra in 1717–31. The commission came from Duke Vittorio Amedeo II, in fulfilment of a vow made to the Virgin Mary in 1706 while the French were besieging the duke and his army in Turin.

The beautiful yellow and white façade is dominated by a large portico designed like a Classical temple, with a 65 m- (213 ft-) high dome immediately beyond. It is flanked by twin bell towers on either side. The interior is magnificent, decorated in light blue and yellow, and contains numerous fine paintings and carvings.

Underneath the basilica lies the great mausoleum which houses the tombs of the kings, princes and princesses of Savoy from the 18th and 19th centuries. Turin's 1949 aircrash victims, including the city's football team, are also remembered on a plaque behind the basilica.

One of the other benefits of visiting the basilica is seeing the views over Turin.

The imposing façade of the 18th-century Baroque Basilica di Superga designed by Filippo Juvarra

The 17th-century Basilica dell'Assunta dominating Sacro Monte, Varallo

Santuario d'Oropa **16**

Via Santuario d'Oropa 480, Comune di Biella. **[** 015 245 59 20. **FS** Biella. **☞** from Biella. **◯** daily. **⚊**

PERCHED ABOVE the wool town of Biella stands the tranquil church and hospice complex of Oropa, a series of three squares surrounded by pale buildings with stone-shingled roofs, cut into the forested hillside.

The sanctuary, which dates largely from the 17th and 18th centuries, was originally found-ed in the 4th century by Sant' Eusebio, Bishop of Vercelli. It was intended as a hospice for the poor, and to honour the "Black Madonna" which he had brought back from the Holy Land. The Madonna, said to be the work of St Luke him-self, is the object of some of the biggest and most important pilgrimages in the region.

The statue of the Madonna is kept in the restored **Chiesa Vecchia** (Old Church), whose façade was designed by Filippo Juvarra (1676–1736). Beyond it, at the top of the complex, rises the imposing mass of the Neo-Classical **Chiesa Nuova** (New Church), which was begun in 1885 but completed only in 1960.

Behind this church, a foot-path leads to the cable car up to Monte Mucrone, from where there is good walking countryside and a small, attrac-tive mountain lake. On a hill

southwest of the complex stand 16 chapels, a dozen of which date from between 1620 and 1720. They contain frescoed scenes which depict the life of the Virgin.

Domodossola **17**

Verbania. **🏛** 20,000. **FS** **☞** **🛈** Stazione entrance, Piazza Matteotti 24 (0324 24 82 65). **⊟** Sat.

AT THE CENTRE of this pretty mountain town of Roman origin lies the **Piazza Mercato**, or market square, framed by attractive arcades and houses dating from the 15th and 16th centuries. The good-value produce at the local market attracts people even from France and Switzerland.

The Ossola valley, where the town lies, sits in an Alpine landscape of pasture and forest sliced by rivers and streams. Pretty villages north of the town include **Crodo**, with its cold-water mineral spas, and **Baceno**, where the 14th–16th-century church contains fine frescoes and wood carvings.

Further north still, the Antigorio and Formazza valleys are planted with fig trees and vineyards. Just before La Frua, spectacular waterfalls from the River Toce drop about 145 m (475 ft) when the waters are not being harnessed for power. The idyllic, wooded Valle Vigezzo, east of Domodossola, also offers some breathtaking scenery.

Varallo **18**

Vercelli. **🏛** 7,900. **FS** **☞** **🛈** Corso Roma 38 (0163 512 80). **⊟** Tue.

THE SMALL TOWN and tourist resort of Varallo lies half-way up the attractive Sesia valley, and boasts a remarkable church, **Santa Maria delle Grazie**. The late 15th-century church is notable for its beau-tiful frescoed wall depicting the Life of Christ and *trompe l'oeil* architectural elements; the paintings are the work of Gaudenzio Ferrari (1484–1546).

A long stairway behind the church (and also a cableway) climbs up to the even more extraordinary **Sacro Monte**, a religious community built at an altitude of about 610 m (2,000 ft). This "Sacred Mount" was founded as a sanctuary of the New Jerusalem in 1486 and sponsored by the Archbishop of Milan, San Carlo Borromeo.

The Basilica dell'Assunta, with a 19th-century façade, is set in a tranquil courtyard with palm trees and a fountain; the interior is a riot of ornate Baroque architecture. Dotted around it are over 40 chapels representing the sacred sites of Jerusalem, with statues and painted figures positioned in front of frescoed backdrops painted by Gaudenzio Ferrari, Tanzio da Varallo and others.

Christ Condemned (16th century) in a chapel at Varallo's Sacro Monte

The interior of the church of San Giulio in the middle of Lake Orta

Lake Orta ⑲

Novara. **FS** 🚌 ⛴ *Orta.*
ℹ️ *Via Panoramica, Orta San Giulio (0322 90 56 14)*

LAKE ORTA IS ONE of Italy's least visited lakes – unjustly, as it is delightfully set among the foothills of the Alps.

The lake's main resort is **Orta San Giulio**, a small town with a historic centre containing handsome palazzi, and houses decorated with wrought-iron balconies. In the lakeside **Piazza Principale** stands the Palazzo della Comunità, a frescoed building of 1582 resting on arcades. At the top of a mound stands the 15th-century church of **Santa Maria Assunta** (rebuilt in the 17th century), with a Romanesque doorway and an interior that is richly decorated with 17th century frescoes and paintings.

Above Orta San Giulio is the sanctuary of **Sacro Monte**, built from 1591 to 1770 and dedicated to St Francis of Assisi. A winding path, offering lovely views of the lake,

climbs to the church. The path is lined by 21 chapels, most of them Baroque, in which frescoes and life-size figure groups by various artists depict scenes from the life of St Francis.

In the middle of the lake rises the picturesque **Isola San Giulio**. The island was said to have been liberated from snakes and monsters by the 4th-century Christian preacher Julius, from whom the island's name derives. A basilica stands on the island to this day; it is notable for its 12th-century black marble pulpit decorated with wild animals and birds, and for the 15th-century frescoes – including one attributed to Gaudenzio Ferrari, of the *Virgin and Child Enthroned*.

Novara ⑳

🏛️ *105,000.* **FS** 🚌 ℹ️ *Corso Baluardo Quintino Sella 40 (0321 39 40 59).* 🚌 *Mon, Thu & Sat.*

Fresco detail of a horseman (17th century) by Morazzone in San Gaudenzio, Novara

NOVARA HAS DISTANT origins as the Roman city of Nubliaria – meaning "surrounded in mist". Nowadays its delightful arcaded streets and

squares, and historic buildings, exude a quiet affluence. Many of the most important buildings stand around Piazza della Repubblica. They include the beautiful Renaissance courtyard of the **Broletto** (town hall), with its graceful 15th-century red-brick arcades and covered stairway. The buildings now house a small **Museo Civico**, comprising an archaeological section, a picture gallery and a modern art gallery.

Across the piazza rises the **Duomo**, rebuilt by the architect Alessandro Antonelli in around 1865 in Neo-Classical style, with a huge central doorway. The interior contains dramatic Renaissance paintings of the Vercelli school and Flemish tapestries, as well as the remains of an earlier sanctuary on this site: these include the frescoed 12th-century chapel of San Siro and the 15th-century cloisters. The octagonal **Baptistry** next door dates in part from the 5th century and is painted with medieval frescoed scenes of the terrible Apocalypse.

A few streets away stands the church of **San Gaudenzio**. It is strikingly crowned by an elongated four-tiered dome and spire, designed by Antonelli, and reminiscent of his Mole Antonelliana in Turin (*see p216*). At the top of the spire, which is 121 m (400 ft) high, is a statue of San Gaudenzio himself. Inside, the late 16th-century church contains a fine collection of Renaissance and Baroque paintings by artists from Piedmont: these include a notable 17th-century battle scene by Tanzio da Varallo, a 16th-century altarpiece by Gaudenzio Ferrari, and a fresco painting by Pier Francesco Morazzone (c.1572–1626).

🏛️ **Museo Civico**
Via Fratelli Roselli 20. 📞 *0321 62 70 37.* 🕐 *Tue–Sun.* ⬛ *public hols.*
📷 ♿ Ⓦ *www.comune.novara.it*
ℹ️ **Baptistry**
Piazza della Repubblica. 📞 *0321 66 16 71.* 🕐 *ask at the Curia Arcivescovile.*

View across Lake Orta to the Isola San Giulio

Vercelli ㉑

🏛 *50,000.* **FS** 🚌 ℹ️ *Viale Garibaldi 90 (0161 25 78 88).* 🗓 *Tue & Fri.*

VERCELLI IS THE RICE capital of Europe, set in a vast plain of paddy fields that give rise to millions of plates of risotto each year. The paddies provide a sight of shimmering sheets of water stretching far into the distance. Vercelli itself also developed its own school of painting in the 16th century, and has one major architectural treasure, the 13th-century **Basilica di Sant'Andrea**.

The Basilica, standing just across from the railway station, is famous as the first example of Italian architecture to be influenced by the Gothic style of northern France – note the beautiful vaulted nave and the flying buttresses, typical Gothic elements. Overall, however, the Basilica remains a stunning achievement in Romanesque architecture, built from 1219 to 1227 as part of an abbey for the papal legate Cardinal Guala Bicheri. The façade, curiously, changes colour halfway up, the blue-grey of the lower part turning to red and white in the twin towers; these are linked by a double arcade. A carving attributed to Antelami (12th century) adorns the central lunette.

The three-aisled interior is gently illuminated through rose windows. The muted decoration is largely focused on the vaulting, which is supported by tall, slender shafts. Off the north side is the simple 13th-century cloister, beautifully framed by arcades rising from clustered columns.

Vercelli's other important historic buildings are not far away, including the imposing 16th-century **Duomo**, the **Ospedale Maggiore** (13th century), and the church of **San Cristoforo**, with frescoes and a particularly fine Madonna (both c.1529) painted by Gaudenzio Ferrari. The **Museo Civico Borgogna** is the best place to admire the masterpieces of the Vercelli school. The main shopping street, Corso Libertà, has a handful of attractive 15th-century houses and courtyards.

🏛 Museo Civico Borgogna
Via Antonio Borgogna 8. 📞 *0161 25 27 76.* 🕐 *Tue–Fri pm, Sat & Sun am.* ⬤ *1 Jan, 15 Aug, 1 Nov, 25 Dec.* 📷 ✓

The 13th-century cloisters of the Basilica di Sant'Andrea in Vercelli

Asti ㉒

🏛 *74,000.* **FS** 🚌 ℹ️ *Piazza Alfieri 34 (0141 53 03 57).* 🗓 *Wed & Sat.*

MOST OFTEN ASSOCIATED only with sweet *spumante* (sparkling) wine, Asti is in fact at the centre of Italy's most prestigious wine region *(see*

Detail of the carving on the 15th-century porch at the entrance to the Duomo in Asti

pp176–7) and also a tranquil and noble city of medieval towers, elegant churches and warm red roofs.

Just north of the main railway station lies the Piazza del Campo del Palio, the largest square in Asti and formerly the site of its annual horse race, now in Piazza Alfieri. The race, held towards the end of September to coincide with the local wine fair, rivals the Palio in Siena *(see p331)* for outrageous horsemanship and medieval pageantry.

Beyond this square lies the triangular-shaped **Piazza Alfieri**. A statue here commemorates the local poet and dramatist Vittorio Alfieri (1749–1803), in whose honour both this square and the main street were renamed.

Corso Alfieri runs the entire length of the old city centre. At its eastern end stands the 15th-century church of **San Pietro in Consavia**, with its terracotta decoration, 17th-century frescoes, and attractive cloister. Beside it is the circular Romanesque **baptistry** which dates from the 10th–12th centuries; it was once the church of the knights of the Order of St John of Jerusalem, who had their headquarters here.

West of Piazza Alfieri is the **Collegiata di San Secondo** (13th–15th century), named after Asti's patron saint, which houses a Renaissance polyptych by Gandolfino d'Asti and 15th-century frescoes. The area around the western section of Corso Alfieri contains a few of the medieval towers for which the town was once famous; they include the Torre dei Comentini, the very elegant Torre Troyana and, at the far

The watery expanses of the rice fields around Vercelli

end, the Torre Ropa. This was built on the ruins of a tower in which San Secondo, a Roman soldier, was held. The nearby 14th-century Gothic **Duomo** has a 15th-century porch and, inside, 18th-century frescoes, stoups made from ancient capitals, and two 12th- to 13th-century carvings on the west corner of the transept.

Cuneo ㉓

🏛 *56,000.* 🚉 🚌 ℹ *Corso Nizza 17 (0171 69 32 58).* 🔄 *Tue.*

CUNEO DERIVES ITS NAME from *cuneo,* meaning wedge-shaped, which describes the sliver of land that the town occupies at the confluence of two rivers, the Gesso and the Stura di Demonte. In early November the town hosts the regional cheese fair, with unusual local cheese varieties.

The market town centres on an enormous main square, **Piazza Galimberti**, with its old arcades, where the traders come to hawk their wares every Tuesday. Much of the town was rebuilt in the 18th and 19th centuries, providing Cuneo with wide, tree-lined boulevards, though the impressive viaduct which takes the railway line into town dates from the 1930s. The deconsecrated 13th-century church of **San Francesco** has a fine 15th-century portal. The 18th-

The Castello di Casotto in the hills above the resort of Garessio

century church of **Santa Croce** has an unusual concave façade by Francesco Gallo.

Cuneo is a good base for exploring the pretty local valleys, such as the Valle Stura where rare flowers grow.

Bossea Caves ㉔

Località Bossea, Comune Frabosa Soprana. 📞 *01/4 34 92 40.* 🚉 *Mondovì.* 🚌 *from Mondovì.* ⭕ *daily for guided tours only.* 📷

SOME 25 KM (16 miles) south of Mondovì, near the end of a scenic route which follows the valley of the Torrente Corsaglia up into the Maritime Alps, are the caves of Bossea, some of the finest in all Italy. The series of caves contains remarkable and beautiful stalactite columns and shapes that have formed over many thousands of years. Guided tours lead through different chambers – some of them surprisingly vast – following the underground rivers and lakes. The skeleton of a prehistoric bear, *Ursus spelaeus,* which was discovered in the caves, may also be seen on display.

Bring a sweater – the temperature rarely rises above 9° C (50° F).

Market day in the enormous Piazza Galimberti at the centre of Cuneo

Garessio ㉕

Cuneo. 🏛 *4,000.* 🚉 🚌 ℹ *Piazza Carrara 131 (0174 811 22).* 🔄 *Fri.*

ONE OF THE PRETTIER resorts of the Maritime Alps, Garessio is no more than a sprinkling of houses spread out over the hills, surrounded by woods of chestnut trees. It is also a popular spa.

According to local legend, the waters here have miraculous powers: in about AD 980 an octogenarian nobleman called Aleramo found instant relief from his painful kidney and circulatory problems by drinking the mineral-rich water. Since then, the waters have been drunk for their remedial properties – linked in particular with the relief of diuretic and digestive problems – and for their refreshing taste.

ENVIRONS: About 10 km (4 miles) west of Garessio stands the **Castello di Casotto**, the dramatically-sited summer palace used by the House of Savoy. The royal family used to come here to enjoy the local mineral water, the attractive scenery and the exceptionally pure air of the hills.

The town of **Ormea**, 12 km (7 miles) southwest, is interesting for its ruined 11th-century castle, its church with late 14th-century Gothic frescoes, and its attractive houses.

♣ Castello di Casotto
Garessio. 📞 *0174 35 11 31.* ⭕ *daily.* 📷

LIGURIA

IGURIA IS A LONG, THIN COASTAL STRIP *nestling at the foot of vine-covered mountains. Here pastel-coloured houses bask in the Mediterranean sun, while their gardens, flourishing in the mild climate, are a riot of colourful plants. In contrast with resorts like Portofino and even San Remo, the bustling city of Genoa, for centuries a trading port of immense power, is the only major population centre.*

Genoa has a long history as a seafaring power, achieving greatness first as a trading post with ancient Greece and Phoenicia, and later, as the capital of a small commercial empire that at one stage eclipsed even Venice. The great sea admiral Andrea Doria came from Genoa, as did the 15th-century explorer of the Americas, Christopher Columbus.

Genoa's rise began in the 12th century, when it succeeded in beating the Saracen pirates that plagued the Ligurian coast. Thereafter, the maritime republic prospered, profiting from the Crusades to set up trading posts in the Middle East and marshalling its naval might to humble its rivals. The golden age lasted from the 16th to the mid-17th century, and included the glorious reign of Andrea Doria who enriched the city by financing the wars of Genoa's European allies through the offices of the city's bank. Factionalism among the ruling aristocracy, however, and foreign conquest, by the French in 1668 and the Austrians in 1734, led to the region's decline. It was only in the early 19th century, with unification fervour spreading thanks to native son Giuseppe Mazzini and the revolutionary Garibaldi, that Liguria ever recaptured a glimpse of its former prominence. Today, sheltered by the steep slopes that rise from the sea, faded, elegant mansions lie along the coast, particularly in San Remo, where aristocrats came to spend the winter at the end of the 19th century.

Green shutters and rich ochre walls characterize the houses of Portofino

◁ Rugged cliffs tumble into the sea along Liguria's Riviera Levante

Exploring Liguria

LIGURIA DIVIDES NEATLY into two parts. The western coastline, known as the Riviera Ponente, is a thin strip of coastal plain stretching across to the French border, while the eastern coastline, or Riviera Levante, is more rugged and picturesque, descending directly into the sea. Between the two lengths of coast lies the region's capital and biggest port, Genoa (Genova). The faded elegance of the tranquil coastal villages contrasts with this cramped and busy port which snakes along the coast, hemmed in between the sea and the mountains rising steeply behind it.

Stag motif of the city of Cervo, above the cathedral doors

Genoese street market selling fruit and vegetables

SIGHTS AT A GLANCE

KEY

Motorway

Major road

Minor road

Scenic route

River

Viewpoint

0 kilometres   25

0 miles   10

Nice
Monaco

The smart resort of San Remo on the Riviera Ponente, west of Genoa

Milano Tortona

MONTE ANTOLA

PENNINO LIGURE

MONTE MAGGIORASCA

BORZONASCA

GENOA ⑨

NERVI   CAMOGLI ⑩

PORTOFINO PENINSULA ⑪ ⑫ RAPALLO

VARESE LIGURE

MONTE GOTTERO

GOLFO DI GENOVA

SESTRI LEVANTE

RIVIERA DI LEVANTE

MONEGLIA

Parma

MARE LIGURE

CINQUE TERRE ⑬

LA SPEZIA

PORTOVENERE ⑭   LERICI ⑮

Massa Lucca Pisa

SEE ALSO

- **Where to Stay** pp554–5
- **Where to Eat** pp589–90

Houses wedged into the cliffs in Riomaggiore, Cinque Terre

GETTING AROUND

If you keep to the coast, transport in Liguria is straightforward. The A10 motorway, becoming the A12 at Genoa, and a mainline railway hug the shore from the French border to Tuscany. The main stations along the route are at Ventimiglia, San Remo, Imperia, Savona, Genoa and La Spezia. There are good road and rail links between Genoa and Milan and Turin. Access to inland Liguria is harder because of the mountains. Bus services link many of the coastal towns with the prettiest hill villages. If you have a car you can explore some of the countryside by following the smaller routes, such as the N28 from Imperia towards Garessio in Piedmont, the N334 from Albisola or the N456 from Voltri towards Milan.

The spectacular gardens of the Villa Hanbury near Ventimiglia

Balzi Rossi **1**

Imperia. **FS** Ventimiglia & Mentone.
🚌 from Ventimiglia to Ponte San Luigi & then a ten-minute walk.

An unassuming promontory is the setting for some of the most important caves in northern Italy. Guided tours lead through the traces of the cave-dwelling civilization of pre-Iron Age Liguria. The caves contain excavated burial sites where the dead were adorned with sea-shells. The **Museo Nazionale dei Balzi Rossi** contains tools, weapons and stone-etched female figures dating from 100,000 years ago. There is also a reproduction of an etching of a horse found in one of the caves.

🏛 Museo Nazionale dei Balzi Rossi

Via Balzi Rossi 9, Frazione di Balzi Rossi. **C** 0184 381 13. ◯ Tue–Sun. ● 1 Jan, 1 May, 25 Dec. 📷

Villa Hanbury **2**

Corso Monte Carlo 43, Località La Mortola. **C** 0184 22 95 07. **FS** Ventimiglia. 🚌 from Ventimiglia. ◯ daily (Nov–Mar: Thu–Tue). 📷 **W** www.cooperativa-omnia.com

In 1867 the English botanist Sir Thomas Hanbury and his brother bought this villa on the Mortola promontory. They took full advantage of the exceptionally mild and sunny Ligurian climate to establish a garden of exotic plants along the sloping pathways of the enchanting seaside villa.

The collection, gathered by Hanbury on trips to Africa and Asia, has grown to number more than 3,000 varieties of tropical flora including rubber trees, palms and wild cacti.

The garden is now run by the state and is one of the most impressive botanical gardens in Italy. Even in winter visitors will find a wealth of colour and vegetation here.

Dolceacqua **3**

Imperia. 🏠 1,800. **FS** 🚌 **i** Via Patrioti Martiri 22 (0184 20 66 66). ◯ Thu.

This pretty wine-producing village, 8 km (5 miles) north of Ventimiglia, is built on either side of the churning River Nervia, its two halves joined by an arching 33-m (108-ft) medieval stone bridge. The highlight is the ruined **castle** (12th–15th century) inhabited for a while in the 16th century by the powerful Doria family from Genoa. The

two square towers at the front dominate the village. The terraced vineyards in the surrounding hills produce bunches of grapes for general consumption as well as for a robust red wine known as Rossese or vino di Dolceacqua.

San Remo **4**

Imperia. 🏠 60,000. **FS** 🚌 **i** Largo Nuvoloni 1 (0184 57 15 71). ◯ Tue & Sat. **W** www.apt.rivieradeifiori.it

The Casinò Municipale in San Remo, completed in 1906

San Remo is a pleasant resort of faded elegance. The composer Tchaikovsky, Alfred Nobel (the father of modern explosives) and the nonsense poet Edward Lear all stayed in the stuccoed mansions of the palm-lined seafront avenue, the Corso Imperatrice. The focus of the town, then as now, is the Casino. A little further down the Corso stands the ornate Russian Orthodox church of San Borilio.

The old town, La Pigna (fir cone), is a huddle of narrow lanes with medieval houses and pastel-coloured shutters. A funicular railway climbs up to Monte Bignone, which has excellent views over the Riviera. On a clear day you can see as far as Cannes.

An enchanting flower market is held on Corso Garibaldi (6–8am, Jun–Oct), while the Italian Song Festival takes place here in February.

Bussana Vecchia **5**

Imperia. Off San Remo–Arma di Taggià road.

Bussana vecchia is a marvellously atmospheric ghost town. In February 1887 an earthquake shook the village,

The village of Dolceacqua with its medieval bridge and ruined castle

reducing its Baroque church and surrounding houses to ruins. (One survivor, Giovanni Torre del Merlo, went on to invent the ice-cream cone.)

The town was rebuilt closer to the sea and since then the original village has been taken over by artists, who have restored some interiors, providing a venue for summer concerts and exhibitions.

Cervo ❻

Imperia. 🏠 1,200. FS 🚌
🛈 Piazza Santa Caterina 2 (0183 40 81 97). 🖰 Thu.

Spectacular rock formations in the grottoes of Toirano

CERVO IS THE PRETTIEST of the many old seafront villages just east of Imperia, with a narrow complex of streets and houses rising dramatically up from the shingle beach. At the top of the village stands the concave Baroque façade of **San Giovanni Battista**. In front of the church, in July and August, they hold charming chamber orchestra performances. The church is also known as the "*dei corallini*", after the coral fishing which once brought prosperity for the local people. Now Cervo is an unassuming but characteristic Ligurian holiday resort, with unspoilt hotels near the beach.

The 5th-century Baptistry at Albenga

San Giovanni Battista at Cervo

Albenga ❼

Savona. 🏠 21,000. FS 🚌 🛈 Viale Martiri della Libertà 1 (0182 55 84 44). 🖰 Wed. ⓦ www.italianriviera.com

UNTIL THE Middle Ages, the Roman port of Albium Ingaunum played an important maritime role. The sea, however, gradually moved further out, leaving the town, now called Albenga, stranded on the Centa River. Most striking now is its Romanesque brick architecture, in particular the three 13th-century towers clustered around the cathedral of **San Michele**. The cathedral's interior was restored to its medieval form in the late 1960s. To the south is an intriguing 5th-century **Baptistry** with a ten-sided exterior and octagonal interior. Inside, the original 5th-century blue and white mosaics of doves represent the 12 apostles. To the north of the cathedral is the small Piazza dei Leoni, named after its three stone lions imported from Rome.

In a 14th-century palace on Piazza San Michele is the **Museo Navale Romano** founded in 1950 following the salvage of a Roman ship that had sunk offshore around 100–90 BC. The museum contains ancient amphorae as well as exhibits salvaged from more recent shipwrecks.

🛈 Baptistry
Piazza San Michele. 📞 0182 512 15. 🕐 Tue–Sun. ● 1 Jan, Easter, 25 Dec. 🖾

🏛 Museo Navale Romano
Piazza San Michele 12. 📞 0182 512 15. 🕐 Tue–Sun. ● 1 Jan, Easter, 25 Dec. 🖾

Grotte di Toirano ❽

Piazzale delle Grotte, Toirano.
📞 0182 980 62. 🚌 from Albenga to Borghetto Santo Spirito. FS to Borghetto Santo Spirito or Loano then bus. 🕐 9am–noon, 2–5pm daily. ● mid-Nov–mid-Dec & 25 Dec. 🖾

BENEATH the delightful medieval hill-town of Toirano lies a series of extraordinary caves containing relics of Paleolithic life dating from 100,000 BC.

Guided tours through the **Grotta della Basura** (Witch's Cave) reveal remarkable prehistoric human and animal footprints, and a collection of ancient bear bones and teeth in the "bear cemetery".

The **Grotta di Santa Lucia**, which can also be visited by guided tour, reveals the full beauty of the luminous yellow and grey stalactites and stalagmites that have formed here over thousands of years.

The **Museo Preistorico della Val Varatella** at the entrance to the Grotta della Basura has a small display of finds from the caves, as well as a model of a prehistoric bear.

🏛 Museo Preistorico della Val Varatella
Piazzale delle Grotte. 📞 0182 980 62. ● for restoration.

Street-by-Street: Genoa 9

THERE IS SOMETHING refreshingly rough-edged about Genoa (Genova in Italian), Italy's most important commercial port. In contrast to the genteel resorts along the neighbouring coast, the narrow streets of the old town are the haunts of sailors and streetwalkers.

With its natural harbour and the mountains to protect it, Genoa rose to prominence as a sea-based power. During the 16th century Andrea Doria cemented Genoa's importance, and also proved an astute patron of the arts.

Palazzo Bianco

Piazza San Matteo
The houses and church of San Matteo were built by the Doria family in 1278. Palazzo Quartara has a bas relief of St George above the doorway.

PIAZZA CAMPETTO

VIA DI SCURRERIA

PIAZZA SAN MATTEO

SALITA SAN M

VIA ARCHIVESCOVATO

← The port and Palazzo Reale

San Lorenzo
The black and white striped Gothic façade of the Duomo dates from the early 13th century.

VIA SAN LORENZO

PIAZZA MATTEOTTI

SALITA POLLAIUOLI

PIA ERB

Palazzo Ducale
Once the seat of the doges of Genoa, this elegant building with its two fine 16th-century courtyards and arcades now contains a major arts and cultural centre.

San Donato has a splendid 12th-century octagonal bell tower.

VICO TRE RE MAGI

Sant'Agostino
The 13th-century church and convent were bombed during World War II, but the bell tower remains. The cloisters now house sculpture like this fragment from the tomb of Margaret of Brabant by Pisano (1312).

KEY

– – –	Suggested route

0 metres   100

0 yards   100

Church of Gesù
This Baroque church, built between 1589 and 1606, is also known as the church of Santi Ambrogio e Andrea.

VISITORS' CHECKLIST

640,000. ✈ Cristoforo Colombo 6 km (4 miles) W. **FS** Stazione Principe, Piazza Acquaverde. ⚓ Stazione Marittima, Ponte dei Mille. ℹ Palazzina S Maria, Area Porto Antico (010 24 87 11); Stazione Principe (010 246 26 33). **W** www.apt.genova.it 📧 Mon, Wed & Thu. 🎉 24 Jun: San Giovanni Battista; Jul: Ballet Festival; Oct: Fiera Nautica.

Piazza De Ferrari is the site of the Neo-Classical Banco di Roma and the Accademia, as well as the restored Teatro Carlo Felice.

The bronze fountain in Piazza De Ferrari was constructed in 1936.

Porta Soprana
The eastern gateway to the city has curved outer walls and stands close to the site of Christopher Columbus's house.

Sant'Andrea
The 12th-century cloisters standing in a small garden are all that remain of the convent that once stood here.

19th-century lion guarding the steps leading to the Duomo

🔒 **San Lorenzo (Duomo)**
Piazza San Lorenzo. ☎ 010 26 57 86. ◷ daily. **Museo del Tesoro** ☎ 010 247 18 31. ◷ Mon–Sat.

The Duomo, with its black and white striped exterior, blends many architectural styles, from the 12th-century Romanesque side portal of San Giovanni to the Baroque touches of some of its side chapels. The three portals at the west end are in French Gothic style.

The most sumptuous of the chapels is dedicated to St John the Baptist, patron saint of the city; it includes a 13th-century sarcophagus that once held the venerated saint's relics.

Steps lead down from the sacristy to the **Museo del Tesoro di San Lorenzo**. It houses such treasures as the Roman green glass dish said to have been used at the Last Supper, and a blue chalcedony plate on which the head of John the Baptist was allegedly served up to Salome.

🚢 **The Port**
The port is the heart of Genoa and the origin of its wealth and power as a seafaring city state in the 11th and 12th centuries. It is a workaday place, given over to container shipping, and ringed by busy roads and 1960s wharves and office buildings.

Among the vestiges of its medieval glory is the **Lanterna** lighthouse (restored in 1543) near the Stazione Marittima. In the old days fires would be lit at the top of the Lanterna to guide ships into port. Today, regeneration of the port is in part due to the modern conference centre designed by Renzo Piano (*see p179*) and to the new aquarium on Ponte Spinola, the largest in Europe. The best way to see the port is from the sea; boats, giving guided tours, depart from Ponte Spinola.

Exploring Genoa

VISITORS ARE WELL REWARDED when they explore Genoa – a city proud of its history and legends. The palaces of the Via Balbi and Via Garibaldi, and the paintings and sculptures dotted around the city in churches and museums, are among the finest in northwestern Italy. The environs, too, provide scenic and relaxing locations for excursions along the coast or in the steep hills behind.

The courtyard of the University on Via Balbi

⛪ Sant'Agostino

Piazza Sarzano 35. **(010 251 12 63.**
◯ *daily pm.* ● *public hols.*
Museo di Architettura e Scultura Ligure ◯ *Tue–Sat & Sun am.*
● *public hols.*

The Gothic church of Sant'Agostino was begun in 1260, but bombed to pieces in World War II. It is now deconsecrated and all that remains of the original building is the fine Gothic bell tower, decorated with coloured tiles. The monastery, of which the church of Sant'Agostino was once a part, was also bombed. What remained were two ruined cloisters – one of which forms the only triangular building in Genoa. The cloisters have recently been reconstructed and converted into the **Museo di Architettura e Scultura Ligure**. It contains the city's collection of architectural pieces and fragments of sculpture, as well as frescoes – all salvaged from Genoa's other destroyed churches. The finest piece is a magnificent fragment from the tomb of Margaret of Brabant. Margaret, who died in 1311, was the wife of Emperor Henry VII who invaded Italy in 1310. Carved by Giovanni Pisano around 1313, the sculptures from her tomb were restored and repositioned in 1987. The figures, whose garments are arranged in simple folds, seem to be helping Margaret to lay down to rest.

♛ Palazzo Reale

Via Balbi 10. **(010 271 02 72.**
◯ *daily am (Mon & Tue pm).* ● *1 Jan, 25 Apr, 1 May, 25 Dec.*

This austere-looking residence, used by the Kings of Savoy from the 17th century onwards, has a highly ornate Rococo interior – notably its ballroom and its Hall of Mirrors. Among the paintings are works by Parodi and Carlone and a *Crucifixion* by Van Dyck. The lovely garden, which slopes down towards the old port, includes an intriguing cobblestone mosaic around the central fountain, depicting houses and animals.

Opposite the palace is the old **University** (1634) designed by the architect Bartolomeo Bianco, as was much of Via Balbi. The large building brilliantly overcomes Genoa's hilly topography, and is constructed on four levels.

♛ Palazzo Bianco

Via Garibaldi 11. **(010 247 63 77.**
◯ *Tue–Sun.* **Palazzo Rosso**
(010 247 63 51. ◯ *Tue–Sun.*

The Palazzo Bianco is situated on Genoa's most beautiful street, the **Via Garibaldi**, where there are numerous fine 16th-century mansions and palazzi. The Palazzo Bianco contains the city's prime collection of paintings, including the works of many Genoese artists such as Luca Cambiaso, Bernardo Strozzi, Domenico Piola and Giovanni Benedetto Castiglione. Better-known artists featured here

---

CHRISTOPHER COLUMBUS IN GENOA

A portrait of Columbus, Villa Doria in Pegli

The name of Christopher Columbus, the explorer of the New World, is in evidence all over Genoa. His statue greets you as soon as you emerge in Piazza Acquaverde from Porta Principe railway station; various public buildings bear his name; even the airport is called Aeroporto Cristoforo Colombo. In the 17th-century Palazzo Belimbau, built on top of the old city walls, is a series of frescoes by the Genoese artist Tavarone celebrating the explorer's life and you can see three of his letters in the Sala del Sindaco in Palazzo Tursi (the city hall) on Via Garibaldi. It is not certain whether Columbus (c.1451–1506) was born in Genoa, in Savona 15 km (9 miles) to the west or outside Italy altogether. However, city registers mention his father, a weaver, and different family homes within the city. The small ivy-clad house next to the Porta Soprana may have been Columbus's childhood home, where he first discovered his passion for the sea.

The house where Columbus may have lived

The romantic gardens at Villa Durazzo-Pallavicini in Pegli

include Filippino Lippi (a lovely *Madonna with Saints*), Veronese, Van Dyck and Rubens. Across the street in the **Palazzo Rosso** are more paintings, including works by Dürer and Caravaggio, as well as ceramics, furniture and coins. Upstairs in the *piano nobile* the rooms are adorned with 17th-century frescoes by Genoese artists such as de Ferrari and Piola.

⛪ Staglieno Cemetery
Piazzale Resasco, Staglieno. 📞 010 87 01 84. ◯ daily. ● public hols. ♿

Fine tomb architecture from the huge Staglieno Cemetery

This grandiose cemetery, just over the hills northeast of Genoa along the Bisagno River, is so big (160 ha, 395 acres) that it has its own internal bus system. Founded in 1844, its tombs and monuments make up an eerie city of miniature cathedrals, Egyptian temples and Art Nouveau palaces. Its most famous resident is Giuseppe Mazzini, the Genoese revolutionary who died not far from Pisa in 1872.

ENVIRONS: Until World War II, **Pegli**, 6 km (4 miles) west of the city centre, was a popular weekend retreat for rich Genoese wanting to get away from it all. Now it forms part of the metropolis, but nevertheless maintains an air of tranquillity thanks to its parks and two villas, the 19th-century **Villa Durazzo-Pallavicini** and the 16th-century **Villa Doria**. The latter now houses a naval history museum celebrating Genoa's glorious past: you can see globes, compasses, astrolabes, maps, model ships and a portrait of Columbus ascribed to Ghirlandaio, probably dating from 1525. The Villa Durazzo-Pallavicini houses an archaeological museum which relates the pre-Roman history of the Ligurian coast. The villa's garden is landscaped with romantic grottoes, pavilions and fountains.

Nervi, 8 km (5 miles) to the east of the city, is another former resort town, famous for its seafront promenade, the **Passeggiata Anita Garibaldi** (named after Garibaldi's Brazilian wife). The walk crosses the Nervi torrent and follows a route that has been cut into the rock face, giving panoramic views

of the coast. The lush **Parco Municipale** is another feature of Nervi. It once formed the grounds of two aristocratic villas – the Villa Serra and the Villa Gropallo. The gardens contain some rare species of exotic and Mediterranean trees.

The Villa Serra on Via Capolungo now houses the **Galleria d'Arte Moderna** featuring modern Italian painting. The **Villa Luxoro** on Via Aurelia is notable for its collection of clocks, fabrics, furniture and lace. The area is also famous as Garibaldi's departure point when he set off for Sicily with his *Mille* (the famous "Thousand" men) to bring about the unification of Italy. A large monument at Quarto dei Mille, about 3 km (2 miles) back towards the city, marks the place where the volunteers met in May 1860 to follow the intrepid revolutionary (see pp58–9).

🏛 Villa Doria
Piazza Bonavino 7, Pegli. 📞 010 696 98 85. ◯ Tue–Sat & 1st & 3rd Sun of month. ● public hols. 🎟 ♿

🏛 Villa Durazzo-Pallavicini
Via Pallavicini 11, Pegli.
📞 010 698 27 76. ◯ Tue, Thu, Fri–Sat & 2nd & 4th Sun of month.
● public hols. 🎟 ♿

🏛 Galleria d'Arte Moderna
Villa Serra, Via Capolungo 3, Nervi.
📞 010 372 60 25. ◯ Tue–Sat.

🏛 Villa Luxoro
Via Mafalda di Savoia 3, Nervi.
📞 010 32 26 73. ◯ Tue–Sat.
● public hols. 🎟

Pini (c.1920) by Rubaldo Merello in the Galleria d'Arte Moderna at Nervi

Pastel-coloured houses near the pebbly beach at Camogli

Camogli ⑩

Genova. ⚲ 6,500. ⬛ 🚌 ⛴
🅸 Via XX Settembre 33 (0185 77 10
66). ⛴ Wed.

BUILT ON A pine-wooded
slope, Camogli is a fishing
village where sea-shells adorn
the pastel-painted house walls,
and the smell of frying fish
wafts out from the small restaurants into the streets. Near
the pebble beach and fishing
port is the medieval Castello
della Dragonara, a castle now
containing the **Acquario
Tirrenico** which displays 22
tanks of sea creatures.
   Camogli celebrates its
famous festival of the Blessing
of the Fish on the second
Sunday of May when sardines
are fried in a huge pan 4 m
(13 ft) in diameter. The fish is
distributed free to all-comers.

🏛 **Acquario Tirrenico**
Castello della Dragonara.
📞 0185 77 33 75. ⬜ Tue–Sun &
public hols. 📷

Portofino Peninsula ⑪

Genova. 🚌 ⛴ Portofino.
🅸 Via Roma 35 (0185 26 90 24).
🅆 www.portofinobayarea.com

PORTOFINO IS THE most
exclusive harbour and
resort town in Italy, crammed
with the yachts of the wealthy.

You can reach Portofino by
road (cars are not allowed
into the village), or boat, from
the resort of Santa Margherita
Ligure. Above the town are
the church of **San Giorgio**,
containing relics said to be of
the dragon-slayer,
and a castle.
   On the other
side of the
peninsula, which
you have to reach
on foot (a two-
hour walk) or
by boat, is the
**Abbazia di
San Fruttuoso**,
named after a
3rd-century saint
whose followers
were shipwrecked here and,
according to legend, protected
by three lions. The white abbey
buildings, set among pines and
olive trees, date mostly from
the 11th century, although the
imposing Torre dei Doria was
added 500 years later. You can

take a boat to try to locate the
Cristo degli Abissi, a bronze
statue of Christ that sits on the
sea bed near San Fruttuoso,
protecting sailors. Further
west along the coast is Punta
Chiappa, a rocky promontory
famous for the changing
colours of the surrounding sea.

🏠 **Abbazia di San Fruttuoso**
San Fruttuoso. 📞 0185 77 27 03.
⬜ Tue–Sun (Dec–Feb: public hols
& the day before only). ⬤ Nov. 📷

Rapallo ⑫

Genova. ⚲ 30,000. ⬛ 🚌 ⛴ 🅸
Via Diaz 9 (0185 23 03 46). ⛴ Thu.

HISTORIANS KNOW Rapallo as
the place where two
post-World War II treaties were
signed, while film buffs might
recognize it from the 1954
movie *The Barefoot Contessa*,
which was shot here. Rapallo
was also a haven for writers
such as DH Lawrence and Ezra
Pound. Its villas still have a
patrician feel to
them, as do the
riding stables,
golf course and
tennis courts.
The palm-lined
esplanade ends
in a small 16th-
century **castle**,
in which art
exhibitions are
occasionally
held. Above
the village is the
16th-century **Santuario di
Montallegro**, which houses
a Byzantine icon said to
possess miraculous powers.

**The 16th-century castle
jutting into Rapallo harbour**

🏠 **Santuario di Montallegro**
Montallegro. 📞 0185 23 90 00.
⬜ daily.

Large yachts moored in Portofino's famous harbour

The dramatic coastline near Corniglia in the Cinque Terre

Cinque Terre ⓭

La Spezia. **FS** *to all towns.*
🚉 *Monterosso, Vernazza.* **🛈** *Piazza
Garibaldi, Monterosso (0187 81 72 04).*
W *www.aptcinqueterre.sp.it*

T HE CINQUE TERRE is a stretch
of rocky coastline on
the Riviera di Levante which
extends from Monterosso
al Mare to Riomaggiore at its
southeastern tip. The name
refers to five self-contained
villages which seem to
dramatically cling to the very
edge of vertiginous cliffs:
Monterosso al Mare, Vernazza,
Corniglia, Manarola and
Riomaggiore. The
villages were once
only accessible by
sea and today
there is still no
road that links
them all. An
ancient foot-
path known
as the Sentiero
Azzurro follows
the coast, joining the villages
and offering wonderful
views of the distinctive
green terraced vineyards
that produce the local dry
white Cinque Terre wines.

These days the villages are
suffering from some depopulation. **Monterosso al Mare**,
on the northwestern edge of
the Cinque Terre, is the
largest of the five villages and
overlooks a wide bay with its
own sandy beach. **Vernazza**,
further down the coast, has
streets linked by steep steps
or *arpaie*. **Corniglia**, perched
at the pinnacle of rocky
terraces, seems untouched by
the passage of time, as does
Manarola which is linked by

the famous Via dell'Amore, or
Lovers' Lane, to **Riomaggiore**,
a 15-minute walk away.

The best way to visit the
villages is by boat (from
La Spezia, Lerici or Porto
Venere) or by train (La
Spezia–Genoa railway line).

Portovenere ⓮

La Spezia. 🏠 *4,600.* 🚉 🚌 **🛈** *Piazza
Bastreri (0187 79 06 91).* 🏛 *Mon.*

N AMED AFTER VENUS herself,
Portovenere is one of the
most romantic villages on the
Ligurian coast with its cluster
of narrow streets lined
with pastel-coloured
houses. In the
upper part of the
village is the
12th-century
church of **San
Lorenzo**. A
sculpture over
the doorway here
depicts the martyr-
dom of the saint who was
roasted alive on a grill. On the
stone promontory that curls

**Above the doorway of San
Lorenzo in Portovenere**

out into the sea stands the
small, black and white 13th-
century church of **San Pietro**.
From here, or from the 16th-
century castle on top of the
cliffs on the northwestern
side of the village, there are
glorious views of the Cinque
Terre and the small island of
Palmaria which lies about
400 m (1,300 ft) offshore.

Lerici ⓯

La Spezia. 🏠 *13,000.* 🚉 🚌 **🛈** *Via
Biagini 2 (0187 96 73 46).* 🏛 *Sat am.*

T HIS STRETCH OF COAST, along
the Gulf of La Spezia or
Poets' Gulf, was once popular
with such literati as Yeats and
DH Lawrence. The village of
San Terenzo, across the bay
from Lerici, was where the
poet Shelley spent the last four
years of his life. It was from his
home, the Casa Magni, that he
set out in 1822 on a voyage to
meet Leigh Hunt in Livorno.
Tragically, he was shipwrecked
near Viareggio and drowned.

Lerici, once a small fishing
village and now a popular
resort, sits on the edge of a
beautiful bay, and has a beach
overlooked by pastel-coloured
houses. The forbidding
medieval **Castello di Lerici**
(13th century), built by the
Pisans and later passed to
the Genoese, dominates the
holiday villas below. Today it
houses a museum of geopale-
ontology and is a venue for
art exhibitions and concerts.

⚓ **Castello di Lerici**
Piazza San Giorgio. **📞** *0187 96 90
42.* ⭕ *Apr–Oct: daily.* 🏛

The harbour of Vernazza in the Cinque Terre

A stunning view of Manarola on the Sentiero Azzurro, Cinque Terre

CENTRAL ITALY

Central Italy at a Glance

T HE CENTRAL REGIONS of Italy are popular
with visitors because they offer a range
of beautiful landscapes and towns rich in
culture and history, including outstanding
churches, towers and palaces. Emilia-
Romagna is home to the impressive Po
Delta that provides a haven for wildlife.
Tuscany is dominated by Florence,
one of Italy's most celebrated centres.
Umbria and Le Marche offer gentle
pastoral countryside and
picturesque hilltowns. The
major sights of this rewarding
area are shown here.

The Leaning Tower *of Pisa
and the Duomo (see pp314–16),
splendid examples of 12th- and
13th-century architecture, are
decorated with Arabic-inspired,
complex geometric patterns.*

*Leaning Tower
of Pisa*

TUSCA
(See pp30

FLORENCE
(See pp262–303)

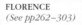

Duomo, Campanile and Baptistry

Uffizi

The Duomo *and the
Baptistry, set in the
heart of Florence,
dominate the city
(see pp272–4). The
dome dwarfs many
surrounding buildings.*

Palazzo Pitti

The Uffizi *contains
a superb collection of
Florentine art from
Gothic to High Renais-
sance and beyond
(see pp278–81).*

The Palazzo Pitti,
begun in 1457 for the
banker Luca Pitti,
became the main resi-
dence of the Medici. It
now houses their treas-
ures (see pp294–5).

| 0 kilometres | 1 |
| 0 miles | 0.5 |

| 0 kilometres | |
| 0 miles | 25 |

◁ **Autumn colour in Tuscany, in the hills of the Val d'Orcia, south of Siena**

The church of San Vitale in Ravenna is a gem of Byzantine art and architecture (see p260). It contains brilliantly preserved mosaics from the 6th century.

EMILIA-ROMAGNA
(See pp246–61)

San Vitale, Ravenna

The Palazzo Ducale in Urbino was built by Duke Federico, the town's 15th-century ruler, to plans by Laurana (see pp360–61). This Renaissance palace now houses the Galleria Nazionale delle Marche.

SAN MARINO

NCE
(set)

Palazzo Ducale, Urbino

UMBRIA
(See pp338–53)

LE MARCHE
(See pp354–63)

Duomo, Siena

Basilica of San Francesco, Assisi

Giotto's fresco cycle from the Basilica of San Francesco in Assisi was executed in the 13th century (see pp344–7). The church is visited by thousands of pilgrims each year.

Siena, a medieval town steeped in tradition, centres around the Campo, the large piazza shaped like a scallop shell (see pp328–33). The lively horse race, the Corsa del Palio, is held here in July and August.

Regional Food: Central Italy

THE FOOD OF TUSCANY, UMBRIA and Le Marche is simple but often hearty. Packed with flavour, it is based on peasant cooking that relies heavily on olive oil, tomatoes, beans, hams and salamis. With Bologna, Italy's gastronomic capital, as its main city, Emilia-Romagna tends to have more elaborate dishes, using ingredients such as cream, interesting meats – including game, Parma ham and mortadella – and good-quality cheeses. Fresh fish and seafood is available along the coasts, but is often more expensive than meat.

Artichoke

Balsamic vinegar from Modena in Emilia-Romagna is renowned throughout the world. Aged for up to fourteen years in oak barrels, the dark, smooth vinegar is used to flavour soups, stews and salad dressings.

Wild boar salami

Mortadella

Cooked ham (*prosciutto cotto*)

Parma ham

Cured meats and hams *form an important part of the cuisine of central Italy. The most famous is Parma ham from Emilia-Romagna, where the pigs are fattened on the whey left over from making Parmesan cheese.*

Panzanella, *a refreshing summer salad, is made of juicy tomatoes, onion, garlic and oil-soaked bread, garnished with fresh basil.*

Tortelloni, *a larger version of tortellini, may be stuffed with meat or cheese and served with a rich sauce.*

Liver paste

Tomato paste

Olive paste

Anchovy paste

Crostini *are delicious snacks made from rounds of toast topped with anchovy, olive, liver or tomato paste. Bruschetta is grilled bread rubbed with garlic and drizzled with olive oil.*

Spaghetti al Ragù *is a traditional dish from Bologna. The pasta is topped with a generous portion of beef and tomato sauce.*

Cannelloni *is another form of stuffed pasta. Large pasta tubes may be filled with meat or cheese and spinach, and then coated with tomato or bechamel sauce before being baked.*

Baccalà *is a simple, flavourful dish of dried salt cod prepared with garlic and garnished with parsley. In Tuscany, tomatoes are often added.*

Bistecca alla Fiorentina*, grilled over an open fire, is a large, tender steak that can be seasoned with oil and herbs and garnished with fresh lemon.*

Scottiglia di Cingbiale *is prepared with wild boar chops. This dish is particularly popular in the Maremma area of southern Tuscany.*

Torta di Limone *is one of the richer desserts that come from Emilia-Romagna. It is prepared with lemons and fresh cream.*

Torta di Riso *is a traditional Tuscan dessert consisting of rice cake served with a simple fruit sauce and seasonal fruit.*

Pecorino

Parmesan

Cheeses *are used in many recipes, but may also be served with fruit as a main course or at the end of a meal.*

Panforte

Panforte *is a dense, dark cake spiced with cinnamon and cloves. Ricciarelli are made from ground almonds, orange peel and honey.*

Ricciarelli

Cantucci *are sweet Tuscan biscuits often served together with vin santo, a traditional dessert wine.*

MUSHROOMS AND TRUFFLES

Wild mushrooms are considered a great delicacy in central Italy, and a range of fresh and dried mushrooms is frequently used in cooking. Fresh mushrooms are available in the autumn when restaurants are often packed with locals tasting seasonal mushroom dishes. Prized black truffles *(tartufi neri)* with a rich flavour and firm texture are expensive and used sparingly, as are funghi porcini. Porcini may be served grilled as a main course, used on pizza, in stuffed pasta or served as a vegetable dish, sautéed gently with garlic.

Chanterelle
(Cantarello or *Gallinaccio)*

Field blewit
(Agarico nudo)

Parasol
(Mazza da Tamburo)

Boletus edulis
(Porcini)

Oyster
(Ostrica)

Black truffle
(Tartufo nero)

The Wines of Central Italy

Roman mosaic of a bird eating grapes

VINEYARDS ARE SEEN EVERYWHERE in Central Italy, from the rolling cypress-fringed hills of Tuscany to the flatter, Lambrusco-producing plains of Emilia-Romagna. The finest red wines are made in the hills of southeastern Tuscany: Chianti Classico, Brunello di Montalcino and Vino Nobile di Montepulciano. Today's innovative mix of modern and traditional techniques is steadily improving the quality of much of the region's wine.

Chianti Classico is the heart of the Chianti zone. Chianti may be light and fruity or dense and long-lived – price is the usual guide. Rocca delle Macie is very reasonably priced.

Vernaccia di San Gimignano is a Tuscan white wine with a long, distinguished history. Traditionally a golden, often oxidized wine, it is now also produced in a fresher style, for early drinking. Teruzzi e Puthod make consistently good Vernaccia.

Vino Nobile di Montepulciano is made from the same grapes as Chianti. It can be of superior quality, hence its claim to be a "noble wine". The vineyards are set around the delightful hilltop village of Montepulciano.

Parma
Modena
Bologna

EMILIA-ROMAGNA

Pistoia
Lucca
Florence
Pisa
Greve
San Gimignano
Siena
TUSCANY
Montepul
Montalcino

Brunello di Montalcino is made from Sangiovese, Brunello being its local name. Its firm tannins may need up to ten years to soften before the rich, spicy flavours are revealed. Rosso di Montalcino, on the other hand, can be enjoyed much younger.

SUPER-TUSCANS

During the 1970s innovative wine makers set out to create new, individual wines even though under the existing rules they would be labelled as simple table wine. A trend which started with Antinori's Tignanello (a Sangiovese-Cabernet Sauvignon blend), this approach has reinvigorated Tuscan wine, to produce some exciting variations.

Sassicaia, a red wine made from the Cabernet Sauvignon grape

0 kilometres 50

0 miles 25

Chianti estate at Badia a Passignano in Tuscany

KEY

- ☐ Chianti
- ☐ Chianti Classico
- ☐ Vernaccia di San Gimignano
- ☐ Brunello di Montalcino
- ☐ Vino Nobile di Montepulciano
- ☐ Orvieto Classico
- ☐ Orvieto
- ☐ Verdicchio dei Castelli di Jesi
- ☐ Lambrusco

Rimini
AN
RINO
Pèsaro

Urbino
LE MARCHE
Jesi
Gubbio
UMBRIA
erugia
Assisi

na

Verdicchio is a dry white wine from Le Marche with a crisp, slightly salty taste. In recent years the introduction of the single vineyard Verdicchio, such as Umani Ronchi's CaSal di Serra, has won much acclaim.

Orvieto Classico is a popular Umbrian white wine. This fresh, dry (Secco) version from the Antinori estate is a good example of a modern-style Orvieto. The wine also comes in a sweeter form, known as Abboccato.

GRAPES OF CENTRAL ITALY

The versatile Sangiovese grape dominates wine making in Central Italy. It is the main grape in Chianti, in Vino Nobile di Montepulciano, in Brunello di Montalcino, and in many of the new-style Super-Tuscan wines. Of the established whites, Trebbiano and Malvasia head the list. Imported varieties such as white Chardonnay and red Cabernet Sauvignon are playing an increasing role, often being used to complement and enhance native varieties.

Sangiovese grapes

HOW TO READ THE LABEL

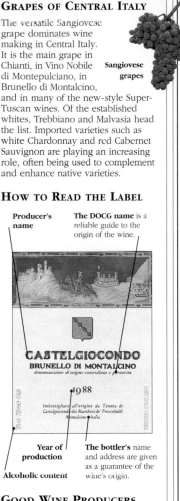

Producer's name

The DOCG name is a reliable guide to the origin of the wine.

CASTELGIOCONDO
BRUNELLO DI MONTALCINO
denominazione di origine controllata e garantita

1988

Imbottigliato all'origine da Tenuta di Castelgiocondo dei Marchesi de' Frescobaldi Montalcino ● Italia

Year of production

The bottler's name and address are given as a guarantee of the wine's origin.

Alcoholic content

GOOD WINE PRODUCERS

Chianti: Antinori, Badia a Coltibuono, Brolio, Castello di Ama, Castello di Rampolla, Fattoria Selvapiana, Felsina Berardenga, Il Palazzino, Isole e Olena, Monte Vertine, Riecine, Rocca delle Macie, Ruffino, Tenuta Fontodi.
Brunello di Montalcino: Argiano, Altesino, Caparzo, Castelgiocondo, Costanti, Il Poggione, Villa Banfi.
Vino Nobile di Montepulciano: Avignonesi, Le Casalte, Poliziano. In **Umbria**: Adanti, Lungarotti.

Good Chianti Vintages
1997, 1995, 1993, 1990, 1988, 1985, 1983, 1975, 1971, 1970, 1967, 1964.

Understanding Architecture in Central Italy

CENTRAL ITALY has countless fine Renaissance buildings, many of them concentrated in and around Florence. Their clear lines, elegant simplicity and harmonious proportions came out of a re-evaluation of the past. Turning their backs on the Gothic style, the architects of the Renaissance returned to Classical Rome for inspiration. Most of the large buildings had been started by the late 15th century, paid for by the Catholic Church or by powerful noble families, such as the Medici of Florence.

The Palazzo Ducale in Urbino (begun 1465)

RELIGIOUS BUILDINGS

Arched bays trisect the façade.

Pope Pius II's coat of arms

One of 12 roundels by Luca della Robbia

Small circular windows

Square plan topped by small dome

Symmetrical floorplan is based on a Greek cross.

Harmonious proportions

Pienza's Duomo was built by Bernardo Rossellino in 1459 for Pope Pius II as part of his vision of the ideal Renaissance city (see p323).

The Pazzi Chapel of Santa Croce in Florence (1433) is one of Brunelleschi's most famous works, decorated with terracotta roundels by Luca della Robbia (see pp276–7).

Santa Maria della Consolazione in Todi, begun in 1508, owes much to the ideas of the architect Bramante (see p349).

TOWN AND COUNTRY HOUSES

The cornice was designed to cast a shadow over the face of the palace around midday.

Square windows are found only on the ground floor.

Wedge-shaped masonry

Strong horizontal line

The Palazzo Strozzi in Florence (1489–1536) is typical of many Tuscan city palaces (see p318). The three storeys are given equal importance, and the massive rusticated stonework conveys the impression of strength and power (see p285).

WHERE TO SEE THE ARCHITECTURE

The simple canons of the Renaissance were interpreted differently away from the hotbed of artistic thought and cultural endeavour of Florence, which has the greatest number of churches and palaces. Alberti's Tempio Malatestiano at Rimini (see p258) evokes the sobriety of ancient Roman architecture yet seeks to

Vista in the Boboli Gardens, Florence

reinterpret it in his own unique fashion. Urbino's Palazzo Ducale (pp360–61) perfects the grace and polish of the era and is a truly noble period residence. On a smaller scale are the planned Renaissance centres of elegant towns such as Ferrara (p253), Pienza (p323) and Urbania (p359). All three centres are examples of enlightened patronage, and pay homage to the art of antiquity.

The weight of the lantern prevents the dome from springing apart.

Timber ribs provide the main support.

Outer shell

Inner shell

Classical triangular pediment

The top edge of the frieze divides the façade in two.

Volute connects the lower and upper parts.

The Duomo in Florence is crowned by the revolutionary dome (1436) by Brunelleschi, which had to be built without scaffolding due to its size. The timber structure is covered by an inner and outer shell (see pp272–3).

The façade of Santa Maria Novella in Florence (1458–70) was designed by Leon Battista Alberti. He incorporated some of the existing Gothic features into an overall design typical of the Renaissance (see pp288–9).

The villa at Poggio a Caiano (1480) was redesigned in the Renaissance by Giuliano da Sangallo (see p318). The graceful, curved staircase was added around 1802.

Clock, a later addition

Classical frieze

Colonnade derived from a Classical temple

Classical portico

EMILIA-ROMAGNA

E MILIA-ROMAGNA *is the heartland of central Italy, a broad corridor through the hills and plains of the Po Valley that marks the watershed between the cold north of the Alps and the hot Mediterranean south. With its rich agricultural land, historical cities and thriving industry, it is one of the most prosperous areas in Italy.*

Most of the major towns in Emilia-Romagna lie near the Via Aemilia, a Roman road built in 187 BC that linked Rimini on the Adriatic coast with the garrison town of Piacenza. Prior to the Romans, the Etruscans had ruled from their capital, Felsina, located on the site of present-day Bologna. After the fall of Rome, the region's focus moved to Ravenna, which became a principal part of the Byzantine Empire administered from Constantinople.

During the Middle Ages pilgrims heading for Rome continued to use the Via Aemilia. Political power, however, passed to influential noble families – the Malatesta in Rimini, the Bentivoglio in Bologna, the d'Este in Ferrara and Modena, and the Farnese in Parma and Piacenza. Great courts grew up around the families, attracting poets such as Dante and Ariosto, as well as painters, sculptors and architects. Many of their works still grace the medieval centres of these towns.

Modern Emilia-Romagna, cobbled together from separate Papal States in 1860, was given its present borders in 1947. Emilia, covering the western half of the region, is traditionally associated with a more northern outlook and a tendency towards the left in politics. Romagna, with its capital at Ravenna, has always turned to the south for artistic, cultural and political inspiration.

The entire region has a reputation as a great gastronomic centre. Agriculture has long thrived on the Po's alluvial fringes, earning the Pianura Padana (Po Plain) epithets such as the "bread basket" and "fruit bowl" of Italy. Pigs still outnumber humans in many areas, and some of the country's most famous staples – Parma ham and Parmesan cheese – originate here.

The medieval Palazzo del Comune in Ferrara

◁ The Fontana del Nettuno (Neptune's Fountain) in Bologna

Exploring Emilia-Romagna

EMILIA-ROMAGNA is a chequerboard of fields and plains between the Po river to the north and the forest-covered Apennine mountain slopes to the south. The best place to begin a tour of the region is centrally situated Bologna. Modena, its long-time rival, boasts one of the country's loveliest Romanesque cathedrals. Parma has a more provincial feel and Ferrara, too, has an easy-going air. Castell'Arquato offers a taste of the smaller villages that dot the hills south of the Po.

Piazza Cavalli, Piacenza's central square

See Also

- **Where to Stay** pp555–7

- **Where to Eat** pp590–91

Reed-lined shores along the Po Delta

GETTING AROUND

Excellent road and rail links, aided by predominantly flat terrain, make this region quick and easy to get around. Bologna is connected by the A1 to Florence and by the A13 to Ferrara and Venice. The busy A1 links Bologna with Milan via Piacenza, Fidenza and Parma. The A15 connects Parma with La Spezia, and the A21 joins Piacenza and Cremona. Fast, frequent train services run along almost parallel routes.

The beach at Cesenatico, north of Rimini on the Adriatic coast

KEY

▬▬	Motorway
▬▬	Major road
▬▬	Minor road
▬▬	Scenic route
～～	River
✿	Viewpoint

0 kilometres   25

0 miles   20

The 13th-century Palazzo Pretorio in Castell'Arquato

Piacenza ❶

🏛 *105,000.* 🚉 🚌 ℹ *Piazzetta dei Mercanti 7 (0523 32 93 24).* 🛒 *Wed & Sat.*

Piacenza traces its history back to Roman times. Located near the Po, it served as a fortified camp protecting the Emilian plain from invasion. The centre is still based on the Roman plan.

Piacenza has a pleasantly understated old centre full of fine medieval and Renaissance buildings. Pride of place goes to two bronze equestrian **statues** in the central Piazza Cavalli, the work of the 17th-century sculptor Francesco Mochi, a pupil of Giam-bologna. Lauded as master-pieces of Baroque sculpture, the statues represent Alessandro Farnese, a soldier of fortune, and his son, Ranuccio: both were rulers of 16th-century Piacenza.

Behind the statues is the red-brick **Palazzo del Comune**, also known as "Il Gotico", an evocatively battlemented Lombard-Gothic palace begun at the end of the 13th century. It is one of Italy's most beautiful medieval buildings.

The **Duomo**, at the end of Via XX Settembre, has a rather leaden Lombard-Romanesque exterior (begun in 1122), and a 14th-century campanile. The interior features Guercino's painted cupola and medieval frescoes that adorn the apse and transepts. There are also frescoed saints near the main door, painted to resemble members of the congregation.

The **Museo Civico** offers an eclectic mixture of sculpture and paintings – the star among these is the *Madonna and Child with John the Baptist* by Botticelli (1444–1510). There is also an armoury and archaeology section. The highlight here is the so-called *Fegato di Piacenza*, an Etruscan bronze representation of the sheep livers once used by priests for divination, inscribed with deities' names.

🏛 Museo Civico
Palazzo Farnese, Piazza Cittadella. 🕐 *0523 32 82 70.* ⏰ *Tue –Sun.* ⬤ *public hols.* 🖼

Castell'Arquato ❷

Piacenza. 🏛 *4,500.* 🚌 ℹ *Viale Remondini 1 (0523 80 30 91).* 🛒 *Mon.*

Tucked into the folded hills between Fidenza and Piacenza, Castell'Arquato is one of the prettiest villages in the countryside south of the Po. Day visitors come at the weekends to escape Emilia's larger cities, thronging the restaurants and bars around the beautiful **Piazza Matteotti**. The best medieval building on the piazza is the 13th-century **Palazzo Pretorio**, a Romanesque basilica. The impressive **Rocca Viscontea** (14th century), a former fortress, is on Piazza del Municipio. It is partly closed for restoration. The village's hilltop site offers good views, particularly over the verdant Arda valley to the east.

Fidenza ❸

Parma. 🏛 *23,000.* 🚉 🚌 ℹ *Piazza Duomo 2 (0524 840 47).* 🛒 *Wed & Sat.*

Like many towns hugging the line of the Po, Fidenza owed its early prominence to the Via Aemilia (the old Roman road). The town assumed greater importance as a medieval way station for pilgrims en route to Rome. Today Fidenza is visited for its superb **Duomo** on Piazza Duomo (13th century), a composite piece of architecture that embraces Lombard, Gothic and transi-tional Romanesque elements. The most immediately eye-catching feature is the opulent façade, probably created by the craftsmen who worked with Benedetto Antelami on Parma's Duomo. Inside, the walls are dotted with fragments of medieval frescoes, while the crypt contains the relics of San Donnino, the Duomo's patron.

Detail from façade of Duomo in Fidenza

Interior of Parma Baptistry

Parma ➍

🏠 175,000. 🚇 🚌 🚏 Via Melloni 1 (0521 21 88 89). 🗓 Wed & Sat; Thu (flea market).

FEW ITALIAN TOWNS are as prosperous as Parma, not only a byword for fine food and good living but also a treasure trove of excellent paintings, superlative sculpture and fine medieval buildings. It boasts one of Italy's top opera houses and a panoply of elegant shops and first-rate bars and restaurants.

The Lombard-Romanesque **Duomo** on Piazza Duomo, among the greatest in northern Italy, is renowned for the painting that fills its main cupola, the *Assumption* (1526–30) by Antonio da Correggio. The nave is adorned with the work of Correggio's pupils. The south transept features a carved frieze of *The Deposition* (1178) by Benedetto Antelami, who was also responsible for much of the exquisite **Baptistry** (1196) just south of the cathedral. The reliefs inside and outside the latter – particularly those describing the months of the year – are among the most important of their age in Italy.

East of the Duomo is the church of **San Giovanni Evangelista** (rebuilt 1498–1510) whose dome features a fresco (c.1520) of the *Vision of St John at Patmos* by Correggio. Frescoes by Parmigianino can be seen here and in the 16th-century church of **Madonna della Steccata** on Via Dante.

🏛 Palazzo Pilotta
Piazzale della Pilotta 15. **Galleria** 📞 0521 23 33 09. 🗓 daily. ⬤ 1 Jan, 1 May, 25 Dec. 🎟 **Museo** 📞 0521 23 37 18. 🗓 daily. ⬤ as above. 🎟

This vast palace was built for the Farnese family during the 1500s and rebuilt after bomb damage from World War II. It comprises several parts, including the **Teatro Farnese** (1628), a copy of Palladio's ravishing theatre in Vicenza, built entirely of wood.

Both Correggio and Parmigianino are represented in the palace's **Galleria Nazionale**, which also houses works by Fra Angelico, El Greco and Bronzino, and two paintings by Ludovico Carracci: the *Apostles at the Sepulchre* and the *Funeral of the Virgin* (both late 16th century).

The **Museo Archeologico Nazionale**, on the lower floor, has exhibits from Velleia, an Etruscan necropolis, and from prehistoric sites in the hills around Parma.

🏛 Camera di Correggio
Via Melloni. 📞 0521 23 33 09. 🗓 daily am. ⬤ 1 Jan, 1 May, 25 Dec. 🎟 🚻

Originally the refectory of the Benedictine convent of San Paolo, this room was frescoed by Correggio in 1518 with mythological scenes.

Campanile and Baptistry in Parma

THE MAKING OF PARMESAN CHEESE AND PARMA HAM

No cheese is as famous or as vital to Italy's cuisine as Parmesan *(Parmigiano)*. There are two types: the superior Parmigiano-Reggiano and the lower-quality Grana. The cheese is made using techniques that have barely altered in centuries. Partially skimmed milk is added to whey, to promote fermentation, and rennet is used to curdle the milk. The cheese is then salted and shaped. Parmesan is not only used in cooking but is delicious eaten on its own, or with pears – an Italian speciality.

Shop selling Parmesan cheese and Parma ham

Parma ham owes its excellence to techniques perfected over many years and to the special conditions in which it is cured. It is made from pigs fattened on whey left over from the making of Parmesan cheese. The meat has a character that requires little more than salt and pepper to produce the famous *prosciutto crudo*. The breezy hills of Langhirino, south of Parma, are ideal for curing the hams, which are aged for up to ten months. Each ham is branded with the five-pointed crown of the old Duchy of Parma.

Flora by Carlo Cignani (1628–1719) in the Galleria Estense in Modena

Modena ⑤

🏛 *175,000.* FS 🚌 ℹ️ *Piazza Grande 17 (059 20 66 60).* 🏛 *Mon.*

To MOST ITALIANS Modena means fast cars, for both Ferrari and Maserati have factories in its industrial outskirts, and opera, since this is the birthplace of Luciano Pavarotti. Monuments to an earlier age, however, make this one of Emilia's most enticing historic destinations. A thriving colony since Roman times, the city rose to medieval prominence on the back of its broad agricultural hinterland and the arrival in 1598 of the d'Este nobles from Ferrara. This family continued to rule the city until the 18th century.

🔒 Duomo

Corso Duomo. 📞 *059 21 60 78.* ⏰ *daily.*

Modena's superlative **Duomo** rises alongside the old Roman Via Aemilia (now Via Emilia). One of the region's greatest Romanesque buildings, it was founded by Countess Matilda of Tuscany, ruler of Modena in the 11th century. It was designed by Lanfranco and dedicated to San Geminiano,

the city's patron saint, whose stone coffin lies under the choir. Its most noticeable feature is the **Torre Ghirlandina** (Apr–Oct: 10am–1pm, 3–7pm Sun), a perilously leaning tower begun at the same time as the Duomo and completed two centuries later. It once housed the *Secchia*, a wooden bucket whose 1325 theft from Bologna allegedly sparked a war between the two cities. It also inspired Tassoni's 17th-century mock epic poem *La Secchia Rapita* (The Stolen Bucket), and became the symbol of a rivalry between the cities.

The large reliefs on the Duomo's impressive main (west) façade are the work of the mysterious 12th-century sculptor Wiligelmus.

The highlight of the rather severe interior is a large carved *tribuna* (rood screen) decorated with 12th-century scenes from the Passion.

🏛 Palazzo dei Musei

Largo di Porta Sant'Agostino 337.
Galleria Estense 📞 *059 22 21 45.* ⏰ *Tue–Sun (Wed, Thu & Sun am only).* ● *1 Jan, 1 May, 25 Dec.* ♿
Biblioteca Estense 📞 *059 22 22 48.* ⏰ *Mon–Sat am.* ● *public hols.*
Northwest of the Duomo, and reached through an attractive warren of old streets, is the Palazzo dei Musei. Formerly an arsenal and workhouse, it is now home to the city's best museums and galleries. Its finest section is the **Galleria Estense**, given over to the d'Este private art collection, which was transferred here when the city of Ferrara, the family's former dominion, became part of the Papal States. Most of the paintings are by Emilian

and Ferrarese artists (notably Reni and the Carracci) but there are also works by Bernini, Velázquez, Tintoretto and Veronese.

Among the permanent displays in the **Biblioteca Estense**, the d'Este Library, are a 1481 edition of Dante's *Divine Comedy*, and dozens of fascinating maps and diplomatic letters, many dating back centuries. A map dated 1501 was among the first to show the 1492 voyage by Columbus to the New World. The jewel of the collection is the magnificent illuminated Borso d'Este Bible, with gloriously decorated pages containing over 1,200 miniatures by 15th-century artists of the Ferrara school, most notably Taddeo Crivelli and Franco Russi.

The Torre Ghirlandina in Modena

ENVIRONS: The **Ferrari** factory, 20 km (12 miles) to the south, was founded by Enzo Ferrari in 1945. The FIAT-owned manufacturer now produces around 2,500 cars annually. The **Galleria Ferrari** has a small exhibition featuring memorabilia, a reconstruction of the founder's study, classic engines and many vintage cars.

🏛 Galleria Ferrari

Via Dino Ferrari 43, Maranello.
📞 *0536 94 32 04.* ⏰ *Tue–Sun.* ● *1 Jan, 25 Dec.* ♿

Ferrari 250 SWB, produced between 1959 and 1962

Ferrara ❻

🏠 140,000. 🚂 🚌 ℹ️ Castello Estense, Largo Castello (0532 20 93 70). 🗓️ Mon & Fri.

THE D'ESTE DYNASTY has left an indelible mark on Ferrara, one of the region's greatest walled towns. The noble family took control of the town under Nicolò II in the late 13th century, holding power until 1598, when the family was forced by the papacy to move to Modena.

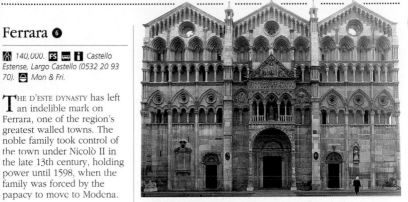

Façade of the Duomo in Ferrara

♟ Castello Estense

Largo Castello. 🎧 0532 29 92 33. ◯ Tue–Sun. ● public hols. 🏷️
The family's dynastic seat, with its moats, towers and battlements (begun 1385), looms over the town centre. Ferrante and Giulio d'Este were

The impressive medieval Castello Estense in Ferrara

incarcerated in its draughty dungeons for plotting to overthrow Alfonso I d'Este. Parisina d'Este, wife of the ruthless Nicolò III, was executed here for having an affair with Ugo, her illegitimate stepson.

🏛 Palazzo del Comune

Piazza Municipale.
Bronze statues of Nicolò III and Borso d'Este, one of Nicolò's reputed 27 children, adorn this medieval palace (begun 1243). Both are copies of the 15th-century originals by Leon Battista Alberti.

🏛 Museo della Cattedrale

Via San Romano. 🎧 0532 20 74 49. ◯ Tue–Sun. ● Mon, public hols. **Donation.**
Ferrara's 12th-century Duomo is a Romanesque-Gothic hybrid designed by Wiligelmus. Fine reliefs on the façade depict

scenes from the Last Judgment. The excellent **museum** (in a deconsecrated church opposite the cathedral) contains a fine set of marble reliefs of the *Labours of the Months* (late 12th century), two painted organ shutters (1469) of *St George* and the *Annunciation* by Cosmè Tura, and the *Madonna of the Pomegranate* (1408) by Jacopo della Quercia.

🏛 Palazzo Schifanoia

Via Scandiana 23. 🎧 0532 641 78. ◯ Tue–Sun. ● public hols. 🏷️
This d'Este summer retreat, begun in 1385, is famous for its Salone dei Mesi (Room of the Months), decorated with beautiful 15th-century murals by Tura and other Ferrarese painters with scenes of the different months. The commissioner, Borso d'Este, appears in many of the panels.

🏛 Museo Archeologico Nazionale

Palazzo di Ludovico il Moro, Via XX Settembre 122. 🎧 0532 662 99. ◯ Tue–Sun. ● public hols. 🏷️ ♿
The most interesting exhibits here are artifacts that were excavated from Spina, a Greco-Etruscan trading post near Comacchio on the Po Delta.

🏛 Palazzo dei Diamanti

Palazzo dei Diamanti, Corso Ercole d'Este 21. 🎧 0532 20 58 44. ◯ Tue–Sun am. ● 1 Jan, 1 May, 25 Dec. 🏷️
Named after the diamond motifs on its façade, this palace houses a modern art gallery, a museum devoted to the Risorgimento, and the Pinacoteca Nazionale, which contains works from leading exponents of the local Renaissance school.

THE D'ESTE FAMILY DYNASTY

During their medieval heyday, the d'Este family presided over one of Europe's leading courts, combining the roles of blood-crazed despots with enlightened Renaissance patrons. Nicolò III, for example, had his wife and her lover brutally murdered. Alfonso I (1503–34) married Lucrezia Borgia, descendant of one of Italy's most notorious families, while Ercole I (1407–1505) attempted to poison a nephew who tried to usurp him (and eventually had him executed). At the same time the d'Este court attracted writers like Petrarch, Tasso and Ariosto, and painters such as Mantegna, Titian and Bellini. Ercole I also rebuilt Ferrara, creating one of Europe's finest Renaissance cities.

Portrait of Alfonso I d'Este by Titian (c.1485–1576)

Street-by-Street: Bologna ❼

Detail of façade from San Petronio

THE HISTORIC city centre of Bologna is a handsome ensemble of brick buildings and charming porticoed streets. Medieval palaces are clustered around the two central squares, Piazza Maggiore and Piazza del Nettuno, flanked to the south by the churches of San Petronio and San Domenico. The university of Bologna is the oldest in Europe and the venerable Archiginnasio was its first official building. Further afield, the skyline is etched by the Asinelli and Garisenda towers, and by the campanile of Santo Stefano.

Fontana di Nettuno
The famous Neptune fountain (1566) was designed by Tommaso Laureti and decorated with magnificent bronze figures by Giambologna.

The Palazzo del Podestà (13th century) was remodelled in 1484.

Tourist information

Railway station
↑ Ferrara

Modena ←

VIA UGO BASSI

VIA DELL'INDIPENDENZA

VIA RIZZOLI

VIA OREFICI

VIA IV NOVEMBRE

PIAZZA MAGGIORE

★ **San Petronio**
The Martyrdom of St Sebastian *(15th century) in the Cappella di San Sebastiano is by Lorenzo Costa of the Ferrarese School.*

Archiginnasio

VIA D'AZEGLIO

VIA DELL'ARCHIGINNASIO

VIA FARINI

Piazza Cavour
The flagged medieval streets and shady porticoed buildings found in this pleasant piazza are typical of Bologna's elegant city centre.

PIAZZA CAVOUR

VIA

VIA GARIBALDI

San Domenico (1251) is dedicated to St Dominic, who is buried here in a magnificent tomb.

STAR SIGHT

★ **San Petronio**

VISITORS' CHECKLIST

400,000. Marconi 9 km (5 miles) NW. Piazza Medaglia d'Oro. Piazza XX Settembre. Piazza Maggiore 6 & Stazione Centrale (051 24 65 41). Fri & Sat. Bologna Music Festival: Mar–Jun; Campionaria: Jun; Bologna Sogna: Jun–Sep.

San Giacomo Maggiore
The Triumph of Death *fresco by Costa (1483–6) adorns the Cappella Bentivoglio.*

San Giacomo Maggiore

Piazza Rossini. 051 22 59 70.
daily.

This Romanesque-Gothic church, begun in 1267 but altered substantially since, is visited mainly for the Cappella Bentivoglio, a superb family chapel founded by Annibale Bentivoglio in 1445 and consecrated in 1486. Pride of place naturally goes to a portrait with subtle characterization of the patrons by Lorenzo Costa (1460–1535), who was also responsible for the frescoes of the *Apocalypse*, the *Madonna Enthroned* and the *Triumph of Death*. The chapel's altarpiece, depicting the *Virgin and Saints with Two Angel Musicians* (1488), is the work of Francesco Francia. The Bentivoglio family is further glorified in the tomb of Anton Galeazzo Bentivoglio (1435) opposite the chapel. It was among the last works of the noted Sienese sculptor, Jacopo della Quercia. The Oratory of Santa Cecilia features frescoes on the lives of Santa Cecilia and San Valeriano by Costa and Francesco Francia (1504–6).

Pinacoteca
Nazionale
Museo di
Anatomia
Umana
Normale

VIA ZAMBONI

VIA BENEDETTO XIV

Ravenna

VIA SAN VITALE

STRADA MAGGIORE

ZZA DI
RTA
GNANA

VIA SANTO STEFANO

Firenze

Torri degli Asinelli e Garisenda
The colossal towers are two of the few remaining towers begun by Bologna's important families in the 12th century.

Abbazia di Santo Stefano
The Fontana di Pilato, or Pilate's fountain, in the courtyard features a basin with Lombard inscriptions from the 8th century.

KEY

– – – Suggested route

0 metres   150
0 yards   150

The Bentivoglio tomb (1435) by Jacopo della Quercia

Exploring Bologna

MONUMENTS TO BOLOGNA's rich cultural heritage are scattered across the city, from the leaning towers and the church of San Petronio in the old centre to the Pinacoteca Nazionale in the university district.

🌃 Torri degli Asinelli e Garisenda

Piazza di Porta Ravegnana. ◯ daily. 🎫
The famous Torri Pendenti, or leaning towers – Torre degli Asinelli and Torre Garisenda – are among the few survivors of the original 200 that once formed the skyline of Bologna. Both were begun in the 12th century, though there were probably earlier towers on the site – Dante mentioned a pair of towers here in his *Inferno*. Torre Garisenda was shortened as a safety measure within only a few years of its construction, and still leans some 3 m (10 ft)

from the vertical. At 97 m (318 ft) tall, Torre Asinelli is the fourth highest tower in Italy after those in Cremona, Siena and Venice. Its 500-step ascent offers fine views over Bologna's pantiled rooftops to the hills beyond.

🏛 Abbazia di Santo Stefano

Via Santo Stefano 24.
🕻 051 22 32 56. ◯ daily.
Santo Stefano is a curious collection of four medieval churches (originally seven) jumbled together under one roof. The 11th-century church of the Crocifisso provides little

Exterior of the Abbazia di Santo Stefano

🏛 SAN PETRONIO

Piazza Maggiore. 🕻 051 22 21 12. ◯ daily. ♿
Dedicated to the city's 5th-century bishop, this church ranks among the greatest of Italy's brick-built medieval buildings. Founded in 1390, it was originally intended to be larger than St Peter's in Rome, but its size was scaled down when the church authorities diverted funds to the nearby Palazzo Archiginnasio. The resulting financial shortfall left the church decidedly lopsided, with a row of columns on its eastern flank that were intended to support an additional internal aisle. The project's financial profligacy, nonetheless, was said to have been instrumental in turning Martin Luther against Catholicism.

The altarpiece of the *Martyrdom of St Sebastian* is from the late Ferrarese School.

The pink and white interior adds to the overall light and airy effect.

The canopied main portal features beautiful biblical reliefs (1425–38) by Jacopo della Quercia.

Gothic Interior
The interior is airy, with graceful pillars supporting the roof. Twenty-two chapels, shielded by screens, open off the nave. In 1547 the Council of Trent (see p168) was temporarily moved here due to the plague.

Entrance

Unfinished upper façade

The meridian line, along the 60th meridian between the north and south poles, was traced in 1655 by the astronomer Gian Domenico Cassini.

The stained glass windows (1464–6) in this chapel are by Jacob of Ulm.

more than a corridor to polygonal San Sepolcro, the most appealing of the quartet. Also dating from the 11th century, its centrepiece is the tomb of St Petronius, a marvellously overstated affair modelled on the Holy Sepulchre of Jerusalem. The courtyard contains the so-called Fontana di Pilato, an 8th-century basin.

Santi Vitale e Agricola dates originally from the 5th century, making it the oldest church in the city. It was rebuilt in the 8th and 11th centuries. Inside are the sarcophagi of Saints Vitalis and Agricola, martyred mainly in the 4th century. Santa Trinità features a small museum of minor paintings and religious artifacts, including wooden statues of the *Adoration of the Magi* painted by Simone dei Crocifissi (c.1370).

Bell tower

Choir Stalls
The exquisite inlaid choir stalls of the Chapel of the Holy Sacrament were made by Raffaello da Brescia in 1521.

�fi Pinacoteca Nazionale

Via delle Belle Arti 56
C 051 243 22.
○ Tue–Sun.
● 1 Jan, 1 May, 15 Aug, 25 Dec.

Bologna's principal art gallery, and one of northern Italy's most important collections, stands on the edge of the city's university district, a bustling area of bars, bookshops and cheap restaurants. The gallery is mainly dedicated to work by Bolognese painters, notably Vitale da Bologna, Guido Reni, Guercino and the Carracci family. Members of the Ferrarese School are also represented, in particular Francesco del Cossa and Ercole de' Roberti. The two highlights are Perugino's *Madonna in Glory* (c.1491) and Raphael's famous *Ecstasy of St Cecilia*, painted around 1515, both artists having worked in Bologna.

The *Ecstasy of St Cecilia* (c.1515) by Raphael in Bologna's Pinacoteca Nazionale

�fi Museo di Anatomia Umana Normale

Palazzo Poggi, Via Zamboni 33. **C** 051 209 93 69. ○ Mon–Fri. ● 25 Dec, 1 Jan, Easter, 1 May, public hols.

Although well off the standard tourist itineraries, the Museum of Human Anatomy is one of the more memorable of Bologna's smaller museums. The collection includes occasionally gruesome visceral waxworks and numerous models of organs, limbs and flayed bodies. Sculpted rather than made from casts, they have an artistic as well as scientific appeal. The models were used as medical teaching aids until the 19th century. The contents of the museum recently moved to Palazzo Poggi, which also contains the Museo Cartageographica.

⋔ San Domenico

Piazza di San Domenico 13.
C 051 640 04 11. ○ daily.
Bologna's San Domenico can lay claim to being the most important of Italy's many Dominican churches. Begun in 1221, after St Dominic's death, it was built to house the body of the saint, who died here and lies buried in a tomb known as the Arca di San Domenico. A magnificent composite work, the tomb's statues were executed by Nicola Pisano; the reliefs of scenes from the *Life of St Dominic* were the work of Nicola Pisano and his assistants; the canopy (1473) is attributed to Nicola di Bari; while the figures of the angels and Saints Proculus and Petronius are early works by Michelangelo. The reliquary (1383) behind the sarcophagus contains St Dominic's head.

Arca di San Domenico in the Basilica di San Domenico

Fresco of Malatesta and St Sigismund (1451) by Piero della Francesca in the Tempio Malatestiano, Rimini

Faenza ⑧

Ravenna. 🚹 54,000. FS 🚌
🅘 Piazza del Popolo 1 (0546 252 31).
🏷 Tue, Thu & Sat.

FAENZA IS SYNONYMOUS with the **faïence** ceramic-ware to which it gave its name. Renowned across Europe for over 500 years, the pottery, with its distinctive blue and ochre colouring, is still made in countless small factories around the town.

The highlight of Faenza is the **Museo Internazionale delle Ceramiche**, one of the largest ceramic collections in Italy. Its exhibits feature not only examples of local ware, but also pottery from other countries and other periods, including Roman ceramics and medieval majolica. There is also a section devoted to the modern ceramic art of Picasso, Matisse and Chagall.

🏛 Museo Internazionale delle Ceramiche
Viale Baccarini 19. 🔇 0546 212 40.
🔾 Tue–Sun. ⬤ 1 Jan, 1 May, 15 Aug, 25 Dec. 🔾 🔾

Rimini ⑨

🚹 130,000. FS 🚌 🅘 Piazza Fellini
3 (0541 569 02). 🏷 Wed & Sat.

RIMINI WAS ONCE a quaint seaside resort, whose innocent charms were celebrated in the early films of Federico Fellini (1920–93), the

director born and raised here. Today it is the largest beach resort in Europe. The seafront, which stretches unbroken for almost 15 km (9 miles), is lined with clubs, restaurants and bars. The crowded beaches are clean and well groomed, though entrance fees are charged at the private beaches.

Rimini's old quarter, by contrast, is pleasantly quiet. Its charming cobbled streets gather around **Piazza Cavour**, dominated by the 14th-century **Palazzo del Podestà**. The town's finest building is the **Tempio Malatestiano**, built as a Franciscan church but converted in 1450 by Leon Battista Alberti, the great Florentine architect, into one of Italy's great Renaissance monuments. The work was commissioned by Sigismondo Malatesta (1417–68), a descendant of Rimini's ruling medieval family, and reputedly one of the most debauched and evil men of

his time. Ostensibly designed as a chapel, the Tempio eventually became little more than a monument to Malatesta. Inside there are sculptures by Agostino di Duccio and a fresco (1451) by Piero della Francesca of Malatesta kneeling before St Sigismund (1451).

The entwined initials of Malatesta and his fourth wife, Isotta degli Atti, provide a recurring decorative motif, and there are reliefs depicting scenes of bacchanalian excess and oddities such as strangely posed elephants (a Malatesta family emblem). All this led Pope Pius II to condemn the building as "a temple of devil-worshippers", and to burn Malatesta's effigy for what the papal charge against him described as acts of "murder, violation, adultery, incest, sacrilege and perjury".

ENVIRONS: Further along the coast, the resorts become relatively quieter. **Cesenatico**, 18 km (11 miles) north, offers all the usual facilities yet the beaches are less crowded.

🏛 Tempio Malatestiano
Via IV Novembre. 🔇 0541 242 44.
🔾 daily. 🔾

Ravenna ⑩

🚹 90,000. FS 🚌 🅘 Via Salara
8–12 (0544 354 04). 🏷 Wed & Sat.

MOST PEOPLE VISIT Ravenna for its superb mosaics from the Byzantine period (see pp260–61), but the town itself is a surprisingly pleasant medley of old streets, fine shops and peaceful piazzas.

Façade of the Renaissance Tempio Malatestiano in Rimini

Piazza del Popolo, Ravenna's central square

The **Museo Nazionale** features a wide range of icons, paintings and archaeological displays. The best place to relax and take a break from sightseeing is Piazza del Popolo, a lovely ensemble of medieval buildings.

🏛 **Museo Nazionale**
Via Fiandrini. ☎ 0544 344 24.
🕐 Tue – Sun. 🎦 ♿

Po Delta ⓫

Ferrara. 🚉 Ferrara Ostellata.
🚌 to Goro or Gorino. ⛴ from Porto Garibaldi, Goro & Gorino.
ℹ Via Buonafede 12, Comacchio (0533 31 01 47).

THE PO IS ITALY'S longest river. Its vast basin covers some 15 per cent of the country and supports around a third of the nation's population. Although ravaged in many places by industrial pollution, at its finest it offers beautifully subtle landscapes – rows of poplar trees across misty fields and long views over soft brown soils. There are also vistas over the shifting sands of its vast delta, an estuary of marshes, dunes and islands.

The Po Delta is known to naturalists as the "Italian Camargue". There are plans to turn the entire region – some 30,000 ha (74,000 acres) – into a national park that would stretch from the edge of the Venetian lagoon to the coastal pine woods that lie around Ravenna.

Wetland areas such as the **Valli di Comacchio** north of Ravenna are already nature reserves, a winter home to thousands of breeding and migrating birds. Ornithologists gather here to

Hen harrier, found in the Po Delta

see gulls, coots, bean geese and black terns, and far rarer species such as the white egret, hen harrier and pygmy cormorant. **Comacchio**, the nearest settlement, is one of several fishing villages dotted around the area. Its most famous catch is eels, often caught using methods like water gates that date back as far as Roman times.

Other nature reserves include the **Bosco della Mesola**, a tract of ancient woodland planted by the Etruscans and cared for by generations of monks. You can walk or cycle through it, with excellent opportunities for seeing large herds of deer.

For a good look at the entire region, follow the N309 – part of the old Via Romea pilgrimage trail to Rome – that runs north to south through some 100 km (62 miles) of the proposed park. Numerous smaller lanes branch off into the wilderness. There are also boat trips to some of the delta's more remote corners: key departure points include the villages of Ca' Tiepolo, Ca' Vernier and Taglio di Po.

The peaceful landscape along the banks of the river in the Po Delta

A Tour of Ravenna

Ravenna rose to power in the 1st century BC under the Emperor Augustus, who built a port and naval base at nearby Classe, currently the site of a major excavation project. As Rome's power declined, Ravenna was made the capital of the Western Empire (AD 402), a role it retained during the Ostrogoth and Byzantine rule in the 5th and 6th centuries. Ravenna is renowned for its early Christian mosaics – the town had converted to Christianity in the 2nd century AD. The mosaics span the years of Roman and Byzantine rule, offering comparisons between Classically inspired designs and later Byzantine motifs.

Mosaic detail from San Vitale

The Good Shepherd ②
This mosaic adorns the tiny Mausoleo di Galla Placidia. Begun in 430, this exquisite building probably never received the remains of Placidia, wife of a barbarian emperor.

San Vitale ①
San Vitale's apse mosaics (526–547) show Christ, San Vitale (being handed a martyr's crown), two angels and Bishop Ecclesius, who began the church (see pp46–7).

Baptism of Jesus ③
The 5th-century Battistero Neoniano (Neonian Baptistry) is named after the bishop who may have commissioned its decoration, including this beautiful mosaic. It was built near the remains of a Roman bathhouse and is Ravenna's oldest monument.

Battistero degli Ariani ⑤

The cupola of this late 5th-century baptistry has a mosaic showing the Apostles ringed around a centrepiece depicting the Baptism of Christ.

VISITORS' CHECKLIST

San Vitale & Mausoleo di Galla Placidia, Via Fiandrini. ☎ *0544 21 99 38.* ⏰ *Apr–Sep: 9am–7pm daily; Oct–Mar: 9:30am–4:30pm (last adm: 15 mins before closing).* ● *1 Jan, 25 Dec.* ♿ **Battistero Neoniano**, Via Battistero. ☎ *0544 21 85 59.* ⏰ *as above.* ● *as above.* ♿ **Sant'Apollinare Nuovo**, Via di Roma. ☎ *0544 390 81.* ⏰ *as above.* ● *as above.* ♿ **Tomba di Dante**, Via Dante Alighieri. ☎ *0544 302 52.* ⏰ *Apr–Sep: 9am–7pm daily; Oct–Mar: 9am–noon, 2–5pm daily (last adm: 15 mins before closing).* ● *1 Jan, 25 Dec.* ♿ **Battistero degli Ariani**, Via degli Ariani. ☎ *0544 344 24.* ⏰ *9am–7pm daily (Oct–Mar: to 1:30pm) (last adm: 15 mins before closing).* ● *1 Jan, 1 May.* ♿ *A combined ticket is available. For reservations (mandatory for Mausoleo di Galla Placidia):* ☎ *800 303 999.* Ⓦ *www.ravennavisitcard.com*

Sant'Apollinare Nuovo ⑥

This glorious 6th-century church, named after Ravenna's first bishop, is dominated by two rows of mosaics. Both show processions of martyrs and virgins bearing gifts for Christ and the Virgin.

Tomba di Dante ④

Dante's wanderings around Italy after his exile from Florence eventually brought him to Ravenna, where he died in 1321. A lamp in his sepulchre (1780) is fed by oil given by the city of Florence.

KEY

— — — Suggested route

🅿 Parking

ℹ Tourist information

0 metres	200
0 yards	200

FLORENCE

*F*LORENCE IS A VAST AND BEAUTIFUL *monument to the Renaissance, the artistic and cultural reawakening of the 15th century. Writers such as Dante, Petrarch and Machiavelli contributed to its proud literary heritage, though it was the paintings and sculptures of artists such as Botticelli, Michelangelo and Donatello that turned the city into one of the world's greatest artistic capitals.*

While the Etruscans had long settled the hills around Fiesole, Florence first sprang to life as a Roman colony in 59 BC. Captured by the Lombards in the 6th century, the city later emerged from the Dark Ages as an independent city state. By the 13th century a burgeoning trade in wool and textiles, backed by a powerful banking sector, had turned the city into one of Italy's leading powers. Political control was wielded first by the guilds, and later by the Florentine Republic. In time, power passed to leading noble families, of which the most influential were the Medici, a hugely wealthy banking dynasty. Florence, and later Tuscany, remained under the family's almost unbroken sway for three centuries. During this time the city was at the cultural and intellectual heart of Europe, its cosmopolitan atmosphere and wealthy patrons providing the impetus for a period of unparalleled artistic growth. Artists, sculptors and architects flocked to the city, filling its streets, churches and palaces with some of the world's greatest Renaissance works. By 1737 the Medici had died out, leaving the city under Austrian (and briefly Napoleonic) control until Italian Unification in 1860. Between 1865 and 1871 Florence was the capital of the new Kingdom of Italy. In recent history its streets and artistic heritage were ravaged by the Arno floods of November 1966.

Florentines strolling in front of Ponte Vecchio (1345), the old bridge lined with shops spanning the Arno

◁ **The dome of Florence's Duomo, completed in 1436, designed by Brunelleschi**

Exploring Florence

Historic Florence is a surprisingly compact area, and the majority of the sights described on the following pages can easily be reached on foot. Most visitors head for the Duomo, the city's geographical and historical focus, ideally placed to explore the Campanile, Baptistry and Museo dell'Opera del Duomo. To the south is Piazza della Signoria, long the city's political heart, flanked by the Palazzo Vecchio, Florence's town hall, and the Uffizi, one of Italy's leading art galleries. To the east lies the church of Santa Croce, home to frescoes by Giotto and the tombs of some of Florence's greatest men. To the west stands Santa Maria Novella, the city's other great church, also adorned with fresco-filled chapels. Across the Ponte Vecchio and the Arno – the river that bisects the city – is the district of Oltrarno, dominated by Santo Spirito and the vast Pitti Palace, containing galleries with works by great Renaissance artists including Raphael and Titian.

Bell tower, Palazzo Vecchio

GETTING AROUND

Florence has an excellent bus service, including electric buses, making public transport both convenient and fast. The compact city centre, which is closed to traffic, is easily negotiated on foot.

KEY

■ Street-by-Street: Around San Marco pp266–7

□ Street-by-Street: Around the Duomo pp270–71

■ Street-by-Street: Around Piazza della Repubblica pp284–5

■ Street-by-Street: Around Oltrarno pp292–3

FS Railway station

P Parking

i Tourist information

— City walls

Ponte Vecchio with Ponte Santa Trinita in the foreground

LOCATOR MAP

SIGHTS AT A GLANCE

Churches

Cappella Brancacci
 pp290–91 **25**
Cappelle Medicee **19**
Convento di San Marco **2**
Duomo and Baptistry
 pp272–4 **7**
Ognissanti **24**
Orsanmichele **8**
Santissima Annunziata **3**
Santa Croce **10**
Santa Felicita **28**
San Lorenzo **18**
Santa Maria Novella **21**
San Miniato al Monte **30**
Santo Spirito **26**

Buildings, Monuments and Squares

Mercato Centrale **20**
Palazzo Antinori **22**
Palazzo Davanzati **16**
Palazzo Rucellai **23**
Palazzo Strozzi **17**
Palazzo Vecchio **15**
Piazza della Signoria **14**
Piazzale Michelangelo **29**
Ponte Vecchio **12**
Spedale degli Innocenti **5**

Museums and Galleries

Bargello **9**
Galleria dell'Accademia **1**
Museo Archeologico **4**
Museo dell'Opera del
 Duomo **6**
Museo di Storia della
 Scienza **11**
Palazzo Pitti pp294–5 **27**
Uffizi pp278–81 **13**

SEE ALSO

- **Street Finder** pp299–303
- **Where to Stay** pp557–9
- **Where to Eat** pp591–3

0 metres		500
0 yards		500

Street-by-Street: Around San Marco

THE BUILDINGS in this part of Florence once stood on the fringes of the city, serving as stables and barracks. The Medici menagerie of lions, elephants and giraffes was housed here. Today it is a student quarter and the streets are often busy with young people attending the university or the Accademia di Belle Arti, the world's oldest art school, founded in 1563.

Santissima Annunziata
This fine Renaissance church has an opulent Baroque interior ❸

Palazzo Pandolfini was designed by Raphael in 1516.

★ **Convento di San Marco**
The Annunciation (c.1445) is an example of Fra Angelico's exquisite fresco decoration ❷

Sant'Apollonia features a fresco of the *Cenacolo* (Last Supper) by Andrea del Castagno (1450).

VIA DELLA DOGANA

VIA CAVOUR

VIA GIORGIO LA PIRA

VIA DEGLI ARAZZIERI

PIAZZA DI SAN MARCO

VIA CESARE BATTISTI

VIA SAN GALLO

VIA RICASOLI

PIAZZA DELLA SANTISSIMA ANNUNZIATA

Luigi Cherubini (1760–1842), the Florentine composer, trained at the Conservatorio.

KEY

– – – Suggested route

Galleria dell'Accademia
This detail is from a 14th-century altarpiece, the Madonna and Saints, *by an unnamed master* ❶

| 0 metres | 50 |
| 0 yards | 50 |

Giambologna's statue of Duke Ferdinando I was cast by Tacca in 1608.

LOCATOR MAP
*See Florence Street Finder
map 2*

Part of the 15th-century *Cassone Adimari* by Lo Scheggia in the Accademia

Spedale degli Innocenti
*Opened in 1444, the city
orphanage by Brunelleschi
was decorated with
cameos by Andrea
della Robbia* ❺

**The Giardino
dei Semplici**
was opened
in 1543.

VIA GINO CAPPONI

**Museo
Archeologico**
*Many of the
Etruscan objects
in the museum
were originally
in the Medici
collections* ❹

STAR SIGHTS

★ **Convento di
San Marco**

★ **Galleria
dell'Accademia**

Galleria dell'Accademia ❶

Via Ricasoli 60. **Map** 2 D4. ⬛ 055
238 86 09 (information); 055 29 48
83 (reservations). ⬜ 8:15am–
6:50pm Tue–Sun (extended hours in
the summer). ⬛ Mon, public hols.
⬛ ⬛ ⬛

THE ACADEMY OF FINE ARTS,
founded in 1563, was the
first school established in
Europe specifically to
teach the techniques of
drawing, painting and
sculpture. The art
collection displayed
here was formed in
1784 to provide
material for
students to study
and copy.

The most
famous work is
Michelangelo's
David (1504), a
colossal (5.2 m/
17 ft) nude of the
biblical hero who
killed the giant Goliath.
The sculpture was com-
missioned by the city for
Piazza della Signoria, but
it was moved to the
Accademia for safe-
keeping in 1873. One
copy now stands in its
original position (*see
pp282–3*) and a second
is on Piazzale Michel-
angelo. The *David*
established Michelangelo,
at the age of 29, as the
foremost sculptor of his time.

Michelangelo's other masterpieces in the Accademia
include the *Quattro Prigioni*
(the Four Prisoners), sculpted
between 1521 and 1523 and
intended to adorn the tomb
of Pope Julius II. The statues

Michelangelo's *David*

were presented to the Medici
family in 1564 by the artist's
nephew, Leonardo. The
muscular figures struggling to
free themselves from the stone
are among the most dramatic
of Michelangelo's works. The
statues were then moved to the
Grotta Grande in the Boboli
Gardens, where casts of the
originals can now be seen.

The Accademia also contains
an important collection of
paintings by 15th- and 16th-
century Florentine artists,
among them Filippino
Lippi, Fra Bartolomeo,
Bronzino and Ridolfo del
Ghirlandaio. The major
works include the
Madonna del Mare
(Madonna of the
Sea), attributed
to Botticelli
(1445–1510), and *Venus
and Cupid* by Jacopo
Pontormo (1494–1556),
based on a preparatory
drawing by Michel-
angelo. Also here is an
elaborately painted
wooden chest, the
Cassone Adimari
(1440–45) by Lo
Scheggia, the step-
brother of Masaccio.
Originally part of
a wealthy bride's
trousseau, it is
decorated with
details of
Florentine life,
clothing and
architecture. A scene of the
bridal party appears on the
chest in front of the Baptistry.

The Salone della Toscana
(Tuscany Room) features
more modest paintings and
sculptures by 19th-century
members of the Accademia
and plaster models by the
sculptor, Lorenzo Bartolini.

The light and airy former library, designed by Michelozzo

Convento di San Marco ❷

Piazza di San Marco. **Map** 2 D4. 📞 *055 28 76 28 (information); 055 29 48 83 (reservations).* ⏰ *7am–noon, 4–8pm.* 🚻 📷 **Museo di San Marco** 📞 *055 238 86 08.* ⏰ *8:30am–1:50pm (later Sat, Sun).* ⚫ *1 Jan, 1 May, 25 Dec, 2nd & 4th Mon and 1st, 2nd & 5th Sun of each month.* 💷 🚫

THE CONVENT OF SAN MARCO was founded in the 13th century and enlarged in 1437 when Dominican monks from nearby

Fiesole moved there at the invitation of Cosimo il Vecchio. He paid a considerable sum to have the convent rebuilt by his favourite architect, Michelozzo, whose simple cloisters and cells provide the setting for a remarkable series of devotional frescoes (c.1438–45) by Florentine painter and Dominican friar Fra Angelico. The convent and art collections form the **Museo di San Marco**.

Michelozzo's magnificent **Chiostro di Sant'Antonino** was named after the convent's first prior, Antonino Pierozzi (1389–1459), who later became the Archbishop of Florence. Most of the faded frescoes in this cloister describe scenes from the saint's life by Bernardino Poccetti. The panels in the corner are by Fra Angelico. A door in the right side of the cloister leads to the **Ospizio dei Pellegrini** (Pilgrims' Hospice). Today it houses the museum's free-standing paintings, including two famous master-

A detail from Fra Angelico's poignant *Deposition* (c. 1440)

pieces: Fra Angelico's moving *Deposition* (c.1435–40), an altarpiece painted for the church of Santa Trinità, and the *Madonna dei Linaiuoli*, commissioned by the Linaiuoli (flaxworkers' guild) in 1433.

In the courtyard, right of the convent's former bell, is the vaulted **Sala Capitolare** (Chapter House), decorated with a noted but over-restored *Crucifixion and Saints* (1440) painted by Fra Angelico.

Covering one wall of the small **Refettorio** (refectory) is a fresco of the *Last Supper* (c.1480) by Domenico Ghirlandaio. Stairs from the courtyard lead to the first floor, where you suddenly see Fra Angelico's *Annunciation* (c.1445), thought by many to be among the city's most beautiful Renaissance paintings. Beyond, ranged around three sides of the cloister, are the **Dormitory Cells**. These 44 tiny monastic cells are frescoed with scenes from *The Life of Christ* by Fra Angelico and assistants (1439–45). The cells numbered 1 to 11 are generally attributed to Fra Angelico personally, as is the lovely fresco of the Madonna and Saints on the right of the corridor *(see p28)*.

Cells 12–14 were once occupied by Savonarola, the zealous Dominican monk who became Prior of San Marco in 1491. Among other deeds, Savonarola incited Florentines to rebel against the Medici and was responsible for the burning of many works of art. Denounced as a heretic, he was burned at the stake in Piazza della Signoria in 1498.

Along the third corridor lies an airy colonnaded hall, formerly a public **library** designed by Michelozzo in 1441 for Cosimo il Vecchio. Beyond it lie two cells (38 and 39) which were used by Cosimo when he went on retreat here. Each is decorated with two frescoes (the other cells have only one), and they are both larger than any of the neighbouring rooms.

Fra Angelico's allegorical fresco, the *Mocking of Christ* (c. 1442), showing Jesus blindfolded and being struck by a Roman guard

The Birth of the Virgin (1514) by del Sarto in Santissima Annunziata

Santissima Annunziata ❸

Piazza della Santissima Annunziata.
Map 2 E4. **☎** 055 239 80 34.
◯ 7:30am–12:30pm, 4pm–6:30pm
daily.

FOUNDED BY the Servite order in 1250, the church of the Holy Annunciation was later rebuilt by Michelozzo between 1444 and 1481. Its atrium contains frescoes by the Mannerist artists Rosso Fiorentino, Andrea del Sarto and Jacopo Pontormo. Perhaps the finest of its panels are *The Journey of the Magi* (1511) and *The Birth of the Virgin* (1514) by Andrea del Sarto.

The heavily decorated, dark interior has a frescoed ceiling completed by Pietro Giambelli in 1669. Here is one of the city's most revered shrines, a painting of the Virgin Mary begun by a monk in 1252 but miraculously completed by an angel, according to devout Florentines. Newly-wed couples traditionally visit the shrine (on the left as you enter the church) to present a bouquet of flowers to the Virgin and to pray for a long, fruitful and fecund marriage.

A door from the north transept leads to the **Chiostrino dei Morti** (Cloister of the Dead), so called because it was originally used as a burial ground. Today it is best known for del Sarto's beautiful fresco, *The Madonna del Sacco* (1525).

The church is situated on the northern flank of **Piazza della Santissima Annunziata**, one of the finest Renaissance squares in Florence. Designed by Brunelleschi, the delicate nine-bay arcade fronts the Spedale degli Innocenti to its right, while at the centre of the square stands a bronze equestrian statue of Duke Ferdinando I. Started by Giambologna, it was finished in 1608 by his assistant Pietro Tacca (who designed the square's bronze fountains).

Museo Archeologico ❹

Via della Colonna 36. **Map** 2 F4.
☎ 055 235 75. ◯ 2–7pm Mon,
9am–7pm Tue–Fri, Sun, 9am–2pm
Sat. ● 2nd & 4th Mon and 1st, 3rd
& 5th Sun of each month. ◉ ♿

THE ARCHAEOLOGICAL MUSEUM in Florence is in a palazzo built by Giulio Parigi for the Princess Maria Maddalena de' Medici in 1620. It now exhibits an outstanding collection of Etruscan, Greek, Roman and Egyptian artifacts, although parts of the collection are being restored following the flood in 1966. The first floor contains a splendid series of Etruscan bronzes as well as the famous *Chimera* (4th century BC), a mythical lion with a goat's head imposed on its body and a serpent for a tail. Equally impressive is the 1st-century *Arringatore* bronze

Etruscan warrior, Museo Archeologico

found near Lake Trasimeno in Umbria. It is inscribed with the name of Aulus Metellus. A large section on the second floor is dedicated to Greek vases, notably the famed François Vase, found in an Etruscan tomb near Chiusi.

Spedale degli Innocenti ❺

Piazza della Santissima Annunziata 12.
Map 2 E4. **☎** 055 249 17 08.
◯ 8:30am–2pm Mon, Tue, Thu–Sat.
● public hols. ♿

Part of Brunelleschi's arcaded loggia, Spedale degli Innocenti

NAMED AFTER Herod's biblical Massacre of the Innocents, the "Hospital" opened in 1444 as Europe's first orphanage. Part of the building is still used for this purpose. Brunelleschi's arcaded loggia is decorated with glazed terracotta roundels, added by Andrea della Robbia around 1498, showing babies wrapped in swaddling bands. At the left end of the portico you can see the *rota*, a rotating stone cylinder on which anonymous mothers could place their unwanted children and ring the bell for them to be admitted to the orphanage.

Within the building lie two elegant cloisters: the **Chiostro degli Uomini** (Men's Cloister), built between 1422 and 1445 and decorated with *sgraffito* roosters and cherubs, and the smaller Women's Cloister (1438). A small upstairs gallery contains a handful of fine works, including terracottas by della Robbia and pictures by Botticelli, Piero di Cosimo and Domenico Ghirlandaio.

Street-by-Street: Around the Duomo

WHILE MUCH OF FLORENCE was rebuilt during the Renaissance, the eastern part of the city retains a distinctly medieval feel. With its maze of tiny alleys, it is an area that would still be familiar to Dante (1265–1321), whose birthplace allegedly lay somewhere among these lanes. The poet would recognize the church of Santa Maria de' Cerchi where he first glimpsed Beatrice, as well as the gaunt outlines of the Bargello. He would also be familiar with the Baptistry, one of the city's oldest buildings, though he would not know the Campanile nor the Duomo, whose foundations were laid in the poet's old age.

Stained glass window from the Duomo

★ Duomo and Baptistry
The exteriors of the Duomo and Baptistry are richly decorated with marbles and reliefs, such as this detail from the Duomo's façade ❼

The Loggia del Bigallo (1358) is where abandoned children were once left. They were then sent to foster homes if they remained unclaimed.

PIAZZA DI SAN GIOVANNI

PIAZZA DEL DUOMO

VIA DELL'OCHE

VIA DE' MEDICI

VIA S. ELISABETTA

VIA ROMA

VIA D. SPEZIALI

VIA DE' CALZAIUOLI

VIA DE' CERCHI

V.D. TAVOLINI

V.D. CIMATORI

Orsanmichele
The church's niche carvings depict patron saints of trade guilds, such as this copy of Donatello's St George ❽

V. DE' LAMBERTI

CALIMALA

VIA PORTA ROSSA

VIA DE

KEY

– – – Suggested route

0 metres   100

0 yards   100

Via dei Calzaiuoli, lined with smart shops, is the city's liveliest street.

Piazza della Signoria

Museo dell'Opera del Duomo
Works from the Duomo, Campanile and Baptistry are displayed in this museum **6**

Pegna sells a range of fine wines, oil and honey.

LOCATOR MAP
See Florence Street Finder map 6

Carving from Luca della Robbia's choir loft in the Museo dell'Opera

Badia Fiorentina,
the abbey church founded in 978, is home to *The Virgin Appearing to St Bernard* (1485) by Filippino Lippi.

Casa di Dante,
a restored medieval house, is reputedly Dante's birthplace.

★ **Bargello**
The city's old prison is home to a rich collection of applied arts and sculpture, including this figure of Mercury by Giambologna (1564) **9**

STAR SIGHTS

★ **Duomo and Baptistry**

★ **Bargello**

Museo dell'Opera del Duomo **6**

Piazza del Duomo 9. **Map** 2 D5 (6 E2). **055 230 28 85.** 9am–6:30pm daily (to 1:40pm Sun) (last adm: 40 mins before closing). 25 Dec, 1 Jan, Easter.

THE CATHEDRAL Works Museum has reopened after extensive remodelling and now a series of rooms is dedicated to the history of the Duomo. The main ground-floor room holds statues from Arnolfo di Cambio's workshop which were once placed in the cathedral's niches. Nearby is Donatello's *St John*. A new room contains 14th- and 15th-century religious paintings and reliquaries.

Michelangelo's *Pietà* has pride of place on the staircase. The hooded figure of Nicodemus is widely believed to be a self portrait.

The first room on the upper floor contains two choir lofts, dating to the 1430s, by Luca della Robbia and Donatello. Carved in crisp white marble and decorated with coloured glass and mosaic, both depict children playing musical instruments and dancing. Other works by Donatello in this room are his statue of *La Maddalena* (1455) and several Old Testament figures.

The room to the left contains an exhibition of the tablets which used to decorate the bell tower. A lower level houses examples of the tools used by Brunelleschi's workmen and a copy of di Cambio's original cathedral façade.

Duomo and Baptistry ❼

Sir John Hawkwood by Paolo Uccello, in the Duomo

Rising above the heart of the city, the richly-decorated Duomo – Santa Maria del Fiore – and its orange-tiled dome have become Florence's most famous symbols. Typical of the Florentine determination to lead in all things, the cathedral is Europe's fourth largest church, and to this day it still remains the city's tallest building. The Baptistry, with its celebrated bronze doors, may date back to the 4th century, making it one of Florence's oldest buildings. The Campanile, designed by Giotto in 1334, was completed in 1359, 22 years after his death.

Campanile
At 85 m (276 ft), the Campanile is 6 m (20 ft) shorter than the dome. It is clad in white, green and pink Tuscan marble.

Gothic windows

The Neo-Gothic marble façade echoes the style of Giotto's Campanile, but was only added in 1871–87.

★ Baptistry
Colourful 13th-century mosaics illustrating the Last Judgment decorate the ceiling above the octagonal font, where many famous Florentines, including Dante, were baptized. The doors are by Andrea Pisano (south) and Lorenzo Ghiberti (north, east).

North Doors

East Doors
(See p274)

Main entrance

South Doors

Campanile Reliefs
Copies of reliefs by Andrea Pisano on the Campanile's first storey depict the Creation of Man, and the Arts and the Industries. The originals are kept in the Museo dell'Opera del Duomo (see p271).

The top of the dome offers spectacular views over the city.

★ Dome by Brunelleschi
Brunelleschi's dome, finished in 1463, was the largest of its time to be built without scaffolding. The outer shell is supported by a thicker inner shell that acts as a platform for it.

The *Last Judgment* frescoes (1572–4) by Vasari were completed by Zuccari.

VISITORS' CHECKLIST

Piazza del Duomo. **Map** 2 D5 (6 E2). [055 230 28 85. 1, 6, 14, 17, 23. **Cathedral** 10am–5pm Mon–Sat (3:30 Thu, 4:45 Sat), 1:30–4:45pm Sun. **Crypt** 10am–5:30pm daily (from 1:30 Sun). **Baptistry** noon–7pm Mon–Sat, 8:30am–2pm Sun. **Dome** 8:30am–7pm Mon–Sat (5:40pm Sat). **Campanile** 8:30am–7.30pm daily. **All buildings** 1 Jan & relig hols.
W www.operaduomo.firenze.it

Bricks were set between marble ribs in a self-supporting herringbone pattern – a technique Brunelleschi copied from the Pantheon in Rome.

Chapels at the East End
The three apses, crowned by smaller copies of the dome, have five chapels each. The 15th-century stained glass is by Ghiberti.

Entrance leading to the dome

The marble sanctuary around the High Altar was created by Baccio Bandinelli in 1555.

Marble Pavement
The colourful, intricately inlaid pavement (16th century) was designed in part by Baccio d'Agnolo and Francesco da Sangallo.

Dante Explaining the Divine Comedy *(1465)*
This painting by Michelino shows the poet outside Florence against a backdrop of Purgatory, Hell and Paradise.

STAR FEATURES

★ Dome by Brunelleschi

★ Baptistry

The East Doors of the Baptistry

Lorenzo Ghiberti's famous bronze Baptistry doors were commissioned in 1401 to mark the city's deliverance from the plague. Ghiberti was chosen to make a set of new doors after a competition that involved seven leading artists, including Donatello, Jacopo

Ghiberti's winning panel

della Quercia and Brunelleschi. The trial panels by Ghiberti and Brunelleschi are so different from Florentine Gothic art of the time, notably in the use of perspective and individuality of figures, that they are often regarded as the first works of the Renaissance.

"GATE OF PARADISE"

Having spent 21 years working on the North Doors, Ghiberti was commissioned to make the East Doors (1424–1452). Michelangelo enthusiastically dubbed them the "Gate of Paradise". The original ten relief panels showing scriptural subjects are now exhibited in the Museo dell'Opera del Duomo *(see p271)*; those on the Baptistry are copies.

Abraham and the Sacrifice of Isaac
The jagged modelled rocks symbolizing Abraham's pain are carefully arranged to emphasize the sacrificial act.

Joseph Sold into Slavery
Ghiberti, a master of perspective, formed the architectural elements in shallower relief behind the figures to create the illusion of depth in the scene.

KEY TO THE EAST DOORS

1	2
3	4
5	6
7	8
9	10

1 Adam and Eve are Expelled from Eden
2 Cain Murders his Brother, Abel
3 The Drunkenness of Noah and his Sacrifice
4 Abraham and the Sacrifice of Isaac
5 Esau and Jacob
6 Joseph Sold into Slavery
7 Moses Receives the Ten Commandments
8 The Fall of Jericho
9 The Battle with the Philistines
10 Solomon and the Queen of Sheba

Detail of carvings by Donatello on the wall of Orsanmichele

Orsanmichele ❽

Via dell'Arte della Lana. **Map** 3 C1
(6 D3). ⬜ 9am–noon (to 1pm Sun),
4–6pm daily. ⬛ 1st and last Mon of
each month, 1 Jan, 1 May, 25 Dec.

BUILT IN 1337 as a grain market, Orsanmichele was later converted into a church which took its name from *Orto di San Michele*, a monastic garden long since vanished. The arcades of the market became windows, which are today bricked in, but the original Gothic tracery can still be seen. The decoration was entrusted to Florence's major *Arti* (guilds). Over 60 years they commissioned sculptures of their patron saints to adorn the 14 exterior niches, though today many of the figures are copies. Among the sculptors were Lorenzo Ghiberti, Donatello and Verrocchio.

The beautifully tranquil interior contains an opulent 14th-century altar by Andrea Orcagna, a *Virgin and Child* by Bernardo Daddi (1348) and a statue of the *Madonna and Child with St Anne* by Francesco da Sangallo (1522).

Bargello ❾

Via del Proconsolo 4. **Map** 4 D1 (6 E3).
📞 055 238 86 06. 🚌 19. ⬜
8:30am–1:50pm daily. ⬛ 1st & 3rd
Sun and 2nd & 4th Mon of each
month, 1 Jan, 1 May, 25 Dec.

FLORENCE'S second-ranking museum after the Uffizi, the Bargello contains a wonderful medley of applied arts and Italy's finest collection of Renaissance sculpture. Begun in 1255, the fortress-like building was initially the town hall (making it the oldest seat of government in the city), but later became a prison and home to the chief of police (the *Bargello*). It also became known for its executions, which took place in the main courtyard until 1786, when the death sentence was abolished by Grand Duke Pietro Leopoldo. Following extensive renovation, the building opened as one of Italy's first national museums in 1865.

The key exhibits range over three floors, beginning with the Michelangelo Room, superbly redesigned after extensive damage during the 1966 flood. Three contrasting works by Michelangelo lie dotted around the room, the most famous a tipsy-looking *Bacchus* (1497), the sculptor's first large free-standing work. Close by is a powerful bust of *Brutus* (1539–40), the only known portrait bust by Michelangelo, and a beautifully delicate circular relief depicting the *Madonna and Child* (1503–5). Countless works by other sculptors occupy the same room. Among them is an exquisite *Mercury* (1564) by the Mannerist genius, Giambologna, as well as several virtuoso bronzes by the sculptor and goldsmith Benvenuto Cellini (1500–71).

Across the courtyard, full of fragments and the coats of arms of the Bargello's various incumbents, two more rooms contain exterior sculptures removed from sites around the city. The courtyard's external staircase leads to the first floor, which opens with a wonderfully eccentric

Donatello's *David* (c.1430) in the Bargello

Brunelleschi's *Sacrifice of Isaac* (1402) in the Bargello

bronze menagerie by Giambologna. To the right is the Salone del Consiglio Generale, a cavernous former courtroom that contains the cream of the museum's Early Renaissance sculpture. Foremost among its highlights is Donatello's heroic *St George* (1416) – the epitome of "youth, courage and valour of arms" in the words of Vasari. Commissioned by the Armourers' Guild, the statue was brought here from Orsanmichele in 1892. At the centre of the room, in direct contrast, is Donatello's androgynous *David* (c.1430), famous as the first free-standing nude by a Western artist since antiquity. Among the room's more easily missed works, tucked away on the right wall, are two reliefs depicting *The Sacrifice of Isaac* (1402). Created by Brunelleschi and Lorenzo Ghiberti respectively, both were entries in the competition to design the Baptistry doors.

Beyond the Salone, the Bargello's emphasis shifts to the applied arts, with room after room devoted to rugs, ceramics, silverware and a host of other beautiful *objets d'art*. The most celebrated of these rooms is the Salone del Camino on the second floor, which features the finest collection of small bronzes in Italy. Some are reproductions of antique models, others are small copies of Renaissance statues. Giambologna, Cellini and Antonio del Pollaiuolo are among those represented.

Bacchus (1497) by Michelangelo

Santa Croce ⑩

WORK BEGAN AROUND 1294 on the gothic church of Santa Croce, which contains tombs and monuments of famous Florentines, such as Michelangelo, Galileo and Machiavelli, as well as radiant early 14th-century frescoes by Giotto and his pupil Taddeo Gaddi. In the cloister alongside the church stands the Cappella de' Pazzi (Pazzi Chapel), a Renaissance masterpiece designed by Filippo Brunelleschi.

Tomb of Leonardo Bruni *(1447)*
Rossellino's effigy of this great humanist was unusual in its sensitive realism and lack of monumental pomp.

Annunciation by Donatello (15th century)

Tomb of Michelangelo *(1570)*
Vasari's tomb figures represent Painting, Sculpture and Architecture.

Tomb of Machiavelli

The Neo-Gothic façade by Niccolò Matas was added in 1863.

Tomb of Galileo

Entrance to church

Exit

Entrance to Cloister and Cappella de' Pazzi

Entrance to Museo

Cimabue's Crucifixion
Badly damaged in the flood of 1966, this 13th-century masterpiece is among the highlights of the museum (museo), as is Taddeo Gaddi's magnificent Last Supper *(c.1355–60).*

★ **Cappella de' Pazzi**
Brunelleschi's domed chapel with Classical proportions was begun in 1443. The roundels (c.1442–52) are by Luca della Robbia.

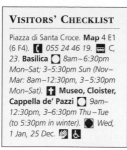

**The Neo-Gothic
campanile** was
added in 1842.

The Cappella Baroncelli,
frescoed by Taddeo Gaddi
between 1332 and 1338,
contains the first true night
scene in Western art.

Sacristy

★ **Cappella Bardi Frescoes**
*Giotto frescoed the Bardi
and Peruzzi chapels to the
right of the high altar
between 1315 and 1330.
This touching scene from
the left-hand wall of the
chapel shows* The Death
of St Francis *(1317).*

Museo di Storia della Scienza ⑪

Piazza de' Giudici 1. **Map** 4 D1 (6 E4).
055 239 88 76. winter:
9:30am–5pm Mon–Wed & Sat (to
1pm Tue); summer: 9:30am–5pm
Mon–Sat (to 1pm Tue & Sat).
public hols.

THIS LIVELY and superbly presented museum devotes two floors to various scientific themes, illustrating each with countless fine displays and a panoply of old and beautifully made scientific instruments. It is also something of a shrine to the Pisa-born scientist Galileo Galilei (1564–1642), and features two of his telescopes, as well as large-scale reconstructions of his experiments into motion, velocity and acceleration. These are sometimes demonstrated by the attendants. Other exhibits come from the Accademia del Cimento (Academy for Experimentation), founded in 1657 by Grand Duke Ferdinand II in memory of Galileo.

**Astrolabe,
Museo di Storia
della Scienza**

The first few rooms are devoted to astronomical, mathematical and navigational instruments, with galleries concentrating on Galileo, telescopes and optical games. Some of the best exhibits are in room 7, which is crammed with early maps, globes and astrolabes, and among the antique microscopes, thermometers and barometers in the rooms beyond. On the

second floor there are some fine old clocks, mathematical instruments, calculators, a horrifying collection of 19th-century surgical instruments, and some graphic anatomical models.

Ponte Vecchio ⑫

Map 4 D1 (6 E4).

PONTE VECCHIO, the oldest surviving bridge in the city, was built in 1345, the last in a succession of bridges and fords on the site that dated back to Roman times. Designed by Giotto's pupil Taddeo Gaddi, it was originally the domain of blacksmiths, butchers and tanners (who used the river for disposing of waste). They were reviled for their noise and stench and were evicted in 1593 by Duke Ferdinando I – replaced by jewellers and goldsmiths. The elevated Corridoio Vasariano runs along the eastern side of the bridge, above the shops. Giorgio Vasari designed the corridor in 1565 to allow the Medici family to move between their residences without having to mix with the public. This was the city's only bridge to escape destruction during World War II and visitors today come as much to admire the views as to browse among the antique shops and specialized jewellery shops. A bust of the famous goldsmith Benvenuto Cellini stands in the middle of the bridge.

Ponte Vecchio viewed from the Ponte Santa Trinita

Uffizi

THE UFFIZI, Italy's greatest art gallery, was built in 1560–80 to house offices *(uffici)* for Duke Cosimo I. The architect Vasari used iron as reinforcement, which enabled his successor, Buontalenti, to create an almost continuous wall of glass on the upper storey. This was used as a gallery for Francesco I to display the Medici art treasures. The collection was divided up in the 19th century: ancient objects went to the archaeological museum and sculpture to the Bargello, leaving the Uffizi with a matchless collection of paintings.

Main staircase

Entrance hall

Entrance

Bacchus *(c.1589)*
Caravaggio's early work depicts the god of wine as a pallid, debauched youth. The mood of dissipation is echoed in the decaying fruit, one of Western art's earliest still-life paintings.

Corridor ceilings are frescoed with 1580s "grotesques" inspired by Roman grottoes.

Annunciation *(1333)*
The Sienese painter Simone Martini was strongly influenced by French Gothic art, and this is one of his masterpieces. The two saints are by Martini's pupil and brother-in-law, Lippo Memmi.

Buontalenti staircase

GALLERY GUIDE
The Uffizi art collection is on the top floor of the building. Greek and Roman sculptures are displayed in the broad corridors (East, Arno, West) running round the inner side of the building. The paintings are hung in rooms off the corridors in chronological order to reveal the development of Florentine art from Byzantine to High Renaissance and beyond. Gothic art is in rooms 2–6; Early Renaissance in 7–14; High Renaissance and Mannerism in 15–29; and later paintings in 30–45.

Ognissanti Madonna *(c.1310)*
Giotto's grasp of spatial depth and substance in this altarpiece was a milestone in the mastery of perspective.

KEY TO FLOORPLAN

☐	East Corridor
☐	West Corridor
☐	Arno Corridor
☐	Gallery rooms 1–45
☐	Non-exhibition space

The Duke and Duchess of Urbino (*c.1465–70*)
*Piero della Francesca's portraits of Federico da Montefeltro
and his wife Battista Sforza were painted after Battista died
aged 26. Her portrait was probably based on her death mask.*

The Tribune,
decorated in
red and gold,
contains the
works most
valued by
the Medici.

The Birth of Venus (*c.1485*)
*Botticelli shows the goddess of love flanked by
Zephyrus, god of the west wind, who blows
the risen Venus to shore on a half-shell. The
myth may symbolize the birth of beauty
through the divine fertilization of matter.*

The Holy Family (*1507*)
*Michelangelo's paint-
ing, the first to break
with the convention
of showing Christ
on the Virgin's lap,
inspired Mannerist
artists through its
expressive handling
of colour and posture.*

**Vasari's Classical Arno
façade (begun 1560)**

The Vasari Corridor
is a passageway
across the Arno to
the Pitti Palace.

**The Venus of
Urbino** (*1538*)
*Titian's sensuous nude,
inspired by Giorgione's
Sleeping Venus, may in
fact be a portrait of a
courtesan deemed
sufficiently beautiful
to be a goddess.*

Exploring the Uffizi

THE UFFIZI offers not only the chance to see the world's greatest collection of Italian Renaissance paintings, but also the opportunity to enjoy masterpieces from as far afield as Holland, Spain and Germany. Accumulated over the centuries by the Medici, the collection was first housed in the Uffizi in 1581, and eventually bequeathed to the Florentine people by Anna Maria Lodovica, the last of the Medici.

Madonna and Child with Angels (1455–66) by Fra Filippo Lippi

GOTHIC ART

PAST THE STATUES and antiquities of room 1, the Uffizi proper opens in style with three altarpieces of the *Maestà*, or Madonna Enthroned, by Giotto, Duccio and Cimabue, some of Italy's greatest 13th-century painters. Each work marks a stage in the development of Italian painting away from the stilted conventions of Byzantium to the livelier traditions of Gothic and Renaissance art. The shift is best expressed in Giotto's version of the subject (known as the *Ognissanti Madonna*), where new feeling for depth and naturalistic detail is shown in the range of emotion displayed by the saints and angels, and by the carefully evoked three-dimensionality of the Virgin's throne.

Giotto's naturalistic influence can also be seen among the paintings of room 4, which is devoted to the 14th-century Florentine School, an interesting counterpoint to the Sienese paintings of Duccio and his followers in room 3. Among the many fine paintings here are works by Ambrogio and Pietro Lorenzetti, and Simone Martini's *Annunciation*.

Room 6 is devoted to International Gothic, a highly decorative style that represented the height of Gothic expression. It is exemplified by Gentile da Fabriano's exquisite, glittering *Adoration of the Magi* painted in 1423.

EARLY RENAISSANCE

A NEW UNDERSTANDING of geometry and perspective during the 15th century increasingly allowed artists to explore the complexities of space and depth. None became more obsessed with these new compositional possibilities than Paolo Uccello (1397–1475), whose picture of *The Battle of San Romano* (1456) in room 7 is one of the gallery's most fevered creations.

Room 7 also contains two panels from 1460 by Piero della Francesca, another artist preoccupied with the art of perspective. The panels, which are among the earliest Renaissance portraits, depict the Duke and Duchess of Urbino on one side and representations of their virtues on the other.

While such works can seem coldly experimental, Fra Filippo Lippi's *Madonna and Child with Angels* (1455–66), in Room 8, is a masterpiece of warmth and humanity.

Sandro Botticelli's allegorical painting, *Primavera* (1480)

Like many Renaissance artists, Lippi uses a religious subject to celebrate earthly delights such as landscape and feminine beauty. A similar approach is apparent in the works of Botticelli, whose famous paintings in rooms 10–14 are for many the highlight of the gallery. In *The Birth of Venus*, for example, Venus takes the place of the Virgin, expressing a fascination with Classical mythology common to many Renaissance artists. The same is true of the *Primavera* (1480), which breaks with Christian religious painting by illustrating a pagan rite of spring.

Detail from *The Annunciation* (1472–5) by Leonardo da Vinci

HIGH RENAISSANCE AND MANNERISM

Room 15 features works attributed to the young Leonardo da Vinci, notably a sublime *Annunciation* (1472–5), which reveals hints of his still emerging style, and the *Adoration of the Magi* (1481), which remained unfinished when he left Florence for Milan to paint *The Last Supper* (1495–8).

Room 18, better known as the Tribune, was designed in 1584 by Buontalenti in order to accommodate the best-loved pieces of the Medici collection. Its most famous work is the so-called Medici Venus (1st century BC), a Roman copy of a Greek statue deemed to be the most erotic in the ancient world. The copy proved equally salacious and was removed from Rome's Villa Medici by Cosimo III to keep it from corrupting the city's art students. Other highlights in

room 18 include Agnolo Bronzino's portraits of *Cosimo I* and *Eleonora di Toledo*, both painted around 1545, and Pontormo's *Charity* (1530) and the portrait of *Cosimo il Vecchio* (1517).

Rooms 19 to 23 depart from the gallery's Florentine bias, demonstrating how rapidly Renaissance ideas and techniques spread beyond Tuscany. Painters from the German and Flemish schools are well-represented, together with painters from Umbria like Perugino, but perhaps the most captivating works are the paintings by Venetian and northern Italian artists such as Mantegna, Carpaccio, Correggio and Bellini.

Room 25, which returns to the Tuscan mainstream, is dominated by Michelangelo's *Holy Family* or Doni Tondo (1456), notable for its vibrant colours and the Virgin's unusually twisted pose. The gallery's only work by Michelangelo, it was to prove immensely influential with the next generation of painters, especially Bronzino (1503–72), Pontormo (1494–1556) and Parmigianino (1503–40). The last of these was responsible for the *Madonna of the Long Neck* (c.1534) in room 29. With its contorted anatomy, unnatural colours and strange composition, this painting is a masterpiece of the style that came to be called Mannerism. Earlier, but no less remarkable masterpieces in rooms 26 and 28 include Raphael's sublime

Madonna of the Goldfinch (1506) by Raphael

Madonna of the Long Neck (c.1534) by Parmigianino

Madonna of the Goldfinch (1506) and Titian's notorious *Venus of Urbino* (1538), censured by Mark Twain as the "foulest, the vilest, the obscenest picture the world possesses". Others hold it to be one of the most beautiful nudes ever painted.

LATER PAINTINGS

Visitors, already sated by a surfeit of outstanding paintings, are often tempted to skim through the Uffizi's final rooms. The paintings in rooms 30 to 35 – which are mainly from the Veneto and Emilia-Romagna – are mostly unexceptional, but the gallery's last rooms (41–45) contain paintings that compare favourably with those that have gone before. Room 43 has three works by Caravaggio: *Medusa* (1596–8), painted for a Roman cardinal; *Bacchus* (c.1589), one of the artist's earliest works; and the *Sacrifice of Isaac* (c.1590), whose violent subject is belied by the painting's gentle background landscape. Room 44, dedicated to Rembrandt and northern European painting, features Rembrandt's *Portrait of an Old Man* (1665) and two self-portraits of the artist as a young and old man (painted in 1634 and 1664, respectively). Canaletto, Goya, Tiepolo and other 18th-century artists bring the gallery to its conclusion.

Piazza della Signoria ⑭

Savonarola (1452–98)

PIAZZA DELLA SIGNORIA and Palazzo Vecchio have been at the heart of Florence's political and social life for centuries. The great bell once used to summon citizens to *parlamento* (public meetings) here, and the square has long been a popular promenade for both visitors and Florentines. The piazza's statues (some are copies) commemorate the city's major historical events, though its most famous episode is celebrated by a simple pavement plaque near the loggia: the execution of the religious leader Girolamo Savonarola who was burnt at the stake.

David
This copy of the famous Michelangelo statue symbolizes triumph over tyranny. The original (see p267) stood in the piazza until 1873.

Heraldic Frieze
The crossed keys on this shield represent Medici papal rule.

Sala dei Gigli

Salone dei Cinquecento *(1495)*
This vast chamber contains a statue of Victory by Michelangelo and frescoes by Vasari describing Florentine triumphs over Pisa and Siena.

Fontana di Nettuno,
Ammannati's fountain (1575) of the Roman sea god surrounded by water nymphs commemorates Tuscan naval victories.

The Marzocco is a copy of the heraldic lion of Florence carved by Donatello in 1420. The original is in the Bargello *(see p275).*

★ **Palazzo Vecchio** *(completed 1332)*
This Republican frieze over the palace entrance is inscribed with the words, "Christ is King", implying that no mortal ruler has absolute power.

★ **The Rape of the Sabine Women by Giambologna**
(1583) The writhing figures in Giambologna's famous statue were carved from a single block of flawed marble.

The Uffizi

The Loggia dei Lanzi
(1382), designed by Orcagna, is named after the Lancers, the bodyguards of Cosimo I who were billeted here.

Roman statues, possibly of emperors, line the Loggia.

★ **Perseus by Cellini**
This bronze statue (1554) of Perseus beheading Medusa was intended to warn Cosimo I's enemies of their probable fate.

STAR FEATURES

★ **Palazzo Vecchio**

★ **Perseus by Cellini**

★ **The Rape of the Sabine Women by Giambologna**

Palazzo Vecchio ⑮

Piazza della Signoria (entrance on via della Ninna). **Map** 4 D1 (6 D3). ℂ 055 276 84 65. ⬚ A, B. ◯ 9am–7pm daily (to 2pm Thu & Sun). Last adm: 45 mins before closing. ● 1 Jan, Easter, 1 May, 15 Aug, 25 Dec. ☒ **Secret Itineraries & Children's Museum** (by reservation only). ℂ 055 276 82 24.

THE "OLD PALACE" still fulfils its original role as town hall. It was completed in 1322 when a huge bell, used to call citizens to meetings or warn of fire, flood or enemy attack, was hauled to the top of the imposing bell tower. While retaining much of its medieval appearance, the interior was remodelled for Duke Cosimo I when he moved into the palace in 1540. The redecoration was undertaken by Vasari, who incorporated bombastic frescoes (1563–5) of Florentine achievements. Michelangelo's *Victory* statue (1525) graces the Salone dei Cinquecento, which also has a tiny study decorated by Florence's leading Mannerist painters in 1569–1573. Other highlights include the Cappella di Eleonora, painted by Bronzino (1540–45); the loggia, with its views over the city; the Sala dei Gigli (Room of Lilies) with Donatello's *Judith and Holofernes* (c.1455) and frescoes of Roman heroes by Ghirlandaio (1485); as well as the recently opened museum for children and the secret rooms and passageways.

A copy of Verrocchio's Putto fountain in Vasari's courtyard

Street-by-Street: Around Piazza della Repubblica

UNDERLYING THE STREET PLAN of modern Florence is the far older pattern of the ancient Roman city. Nowhere is this more evident than in the grid of narrow streets around Piazza della Repubblica, site of the old Roman forum. This pivotal square housed the city's main food market until the 1860s, when redevelopment tidied up the area, and added the triumphal arch that now stands in today's café-filled square.

Santa Trìnita has frescoes by Ghirlandaio on the Life of St Francis (1486), depicting events that took place in this area. Here, a child is revived after falling from the Palazzo Spini-Ferroni.

Palazzo Spini-Ferroni

Ponte Santa Trìnita was built in wood in 1290 and then rebuilt by Ammannati in 1567 to celebrate the defeat of Siena.

Palazzo Strozzi
This monumental palazzo dominates the square 🔟

Santi Apostoli
was reputedly founded by Charlemagne.

Palazzo Davanzati
Frescoes with exotic birds decorate the Sala dei Pappagalli, which was once the dining room of this 14th-century palazzo 🔟

KEY

— — — Suggested route

```
0 metres          200
0 yards           200
```

LOCATOR MAP
*See Florence Street Finder
maps 5, 6*

Piazza della Repubblica,
which dates from the
19th century, is lined by
some of Florence's
oldest and best
known cafés.

Mercato Nuovo,
the "New Market"
(1547), now deals
mainly in souvenirs.

**Palazzo di Parte
Guelfa** was the
headquarters of
the Guelphs, the
dominant
political party
of medieval
Florence.

Ponte Vecchio
(See p277)

Detail of a frieze illustrating a medieval romance in Palazzo Davanzati

Palazzo Davanzati ⑯

Via Porta Rossa 13. **Map** 3 C1 (5 C3).
📞 055 238 86 10. ⬤ *for renovation.*

THIS WONDERFUL MUSEUM,
also known as the Museo
dell'Antica Casa Fiorentina,
uses original fittings and
furniture to recreate a typical
well-to-do 14th-century town
house. Due to structural
problems, the museum is
currently closed to the public,
but a small exhibition,
including photographs and a
few items from the museum,
has been organized in the
entrance of the building.

Pelting holes in the vaulted
ceiling of the entrance courtyard were designed to drop
missiles on unwanted
visitors. In one corner of
the inner courtyard is a
well and a pulley system
to raise buckets of water to
each floor – something of a
luxury since most medieval
households had to fetch their
water from a public fountain.

Palazzo Strozzi ⑰

Piazza degli Strozzi. **Map** 3 C1 (5 C3).
**Piccolo Museo di Palazzo
Strozzi** ⬤ *for restoration.*

SHEER SIZE accounts for
the impact of the Palazzo
Strozzi, and although it is
only three storeys high, each
floor exceeds the height of
a normal palazzo. It was

commissioned by the wealthy
banker Filippo Strozzi, who
had 15 buildings demolished
to make way for the palazzo.
He hoped it would rival the
Medici palaces elsewhere in
the city. Strozzi died in 1491,
just two years after the first
stone was laid.

Work on the building con-
tinued until 1536, with three
major architects contributing
to its design – Giuliano da
Sangallo, Benedetto da Maiano
and Simone del Pollaiuolo
(also known as Cronaca).
The exterior, built of huge
rusticated masonry blocks,
remains unspoiled. Look out
for the original Renaissance
torch-holders, lamps and the
rings for tethering horses that
still adorn the corners and
façades. A small museum off
the courtyard records the
building's history, but the
palace is now primarily used
as an exhibition venue and a
large antique fair is held here
biennially in late September.

**Exterior of Palazzo Strozzi, with
masonry block rustication**

San Lorenzo ⑱

SAN LORENZO was the parish church of the Medici family, and in 1419 Brunelleschi was commissioned to rebuild it in the Classical style of the Renaissance. Almost a century later Michelangelo submitted some plans for the façade, and began work on the Medici tombs in the Sagrestia Nuova. He also designed a library, the Biblioteca Mediceo-Laurenziana, to house the family's collection of manuscripts. The lavish family mausoleum, the Cappella dei Principi, was started in 1604.

Cappella dei Principi
The Medici mausoleum, behind the high altar, was begun in 1604 by Matteo Nigetti, and forms part of the Cappelle Medicee.

The huge dome by Buontalenti echoes that of the Duomo *(see pp272–3).*

The Old Sacristy was designed by Brunelleschi and decorated by Donatello.

Campanile

Biblioteca Staircase
Michelangelo's Mannerist staircase, one of the artist's most innovative designs, was built by Ammannati in 1559.

Michelangelo designed the desks and ceiling of the Biblioteca, where exhibitions of Medici manuscripts are often held.

The cloister garden is planted with box hedges, pomegranate and orange trees.

The Martyrdom of St Lawrence
Bronzino's vast Mannerist fresco of 1659 is a bravura, choreographed study of the human form, rather than a reverential response to the agony of the saint.

Entrance to church

A simple stone slab marks
the unostentatious grave of
Cosimo il Vecchio
(1389–1464), founder
of the Medici dynasty.

The Cappelle Medicee
complex comprises the
Cappella dei Principi and its
crypt, the Sagrestia Nuova
(see p287).

Pulpits by Donatello
*The bronze pulpits in the
nave were Donatello's last
works. Completed by his
pupils in 1460, the reliefs
capture the flinching pain of
Christ's Passion and the
glory of the Resurrection.*

**St Joseph and Christ
in the Workshop**, a
striking work showing
the young Christ with
his father, is by Pietro
Annigoni (1910–88),
one of the few modern
artists whose work is
seen in Florence.

Michelangelo submitted
several designs for the
façade of San Lorenzo, but
it remains unfinished.

*The Tomb of the Duke of Nemours
(1520–34) by Michelangelo in the
Cappelle Medicee's New Sacristy*

Cappelle
Medicee ⑲

Piazza di Madonna degli Aldobrandini.
Map 1 C5 (6 D1). 📞 055 238 86
02; 055 29 48 83 (reservations). 🚌
many routes. 🕐 8:30am–5pm daily
(1:50pm public hols) (last adm: 30
mins before closing). ● 1st, 3rd,
& 5th Mon of each month, 1 Jan,
1 May, 25 Dec. 🎟️ 📷 ♿

THE MEDICI CHAPELS divide
into three distinct areas.
Beyond the entrance hall lies
a low-vaulted crypt, a suitably
subdued space for the brass-
railed tombs of many lesser
members of the Medici
family. From here steps lead
to the octagonal **Cappella dei
Principi** (Chapel of Princes),
a vast family mausoleum
begun by Cosimo I in 1604.
The ceiling is garishly frescoed
and the walls are smothered
in huge swathes of semi-
precious *pietre dure* (inlaid
stone). Spaced around the

walls are the tombs of six
Medici Grand Dukes. A corridor leads to Michelangelo's
New Sacristy, designed as a
counterpoint to Brunelleschi's
Old Sacristy in San Lorenzo.
Three groups of statues, all
carved by Michelangelo
between 1520 and 1534, stand
around the walls: that on
the near left hand wall is *The
Tomb of the Duke of Urbino*
(grandson of Lorenzo the
Magnificent). Opposite is *The
Tomb of the Duke of Nemours*
(Lorenzo's third son). Close
to the unfinished *Madonna
and Child* (1521) is the simple
tomb containing Lorenzo the
Magnificent and his murdered
brother, Giuliano (died 1478).

Mercato Centrale ⑳

Piazza del Mercato Centrale. **Map** 1 C4
(5 C1). 🕐 7am–2pm Mon–Sat.

AT THE HEART of the San
Lorenzo street market is
the bustling Mercato Centrale,
Florence's busiest food
market. It is housed in a vast
two-storey building of cast-
iron and glass, built in 1874
by Giuseppe Mengoni.
   The ground floor stalls sell
meat, poultry, fish, salamis,
hams, cheeses and excellent
olive oils. There are also
Tuscan takeaway foods such as
porchetta (roast suckling pig),
lampredotto (pig's intestines)
and *trippa* (tripe). Fresh fruit,
vegetables and flowers are sold
on the top floor: look out for
wild mushrooms and truffles
in the autumn, and broad
beans, peas and baby
artichokes in early spring.

Yellow courgette flowers and other vegetables in the Mercato Centrale

Santa Maria Novella ㉑

THE CHURCH of Santa Maria Novella was built by the Dominicans between 1279 and 1357. The lower Romanesque part of its façade was incorporated into one based on Classical proportions by the pioneering Renaissance architect Leon Battista Alberti in 1456–70. The Gothic interior contains superb frescoes, including Masaccio's powerful *Trinity*. The famous Green Cloister, frescoed with perspective scenes by Paolo Uccello, and the dramatically decorated Spanish Chapel now form a museum.

The arcade arches are emphasized by grey and white banding.

Monastic buildings

The Nave
The piers of the nave are spaced closer together at the altar end. This trick of perspective creates the illusion of an exceptionally long church.

Cappellone degli Spagnuoli, the chapel used by the Spanish courtiers of Eleonora of Toledo, has frescoes of salvation and damnation.

Chiostro Verde takes its name from the green base used in Uccello's frescoes, which were sadly damaged by the 1966 floods.

Trinity by Masaccio
This pioneering fresco (c.1428) is renowned as a masterpiece of perspective and portraiture. The kneeling figures flanking the arch are the painting's sponsors, judge Lorenzo Lenzi and his wife.

Entrance

Entrance to museum

Cappella Strozzi
The 14th-century frescoes by Nardo di Cione and his brother Andrea Orcagna were inspired by Dante's epic poem, The Divine Comedy.

Ghirlandaio's *Madonna della Misericordia* (1472) in Ognissanti

The Strozzi Tomb is
by Benedetto
da Maiano
(1493).

**Cappella di
Filippo Strozzi**
features Filippino
Lippi's frescoes of St John
raising Drusiana from the dead
and St Philip slaying a dragon.

Cappella Tornabuoni
*Ghirlandaio's famous fresco
cycle,* The Life of John the
Baptist *(1485), peoples the
biblical episodes with
Florentine aristocrats in
contemporary dress.*

Palazzo Antinori ㉒

Via de' Tornabuoni. **Map** 1 C5 (5 C2).
⬤ *to the public.* **Cantinetta
Antinori** ☎ *055 29 22 34,* 🕐
12:30–2:30pm, 7–10:30pm Mon–Fri.

PALAZZO ANTINORI was built
in 1461–6 and is one of
the finest small Renaissance
palazzi in Florence. It was
acquired by the Antinori in
1506 and has remained with
the family ever since. The
dynasty owns many estates
all over Tuscany and Umbria,
producing a range of wines,
oils and liqueurs that can be
sampled – along with fine
Tuscan dishes – in the wine
bar off the main courtyard,
called the Cantinetta Antinori.

Palazzo Rucellai ㉓

Via della Vigna Nuova 16. **Map** 1 C5
(5 B2). ⬤ *to the public.*
Archivio Alinari Largo Fratelli Alinari
15. ☎ *055 239 51.* 🕐 *9am–6pm
Mon–Fri.* ⬤ *public hols.* 🎫

BUILT IN 1446–57, this is
one of the most ornate
Renaissance palaces in the
city. It was commissioned
by Giovanni Rucellai,
whose enormous wealth
derived from the import of
a rare and costly red dye
made from lichen found
only on Majorca. The dye
was called *oricello,* from which
the name Rucellai is derived.

Giovanni commissioned
several buildings from the
architect Leon Battista Alberti,
who designed this palace as a
virtual textbook illustration of
the major Classical orders.

The palazzo used to house
the Museo Alinari, but the
collection has recently moved
to Largo Alinari 15 and is now
known as the Archivio Alinari.
The Alinari brothers began
taking pictures of Florence in
the 1840s. They supplied high-
quality prints, postcards and
art books to foreigners on the
Grand Tour who flocked to
Florence in the 19th century.
The museum offers a vivid
insight into the social history
of Florence at that time.

Ognissanti ㉔

Borgo Ognissanti 42. **Map** 1 B5 (5 A2).
☎ *055 239 87 00.* 🕐 *8am–noon,
4–7pm Mon–Sat, 4–6pm Sun.* ⬤
first and last Mon of each month. ♿

OGNISSANTI, or All Saints,
was the parish church of
the Vespucci, one of whose
members, the 15th-century
navigator Amerigo, gave his
name to the New World. The
young Amerigo is depicted in
Ghirlandaio's fresco of the
Madonna della Misericordia
(1472) in the second chapel
on the right between the Virgin
and the man in the red cloak.
Amerigo realized that the land
discovered by Columbus was
a new continent and made
two voyages there. The letters
he sent back enabled carto-
graphers to draw the first maps
of the new land.

Ognissanti is also the burial
place of Botticelli. His fresco
of *St Augustine* (1480) is on
the south wall. Alongside the
church is a cloister and refectory with Ghirlandaio's fresco
of *The Last Supper* (1480).

Cappella Brancacci ㉕

THE CHURCH of Santa Maria del Carmine is famous for the Brancacci Chapel, which contains frescoes on *The Life of St Peter* commissioned by the Florentine merchant Felice Brancacci around 1424. Although the paintings were begun by Masolino in 1425, many of the scenes are by his pupil, Masaccio (who died before completing the cycle) and by Filippino Lippi, who completed the work in 1480. Masaccio's revolutionary use of perspective, his narrative drama and the tragic realism of his figures placed him in the vanguard of Renaissance painting. Many great artists, including Leonardo and Michelangelo, later visited the chapel to study his pioneering work.

St Peter Healing the Sick
Masaccio's realistic portrayal of cripples and beggars was revolutionary in his time.

In every scene, St Peter is distinguished from the crowds as the figure in the orange cloak.

The grouping of stylized figures in Masaccio's frescoes reflects his interest in the sculpture of Donatello.

Masaccio's simple style allows us to focus on the figures central to the frescoes without distracting detail.

Expulsion of Adam and Eve
Masaccio's ability to express emotion is well illustrated by his harrowing portrait of Adam and Eve being driven out of the Garden of Eden, their faces wracked by misery, shame and the burden of self-knowledge.

KEY TO THE FRESCOES: ARTISTS AND SUBJECTS

☐ Masolino

☐ Masaccio

☐ Lippi

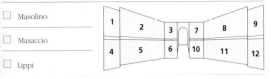

VISITORS' CHECKLIST

Piazza del Carmine. **Map** 3 A1 (5 A4). 📞 055 238 21 95; 055 29 48 83 (reservations). 🚌 D. 🕐 10am–5pm Mon, Wed–Sat, 1–5pm Sun. 🔴 public hols. 🏷

1 Expulsion of Adam and Eve
2 The Tribute Money
3 St Peter Preaching
4 St Peter Visited by St Paul
5 Raising the Emperor's Son; St Peter Enthroned
6 St Peter Healing the Sick

7 St Peter Baptizing the Converts
8 St Peter Healing the Cripple; Raising Tabitha
9 Temptation of Adam and Eve
10 St Peter and St John Giving Alms
11 Crucifixion; Before the Proconsul
12 The Release of St Peter

Masolino's *Temptation of Adam and Eve* is gentle and decorous, in contrast with the emotional force of Masaccio's painting on the opposite wall.

Woman in a Turban
The freshness of Masaccio's original colours is seen in this rediscovered roundel, hidden behind the altar for 500 years.

St Peter is depicted against a background of Florentine buildings.

Two Figures
Masolino's work tends to be more formal, less naturalistic and less animated than that of Masaccio.

Before the Proconsul
Filippino Lippi was called in to complete the cycle of frescoes in 1480. He added this emotional scene showing the Proconsul sentencing St Peter to death.

Street-by-Street: Oltrarno

**Medici coat
of arms**

FOR THE MOST PART, the Oltrarno is a homely area of small houses, quiet squares and shops selling antiques, bric-a-brac and foodstuffs. The Via Maggio, a busy thoroughfare, breaks this pattern, but step into the side streets and you escape the bustle to discover a corner of old world Florence. The restaurants serve authentic, reasonably priced food, and the area is full of studios and workshops restoring antique furniture. Among the things to see are Santo Spirito and Palazzo Pitti, one of the city's largest palaces, whose medley of museums contains an art collection second only to that of the Uffizi.

Santo Spirito
Brunelleschi's simple church was completed after the architect's death ㉖

Ponte Santa Trinita

Cenacolo di Santo Spirito, the old refectory of a monastery that once stood here, contains a dramatic fresco attributed to Orcagna (c.1360).

Palazzo Guadagni (1500) was the first in the city to be built with a rooftop loggia, setting a trend among the aristocracy.

Palazzo di Bianca Cappello (1579) is covered in ornate *sgraffito* work and was the home of the mistress of Grand Duke Francesco I.

Masks and murals are handmade at this shop, Frieze of Papier Mâché.

LUNGARNO GUICCIARDINI

VIA DI SANTO SPIRITO

VIA DE' COVERELLI

PIAZZA DE' FRESCOBALDI

VIA DEL PRESTO DI SAN MARTINO

VIA DE' VEL

VIA SGUAZZA

VIA MAGGIO

VIA DE' MICHELOZZI

PIAZZA DI S. SPIRITO

SDRUCCIOLO DE' PITTI

VIA TOSC

BORGO TEGOLAIO

V. DELLE CALDAIE

VIA MAZZETTA

PIAZZA DI S. FELICE

PIAZZA DE'

LOCATOR MAP
See Florence Street Finder
maps 3, 5

The 16th-century fountain
and gargoyle in Piazza de' Frescobaldi were
designed by Buontalenti, as was the façade
(1593–4) of the nearby church of Santa Trinita.

Ponte Vecchio
(see p277)

Palazzo Guicciardini
was the birthplace of historian Francesco Guicciardini.

★ **Palazzo Pitti**
Several museums are contained in this massive palazzo, including an outstanding collection of paintings. This painting of Palazzo Pitti was made by Giusto Utens in 1599 ㉗

KEY

– – – Suggested route

0 metres 100
0 yards 100

STAR SIGHTS

★ **Palazzo Pitti**

Santo Spirito ㉖

Piazza di Santo Spirito. Map 3 B2
(5 B4). 🚌 D. 📞 055 21 00 30.
🕐 8am–noon, 4–6pm Thu–Tue,
8:30am–noon Wed.

THE AUGUSTINIAN foundation of this church dates from 1250. The present building, dominating the northern end of the pretty Piazza di Santo Spirito, was designed by the architect Brunelleschi in 1435, but not completed until the late 15th century. The unfinished, modest façade was added in the 18th century.

Inside, the harmony of the proportions has been somewhat spoiled by the elaborate Baroque baldacchino and the High Altar, which was finished in 1607 by Giovanni Caccini. The church has 38 side altars, decorated with 15th- and 16th-century Renaissance paintings and sculpture, among them works by Cosimo Rosselli, Domenico Ghirlandaio and Filippino Lippi. The latter painted a magnificent *Madonna and Child* (1466) for the Nerli Chapel in the south transept.

In the north aisle, a door beneath the organ leads to a vestibule with an ornate coffered ceiling. It was designed by Simone del Pollaiuolo, more commonly known as Cronaca, in 1491. The sacristy adjoining the vestibule, in which 12 huge columns are crammed into a tiny space, was designed by Giuliano da Sangallo in 1489.

Interior of Santo Spirito with colonnaded aisle

Palazzo Pitti ㉗

THE PALAZZO PITTI was originally built for the banker Luca Pitti. The huge scale of the building, begun in 1457 and attributed to Brunelleschi, illustrated Pitti's determination to outrival the Medici family through its display of wealth and power. Ironically, the Medici later purchased the palazzo when building costs bankrupted Pitti's heirs. In 1550 it became the main residence of the Medici, and subsequently all the rulers of the city lived here. Today the richly decorated rooms exhibit countless treasures from the Medici collections.

Judith (1620–30) by Artemisia Gentileschi

The Three Ages of Man (c.1510), attributed to Giorgione

GALLERIA PALATINA

THE PALATINE GALLERY, which forms the heart of the Pitti museum complex, contains countless masterpieces by artists such as Botticelli, Titian, Perugino, Andrea del Sarto, Tintoretto, Veronese, Giorgione and Gentileschi. The works of art, accumulated by the Medici family and the house of Habsburg-Lorraine, are still hung much as the grand dukes wished, regardless of subject or chronology. The gallery consists of 11 main salons, the first five of which are painted with allegorical ceiling frescoes glorifying the Medici. Begun by Pietro da Cortona in 1641, they were completed in 1665

by his pupil Ciro Ferri. Room 1 (Sala di Venere) contains Antonio Canova's statue of the *Venus Italica* (1810), commissioned by Napoleon to replace the *Venus de' Medici* (which was to be taken to Paris). Room 2 (Sala di Apollo) features Titian's *Portrait of a Gentleman* (1540), perhaps the finest of several paintings by the artist in the gallery. Still finer pictures adorn rooms 4 and 5, including some by Perugino, Andrea del Sarto and a host of paintings by Raphael. The most beautiful of the last group are

Madonna of the Chair (c.1515) by Raphael

Raphael's High Renaissance *Madonna della Seggiola* or Madonna of the Chair (c.1514–15), and the *Donna Velata* or Veiled Woman (c.1516), whose model was reputedly the artist's mistress. Other paintings in the remaining gallery rooms include Fra Filippo Lippi's lovely *Madonna and Child*, painted in the mid-15th century, and Caravaggio's *The Sleeping Cupid* (1608).

Galleria Palatina

The Museo degli Argenti, or the silverware museum, also displays precious *objets d'art*.

The Boboli Gardens

Entrance to museums and galleries

Brunelleschi designed the palace façade, which was eventually extended to three times its original length.

Appartamenti Monumentali

The Galleria d'Arte Moderna is a 30-room gallery featuring paintings from the years 1784 to 1924.

The Palmieri Rotonda by Giovanni Fattori (1825–1908)

APPARTAMENTI REALI

THE ROYAL APARTMENTS on the first floor of the south wing of the palazzo were built in the 17th century. They are decorated with frescoes by various Florentine artists, a series of portraits of the Medici by the Flemish painter Justus Sustermans, who worked at the court between 1619 and 1681, and a group of 18th-century Gobelins tapestries. In the late 18th and early 19th centuries, the apartments were revamped

The Throne Room of the Appartamenti Reali

Galleria del Costume

Piazza della Signoria depicted in precious stones

in Neo-Classical style by the Dukes of Lorraine when they succeeded the Medici dynasty as the rulers of Florence.

The apartments are lavishly appointed with ornate gold and white stuccoed ceilings and rich decoration, notably the walls of the Parrot Room, which are covered with an opulent crimson fabric detailed with a bird design. The Tapestry Rooms are hung with 17th- and 18th-century tapestries of French, Belgian and Italian manufacture. The apartments reflect the tastes of three distinct historical periods.

OTHER COLLECTIONS

THE MUSEO degli Argenti (Silverware Museum) is housed in rooms formerly used by the Medici as summer apartments. The family's lavish taste is reflected in the vast array of precious objects on display. These embrace beautiful examples of Roman glassware, ivory, carpets, crystal, amber, and fine works by Florentine and German goldsmiths. Pride of place goes to 16 *pietre dure* vases (decorated with hard or semi-precious inlaid stones), once owned by Lorenzo the Magnificent.

The Galleria del Costume, which opened in 1983, reflects the changing taste in the courtly fashion of the late 18th century up to the 1920s.

The highlights of the Galleria d'Arte Moderna (Modern Art Gallery) are the wonderful paintings of the *Macchiaioli* (spot-makers), who were a group of Tuscan artists with a style very similar to that of the French Impressionists.

THE BOBOLI GARDENS

A copy of Giambologna's *Oceanus Fountain* (1576)

The Boboli Gardens, a lovely place to escape the rigours of sightseeing, were laid out for the Medici after they bought the Palazzo Pitti in 1549. An excellent example of stylized Renaissance gardening, they were opened to the public in 1766. The more formal parts of the garden, nearest the palazzo, consist of box hedges clipped into symmetrical geometric patterns. These lead to wilder groves of ilex and cypress trees, planted to create a contrast between artifice and nature. Countless statues adorn the gardens, particularly along the Viottolone, an avenue of cypress trees planted in 1637. High above the gardens stands the Forte di Belvedere, designed by Buontalenti in 1590 for the Medici Grand Dukes.

The Virgin from *The Annunciation* (1528) by Pontormo

Santa Felìcita ㉘

Piazza di Santa Felìcita. **Map** 3 C2 (5 C5). 🚌 *D.* 📞 *055 21 30 18.* ⏰ *9am–noon, 3:30–6pm Mon–Sat; 4:30–6pm Sun.* ♿

THERE HAS BEEN a church on this site since the 4th century. The present structure, begun in the 11th century, was remodelled in 1736–9 by Ferdinando Ruggieri, who retained Vasari's earlier porch (added in 1564) as well as many of the church's original Gothic features.

The Capponi family chapel to the right of the entrance contains two works by Jacopo da Pontormo: *The Deposition* and *The Annunciation* (1525–28). The frescoes' strange composition and remarkable colouring make them two of Mannerism's greatest masterpieces.

Piazzale Michelangelo ㉙

Piazzale Michelangelo. **Map** 4 E3. 🚌 *12, 13.*

OF ALL THE GREAT Florentine viewpoints – such as the Duomo and Campanile – none offers such a magnificent panorama of the city as Piazzale Michelangelo. Laid out in the 1860s by Giuseppe Poggi, and dotted with copies of Michelangelo's statues, its lofty balconies attract countless visitors and the inevitable massed ranks of souvenir sellers. However, this bustling square remains an evocative spot, especially at dusk, when the sun sets over the Arno and distant Tuscan hills.

San Miniato al Monte ㉚

Via del Monte alle Croci. **Map** 4 E3. 📞 *055 234 27 31.* 🚌 *12, 13.* ⏰ *8am–7:30pm daily (Oct–Mar: 8am–5:30pm).* 🌑 *public hols.* ♿

SAN MINIATO is one of the most beautiful Romanesque churches in Italy. Begun in 1018, it was built over the shrine of San Miniato (St Minias), a rich Armenian merchant beheaded for his beliefs by Emperor Decius in the 3rd century. The façade, begun around 1090, has the geometric marble patterning typical of Pisan-Romanesque architecture. The statue on the gable shows an eagle carrying a bale of cloth, the symbol of the powerful Arte di Calimala (guild of wool importers), who financed the church in the

The façade of the church of San Miniato al Monte

Middle Ages. The 13th-century mosaic shows Christ, the Virgin and St Minias. The same protagonists appear in the apse mosaic inside the church, which sits above a crypt supported by columns salvaged from ancient Roman buildings. The floor of the nave is covered with seven mosaic panels of animals and signs of the Zodiac (1207).

Other highlights in the church include Michelozzo's free-standing Cappella del Crocifisso (1448) and the Renaissance Cappella del Cardinale del Portogallo (1480) with terracotta roundels (1461) on the ceiling by Luca della Robbia. There is a fresco cycle of *Scenes from the Life of St Benedict* (1387) by Spinello Aretino in the sacristy.

Ponte Vecchio and the Arno from the heights of Piazzale Michelangelo

FLORENCE STREET FINDER

Map references given for sights in the Florence section refer to the maps on the following pages. Where two references are provided, the one in brackets relates to the large-scale maps, 5 and 6. References are also given for Florence hotels (see pp557–9) and restaurants (see pp591–3), and for useful addresses in the Travellers' Needs and Survival Guide sections at the back of the book. The map below shows the area of Florence covered by the Street Finder. The symbols used for sights and other features on the Florence Street Finder maps are listed below. Streets in Florence have double sets of numbers: red numbers are for businesses, and black or blue for domestic residences.

Scale of Maps 1–2 & 3–4

| 0 metres | 250 |
| 0 yards | 250 |

1:12,000

Scale of Maps 5–6

| 0 metres | 150 |
| 0 yards | 150 |

1:7000

| 0 kilometres | 1 |
| 0 miles | 0.5 |

Key to Street Finder

▢ Major sight	🛈 Tourist information	⊠ Post office
▢ Place of interest	✚ Hospital with casualty unit	═ Railway line
FS Railway station	🚔 Police station	One-way street
🚌 Bus terminus	✝ Church	City walls
P Parking	✡ Synagogue	

SEE PAGES
5, 6 FOR
ENLARGEMENT
OF THIS AREA

TUSCANY

R ENOWNED FOR ITS ART, *history and evocative landscape, Tuscany is a region where the past and present merge in pleasant harmony. Hill-towns gaze across the countryside from on high, many encircled by Etruscan walls and slender cypress trees. Handsome palaces testify to the region's wealth while medieval town halls indicate a long-standing tradition of democracy and self-government.*

In the countryside, among the vineyards and olive groves, there are hamlets and farmhouses, as well as fortified villas and castles that symbolize the violence and intercommunal strife that tore Tuscany apart during the Middle Ages. Several imposing castles and villas were built for the Medici family, the great patrons of the Renaissance who supported eminent scientists, such as Galileo.

Northern Tuscany, and the heavily populated plain between Florence and Lucca, is dominated by industry, with intensively cultivated land between the cities and the wild mountainous areas.

The area centred around Livorno and Pisa is now the region's economic hub. Pisa, at the height of its powers, dominated the western Mediterranean from the 11th to the 13th centuries. Its navy opened up extensive trading routes with North Africa, and brought to Italy the benefits of Arabic scientific and artistic achievement. During the 16th century the Arno estuary began to silt up, ending Pisan power.

At the heart of central Tuscany lies Siena, which was involved in a long feud with Florence. Its finest hour came with its victory in the Battle of Montaperti in 1260, but it was devastated by the Black Death in the 14th century and finally suffered a crushing defeat by Florence in the siege of 1554–5.

Northeastern Tuscany, with its mountain peaks and woodland, provided refuge for hermits and saints, while the east was home to Piero della Francesca, the early Renaissance painter whose timeless and serene works are imbued with an almost religious perfection.

A timeless view and way of life in Casole d'Elsa, near San Gimignano in central Tuscany

◁ The complex architecture of Pisa's Duomo (begun in 1063) and the Leaning Tower (begun in 1173)

Exploring Tuscany

Tuscan cities such as Florence, Siena and Pisa, together with smaller towns like Lucca, Cortona and Arezzo, contain some of Italy's most famous artistic treasures. Medieval villages such as San Gimignano, with its famous towers, or Pienza, a tiny Renaissance jewel, sit at the heart of the glorious pastoral countryside for which the region is equally renowned. Elsewhere landscapes range from the spectacular mountains of the Alpi Apuane to the gentle hills of Chianti.

SIGHTS AT A GLANCE

View of Cortona in eastern Tuscany

0 kilometres   25

0 miles   20

SEE ALSO

• *Where to Stay* pp559–61

• *Where to Eat* pp593–5

Cypress trees, a classic feature of the Tuscan landscape

GETTING AROUND

Motorways or fast dual carriageways link Florence, the hub of Tuscany's road and rail network, to Siena, Pisa, Lucca and the south. The Via Aurelia and A12 motorway serve the Tuscan coast. Rural roads, however, can be slow and winding. Rail links are good, and connect most major towns.

KEY

▬	Motorway
▬	Major road
▬	Minor road
▬	Scenic route
≈	River
❋	Viewpoint

Carrara ❶

Massa Carrara. 🏔 70,000. FS 🚌
ℹ Viale XX Settembre (località
Stadio) (0585 84 44 03). 🅰 Mon.

INTERNATIONALLY renowned for
its marble quarries, Carrara's
almost flawless white stone
has been prized for centuries
by famous sculptors from
Michelangelo to Henry Moore
(the stone for Michelangelo's
David came from Carrara). The
region's 300 or more quarries
date back to Roman times,
making this one of the oldest
industrial sites in continuous
use in the world. Many of the
town's marble-sawing mills
and workshops welcome
visitors, offering them the
chance to see the ways in
which marble and quartz are
worked. These techniques –
along with marble artifacts old
and new – can be seen at the
Museo Civico del Marmo.

Local marble is put to good
use in the town's **Duomo** in
Piazza del Duomo, particularly
in the fine Pisan-Romanesque
façade with its delicate rose
window. The cathedral square
also contains Michelangelo's
house, used by the sculptor

A quarry in the marble-bearing hills around Carrara

during his visits to select blocks
of marble. The town has some
lovely corners to explore, in
particular the elegant Piazza
Alberica. Most visitors head
for the stone quarries that are
open to the public at nearby
Colonnata and at **Fantiscritti**
(take one of the regular town
buses or follow the signs to
the "Cave di Marmo"). The
latter features a small museum
with displays of various marble
quarrying techniques.

🏛 **Museo Civico del Marmo**
Viale XX Settembre. 📞 0585 84 57
46. 🕐 Mon–Sat (Nov–Apr: am only).

Garfagnana ❷

Lucca. FS 🚌 Castelnuovo di
Garfagnana. ℹ Castelnuovo di
Garfagnana (0583 64 43 54).

A LOVELY VERDANT, silent
valley wedged between
the Orecchiella mountains
and the Alpi Apuane, the
Garfagnana region can be
explored from **Seravezza**,
Barga or **Castelnuovo di
Garfagnana**. While the town
of Barga makes the prettiest
base, thanks to its tawny
stone cathedral and charming
streets, Castelnuovo is more
convenient for drives and
walks in the surrounding
mountains. **San Pellegrino in
Alpe** in the Orecchiella has a
fascinating folklore museum,
the **Museo Etnografico**. It is
easily seen in conjunction with
the **Orto Botanico Pania di
Corfino** at the headquarters
of the **Parco dell'Orecchiella**
at Pania di Corfino, with its
collection of local Alpine trees.

To the west is the Parco
Naturale delle Alpi Apuane, an
area whose spectacular jagged
peaks and wooded valleys are
criss-crossed by hiking trails
and scenic mountain roads.

🏛 **Museo Etnografico**
Via del Voltone 15, San Pellegrino in
Alpe. 📞 0583 64 90 72.
🕐 Tue–Sun. 🔴 public hols. 📷
🌿 **Parco dell'Orecchiella**
Centro Visitatori, Orecchiella.
📞 0583 61 90 98. 🕐 Jul–Aug:
daily; Jun & Sep: Sat–Sun; Apr–May &
Oct–Nov: Sun. ♿
🌿 **Orto Botanico Pania
di Corfino**
Parco dell'Orecchiella. 📞 0583 61 90
98. 🕐 May–Sep: Sun (Jul–Aug: daily).

The Parco Naturale delle Alpi Apuane on the edge of the Garfagnana

One of many seaside cafés lining the waterfront in the popular beach resort of Viareggio

Bagni di Lucca ❸

Lucca. 🏛 7,400. 🚌 ℹ️ Via del Casino 4 (0583 879 46). 🛒 Wed & Sat.

ALL OVER TUSCANY there are hot springs of volcanic origin, like Bagni di Lucca. The Romans first exploited the springs and built bath complexes where army veterans, who settled in towns including Florence and Siena, could relax. More spas came into prominence in the Middle Ages and the Renaissance, and have continued to be recommended for relieving a variety of ailments, such as arthritis.

Tuscan spas really came into their own in the early 19th century when Bagni di Lucca reached its heyday as one of Europe's most fashionable spas, frequented by emperors, kings and aristocrats. Visitors came not only for thermal cures, but also for the **Casino** (1837), one of Europe's first licensed gambling houses. These days the town is rather sleepy, and its main sights are the 19th-century monuments, including the Neo-Gothic **English Church** (1839) on Via Crawford and the **Cimitero Anglicano** (Protestant Cemetery) on Via Letizia.

ENVIRONS: Southeast of Bagni di Lucca lies another popular spa town, **Montecatini Terme**. Developed in the 18th century, this town is one of the most interesting with a wide range of spa architecture, from Neo-Classical to Art Nouveau spa establishments.

Viareggio ❹

Lucca. 🏛 55,000. 🚆 🚌 ℹ️ Viale Carducci 10 (0584 87 62 23). 🛒 Thu.

KNOWN FOR ITS CARNIVAL, held in January and early February, this is also the most popular of the resorts on the Versilia coast. Its famous "Liberty" (Art Nouveau) style of architecture can be seen in the grand hotels, villas and cafés built in the 1920s after the resort's original boardwalk and timber chalets went up in flames in 1917. The finest example of the architecture is the **Gran Caffè Margherita** at the end of Passeggiata Margherita, designed by the prolific father of Italian Art Nouveau, Galileo Chini.

Torre del Lago Puccini ❺

Lucca. 🏛 11,000. 🚆 🚌 ℹ️ Via Marconi 225 (0584 35 98 93). 🛒 Fri & Sun.

A GLORIOUS AVENUE of lime trees, the Via dei Tigli, connects Viareggio with Torre del Lago Puccini, once the home of the opera composer Giacomo Puccini (1858–1924). He and his wife are buried in their former home, now the **Museo Villa Puccini**, a small museum that features the piano on which the maestro composed many of his works. Equal prominence is given to the villa's original fittings, including the gun room that housed Puccini's hunting rifle. **Lago Massaciuccoli**, a nature reserve for rare and migrant birds, provides a pretty backdrop for open-air performances of Puccini's works.

🏛 Museo Villa Puccini
Piazzale Belvedere Puccini.
📞 0584 34 14 45. ⏰ daily (winter: Tue–Sun). 🎫 ♿

Near Puccini's lakeside home at Torre del Lago Puccini

Street-by-Street: Lucca ⑥

Lucca's regular grid of streets still follows the pattern of the former Roman colony founded in 180 BC. Great, solid ramparts, built in the 16th to 17th century, help to shut out traffic, making the city a pleasant place to explore on foot. San Michele in Foro – one of the town's many fine Pisan-Romanesque churches – stands on the site of the Roman forum (foro), the city's main square laid out in ancient times. It is still Lucca's main square today.

San Frediano
Palazzo Pfanner

VIA CALDERIA
VIA BUIA
VIA S. LUCIA

Casa di Puccini
Giacomo Puccini (1858–1924), composer of some of the world's most popular operas, including La Bohème, *was born in this house.*

Tourist information

PIAZZA SAN MICHELE

VIA VENETO
VIA FILLUNGO
VIA ROMA
VIA BECCHERIA
VIA SANTA CRO
VIA CENAMI
B.

VIA XX SETTEMBRE

PIAZZA NAPOLEONE

VIA DEL BATTISTERO

Piazza Napoleone
This sprawling square is named after Napoleon, whose sister, Elisa Baciocchi, ruled Lucca from 1805 to 1815.

PIAZZA DEL GIGLIO

VIA DEL DUOMO

PIAZZA ANTELMINELLI

PIAZZA SAN MARTINO

Railway station

★ **San Michele in Foro**
The extraordinary Pisan-Romanesque façade (11th to 14th century) has three tiers of twisted or carved columns, each one different from the rest.

San Giovanni

The Museo dell'Opera del Duomo, a new museum, features treasures removed from San Martino.

In Via Fillungo,
Lucca's main
shopping street,
several shop fronts
are decorated
with Art Nouveau
details.

Anfiteatro Romano

Torre dei Guinigi

Villa Bottoni

Pinacoteca Nazionale

Giardino Botanico

n Martino
a's beautiful 11th-century
mo is one of the outstand-
xamples of the exuberant
n-Romanesque style.

Apostles from the mosaic on the façade of San Frediano in Lucca

🏛 San Frediano
Piazza San Frediano. ⭕ *daily.*
San Frediano's striking façade
features a colourful 13th-
century mosaic, *The Ascension*,
a fine prelude to the church's
wonderfully atmospheric interior. Pride of place goes to a
splendid Romanesque font on
the right, its sides carved with
scenes from the Life of Christ
and the story of Moses. In the
second chapel in the north
aisle, Aspertini's frescoes
(1508–9) tell the story of
Lucca's precious relic, the
Volto Santo – a carving said
to date from the time of the
Crucifixion. The fine altarpiece
(1422) in the fourth chapel of
San Frediano's north aisle is
by Jacopo della Quercia.

🏛 San Michele in Foro
Piazza San Michele. ⭕ *daily.*
Built on the site of the old
Roman forum *(foro)*, San
Michele's wonderfully rich
mixture of twisted marble
columns and Cosmati work
(inlaid marble) adorns one of
the most exuberant Pisan-
Romanesque façades in
Tuscany. Built between the
11th and 14th centuries, its
decoration is overwhelmingly
pagan. Only the huge winged
figure of St Michael on the
pediment marks this out as a
church. The interior has little

of interest except for the
beautiful painting of *Saints*
Helena, Jerome, Sebastian
and Roch by Filippino Lippi
(1457–1504).

🎹 Casa di Puccini
Via di Poggio. 📞 *0583 58 40 28.*
⭕ *Tue–Sun.* ⬤ *1 Jan, 25 Dec.* 🎫
The fine 15th-century house
in which Giacomo Puccini
(1858–1924) was born is now
a shrine to the great opera
composer. It contains portraits
of Puccini, costume designs
for his operas and the piano
he used when composing his
last opera, *Turandot.*

🎹 Via Fillungo
Lucca's principal shopping
street winds its way through
the heart of the city towards
the Anfiteatro Romano. A good
place to stroll, its northern
end has several shops with
Art Nouveau ironwork, and
halfway down lies the de-
consecrated church of San
Cristoforo, built in the 13th
century, with a lovely interior.

One of the many bars and shops
along Via Fillungo

Exploring Lucca

L UCCA'S PEACEFUL NARROW LANES wind among the medieval buildings, opening suddenly to reveal churches, tiny piazzas, and many other reminders of the city's long history, including a Roman amphitheatre.

Medieval buildings mark the outline of Lucca's old Roman amphitheatre

⋔ Anfiteatro Romano
Piazza del Anfiteatro.
Roman *Luca* was founded in 180 BC, and stones from the ancient Roman amphitheatre have been ransacked over the centuries to build churches and palaces, leaving only a handful of original fragments studded into today's arena-shaped Piazza del Mercato. Slum housing clogged the piazza until 1830, when it was cleared on the orders of Marie Louise, the city's Bourbon ruler of that time. It was then that the amphitheatre's original shape was revealed, a graphic and evocative reminder of Lucca's rich Roman heritage. Low archways at the piazza's cardinal points mark the gates through which beasts and gladiators would once have entered the arena.

🏛 Museo dell'Opera del Duomo
Via Arcivescovado. [0583 49 05 30. ⬚ daily. 📷 ♿ ⚡
The museum, housed in the former Archbishop's Palace (14th century), displays the treasures of the Duomo of San Martino. These include the 11th-century carved stone heac

---

⛪ SAN MARTINO
Piazza San Martino. [0583 95 70 68. ⬚ daily.
Lucca's extraordinary cathedral, dedicated to St Martin, was built subsequent to the campanile, hence the façade's cramped and asymmetric appearance. The main portals contain outstanding 13th-century carvings by Nicola Pisano and Guidetto da Como. The Tempietto inside houses the Volto Santo, a revered 13th-century effigy believed by medieval pilgrims to have been carved at the time of the Crucifixion.

Façade
The cathedral façade is decorated with Romanesque sculptures and colonnading (1204)

The campanile was begun in 1060 as a defensive tower.

Domed chapels encircling the apse

Ghirlandaio's painting of *The Madonna and Saints* (1449–94) is in the Sacristy.

Romanesque blind arcades and carved capitals

Tomb of Ilaria del Carretto
This beautiful portrait in marble by Jacopo della Quercia (1405–6) is of the youthful bride of Paolo Guinigi.

Matteo Civitali's marble Tempietto (1184)

Circular clerestory windows, in the nave and above the aisle roof, illuminate the church's unusually tall nave.

Nicola Pisan (1200–78) carve the *Journey of th Magi* and *Depositio* on the left porta

Baroque gods and goddesses in the garden of the Palazzo Pfanner

of a king, removed from the cathedral façade, and a rare 12th-century Limoges casket, possibly created for a relic of St Thomas à Becket. The Croce dei Pisani, made by Vincenzo di Michele in 1411, is a sublime masterpiece of the goldsmith's art. It shows Christ on the Tree of Redemption, surrounded by angels, the Virgin, St John and the other Evangelists.

⚱ Palazzo Pfanner

Gardens **(** *0583 49 12 43.*
☐ *Mar–Oct: daily; Nov–Feb: by appt.*
This elegant, imposing house (1667) has a beautiful outside staircase. It also boasts one of Tuscany's most delightful formal gardens. Laid out in the 18th century, the garden's central avenue is lined with Baroque statues of the gods and goddesses of ancient Roman mythology. The garden can also be viewed while walking along the ramparts.

The house itself contains a collection of court costume of the 18th and 19th centuries. Many garments are made of silk, whose production accounted for much of Lucca's medieval wealth.

⚱ Ramparts

One of the pleasures of visiting Lucca is strolling along the ramparts – the magnificent city walls, whose tree-lined promenade offers some entrancing views of the city.

Work on the ramparts began around 1500, when advances in military technology made the old medieval defences ineffective. On their completion in 1645, the walls were some of the most advanced of their time. One of their most curious features was the open space that lay beyond them, and which survives to this day, cleared to prevent the enemy taking cover in trees and undergrowth. Ironically, the walls never actually had to be defended, and they were eventually converted into a public park in the early 19th century.

Part of the imposing 17th-century ramparts that encircle Lucca

🔒 Santa Maria Forisportam

Piazza di Santa Maria Forisportam.
☐ *daily.*
This church was built at the end of the 12th century, beyond the Roman walls of Lucca. Its name, Forisportam, means "outside the gate". The unfinished marble façade, in Pisan-Romanesque style, has blind arcading. Above the central portal is a relief of the *Coronation of the Virgin* (17th century). The interior was redesigned in the early 16th century, resulting in the nave and transepts being raised. The fourth altar of the south aisle contains a painting of *St Lucy*, and the north transept has an *Assumption*, both by Guercino (1591–1666).

🏛 Museo Nazionale di Villa Guinigi

Via della Quarquonia. **(** *0583 49 60 33.* ☐ *Tue–Sun.* ⬤ *25 Dec.* 🈂
This massive Renaissance villa was built in 1418 for Paolo Guinigi, leading light of the powerful noble family who ruled Lucca in the early 15th century. A familiar landmark of the city is the battlemented tower, the Torre dei Guinigi, with oak trees growing at the top. It offers good views over the city and the Apuan Alps. The garden features traces of a Roman mosaic, together with a pride of Romanesque lions removed from the city's walls.

Romanesque lion in the Museo Nazionale Guinigi

Inside, the museum's first floor is devoted to sculptures and archaeological displays. The highlights are works by Matteo Civitali, Jacopo della Quercia and fine Romanesque reliefs removed from several of Lucca's churches. Most of the paintings in the gallery on the floor above are by minor local artists, with the exception of two works by Fra Bartolomeo (c.1472–1517): *God the Father with Saints Catherine and Mary Magdalene* and the *Madonna della Misericordia*. The floor also has furnishings, church vestments and choir stalls from Lucca's cathedral, inlaid with marquetry views of the city carved in 1529.

Pisa

Inlaid marble, Duomo façade

For much of the Middle Ages, Pisa's powerful navy ensured its dominance of the western Mediterranean. Trading links with Spain and North Africa in the 12th century brought vast mercantile wealth and formed the basis of a scientific and cultural revolution that is still reflected in Pisa's splendid buildings – especially the Duomo, Baptistry and Campanile (Leaning Tower). Pisa's decline began in 1284, with its defeat by Genoa, and was hastened by the silting up of the harbour. The city fell to the Florentines in 1406, but suffered its worst crisis in 1944 when it fell victim to Allied bombing.

A detail from the Duomo pulpit

The Baptistry, Duomo and Leaning Tower in Pisa's Campo dei Miracoli

⛫ Leaning Tower
See p316.
🖳 http://torre.duomo.pisa.it

⛪ Duomo and Baptistry
Piazza Duomo. 📞 050 56 09 21.
🔾 *daily.* 🖳 www.duomo.pisa.it
Pisa's famous Leaning Tower is now the best-known building in the Campo dei Miracoli (Field of Miracles). Originally, however, it was intended as a campanile to complement the Duomo, which was begun by Buscheto in 1064. Today the Duomo stands as one of the finest Pisan-Romanesque buildings in Tuscany, its wonderful four-tiered façade a

medley of creamy colonnades and intricate blind arcades. Buscheto's tomb is in the left arch of the façade. Other important features of the exterior include the Portale di San Ranieri (leading to the south transept) and the bronze doors (1180), decorated with reliefs cast by Bonanno Pisano, the first architect of the Leaning Tower. Inside, the highlights are the carved pulpit (1302–11) by Giovanni Pisano, the *Tomb of Emperor Henry VII* (1315) by Tino da Camaino, and a mosaic of *Christ in Majesty* in the apse, completed by Cimabue in 1302.

The circular Baptistry, a graceful counterpoint to the Duomo, was begun in 1152 along Romanesque lines, and finished a century later – after a delay caused by a shortage of money – in a more ornate Gothic style by Nicola and Giovanni Pisano. The former was responsible for the magnificent marble pulpit (1260) in the interior, carved with reliefs of the *Nativity*, the *Adoration of the Magi*, the *Presentation*, the *Crucifixion* and the *Last Judgment*. The pillars that support the pulpit feature statues of the Virtues. The inlaid marble font (1246) is by Guido da Como.

⛫ Camposanto
Piazza dei Miracoli. 📞 050 56 05 47.
🔾 *daily.* ⬤ *1 Jan, 25 Dec.*
The Camposanto (cemetery) is the fourth element in the Campo dei Miracoli's lovely ensemble. Begun in 1278 by Giovanni di Simone, the vast marble arcades of this long, rectangular building are said to enclose soil from the Holy Land. Bombs in World War II all but destroyed its once famous frescoes, leaving only traces of *The Triumph of Death* (1360–80). Nearby is the Orto Botanico, allegedly Europe's oldest botanical garden.

A fresco from the *Triumph of Death* cycle in the Camposanto

Santa Maria della Spina alongside the River Arno in Pisa

VISITORS' CHECKLIST

🏛 100,000. ✈ Galileo Galilei
5 km (3 miles) S. 🚉 Pisa Centrale,
Piazza della Stazione. 🚌 Piazza
Sant'Antonio. 🛈 Piazza del
Duomo (050 56 04 64). Piazza
della Stazione (050 422 91).
🛒 Wed & Sat. 🎭 Regata di
San Ranieri: 17 Jun; Gioco del
Ponte: last Sun in Jun.

🏛 Museo dell'Opera del Duomo

Piazza del Duomo 6. 📞 050 56 05
47. 📞 daily. 🎫 ♿

Housed in the cathedral's 13th-century former Chapter House, this excellent modern museum displays exhibits removed over the years from the Duomo, Baptistry and Camposanto. Among the highlights is an imposing 10th-century hippogriff (half horse, half griffin). Cast in bronze by Moorish craftsmen, this statue was looted by Pisan adventurers during the wars against the Saracens. There are also works by both Nicola and Giovanni Pisano, notably Giovanni's ivory *Virgin and Child* (1300), carved for the Duomo's high altar. Other exhibits include paintings, Roman and Etruscan remains, and ecclesiastical treasures.

10th-century bronze hippogriff

🏛 Museo Nazionale di San Matteo

Lungarno Mediceo, Piazza San Matteo
1. 📞 050 54 18 65. ⏰ Tue–Sun. 🎫

This museum is located on the banks of the Arno in San Matteo, an elegantly fronted medieval convent that also served as a prison in the 19th century. Much of the building has been closed for years, with the result that several of the rooms have no numbers and some of the exhibits are poorly labelled. Nevertheless, the museum presents a unique opportunity to examine the complete sweep of Pisan and Florentine art from the 12th to the 17th centuries.

The first rooms are devoted to sculpture and early Tuscan paintings. The best exhibits include a 14th-century polyptych by Francesco Traini of *Scenes from the Life of St Dominic*, Simone Martini's fine polyptych of *The Madonna and Saints* (1321), and a 14th-century statue of the *Madonna del Latte*, attributed to Andrea Pisano, another member of Pisa's talented school of medieval sculptors. The half-length statue, in gilded marble, shows Christ feeding at his mother's breast. In room 6 are some of the highlights of the museum, including Masaccio's *St Paul* (1426), Gentile da Fabriano's radiant 15th-century *Madonna of Humility*, and Donatello's reliquary bust of *San Rossore* (1424–7). Additional rooms contain paintings by Guido Reni, Benozzo Gozzoli, Rosso Fiorentino, and an important picture of *Christ* attributed to Fra Angelico (c.1395–1455).

🔒 Santa Maria della Spina

Lungarno Gambacorti. 📞 050 53 24
74. ⏰ by permission only.

The roofline of this tiny church, located just beyond the Ponte Solferino, bristles with spiky Gothic pinnacles, miniature spires and niches sheltering statues of apostles and saints. The decoration reflects the history of the church, which was built between 1230 and 1323 to house a thorn *(spina)* from Christ's Crown of Thorns, the gift of a Pisan merchant. The church was once even closer to the Arno, but was rebuilt on the present site in 1871 to protect it from flooding.

🏛 Piazza dei Cavalieri

The huge building on the north side of this square is the Palazzo dei Cavalieri, home to one of Pisa University's most prestigious colleges: the Scuola Normale Superiore. Designed by Vasari in 1562, the building, which is covered in exuberant black and white *sgraffito* decoration (designs scratched into wet plaster), served as the headquarters of the Cavalieri di Santo Stefano, an order of knights created by Cosimo I in 1561. The imposing statue outside depicts Cosimo I.

The Virgin and Child (1321) by Simone Martini in the Museo Nazionale

The Leaning Tower of Pisa

BEGUN IN 1173 on sandy silt subsoil, the Leaning Tower (Torre Pendente) started to tilt even before the third storey was finished in 1274. Despite the shallow foundations, construction continued and the structure was completed in 1350. The tower's apparent flouting of the laws of gravity has attracted many visitors over the centuries, including the Pisan scientist Galileo, who climbed to the top to conduct his experiments on the velocity of falling objects. In recent years engineering interventions have decreased the lean by 38 cm (14 in), and a ceremony in mid-2001 symbolically reopened the tower.

Galileo Galilei
(1564–1642)

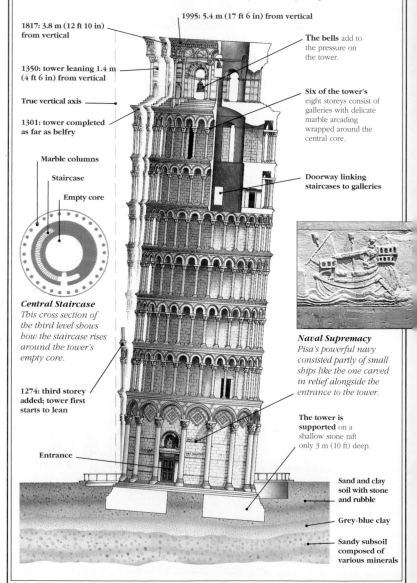

1995: 5.4 m (17 ft 6 in) from vertical

1817: 3.8 m (12 ft 10 in) from vertical

1350: tower leaning 1.4 m (4 ft 6 in) from vertical

True vertical axis

1301: tower completed as far as belfry

Marble columns

Staircase

Empty core

Central Staircase
This cross section of the third level shows how the staircase rises around the tower's empty core.

1274: third storey added; tower first starts to lean

Entrance

The bells add to the pressure on the tower.

Six of the tower's eight storeys consist of galleries with delicate marble arcading wrapped around the central core.

Doorway linking staircases to galleries

Naval Supremacy
Pisa's powerful navy consisted partly of small ships like the one carved in relief alongside the entrance to the tower.

The tower is supported on a shallow stone raft only 3 m (10 ft) deep.

Sand and clay soil with stone and rubble

Grey-blue clay

Sandy subsoil composed of various minerals

Vinci ❽

Florence. 🏠 1,500. 🚌 🚉 Wed.

Famous as the birthplace of Leonardo da Vinci (1452–1519), this hilltop town celebrates the genius in the **Museo Leonardiano**, housed in the 13th-century castle. Among the displays are wooden models of Leonardo's machines and inventions, most of them based on drawings from his notebooks, shown alongside. These include a bicycle, his conception of a car, an armoured tank and even a machine-gun.

🏛 Museo Leonardiano
Castello dei Conti Guidi.
📞 0571 560 55. ◯ daily. 🎫

Model bicycle based on designs by Leonardo, Museo Leonardiano

Pistoia ❾

🏠 93,000. 🚉 🚌 ❶ Palazzo dei Vescovi, Piazza del Duomo (0573 216 22). 🛒 Wed & Sat.

Pistoia's citizens were once known for violence and intrigue, a reputation grounded in the medieval disputes between the city's rival factions, the Bianchi and Neri (Whites and Blacks). Their favoured weapon was a tiny, locally made dagger known as a *pistola*. Long a centre of metalwork, everything from buses to mattress springs are now made here. In the centre, several fine historic buildings are preserved.

❶ Duomo
Piazza del Duomo. ◯ daily.
Piazza del Duomo, Pistoia's main square, is dominated by the Duomo (San Zeno) and its bulky 12th-century campanile, originally built as a watchtower in the city walls. The interior of the Duomo is

Detail of frieze (1514–25) by Giovanni della Robbia, Ospedale del Ceppo

rich in funerary monuments. The finest of these, in the south aisle, is the tomb of Cino da Pistoia. He was a friend of Dante and fellow poet, and is depicted in a relief (1337) lecturing to a class of young boys.

Nearby is the chapel of St James and its extraordinary silver altar decorated with more than 600 statues and reliefs. Although the earliest of these dates from 1287, the altar was not completed until 1456. One of the craftsmen involved was Brunelleschi, who began his career as a silversmith before turning to architecture. Also in the Piazza del Duomo is the octagonal Baptistry, completed in 1359.

❶ Ospedale del Ceppo
Piazza Giovanni XXIII.
This hospital and orphanage, founded in 1277, was named after the *ceppo* (hollowed-out tree trunk) that was used to collect donations for its work. The main façade features coloured terracotta panels (1514–25) by Giovanni della Robbia illustrating the *Seven Works of Mercy*. The portico is by Michelozzo.

The Pisan-Romanesque façade of Pistoia's Duomo (San Zeno)

❶ Cappella del Tau
Corso Silvano Fedi 70.
📞 0573 322 04. ◯ Mon–Sat am.
The Cappella del Tau (1360) is so called because the monks who built it wore on their cloaks the letter T (*tau* in Greek), symbolizing a crutch and their work with the sick and disabled. Inside there are frescoes by Niccolò di Tommaso on *The Creation* and the *Life of St Anthony Abbot* (1370). Two doors down, the **Palazzo Tau** has work by Marino Marini, Pistoia's best-known 20th-century artist.

The Fall (1372) by Niccolò di Tommaso in the Cappella del Tau

❶ San Giovanni Fuorcivitas
Via Cavour. ◯ daily.
Built in the 12th to 14th centuries, the striking church of San Giovanni Fuorcivitas (literally "St John Outside the City") once stood beyond the city walls. Its north flank is clad in banded marble and there is a Romanesque relief of the Last Supper over the portal. Inside, the holy water stoup, carved in marble with figures of the Virtues, is by Giovanni Pisano (1245–1320). A masterly pulpit, carved in 1270 with scenes from the New Testament, is by Guglielmo da Pisa. Both are among the finest works of this period, when artists were reviving the art of carving.

Prato ❿

🏛 170,000. 🚌 **ℹ** Piazza delle
Carceri 15 (0574 241 12). 🛒 Mon.

WHILE TEXTILE factories gird
Prato's outskirts, the city's
historic centre retains several
important churches and museums. The **Duomo** (begun
1211) is flanked by the Pulpit
of the Holy Girdle (1434–8),
designed by Donatello and
Michelozzo, used once a year
to display a girdle, reputedly
given to Thomas the Apostle
before the Assumption of the
Virgin. Inside the Duomo is a
masterpiece by Fra Filippo
Lippi, *The Life of John the
Baptist* (1452–66), and a fresco
cycle (1392–5) by Agnolo
Gaddi describing how the
Virgin's girdle reached Prato.
The *Madonna del Ceppo* (15th
century), also painted by Lippi,
is kept in the **Museo Civico**.

Other sights include **Santa
Maria delle Carceri** in Piazza
delle Carceri, a Renaissance
church designed by Giuliano
da Sangallo; the **Castello dell'
Imperatore**, a fortress built
by Emperor Frederick II in
1237; and the **Museo del
Tessuto**, which traces the history of Prato's textile industry.

🏛 **Museo Civico**
Palazzo Pretorio, Piazza del Comune.
📞 0574 61 63 02.
⬤ for restoration.
⚜ **Castello dell'Imperatore**
Piazza delle Carceri. ◯ Wed–Mon.
🏛 **Museo del Tessuto**
Piazza del Comune.
📞 0574 531 71. ◯ Mon, Wed–Sat.

***Madonna del Ceppo* by Fra Filippo
Lippi in Prato's Museo Civico**

**Buontalenti's Villa di Artimino, or
"Villa of a Hundred Chimneys"**

Artimino ⓫

Prato. 🏛 400. 🚌

A SMALL FORTIFIED hamlet,
Artimino is remarkable for
the unspoiled Romanesque
church of **San Leonardo**.
Outside the walls lies the
Villa di Artimino, designed
by Buontalenti in 1594 for
Grand Duke Ferdinando I.
Also known as the "Villa of
a Hundred Chimneys" – after
the chimney pots crowding
the roofline – it houses the
**Museo Archeologico
Etrusco**, a collection of
archaeological exhibits.

ENVIRONS: For lovers of
Pontormo's paintings, the
church of **San Michele** in
Carmignano, 5 km (3 miles)
north of Artimino, contains
The Visitation (1530). East of
here lies the villa of **Poggio
a Caiano**. Built in 1480 by
Giuliano da Sangallo for
Lorenzo de' Medici *(see
p245)*, it was the first Italian
villa to be designed in the
Renaissance style.

🏰 **Villa di Artimino**
Viale Papa Giovanni 23. **Villa** 📞 055
879 20 30. ◯ by appt. **Museum**
📞 055 871 80 81. ◯ 9am–4pm
(12.30pm Sun) Thu–Tue. 🧳
🏰 **Poggio a Caiano**
Piazza Medici. 📞 055 87 70 12.
◯ Tue – Sun. 🧳 ♿ 📷

San Miniato ⓬

Pisa. 🏛 3,900. 🚌 **ℹ** Piazza del
Popolo 3 (0571 427 45). 🛒 Tue.

THIS HILLTOP TOWN manages
to remain aloof from the
vast industrial sprawl of the
Arno valley. Its key building

is the semi-derelict Rocca
(castle), built for Frederick II,
German Holy Roman Emperor,
in the 13th century. Close by
stands the **Museo Diocesano**,
which is home to a *Crucifixion*
(c.1430) attributed to Filippo
Lippi, a terracotta bust of
Christ attributed to Verrocchio
(1435–88), and the *Virgin of
the Holy Girdle* by Andrea del
Castagno (c.1417–57). Next
door, the red-brick Romanesque façade of the **Duomo**
dates from the 12th century.
Its strange inset majolica plates,
evidence of trade with Spain
or North Africa, probably
represent the North Star and
the constellations of Ursus
Major and Minor (all three
were key points of reference
for early navigators).

🏛 **Museo Diocesano**
Piazza Duomo. 📞 0571 41 82 71.
◯ Easter–5 Jan: Sat & Sun;
6 Jan–Easter: Tue–Sat. 🧳

Façade of the Duomo in San Miniato

Fiesole ⓭

Florence. 🏛 15,000. 🚌 **ℹ** Via
Portigiani 3/5 (055 59 87 20). 🛒
Sat.

FIESOLE STANDS IN rolling hilly
countryside 8 km (5 miles)
north of Florence. Idyllically
situated among olive groves,
it is a popular retreat from
the city thanks to its hilltop
position which attracts cool
breezes. Founded in the 7th
century BC, the original Etruscan colony was a powerful
force in central Italy, only

A view over the hills and rooftops of Fiesole from Via di San Francesco

surrendering its supremacy after the foundation of Florence (1st century BC).

The recently restored **Duomo** of San Romolo in Piazza Mino da Fiesole was begun in 1028. It has a massive bell tower and a bare Romanesque interior. Behind the Duomo, an archaeological area contains the remains of a 1st-century BC **Roman theatre**, traces of **Etruscan walls** from the 4th century BC, and the **Museo Faesulanum**, with a collection of bronzes, ceramics and jewellery dating from the Bronze Age.

Via di San Francesco, a steep lane offering lovely views, leads to the Franciscan friary of **San Francesco** (14th century) and the interesting 9th-century church of **Sant'Alessandro**, with a Neo-Classical façade.

Via Vecchia Fiesolana leads to the hamlet of **San Domenico**, where the 15th-century church of the same name contains a painting of the *Madonna with Angels and Saints* (c.1430) by Fra Angelico and the Chapter House contains a fresco of *The Crucifixion* (c.1430), also by him. Close by, on the Via della Badia dei Roccettini, is the **Badia Fiesolana**, a pretty Romanesque church with a striped marble façade and interior of local grey sandstone, *pietra serena*.

🏛 **Museo Faesulanum**
Via Portigiani 1. 📞 055 594 77.
⭘ *daily (Oct–Mar: Wed–Mon).* 🏷

Arezzo ⑭

🏠 *92,000.* 🚌 ℹ️ *Piazza della Repubblica (05/5 208 39).* 🚌 *Sat.*

Arezzo is one of Tuscany's wealthiest cities, its prosperity based on a thriving jewellery industry. Although much of its medieval centre was destroyed during World War II, resulting in extensive rebuilding and many medieval alleys being replaced by broad avenues, the city preserves some outstanding sights: foremost are Piero della Francesca's famous frescoes in the church of **San Francesco** *(see pp320–21)*. Close to the church on Corso Italia, the main street, stands the **Pieve di Santa Maria**, which boasts one of the most ornate Romanesque façades in the region. To its rear stretches the steeply sloping **Piazza Grande**, flanked by an arcade (1573) designed by Vasari, and by

the **Palazzo della Fraternità dei Laici** (1377–1552). The latter features a *Madonna* relief by Bernardo Rossellino. The huge **Duomo** to the north is best known for its 16th-century stained glass and a small fresco of *Mary Magdalene* by Piero della Francesca (1416–92). The **Museo del Duomo** features three wooden crucifixes, dating from the 12th and 13th centuries, a bas relief of *The Annunciation* (1434) by Rossellino and paintings by Vasari. More works by Vasari can be seen in the **Casa di Vasari**, a house built by the artist in 1540. Still more frescoes by him are displayed in the **Museo d'Arte Medio-evale e Moderna**, a museum that is famed for its excellent collection of majolica pottery.

The **Fortezza Medicea**, a ruined Medici castle built by Antonio da Sangallo during the 16th century, has fine views.

🏛 **Museo del Duomo**
Piazzetta del Duomo 13. 📞 *0575 239 91.* ⭘ *Thu–Sat am by appt.* 🏷
🏠 **Casa di Vasari**
Via XX Settembre 55. 📞 *0575 40 90 40.* ⭘ *Wed–Mon.*
🏛 **Museo d'Arte Medioevale e Moderna**
Via di San Lorentino 8. 📞 *0575 40 90 50.* ⭘ *Tue–Sun.* 🏷
⚓ **Fortezza Medicea**
Parco il Prato. 📞 *0575 37 76 66.* ⭘ *daily.* 🏷

The monthly antiques market held in Arezzo's Piazza Grande

Arezzo: San Francesco

THE 13TH-CENTURY CHURCH of San Francesco houses one of Italy's greatest fresco cycles, the *Legend of the True Cross* (1452–66), Piero della Francesca's masterpiece. The scenes, on the walls of the choir, are now visible again after a long restoration. They describe the history of the Cross used to crucify Christ, from sprig to Tree of Knowledge, to its use as a bridge during the reign of Solomon, and ultimately its discovery by Helena, mother of Constantine, the first Christian emperor.

A Group of Onlookers
These figures kneel in wonder while Heraclius returns the True Cross to Jerusalem.

Excavation of the Cross
The town, meant to be Jerusalem, gives a fair representation of 15th-century Arezzo.

The Cross returns to Jerusalem.

The Defeat of Chosroes depicts the defeat of a Persian king who had stolen the Cross.

Judas reveals where the Cross is hidden.

KEY TO FRESCOES

1 The Death of Adam; a sprig from the Tree of Knowledge is planted over his grave; 2 The Queen of Sheba visits Solomon and foresees that a bridge made from the Tree will be used to crucify the greatest king in the world; 3 Solomon, assuming he is the greatest king in the world, orders the bridge to be buried; 4 The Annunciation: Christ's death is foreshadowed in the panel's cruciform structure; 5 Constantine has a vision of the Cross and hears a voice saying "In this sign you shall conquer"; 6 Constantine defeats his rival Maxentius; 7 The Levite Judas is tortured and reveals the location of the True Cross; 8 Three crosses are dug up; Constantine's mother Helena recognizes the True Cross; 9 The Persian king Chosroes is defeated after stealing the Cross; 10 The True Cross is returned to Jerusalem.

Painted Crucifix
The 13th-century Crucifix forms the focal point of the fresco cycle. The figure at the foot of the Cross represents St Francis, to whom the church is dedicated.

The Death of Adam
Piero's vivid portrayal of Adam and Eve in old age shows an adept treatment of anatomy. He was one of the first Renaissance artists to paint nude figures.

The prophets appear to play no part in the narrative cycle; their presence may be for purely decorative reasons.

VISITORS' CHECKLIST

Piazza San Francesco. 0575 206 30; 0575 900 404 (booking mandatory). 8:30am–noon, 2:30–6:30pm daily.

The buildings in the fresco reflect the newly fashionable styles of Renaissance architecture.

The wood of the Cross is buried in a pit.

Constantine dreams of the Cross on the eve of battle against rival emperor Maxentius.

Constantine leads his cavalry into battle.

The Queen of Sheba recognizes the wood of the Cross.

Solomon's Handshake
The handshake between the Queen of Sheba and Solomon, King of Israel, portrays 15th-century hopes for a union between the Orthodox and Western churches.

Piero's *The Resurrection* (1463) in Sansepolcro

Sansepolcro ⑮

Arezzo. 🏠 *16,000.* 🚌 🛈 *Piazza Garibaldi 2 (0575 74 05 36).* 🖴 *Tue, Sat.*

SANSEPOLCRO IS the birthplace of Piero della Francesca (1410–92). The town's **Museo Civico** contains two of his masterpieces: *The Resurrection* (1463) and the *Madonna della Misericordia* (1462). It also has a 15th-century *Crucifixion* by Luca Signorelli. In the church of **San Lorenzo** on Via Santa Croce there is a *Deposition* in the Mannerist style by Rosso Fiorentino (1494–1541).

Another renowned painting by Piero della Francesca, the *Madonna del Parto* (1460), can be seen at Via Reglia 1 in Monterchi, 13 km (8 miles) southwest of Sansepolcro.

🏛 **Museo Civico**
Via Aggiunti 65. (*0575 73 22 18.* ◻ *daily.* ● *public hols.* 📷

Cortona ⑯

Arezzo. 🏠 *23,000.* 🚆 🚌 🛈 *Via Nazionale 42 (0575 63 03 52).* 🖴 *Sat.*

CORTONA WAS FOUNDED by the Etruscans and apart from being one of the oldest hill-towns in Tuscany, it is also one of the most scenic. A major power in the Middle Ages, it was able to hold its own against Siena and Arezzo. Today it is a charming maze of old streets and medieval

buildings, like the **Palazzo Comunale** on Piazza Signorelli. The town's early history is traced in the **Museo dell'Accademia Etrusca**, which contains Etruscan artifacts and a wide variety of Egyptian and Roman remains. The small **Museo Diocesano** features several fine paintings, in particular a *Crucifixion* by the Renaissance artist Pietro Lorenzetti, a *Deposition* (1502) by Luca Signorelli, and a sublime *Annunciation* (c.1434) by Fra Angelico. Signorelli, born in Cortona, is buried in the church of **San Francesco** (built in 1245), which contains an *Annunciation* painted in Baroque style by Pietro da Cortona, another native artist. The other well-known church in Cortona is the **Madonna del Calcinaio** (1485), a gem of Renaissance architecture located on the southern outskirts of town.

The 13th-century Palazzo Comunale in Cortona

🏛 **Museo dell'Accademia Etrusca**
Palazzo Casali, Piazza Signorelli 9. (*0575 63 04 15.* ◻ *Tue–Sun.* 📷
🏛 **Museo Diocesano**
Piazza del Duomo 1. ◻ *0575 628 30.* ◻ *Tue–Sun.* 📷

Chiusi ⑰

Siena. 🏠 *10,000.* 🚆 🚌 🛈 *Piazza Duomo 1 (0578 22 76 67).* 🖴 *Tue.*

CHIUSI IS NOW a largely modern town, but in the past it was one of the most powerful cities in the Etruscan league, reaching the height of its influence in the 7th and 6th centuries BC *(see p41)*. Numerous Etruscan tombs lie dotted in the surrounding countryside, the source of the exhibits in the town's **Museo Nazionale Etrusco**. Founded in 1871, the museum is packed with cremation urns, vases decorated with black figures and Bucchero ware, burnished to resemble bronze.

The Romanesque **Duomo** in Piazza del Duomo incorporates recycled Roman pillars and capitals. The wall decorations in the nave, resembling frescoes, were painted by Arturo Viligiardi in 1887. There is a Roman mosaic underneath the high altar. Visits can be made to several Etruscan tombs under the town from the **Museo della Cattedrale**, a museum in the cloister of the Duomo that also features displays of Roman, Lombardic and medieval sculpture from the region.

🏛 **Museo Nazionale Etrusco**
Via Porsenna 17. (*0578 201 77.* ◻ *daily.* 📷
🏛 **Museo della Cattedrale**
Piazza del Duomo. (*0578 22 64 90.* ◻ *daily.* 📷

Etruscan frieze in the Museo Nazionale Etrusco in Chiusi

Pienza's Piazza Pio II, designed by Bernardo Rossellino (1459)

in the building before it was even completed. Today the church's eastern end suffers from severe subsidence.

⌂ Palazzo Piccolomini
Piazza Pio II. **[** *0578 74 85 03.*
○ *Tue – Sun.* 🈺

Montepulciano ⓲

Siena. 🏠 *14,000.* 🚌 **ℹ** *Via di Gracciano 59 (0578 75 73 41).* 🛒 *Thu.*

This is one of Tuscany's highest hill-towns, its walls and fortifications offering broad views over Umbria and southern Tuscany, and the vineyards providing the Vino Nobile wine that has made its name famous. The streets are brimming with Renaissance palazzi. The steep main street, the Corso, climbs to the **Duomo** (1592–1630), the setting for one of the master-pieces of the Sienese School, the *Assumption* (1401) by Taddeo di Bartolo. The High Renaissance church, **Tempio di San Biagio** (1518–34), lies off the road to Pienza.

Pienza ⓳

Siena. 🏠 *2,300.* 🚌 **ℹ** *Corso il Rossellino 59 (0578 74 90 71).* 🛒 *Fri.*

Pienza is a delightful village whose intimate little centre was almost completely re-designed in the 15th century by Pope Pius II. Born as Aeneas Sylvius Piccolomini in 1405, when the village was known as Corsignano, he became a leading Humanist scholar and philosopher. Elected pope in 1458, Pius II decided to rebuild his birth-place a year later, renaming it Pienza in his own honour. The Florentine architect and sculptor, Bernardo Rossellino, was commissioned to build a cathedral, papal palace and

town hall (all completed in the three years from 1459 to 1462), but the grander scheme for a planned model Renais-sance town was never realized. Some idea of what might have been, however, can still be gained from the **Palazzo Piccolomini**, the former papal palace, which continued to be inhabited by Pius's descendants until 1968. The rooms open to the public include Pius's bedroom and library, though the highlight of a visit is the superb panorama from the loggia and arcaded courtyard at the palace's rear.

Pleasant walks and more great views can be had from the village walls. The airy **Duomo** *(see p244)* next door contains six altarpieces of the *Madonna and Child*, each commissioned from the leading Sienese painters of the day. Rossellino was forced to build the Duomo on a cramped site with poor foundations, and cracks appeared

Montalcino ⓴

Siena. 🏠 *5,100.* 🚌 **ℹ** *Costa del Municipio 8 (0577 84 93 31).* 🛒 *Fri.*

Hilltop montalcino sits at the heart of vineyards that produce Brunello, one of Italy's finest red wines. It can be sampled in the Enoteca (wine shop) situated in the 14th-century **Fortezza** with its impressive ramparts. The town's timeless streets are a pleasure to wander, and there are some buildings of interest. On the way from the fortress into town is the monastery of Sant' Agostino and its 14th-century church with an attrac-tive rose window and, just beyond, the Palazzo Vescovile. On Piazza del Popolo the slim tower of the Palazzo Communale, constructed in the 13th and 14th centuries, stands tall above the town.

♜ Fortezza
Piazzale della Fortezza. **[** *0577 84 92 11.* 🈺 *for ramparts.*
Enoteca **○** *Apr–Oct: 9am–8pm daily; Nov–Mar: 9am–6pm Tue – Sun.*

The Tempio di San Biagio on the outskirts of Montepulciano

The landscape of the Crete Senesi

Crete Senesi ㉑

Asciano. FS 🚌 ℹ️ *Corso Matteotti (0577 71 95 10).*

To the south of Siena and central Tuscany is the area known as the Crete Senesi, which is characterized by round clay hillocks eroded by heavy rain over the centuries. Dubbed the "Tuscan desert", it is almost completely barren. Cypress and pine trees, planted to provide windbreaks along roads and around isolated farm houses, are an important feature in this empty, primeval landscape. Shepherds tend flocks of sheep here; the milk is used to produce the strongly flavoured *pecorino* cheese that is popular throughout Tuscany.

Siena ㉒

See pp328–33.

Monteriggioni ㉓

Siena. 👥 *7,000.* 🚌

Monteriggioni is a gem of a medieval hilltop town. It was built in 1203 and ten years later became a garrison town. It is completely encircled by high walls with 14 heavily fortified towers, built to guard the northern borders of Siena's territory against invasion by Florentine armies.

Dante was sufficiently impressed to use Monteriggioni as a simile for the deepest abyss at the heart of his *Inferno*, which compares the town's "ring-shaped citadel... crowned with towers" with

giants standing in a moat. The perfectly preserved walls are best viewed from the Colle di Val d'Elsa road. Within the walls, the sleepy town consists of a large piazza, a pretty Romanesque church (on the piazza), a few houses, a couple of craft shops, restaurants, and shops selling many of the locally produced Castello di Monteriggioni wines.

Environs: West of Monteriggioni by 3 km (2 miles) lies the former Cistercian Abbey of **Abbadia dell' Isola** (12th century). This Romanesque church was largely rebuilt in the 18th century, after the cupola fell apart. It contains frescoes by Taddeo di Bartolo and Vincenzo Tamagni and a Renaissance altarpiece.

Detail from the pulpit in Volterra's Duomo

San Gimignano ㉔

See pp334–5.

Volterra ㉕

Pisa. 👥 *13,000.* 🚌 ℹ️ *Via Giusto Turazza 2 (0588 861 50).* 🛒 *Sat.*

Like many Etruscan cities, Volterra is situated on a high plateau, offering fine views over the surrounding hills. In many places the ancient Etruscan walls still

survive. The famous **Museo Guarnacci** contains one of the best collections of Etruscan artifacts in Italy. Of special interest is the group of over 600 Etruscan cinerary urns, made from alabaster or terracotta, many of which were gathered from local tombs.

The **Palazzo dei Priori**, the medieval seat of government on Piazza dei Priori, is the oldest of its kind in Tuscany. It was begun in 1208 and there are 14th-century frescoes inside. The Pisan-Romanesque **Duomo**, located on Piazza San Giovanni, has a fine 13th-century pulpit with sculptured panels.

Volterra's excellent art gallery and museum, the **Pinacoteca e Museo Civico**, features works by Florentine artists. *Christ in Majesty* (1492) by Ghirlandaio shows Christ hovering above an idealized Tuscan landscape. Luca Signorelli's *Virgin and Child with Saints* (1491) states his debt to Roman art through the reliefs on the base of the Virgin's throne. Painted in the same year, his *Annunciation* is a beautifully balanced composition. Another highlight is Rosso Fiorentino's Mannerist painting, *The Deposition* (1521).

The city is famous for its craftsmen who have been carving elaborate statues and *objets d'art* from locally mined alabaster for 2,500 years.

The beautifully preserved walls of Monteriggioni in central Tuscany

The ruined abbey at San Galgano, surrounded by dense woodland

🏛 **Museo Guarnacci**
Via Don Minzoni 15. ☎ *0588 863 47.*
⬜ *daily.* ● *1 Jan, 25 Dec.* 🌀
🏛 **Pinacoteca e Museo Civico**
Via dei Sarti 1. ☎ *0588 875 80.*
⬜ *daily.* ● *1 Jan, 25 Dec.* 🌀

San Galgano ㉖

Siena. 🚌 *from Siena.* ☎ *0577 75 66 11.* **Abbey & oratory** ⬜ *daily.*

THE REMOTE Cistercian abbey at San Galgano lies in a superb setting. San Galgano (1148–81) was a brave but dissolute young knight who turned to God, renouncing the material world. When he tried to break his sword against a rock as a symbol of his rejection of war, it was swallowed by the stone. This he interpreted as a sign of God's approval. He built a hut on a hill above the abbey (the site of today's beehive-shaped chapel at **Montesiepi**, built c.1185). Here he later died a hermit. Pope Urban III declared him a saint and an example to Christian souls.

The abbey, begun in 1218, is Gothic in style, reflecting the French origins of the Cistercian monks who designed it. They avoided contact with the outside world and divided their lives between prayer and labour. Despite an emphasis on poverty, the monks became wealthy from the sale of wood, and by the middle of the 14th century the abbey was corruptly administered and gradually fell into decline.

In the late 14th century, the English mercenary Sir John Hawkwood sacked the abbey and by 1397 the abbot was its sole occupant. It was eventually dissolved in 1652.

St Galgano's sword stands embedded in a stone just inside the door of the circular **oratory**. The 14th-century stone walls of the side chapel are covered with worn frescoes showing scenes from Galgano's life by Ambrogio Lorenzetti (1344).

Massa Marittima ㉗

Grosseto. 🏠 *9,500.* 🚌 **🚶** *Amatur, Via Norma Parenti 22 (0566 90 27 56).* 🏪 *Wed.*

SET IN THE Colline Metallifere (metal-bearing hills) where lead, copper and silver ores were mined as early as Etruscan times, Massa Marittima is far from being a grimy industrial town. Excellent examples of Romanesque architecture survive from the period when the town became an independent republic (1225–1335). The Romanesque-Gothic **Duomo** in Piazza Garibaldi is dedicated to St Cerbone, a 6th-century saint whose story is sculpted in stone above the main portal. Inside the building, the *Maestà* is attributed to Duccio (c.1316).

The interesting **Museo della Miniera** (museum of mining) is located partially inside a former mine shaft and has exhibits that explain mining techniques, tools and locally found minerals.

The **Museo Archeologico**, housed in a 13th-century building, has material from Paleolithic to Roman times. There is also a picture gallery.

🏛 **Museo della Miniera**
Via Corridoni. ☎ *0566 90 22 89.* ⬜ *Tue–Sun (Jul & Aug: daily).* ● *Feb.* 🌀
🏛 **Museo Archeologico**
Palazzo del Podestà, Piazza Garibaldi.
☎ *0566 90 22 89.* ⬜ *Tue–Sun.* 🌀

View across the rooftops of Massa Marittima

Denuded hillocks of clay in the Crete Senesi area southeast of Siena

Street-by-Street: Siena ㉒

Unicorn
Contrada

Sᴵᴇɴᴀ'ꜱ ᴘʀɪɴᴄɪᴘᴀʟ ꜱɪɢʜᴛꜱ cluster in the maze of narrow streets and alleys around the fan-shaped Piazza del Campo. One of Europe's greatest medieval squares, the piazza sits at the heart of the city's 17 *contrade*, a series of parishes whose ancient rivalries are still acted out in the twice-yearly Palio *(see p331)*. Loyalty to the *contrada* of one's birth is fierce, and as you wander the streets you will see the parishes' animal symbols repeated on flags, plaques and carvings. Siena's hilly position also means that city walks offer delightful hidden corners and countless sudden views.

The Duomo dominating Siena's skyline

Via della Galluzza leads to the house of St Catherine.

The Baptistry has fine frescoes and a font with reliefs by Donatello, Jacopo della Quercia and Ghiberti.

★ Duomo
Striped black and white marble pillars, surmounted by a carved frieze of the popes, support the Duomo's vaulted ceiling, painted blue with gold stars to resemble the night sky.

Each tier of the Duomo's bell tower has one more window than the floor below.

Bus station

Railway station

VIA D. GALLUZZA

PIAZZA INDIPENDENZA

VIA DI DIACCETO

VIA DI CITTA

VIA DI FONTEBRANDA

VIA DEI PELLEGRINI

VIA FRANCIOSA

PIAZZA SAN GIOVANNI

VIC. D. CAMPANE

VIA DEL FUSARI

VIA DEL POGGIO

VIA DI CITTA

PIAZZA DEL DUOMO

VIA DEL CAPITANO

Museo dell'Opera del Duomo
Duccio's Maestà, one of the greatest Sienese paintings, was paraded around Siena's streets on its completion in 1311, and influenced the city's painters for decades to come.

KEY

‒ ‒ ‒   Suggested route

| 0 metres | 300 |
| 0 yards | 300 |

Loggia della Mercanzia

Built in 1417, the arcade is where Siena's medieval merchants and money dealers carried out their business.

The Logge del Papa, or Pope's colonnade, was built in honour of Pius II in 1462.

Tourist information

Drummer in Siena's Palio

Piazza del Campo

Italy's loveliest piazza occupies the site of the old Roman forum, and for much of Siena's early history was the city's principal marketplace. It began to assume its present shape in 1293, when the Council of Nine, Siena's ruling body at the time, began to acquire land with a view to creating a grand civic piazza. The red brick paving was begun in 1327 and completed in 1349, its distinctive nine segments designed to reflect the authority of the Council of Nine and to symbolize the protective folds of the Madonna's cloak. The piazza has been the focus of city life ever since, a setting for executions, bullfights and the twice-yearly drama of the Palio *(see p331)*, a festival centred around a bareback horse race. Cafés, restaurants and fine medieval palazzi now line the Campo's fringes, dominated by the **Palazzo Pubblico** (1297–1342) and **Torre del Mangia**, built in 1348 *(see p330)*. This imposing ensemble tends to overshadow the little **Fonte Gaia** on the piazza's northern edge. The fountain is a 19th-century copy of an original carved by Jacopo della Quercia in 1409–19. Its reliefs depict the *Virtues, Adam and Eve*, and the *Madonna and Child* (the originals are on the rear loggia of the Palazzo Pubblico). The fountain's water is still supplied by a 500-year-old aqueduct.

Fonte Gaia

These reliefs are 19th-century copies of originals by Jacopo della Quercia.

★ Palazzo Pubblico

The graceful Gothic town hall was completed in 1342. At 102 m (330 ft), the bell tower, Torre del Mangia, is the second highest medieval tower ever built in Italy.

STAR SIGHTS

★ Duomo

★ Palazzo Pubblico

The Piazza del Campo and Fonte Gaia from the Torre del Mangia

Exploring Siena

ONCE A CAPITAL to rival Florence, Siena is Italy's prettiest medieval town, still endowed with the grandeur of the age in which it was at its peak (1260–1348). Begin an exploration of its historic centre in Piazza del Campo and the surrounding maze of medieval alleys.

Lorenzetti's *Allegory of Good Government* (1338), Palazzo Pubblico

🏛 Palazzo Pubblico

Piazza del Campo 1.   📞 *0577 29 22 63.* **Museo Civico & Torre del Mangia** 🕐 *daily.* 📷

Although it continues in its ancient role as Siena's town hall, the Palazzo Pubblico's medieval rooms, some decorated with paintings of the Sienese School, are open to the public. The **Museo Civico** is housed here. The main council chamber, or Sala del Mappamondo, is named after a map of the world painted by Ambrogio Lorenzetti in the early 14th century. One wall is covered by Simone Martini's recently restored fresco of the *Maestà* (1315), which depicts the Virgin in Majesty as the Queen of Heaven, attended by the Apostles, saints and angels. Opposite is a fresco (attributed to Simone Martini, but possibly later) of the mercenary *Guidoriccio da Fogliano* (1330). The walls of the chapel alongside are covered with frescoes of the *Life of the Virgin* (1407) by Taddeo di Bartolo, and the choir stalls

(1428) are decorated with wooden panels inlaid with biblical scenes. The Sala della Pace contains the famous *Allegory of Good and Bad Government* (1338–40), a pair of frescoes by Ambrogio Lorenzetti. They form one of the most important series of secular paintings from the Middle Ages. In the *Good Government* fresco civic life flourishes, while the *Bad Government*, presided over by a demon, reveals rubbish-strewn streets and ruins.

The Sala del Risorgimento is covered with late 19th-century frescoes illustrating the events leading up to the unification of Italy under King Vittorio Emanuele II.

In the palace courtyard is the entrance to the magnificent **Torre del Mangia**, the palace's huge bell tower. Rising 102 m (330 ft), it is a prominent feature of

Siena's skyline. Built by the brothers Muccio and Francesco di Rinaldo between 1338 and 1348, it was named after the first bell-ringer, whose idleness led to the nickname *Mangia-guadagni* (literally "eat the profits"). There are 505 steps to the top of the tower, which has wonderful views.

🏛 Casa di Santa Caterina

Costa di Sant'Antonio. 📞 *0577 441 77.* 🕐 *daily.*

Siena's patron saint, Catherine Benincasa (1347–80), was the daughter of a tradesman. At the age of eight she devoted herself to God and had many visions, as well as later receiving the stigmata (wounds of Christ). Like her namesake, St Catherine of Alexandria, she was believed to have been betrothed to the Christ child in a vision – a scene which inspired many artists. Her eloquence persuaded Pope Gregory XI to return the seat of the papacy to Rome in 1376, after 67 years of exile in Avignon. St Catherine died in Rome and was canonized in 1461.

Today Catherine's house is surrounded by chapels and cloisters. Among them is the Church of the Crucifixion, which was built in 1623 in her orchard to house the late 12th-century Crucifixion, in front of which she received the stigmata in 1375. The house is decorated with paintings of events from her life by artists including her contemporaries Francesco Vanni and Pietro Sorri.

Cloister of Casa di Santa Caterina, birthplace of Siena's patron saint

⚏ Palazzo Piccolomini

Via Banchi di Sotto 52. **C** *0577 24 71 45.* ☐ *Mon–Sat am.*

Siena's most imposing private palazzo was built for the wealthy Piccolomini family in the 1460s by the Florentine architect and sculptor Bernardo Rossellino. It now contains the Sienese state archives, account books and taxation documents dating back to the 13th century. Some of the leading artists of their day were employed to paint the wooden bindings used to enclose the tax and account records. The paintings, now on display in the Sala di Congresso, often show scenes of Siena itself, bristling with towers, or episodes from the city's past.

Other records include a will attributed to Boccaccio and the council's contract with Jacopo della Quercia for the Fonte Gaia *(see p329).*

A detail from Martini's *Blessed Agostino Novello* (c.1330)

⚏ Pinacoteca Nazionale

Via San Pietro 29. **C** *0577 28 11 61.* ☐ *daily.* 🖼 🚻

This fine gallery, which is housed in the 14th-century Palazzo Buonsignori, contains an unsurpassed collection of paintings by artists of the Sienese School. Arranged in chronological order, from the 13th century through to the Mannerist period (1520–1600), highlights include Duccio's *Madonna dei Francescani* (1285) and Simone Martini's masterpiece *The Blessed Agostino Novello and Four of His Miracles* (c.1330). Pietro Lorenzetti's *Two Views*, from the 14th century, are early examples of landscape painting, and Pietro da Domenico's *Adoration of the Shepherds* (1510) shows how the art of

The austere exterior of the church of San Domenico (begun 1226)

Siena remained visibly influenced by its Byzantine roots long after the naturalism of the Renaissance had reached across the rest of Europe.

⚏ San Domenico

Piazza San Domenico. ☐ *daily.*

The preserved head of the city's patroness, St Catherine of Siena (1347–80), can be seen in a gilded tabernacle on the altar of a chapel dedicated to her in the huge, barn-like Gothic church of San Domenico (begun 1226). The chapel itself was built in 1460 for this purpose and is dominated by Sodoma's frescoes (1526), to the right and left of the altar, which show Catherine in states of religious fervour. The church has the only portrait of St Catherine considered authentic, painted by her friend Andrea Vanni.

THE SIENESE PALIO

The Palio is Tuscany's most celebrated festival and it occurs in the Campo each year on 2 July and 16 August at 7pm. It is a bareback horse race first recorded in 1283, but it may have had its origins in Roman military training. The jockeys represent ten of Siena's 17 *contrade* (districts); the horses are chosen by the drawing of lots and are blessed at the local *contrada* churches. Preceded by days of colourful pageantry, costume processions and heavy betting, the races themselves last only 90 seconds each. Thousands of spectators crowd into the piazza to watch the race, and rivalry between competitors is intense. The winner is rewarded with a silk *palio* (banner). Festivities for the winners can last for weeks.

A *contrada* symbol

The Sienese displaying their flag-throwing skills before the Palio

Siena: Duomo

A symbol of
the Risen Christ
on the façade

SIENA'S DUOMO (1136–1382) is one of Italy's greatest cathedrals, a spectacular mixture of sculpture, paintings and Pisan-influenced Romanesque-Gothic architecture. Had 14th-century plans to create a new nave come to fruition, the building would have become the largest church in Christendom. In the event the plan came to nothing, abandoned when the plague of 1348 virtually halved the city's population. Among the Duomo's treasures are sculptural masterpieces by Nicola Pisano, Donatello and Michelangelo, a fine inlaid pavement and a magnificent fresco cycle by Pinturicchio.

Baptismal Font
This Renaissance font by della Quercia and Donatello stands in the Baptistry.

Pulpit Panels
Carved in 1265–8 by Nicola Pisano, with help from Arnolfo di Cambio and his son Giovanni, the panels on the octagonal pulpit depict scenes from the Life of Christ.

In the nave, black and white marble pillars support the vault.

Chapel of St John the Baptist

The north aisle contains sculptures by Michelangelo of Saints Peter, Pius, Gregory and Paul (1501–4).

Inlaid Marble Floor
The Massacre of the Innocents *is one of a series of scenes in the inlaid marble floor. The marble is usually uncovered during September each year.*

Piccolomini Library
Pinturicchio's frescoes (1509) portray the life of the Piccolomini pope, Pius II. Here he presides at the betrothal of Frederick III to Eleonora of Portugal.

The Museo dell'Opera del Duomo occupies the side aisle of the unfinished nave, which was roofed over to house the museum.

The Campanile was added in 1313.

Archway leading to the Baptistry

VISITORS' CHECKLIST

P. del Duomo. 0577 28 30 48.
Pollicino. 9am–7:30pm daily (Nov–Mar: 7:30am–1pm, 2:30–5pm daily). Piccolomini Library 2:30–7:30pm (Nov–Mar: to 5pm). (also allows access to Museo dell'Opera.)

Façade gives indication of planned size of nave

The unfinished nave, if completed, would have measured 50 m (162 ft) in length and 30 m (97 ft) in breadth.

Entrance to Duomo

The doors were built in 1284–97, the rest of the façade a century later.

Façade Statues
Many façade statues have been replaced by copies; the originals are in the Museo dell'Opera del Duomo.

Museo dell'Opera del Duomo

Piazza del Duomo 8. 0577 28 30 48. daily. public hols.
Part of this museum is devoted to sculpture removed from the exterior of the Duomo, including a Renaissance tondo of a *Madonna and Child*, probably by Donatello, as well as several badly eroded Gothic statues by Giovanni Pisano and Jacopo della Quercia. The highlight is Duccio's huge *Maestà* (1308–11), one of the Sienese School's finest works. It depicts the Madonna and Child on one side, and scenes from the Life of Christ on the other. It was originally placed on the Duomo's high altar, where it replaced the striking *Madonna of the Large Eyes* (1220–30) by an anonymous Sienese painter, also in the museum.

Statues from the Duomo now on show in the Museo dell'Opera

Fortezza Medicea

Viale Maccari. **Fortezza** daily. **Enoteca** 0577 28 84 97. 3pm–midnight Mon–Sat.
This huge red-brick fortress was built for Cosimo I by Baldassarre Lanci in 1560, following Siena's defeat by the Florentines in the 1554–5 war. After an 18-month siege, during which more than 8,000 Sienese died, the town's banking and wool industries were suppressed by the Florentine masters and all major building work ended.

The fortress now houses the Enoteca Italica, a wine shop offering visitors the chance both to taste and to buy from a comprehensive list of quality wines from all over Italy.

Street-by-Street: San Gimignano ㉔

THE THIRTEEN TOWERS that dominate San Gimignano's majestic skyline were built by noble families in the 12th and 13th centuries, when the town's position – on the main pilgrim route from northern Europe to Rome – brought it great prosperity. The plague of 1348, and the diversion of the pilgrim route, led to its decline as well as its preservation. Today only one of the towers, the Torre Grossa, is open to the public. For a small town, San Gimignano is rich in works of art, good shops and restaurants.

San Gimignano's famous skyline, almost unchanged since the Middle Ages

Collegiata
This 11th-century church's interior is full of frescoes, including The Creation *(1367) by Bartolo di Fredi.*

Sant'Agostino

Tourist information

VIA SAN MATTEO

VIA CAPASSI

VIA DIACCETO

PIAZZA NOMI

PIAZZA DEL DUOMO

PIAZZA DELLA CISTERN

VIA DELLA COSTERELLA

VIA DI QUERCECCHIO

VIA BERIGNANO

VIA SAN GIOVANNI

Palazzo del Popolo
The council chamber of the town hall (1288–1323) features a large Maestà *(1317) by Lippo Memmi.*

The Annunciation by Ghirlandaio
This painting, completed in 1482, is located in a courtyard loggia alongside the Collegiata.

Bus station ↙

Via San Giovanni
is lined with shops selling local goods.

**Among the Piazza del
Duomo's** historic buildings
is the Palazzo Vecchio
del Podestà (1239),
whose tower is
probably the
town's oldest.

**Piazza della
Cisterna**
*This square is
named after
the well at its
centre and
is the heart
of the old
town.*

L CASTELLO

OCENTI

ANDORNELLA

**The Museo
Civico** provides
access to the tallest of
the town's 13 remaining towers.

KEY

– – – Suggested route

metres   250

yards   250

🏛 Museo Civico

Palazzo del Popolo, Piazza del
Duomo. [📞] 0577 94 00 08.
Museum & tower 🕐 daily. 🎫
Frescoes in the courtyard of
this museum feature the coats
of arms of city mayors and
magistrates, as well as a 14th-
century *Virgin and Child* by
Taddeo di Bartolo.

The first public room is
the Sala di Dante, where an
inscription recalls a visit by
the poet in 1300. The walls
are covered with hunting
scenes and a huge *Maestà*
fresco (1317) by Lippo
Memmi. The floor above has
an art collection, which
includes excellent works
by Pinturicchio, Bartolo
di Fredi, Benozzo Gozzoli
and Filippino Lippi. The
famous *Wedding Scene*
frescoes by Memmo di
Filippucci (early 14th
century) show a couple
sharing a bath and going
to bed – an unusual
record of life in 14th-
century Tuscany.

⛪ Collegiata

Piazza del
Duomo. 🕐 daily.
This 12th-century
Romanesque church
contains a feast of
frescoes. In the
north aisle the
frescoes comprise
26 episodes from
the Old Testament
(1367) by Bartolo di Fredi.
The opposite wall features
scenes from the *Life of Christ*
(1333–41) by Lippo Memmi,
while at the back of the church

**Bartolo di Fredi's
Christ, Sant'Agostino**

The ceiling of the Collegiata,
painted with gold stars

there are scenes from the *Last
Judgment* painted by Taddeo
di Bartolo. Frescoes (1475) by
Ghirlandaio adorn both the
tiny Chapel of Santa Fina and
the nearby loggia.

⛪ Sant'Agostino

Piazza Sant'Agostino. 🕐 daily.
Consecrated in 1298, this
church has a simple façade,
contrasting markedly with the
heavily decorated Rococo
interior (c.1740) by Vanvitelli.
Above the main altar is
the *Coronation of the
Virgin* by Piero del
Pollaiuolo, dated
1483. The choir is
entirely covered in
a cycle of frescoes
of *The Life of St
Augustine* (1465)
executed by the
Florentine artist
Benozzo Gozzoli.
In the Cappella di San
Bartolo, on the right of the
main entrance, is an elaborate
marble altar completed by
Benedetto da Maiano in 1495.

Fresco from the early 14th-century *Wedding Scene* cycle by
Memmo di Filippucci in the Museo Civico

Elba ㉘

Livorno. 🏘 *30,000.* 🚢 *Portoferraio* 🚌 ℹ️ *Calata Italia 26 (0565 91 46 71).* 🚃 *Portoferraio: Fri.*

ELBA'S MOST FAMOUS resident was Napoleon, who spent nine months here after the fall of Paris in 1814. Today Italy's third largest island is mainly populated by holiday-makers, who come by ferry from Piombino, 10 km (6 miles) away on the mainland. The main town is Porto-ferraio, with an old port and a modern seafront of hotels and fish restaurants.

The landscape of the island is varied. On the west coast, which tends to be a little quieter, there are sandy beaches suitable for all water sports. The east coast, centred on the town of Porto Azzurro, the island's second port, is more rugged, with high cliffs and stony beaches. Inland, olive groves and vineyards line hillsides, and vegetation covers the mountains. A good way to see the interior is to take the road from Marciana Marina to the old medieval village of Marciana Alta. Close by, a minor road leads to a cable car that runs to Monte Capanne (1,018 m/3,300 ft), a magnificent viewpoint.

Marciana Marina on Elba

Sovana ㉙

Grosseto. 🏘 *100.*

SOVANA IS ONE of southern Tuscany's prettiest villages. Its single little street ends in Piazza del Pretorio, home to the ancient church of Santa

View over Pitigliano and the town's dramatic cliffs and caves

Maria, whose lovely interior contains frescoes and a 9th-century altar canopy. A lane beyond leads through olive groves to the Romanesque Duomo, filled with reliefs and carvings from an earlier church on the site. Tuscany's finest Etruscan tombs lie in the sur-rounding countryside, many of them clearly signed and easily visited from the village.

Maremma ㉛

Grosseto. ℹ️ *Maremma Centro Visite, Alberese (0564 40 70 98).* **Marginal Areas** 🚪 *to entrances from Alberese.* 🔲 *daily.* 🎫 📷 **Inner Park Areas** 🚌 *from Alberese to tour departure point.* 🔲 *9am–1 hr before sunset Wed, Sat, Sun, public hols.* 🎫 *only Jun–Sep: walking tours at 7am (4 hrs) & 4pm (3 hrs).* 📷

THE ETRUSCANS, followed by the Romans, were the first to cultivate the marshes and low hills of the Maremma. Following the collapse of the Roman Empire, however, the area fell prey to flooding and malaria, twin scourges that left it virtually uninhabited until the 18th century. The land has since been reclaimed, the irrigation canals unblocked and farming developed on the fertile soil. The stunning Parco Naturale della Maremma was set up in 1975 to preserve the area's native flora and fauna, and to prevent development on one of Italy's few pristine stretches of coastline. Entrance to much of the park is restricted to access on foot or by a park bus from Alberese. Other more marginal areas, however, such as the excellent beach at Marina di Alberese and the countryside around Talamone in the south, are easier to see.

Pitigliano ㉚

Grosseto. 🏘 *4,400.* 🚌 ℹ️ *Via Roma 6 (0564 61 70 19).* 🚃 *Wed.*

PITIGLIANO IS spectacularly situated high above the cave-riddled cliffs of the Lente valley. Its maze of tiny medieval streets includes a small Jewish ghetto, formed in the 17th century by Jews

Irrigated salt marsh

Trappola

Fiume Ombrone

Beaches

The Ombrone estuary is a mixture of pines, marsh and dunes and is home to birds such as the flamingo, sea eagle, roller and bee-eater.

KEY

═══	Roads
▬▬	Paths
═══	Canals and rivers
– –	Itineraries

0 kilometres   2

0 miles   1

fleeing from Catholic persecution. The **Palazzo Orsini** has its water supply brought in by an impressive aqueduct, built in 1545. It houses the **Museo Zuccarelli** with its small exhibition of work by artist Francesco Zuccarelli (1702–88), who lived locally. He also painted two of the altarpieces in the medieval **Duomo** in Piazza San Gregorio. The **Museo Etrusco** contains finds from ancient local settlements.

🏛 **Museo Zuccarelli**
Palazzo Orsini, Piazza della Fortezza Orsini 4. ☎ 0564 61 55 68.
☐ Mar–Jul: Tue–Sun; Aug: daily; Sep–Dec: Sat & Sun. ◪
🏛 **Museo Etrusco**
Piazza della Fortezza Orsini.
☎ 0564 61 70 19. ☐ Tue–Sun.

Monte Argentario ❷

Grosseto. 🏘 13,000. 🚊 ❶ Corso Umberto 55, Porto Santo Stefano (0564 81 42 08). ☐ Tue.

MONTE ARGENTARIO was an island until the early 1700s, when the shallow waters separating it from the mainland began to silt up, creating two sandy spits of land, known as *tomboli*, which enclose the Orbetello lagoon. Today the lagoon hosts a beautiful nature reserve. **Orbetello** itself, a lively and relatively unspoilt little town, was linked to the island in 1842, when a dyke was constructed from the mainland. The harbour towns of **Porto Ercole** and **Porto Santo Stefano** are up-market

Porto Ercole, Monte Argentario

resorts, busy with visitors in summer. Interior roads – notably the Strada Panoramica – offer peaceful drives past rocky coves and bays.

Entry tickets are sold at Alberese's park headquarters.

Wild Boar
The most impressive of the Maremma's many wild animals is the indigenous wild boar, a smaller creature than the Eastern European boar found elsewhere in Tuscany.

San Rabano, a ruined Cistercian abbey (12th century), is close to the park's highest point.

Pine nuts for cooking are still collected from the park's woodlands.

The Uccellina Hills are crowned by old Spanish watchtowers, pinewoods and scented *macchia*.

Birds of prey, such as the hobby and peregrine, hunt in more remote parts of the park.

 Stazione di Alberese

Unspoilt coastline

Marked Footpaths
Several gentle footpaths are marked around the park, but in practice you can wander almost at will among most of its dunes and pinewoods.

This fishing village is set against pretty countryside.

Stazione di Talamone

Rocca di Talamone

UMBRIA

·······································

LONG DISMISSED AS *Tuscany's "gentler sister", Umbria has recently emerged from the shadow of its more famous western neighbour. Forming an expanse of gentle pastoral countryside and high mountain wilderness, the picturesque region has been dubbed the "Green Heart of Italy". Umbria is also well known for the beauty and profusion of its medieval hill-towns.*

The region was inhabited in the 8th century BC by the Umbrians, a peaceable farming tribe, and later colonized by the Etruscans and Romans. In the Middle Ages, the Lombards established a dukedom centred around Spoleto. By the 13th century much of the region was scattered with independent city-states, most of them eventually absorbed by the Papal States, where they remained until Italian unification in 1860.

Today the old towns are Umbria's chief glory. In Perugia, the region's capital, and the smaller centres of Gubbio, Montefalco and Todi, there are numerous Romanesque churches, civic palaces, vivid fresco cycles and endless medieval nooks and crannies. Spoleto, renowned for its summer arts festival, blends grandiose medieval monuments with Roman remains and some of Italy's oldest churches. The surrounding Vale of Spoleto is a chequerboard of agricultural countryside and fascinating traditional villages.

Assisi, the birthplace of St Francis, contains the Basilica di San Francesco, frescoed in part by Giotto. At Orvieto, magnificently situated on its volcanic crag, there are Etruscan remains and one of Italy's finest Romanesque-Gothic cathedrals.

Umbria's oak woods, ice-clear streams and rich soils yield many delicacies. Chief among these are trout and truffles, olive oils to rival those of Tuscany, prized lentils from Castelluccio, cured meats from Norcia and tangy mountain cheeses. A variety of well-regarded wines are produced from the vineyards of Torgiano and Montefalco.

A shop in Norcia selling a selection of Italy's finest hams, sausages and salamis

◁ A street scene in the ancient town of Todi

Exploring Umbria

ASSISI AND SPOLETO, Umbria's loveliest towns, are the most convenient and charming bases for exploring the region. Both these medieval gems are unmissable, as is the old centre of Perugia, the region's capital, and the alluring hill-towns of Gubbio, Spello, Montefalco and Todi. Umbria's landscapes are as compelling as its towns, from the eerie wastes of the Piano Grande and the mountain splendour of the Monti Sibillini national park (best reached from Norcia) to the gentler countryside of the Valnerina and the beach-fringed shores of Lake Trasimeno.

SIGHTS AT A GLANCE

Assisi pp344–5 ❷
Gubbio ❶
Lake Trasimeno ❹
Montefalco ❽
Monti Sibillini ❿
Norcia ⓫
Orvieto ❺
Perugia ❸
Spello ❾
Spoleto ❼
Todi ❻
Valnerina ⓬

SEE ALSO

• **Where to Stay** pp561–3

• **Where to Eat** pp595–7

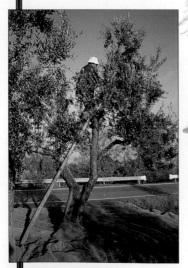

Olive harvest in the Umbrian
countryside near Orvieto

GETTING AROUND

Excellent road, rail and bus links exist in the region. The A1 from Florence passes Orvieto, which is linked to Todi by the N448. The N75 connects Perugia, Assisi and Spello, then the N3 continues to Trevi, Spoleto and Terni. Rome–Florence trains serve Orvieto, and Rome–Ancona trains serve Spoleto, with branch lines connecting Perugia, Spello and Assisi.

The hill-town of Castelluccio, east of Norcia, and the Monti Sibillini

A side street in the medieval town of Gubbio in northern Umbria

KEY

- Motorway
- Major road
- Minor road
- Scenic route
- River
- Viewpoint

0 kilometres 25

0 miles 15

Gubbio ❶

Perugia. 🏛 33,000. 🚉 Fossato di Vico-Gubbio. 🚌 ℹ️ Piazza Oderesi 6 (075 922 06 93). 🗓 Tue.

GUBBIO VIES with Assisi for the title of Umbria's most medieval town. The beauty of its twisting streets and terracotta-tiled houses is enhanced by the forest-swathed Apennines. Founded by the Umbrians in the 3rd century BC as Tota Ikuvina, it assumed greater prominence in the 1st century AD as the Roman colony, Eugubium. It emerged as an independent commune in the 11th century having spread up the slopes of Monte Ingino. From 1387 to 1508 Gubbio was ruled from Urbino by the Dukes of Montefeltro.

The 13th-century **Duomo** is distinguished by a wagon-vaulted ceiling whose curved arches symbolize hands in prayer. Medieval Via dei Consoli leads to the 13th-century **Palazzo del Bargello** – a stone-faced building formerly the headquarters of the chief of police. Also here is the **Fontana dei Matti** (Fountain of the Mad), named after the tradition that anyone who walks around it three times will go insane.

Macabre legends surround the walled-up **Porte della Morte** (Doors of Death) that can be seen in Via dei Consoli and elsewhere in the town. Reputedly used for the passage of coffins from houses, the doors, once tainted, were sealed and never used again.

It is now thought their purpose was probably defensive. In the lower town, the church of **San Francesco** (1259–82)

Façade of the Palazzo dei Consoli in Gubbio

The interior of Perugia's San Pietro, rebuilt in the 15th century

is known for 17 faded frescoes showing scenes from the *Life of the Virgin*, painted between 1408 and 1413 by Ottaviano Nelli. Opposite is the **Tiratoio** (Weavers' Loggia). Wool was stretched out to dry in its shady arcade. West of here are the ruins of a 1st-century AD Roman amphitheatre.

🏛 Palazzo dei Consoli

Piazza Grande. 📞 075 927 42 98. 🗓 daily. 🔴 1 Jan, 1 May, 25 Dec. 🎟
Dominating the skyline of Gubbio is this mighty civic palace, begun in 1332 by Gattapone. Its Salone dell'Arengo houses the Museo Civico, best known for the Eugubine Tablets (250–150 BC). Discovered in 1444, the seven bronze slabs are inscribed with Etruscan and Roman characters, probably a phonetic translation of prayers and rituals from the ancient Umbrian and Etruscan languages. Upstairs a small art gallery contains works by local painters.

One of the Eugubine Tablets in Gubbio

🏛 Palazzo Ducale

Via Federico da Montefeltro. 📞 075 927 58 72. 🗓 Tue–Sun. 🔴 Mon, 1 Jan, 1 May, 25 Dec. 🎟 ♿
Attributed to Francesco di Giorgio Martini, this palace was built in 1470 for the Montefeltro as a copy of the family home in Urbino *(see pp360–61)*. It also has a pretty Renaissance courtyard.

Assisi ❷

See pp344–5.

Perugia ❸

🏛 160,000. 🚉 🚌 ℹ️ Piazza IV Novembre 3 (075 572 33 27). 🗓 daily.

PERUGIA'S OLD CENTRE hinges around the pedestrianized Corso Vannucci, named after the local painter Pietro Vannucci (Perugino). At its northern end is Piazza IV Novembre, dominated by the **Fontana Maggiore**, a 13th-century fountain by Nicola and Giovanni Pisano.

To the rear rises Perugia's 15th-century **Duomo**, its entrance flanked by a statue of Pope Julius II (1555) and a pulpit built for Siena's San Bernardino (1425). Its Cappella del Santo Anello contains the Virgin's "wedding ring", a weighty piece of agate said to change colour according to the character of the person wearing it. The third pillar in the south nave holds a Renaissance painting of the *Madonna delle Grazie* by Gian Nicola di Paolo. The figure is credited with miraculous powers, and mothers bring newly baptized children to kneel before it. Buried in the transepts are Popes Urban IV and Martin IV.

Away from the Corso is the **Oratorio di San Bernardino** (1457–61) on Piazza San Francesco, with a colourful façade by Agostino di Duccio.

Beyond the old city walls on Borgo XX Giugno stands **San Pietro**, Perugia's most extravagantly decorated church. Founded in the 10th century and rebuilt in 1463, the best feature of the fine interior is the wooden choir (1526).

Piazza Giordano Bruno is home to **San Domenico** (1305–1632), Umbria's largest church, which is known for the Gothic tomb of Benedict XI (c.1304) and decoration by Agostino di Duccio.

🏛 Museo Archeologico Nazionale dell'Umbria
San Domenico, Piazza Giordano Bruno.
[075 572 71 41. ◯ daily (Sun am).
● 1 Jan, 1 May, 25 Dec. 🖼 ♿
Housed in the cloisters of San Domenico, this museum exhibits prehistoric, Etruscan and Roman artifacts.

🏛 Palazzo dei Priori
Corso Vannucci 19.
[075 574 12 47.
◯ daily. ● 1 Jan, 1 May, 25 Dec & 1st Mon each month. 🖼 ♿
The monumental walls and bristling crenellations of this palace mark it as Umbria's finest public building (see pp50–51). Among its finely decorated rooms is the Sala dei Notari (c.1295), the former lawyers' hall, which is vividly frescoed with scenes from the Old Testament – the work of a follower of Pietro Cavallini. The raised doorway is guarded by a pair of large bronzes made in 1274: a Guelph lion and a griffin, the medieval

Entrance of Palazzo dei Priori, Perugia

Colourful façade of Perugia's Oratorio di San Bernardino

Medieval street in Perugia

emblem of Perugia. The Sala di Udienza del Collegio della Mercanzia, built around 1390, was formerly used by the Merchants' Guild. This room is late Gothic in style, with exquisite panelling and 15th-century inlaid wood.

Also in the palace is the Collegio del Cambio, Perugia's former money exchange, which was begun in 1452. This room was used by the Bankers' Guild. Its walls are covered with superlative frescoes (1498–1500) by Perugino, works that are devoted to a mixture of Classical and religious scenes. A glum self-portrait scowls down from the centre of the left wall, while the hand of Perugino's pupil Raphael may be evident in some panels on the right wall.

🏛 Galleria Nazionale dell'Umbria
Palazzo dei Priori, Corso Vannucci 19.
[075 574 12 47. ◯ daily.
● 1 Jan, 25 Dec. 🖼 ♿
Umbria's greatest collection of paintings is displayed here on the third floor of the palace. Most of the works are 13th- to 18th-century paintings by local artists, but the highlights are altarpieces by Piero della Francesca and Fra Angelico.

Lake Trasimeno ❹

Perugia. 🚆 🚌 Castiglione del Lago.
🛈 Piazza Mazzini 10, Castiglione del Lago (075 965 24 84).

EDGED WITH LOW HILLS and gentle farming country, this is Italy's fourth-largest lake. Its miles of placid water and reed-lined shores have a tranquil, melancholy beauty.

Drainage of the lake began under the Romans, but today the lake is gently drying up of its own accord. The town of **Castiglione del Lago**, jutting out on a fortified promontory, has an easy-going atmosphere and small sandy beaches. The 16th century **castle** is used for summer concerts. The church of **Santa Maria Maddalena**, begun in 1836, has a fine Madonna and Child (c.1500) by Eusebio di San Giorgio.

Passignano sul Trasimeno has a bustling promenade and, like Castiglione, it offers boat trips to **Isola Maggiore**. The island's charming village is known for lace-making.

THE BATTLE OF LAKE TRASIMENO

In 217 BC the Romans suffered one of their worst ever military defeats on the shores of Lake Trasimeno. The Carthaginian general, Hannibal, lured the Romans (who were led by the consul Flaminius) into a masterful ambush close to present-day Ossaia (Place of Bones) and Sanguineto (Place of Blood). Some 16,000 legionaries perished, hacked down on the lake's marshy fringes. Hannibal, by contrast, lost only 1,500 men. Today you can explore the battlefield, which includes over 100 mass graves found near Tuoro sul Trasimeno.

19th-century engraving of General Hannibal

Assisi: Basilica di San Francesco

THE BURIAL PLACE of St Francis, this basilica was begun in 1228, two years after the saint's death. Over the next century its Upper and Lower Churches were decorated by the foremost artists of their day, among them Cimabue, Simone Martini, Pietro Lorenzetti and Giotto, whose frescoes on the *Life of St Francis* are some of the most renowned in Italy. The basilica, which dominates Assisi, is one of the great Christian shrines and receives vast numbers of pilgrims throughout the year.

The campanile was built in 1239.

The choir (1501) features a 13th-century stone papal throne.

Faded paintings by Roman artists line the walls above Giotto's *Life of St Francis*.

St Francis
Cimabue's simple painting (c.1280) captures the humility of the revered saint, who stood for poverty, chastity and obedience.

Steps to the Treasury

The crypt contains the tomb of St Francis.

★ Frescoes by Lorenzetti
The bold composition of Pietro Lorenzetti's fresco, entitled The Deposition *(1323), is based around the truncated Cross, focusing attention on the twisted figure of Christ.*

Lower Church
Side chapels were created here in the 13th century to accommodate the growing number of pilgrims.

STAR FEATURES

- ★ Frescoes by Giotto
- ★ Frescoes by Lorenzetti
- ★ Cappella di San Martino

Upper Church
The soaring Gothic lines of the 13th-century Upper Church symbolized the heavenly glory of St Francis. This style also influenced later Franciscan churches.

The façade
and its rose window are early examples of Italian Gothic.

Entrance to Upper Church

Entrance to Lower Church

★ **Frescoes by Giotto**
The Ecstasy of St Francis is one of 28 panels that make up Giotto's cycle on the Life of St Francis *(c.1290–95).*

★ **Cappella di San Martino**
The frescoes in this chapel on the Life of St Martin *(1315) are by the Sienese painter Simone Martini. This panel shows the* Death of the Saint. *Martini was also responsible for the fine stained glass in the chapel.*

Assisi ❷

Perugia. 🏠 25,000. **FS** 🚌 **i** *Piazza del Comune (075 81 25 34).* 🛒 *Sat.*

THIS BEAUTIFUL medieval town, with its geranium-hung streets, lovely views and fountain-splashed piazzas, is heir to the legacy of St Francis (c.1181–1226), who is buried in the **Basilica di San Francesco**. Sadly the town suffered serious damage when it was hit by an earthquake on 26 September 1997, but restoration was relatively swift – completed in approximately two years. The tourist office can give information on which sights are open to visitors.

Piazza del Comune, Assisi's main square, is dominated by the columns of the **Tempio di Minerva**, a Roman temple-front from the Augustan age. The Palazzo Comunale, opposite, is home to the **Pinacoteca Comunale**, an art gallery with works by local medieval artists.

Down Corso Mazzini lies the **Basilica di Santa Chiara**, the burial place of St Clare – Francis's companion and the founder of the Poor Clares (an order of nuns). One of its chapels contains the crucifix that is said to have bowed its head and ordered Francis to "Repair God's church". It came from **San Damiano**, a sublime church set amid olive groves south of the Porta Nuova.

The **Duomo (San Rufino)**, built during the 12th and 13th centuries, has a superb Roman-esque façade. Inside is a small museum of paintings, and there are archaeological items in the crypt. From the Duomo, Via Maria delle Rose leads to the **Rocca Maggiore** (rebuilt in 1367), an evocative if much-restored castle.

Thirteenth-century **San Pietro**, on Piazza San Pietro, is a simple and carefully restored Romanesque church. The nearby **Oratorio dei Pellegrini**, a 15th-century pilgrims' hospice, contains well-preserved frescoes by Matteo da Gualdo.

Giotto's fresco, *St Francis Appearing to the Friars at Arles* (c.1295), in the Basilica di San Francesco, Assisi

Orvieto ❺

Terni. 🏠 22,000. ☰☰ 🚌 ℹ️ *Piazza Duomo 24 (0763 34 17 72).* 🗓️ *Thu & Sat.*

ORVIETO IS MAGNIFICENT from any angle. Perched on a 300-m (984-ft) plateau, it looks down from its cliff-edged balcony over a vineyard-spotted plain. Visitors flood into the town to admire the **Duomo**, among the greatest of all Italy's Romanesque-Gothic cathedrals.

The tiny 13th-century church of **San Lorenzo in Arari** is at the end of Via Scalza. Its walls feature frescoes describing the martyrdom of St Lawrence, who was grilled to death. The altar is made from an Etruscan sacrificial slab. Via Malabranca leads to **San Giovenale** at Orvieto's western tip, a church that is beautifully and almost completely covered in detailed frescoes from the 15th and 16th centuries. It offers broad views over the surrounding countryside. **Sant'Andrea**, in Piazza della Repubblica, is distinguished by a curious 12-sided campanile, part of the original 12th-century building.

🏛 Museo dell' Opera del Duomo

Piazza Duomo. ☎ *0763 34 24 77.* ⏰ *phone to check times.*

This interesting little museum contains an eclectic collection of treasures given to the Duomo. Among the highlights are paintings by Lorenzo Maitani (died 1330) and sculptures by Andrea Pisano (c.1270–1348).

🏛 Museo Archeologico Faina and Museo Civico

Piazza Duomo 29. ☎ *0763 34 15 11.* ⏰ *daily; Oct–Mar: Tue–Sun.* ● *1 Jan, 25 Dec.* 📷 🎫 📷 ♿

The first of these two museums has a well-known, low-key collection of Etruscan remains including many Greek vases

View into the Pozzo di San Patrizio in Orvieto

that were found in Etruscan tombs in the area. The Museo Civico contains ancient Greek artifacts, as well as Etruscan copies of Greek works.

🏛 Museo d'Arte Moderna "Emilio Greco"

Palazzo Soliano, Piazza Duomo. ☎ *0763 34 46 05.* ⏰ *daily.* ● *1 Jan, 25 Dec.* 📷 ♿

This museum is devoted to the modern Sicilian sculptor, Emilio Greco, who made the bronze doors (1964–70) of the Duomo in Orvieto.

🅰 DUOMO OF ORVIETO

Piazza Duomo. ☎ *0763 34 11 67.* ⏰ *daily.* ♿ 📷

Some 300 years in the building, Orvieto's Duomo (begun 1290), with its breathtaking façade, is one of Italy's greatest cathedrals. It was inspired by the Miracle of Bolsena in which real blood from a consecrated host supposedly fell on the altar cloth of a church in nearby Bolsena.

Carved choir stalls

The exterior is characterized by horizontal bands of white travertine and blue-grey basalt.

14th-century rose window by Orcagna

The reliquary of the Corporal contains the altar cloth from Bolsena.

Cappella del Corporale
This chapel contains Lippo Memmi's Madonna dei Raccomandati *(1320). There are also frescoes (1357–64) by Ugolino di Prete Ilario of the* Miracle of Bolsena *and* Miracles of the Sacrament.

Bronze doors by Emilio Greco (1964–70)

🛁 Pozzo di San Patrizio

Viale San Gallo. **[** 0763 34 37 68.
◯ daily. ● 1 Jan, 25 Dec. 🌐

Orvieto's vast well was commissioned in 1527 by Pope
Clement VII and designed
by the Florentine architect
Antonio da Sangallo to provide the town with a water
supply in case of attack. Two
248-step staircases drop into
its dank interior, cleverly
arranged as a double helix
(spiral) so as not to intersect.
The 62-m (203-ft) shaft, built
from tufa blocks and bricks,
took ten years to complete.

⋔ Necropoli Etrusca – Crocefisso del Tufo

Strada Statale 71 to Orvieto Scalo, km
1,600. **[** 0763 34 36 11. ◯ daily.
🌐 ♿

This Etruscan necropolis from
the 6th century BC has burial
chambers built of blocks of
tufa. Etruscan letters, thought
to be the names
of the deceased,
are inscribed on
the tombs.

Cappella Nuova
*Luca Signorelli's great fresco
cycle of the* Last Judgment
*(1499–1504) features prominently in this chapel. Fra
Angelico and Benozzo Gozzoli
worked here before Signorelli.*

The Façade
*There are detailed carvings
(c.1320–30) at the base of its
four main pilasters. By Lorenzo
Maitani, they depict scenes from
the Old and New Testaments,
including hell and damnation.*

**View of the hill-town of Todi in
southern Umbria**

Todi ❻

Perugia. 🏠 17,000. 🚉 🚌
ℹ Piazza Umberto I 6 (075 894 33 95).
🚍 Sat.

LOOKING DOWN over the Tiber
valley from its hilltop
eyrie, Todi is one of the most
strikingly situated of Umbria's
famous hill-towns. An ancient
Etruscan, and then Roman
settlement, it still preserves
an uncorrupted medieval air,
with several tiny churches,
three austere public palaces
and many sleepy corners.

Most people are drawn here
by the **Piazza del Popolo**,
the main square, flanked by
the lovely plain-faced **Duomo**.
Built in the 13th century on
the site of a Roman temple to
Apollo, it has a dusky
interior and one of
Umbria's finest choirs
(1521–30). Note Ferraù da
Faenza's huge painting (1596)
on the rear wall, a less than
totally successful copy of
Michelangelo's *Last Judgment*,
and the altarpiece at the end
of the right aisle by
Giannicola di Paolo (a
follower of Perugino).

Also flanking the
piazza are the **Palazzo
dei Priori** (1293–
1337) and the
linked **Palazzo
del Capitano**
(1290) and
**Palazzo del
Popolo** (1213).
In the Palazzo del
Capitano, distinguished by its
redoubtable
medieval interior,
lies the **Museo**

Etrusco-Romano. The
museum contains a collection
of local Etruscan and Roman
artifacts. There are altarpieces
and sacred objects in the
Pinacoteca Comunale, also
housed in the palace.

A few steps from the piazza
rises **San Fortunato** (1292–
1462), named after Todi's first
bishop, with a florid Gothic
doorway (1415–58). The high
vaulted plan is based on
German Gothic "hall" churches
and the "barn" churches of
Tuscany, characterized by a
low-pitched vault, polygonal
apse and naves and aisles of
equal height. The choir (1590)
is superb, but the church's
most famous work is a
Madonna and Child (1432) by
Masolino da Panicale (fourth
chapel on the right). The crypt
contains the tomb of Jacopone
da Todi (c.1228–1306), a noted
medieval poet and mystic.

To the right of the church
are some shady gardens, from
which a path (past the tiny
castle) drops through the trees
to emerge in front of **Santa
Maria della Consolazione**
(1508–1607), near the N79.
One of central Italy's finest
Renaissance churches, and
based on a Greek cross, it
may have been built to a plan
by Bramante. The stark, chill
interior is overshadowed by
the harmonious exterior.

🏛 Museo Etrusco-Romano and Pinacoteca Comunale

Palazzi Comunali. **[** 075 895 61.
◯ Tue–Sun (Apr: daily). 🌐 ♿

Santa Maria della Consolazione in Todi

Spoleto ❼

Perugia. 🏘 38,000. FS ▣
ℹ️ Piazza della Libertà 7 (0743 22
03 11). 🛒 Tue & Fri.

FOUNDED BY THE UMBRIANS,
Spoleto became one of
central Italy's most important
Roman colonies, a prominence
maintained by the Lombards,
who in the 7th century made
it the capital of one of their
three Italian dukedoms. After
a period as an independent
city state, the town fell to the
papacy in 1354.

Spoleto, within its wooded
setting, is the loveliest of the
Umbrian hill-towns. Its urbane
atmosphere is enhanced by its
superb monuments and by the
Festival dei Due Mondi, one of
Europe's leading arts festivals
held annually in June and July.

At the southern end of
Piazza del Mercato is the

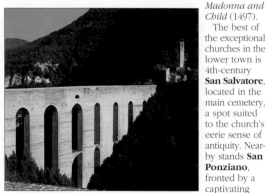

Ponte delle Torri, Spoleto

Arco di Druso, a 1st-century
AD Roman arch. It is flanked
by the church of **Sant'Ansano**,
whose crypt is covered in
frescoes that may date from
the 6th century. Via Aurelio
Saffi, at the piazza's northern
end, leads to **Sant'Eufemia**.
This utterly simple 10th-
century Romanesque church
is known for its matroneum
(women's gallery), once used
to segregate the congregation.

A short way beyond, the
fan-shaped Piazza del Duomo
opens out to reveal Spoleto's
12th-century **Duomo**, graced
with one of the most elegant
façades in Italy. Filling the
apse of the Baroque interior
is a great, newly-restored
fresco cycle. The final work of
Fra Lippo Lippi, from 1467–9,
it describes episodes from
the *Life of the Virgin*. The
Cappella Erioli is adorned
with Pinturicchio's unfinished
*Madonna and
Child* (1497).

The best of
the exceptional
churches in the
lower town is
4th-century
San Salvatore,
located in the
main cemetery,
a spot suited
to the church's
eerie sense of
antiquity. Near-
by stands **San
Ponziano**,
fronted by a
captivating
three-tiered

Façade of San Pietro in Spoleto

Romanesque façade typical of
Umbria. It has a 10th-century
crypt, supported by odd little
columns and decorated with
Byzantine frescoes.

Romanesque **San Gregorio**
in Piazza Garibaldi dates from
1069, but its cramped façade
and stolid campanile incorporate fragments of Roman
buildings. Inside is a raised
presbytery and a lovely
multi-columned crypt. Well-
preserved patches of fresco dot
the walls, interspersed with
austere stone confessionals.
Some 10,000 Christian martyrs
are supposedly buried near the
church. They were reputedly
slaughtered in the town's
Roman **amphitheatre**, traces
of which can be seen in the
barracks on Via del Anfiteatro.

🜛 Ponte delle Torri
This magnificent 14th-century
aqueduct, the "bridge of
towers", is 80 m (262 ft)
high. Designed by
Gattapone (from

ROMANESQUE CHURCHES IN UMBRIA

Umbria's church-building tradition had its roots in ancient
Roman basilicas and in the chapels built over the shrines of its
many saints and martyrs. The region's Romanesque façades are
usually divided into three tiers, often with three rose windows
arranged above a trio of arched portals.
The three doors usually correspond to
the interior's nave and two aisles, which
derive from the simple barn-like plan
of Roman basilicas. Inside, the
presbytery is often raised in
order to allow for the building
of a crypt, which usually contained the relics of a saint or
martyr. Many of the churches
took centuries to build, or
were repeatedly modified
over time, often acquiring
elements of Gothic, Baroque
or Renaissance styles.

San Lorenzo di Arari in
Orvieto takes its name from an
Etruscan altar (arari). This
14th-century church has a
very simple façade (see p348).

12th-century
campanile

Renaissance
portico

Spoleto's Duomo (1198) has
eight rose windows, a mosaic
(1207) and a Renaissance
portico (1491). The tower was
built from old Roman remains.

Gubbio), it is the town's single most famous monument. From the bridge, there are views of the bastions of the **Rocca Albornoz**, a huge papal fortress built in 1359–64, also by Gattapone. Unfortunately, the fortress is closed to the public. Across the bridge a path leads to the Strada di Monteluco and the church of **San Pietro**, which is renowned for the fascinating 12th-century carvings on its façade.

🏛 Pinacoteca Comunale
Palazzo Comunale, Piazza del Municipio.
📞 0743 21 81. ☐ Tue–Sun.
● 1 Jan, 25 Dec. 🗾

Spoleto's art gallery has four beautifully appointed rooms with works by Perugino and his Spoletan protégé, Lo Spagna (c.1450–1528), including a painting of the Madonna and Child with Saints.

Montefalco ❽

Perugia. 🕍 4,900. 🚌 🚐 Mon.

MONTEFALCO, whose name (Falcon's Mount) draws inspiration from its lofty position and sweeping views, is the best of the fascinating villages in the Vale of Spoleto. Criss-crossed by streets almost too narrow for cars, it takes less than five minutes to walk through the village. Yet you might happily spend a morning here, most of it in the polished, new **Museo Civico** housed in the former church

A panel from Gozzoli's fresco cycle (1452) in Montefalco's Museo Civico

of San Francesco. Its highlight is Benozzo Gozzoli's *Life of St Francis* (1452), a radiant fresco cycle that borrows heavily from Giotto's cycle in Assisi *(see pp344–7)*. Other painters represented here are Perugino, Tiberio d'Assisi and Nicolò Alunno, all leading medieval Umbrian artists.

The simple Gothic church of **Sant'Agostino** (begun 1279) on Corso Mameli is dotted with frescoes from the 14th–16th centuries. The church also contains three mummies.

In the main square local wines on sale include the rich, red Sagrantino di Montefalco. Just outside the town walls, the church of **Sant'Illuminata** is covered with charming frescoes, the work of the local 16th-century artist Francesco

Melanzio. About 2 km (1 mile) beyond, the prettily situated church of **San Fortunato** is decorated with frescoes by Gozzoli and Tiberio d'Assisi.

ENVIRONS: The village in the Vale of Spoleto with the most spectacular setting is **Trevi**. The churches of **San Martino** (16th century), on Passeggiata di San Martino, and **Madonna delle Lacrime** (1487–1522), south of Trevi on the road into the village, contain paintings by Perugino and Tiberio d'Assisi, among others.

🏛 Museo Civico di San Francesco
Via Ringhiera Umbra 9. 📞 0742 37 95 98. ☐ Mar–Oct: daily; Nov–Feb: Tue–Sun.
● 1 Jan, 25 Dec. 🗾 ⚙

11th-century campanile
Carved figures

The Duomo (1253) in Assisi is a fine example of the three-tiered façades found across central Italy (see p345). It has a pointed arch and a row of arcading.

Rose window
Rounded portal

Todi's Duomo was begun in the 12th century, but work on its windows and portals continued until the 17th century (see p349).

18th-century rose window

San Michele (c.1195) in Bevagna has a beautiful portal that combines both Romanesque and old Roman fragments (see p352).

Spello ❾

Perugia. 🏘 8,000. FS 🚌
ℹ Piazza Matteotti 3 (0742 30
10 09). 🔄 Wed.

SPELLO IS ONE of the better
known villages in the Vale
of Spoleto. It is renowned for
a fresco cycle by Pinturicchio
in the Cappella Baglioni of
the church of **Santa Maria
Maggiore** (12th–13th century)
on Via Consolare. Executed
around 1500, the frescoes
depict scenes from the New
Testament. Towards the centre
of the village is the Gothic
church of **Sant'Andrea** (13th
century) on Via Cavour. This
road becomes Via Garibaldi,
which leads to **San Lorenzo**,
a Baroque gem of a church
dating from the 12th century.

Spello also boasts Roman
ruins from the age of Augustus:
the **Porta Consolare** at the
end of Via Consolare, and the
twin-towered **Porta Venere**
by Via Torri di Properzio.

The road to Assisi over
Monte Subasio offers stunning views from the top of
the mountain above Spello.

ENVIRONS: The least known
village in the Vale of Spoleto
is **Bevagna**. Like Spello, it
sprang to life as a way-station
on the Via Flaminia (the
Roman road that ran through
this part of Umbria). The
medieval Piazza Silvestri is
the setting for two
Romanesque
churches.

The lofty peaks of the Monti
Sibillini in eastern Umbria

San Silvestro (1195) is the
more atmospheric of the pair,
thanks to its shadowy interior
and ancient crypt, but **San
Michele** (late 12th century)
has an elegant portal, famed
for the little gargoyles on either
side. Both churches are the
work of Maestro Binello.

Monti Sibillini ❿

Macerata. FS Spoleto, 🚌 Visso.
ℹ Largo Giovanni Battista Antinori 1,
Visso (0737 955 26).

RECENTLY AWARDED national
park status, the Monti
Sibillini in eastern Umbria
provide the region's wildest
and most spectacular scenery.
A range 40 km (25 miles) long,
the mountains form part of
the Apennines, a chain that
runs the length of the Italian
peninsula. **Monte
Vettore** is the
loftiest

Pinturicchio's *Annunciation* (c.1500) in Spello's Santa Maria Maggiore

point, and the peninsula's
third highest; it stands at
2,476 m (8,123 ft), a great
whale-backed peak close to
the cave of the mythical sybil
that gave the region its name.

Good maps and trails make
this a superb walking area,
while drivers can follow hair-
pin roads to some of Italy's
most magical landscapes.
Chief of these is the **Piano
Grande**, a huge upland plain
surrounded by a vast amphitheatre of mountains. Bare
but for flocks of sheep and
bedraggled haystacks, the plain
blazes with wild flowers in
spring and with lentils later in
the year. The only habitation
is **Castelluccio**, a beautiful,
neglected mountain village
now being restored. It can be
reached by road from Norcia
and Arquata del Tronto.

Shop front in Norcia displaying
the town's varied meats

Norcia ⓫

Perugia. 🏘 4,700. 🚌 ℹ Piazza
San Benedetto (0743 82 81 73).
🔄 Thu.

THE BIRTHPLACE of St
Benedict, Norcia is a
robust mountain town and an
excellent base for exploring
Valnerina and Monti Sibillini.
One of Italy's culinary capitals,
it is renowned for truffles and
for some of Italy's best hams,
sausages and salamis. Indeed,
the Italian word for a pork
butcher's *(norcineria)* derives
from the name of the town.

Norcia's main sights are in
Piazza San Benedetto. On
the eastern flank, the church
of **San Benedetto** has a 14th-
century portal adorned with
statues of Benedict and his
sister (Santa Scolastica). Legend
claims that the church marks
the site of Benedict's birth –

The 8th-century monastery of San Pietro in Valle, set in the beautiful Valnerina

indeed there are the remains of a 5th-century building in the crypt. However, the church was more likely to have been built over the site of an old Roman temple, since the forum of the Roman colony of Nursia once occupied this spot.

Left of the church stands the newly renovated **Palazzo Comunale**, a monument to the town's period as a free commune during the 13th and 14th centuries. On the opposite side of the square, still dominating the town, rises the **Castellina** (1554), a blunt papal fortress designed by Vignola to help impose order on an unruly mountain district. The **Duomo** (1560), to the left of the Castellina, has been ravaged by earthquakes over the centuries. Indeed, Norcia has been the victim of successive earthquakes and

its houses are low and heavily buttressed with thick walls to protect them from further damage. **Sant'Agostino** on Via Anicia features a range of good 16th-century frescoes. A little way beyond, the **Oratorio di Sant'Agostinaccio** in Piazza Palatina contains a superb 17th-century cciling. Via Umberto shelters the **Edicola** (1354), a strange tabernacle believed to have been carved for a Holy Week procession.

Valnerina ⑫

Perugia. **FS** *Spoleto, then bus.* **ℹ** *Piazza Garibaldi, Cascia (0743 711 47).*

THE VALNERINA (Little Valley of the River Nera) curves through a broad swathe of eastern Umbria, draining the

mountains around Norcia and the Sibillini before emptying into the Tiber. It is edged with craggy, tree-covered slopes and dotted with upland villages and fortified hamlets.

The high spot is **San Pietro in Valle**, an idyllically situated monastery in the hills above the village of Colleponte. Founded in the 8th century, it is one of the few surviving memorials to the Lombards, whose central Italian duchy had its capital in Spoleto. The main body of the monastery church dates from this period, as does the high altar. The nave walls are covered in a wealth of 12th-century frescoes. Some of the best Romanesque carvings in Umbria can be found here.

More popular than the monastery are the **Cascate delle Marmore** near Terni, among Europe's highest waterfalls at 165 m (541 ft). Created by the Romans during drainage work, their waters are now diverted to produce hydroelectric power on all but a few special days. You can view the falls from Marmore village or the N209.

⌂ San Pietro in Valle
Località Ferentillo, Terni. **C** *0744 78 03 16.* ◯ *daily.*
Cascate delle Marmore
7 km (4 miles) along N209 Valnerina, Terni. ◯ *sporadically. Ask at tourist information.*

Piazza San Benedetto and the church of San Benedetto in Norcia

LE MARCHE

Tucked away *in a remote corner between the Adriatic Sea and the Apennine mountains, Le Marche (the Marches) is an enchanting rural patchwork of old towns, hill country and long, sandy beaches. In pre-Christian times the area was settled by the Piceni, a tribe eventually assimilated by the Romans.*

In the 4th century BC, exiles from Magna Graecia colonized much of the region. The most notable town was Ancona, also the northernmost point of Greek influence on the Italian peninsula. During the early Middle Ages the region marked the edge of the Holy Roman Empire, giving rise to its present name (*march* meant border area).

The region's historical peak was reached in the 15th century under Federico da Montefeltro, whose court at Urbino became one of Europe's leading cultural centres. Much of Urbino's former grandeur survives, particularly in Federico's magnificent Renaissance Palazzo Ducale, now home to a regional art collection. Ascoli Piceno is almost as enchanting as Urbino, its central Piazza del Popolo among the most evocative old squares in Italy. Smaller towns like San Leo and Urbania and the republic of San Marino also boast fine medieval monuments.

Today probably as many people come to Le Marche for its beaches and towns as for its hilly, unspoilt interior. Especially beautiful are the snowcapped peaks of the Monti Sibillini, situated in magnificent walking and skiing country.

Regional cuisine encompasses the truffles and robust cheeses of the mountains, tender hams and salamis, *olive ascolane* (olives stuffed with meat and herbs) and *brodetto*, fish soup made in several versions up and down the coast. Dry, white Verdicchio is the best known wine, although more unusual names, such as Bianchello del Metauro, are gaining in popularity.

A field of poppies and olive trees in the heart of Le Marche's countryside

◁ **Medieval gates and ramparts surrounding the hilltop republic of San Marino**

Exploring Le Marche

THE MEDIEVAL TOWNS of Urbino and Ascoli Piceno are the highlights of the region, but the rolling hills of the interior contain an abundance of smaller towns and all but undiscovered villages. San Leo, with its dramatic fortress, is one of the best. Most of the countryside is a pretty mixture of woods and remote hills, rising in the west to the majestic Monti Sibillini. Ancona and the attractive town of Pèsaro are the pivotal points of the vast coastline.

Rolling countryside between
Loreto and Ascoli Piceno

KEY

▰▰▰	Motorway
▬▬▬	Major road
▭▭▭	Minor road
▬▬▬	Scenic route
≈≈≈	River
☀	Viewpoint

View of Ascoli Piceno, one of the prettiest towns in Le Marche

SIGHTS AT A GLANCE

Ancona **9**
Ascoli Piceno **12**
Conero Peninsula **10**
Fano **4**
Grotte di Frasassi **7**
Jesi **8**
Loreto **11**
Pèsaro **3**
San Marino **2**
San Leo **1**
Urbania **6**
Urbino pp360–61 **5**

The rocky reef near Portonovo on the Conero Peninsula

GETTING AROUND

The A14 provides easy access to the coastal resorts. Dual-carriageway spurs from the A14 lead to Urbino, Jesi and Ascoli Piceno, but north south roads in the interior can be slow. Bus services are generally good, but in the interior can be infrequent. The railway service along the coast is excellent, with a good service through the heart of the region, though it can be slow.

A market scene in Fano

0 kilometres   25

0 miles   10

The bell tower of the Duomo rising above the village of San Leo

San Leo ❶

Pèsaro. **i** *Piazza Dante 10 (0541 91 62 31).* 🚌 *from Rimini, change at Villanova.*

FEW CASTLES are as impressive as the great **fortress** that towers over the village of San Leo. Dante used this crag-top site as a model for the landscapes of *Purgatorio*, while Machiavelli considered the citadel to be the finest piece of military architecture in Italy. Its rocky ramparts once contained the Mons Feretrius, a Roman temple dedicated to Jupiter.

An earlier Roman fortress on the site became a papal prison in the 18th century. Its most famous inmate was the larger-than-life Conte di Cagliostro. A swindler, womanizer, necromancer, quack and alchemist, Cagliostro was imprisoned for heresy in the 1790s. His cell was specially built so that its window faced the village's two churches. It is still visible, together with a small picture gallery, state rooms, and the majestic Renaissance ramparts, built by Francesco di Giorgio Martini for the dukes of Montefeltro in the 15th century.

Duty-free shop in San Marino

The captivating village has a quaint cobbled square with a superb 9th-century **Pieve** (parish church). Built partly with stone from the ruined Mons Feretrius, the church was raised over the site of a 6th-century chapel.

Just behind lies the 12th-century **Duomo**, a fine Romanesque building with Corinthian capitals and Roman columns from the Mons Feretrius. The lid of St Leo's sarcophagus is in the crypt. Ancient pagan carvings can be seen on the wall behind the altar.

⚓ Fortress
Via Leopardi. **C** *0541 91 62 31.* ◻ *daily.*

San Marino ❷

🏛 *26,000.* 🚌 *San Marino Città (fr Rimini).* **i** *Contrada Omagnano 20, San Marino (0549 88 23 90).*

EUROPE'S OLDEST republic, tiny San Marino was reputedly founded by St Marinus, a 4th-century monk and stonemason forced to flee the religious persecution of the Emperor Diocletian. With him was St Leo, the founder of the nearby town of San Leo. Dramatically situated on the slopes of Monte Titano, the country has its own mint, stamps, football team – even its own 1,000-strong army.

There are no customs formalities in this small country, whose borders are just 12 km (7 miles)

apart at the widest point. Sadly, the capital, also known as **San Marino**, is thronged with visitors for much of the year and its streets are clogged with souvenir stalls. Garibaldi, who sought shelter here after fleeing Venice in 1849, is honoured by a monument in Piazza Garibaldi. **Borgomaggiore**, the largest town, lies at the foot of Monte Titano, with a cable car to the capital above.

Pèsaro ❸

🏛 *85,000.* 🚉 🚌 **i** *Piazza della Libertà 164 (0721 693 41).* 🅰 *Tue & 1st Thu of month.*

Detail of the *Coronation of the Virgin* by Bellini (c.1470) in the Musei Civici

ONE OF THE ADRIATIC's larger seaside resorts, Pèsaro has managed to retain a stylish air. Behind the promenade and the wall of white stucco hotels is a lively, attractive medieval area.

The art gallery of the **Musei Civici** contains Giovanni Bellini's sumptuous polyptych, the *Coronation of the Virgin* (c.1470). The museum also features Renaissance ceramics.

The **Museo Archeologico Oliveriano** presents historical displays from Roman remains to Iron Age artifacts from the necropolis of nearby Novilara.

The best of the town's churches is **Sant'Agostino** on Corso XI Settembre, remarkable for its choir stalls, each a patchwork of inlaid landscapes and narrative scenes.

Pèsaro is also a point of musical pilgrimage. In 1792 the composer Gioacchino Rossini was born here. His home, **Casa Rossini**, contains memorabilia, while his piano and some original manuscripts lie in the **Conservatorio Rossini**. His operas are performed in the **Teatro Rossini** in Piazza Lazzarini during the annual August music festival.

🏛 **Musei Civici**
Piazza Mosca 29. [0721 312 13.
◯ Tue, Wed am; Thu–Sun. 📷

🏛 **Museo Archeologico Oliveriano**
Via Mazza 97. [0721 333 44.
◯ Mon–Sat am by appt. ♿

🏠 **Casa Rossini**
Via Rossini 34. [0721 38 73 57.
◯ Tue–Sun. 📷

🏠 **Conservatorio Rossini**
Piazza Olivieri 5. [0721 336 70.
◯ Mon–Sat am, but phone first to arrange. ● public hols.

Fano ❹

Pèsaro. 🚶 54,000. FS 🚌 ⛴
ℹ Via Cesare Battisti 10 (0721 80 35 34). 🎪 Wed & Sat.

ANCIENT FANO stands out from the string of beach resorts south of Pèsaro, thanks to its fine old centre and historic monuments. Named after Fanum Fortunae, a pagan temple to the goddess Fortuna, it became the terminus of the Via Flaminia (an important consular road from Rome) and the largest Roman colony on the Adriatic coast. The **Arco d'Augusto** (AD 2), on Via Arco d'Augusto, is Fano's most significant ancient monument, having narrowly escaped destruction at the hands of Federico da Montefeltro in 1463. He destroyed its upper section while besieging the town as a papal *condottiere*.

The 16th-century **Fontana della Fortuna**, in Piazza XX Settembre, is dedicated to the goddess Fortuna. The large **Palazzo Malatesta** that rises up to its rear was built around 1420 and enlarged in 1544 for Fano's rulers, the Rimini-based Malatesta family. Inside is the small **Museo Civico** and the **Pinacoteca Malatestiana**, with works by Guercino, Guido Reni and the Venetian artist, Michele Giambono.

🏛 **Museo Civico and Pinacoteca Malatestiana**
Piazza XX Settembre.
[0721 82 83 62. ◯ Tue–Sun (Oct–Mar: Tue–Sun am). ● 1 Jan, 25, 26 Dec. 📷

Entrance to the Palazzo Ducale in Urbania

Urbino ❺

See pp360–61.

Urbania ❻

Pèsaro. 🚶 7,200. 🚌 ℹ Corso Vittorio Emanuele 24 (0722 31 31 40). 🎪 Thu.

URBANIA, WITH ITS elegant arcaded centre, takes its name from Pope Urban VIII (1623–44), who entertained the notion of converting the old medieval village known as Castel Durante into a model Renaissance town.

Its chief attraction is a monument from an earlier age, the huge **Palazzo Ducale**, built by the dukes of Montefeltro as one of several residential alternatives to the Palazzo Ducale in nearby Urbino. It was begun in the 13th century, and then rebuilt in the 15th and 16th centuries. Beautifully situated alongside the Metauro river, it houses a small art gallery, a modest museum, old maps and globes, and the remnants of Duke Federico's famous library.

🏛 **Palazzo Ducale**
Palazzo Ducale. [0722 31 31 51.
◯ Tue–Sun (Oct–Mar: ask at library). ● public hols. 📷

Fontana della Fortuna in Fano

Urbino: Palazzo Ducale

ITALY'S MOST BEAUTIFUL Renaissance palace was built for Duke Federico da Montefeltro, the ruler of Urbino between 1444 and 1482, known for his prowess as a mercenary soldier. Federico was also a man of the arts, and his palace, with its library, paintings and refined architecture, is a monument to courtly life and to the artistic and intellectual ideals of the Renaissance.

★ The Flagellation by Piero della Francesca
Dramatic perspective creates an unsettling effect in this 15th-century painting of the scourging of Christ.

Towers attributed to Laurana

The palace rising above Urbino

The simple east side of the palace was designed by Maso di Bartolomeo before 1460.

Cortile d'Onore
This early Renaissance courtyard was designed by the Dalmatian-born artist Luciano Laurana (1420–79).

M
entra

The Libr
was one
Europe's
in its day

Ideal City
Attributed to Luciano Laurana, this 15th-century painting of an imaginary Renaissance city is notable for its measured perspective and lack of people.

★ **Studiolo**
*The former study of Federico
da Montefeltro is decorated with
intarsia (inlaid wood), some
of it designed by Botticelli.*

**Duke Federico by
Pedro Berruguete**
*The duke, shown
here with his son in
this 15th-century
painting, was always
portrayed in left
profile after an
injury to his face.*

**Hanging
garden**

The rooms in
this wing are
known as the
Appartamento
della Duchessa.

★ **La Muta by Raphael**
The Mute Woman *may be a
portrait of Maddalena Doni,
a Florentine noblewoman.*

Urbino ❺

Pèsaro. ▦ 16,000. ▦ ℹ Via
Puccinotti 37 (0722 26 13). ⊟ Sat.

AMID URBINO'S TANGLE of
medieval and Renaissance
streets stands the Neo-Classical
Duomo, on Piazza Federico,
built in 1789. Of special interest
is the painting of the *Last
Supper* by Federico Barocci
(c.1535–1612). The
Museo Diocesano
contains a collection
of ceramics, glass and
religious artifacts.
    Urbino's famous son,
the painter Raphael
(1483–1520), lived in
the **Casa Natale di
Raffaello**. It has a
highly evocative
interior, especially the
kitchen and courtyard.
    In Via Barocci stands
the medieval **Oratorio
di San Giuseppe**,
known for its *presepio*
(Christmas crib), and
the 14th-century
**Oratorio di San
Giovanni Battista**,
whose interior is
smothered in 15th-
century frescoes of the
Crucifixion and the *Life of John
the Baptist* by Giacomo and
Lorenzo Salimbeni.
    The 15th-century **Fortezza
dell'Albornoz** on Viale Bruno
Buozzi is the defensive focus of
Urbino's surviving 16th-century
walls and bastions.

🏛 **Museo Diocesano**
Piazza Pascoli 2. ☎ 0722 28 50.
☐ Mon–Sat (Oct–Mar: ask Duomo
custodian). ▨ ♿
🏠 **Casa Natale di Raffaello**
Via di Raffaello 57. ☎ 0722 32 01 05.
☐ daily (Sun am only). ● 1 Jan,
25 Dec. ▨

A street scene in the medieval
town of Urbino

Fresh seafood and fishing boats in the harbour at Ancona

Grotte di Frasassi ⑦

Ancona. 🅲 *0732 972 11.* 🆁🆂 *Genga San Vittore Terme.* ⭕ *for guided tours only (1 hr 15 mins).* ⬤ *1 Jan, 10–30 Jan, 4 Dec, 25 Dec.* 📷 🅹

SOME OF EUROPE'S largest publicly accessible caverns lie in the cave network gouged out by the River Sentino southwest of Jesi. Of the vast network of 18 km (11 miles), an area of about 1,000 m (3,281 ft) is open to the public. The colossal **Grotta del Vento** is large enough to contain Milan cathedral – its ceiling extends to a height of 240 m (787 ft). This cavern has been used for a range of experiments, from sensory deprivation to an exploration of the social consequences of leaving a group of people alone in its depths for long periods.

Jesi ⑧

Ancona. 🏛 *41,000.* 🆁🆂 🚌
ℹ️ *Piazza della Repubblica 11 (0731 597 88).* 🚌 *Wed & Sat.*

PERCHED ON A LONG, rocky ridge, Jesi lies in the heart of the verdant hill country where Verdicchio is produced. A crisp, white wine renowned for centuries, Verdicchio is bottled in unique containers – glass models of the terracotta amphorae once used to export the wine to ancient Greece. No wine is made in Jesi itself, but there are many vineyards in the surrounding countryside.

Housed in the town's 18th-century Palazzo Pianetti is the **Pinacoteca e Musei Civici,** which contains fine late-period paintings by Lorenzo Lotto. Almost as alluring as the gallery's paintings, however, is the great central salon – an orgy of Rococo decoration that once formed the centrepiece of the Palazzo Pianetti. The nearby **Palazzo della Signoria** features an interesting little collection of archaeological finds, while beyond the old town's Renaissance walls stands the 14th-century church of **San Marco,** known for its collection of well-preserved Giottesque frescoes.

🏛 **Pinacoteca e Musei Civici**
Via XV Settembre. 🅲 *0731 53 83 43.* ⭕ *Tue–Sun.* 📷
🏛 **Palazzo della Signoria**
Piazza Colocci. 🅲 *0731 53 83 45.* ⭕ *phone to check times.*

Ancona ⑨

🏛 *98,000.* ✈ 🆁🆂 🚌 ⛴
ℹ️ *Via Thaon de Revel 4 (071 35 89 91).* 🚌 *Tue & Fri.*

THE CAPITAL OF LE MARCHE and its largest port (with ferries to and from Greece and Croatia), Ancona dates back to at least the 5th century BC, when it was settled by Greek exiles from Siracusa. Its name derives from *ankon* (Greek for elbow), a reference to the rocky spur that juts into the sea to form the town's fine natural harbour.

Heavy bombing during World War II destroyed much of the medieval town. The 15th-century **Loggia dei Mercanti** (merchants' exchange) on Via della Loggia survives as a monument to the town's medieval heyday.

Just north of the loggia is the Romanesque church of **Santa Maria della Piazza,** with a lovely façade. The nearby **Pinacoteca Comunale F Podesti e Galleria d'Arte Moderna** includes canvases by Titian and Lorenzo Lotto. In the **Museo Archeologico Nazionale delle Marche** there are displays of Greek, Gallic and Roman art. The **Arco di Traiano,** by the harbour, was erected in AD 115 and is one of Italy's better preserved Roman arches.

An impressive cavern in the cave system of the Grotte di Frasassi

The beach at the village of Sirolo on the Conero Peninsula

🏛 **Pinacoteca Comunale
F Podesti e Galleria d'Arte
Moderna**
Via Pizzecolli 17. 📞 071 222 50 41.
⬤ Tue–Sat daily (Sun pm & Mon
am). ⬤ public hols. 🈳 ⬤

🏛 **Museo Archeologico
Nazionale delle Marche**
Palazzo Ferretti, Via Ferretti 1. 📞 071
207 53 90. ⬤ Tue–Sun (Oct–May
am only). ⬤ 1 Jan, 25 Dec. 🈳 ⬤

Concro Peninsula ⑩

Ancona. 🚉 🚢 Ancona.
🚌 from Ancona to Sirolo or
Numana. 🈽 Via Thaon de Revel 4,
Ancona (071 35 89 91).

THE BEAUTIFUL cliff-edged
Conero Peninsula is the
only natural feature to disturb
the almost unbroken line of
beaches along the coast of Le
Marche. Easily accessible from
Ancona to the north, it is a
semi-wild area known for its
scenery, its wines (notably
Rosso del Conero) and for a
collection of coves, beaches
and picturesque little resorts.

The best of these resorts is
Portonovo, above whose
beach stands **Santa Maria di
Portonovo**, a pretty 11th-
century Romanesque church
mentioned by Dante in Canto
XXI of *Paradiso*. The villages
of **Sirolo** and **Numana** are
busier and more commercial-
ized, but you can escape the
summer crowds by hiking the
flower-swathed slopes of
Monte Conero, which stands
at 572 m (1,877 ft), or by
taking a boat trip to the smaller
beaches beyond the resorts.

Loreto ⑪

Ancona. 🚉 11,000. 🚆 🚌 🈽 Via
Solari 3 (071 97 02 76). 🚢 Fri.

LEGEND HAS IT that in 1294
the house of the Virgin
Mary (**Santa Casa**)
miraculously up-
rooted itself from
the Holy Land and
was brought by
angels to a laurel
grove *(loreto)* south
of Ancona. Each
year several million
pilgrims visit the

Santa Casa in Loreto

Santa Casa in Loreto and its
Basilica. Begun in 1468, the
latter was designed and built
in part by Renaissance architects Bramante, Sansovino and
Giuliano da Sangallo. Its
paintings include works by
Luca Signorelli. The **Museo-
Pinacoteca** has 16th-century
paintings by Lorenzo Lotto.

🈽 **Basilica and Santa Casa**
Piazza Santuario. 📞 071 97 01 04.
⬤ daily. ⬤

🏛 **Museo-Pinacoteca**
Palazzo Apostolico.
📞 071 97 77 59. ⬤ Tue–Sun daily.
⬤ Easter, 1 May, 15 Aug. 🈳

Ascoli Piceno ⑫

🚉 54,000. 🚌 🈽 Piazza del Popolo
(0736 25 30 45). 🚢 Wed & Sat.

THIS ALLURING TOWN takes its
name from the Piceni, a
tribe eventually conquered
by the Romans in 89 BC.
The gridiron plan of Roman

Asculum Picenum is visible in
the streets today, but it is the
town's medieval heritage that
attracts most visitors.

The enchanting **Piazza del
Popolo** is dominated by the
13th-century **Palazzo dei
Capitani del Popolo**, whose
façade was designed by Cola
dell'Amatrice, and the church
of **San Francesco**, a large and
faintly austere Gothic ensemble
built between 1262 and 1549.

Via del Trivio leads north to
a medieval district overlooking
the River Tronto. Along Via
Cairoli lies the 13th-century
Dominican church of **San
Pietro Martire**. Opposite is
the church of **Santi Vincenzo
e Anastasio** (11th century),
with an ancient crypt built over
a spring said to cure leprosy.

Around Piazza dell'Arringo
is the 12th-century **Duomo**,
spoiled by a Baroque overlay.
Its Cappella del Sacramento
contains a polyptych by
the 15th-century artist
Carlo Crivelli. The
Pinacoteca Civica
has more works
by Crivelli and by
Guido Reni, Titian
and Alemanno.
The **Museo
Archeologico**
contains Roman,
Piceni and Lombard artifacts.

🏛 **Pinacoteca Civica**
Palazzo Comunale, Piazza Arringo.
📞 0736 29 82 13. ⬤ daily.
⬤ 1 Jan, 25 Dec. 🈳 ⬤

🏛 **Museo Archeologico**
Palazzo Panighi, Piazza Arringo.
📞 0736 25 35 62. ⬤ daily.
⬤ 1 Jan, 1 May, 25 Dec. 🈳 ⬤

A view of the medieval town of
Ascoli Piceno

ROME AND LAZIO

Rome and Lazio at a Glance

THE FIRST SETTLEMENTS IN THE REGION can be traced back to the early Etruscan civilization in northern Lazio. Rome grew to rule a vast empire and, as the empire began to divide, the region became the centre of the Christian world. Artists and architects flocked to work for the popes and their families, notably in the Renaissance and Baroque periods when some magnificent architectural works were created. The legacy of this uninterrupted history can be seen all over the city and the surrounding area.

St Peter's, with its majestic dome by Michelangelo, is a magnificent and sumptuous 16th-century basilica (see pp408–9).

Piazza Navona, flanked by cafés, contains three Baroque fountains, including the colossal Fontana dei Quattro Fiumi, one of Bernini's finest works (see p389).

St Peter's

PIAZZA
NAVONA
(See pp386–9

Fontana dei Quattro Fiumi

THE VATICAN
AND TRASTEVERE
(See pp404–19)

Santa Maria in Trastevere, probably the first Christian church in Rome, holds some remarkable mosaics such as this detail from Cavallini's Life of the Virgin *which dates from 1291 (see p418).*

RITORIA

E PATER POST TEMPO

Santa Maria in
Trastevere

LAZIO
(See pp444–55)

Cerveteri tombs

ROME
(See main map)

0 kilometres   15

0 miles   10

Cerveteri is one of the many necropolises left by the Etruscan civilization in northern Lazio. The larger tumulus tombs often contained frescoes and utensils useful for the afterlife (see p450).

◁ Bernini's allegorical Fountain of the Four Rivers at the centre of Piazza Navona

The Pantheon, built between AD 118–125, is a marvel of Roman engineering with its huge dome hidden behind the Classical portico (see p394).

SEE ALSO

• *Where to Stay* pp565–9

• *Where to Eat* pp599–602

NORTHEAST ROME
(See pp396–403)

Santa Maria Maggiore's richly decorated interior blends different architectural styles, such as this baldacchino from the 18th century (see p403).

Santa Maria Maggiore

THE ANCIENT CENTRE
(See pp372–85)

Pantheon

Capitoline Museums

Colosseum

San Giovanni in Laterano

AVENTINE AND LATERAN
(See pp420–27)

San Giovanni in Laterano, the Cathedral of Rome, incorporates the elaborate Corsini Chapel built in the 1730s (see p426).

The Capitoline Museums have held treasures of the Classical world since the Renaissance, including this colossal 4th-century head of Constantine (see pp376–7).

| 0 metres | 750 |
| 0 yards | 750 |

The Colosseum was constructed in AD 80 by Emperor Vespasian. His aim was to gain popularity by staging deadly gladiatorial combats and wild animal fights for public viewing (see p383).

Regional Food: Rome and Lazio

Sage
leaves

THE TRADITIONAL *cucina romanesca* has
always relied on fresh seasonal produce
from the nearby countryside bought in the
local markets. Mushrooms, in autumn, and
artichokes, in spring, are served in dozens of
different ways, and the *mesticanza*, a fresh mix
of salad leaves including the peppery *rughetta*
(rocket) and *puntarelle* (curly endive shoots),
is also delicious when it is in season in the
summer months. Many of the genuinely
Roman dishes are highly seasoned with
onions, garlic, rosemary, sage and bay leaves. The
typical Roman meat dish, based on the so-called *quinto
quarto* (fifth quarter) – head, tail, trotters and so on – is
flavoured with olive oil, herbs, *pancetta* (bacon) and
guanciale (pig's cheek) and is a culinary delight.
Pecorino, a tangy sheep's milk cheese, is often
sprinkled onto dishes as seasoning and the blander
ricotta is a filling for pizzas as well as the Roman
dessert *torta di ricotta*.

Supplì di Riso *are fried rice
croquettes stuffed with* mozzarella. *They are typically Roman
and make an excellent snack.*

Batter-fried
artichoke
hearts

Batter-fried
courgette
flowers

An antipasto *starts the meal and is usually a selection of
appetizers based on the vegetables that are in season. The
vegetables may be fresh, grilled or preserved in aromatic oils
or vinegar. Artichoke hearts and courgette flowers are excellent
in spring, and are used in a variety of dishes, including the
fritto misto, a selection of local ingredients fried in batter.*

Filetti di Baccalà*, deep-fried
cod fillets which were originally
a Jewish speciality, have become
a feature of Roman cuisine.*

Gnocchi alla Romana*, small
semolina dumplings, can be
eaten with tomato sauce or
just with butter.*

Risotto alla Romana *is a
rice dish made with a sauce of
liver, sweetbreads and Marsala,
a fortified wine from Sicily.*

Bucatini all'Amatriciana *is
hollow spaghetti-like pasta
with bacon, tomatoes and onion
sprinkled with* pecorino *cheese.*

Spaghetti alla Carbonara*,
devised in Rome, is made with
bacon, eggs, Parmesan cheese
and, if desired, black pepper.*

Coda alla Vaccinara *is a traditional Roman dish made from braised oxtail served with herbs and a tomato sauce.*

Torta di Ricotta*, a popular dessert from Rome, is a delicious cheesecake filled with ricotta, Marsala and lemon.*

Saltimbocca alla Romana *is a tasty dish of veal with ham and sage. It can also be served rolled and skewered.*

Fave al Guanciale *are young spring broad beans, simmered in olive oil with pig's cheek (guanciale) and onion.*

WHAT TO DRINK IN ROME AND LAZIO

Vines thrive in the warm climate and fertile land of Lazio, keeping up the wine-producing tradition that was started around the hills of Rome over 2,000 years ago by the ancient Romans. Today, wine is usually drunk with meals as a matter of course and the region offers abundant supplies of inexpensive dry white wine for the city's restaurants and cafés. Of local bottled white wines, Frascati is the best known, but Castelli Romani, Marino, Colli Albani and Velletri are very similar in style. All are made from one grape variety, the Trebbiano, though better quality versions contain a dash of Malvasia for perfume and flavour. Local red wine is rarer and most reds come from other parts of Italy. As well as the usual range of digestives and apéritifs, such as Campari, beer is also widely available and the popular Italian lager is Nastro Azzurro. Fruit juices are also good and bars squeeze fresh orange juice *(spremuta)*. Rome's drinking water, another debt to the ancient Romans, is particularly good, fresh and sweet, and in abundant supply.

Frascati, the best known local white

Torre Ercolana*, one of the few red wines produced in Lazio, is made in small quantities and generally regarded as one of the region's best wines. It is made from both the local Cesanese grapes and the more robust Cabernet, and should be kept to age for at least five years.*

Drinking water *in Rome, unlike many other Mediterranean cities, is excellent. The city benefits from a constant supply of fresh drinking water, piped down from the hills through a system of pipes and aqueducts that has changed very little since ancient Roman times. At regular intervals throughout the city, ornate fountains pump delicious fresh water for general use as well as for drinking. Only if there is a sign saying* acqua non potabile *is the water not safe to drink.*

One of Rome's many fresh water drinking fountains

Coffee *is almost more important to Roman life than wine. Take espresso for a shot of neat strong black coffee at any time of the day, sit with a milky cappuccino for breakfast or mid-afternoon, or take a caffelatte in a glass for extra milk.*

Espresso   **Cappuccino**   **Caffelatte**

Understanding Architecture in Rome and Lazio

THE ARCHITECTURE of Imperial Rome, a combination of Etruscan and Classical Greek styles, gradually developed new and uniquely Roman forms based on the arch, the vault and the dome. During the early Christian period simple, rectangular basilicas were built, forms which by the 12th century had been incorporated into the stark Romanesque style. The Renaissance, inspired by the example of Florence, saw a return to Classical ideals of simplicity and harmonious proportions, though it was to be in the flamboyance of the 17th-century Baroque that Rome once again found great architectural expression.

The extravagant Baroque style of the Fontana di Trevi, Rome

FROM ETRUSCAN TO CLASSICAL ROME

The Podium made the temple more prominent.

A portico was a porch with columns.

The arch became a feature of Roman architecture.

Reliefs were scavenged from earlier monuments.

Three naves divided the interior of the basilica.

Etruscan temples, *based on Greek models, inspired early Roman architecture. A front portico was the only entrance.*

The Arch of Constantine *(AD 315) is typical of triumphant Imperial Roman architecture (see p379). It stands at a colossal 25 m (82 ft).*

Early Christian basilicas *(4th century) were based on a rectangular floorplan.*

FROM RENAISSANCE TO BAROQUE

Doric columns recall Classical architecture.

Bramante adopted the circular form of ancient temples.

Rustication, massive blocks divided by deep joints, was used for palazzi.

Ionic pilasters lend an air of elegance to the imposing upper storeys.

The elliptical staircase was a typical feature of Mannerist houses.

The Tempietto at San Pietro in Montorio, Rome (1502) is a model of Renaissance architecture: simple and perfectly proportioned (see p419).

Palazzo Farnese *at Caprarola, a pentagonal building completed in 1575 (see p449), combines some Mannerist tricks of architecture with the strict geometric proportions characteristic of the Renaissance.*

WHERE TO SEE THE ARCHITECTURE

A walk through the back streets of the centre of Rome will reveal masterpieces of virtually every architectural age. The most ancient treasures are seven obelisks stolen from Egypt. One stands on the back of Bernini's elephant *(see p394)*. Highlights from Ancient Rome include triumphal arches and temples such as the Pantheon *(see p394)*. Romanesque elements survive in the church of San Clemente *(see p425)*, while the Renaissance finds expression in the dome of St Peter's *(see pp408–9)*. Magnificent Baroque treasures dot the entire city, in particular flamboyant fountains that adorn the squares. Outside the city the outstanding sights are the late Renaissance villas such as Caprarola *(see p449)*.

Part of Bernini's elephant supporting an ancient Egyptian obelisk

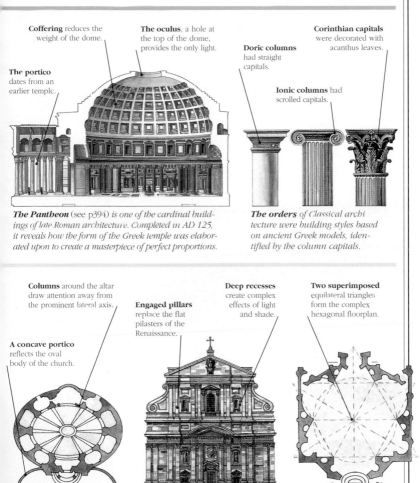

Coffering reduces the weight of the dome.

The oculus, a hole at the top of the dome, provides the only light.

The portico dates from an earlier temple.

The Pantheon (see p394) is one of the cardinal buildings of late Roman architecture. Completed in AD 125, it reveals how the form of the Greek temple was elaborated upon to create a masterpiece of perfect proportions.

Corinthian capitals were decorated with acanthus leaves.

Doric columns had straight capitals.

Ionic columns had scrolled capitals.

The orders of Classical architecture were building styles based on ancient Greek models, identified by the column capitals.

Columns around the altar draw attention away from the prominent lateral axis.

A concave portico reflects the oval body of the church.

Engaged pillars replace the flat pilasters of the Renaissance.

Deep recesses create complex effects of light and shade.

Two superimposed equilateral triangles form the complex hexagonal floorplan.

The oval floorplan of the Baroque Sant'Andrea al Quirinale (see p401) makes ingenious use of restricted space.

The Gesù façade (1584) epitomizes Counter-Reformation architecture and has been imitated throughout the Catholic world (see p393).

Sant'Ivo alla Sapienza's floorplan (1642) favoured grandiose design over Classical form (see p390).

THE ANCIENT CENTRE

THE CAPITOL, the southern summit of the Capitoline Hill, was the symbolic centre of the Roman world and home to the city's three most important temples. These were dedicated to the god Jupiter Optimus Maximus, protector of Rome, Minerva, goddess of wisdom and war, and Juno Moneta, a guardian goddess. Below the Capitol lies

Capitoline Wolf with Romulus and Remus

the Forum, once the focus of political, social, legal and commercial life; the Imperial Fora, built when Rome's population grew; and the Colosseum, the centre of entertainment. Overlooking the Forum is the Palatine Hill, where Romulus is said to have founded Rome in the 8th century BC, and emperors lived for over 400 years.

SIGHTS AT A GLANCE

Churches
Santa Maria in Aracoeli ❸

Museums and Galleries
Capitoline Museums pp376–7 ❶

Historic Piazzas
Piazza del Campidoglio ❷

Ancient Sites and Buildings
Arch of Constantine ❿

Colosseum p383 ❾
Forum of Augustus ❺
Forum of Caesar ❼
Mamertine Prison ❻
Palatine pp384–5 ⓫
Roman Forum pp380–81 ❽
Trajan's Forum and Markets ❹

GETTING THERE

The Capitoline is in walking distance of Piazza Venezia, the hub of the city bus routes, while the Forum, Colosseum and Palatine are close to Metro Colosseo. Buses 87 and 186 link Piazza Venezia and the Colosseum with Corso Rinascimento, in the heart of the *centro storico*.

KEY

▦	Street-by-Street: The Capitoline Hill *pp374–5*
M	Metro station
i	Tourist information

0 metres 250
0 yards 250

◁ **View of the Colosseum rising behind the Forum**

Street-by-Street: The Capitoline Hill

THE CAPITOL, citadel of ancient Rome, was designed by Michelangelo in the 16th century. He was responsible for the trapezoid Piazza del Campidoglio as well as the Cordonata, the broad flight of steps leading up to it. The piazza is flanked by Palazzo Nuovo and Palazzo dei Conservatori, housing the Capitoline Museums, with their fine collections of sculpture and paintings. It is also well worth walking behind the museums to the Tarpeian Rock, for a fine view of the Forum lying below.

The Victor Emmanuel Monument was begun in 1885 and inaugurated in 1911 in honour of Victor Emmanuel II, the first king of unified Italy.

San Marco, dedicated to the patron saint of Venice, has splendid 9th-century mosaics in the apse.

PIAZZA VENEZIA

Palazzo Venezia, once the home of Mussolini, now holds a museum of fine and decorative arts. Exhibits include this medieval gilt and enamel angel.

The Aracoeli Staircase was completed in 1348 to commemorate the end of plague.

The Cordonata is presided over by the colossal statues of Castor and Pollux.

VIA DEL TEATRO DI MARCELLO

★ **Capitoline Museums**
The collections of art and ancient sculpture include this statue of the Emperor Marcus Aurelius, a replica of which stands in the centre of the piazza ❶

STAR SIGHT

★ Capitoline Museums

KEY

– – –　Suggested route

0 metres	75
0 yards	75

Santa Maria in Aracoeli
The brick façade hides treasures such as this 15th-century fresco of the Funeral of San Bernardino by Pinturicchio **3**

LOCATOR MAP
See Rome Street Finder
map 3

Palazzo Nuovo
was made into a public museum in 1734.

Palazzo Senatorio, the splendid Renaissance seat of the city government, is built on the ruins of the ancient Tabularium.

Piazza del Campidoglio
Michelangelo designed the geometric paving and the façades of the buildings **2**

Palazzo dei Conservatori

The Temple of Jupiter, represented on this coin, was dedicated to Jupiter Optimus Maximus, the most important of the Roman gods. He was believed to have the power to protect or destroy the city.

The Tarpeian Rock is a cliff from which traitors were believed to have been thrown to their death in ancient Rome.

Steps to the Capitoline

Capitoline Museums **1**

See pp376–7.

Piazza del Campidoglio **2**

Map 3 B5. 🚌 40, 64, 70, 75.

WHEN EMPEROR CHARLES V announced he was to visit Rome in 1536, Pope Paul III Farnese asked Michelangelo to give the Capitoline a face-lift. He redesigned the piazza, renovated the façades of its palaces and built a new stair-case, the Cordonata. This gently rising ramp is now crowned with the massive statues of Castor and Pollux.

Santa Maria in Aracoeli **3**

Piazza d'Aracoeli. **Map** 3 B5.
📞 06 679 81 55. 🚌 64, 70, 75.
🕐 6:30am–6pm daily.

THIS CHURCH STANDS on the site of the Temple of Juno on the northern summit of the Capitoline Hill, and dates back at least to the 6th century. The church is famous today for its ornate gilded ceiling and a very fine series of frescoes by Pinturicchio, dating from the 1480s. They depict scenes from the life of San Bernardino of Siena. The miracle-working *Santo Bambino* figure was stolen in 1994 but has been replaced by a replica.

The marble staircase and austere façade of Santa Maria in Aracoeli

Capitoline Museums: ❶
Palazzo Nuovo

A COLLECTION of Classical sculptures has been kept on the Capitoline Hill since Pope Sixtus IV donated a group of bronze sculptures to the city in 1471. Paintings as well as sculpture are now housed in two palaces designed by Michelangelo. The Palazzo Nuovo, first opened to the public in 1734 by Pope Clement XII, contains a fine selection of Greek and Roman sculptures.

LOCATOR MAP

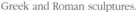

Discobolus
The twisted torso was part of a Greek statue of a discus thrower. An 18th-century sculptor turned him into a wounded warrior.

Mosaic of the Doves
This 1st-century AD naturalistic mosaic once decorated the floor of Hadrian's Villa at Tivoli (see p452).

Alexander Severus as Hunter
In this marble of the 3rd century AD, the emperor's pose is a pastiche of the mythical hero, Perseus, holding up the head of Medusa the Gorgon after he had killed her.

Hall of the Philosophers
The hall contains Roman copies of portrait busts of Greek politicians, scientists and poets. These adorned the homes of wealthy Romans.

Stairs to ground floor

Stairs to first floor

Courtyard

Main entrance

Dying Galatian
Great compassion is conveyed in this Roman copy of a Greek work of the 3rd century BC.

KEY TO FLOORPLAN

☐ Ground floor
☐ First floor
☐ Second floor
☐ Non-exhibition space

Palazzo dei Conservatori

THE PALAZZO DEI CONSERVATORI was the seat of the city's magistrates during the late Middle Ages. Its frescoed halls are still used occasionally for political meetings and the ground floor houses the municipal registry office. While much of the palazzo is given over to sculpture, including fragments of a huge sculpture of Constantine, the art galleries on the second floor hold works by Veronese, Tintoretto, Caravaggio, Van Dyck and Titian.

VISITORS' CHECKLIST

Musei Capitolini, Piazza del Campidoglio. **Map** 3 B5.
06 67 10 20 71.
40, 63, 64, 70, 75, 81, 87 and many other routes through Piazza Venezia. 9:30am – 7pm Tue–Sun (to 11pm Sat). 1 Jan, 1 May, 25 Dec. entrance ticket is valid for both museums.

St John the Baptist
Caravaggio's sensual portrait (1595–6) of the young saint caressing a sheep is a highly unorthodox image of Christ's forerunner.

Medusa
This bust by Bernini of the mythological Medusa is in Room 5.

Second-floor art gallery

Roman Garden

First floor

Courtyard

Stairs to first floor

Stairs to ground floor

The Rape of the Sabine Women
Pietro da Cortona glamorized the mass abduction of Sabine women by the Romans in this painting of 1629.

Spinario
This is a charming bronze sculpture from the 1st century BC of a boy trying to remove a thorn from his foot.

Main entrance

Trajan's Forum and Markets ❹

Map 3 B4. **Trajan's Forum**, Via dei Fori Imperiali. ● *to the public.* **Trajan's Markets**, Via IV Novembre. 📞 *06 679 00 48.* 🕙 *10am–6pm Tue–Sun.* ● *Mon, public hols.* 📷 📹

TRAJAN BEGAN to build his forum in AD 107 to commemorate his final conquest of Dacia (present day Romania) after successful campaigns in AD 101–2 and 105–6. His new forum was the most ambitious yet, with a vast colonnaded open space centring on an equestrian statue of the emperor, a huge basilica, and two big libraries. Dominating the ruins today is **Trajan's Column**, which originally stood between the two libraries.

Trajan's Column

Spiralling up its 30 m (98 ft) high stem are minutely detailed scenes from the Dacian campaigns, beginning with the Romans preparing for war and ending with the Dacians being ousted from their homeland. The subtly modelled reliefs were designed to be seen from viewing platforms on the libraries, and are consequently difficult to interpret from ground level. If you want to examine the scenes in detail there are casts in the Museo della Civiltà Romana (see p432). The **market** complex, which is situated directly behind the forum, was begun slightly earlier. Like the forum it was probably designed by Apollodorus of Damascus, and was the

Via Biberatica, the main street through Trajan's Markets

ancient Roman equivalent of the modern shopping centre. There were around 150 shops selling everything from oriental silks and spices to fruit, fresh fish and flowers. It was also here that the *annone*, or corn dole, was distributed. This was a free ration of corn given to Roman men, a practice which was introduced in the Republic by politicians who wanted to buy votes and prevent unrest during periods of famine.

RECONSTRUCTION OF TRAJAN'S MARKETS

Cross vaulting

The Main Hall had 12 shops on two storeys. The corn ration was distributed from the upper floor.

Amphorae, used for storing wine and oil, were discovered on the upper corridor

The terrace has a good view of Trajan's Forum

The shops on the ground floor were cool, and probably sold vegetables, fruit and flowers.

Staircase

Via Biberatica is named after the drinking inns that once lined it.

Large hall with semi-domed ceiling

Forum of Augustus ❺

Piazza del Grillo 1. **Map** 3 B5.
🚌 87, 186. ⭕ by appt. 🎟 includes entry to Trajan's Markets.

THE FORUM of Augustus, which once stretched from a high wall at the foot of sleazy Suburra to the edge of Caesar's Forum, was built to celebrate Augustus's victory in 41 BC over Brutus and Cassius, the assassins of Julius Caesar. As a consequence the temple in its centre was dedicated to Mars the Avenger. The temple, with its cracked steps and four Corinthian columns, is easily identified. Originally it had a statue of Mars that looked very like Augustus, but in case anyone failed to notice the resemblance, a colossal statue of the emperor himself was placed against the wall of the Suburra quarter.

19th-century engraving of the Mamertine Prison

Mamertine Prison ❻

Clivo Argentario 1. **Map** 3 B5.
📞 06 69 94 10 20. 🚌 84, 85, 87, 175, 186. ⭕ 9am–noon, 2–5pm daily. **Donation.** 📷

BELOW THE 16th-century church of San Giuseppe dei Falegnami is a dank dungeon in which, according to Christian legend, St Peter and St Paul were imprisoned. They are said to have caused a spring to bubble up into the

Podium of the Temple of Mars the Avenger, Forum of Augustus

cell, and to have used the water to baptize two prison guards. The prison was in an old cistern with access to the city's main sewer (the Cloaca Maxima). The lower cell was used for executions, and corpses were thrown into the sewer. However, the inmates, who received no food, often died of starvation.

Forum of Caesar ❼

Via del Carcere Tulliano. **Map** 3 B5.
📞 06 679 07 95. 🚌 84, 85, 87, 175, 186, 810, 850. ⭕ by appt only: permit needed (see p614).

THE FIRST of Rome's Imperial fora was built by Julius Caesar to relieve congestion in the Roman Forum when Rome's population boomed. He spent a fortune – most of it booty from his recent conquest of Gaul – buying up and demolishing houses on the site. Pride of place went to a temple dedicated in 46 BC to Venus Genetrix (Venus the Ancestor) as Caesar claimed to be descended from the goddess. The temple contained statues of Caesar and Cleopatra as well as of Venus, but all that remains today is a platform and three Corinthian columns. The forum was once enclosed by a double colonnade, under which was sheltered a row of shops. However, this burned down in AD 80 and was rebuilt by Domitian and Trajan. The latter also added the

Basilica Argentaria – which became an important financial exchange – as well as shops and a heated public lavatory.

Roman Forum ❽

See pp380–81.

Colosseum ❾

See p383.

Arch of Constantine ❿

Between Via di San Gregorio and Piazza del Colosseo. **Map** 7 A1.
🚌 75, 85, 87, 110, 175, 673, 810.
🚃 3 Ⓜ Colosseo.

THIS TRIUMPHAL ARCH is one of Imperial Rome's last monuments, built in AD 315, a few years before Constantine moved the capital of the Empire to Byzantium. It was built to celebrate Constantine's victory in AD 312 over his co-emperor Maxentius at the Battle of the Milvian Bridge. Constantine attributed the victory to a dream in which he was told to mark his men's shields with *chi-rho*, the first two Greek letters of Christ's name. Christian tradition prefers a version in which the emperor has a vision of the Cross, mid-battle. There is nothing Christian about the arch: most of the reliefs were from earlier pagan monuments.

Palatine ⓫

See pp384–5.

The north side of the Arch of Constantine

Roman Forum ⑧

IN THE EARLY REPUBLIC, the Forum was a
chaotic place, with food stalls and brothels
as well as temples and the Senate House. By
the 2nd century BC it was decided that Rome
required a more salubrious centre, and the
food stores were replaced by business
centres and law courts. The Forum
remained the ceremonial centre
of the city under the Empire,
with emperors renovating
old buildings and erecting
new temples and
monuments.

**Arch of
Septimius Severus**
*This triumphal arch
was erected in AD 203,
the 10th anniversary
of Emperor Septimius
Severus' accession.*

**The Temple of Antoninus
and Faustina** is now
incorporated into the
church of San
Lorenzo in
Miranda.

**Temple
of Saturn**

The Rostra was the
orator's tribune from
which speeches
were made.

VIA DELLA CURIA

VIA SACRA

The Curia, or
ancient Roman
Senate House,
has been
reconstructed.

Basilica Julia
*Named after Julius
Caesar, who began its
construction in 54 BC,
this was the seat of the civil
magistrates court.*

Basilica Aemilia
was a meeting hall
for business and
money exchange.

**Temple
of Vesta**

Temple of Castor and Pollux
*Although there has been a temple
here since the 5th century BC, the
columns and elaborate cornice
date from AD 6 when the
temple was rebuilt.*

STAR SIGHTS

★ **House of the Vestal
Virgins**

★ **Basilica of Constan-
tine and Maxentius**

★ **House of the
Vestal Virgins**
*The priestesses who
tended the sacred
flame in the Temple
of Vesta lived here.
The house was a
large rectangular
building around a
central garden.*

**★ Basilica of Constantine
and Maxentius**
*The basilica's three vast
barrel vaults are all that
remain of the Forum's
largest building. Like other
basilicas, it was used for the
administration of justice
and conducting business.*

**The Temple of
Romulus**, now part
of the church of Santi
Cosma e Damiano which
stands behind it, retains
its original 4th-century
bronze doors.

Arch of Titus
*This arch was erected
by Emperor Domitian
in AD 81 to commem-
orate the sack of
Jerusalem by his
father Vespasian
and brother Titus,
13 years earlier.*

Antiquarium Forense
*This small museum contains
finds from the Forum.
Exhibits range from Iron
Age burial urns to this
frieze of Aeneas from
the Basilica Aemilia.*

**The Temple of Venus
and Rome** was built in
AD 135, and was largely
designed by Hadrian.

VIA DEI FORI IMPERIALI

VIA SACRA

VIA SACRA

Colosseum

Palatine

**Santa
Francesca
Romana**
*The Romanesque
bell tower of
Santa Francesca
Romana towers
over one of a
number of
churches built
among the ruins
of the Forum.*

THE VESTAL VIRGINS

The cult of Vesta, the goddess of fire, dates
back to at least the 8th century BC. Romulus
and Remus were allegedly born of the Vestal
priestess Rhea and the god Mars. Six virgins kept
the sacred flame of Vesta burning in her circular
temple. The girls, who came from noble families,
were selected when they were between six and
ten years old, and served for 30 years. They had
high status and financial security, but were buried
alive if they lost their virginity and whipped by
the high priest if the sacred flame died out.
Although they were permitted to marry after
finishing their service, few did so.

**Honorary
statue of a
Vestal Virgin**

Exploring the Roman Forum

To APPRECIATE THE LAYOUT of the Roman Forum before wandering through its confusing patchwork of ruined temples, triumphal arches and basilicas, it is best to view the whole area from the Capitoline Hill above. From there you can make out the more substantial ruins, and the course of the Via Sacra (Sacred Way), the route followed through the Forum by religious and triumphal processions making their way up to the Capitol to give thanks at the Temple of Jupiter (see p375).

Corinthian columns of the Temple of Castor and Pollux

The Main Sights

The first building you come to on entering the Forum is the **Basilica Aemilia**. A rectangular hall built in 179 BC, it was a meeting place for moneylenders, businessmen and tax collectors. Although little more remains of it than a pastel marble pavement fringed with column stumps, you can still find splashes of verdigrised bronze, reputedly the remains of coins which melted when the Visigoths invaded Rome and burnt down the basilica in the 5th century.

Inside the Curia – the stark brick building next to the basilica – are the **Plutei of Trajan**, relief panels commissioned by either Trajan or Hadrian to decorate the Rostra, the public oratory platform. On one panel are piles of books holding tax records, which Trajan had destroyed in order to free citizens from debts. The **Arch of Septimius Severus** is the best preserved of the Forum's monuments. The marble relief panels depict the military triumphs of the emperor in Parthia (modern-day Iran and Iraq) and Arabia.

The **Temple of Saturn** was the focus of the annual Saturnalia celebrations, when, for up to a week in December, schools closed, slaves dined with their masters, presents were exchanged and a fair and market were held.

Soaring above the remains of the Basilica Julia are three delicately fluted columns and a finely carved slab of entablature taken from the **Temple of Castor and Pollux**. This striking relic is dedicated to the twin brothers of Helen of Troy, who were supposed to have appeared at the battle of Lake Regillus in 499 BC, aiding the Romans in their defeat of the Etruscans.

Restored section of Temple of Vesta

The elegant circular **Temple of Vesta** was one of ancient Rome's most sacred shrines and was dedicated to the goddess of the hearth. The flame, kept alive by the Vestal Virgins, symbolized the perpetuity of the state and its extinction prophesied doom for the city. The building was

partly reconstructed in 1930, but the circular form goes back to the Latin mud huts which originally occupied the site. Just behind is the **House of the Vestal Virgins**, the living quarters of the priestess and the Vestals. This enormous complex of 50 rooms was once annexed to the Temple. Best preserved are the rooms overlooking a pretty courtyard, ornamented with statues of Vestals, ponds of waterlilies and rose trees.

On the other side of the Forum lie the impressive remains of the **Basilica of Constantine**. It was begun in AD 308 by Maxentius, and is therefore also known as the Basilica of Maxentius.

Constantine completed it after he defeated his rival at the battle of Milvio in AD 312. The stark remains of the huge arches and ceilings give an indication of the original scale and grandeur of the forum's public buildings. Three enormous coffered vaults remain, which originally measured up to 35 m (115 ft) and were faced with marble. The interior walls, which held niches for statues, were also covered with marble below and stucco above. Remains of a spiral staircase which once led to the roof can be found scattered on the ground.

The basilica's apse and hexagonal arches were often used as models by Renaissance architects striving to recreate a Classical symmetry and nobility in their work. They include Michelangelo, who allegedly studied the basilica's architecture when working on the dome of St Peter's.

Central courtyard of the House of the Vestal Virgins

Colosseum ❾

Gladiator's shield

Rome's greatest amphitheatre was commissioned by Emperor Vespasian in AD 72. Deadly gladiatorial combats and wild animal fights were staged by emperors and wealthy citizens, largely to gain popularity. Slaughter was on a huge scale: at the inaugural games in AD 80, over 9,000 wild animals were killed. The Colosseum could hold up to 55,000 people, who were seated according to rank.

Internal Corridors
These allowed the large and often unruly crowd to move freely and be seated quickly.

The Colossus of Nero
This gilt bronze statue from Nero's palace, over which the Colosseum was built, may have given the amphitheatre its name.

The Velarium, a huge sailcloth awning which sheltered spectators from the sun, was supported by poles on the upper storey.

Entry routes and stairs led to seats at the various levels. The emperor and consul had their own, separate entrances.

Corinthian columns

Ionic columns

Doric columns

The arena floor covered a network of lifts and cages for wild animals.

Entrances

Doric, Ionic and Corinthian Tiers
The tiers inspired many Renaissance architects, who also plundered the building, using its travertine to build palaces and part of St Peter's.

Roman Gladiators
These were originally soldiers in training. Their combat became a sport, and slaves, prisoners of war or criminals were forced to fight men or wild animals to the death.

Emperor Vespasian
He ordered the Colosseum to be built on the site of Nero's palace, to dissociate himself from the hated tyrant.

Palatine ⑪

THE PALATINE, once the residence of emperors and aristocrats, is the most pleasant of Rome's ancient sites. The ruins range from the simple house in which Augustus is thought to have lived, to the Domus Flavia and Domus Augustana, the public and private wings of a luxurious palace built by Domitian.

Statue of the Goddess Cybele

The Huts of Romulus, indicated by holes left by the supporting posts, were reputedly founded by Romulus in the 9th century BC.

Temple of Cybele, Goddess of fertility

The House of Augustus is thought to have been the public part of the emperor's modest home.

★ House of Livia
Many of the wall paintings have survived in the private quarters of the house where Augustus is believed to have lived with his wife Livia.

★ Domus Flavia
The courtyard of the Domus Flavia was lavishly paved with coloured marble. The Roman poets praised this villa as the most splendid.

Domus Augustana was the private home of the emperors.

STAR SIGHTS

★ Domus Flavia

★ House of Livia

0 metres		75
0 yards		75

Emperor Septimius Severus
During his reign (AD 193–211), he extended the Domus Augustana and built an impressive bath complex.

Cryptoporticus
This underground gallery, elaborately decorated with stuccoed walls, was built by Emperor Nero.

VISITORS' CHECKLIST

Via di San Gregorio or near the Arch of Titus on Via Sacra.
Map 6 F1. 🄲 *06 39 74 99 07.*
🚌 *75, 85, 87, 117, 175, 186, 810, 850.* Ⓜ *Colosseo.* 🚋 *3.*
⭘ *9am–1 hr before sunset daily.*
⬤ *1 Jan, 1 May, 25 Dec.*
🎫 *includes entry to the Palatine Museum.* 📷 🅿 🄽 🄰

The courtyard of the Domus Flavia was lined by Domitian with mirror-like marble, so he could spot would-be assassins.

The exedra of the stadium may have housed a balcony.

Forum entrance

Stadium
Part of the Imperial palace, this enclosure may have been used by the emperors as a private garden.

The Palace of Septimius Severus
This extension of the Domus Augustana projected beyond the hillside, supported on giant arches.

A HISTORY OF THE PALATINE HILL

Romans of the Decadence by Thomas Couture (1815–79)

The Founding of Rome
According to legend the twins Romulus and Remus were brought up on the Palatine by a wolf. Here Romulus, having killed his brother, is said to have founded the village that was destined to become Rome. Traces of mud huts dating back to the 8th century BC have been found on the hill, lending archaeological support to the legend.

The Republic
By the 1st century BC the Palatine was the most desirable address in Rome and home to the leading citizens of the Republic. Its residents, including the erotic poet Catullus and the orator Cicero, were notoriously indulgent, and their villas were magnificent dwellings with doors of ivory, floors of bronze and frescoed walls.

The Empire
Augustus was born on the Palatine in 63 BC, and lived there in a modest house after becoming emperor. The hill was therefore an obvious choice of abode for future emperors. Domitian's ambitious house, the Domus Flavia (1st century AD), and its private quarters, the Domus Augustana, remained the official residence of future emperors (who were referred to as *Augustus*) for more than 300 years.

AROUND PIAZZA NAVONA

Detail of an 18th-century street shrine

THE AREA around Piazza Navona, known as the *centro storico*, has been inhabited for at least 2,000 years. Piazza Navona stands above an ancient stadium; the Pantheon has been a temple since AD 27; and the Theatre of Marcellus in the Ghetto has been converted into exclusive flats. The area's heyday began in the 15th century, when the papacy returned to Rome. Throughout the Renaissance and Baroque eras princes, popes and cardinals settled here, as did the artists and artisans they commissioned to build and adorn lavish palaces, churches and fountains.

SIGHTS AT A GLANCE

Churches and Temples
Chiesa Nuova **6**
Gesù **13**
La Maddalena **20**
Sant'Ignazio di Loyola **17**
Sant'Ivo alla Sapienza **2**
San Luigi dei Francesi **3**
Santa Maria sopra Minerva **15**
Santa Maria della Pace **5**

Museums and Galleries
Palazzo Doria Pamphilj **14**
Palazzo Spada **10**

Ancient Sites and Buildings
Area Sacra di Largo Argentina **12**
Pantheon **16**

Historic Buildings
Palazzo Altemps **4**
Palazzo della Cancelleria **7**
Palazzo Farnese **9**

Historic Piazzas and Areas
Campo de' Fiori **8**
Ghetto and Tiber Island **11**
Piazza Colonna **18**
Piazza di Montecitorio **19**
Piazza Navona **1**

GETTING THERE

Corso Vittorio Emanuele II and Corso Rinascimento are main bus arteries, but only minibus 116 runs in the *centro storico*.

KEY

Street-by-Street: Around Piazza Navona *pp388–9*

Street-by-Street: Around the Pantheon *pp392–3*

P Parking

i Tourist information

0 metres   250
0 yards   250

◁ **Piazza Navona, with the Fontana del Moro (1653) and the 17th-century church of Sant'Agnese in Agone**

Street-by-Street: Around Piazza Navona

No OTHER PIAZZA in Rome can rival the theatricality of Piazza Navona. The luxurious cafés are the social centre of the city, and day and night there is always something going on in the pedestrian area around the three flamboyant Baroque fountains. The Baroque is also represented in many of the area's churches. To discover an older Rome, walk along Via del Governo Vecchio to admire the façades of Renaissance buildings, browse in the fascinating antiques shops and lunch in one of the many trattorias.

The Vatican

The Torre dell'Orologio by Borromini (1648) formed part of the Oratorio dei Filippini.

Chiesa Nuova
This church was rebuilt in 1575 for the order founded by San Filippo Neri **6**

VIA DEL CORALLO

VIA DEL GOVERNO VECCHIO

VIA DI PARIONE

CORSO VITTORIO EMANUELE II

VIA DI SANT'

PIAZZA DI PASQUINO

At the Oratorio dei Filippini (1637) biblical stories were sung and the congregation responded with a chorus: the origin of the oratorio.

Via del Governo Vecchio preserves a large number of fine Renaissance houses.

Santa Maria della Pace
This Renaissance church has frescoes of the Four Sibyls by Raphael and a refined courtyard by Bramante. The Baroque portico is by Pietro da Cortona **5**

Pasquino is a 3rd-century BC Hellenistic statue of Menelaus. Romans have been hanging satirical verses at its feet since the 16th century.

Palazzo Pamphilj

Fontana del Moro

Campo de' Fiori

STAR SIGHTS

★ **Piazza Navona**

Palazzo Braschi, a late 18th-century building designed by Cosimo Morelli, has a splendid balcony overlooking the piazza.

Sant'Andrea della Valle, begun in 1591, has a flamboyant Baroque façade flanked by angels with outstretched wings by Ercole Ferrata. The church is the setting of the first act of Puccini's *Tosca*.

KEY

– – – Suggested route

0 metres   75

0 yards   75

Sant'Agnese in Agone
by Borromini (1657)
is allegedly built
on the site where,
in AD 304, the
young St Agnes
was exposed
naked to force
her to renounce
her faith.

**Fontana dei
Quattro Fiumi**

LOCATOR MAP
*See Rome Street Finder
map 2*

San Luigi dei Francesi
*This church, which was
completed in 1589, is best
known for three paintings
by Caravaggio* ❸

Palazzo Madama,
the seat of the Italian
Senate, was originally built
for the Medici family in
the 16th century, on the
site of one of their banks.

Sant'Ivo alla Sapienza
*This tiny domed church is one
of Borromini's most original
creations. He worked on it
between 1642 and 1650* ❷

★ **Piazza Navona**
*The piazza is lined with palaces and
pavement cafés, and punctuated by
flamboyant Baroque fountains* ❶

**Largo
di Torre
Argentina**

Piazza Navona ❶

Map 2 F3. 🚌 *40, 46, 62, 64, 81, 87,
116, 492, 628, 810.*

ROME'S MOST BEAUTIFUL
Baroque piazza follows
the shape of a 1st-century AD
stadium built by Domitian,
which was used for athletic
contests *(agones)*, chariot races
and other sports. Traces of the
stadium are still visible below
the church of Sant'Agnese in
Agone, which is dedicated to
a virgin martyred on the site
for refusing to marry a pagan.

The piazza began to take
on its present appearance in
the 17th century, when Pope
Innocent X, whose family
palazzo was on the piazza,
commissioned a new
church, palace and
fountain. The fountain,
the Fontana dei Quattro
Fiumi, is Bernini's most
magnificent, with statues
of the four great rivers of
the world at that time (the
Nile, the Plate, the Ganges
and the Danube) sitting
on rocks below an obelisk.
Bernini also designed the
muscle-bound Moor in the
Fontana del Moro, though
the present statue is a copy.
Until the 19th century, the
piazza was flooded in August
by stopping the fountain outlets. The rich would splash
around in carriages, while
street urchins paddled. Even
today the piazza remains
the social centre of the city.

**Symbolic figure of the River Nile on
Bernini's Fontana dei Quattro Fiumi**

Sant'Ivo alla Sapienza ❷

Corso del Rinascimento 40. **Map** 2 F4.
📞 06 686 49 87. 🚌 40, 46, 64, 70, 81, 87, 116, 186, 492, 628. ⏰ 10am–4pm (to 1pm Sat) Mon–Sat, 9am–noon Sun. 📷 Jul–Aug. 🅰 ♿

HIDDEN IN the courtyard of Palazzo della Sapienza, seat of the old University of Rome, Sant'Ivo's spiral belfry is nevertheless a distinctive landmark on Rome's skyline. Built by Borromini in 1642–60, the church is astonishingly complex, an ingenious combination of concave and convex surfaces. The work spanned the reigns of three popes, and incorporated in the design are their emblems: Urban VIII's bee, Innocent X's dove and olive branch and the star and hills of Alexander VII.

San Luigi dei Francesi ❸

Via Santa Giovanna d'Arco. **Map** 4 F4 & 12 D2. 📞 06 688 27 1. 🚌 70, 81, 87, 116, 186, 492, 628. ⏰ 8:30am–12:30pm, 3:30–7pm daily. 📷 Thu pm. 🅰

THE FRENCH NATIONAL church in Rome, San Luigi is a 16th-century building, best known for three magnificent canvases by Caravaggio in the Cerasi chapel. Painted between 1597 and 1602, these were Caravaggio's first significant religious works: *The Calling of St Matthew, Martyrdom of St Matthew* and *St Matthew and the Angel.* The first version of this last was initially rejected because it depicted the saint as an old man with dirty feet.

Detail from Caravaggio's *The Calling of St Matthew* (1597–1602) in San Luigi dei Francesi

Side relief of the Ludovisi Throne, on display in the Palazzo Altemps

Palazzo Altemps ❹

Via di Sant'Apollinare 46. **Map** 2 F3.
📞 06 39 74 99 07. 🚌 70, 81, 87, 115, 280, 628. ⏰ 9am–8pm Tue–Sun. 🅰

AN EXTRAORDINARY collection of Classical sculpture is housed in this branch of the Museo Nazionale Romano *(see p402).* Restored as a museum during the 1990s, the palazzo was originally built for Girolamo Riario, nephew of Pope Sixtus IV in 1480. In the popular uprising that followed the pope's death in 1484, the building was sacked and Girolamo fled the city. In 1568 the palazzo was bought by Cardinal Marco Sittico Altemps and renovated in the 1570s by Martino Longhi the Elder, who added the obelisk-crowned belvedere and marble unicorn.

The Altemps family were avid collectors; the courtyard and its staircase are lined with ancient sculptures, which complement the Ludovisi sculptures. One of the highlights is the statue of *Galatea's Suicide*, a marble copy of the bronze original, in the Salone del Camino. Also on the first floor is the Greek, 5th-century BC Ludovisi Throne. One of the carved reliefs shows a woman representing Aphrodite.

Galatea's Suicide in the Palazzo Altemps

Santa Maria della Pace ❺

Vicolo del Arco della Pace 5. **Map** 2 E3. 📞 06 686 11 56. 🚌 46, 62, 64, 70, 81, 87, 116, 492, 628, 810. ⏰ 10am–6pm daily (to 10pm Sat, to 1pm Sun). 🅰 ♿

NAMED BY POPE Sixtus IV to celebrate the peace he hoped to bring to Italy, this church dates from the 1480s and contains a beautiful fresco by Raphael. Bramante's refined cloister was added in 1504, while the façade was designed in 1656 by Pietro da Cortona.

Chiesa Nuova ❻

Piazza della Chiesa Nuova. **Map** 2 E4. 📞 06 687 52 89. 🚌 46, 64. ⏰ 8am–noon, 4:30–7pm daily. 📷 ♿

SAN FILIPPO NERI commissioned this church in 1575 to replace the dilapidated one his Order had been given by Pope Gregory XIII. Neri required his followers to humble themselves, and set aristocratic young men to work as labourers on the church. Against his wishes, the nave, apse and dome were richly frescoed after his death by Pietro da Cortona. There are three paintings by Rubens around the altar. The first versions were rejected, so Rubens repainted them on slate, placing the originals above his mother's tomb.

Palazzo della Cancelleria ❼

Piazza della Cancelleria. **Map** 2 E4. 📞 06 69 89 34 91. 🚌 46, 62, 64, 70, 81, 87, 116, 492. ⏰ by appt only.

A SUPREME EXAMPLE of the confident delicacy of early Renaissance architecture, this palazzo was begun in 1485, and was allegedly financed by the gambling proceeds of Raffaele Riario, a nephew of Pope Sixtus I. In 1478 Riario was involved in the Pazzi conspiracy against the Medici, and when Giovanni de' Medici became Pope Leo XIII in 1513, he took belated revenge, seizing the Riario palace and turning it into the papal chancellery.

Tiber Island, with Ponte Cestio, built in 46 BC, linking it to Trastevere

Campo de' Fiori ❽

Map 2 F4. 🚌 116 & routes to Corso Vittorio Emanuele II.

CAMPO DE' FIORI (field of flowers), was one of the liveliest and roughest areas of medieval and Renaissance Rome. Cardinals and nobles mingled with fishmongers and foreigners in the piazza's market; Caravaggio killed his opponent after losing a game of tennis on the square; and the goldsmith Cellini murdered a business rival nearby. Today, the area continues to be a hub of secular activity. The colourful market, trattorias and down to-earth bars retain the original animated atmosphere.

In the Renaissance the piazza was surrounded by inns, many of which were owned by the 15th-century courtesan Vannozza Catanei, mistress of Pope Alexander VI.

The square was also a place of execution. The statue in its centre is the philosopher Giordano Bruno, burned at the stake for heresy on this spot in 1600 for suggesting the earth moved around the sun.

Palazzo Farnese ❾

Piazza Farnese. Map 2 E5. 🚌 23, 116, 280 & routes to Corso Vittorio Emanuele II. ⬤ to the public

ORIGINALLY CONSTRUCTED for Cardinal Alessandro Farnese, who became Pope Paul III in 1534, this palazzo was started by Antonio da Sangallo the Younger, and continued after his death by Michelangelo, who created the cornice on the façade and the courtyard's third storey.

The palace, now the French Embassy, is closed to the public, but when the chandeliers are lit at night you may be able to glimpse the ceiling of the Galleria, an illusionistic masterpiece by Annibale Carracci (1597–1603) based on Ovid's *Metamorphoses*.

Palazzo Spada ❿

Piazza Capo di Ferro 13. Map 2 F5. 📞 06 686 11 58. 🚌 23, 116, 280 & routes to Largo di Torre Argentina. ⬤ 9am–7pm Tue–Sat, 9am–1pm Sun. ⬤ 1 Jan, 1 May, 25 Dec. 🎫 📷 ⬜ W www.galleriaborghese.it

A STUCCO extravaganza studded with reliefs of illustrious Romans, this palazzo was built in 1550, but bought in 1637 by Cardinal Bernardino Spada. A keen patron of the arts, he commissioned Borromini to create an illusionistic tunnel that appears four times longer than it is. The cardinal's art collection, in the Galleria Spada, includes works by Guercino, Dürer and Artemisia Gentileschi.

Ghetto and Tiber Island ⓫

Map 3 A5. 🚌 23, 63, 280, 780 and routes to Largo di Torre Argentina

THE FIRST JEWS came to Rome as traders in the 2nd century BC and were greatly appreciated for their financial and medical skills during the Roman Empire. Persecution began in the 16th century, when Pope Paul IV forced all of the Jews to live within a walled enclosure, an area later to form the hub of the present-day Ghetto.

Today Via del Portico d'Ottavia, the district's main street, leads to Rome's central synagogue, passing restaurants and shops selling Roman Jewish food. Ponte Fabricio links the Ghetto with Tiber Island, a centre of healing since 293 BC when a Temple to Aesculapius was founded. The island is now home to a hospital.

Fruit stalls at Campo de' Fiori's lively morning market

Street-by-Street: Around the Pantheon

THE MAZE OF NARROW STREETS around the Pantheon is a mixture of lively restaurants and cafés, and some of Rome's finest sights. This is also the city's financial and political district, home to Parliament, government offices and the stock exchange. The Pantheon itself, with its awe-inspiring domed interior, has long been a symbol of the city.

Sant'Ignazio di Loyola
This church has a superb illusionistic ceiling painted by Andrea Pozzo in 1685 **17**

The Temple of Hadrian now forms the façade of the Stock Exchange.

Piazza della Minerva centres on Bernini's outlandish sculpture of an elephant supporting an Egyptian obelisk.

★ Palazzo Doria Pamphilj
Among the masterpieces in the art gallery of this vast family palazzo is this Salomé by Titian painted in 1516 **14**

PIAZZA DI SANT'IGNAZIO

VIA DI SANT'IGNAZIO

PIAZZA DEL COLLEGIO ROMANO

VIA DELLA GATTA

VIA DEL SEMINARIO

PIAZZA DELLA ROTONDA

VIA DEL PIÈ DI MARMO

PIAZZA DELLA MINERVA

VIA DEL GESÙ

VIA DEL PLEBISCIT

★ Pantheon
The Pantheon, a temple to "all the gods", is Rome's best-preserved ancient building. It was built in the 1st century AD, probably to a design by Emperor Hadrian **16**

Santa Maria sopra Minerva
This is one of Rome's few Gothic churches, with works by Michelangelo, Bernini and Filippino Lippi **15**

Key	
– – –	Suggested route

LOCATOR MAP
*See Rome Street Finder
map 3*

Via della Gatta is overlooked
by this marble statue of a cat
(*gatta*) that gives the narrow
street its name.

The Pie' di Marmo,
an ancient marble
foot, is probably
part of a giant
statue from
the temple to
the Egyptian
goddess Isis.

Palazzo Altieri incorporates
the hovel of an old woman
who refused to allow her
house to be demolished
when this palace was built
in the 17th century.

Gesù
*Built in the late 16th
century, this Jesuit
church served as a model
for the Order's churches
throughout the world* ⑬

STAR SIGHTS

★ **Pantheon**

★ **Palazzo Doria
Pamphilj**

0 metres   75
0 yards   75

Area Sacra di Largo Argentina ⑫

Largo di Torre Argentina. **Map** 2 F5.
🚌 40, 46, 62, 64, 70, 81, 87, 186,
492. ⭕ with permit only (see p614).

THE REMAINS of four temples
were discovered in the
1920s at the centre of Largo
Argentina, now a busy bus
terminus and traffic junction.
They date from the era of the
Republic, and are among the
oldest found in Rome. For the
purpose of identification, they
are known as A, B, C and D.
The oldest (temple C) dates
from the early 3rd century BC.
It was placed on a high platform preceded by an altar and
is typical of Italic temple
plans as opposed to the
Greek model. Temple A is
from the 3rd century BC,
but in medieval times the
small church of San Nicola di
Cesarini was built over its
podium and the remains of
its two apses are still visible.
The column stumps to the
north belonged to a great
portico, known as the
Hecatostylum (portico
of 100 columns). In
Imperial times two
marble latrines were
built here – the
remains of one are
visible behind temple A.
Behind temples B and C,
near Via di Torre Argentina,
are the remains of a great
platform of tufa blocks. These
have been identified as part
of the Curia of Pompey, a
rectangular building where
the Senate met, and where
Julius Caesar was assassinated
by Brutus, Cassius and their
followers on 15 March 44 BC.

**Area Sacra, with the ruins of
circular temple B**

**Baroque *Triumph of Faith over
Idolatry* by Pierre Legros, Gesù**

Gesù ⑬

Piazza del Gesù. **Map** 3 A4.
📞 06 69 70 01. 🚌 H, 46, 62, 64,
70, 81, 87, 186, 492, 628 & other
routes. ⭕ 6am–12:30pm, 4–7:15pm
daily. 📷

BUILT BETWEEN 1568 and
1584, the Gesù was Rome's
first Jesuit church. The Jesuit
order was founded in Rome
in 1537 by a Basque soldier,
Ignatius Loyola, who became
a Christian after he was
wounded in battle. The order
was austere, intellectual and
heavily engaged in missionary
activity and religious wars.

The much-imitated design
of the Gesù typifies Counter-
Reformation architecture, with
a large nave with side pulpits
for preaching to crowds, and
a main altar as the centrepiece
for the mass. The illusionistic
decoration on the nave ceiling
and dome was added by Il
Baciccia in the 17th century.

The nave depicts the
Triumph of the Name of Jesus
and its message is clear: faithful, Catholic worshippers will
be joyfully uplifted to heaven
while Protestants and heretics
are flung into the fires of hell.
The message is reiterated in
the Cappella di Sant'Ignazio, a
rich display of lapis lazuli, ser-
pentine, silver and gold. The
Baroque marble by Legros,
Triumph of Faith over Idolatry,
shows a female "Religion"
trampling on the head of the
serpent Idolatry, while in Théu-
don's *Barbarians Adoring the
Faith*, an angel aims a kick towards a decrepit old barbarian
couple entangled with a snake.

Palazzo Doria Pamphilj ⓮

Piazza del Collegio Romano 2.
Map 5 A4. 📞 *06 679 73 23.*
🚌 *64, 70, 81, 85, 117, 119, 492.*
⏰ *10am–5pm Fri–Wed.* ⏰ *1 Jan,
1 May, 25 Dec.* 📷 ♿ 🎧 *by appt
for private apartments.*

Palazzo doria pamphilj is a vast edifice whose oldest parts date from 1435. When the Pamphilj family took over in 1647 they built a new wing, a splendid chapel and a theatre.

The family art collection has over 400 paintings dating from the 15th–18th centuries, including a portrait of Pope Innocent X by Velázquez and works by Titian, Guercino, Caravaggio and Claude Lorrain. The opulent rooms of the private apartments retain many of their original furnishings, including Brussels and Gobelins tapestries, Murano chandeliers and a gilded crib.

Velázquez's *Pope Innocent X* (1650)

Santa Maria sopra Minerva ⓯

Piazza della Minerva 42. **Map** 4 F4.
📞 *06 679 39 26.* 🚌 *116 & many
other routes.* ⏰ *7am–7pm daily.*

One of rome's rare Gothic buildings, this church was built in the 13th century over what was thought to be the ruins of a Temple of Minerva. It was a stronghold of the Dominicans, who produced some of the Church's most infamous inquisitors, and who tried the scientist Galileo in the adjoining monastery.

Inside, the church has a superb collection of art and sculpture, ranging from 13th-century Cosmatesque tombs to

a bust by Bernini. Highlights include Antoniazzo Romano's *Annunciation* featuring Cardinal Juan de Torquemada, uncle of the vicious Spanish Inquisitor, and the Carafa Chapel whose frescoes by Filippino Lippi have recently been restored.

In the Aldobrandini Chapel are the tombs of the 16th-century Medici popes, Leo X and his cousin Clement VII, and near the steps of the choir is a stocky *Risen Christ*, begun by Michelangelo.

The church also contains the tombs of many famous Italians, such as St Catherine of Siena who died in 1380 and Fra Angelico, the Dominican friar and painter, who died in 1455. Outside, Bernini's spectacular sculpture of an elephant holds an obelisk on its back.

Simple vaulted nave of Santa Maria sopra Minerva

Interior of the Pantheon, burial place for Italian monarchs

Pantheon ⓰

Piazza della Rotonda. **Map** 3 F4. 📞 *06
68 30 02 30.* 🚌 *116 & many routes.*
⏰ *8:30am–7:30pm daily (6pm Sun).*
⏰ *1 Jan, 1 May, 25 Dec.* 📷 ♿

The pantheon, the Roman "temple of all the gods", is the most extraordinary and best preserved ancient building in Rome. The first temple on the site was a conventional rectangular affair erected by Agrippa between 27 and 25 BC; the present structure was built and possibly designed by Emperor Hadrian in AD 118.

The temple is fronted by a massive pedimented portico screening what appears to be a cylinder fused to a shallow dome. Only from the inside can the true scale and beauty of this building be appreciated: a vast hemispherical dome equal in radius to the height of the cylinder giving perfectly harmonious proportions to the building. A circular opening, the *oculus*, lets in the only light.

In the 7th century Christians claimed to be plagued by demons as they passed by, and permission was given to make the Pantheon a church. Today it is lined with tombs, ranging from a restrained monument to Raphael to huge marble and porphyry sarcophagi holding the bodies of Italian monarchs.

Sant'Ignazio di Loyola ⑰

Piazza di Sant'Ignazio. **Map** 3 A4.
📞 06 679 44 06. 🚌 117, 119, 492.
🕐 7:30am–12:30pm, 4–7:15pm
daily. 📷 ✝

Tʜɪs ᴄʜᴜʀᴄʜ was built by
Pope Gregory XV in 1626
in honour of St Ignatius of
Loyola, founder of the Society
of Jesus (Jesuits) and the man
who most embodied the zeal
of the Counter-Reformation.
    Together with the Gesù (see
p393), Sant'Ignazio forms the
nucleus of the Jesuit area of
Rome. It is one of the most
extravagant Baroque churches
and its vast interior is plated
with precious stones, marble,
stucco and gilt, creating a
thrilling sense of theatre. The
church has a Latin-cross plan,
with an apse and many side
chapels. A cupola was planned
but never built, as the nuns
from a nearby convent
objected that it would obscure
the view from their roof
garden. Instead the space was
filled by a perspective painting
of a dome on a flat disc.
    Even more striking is the
illusionistic ceiling created by
the Jesuit artist Andrea Pozzo
in 1685, a propagandist
extravaganza extolling the
success of Jesuit missionaries
throughout the world. Above
four women, representing
Asia, Europe, America and
Africa, lithe angels and
beautiful youths are sucked
into a heaven of fluffy clouds.

**Detail from the AD 180 Column of
Marcus Aurelius, Piazza Colonna**

Piazza Colonna ⑱

Map 3 A3. 🚌 95, 116, 492.

Hᴏᴍᴇ ᴛᴏ Palazzo Chigi,
official residence of the
prime minister, Piazza Colonna
is dominated by and named
after the majestic Column of
Marcus Aurelius. This was
erected after the death of
Marcus Aurelius in AD 180 to
commemorate his victories
over the barbarian tribes of
the Danube. It is clearly an
imitation of Trajan's Column
(see p378) with scenes from
the emperor's wars spiralling
in reliefs up the column. The
80-year lapse between the
two works produced a great
artistic change: the wars of
Marcus Aurelius are rendered
with simplified pictures in
stronger relief, sacrificing
Classical proportions for the
sake of clarity and immediacy.

Piazza di Montecitorio ⑲

Map 3 A3. 📞 06 676 01. 🚌 116.
🕐 10am–5:30pm 1st Sun of month.

Tʜᴇ ᴏʙᴇʟɪsᴋ in the centre of
Piazza Montecitorio formed
the spine of a giant sundial
brought back from Heliopolis
in Egypt by Augustus. It vanished some time in the 9th
century, and was rediscovered
under medieval houses during
the reign of Julius II (1503–13).
    The piazza is dominated by
the rugged façade of Palazzo
di Montecitorio, designed by
Bernini and completed in
1697, after his death, by Carlo
Fontana. It has been the seat
of Italy's Chamber of Deputies
since the late 19th century.

La Maddalena's stuccoed façade

La Maddalena ⑳

Piazza della Maddalena. **Map** 3 A3.
📞 06 679 77 96. 🚌 116 & many
other routes. 🕐 8am–noon,
5–7:30pm daily. 📷

Sɪᴛᴜᴀᴛᴇᴅ ɪɴ a small piazza
near the Pantheon, the
Maddalena's Rococo façade,
built in 1735, epitomizes the
love of light and movement
of the late Baroque. The
façade has been restored,
despite the protests of Neo-
Classicists who dismissed its
painted stucco as icing sugar.
    The diminutive dimensions
of the church did not deter
17th- and 18th-century
decorators from filling the
interior with paintings and
ornaments from the floor to
the top of the elegant cupola.

Baroque illusionistic ceiling by Andrea Pozzo in Sant'Ignazio di Loyola

NORTHEAST ROME

THIS AREA stretches from the exclusive shopping streets around Piazza di Spagna to the Esquiline Hill, once bourgeois, but now a poor, often seedy area full of early Christian churches. The Piazza di Spagna and Piazza del Popolo district grew up in the 16th century, when the increase in the influx of pilgrims

Lion fountain in Piazza del Popolo

was such that a road was built to channel them as quickly as possible to the Vatican. About the same time, the Quirinal Hill became the site of a papal palace. When Rome became capital of Italy in 1870, Via Veneto became a lavish residential area, and the Esquiline was covered with apartments for the new civil servants.

SIGHTS AT A GLANCE

Churches
Sant'Andrea al Quirinale ➆
San Carlo alle Quattro Fontane ➇
Santa Maria della Concezione ➉
Santa Maria Maggiore ⑮
Santa Maria del Popolo ➂
Santa Maria della Vittoria ⑪
San Pietro in Vincoli ⑭
Santa Prassede ⑬

Museums and Galleries
Museo Nazionale Romano ⑫
Palazzo Barberini ➈

Ancient Sites and Buildings
Ara Pacis ➃
Mausoleum of Augustus ➄

Historic Buildings
Villa Medici ➁

Piazzas and Fountains
Piazza di Spagna and the Spanish Steps ➀
Trevi Fountain ➅

GETTING THERE
Metro stations Repubblica, Barberini and Spagna (line A) cover the area between Termini and Piazza del Popolo. Bus 16 runs from Termini to Santa Maria Maggiore and down Via Merulana.

KEY

Street-by-Street: Piazza di Spagna pp398–9

FS Railway station

M Metro station

P Parking

i Tourist information

City walls

0 metres 250
0 yards 250

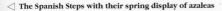

◁ **The Spanish Steps with their spring display of azaleas**

Street-by-Street: Piazza di Spagna

THE NETWORK OF NARROW STREETS around Piazza di Spagna forms one of the most exclusive areas in Rome, drawing droves of tourists and Romans to the elegant shops around Via Condotti. The square and its nearby coffee houses have long attracted those who want to see and be seen. In the 18th century the area was full of hotels for frivolous aristocrats doing the Grand Tour, as well as artists, writers and composers, who took the city's history and culture more seriously.

Caffè Greco is an 18th-century café once frequented by writers and musicians such as Keats, Goethe, Byron, Liszt and Wagner.

Spagna

VIALE TRINITÀ DEI MONTI

Trinità dei Monti is a 16th-century church at the top of the Spanish Steps. There are fine views of Rome from the stairway.

Babington's Tea Rooms, founded by two English spinsters in 1896, still serves English teas.

PIAZZA DI SPAGNA

PIAZZA MIGNANELLI

VIA CONDOTTI

★ **Piazza di Spagna and the Spanish Steps**
These have been at the heart of tourist Rome since the 18th century ❶

VIA DI PROPAGANDA

The Keats-Shelley Memorial House, where the poet Keats died in 1821, is now a museum honouring English Romantic poets.

The Colonna dell' Immacolata, erected in 1857, commemorates Pope Pius IX's doctrine of the Immaculate Conception.

The Collegio di Propaganda Fide, built for the Jesuits in 1662, has a superb façade designed by Francesco Borromini.

KEY

– – – Suggested route

0 metres   75
0 yards   75

LOCATOR MAP
See Rome Street Finder map 3

Sant'Andrea delle Fratte
contains two angels by
Bernini (1669) made for
Ponte Sant'Angelo, which Pope
Clement X thought
too lovely to expose
to the weather.

**The Fontana della Barcaccia at the
foot of the Spanish Steps**

Piazza di Spagna and the Spanish Steps ❶

Map 3 A2. 🚌 116, 117. Ⓜ Spagna.

SHAPED LIKE a crooked bow
tie, and surrounded by
muted, shuttered façades,
Piazza di Spagna is crowded
all day and (in summer) most
of the night. The most famous
square in Rome, it takes its
name from the Palazzo di
Spagna, built in the 17th
century to house the Spanish
Embassy to the Holy See.

The piazza has long been
the haunt of foreign visitors
and expatriates. In the 18th
and 19th centuries the square
stood at the heart of the city's
main hotel district. Some of the
travellers came in search of
knowledge and inspiration,
although most were more
interested in collecting statues
to adorn their family homes.

When the Victorian novelist
Charles Dickens visited, he
reported that the Spanish Steps
were crowded with models
dressed as Madonnas, saints
and emperors, hoping to attract
the attention of foreign artists.

The steps were built in the
1720s to link the square with
the French church of Trinità
del Monti above. The French
wanted to place a statue of
Louis XIV at the top, but the
pope objected, and it was not
until the 1720s that the Italian
architect Francesco de Sanctis
produced the voluptuous
Rococo design which satisfied
both camps. The Fontana
Barcaccia, sunk into the
paving at the foot of the steps
due to low water pressure,
was designed by Bernini's
less famous father, Pietro.

Villa Medici ❷

Accademia di Francia a Roma, Viale
Trinità dei Monti 1. **Map** 3 B1.
📞 06 679 83 81. 🚌 117.
Ⓜ Spagna. **Accademia and
gardens** 🕐 10.30am, 11.30am Sat,
Sun spring & autumn. 🎫 🎥 only.

SUPERBLY POSITIONED on the
Pincio Hill, this 16th-century
villa has retained the name
that it assumed when Cardinal
Ferdinando de' Medici bought
it in 1576. It is now home to
the French Academy, which
was founded in 1666 to give
artists the chance to study in
Rome. From 1803 musicians
were also allowed to study
here: both Berlioz and
Debussy were students.

The villa is only open for
exhibitions, but the formal
gardens, with a gorgeously
frescoed pavilion, and copies
of ancient statues, can be
visited in certain months.

STAR SIGHT

★ Piazza di Spagna and
the Spanish Steps

19th-century engraving of the inner façade of the Villa Medici

Pinturicchio's fresco of the *Delphic Sibyl* (1509) in Santa Maria del Popolo

Santa Maria del Popolo ③

Piazza del Popolo 12. **Map** 2 F1. 📞 06 361 08 36. 🚌 95, 117, 119, 490, 495, 628, 926. Ⓜ Flaminio. ⏰ 7am–noon, 4–7pm Mon–Sat, 7:30am–1:30pm, 4:30–7:30pm Sun. 📷

SANTA MARIA DEL POPOLO was one of the first Renaissance churches in Rome, commissioned by Pope Sixtus IV della Rovere in 1472. Lavish endowments by Sixtus's descendants and other powerful families have made it one of Rome's greatest artistic treasures.

Shortly after Sixtus died in 1484, Pinturicchio and his pupils frescoed two chapels (first and third right) for the della Rovere family. On the altar of the first chapel there is a lovely *Nativity* from 1490 that depicts a stable at the foot of a Classical column.

In 1503 Sixtus IV's nephew Giuliano became Pope Julius II and had Bramante build a new apse. Pinturicchio was called in again to paint its vaults with Sibyls and Apostles framed in an intricate tracery of freakish beasts.

In 1513 Raphael created the Chigi chapel (second left) for the wealthy banker Agostino Chigi. The design is an audacious Renaissance fusion of the sacred and profane; there are pyramid-like tombs and a ceiling mosaic of God holding the signs of the zodiac describing Chigi's horoscope. Raphael died before the chapel was finished and it was completed by Bernini who added the dynamic statues of Daniel and Habakkuk. In the Cerasi chapel, left of the altar, there are two realistic works painted by Caravaggio in 1601: the *Conversion of St Paul* and the *Crucifixion of St Peter*. The artist uses daringly exaggerated lighting effects and foreshortening techniques to intensify the dramatic effect.

Detail of the Ara Pacis frieze

Ara Pacis ④

Via di Ripetta. **Map** 2 F2. 📞 06 36 00 34 71. 🚌 70, 81, 117, 119, 186. ● for restoration.

PAINSTAKINGLY reconstructed over many years from scattered fragments, the exquisitely carved Ara Pacis (Altar of Peace) celebrates the peace created throughout the Mediterranean by Emperor Augustus. Commissioned by the Senate in 13 BC and completed four years later, the altar stands in a square enclosure of Carrara marble, carved with realistic reliefs of such high quality that experts think the craftsmen may have been Greek.

The reliefs on the north and south walls depict a procession that took place on 4 July, 13 BC, in which the members of the emperor's family can be identified, including Augustus's grandson, Lucius, who is the toddler clutching at the skirts of his mother, Antonia.

Mausoleum of Augustus ⑤

Piazza Augusto Imperatore. **Map** 2 F2. 📞 06 67 10 38 19. 🚌 81, 117, 492, 628, 913, 926. ⏰ by appt only: permit needed (see p614). 📷 ◻ ♿

NOW JUST A WEEDY mound ringed with cypresses and strewn with litter, this was once the most prestigious burial place in Rome. Augustus had the mausoleum built in 28 BC, the year before he became sole ruler, as a tomb for himself and his descendants. The circular building was 87 m (270 ft) in diameter with two obelisks (now in Piazza del Quirinale and Piazza dell' Esquilino) at the entrance. Inside were four concentric passageways linked by corridors where urns holding the ashes of the Imperial family were placed, including those of Augustus who died in AD 14.

Trevi Fountain ⑥

Piazza di Trevi. **Map** 3 B3. 🚌 116 & many other routes.

NICOLA SALVI's theatrical design for Rome's largest and most famous fountain was completed in 1762. The central figures are Neptune, flanked by two Tritons, one trying to

Rome's largest and most famous fountain, the Trevi

master an unruly sea-horse, the other leading a quieter beast, symbolizing the two contrasting moods of the sea.

The site originally marked the terminal of the Aqua Virgo aqueduct, built by Augustus' right-hand man and son-in-law, Agrippa, in 19 BC to channel water to Rome's new bath complexes. One of the reliefs on the first storey shows a young girl, Trivia, after whom the fountain may have been named. She is said to have first shown the spring, 22 km (14 miles) from the city, to thirsty Roman soldiers.

Interior, Sant'Andrea al Quirinale

Sant'Andrea al Quirinale ❼

Via del Quirinale 29. **Map** 3 C3.
[06 48 90 31 87. **🚌** 116, 116T, 117. **◯** 9am–noon, 4–7pm Wed–Mon. **●** Aug pm. **∅**

SANT'ANDREA was designed for the Jesuits by Bernini and executed by his assistants between 1658 and 1670. The site was wide but shallow, so Bernini took the radical step of pointing the long axis of his oval plan towards the sides, and leading the eye round to the altar by means of a strong horizontal cornice. At the altar he combined sculpture and painting to create a theatrical crucifixion of Sant'Andrea (St Andrew); the diagonally crucified saint on the altarpiece looks up at a stucco effigy of himself ascending to the lantern, where the Holy Spirit and cherubs await him in heaven.

The dome of San Carlo alle Quattro Fontane, by Borromini

San Carlo alle Quattro Fontane ❽

Via del Quirinale 23. **Map** 3 C3. **[**
06 488 32 61. **🚌** 116T & routes to Piazza Barberini. **M** Barberini. **◯** 10am–1pm & 3 6pm Mon–Fri; 10am–1pm Sat & Sun.

IN 1638, Borromini was commissioned by the Trinitarians to design a church and convent on a tiny cramped site at the Quattro Fontane crossroads. The church, so small that it is said it would fit inside one of the piers of St Peter's, is designed with bold, fluid curves on both the façade and interior to give light and life to the diminutive building. The dome, with its concealed windows, illusionistic coffering and tiny lantern designed to make it look higher than it really is, is a cunning feature.

Ceiling fresco detail in Palazzo Barberini (1633)

Palazzo Barberini ❾

Via delle Quattro Fontane 13. **Map** 3 C2. **[** 06 481 45 91. **🚌** 52, 53, 61, 62, 63, 80, 95, 116, 175, 492, 590. **M** Barberini. **◯** 9am–7pm Tue–Sun. **●** Mon & public hols. **🎟 ∅ ▯ ▲** **♿** (lift). **w** www.galleriaborghese.it

WHEN MAFFEI BARBERINI became Pope Urban VIII in 1623, he decided to build a grand family palazzo. Designed by Carlo Maderno as a typical country villa on the fringes of the city, it now overlooks Piazza Barberini, where traffic hurtles around Bernini's Triton fountain. Maderno died shortly after the foundations had been laid, and Bernini and Borromini took over.

The most dazzling room is the Gran Salone, with an illusionistic ceiling frescoed by Pietro da Cortona in 1633–9. The palazzo also houses part of the Galleria Nazionale d'Arte Antica with works by Filippo Lippi, Titian, Artemisia Gentileschi and Caravaggio. The most famous is a portrait of a courtesan, reputedly Raphael's lover, *La Fornarina*, said to be the daughter of a baker, although not painted by the artist himself.

Santa Maria della Concezione ❿

Via Veneto 27. **Map** 3 C2. **[** 06 487 11 85. **🚌** 52, 53, 61, 62, 63, 80, 95, 116, 175. **M** Barberini. **Crypt ◯** 9am–noon, 3–6pm Fri–Wed. **🎟**

BELOW THIS UNASSUMING church on Via Veneto is a crypt decked with the dismembered skeletons of 4,000 Capuchin monks. They form a macabre reminder of the transience of life, with vertebrae wired together to make sacred hearts and crowns of thorns, and, in one chapel, the poignant skeleton of a tiny Barberini princess.

Santa Maria della Vittoria ⓫

Via XX Settembre 17. **Map** 4 D2.
06 482 61 90. 61, 62, 84, 175, 910. **M** Repubblica. 7am–noon, 3:30–7pm daily. August.

SANTA MARIA DELLA VITTORIA is an intimate Baroque church with a lavish, candlelit interior. Inside the Cornaro chapel is one of Bernini's most ambitious sculptures, the *Ecstasy of St Teresa* (1646). The physical nature of St Teresa's ecstasy is apparent as she appears collapsed on a cloud with her mouth half open and eyes closed, struck by the arrow of a smiling angel. Ecclesiastical members, past and present, of the Venetian Cornaro family, who commissioned the chapel, sit in boxes as if watching and discussing the scene being played out in front of them.

Bernini's *Ecstasy of St Teresa* in Santa Maria della Vittoria

Museo Nazionale Romano ⓬

Palazzo Massimo, Largo di Villa Peretti 1 (1 of 5 sites). **Map** 4 E3. 06 481 55 76. all routes to Termini. **M** Repubblica. 9am–6.45pm Tue–Sun. ticket valid for all sites.

FOUNDED IN 1899, the Museo Nazionale Romano – one of the world's leading museums of Classical art – houses most of the antiquities found in Rome since 1870, as well as important older collections.

During the 1990s it underwent a major reorganization and now has five branches: the Palazzo Altemps (see p390); the Baths of Diocletian; the Aula Ottagona, the Crypta; Balbi, and the Palazzo Massimo. In the latter, exhibits dating from the 2nd century BC to the late 4th century AD are displayed in a series of rooms over three floors. Highlights of the collection include the exquisite *Quattro Aurighe* mosaics from a villa in northern Rome, a Greek statue, the *Generale di Tivoli*, depicting a Roman soldier from the Asian wars, and the famous statue of Emperor Augustus.

One of the finely detailed Quattro Aurighe mosaics on display at the Museo Nazionale Romano

Santa Prassede ⓭

Via Santa Prassede 9a. **Map** 4 D5. 06 488 24 56. 16, 70, 71, 75, 714. **M** Vittorio Emanuele. 7am–noon, 4–6:30pm daily.

THE CHURCH was founded by Pope Paschal II in the 9th century and decorated by Byzantium artists with the most important, glittering mosaics in Rome. In the apse Christ stands between Santa Prassede and her sister, dressed as Byzantine empresses, among white-robed elders, lambs, feather-mop palms and bright red poppies. The Cappella di San Zeno is even lovelier, a jewel-box of

9th-century mosaic, Santa Prassede

a mausoleum, built by Pope Paschal II for his mother, Theodora. Her square halo shows that she was still alive when the mosaic was created.

San Pietro in Vincoli ⓮

Piazza di San Pietro in Vincoli. **Map** 4 D5. 06 488 28 65. 75, 84, 117. **M** Colosseo. 7am–12:30pm, 3:30–7pm (Oct–Mar: 6pm) Mon–Sat, 8:45am–11:45am Sun.

THE CHURCH'S NAME means St Peter in Chains, so called because it houses what are said to be the chains with which St Peter was shackled in the Mamertine Prison (see p379). According to tradition, one set of chains was sent to Constantinople by Empress Eudoxia; when it was returned to Rome some years later it miraculously fused with its partner.

San Pietro is now best known for the Tomb of Julius II, commissioned from Michelangelo by the pope in 1505. Much to the artist's chagrin, Julius soon became more interested in the building of a new St Peter's and the tomb project was laid to one side. After the pope died in 1513, Michelangelo resumed work on the tomb, but had only completed the statues of the *Dying Slaves* (now in found in Paris and Florence) and *Moses* when he was called away to paint the *Last Judgment* in the Sistine Chapel.

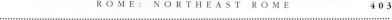

Santa Maria Maggiore ⓯

A CONFIDENT BLEND of architectural styles, ranging from Early Christian to late Baroque, Santa Maria is also famous for its superb mosaics. Founded in about AD 420, it retains the original colonnaded triple nave, lined with panels of rare 5th-century mosaics. The Cosmatesque marble floor and bell tower are medieval, as are the spectacular mosaics on the triumphal arch and in the loggia. The lavish coffered ceiling is Renaissance; the façades, domes and chapels Baroque.

VISITORS' CHECKLIST

Piazza di Santa Maria
Maggiore. **Map** 4 E4.
☎ 06 48 31 95. 🚌 16, 70,
71, 714. 🚋 14. Ⓜ Cavour.
🕐 7am–7pm daily.
🔠 📷

Coronation of the Virgin
This is one of the wonderful 13th-century mosaics in the apse by Jacopo Torriti.

Bell tower

5th-century mosaics

Tomb of Cardinal Rodriguez
This Gothic tomb, which dates from 1299, contains magnificent marblework by the Cosmati.

18th-century façade by Ferdinando Fuga

13th-century mosaics

Cappella Sistina
This chapel was built for Pope Sixtus V (1584–7) by Domenico Fontana and was opulently covered with ancient marble. It houses the pope's tomb.

Cappella Paolina
Flaminio Ponzio, architect of the Villa Borghese, designed this sumptuous chapel in 1611 for Pope Paul V who is buried here.

Column in Piazza Santa Maria Maggiore
In 1611 a bronze of the Virgin and Child was added to this ancient marble column which came from the Basilica of Constantine.

THE VATICAN AND TRASTEVERE

VATICAN CITY, the world capital of Catholicism, is the world's smallest state. It occupies 43 ha (106 acres) within high walls watched over by the Vatican guard. It was the site where St Peter was martyred (c.AD 64) and buried, and it became the residence of the popes who succeeded him. The papal palaces, next to the great basilica of St Peter's, are home to the Sistine Chapel

Pope Urban VIII's coat of arms in St Peter's

and the eclectic collections of the Vatican Museums, as well as being the residence of the pope. Neighbouring Trastevere is quite different, a picturesque old quarter, whose inhabitants consider themselves to be the only true Romans. Sadly, the proletarian identity of the place is in danger of being destroyed by the proliferation of trendy restaurants, clubs and shops.

SIGHTS AT A GLANCE

GETTING THERE
The quickest way to the Vatican is by Metro Line A to Ottaviano San Pietro, just north of Piazza San Pietro. The 40 and 64 buses link it with Termini. Trastevere is a short walk from Campo de' Fiori across Ponte Sisto.

Churches
San Francesco a Ripa ⑨
San Pietro in Montorio and
  the Tempietto ⑩
Santa Cecilia in Trastevere ⑧
Santa Maria in Trastevere ⑦
St Peter's pp408–9 ②

Museums and Galleries
Palazzo Corsini and
  Galleria Nazionale
  d'Arte Antica ⑤
Vatican Museums pp410–17 ③

Historic Buildings
Castel Sant'Angelo ①
Villa Farnesina ④

Parks and Gardens
Botanical Gardens ⑥

KEY

▨	A Tour of the Vatican pp406–7
🅿	Parking
ℹ	Tourist information
---	City walls

0 metres   250
0 yards   250

◁ **View of St Peter's with the Ponte Sant'Angelo in the foreground**

A Tour of the Vatican

THE VATICAN, a sovereign state since February 1929, is ruled by the pope, Europe's only absolute monarch. About 500 people live here and, as well as accommodation for staff and ecclesiasts, the city has

Crucifix in the Vatican its own post office, banks, currency, judicial system, radio station, shops and a daily newspaper, *l'Osservatore Romano*.

Vatican Radio broadcasts in 20 languages throughout the world from this tower, part of the 9th-century Leonine Wall.

★ St Peter's
Most of the great architects of the Renaissance and Baroque had a hand in the design of the Basilica of St Peter's, the most famous church in Christendom (see pp408–9).

★ Sistine Chapel
Michelangelo frescoed the ceiling with scenes from Genesis (1508–12), and the altar wall with the Last Judgment (1534–41). The chapel is used by cardinals when electing a new pope (see p414).

The Papal Audience Chamber

Information office

PIAZZA DEL SANT'UFFIZIO

★ Raphael Rooms
Raphael frescoed this suite in the early 16th century. Works like The School of Athens *established his reputation, to equal that of his contemporary Michelangelo (see p417).*

Piazza San Pietro was laid out by Bernini between 1656 and 1667.

To Via della Conciliazione

This staircase leading down from the museums, designed in 1932 by Giuseppe Momo, is in the form of a double helix, consisting of two spirals: one to walk up and one to walk down.

LOCATOR MAP
See Rome Street Finder map 1

Entrance to Vatican Museums

★ **Vatican Museums**
This marble group of the Laocoön (AD 1) is one of many prestigious works of art in the Vatican (see p410).

The Cortile della Pigna is named after a bronze pine cone from an ancient fountain.

The Vatican Gardens, open for guided tours, make up a third of the Vatican's territory.

metres   75
yards   75

Castel Sant'Angelo ❶

Lungotevere Castello. **Map** 2 D3.
☎ 06 39 96 76 00. 🚌 23, 34, 280.
🕐 9am–8pm Tue–Sun (last entry 7pm). 🌑 public hols. 🗓 🎧 🎁 🖥 🚻

THE MASSIVE FORTRESS of Castel Sant'Angelo takes its name from the vision of the Archangel Michael by Pope Gregory the Great in the 6th century as he led a procession across the bridge, praying for the end of the plague.

The castle began life in AD 139 as the Emperor Hadrian's mausoleum. Since then it has been a bridgehead in the Emperor Aurelian's city wall, a medieval citadel and prison, and a place of safety for popes during times of political unrest. A corridor links it with the Vatican Palace, providing an escape route for the pope. From dank cells to fine apartments of Renaissance popes, the museums cover all aspects of the castle's history, including the Sala Paolina, with illusionistic frescoes (1546–8) by Pellegrino Tibaldi and Perin del Vaga and the Courtyard of Honour.

St Peter's ❷

See pp408–9.

Vatican Museums ❸

See pp410–17.

View of Castel Sant'Angelo from the Ponte Sant'Angelo

STAR SIGHTS

★ **St Peter's**

★ **Vatican Museums**

★ **Sistine Chapel**

★ **Raphael Rooms**

St Peter's ❷

CATHOLICISM'S most sacred shrine, the sumptuous, marble-caked basilica of St Peter's draws pilgrims and tourists from all over the world. It holds hundreds of precious works of art, some salvaged from the original 4th-century basilica built by Constantine, others commissioned from Renaissance and Baroque artists. The dominant tone is set by Bernini, who created the baldacchino twisting up below Michelangelo's huge dome. He also created the Cathedra in the apse, with four saints supporting a throne that contains fragments once thought to be relics of the chair from which St Peter delivered his first sermon.

Dome of St Peter's
The 136.5 m (448 ft) high dome, designed by Michelangelo, was not completed in his lifetime.

Baldacchino
Commissioned by Pope Urban VIII in 1624, Bernini's extravagant Baroque canopy stands above St Peter's tomb.

A staircase of 537 steps leads to the summit of the dome.

The church is 186 m (615 ft) long.

Entrance to Historical Artistic Museum and Sacristy

The Papal Altar stands over the crypt where St Peter is reputedly buried

HISTORICAL PLAN OF THE BASILICA OF ST PETER'S

St Peter was buried in AD 64 in a necropolis near the site of his cruci-fixion in the Circus of Nero. In AD 324 Constantine constructed a basilica over the tomb. The old church was rebuilt in the 15th century, and throughout the 16th and 17th cen-turies various archi-tects developed the existing structure. The new church was inaugurated in 1626.

KEY

- ■ Circus of Nero
- ■ Constantinian
- ■ Renaissance
- ■ Baroque

Monument to Pope Alexander VII
Bernini's last work in St Peter's was finished in 1678 and shows the Chigi pope among the allegorical figures of Truth, Justice, Charity and Prudence.

The Grottoes
A fragment of this 13th-century mosaic by Giotto, salvaged from the old basilica, is now in the Grottoes, where many popes are buried.

Two minor cupolas by Vignola (1507–73)

The foot of St Peter by Arnolfo di Cambio, 13th century, has worn thin from the touch of pilgrims over the centuries.

Michelangelo's Pietà
Protected by glass since an attack in 1972, the Pietà was created in 1499 when Michelangelo was only 25.

From this Library window, the pope blesses the faithful gathered in the piazza below.

Façade by Carlo Maderno (1614)

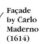

The Holy Door is used only in Holy Years.

Filarete Doors
These bronze doors from the old basilica were decorated with biblical reliefs by Filarete between 1439 and 1445.

Entrance

Markings on the floor of the nave show how other churches compare in length.

Atrium by Carlo Maderno

Piazza San Pietro
On Sundays, religious festivals and special occasions such as canonizations, the pope blesses the crowds from a balcony.

Vatican Museums ❸

Home to the Sistine Chapel and Raphael Rooms as well as to one of the world's most important art collections, the Vatican Museums are housed in palaces originally built for Renaissance popes such as Julius II, Innocent VIII and Sixtus IV. Most of the later additions were made in the 18th century, when priceless works of art accumulated by earlier popes were first put on show.

Etruscan Museum
The Etruscan collection includes a woman's gold clasp (fibula) from the 7th-century BC Regolini-Galassi tomb at Cerveteri, north of Rome.

Gallery of Maps
The Siege of Malta is one of 40 maps of the Church's territories, frescoed by the 16th-century cartographer Ignazio Danti on the gallery's walls.

Gallery of the Candelabra

Raphael Rooms
This is a detail of the Expulsion of Heliodorus from the Temple, one of many frescoes painted by Raphael and his pupils for Julius II's private apartments (see p417).

Gallery of Tapestries

Stairs down

Upper floor

Sala dei Chiaroscuri

Raphael Loggia

Sistine Chapel
(see p414)

Borgia Apartment
Pinturicchio and his assistants frescoed these rooms for Alexander VI in 1492–95.

GALLERY GUIDE
The museum complex is vast: the Sistine Chapel is 20–30 minutes' walk from the entrance, so allow plenty of time. There is a strict one-way system, and it is best to be selective or choose one of four colour-coded itineraries, which vary from 90 minutes to a five-hour marathon.

Modern religious art on view here was sent to the popes by artists worldwide, such as Bacon, Ernst and Carrà.

Pio-Clementine Museum
The finest of the Vatican's Classical statues are on display here, like the Apollo Belvedere, *a Roman copy in marble of a 4th-century BC Greek bronze.*

Gregorian Profane Museum

Stairs up to Etruscan Museum

Entrance

Lower floor

Cortile Ottagonale

Braccio Nuovo

Chiaramonti Museum

The Lapidary Gallery
contains inscriptions from pagan and Christian catacombs, but is closed to the public.

VISITORS' CHECKLIST

Città del Vaticano (entrance in Viale Vaticano). **Map** 1 B2.
06 69 88 33 33. 49 to entrance, 23, 81, 492, 990.
Ottaviano San Pietro, Cipro Musei Vaticani. 8:45am–4:45pm Mon–Fri (Nov–Feb: to 1:45pm), 8:45am–1:45pm Sat, last Sun of month (last entry: 1 hr before closing). religious and public hols. Special permit required for Raphael Loggia, Vatican Library, Lapidary Gallery & Vatican Archives. free last Sun of month. special routes.
W www.vatican.va

Egyptian Museum
The collection of Egyptian artifacts includes this painted bas-relief from a 2400 BC tomb. The museum was organized by Father Ungarelli, a 19th-century Egyptologist.

Pio-Christian Museum
Early Christianity adopted Classical images so that its doctrines could be more easily understood. This 4th-century statue of Christ as the Good Shepherd derives from the pastoral figure of the shepherd.

Pinacoteca
The Vatican's art gallery has 15th- to 19th-century works, and is particularly strong on the Renaissance. This unfinished painting of St Jerome by Leonardo da Vinci reveals his mastery of anatomy.

KEY TO FLOORPLAN
- Egyptian and Assyrian art
- Greek and Roman art
- Etruscan art
- Early Christian and medieval art
- 15th- to 19th-century art
- Modern religious art
- Lapidary Gallery
- Non-exhibition space

Exploring the Vatican's Collections

THE VATICAN'S GREATEST TREASURES are its superlative Greek and Roman antiquities, together with the magnificent artifacts excavated from Egyptian and Etruscan tombs during the 19th century. Some of Italy's greatest artists, such as Raphael, Michelangelo and Leonardo da Vinci, are represented in the Pinacoteca (art gallery) and parts of the former palaces, where they were employed by popes to decorate sumptuous apartments and galleries.

Head of an athlete in mosaic from the Baths of Caracalla, AD 217

EGYPTIAN AND ASSYRIAN ART

THE EGYPTIAN COLLECTION contains finds from 19th- and 20th-century excavations in Egypt, as well as statues that were brought to Rome in Imperial times. There are also Roman imitations of Egyptian art from Hadrian's Villa (see p452) and from temples in Rome devoted to Egyptian gods and goddesses, such as Isis and Serapis.

The genuine Egyptian works, displayed on the lower floor next to the Pio-Clementine Museum, include statues, mummies, mummy cases and a Book of the Dead. One of the main treasures is a colossal granite 13th-century statue of Queen Mutuy, the mother of Rameses II, which was found on the site of the Horti Sallustiani gardens near Via Veneto. Also noteworthy are the head of a statue of Montuhotep IV (20th century BC), the beautiful mummy case of Queen Hetep-heret-es, and the tomb of Iri, who was the guardian of the Pyramid of Cheops. This dates back to the 22nd century BC.

Roman copy of the Greek *Doryphoros*

GREEK, ETRUSCAN AND ROMAN ART

THE GREATER PART of the Vatican Museums is dedicated to Greek and Roman art. However, the Etruscan Museum houses a superb collection of Etruscan (see p40) and pre-Roman artifacts from Etruria and the Greek colonies of southern Italy. Here, the most famous exhibits are the gold jewellery and bronze throne, bed and funeral cart, found in the 650 BC Regolini-Galassi tomb in Cerveteri (see p450).

Prize Greek and Roman pieces form the nucleus of the Pio-Clementine Museum. These include high-quality Roman copies of 4th-century BC Greek statues, such as the *Apoxyomenos* (an athlete wiping his body after a race) and the *Apollo del Belvedere*. The splendid *Laocoön* (1st century AD), originally from Rhodes, was found in 1506 in the ruins of Nero's Golden House. Works such as these inspired Michelangelo and other Renaissance artists.

The much smaller Chiaramonti Museum is lined with ancient busts, and its extension, the Braccio Nuovo, has a 1st-century BC statue of Augustus from the villa of his wife Livia. It is based on the *Doryphoros* (spear-carrier) by the 5th-century BC Greek sculptor Polyclitus. There is also a Roman copy of this on display opposite. The Gregorian Profane Museum, housed in a new wing, follows the evolution of Roman art from reliance on Greek models to a recognizably Roman style.

In this museum, original Greek works include large marble fragments from the Parthenon in Athens. Among the Roman pieces are two reliefs, the *Rilievi della Cancelleria*, commissioned by Domitian in AD 81 to glorify the military parades of his father, Emperor Vespasian. There are also fine Roman floor mosaics, two from the Baths of Caracalla (see p427), and one, in the Round Room, dated 3rd century AD, from the Baths of Otricoli in Umbria.

In the Vatican Library is the 1st-century AD *Aldobrandini Wedding*, a beautiful Roman fresco depicting a bride being prepared for her marriage.

Roman mosaic from the Baths of Otricoli, Umbria, in the Round Room

EARLY CHRISTIAN AND MEDIEVAL ART

THE MAIN COLLECTION of early Christian antiquities is in the Pio-Christian Museum, which contains inscriptions and sculpture from catacombs and early Christian basilicas. The sculpture consists chiefly of reliefs from sarcophagi, though the most striking work is a free-standing 4th-century statue of the *Good Shepherd*. The sculpture's chief interest lies in the way it blends Biblical episodes with pagan mythology. The idealized pastoral figure of the shepherd became Christ himself, while bearded philosophers turned into the Apostles.

The first two rooms of the Pinacoteca are dedicated to late medieval art, mostly wooden altarpieces painted in tempera. The outstanding work is Giotto's *Stefaneschi Triptych* of about 1300 which decorated the main altar of the old St Peter's.

The Vatican Library has a number of medieval treasures including reliquaries, textiles, enamels and icons.

Pietà (c.1471–4) by the Venetian artist Giovanni Bellini in the Pinacoteca

Detail of Giotto's *Stefaneschi Triptych* (1330) in the Pinacoteca

15TH- TO 19TH-CENTURY ART

MANY RENAISSANCE popes were connoisseurs of the arts who considered it their duty to sponsor the leading painters, sculptors and goldsmiths of the age. The galleries around the Cortile del Belvedere were decorated by great artists between the 16th and the 19th centuries.

The Gallery of Tapestries is hung with tapestries woven in Brussels to designs by students of Raphael. The Apartment of Pope Pius V has beautiful 15th-century Flemish tapestries, and the Gallery of Maps is frescoed with 16th-century maps of ancient and contemporary Italy.

Alongside the Raphael Rooms (*see p417*) are the Room of the Chiaroscuri and Pope Nicholas V's private chapel. This was frescoed be-tween 1447 and 1451 by Fra Angelico. Also worth seeing is the Borgia Apartment, decorated in the 1490s by Pinturicchio and his pupils for the Borgia pope, Alexander VI. Another set of fascinating frescoes can

Pinturicchio's *Adoration of the Magi* (1490), Borgia Apartment

be found in the Loggia of Raphael, but a visit here requires special permission.

The Pinacoteca has many important Renaissance works. Highlights from the 15th century are a fine *Pietà* by Giovanni Bellini, part of his *Coronation of the Virgin* altar-piece in Pèsaro (*see p358*); and Leonardo da Vinci's unfinished *St Jerome*, discovered, after being long lost, in two halves. One was being used as a coffer lid in an antique shop, the other as the seat of a stool in a shoemaker's. Exceptional pieces from the 16th century include eight tapestry cartoons, the *Transfiguration* and *Madonna of Foligno* by Raphael, in a room devoted to the artist; a *Deposition* by Caravaggio; an altarpiece by Titian; and *St Helen* by Veronese, which shows the saint as a gorgeously dressed aristocrat.

Sistine Chapel: The Ceiling

MICHELANGELO FRESCOED the ceiling for Pope Julius II between 1508 and 1512, working on specially designed scaffolding. The main panels, which chart the Creation of the World and Fall of Man, are surrounded by subjects from the Old and New Testaments – except for the Classical Sibyls who are said to have foreseen the birth of Christ. In the 1980s the ceiling was restored revealing colours of an unsuspected vibrancy.

Libyan Sibyl
The pagan prophetess reaches for the Book of Knowledge. Like most female figures Michelangelo painted, the beautiful Libyan Sibyl was probably modelled on a man.

Illusionistic architecture

Creation of the Sun and Moon
Michelangelo depicts God as a dynamic but terrifying figure commanding the sun to shed light on the earth.

KEY TO CEILING PANELS

GENESIS: 1 God Dividing Light from Darkness; **2** Creation of the Sun and Moon; **3** Separating Waters from Land; **4** Creation of Adam; **5** Creation of Eve; **6** Original Sin; **7** Sacrifice of Noah; **8** The Deluge; **9** Drunkenness of Noah.

ANCESTORS OF CHRIST: 10 Solomon with his Mother; **11** Parents of Jesse; **12** Rehoboam with Mother; **13** Asa with Parents; **14** Uzziah with Parents; **15** Hezekiah with Parents; **16** Zerubbabel with Parents; **17** Josiah with Parents.

PROPHETS: 18 Jonah; **19** Jeremiah; **20** Daniel; **21** Ezekiel; **22** Isaiah; **23** Joel; **24** Zechariah.

SIBYLS: 25 Libyan Sibyl; **26** Persian Sibyl; **27** Cumaean Sibyl; **28** Erythrean Sibyl; **29** Delphic Sibyl.

OLD TESTAMENT SCENES OF SALVATION: 30 Punishment of Haman; **31** Moses and the Brazen Serpent; **32** David and Goliath; **33** Judith and Holofernes.

Original Sin
This shows Adam and Eve tasting the forbidden fruit from the Tree of Knowledge, and their expulsion from Paradise. Michelangelo represents Satan as a snake with the body of a woman.

The Ignudi are athletic male nudes whose significance is uncertain.

RESTORATION OF THE SISTINE CEILING

The recent restorers of the Sistine Chapel used computers, photography and spectrum technology to analyse the fresco before cleaning began. They separated Michelangelo's work from that of later restorers and discovered that the restorers had attempted to clean the ceiling with materials ranging from bread to retsina wine. The new restoration revealed the familiarly

A restorer cleaning the Libyan Sibyl

dusky, eggshell-cracked figures to have creamy skins, lustrous hair and to be dressed in brightly-coloured, luscious robes: "a Benetton Michelangelo" mocked one critic, claiming that a layer of varnish which the artist had added to darken the colours had been removed. However, after examining the work, most experts agreed that the new colours probably matched those painted by Michelangelo.

The lunettes are devoted to frescoes of the ancestors of Christ, like Hezekiah.

Sistine Chapel: The Walls

THE MASSIVE WALLS of the Sistine Chapel, the main chapel in the Vatican Palace, were frescoed by some of the finest artists of the 15th and 16th centuries. The 12 paintings on the side walls, by artists including Perugino, Ghirlandaio, Botticelli and Signorelli, show parallel episodes from the life of Moses and of Christ. The decoration of the chapel walls was completed between 1534 and 1541 by Michelangelo, who added the great altar wall fresco, the *Last Judgment*.

KEY TO THE FRESCOES: ARTISTS AND SUBJECTS

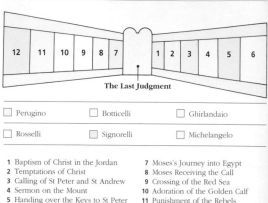

The Last Judgment

☐ Perugino   ☐ Botticelli   ☐ Ghirlandaio
☐ Rosselli   ☐ Signorelli   ☐ Michelangelo

1 Baptism of Christ in the Jordan
2 Temptations of Christ
3 Calling of St Peter and St Andrew
4 Sermon on the Mount
5 Handing over the Keys to St Peter
6 Last Supper
7 Moses's Journey into Egypt
8 Moses Receiving the Call
9 Crossing of the Red Sea
10 Adoration of the Golden Calf
11 Punishment of the Rebels
12 Last Days of Moses

THE LAST JUDGMENT BY MICHELANGELO

REVEALED IN 1993 after a year's restoration, the *Last Judgment* is considered to be the masterpiece of Michelangelo's mature years. It was commissioned by Pope Paul III Farnese, and required the removal of some earlier frescoes and two windows over the altar. A new wall was erected which slanted inwards to stop dust settling on it. Michelangelo worked alone on the fresco for seven years, until its completion in 1541.

The painting depicts the souls of the dead rising up to face the wrath of God, a subject that is rarely used for an altar decoration. The pope chose it as a warning to Catholics to adhere to their faith in the turmoil of the Reformation. In fact the work conveys the artist's own tormented attitude to his faith. It offers neither the certainties of Christian orthodoxy, nor the ordered view of Classicism.

In a dynamic, emotional composition, the figures are caught in a vortex of motion. The dead are torn from their graves and hauled up to face Christ the Judge, whose athletic, muscular figure is the focus of all the painting's movement. Christ shows little sympathy for the agitated saints around him, clutching the instruments of their martyrdom. Neither is any pity shown for the damned, hurled down to the demons in hell. Here Charon, pushing people off his boat into the depths of Hades, and the infernal judge Minos, are taken from Dante's *Inferno*. Minos has ass's ears, and is a portrait of courtier Biagio da Cesena, who had objected to the nude figures in the fresco. Michelangelo's self-portrait is on the skin held by the martyr St Bartholomew.

Souls meeting the wrath of Christ in Michelangelo's *Last Judgment*

Raphael Rooms

POPE JULIUS II'S PRIVATE APARTMENTS were built above those of his hated predecessor, Alexander VI, who died in 1503. Julius was impressed with Raphael's work and chose him to redecorate the four rooms (stanze). Raphael and his pupils began in 1508, replacing works by better-known artists, including Raphael's teacher, Perugino. The new frescoes quickly established the young artist's reputation in Rome, but the project took 16 years to complete and he died before it was finished.

Detail from Raphael's *The Mass of Bolsena* (1512)

HALL OF CONSTANTINE

THE FRESCOES IN THIS ROOM were started in 1517 and completed in 1525, five years after Raphael's death, and are largely the work of the artist's pupils. The theme of the decoration is the triumph of Christianity over paganism, and the four major frescoes show scenes from the life of Constantine, the first Christian emperor. These include the *Vision of the Cross* and the emperor's victory over his rival, Maxentius, at *The Battle of the Milvian Bridge*, for which Raphael had provided a preparatory sketch.

ROOM OF HELIODORUS

RAPHAEL DECORATED this private antechamber between 1512 and 1514. The main frescoes all contain thinly veiled references to the protective powers of the papacy. The room's name refers to the fresco on the right, *The Expulsion of Heliodorus from the Temple*, showing Heliodorus felled by a horseman as he tries to rob the Temple in Jerusalem. It alludes to Pope Julius II's victory over foreign armies in Italy. *The Mass of Bolsena* on the left wall refers to a miracle that occurred in 1263, in which a priest who doubted the doctrine of the Holy Host was said to have seen blood issue from it at the moment of sacrifice.

ROOM OF THE SEGNATURA

COMPLETED BETWEEN 1508 and 1511, the frescoes here are the most harmonious in the series. The scheme followed by Raphael, dictated by Pope Julius II, reflected the Humanist belief that there could be perfect harmony between Classical culture and Christianity in the search for truth. The most famous work, *The School of Athens*, centres on the debate about truth between the Greek philosophers Plato and Aristotle. Raphael depicted some of his contemporaries as philosophers, including Leonardo da Vinci, Bramante and Michelangelo.

KEY TO FLOORPLAN

① Hall of Constantine
② Room of Heliodorus
③ Room of the Segnatura
④ Room of the Fire in the Borgo

ROOM OF THE FIRE IN THE BORGO

THIS WAS ORIGINALLY the dining room, but when the decoration was completed under Pope Leo X, it became a music room. All the frescoes exalt the reigning pope by depicting events in the lives of his 9th-century namesakes, Leo III and IV. The main frescoes were designed by Raphael, but finished by his assistants between 1514 and 1517. The most famous, *The Fire in the Borgo*, shows a miracle of 847, when Pope Leo IV put out a fire by making the sign of the cross. Raphael draws a parallel between this and the legendary flight of Aeneas from Troy, recounted by Virgil. Aeneas appears in the foreground, carrying his father Anchises on his back.

The School of Athens (1511) showing philosophers and scholars

Villa Farnesina ❹

Via della Lungara 230. **Map** 2 E5.
📞 06 68 02 72 68. 🚌 23, 280.
🕐 9am–1pm Mon–Sat. 🎨

THE FABULOUSLY WEALTHY
Sienese banker Agostino
Chigi commissioned this villa
in 1508 from his fellow
Sienese Baldassare Peruzzi.
Chigi's main home was across
the Tiber, and the villa was
designed purely for lavish
banquets. Artists, poets,
cardinals, princes and the
pope himself were entertained
here in magnificent style.
Chigi also used the villa for
sojourns with the courtesan
Imperia, who allegedly inspired one of the *Three Graces*
painted by Raphael in the
Loggia of Cupid and Psyche.

The simple, harmonious
design of the Farnesina, with
a central block and projecting
wings, made it one of the first
true villas of the Renaissance.
Peruzzi decorated some of
the interiors himself, such as
the Sala della Prospettiva
upstairs, in which the illusionistic frescoes create the
impression of looking out
over 16th-century Rome
through a marble colonnade.

Other frescoes, by Sebastiano
del Piombo and Raphael and
his pupils, illustrate Classical
myths, while the vault of the
main hall, the Sala di Galatea,
is adorned with astrological
scenes showing the position
of the stars at the time of
Chigi's birth. After his death
the business collapsed, and in
1577 the villa was sold off to
the Farnese family.

**Raphael's *Three Graces* in the
Villa Farnesina**

**Queen Christina of Sweden's
bedroom in the Palazzo Corsini**

Palazzo Corsini and Galleria Nazionale d'Arte Antica ❺

Via della Lungara 10. **Map** 2 D5. 📞
06 328 10. 🚌 23, 280. 🕐 9am–
7pm Tue–Sat (to 2pm Sat), 9am–1pm
Sun & public hols (last adm: 30 mins
before closing). 🕐 1 Jan, 1 May,
15 Aug, 25 Dec. 🎨 🔖 ♿ 🚫
🌐 www.galleriaborghese.it

BUILT FOR Cardinal Domenico
Riario in 1510–12, the
Palazzo Corsini has numbered
Bramante, the young Michelangelo, Erasmus and the
mother of Napoleon among
its guests. Queen Christina of
Sweden died here in 1689.
The palazzo was rebuilt by
Ferdinando Fuga, who
planned the façade to be
viewed from an angle, as Via
della Lungara is too narrow
for a full frontal view.

When the palazzo was
bought by the state in 1893,
the Corsini family donated
their collection of paintings,
which formed the core of the
national art collection, and
was soon augmented. The
collection is now split between
Palazzo Barberini and Palazzo
Corsini. Although the best
works are in the Barberini,
there are paintings by Van
Dyck, Rubens, Murillo, and,
notably, an androgynous
St John the Baptist (c.1604)
by Caravaggio and a *Salome*
(1638) by Reni. The strangest
work is a portrait of the rotund
Queen Christina as the goddess
Diana by J Van Egmont.

Botanical Gardens ❻

Largo Cristina di Svezia 24. **Map** 2 D5.
📞 06 49 91 71 06. 🚌 23, 280. 🕐
9:30am–6:30pm (Oct–Mar: 5:30pm)
Tue–Sun. 🕐 public hols. 🎨 🎨

SEQUOIAS, PALM TREES, orchids
and bromeliads are among
the 7,000 plants from all over
the world represented in the
Botanical Gardens (Orto
Botanico). Indigenous and
exotic species are grouped to
illustrate their botanical families and their adaptation to
different climates and eco-
systems. There are also some
curious plants like the ginkgo
that have survived almost
unchanged from earlier eras.

**Palm trees in the Botanical
Gardens, Trastevere**

Santa Maria in Trastevere ❼

Piazza Santa Maria in Trastevere.
Map 5 C1. 📞 06 581 48 02.
🚌 H, 23, 280. 🕐 7:30am–1pm,
4–7pm daily. 📷 ♿ 🚪

SANTA MARIA IN TRASTEVERE
was probably the first
Christian place of worship in
Rome, founded by Pope
Callixtus I in the 3rd century,
when emperors were still
pagan and Christianity a
minority cult. According to
legend, it was built on the
site where a fountain of oil
had miraculously sprung up
on the day that Christ was
born. The basilica became
the focus of devotion to the
Madonna, and although
today's church, and its
remarkable mosaics, date
largely from the 12th and
13th centuries, images of the

Apse mosaic of the *Coronation of the Virgin*, Santa Maria in Trastevere

Virgin continue to dominate. The façade mosaics probably date from the 12th century, and show Mary, Christ and ten lamp-bearing women. Inside in the apse is a stylized 12th-century *Coronation of the Virgin*, and below, a series of realistic scenes from the life of the Virgin by the 13th-century artist Pietro Cavallini. The oldest image of the Virgin is a 7th-century icon, the *Madonna di Clemenza*, which depicts her as a Byzantine empress flanked by a guard of angels. It sits above the altar in the Cappella Altemps.

Santa Cecilia in Trastevere ❽

Piazza di Santa Cecilia. **Map** 6 D2.
📞 06 589 92 89. 🚌 H, 23, 44, 280.
🕐 9am–12.30pm, 3–7pm daily (to 5:30pm in winter). **Cavallini fresco**
🕐 10–11:30am Tue & Thu, 11.30am–12 noon Sun.

ST CECILIA, aristocrat and patron saint of music, was martyred here in AD 230. After an unsuccessful attempt to suffocate her by locking her in the hot steam bath of her house for three days, she was beheaded. A church was built, possibly in the 4th century, on the site of her house (still to be seen beneath the church, along with the remains of a tannery). Her body was lost, but it turned up again in the Catacombs of San Callisto *(see p432)*. In the 9th century it was reburied here by Pope Paschal I, who rebuilt the church.

A fine apse mosaic survives from this period. The altar canopy by Arnolfo di Cambio and the fresco of *The Last Judgment* by Pietro Cavallini can be reached through the adjoining convent; they date from the 13th century, one of the few periods when Rome had a distinctive artistic style.

In front of the altar is a delicate statue of St Cecilia by Stefano Maderno, which is based on sketches made of her perfectly preserved relics when they were briefly disinterred in 1599.

San Francesco a Ripa ❾

Piazza San Francesco d'Assisi 88.
Map 6 D2. 📞 06 581 90 20.
🚌 H, 23, 44, 75, 280. 🕐 7:30am–noon, 4–7pm daily. ♿

ST FRANCIS OF ASSISI lived here in a hospice when he visited Rome in 1219 and his stone pillow and crucifix are preserved in his cell. The church was built by a follower, a local nobleman called Rodolfo Anguillara, who is

portrayed on his tombstone wearing the Franciscan habit.

Entirely rebuilt in the 1680s by Cardinal Pallavicini, the church is rich in 17th- and 18th-century sculptures. Not to be missed in the Altieri chapel (fourth left, along the nave) is Bernini's exquisite late work, the *Ecstasy of Beata Ludovica Albertoni* (1674).

San Pietro in Montorio and the Tempietto ❿

Piazza San Pietro in Montorio 2. **Map** 5 B1. 📞 06 581 39 40. 🚌 44, 75, 100. 🕐 7:30am–noon, 4–6pm daily. **Tempietto** 🕐 9:30am–12:30pm, 2–4pm (4–6pm in summer) Tue–Sun. 📷

Bramante's circular Tempietto at San Pietro in Montorio

THE TEMPIETTO, a diminutive masterpiece of Renaissance architecture completed by Bramante in 1502, stands in the courtyard of San Pietro in Montorio. The name means "little temple" and its circular shape echoes early Christian *martyria*, chapels built on the site of a saint's martyrdom. This was erroneously thought to be the spot in Nero's Circus where St Peter was crucified. Bramante ringed the chapel with Doric columns, a Classical frieze and fine balustrade.

Bernini's *Ecstasy of Beata Ludovica Albertoni*, San Francesco a Ripa

AVENTINE AND LATERAN

Mosaic fragment, Baths of Caracalla

THIS IS ONE of the greenest parts of the city, taking in the Celian and Aventine Hills, as well as the very congested area around San Giovanni in Laterano. The Celian, now scattered with churches, was a fashionable place to live in Imperial Rome. Some of the era's splendour is still apparent in the ruins of the Baths of Caracalla.

Behind the Baths rises the Aventine Hill, a peaceful, leafy area, with the superb basilica of Santa Sabina, and lovely views across the river to Trastevere and St Peter's. In the valley below, cars and Vespas skim around the Circus Maximus, following the ancient charioteering track, while to the south lies Testaccio, a lively working-class district.

SIGHTS AT A GLANCE

Churches
San Clemente ⑥
San Giovanni in Laterano ⑦
Santa Maria in Cosmedin ②
Santa Maria in Domnica ③
Santi Quattro Coronati ⑤
Santa Sabina ⑪
Santo Stefano Rotondo ④

Ancient Sites and Buildings
Baths of Caracalla ⑧
Temples of the Forum Boarium ①

Monuments and Tombs
Protestant Cemetery ⑩
Pyramid of Caius Cestius ⑨

KEY

	Street by Street: Piazza della Bocca della Verità pp422–3
FS	Railway station
M	Metro station
P	Parking
i	Tourist information

GETTING THERE

Bus 95 runs from Piramide to Piazza della Bocca della Verità. The Celian is near Metro Colosseo and Circo Massimo; tram 3 and buses 81, 160 and 715 are all good routes to the Aventine area.

0 metres   250
0 yards   250

◁ Pines and orange trees in the Aventine's Parco Savelli, with the dome of St Peter's in the distance

Street-by-Street: Piazza della Bocca della Verità

THE SITE OF ROME'S FIRST PORT and its busy cattle
market, this is an odd little corner of the city,
stretching from the heavily trafficked road running
along the Tiber to the southern spur of the Capitoline
Hill, a place of execution from ancient times until the
Middle Ages. Although best known for the Bocca della
Verità (Mouth of Truth) in Santa Maria in Cosmedin,
which is supposed to snap shut on the hands of liars,
there are many other sites in the area, notably two
temples from the Republican era. In the 6th century
the area became home
to a Greek community
who founded the
churches of San Giorgio
in Velabro and Santa
Maria in Cosmedin.

The Casa dei Crescenzi, studded
with ancient fragments, incorporates
the ruins of a 10th-century tower
built by the powerful Crescenzi
family to guard the river Tiber.

Sant'Omobono stands
on an archaeological
site where finds date
back to the 6th century.

**★ Temples of the
Forum Boarium**
*These two buildings
are the best preserved
of Rome's Republican
temples* ❶

Ponte Rotto, as this forlorn ruined
arch in the Tiber is called, simply
means "broken bridge". Built in the
2nd century BC, its original name
was the Pons Aemilius.

The Fontana dei Tritoni,
built by Carlo Bizzaccheri
in 1715, shows the strong
influence of Bernini.

★ Santa Maria in Cosmedin
*The Bocca della Verità, a
medieval drain cover, is
set into the portico* ❷

San Giovanni Decollato
belonged to a confraternity
that encouraged condemned
prisoners to repent.

KEY

– – – Suggested route

0 metres   75
0 yards   75

VIA DI SAN GIOVANNI DECOLLATO
LUNGOTEVERE DEI PIERLEONI
TEVERE
PONTE PALATINO
PIAZZA DELLA BOCCA DELLA VERITÀ
VIA DELLA G

Santa Maria della Consolazione was named after an image of the Virgin placed here in 1385 to give consolation to the condemned.

LOCATOR MAP
See Rome Street Finder map 6

San Teodoro is a circular church on the edge of the Palatine with exceptional 6th-century apse mosaics.

San Giorgio in Velabro, a 7th-century basilica, was damaged in an explosion in 1994, and has now been restored.

Arco degli Argentari

The 4th-century Arch of Janus, a four-faced marble-plated arch at the edge of the Forum Boarium market, was an ideal place for merchants and customers to do business in the shade.

VIA DEI FIENILI

VIA DI SAN TEODORO

DEI CERCHI

★ STAR SIGHTS

★ Santa Maria in Cosmedin

★ Temples of the Forum Boarium

Temples of the Forum Boarium ❶

Piazza della Bocca della Verità.
Map 6 E1. 🚌 *23, 44, 81, 95, 160, 170, 280, 628, 715, 716.*

THESE WONDERFULLY well-preserved Republican temples are at their best in moonlight, standing in their grassy enclave beside the Tiber sheltered by umbrella pines. During the day, they look less romantic, stranded in a sea of traffic. They date from the 2nd century BC, and were saved from ruin by being consecrated as Christian churches in the Middle Ages by the Greek community then living in the area. The rectangular temple, formerly known as the Temple of Fortuna Virilis, was probably dedicated to Portunus, the god of rivers and ports. Set on a podium it has four Ionic travertine columns fluted at the front and 12 half-columns embedded in the tufa wall of the *cella* – the room that housed the image of the god. In the 9th century the Temple was converted into the church of Santa Maria Egiziaca, after a 5th-century prostitute who reformed and became a hermit.
 The smaller circular Temple, which is made of solid marble and surrounded by 20 fluted columns, was dedicated to Hercules, though it was long believed to be a Temple of Vesta because of its similarity to the one in the Forum.

The Ionic façade of the Republican era Temple of Portunus

Apse mosaic from the 9th century of the Virgin and Child in Santa Maria in Domnica

Santa Maria in Cosmedin ❷

Piazza della Bocca della Verità. **Map** 6 E1. 🎧 *06 678 14 19.* 🚌 *23, 44, 81, 95, 160, 170, 280, 628, 715, 716.* ⏲ *9am–6pm daily (10am–noon, 3–5pm winter).* 🚻 🚻 🚻

T HIS BEAUTIFUL church was built in the 6th century on the site of the ancient city's food market. The Romanesque bell tower and portico were added during the 12th century. In the 19th century a Baroque façade was removed and the church restored to its original simplicity. It contains many fine examples of Cosmati work, in particular the mosaic pavement, the raised choir, the bishop's throne, and the canopy over the main altar.

Set into the wall of the portico is the Bocca della Verità (Mouth of Truth), a grotesque marble face, thought to have

The nave of Santa Maria in Cosmedin with its Cosmati floor

been an ancient drain cover. Medieval tradition had it that the jaws would snap shut on liars – a useful way of testing the faithfulness of spouses.

Santa Maria in Domnica ❸

Piazza della Navicella 12. **Map** 7 B2. 🎧 *06 700 15 19.* 🚌 *81, 117, 673.* Ⓜ *Colosseo.* ⏲ *9am–noon daily (pm sometimes).* 📷 🚻

S ANTA MARIA IN DOMNICA was probably founded in the 7th century, and renovated in the 9th century. By this time the Romans had lost the art of making mosaics, so Pope Paschal I imported mosaicists from Byzantium. They created an exquisite apse mosaic showing the Virgin, Child and angels in a delicate garden of paradise. Paschal I is kneeling at the Virgin's feet wearing a square halo, indicating that he was alive when it was made.

In 1513 Andrea Sansovino added a portico decorated with lions' heads, a punning homage to Pope Leo X.

Santo Stefano Rotondo ❹

Via di Santo Stefano Rotondo 7. **Map** 9 B2. 🎧 *06 42 11 99.* 🚌 *81, 117, 673.* ⏲ *2–4pm Mon, 9am–1pm, 2–4pm Tue–Sat (2–6pm in summer).*

S ANTO STEFANO ROTONDO was built between 468 and 483 on a circular plan with four chapels in a cruciform shape.

Its circular inner area is enclosed by two concentric corridors. A third, outer corridor was demolished on the orders of Leon Battista Alberti in 1453. In the 16th century Niccolò Pomarancio, Antonio Tempesta and others covered the walls with 34 frescoes detailing the martyrdoms of saints by Roman emperors.

Cloister of Santi Quattro Coronati

Santi Quattro Coronati ❺

Via dei Santi Quattro Coronati 20. **Map** 7 C1. 🎧 *06 70 47 54 27.* 🚌 *85, 117, 850.* 🚋 *3.* ⏲ *9:30am–noon, 3:30–6pm daily.* 📷 🚻

T HIS FORTIFIED convent was built in the 4th century to house the relics of four Persian stonemasons, martyred after they refused to make a statue honouring the pagan god Aesculapius. It was rebuilt after invading Normans set fire to it in 1084.

Highlights are a delightful garden cloister and the Chapel of St Sylvester, where 12th-century frescoes recount the legend of Constantine's conversion to Christianity.

San Clemente ➏

IN 1857 FATHER MULLOOLY, the Irish Dominican prior of San Clemente, began excavations beneath the existing 12th-century basilica. Directly underneath he and his successors discovered a 4th-century church, and below that a number of ancient Roman buildings. Both basilicas are dedicated to St Clement, the fourth pope. On the lowest level is a temple devoted to the cult of Mithras, a mystical all-male religion imported from Persia which rivalled Christianity for popularity.

VISITORS' CHECKLIST

Via di San Giovanni in Laterano.
Map 7 B1. **C** 06 70 45 10 18.
85, 87, 117, 186, 810, 850.
M Colosseo. 3. 9am–12:30pm, 3–6pm daily (from 10am Sun). to excavations.

Cappella di Santa Caterina
Recently restored frescoes by the 15th-century artist Masolino da Panicale show scenes from the life of St Catherine of Alexandria.

Entrance

Apse Mosaic
The 12th-century Triumph of the Cross *includes finely detailed animals and acanthus leaves.*

12th-century basilica

18th-century façade

Piscina

4th-century basilica

Paschal Candlestick
This splendid 12th-century spiralling candlestick, striped with glittering multi-coloured mosaic, is the work of the Cosmati.

Schola Cantorum

Temple of Mithras

Life of San Clemente
Faded frescoed episodes from the life of the fourth pope decorate the lower church. This one tells the story of a boy found alive in his tomb under the sea.

Triclinium
An altar to the god Mithras, showing him slaying a bull, stands in the dank triclinium, a room used for ritual banquets by cult members.

San Giovanni in Laterano ❼

SAN GIOVANNI, the cathedral of Rome, was founded by Emperor Constantine in the early 4th century. It has been rebuilt several times, notably in 1646 when Borromini restyled the interior, but retains its original basilica form. Before the papacy moved to Avignon in 1309, the adjoining Lateran Palace was the official papal residence. The present structure dates from 1589, but older parts survive, like the Scala Santa (Holy Staircase) which Christ is said to have climbed at his trial.

Baptistry
Though much restored, the octagonal baptistry contains some beautiful 5th-century mosaics.

North façade

Apse

East Façade
The main entrance, on the east façade (1735), is adorned with statues of Christ and the Apostles.

Museum entrance

Lateran Palace

Papal Altar
The Gothic baldacchino, which rises over the papal altar, is decorated with 14th-century frescoes.

On Maundy Thursday the pope, as Bishop of Rome, gives a blessing from the loggia of the city's main cathedral.

The Corsini Chapel
was built in the 1730s for Pope Clement XII Corsini, who lies buried in a porphyry tomb from the Pantheon.

Main entrance

Boniface VIII Fresco
Possibly by Giotto, this fragment shows the pope announcing the Holy Year of 1300, which attracted around two million pilgrims.

Cloisters
Built by the Vassalletto family in about 1220, the cloisters are remarkable for their twisted columns and inlaid marble mosaics.

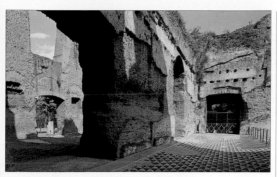

Part of one of the gymnasia in the Baths of Caracalla

Baths of Caracalla ⑧

Viale delle Terme di Caracalla 52.
Map 7 A3. **[** 06 575 86 26. **[**] 160,
628. **[]** 3. **[** 9am–1 hr before
sunset Tue–Sun, 9am–2pm Mon.
[1 Jan, 1 May, 25 Dec. **[] [] []**

REARING UP at the foot of the Aventine Hill are the monolithic red-brick ruins of the Baths of Caracalla. Begun by Emperor Septimius Severus in AD 206, and completed by his son Caracalla in AD 217, they remained in use until the 6th century, when the Goths sabotaged the city's aqueducts.

Going for a bath was one of the social events of the day in ancient Rome. Large complexes such as Caracalla, with a capacity for 1,600 bathers, were not simply places to have a natter and get washed, but also areas which offered an impressive array of facilities: art galleries, gymnasia, gardens, libraries, conference rooms, lecture rooms and shops selling food and drink.

A Roman bath was a long and complicated business, beginning with a form of Turkish bath, followed by a spell in the *caldarium*, a large hot room with pools of water to moisten the atmosphere. Then came the lukewarm *tepidarium*, followed by a visit to the large central meeting place known as the *frigidarium*, and finally a plunge into the *natatio*, an open-air swimming pool. For the rich, this was followed by a rub-down with scented woollen cloth.

Most of the rich marble decorations of the baths were scavenged by the Farnese family in the 16th century to adorn the rooms of Palazzo Farnese *(see p391)*. There are, however, statues and mosaics from the Baths in the Museo Nazionale Archeologico in Naples *(see pp474–5)* and in the Vatican's Gregorian Profane Museum *(see p412)*.

So dramatic is the setting that until recently it was the regular venue for the open-air opera season in August.

Pyramid of Caius Cestius ⑨

Piazzale Ostiense. **Map** 6 F4
[**] 23, 95, 280. **[] 3. **[M]** Piramide.

CAIUS CESTIUS was a wealthy but unimportant 1st-century BC *praetor*, or senior magistrate. At the time, inspired by the Cleopatra scandals, there was a craze for all things Egyptian, and Caius decided to commission himself a pyramid as a tomb. Set into the Aurelian Wall near Porta San Paolo, it is built of brick and faced with white marble; according to an inscription, it took just 330 days to build in 12 BC.

The Pyramid of Caius Cestius on Piazzale Ostiense

Protestant Cemetery ⑩

Cimitero Acattolico, Via di Caio Cestio.
Map 6 E4. **[** 06 574 19 00. **[**] 23,
280. **[]** 3. **[** 9am–5:30pm Tue–Sun
(Oct–Mar: to 4:30pm) (last adm. 30
mins before closing). **Donation.** **[]**

NON-CATHOLICS have been buried in this peaceful cemetery behind the Aurelian Wall since 1738. In the oldest part (on the left as you enter) is the grave of the poet John Keats, who died in 1821 in a house on Piazza di Spagna *(see p398)*. He wrote his own epitaph: "Here lies one whose name was writ in water". Not far away from here rest the ashes of Percy Bysshe Shelley, who drowned in 1822.

The interior of Santa Sabina

Santa Sabina ⑪

Piazza Pietro d'Illiria 1. **Map** 6 E4.
[06 579 46 00. **[**] 23, 44, 95,
170, 781. **[** 6:30am–12:45pm,
3:30–7pm daily. **[] []**

HIGH ON THE AVENTINE stands an early Christian basilica, founded by Peter of Illyria in AD 425 and later given to the Dominican order. It was restored to its original simplicity in the early 20th century. Light filters through 9th-century windows on to a nave framed by pale Corinthian columns. Above the main door is a blue and gold 5th-century mosaic inscription to Peter. In the side portico outside is a 5th-century panelled door carved with biblical scenes, notably one of the oldest images of the Crucifixion (top left-hand corner).

Further Afield

IT IS WELL WORTH making the effort to see some of Rome's outlying sights. Highlights are the Villa Giulia, home to a magnificent Etruscan museum, and the Museo Borghese on the splendid Villa Borghese estate, with its extraordinary collection of virtuoso statues by Bernini. Other sights range from ancient churches and catacombs to the more modern suburb of EUR, a strange architectural medley begun by Mussolini in the 1930s.

KEY

▩	Central Rome
▢	Suburbs
▭	Motorway
▬	Major road
═	Minor road
⋯	City walls

10 km = 6 miles

Villa Borghese ❶

Map 3 B1. 🚌 *52, 53, 88, 95, 116, 490.* 🚊 *3, 19.* **Park** ○ *dawn–sunset daily.*

THE VILLA AND ITS PARK were designed in 1605 for Cardinal Scipione Borghese, the sybaritic nephew of Pope Paul V. An extravagant patron of the arts, he amassed one of Europe's finest collections of paintings, statues and antiquities, many of which are still displayed in the villa which he built especially to house his antique sculptures.

The **park** was one of the first of its kind in Rome, its formal gardens divided by avenues and graced with statues. It contained 400 newly planted trees, garden sculpture by Bernini's father, Pietro, along with many ingenious fountains, "secret" flower gardens, enclosures of exotic animals and birds, and even a grotto with artificial rain. There was also a speaking robot and a trick

chair, which trapped anyone who sat in it. At first the grounds were open to the public, but after a visitor was shocked by the collection of erotic paintings, Paul V decided to keep the park private.

In 1773 work began on redesigning the park in the wilder, Romantic style made fashionable by landscape artists like Claude Lorrain and Poussin. Over the next few

Temple of Aesculapius, an 18th-century folly, at the Villa Borghese

years mock-Classical temples, fountains and *casine* (summer-houses) were added. In 1901, the park and villa were acquired by the state, and in 1911 the area was chosen as the site for the International Exhibition. Pavilions were built by many of the world's nations, the most impressive of which is the **British School at Rome** by Edwin Lutyens. In the northeastern corner of the park lie the Museo Zoologico and a small redeveloped zoo, known as the Bioparco, where the emphasis is on conservation. Today the estates of the Villa Borghese, Villa Giulia and the Pincio gardens form one vast park, with the **Giardino del Lago**, at its centre, named after an artificial boating lake. Its main entrance is marked by an 18th-century copy of the Arch of Septimius Severus, while on the lake's island is a fake Ionic temple to the Greek god of health, Aesculapius, designed by the 18th-century architect Antonis Aspurucci.

A circular Temple of Diana folly lies between the Porta Pinciana, at the top of Via Veneto, and Piazza di Siena, a grassy amphitheatre which hosts Rome's international horse show in May. Its umbrella pines inspired the composer Ottorino Respighi to write *The Pines of Rome* (1924). The open-air opera season is also held in the park.

To the northwest of the park is the Galleria Nazionale d'Arte Moderna, which houses a large but somewhat uninspiring collection of 19th- and 20th-century paintings.

Sacred and Profane Love by Titian (1514), in the Galleria Borghese

Museo e Galleria Borghese ❷

Villa Borghese, Piazzale Scipione Borghese 5. **06 328 10.** ▦ 52, 53, 116, 910. ▦ 3, 19. ◯ 9am–7pm Tue–Sat, 9am–8pm Sun (reservations needed for Sat & Sun). ◯ public hols. ▨ ◉ ◉ ▢ ◉

SCIPIONE BORGHESE'S villa was designed in 1605 as a typical Roman country house, with its wings projecting into the surrounding gardens. It was built by Flaminio Ponzio, Pope Paul V's architect, and was used by Scipione for entertaining guests and for displaying his impressive collection of paintings and sculpture. Between 1801 and 1809 Prince Camillo Borghese, husband to Napoleon's sister Pauline, unfortunately sold many of the family paintings

to his brother-in-law, and swapped 200 of Scipione's Classical statues for an estate in Piedmont. These statues are still in the Louvre and, as a consequence, the remaining antique Classical collection is less interesting than it might once have been. However, the hedonistic cardinal was an enthusiastic patron of the arts and the sculptures he commissioned from artists such as the young Bernini now rank among their most famous works.

The eight rooms of the ground floor of the Villa Borghese are set around a central hall, the Salone. The most famous statue is one of Bernini's finest works, *Apollo and Daphne* (1624) in room 3, which shows the nymph Daphne with bay leaves sprouting from her out-stretched fingers, roots growing from her toes and rough bark enfolding her smooth body, as she begins to metamorphose into a laurel tree to escape being abducted by the god Apollo. Abduction is also the theme of *The Rape of Proserpina*, again by Bernini, in room 4. Depicting Pluto, the god of the underworld, carrying Proserpina, daughter of Ceres, off to be his bride, the sculpture is a virtuoso piece in which Bernini contrasts the taut musculature of Pluto with the soft yielding flesh of Proserpina, whose thigh dimples in his iron grip.

The third famous Bernini piece, which dates from 1623, is *David* in room 2. The artist captures the tensed, grimacing youth the moment before he releases the stone that slew Goliath. It is said that Pope Urban VIII held a mirror up to Bernini so that the sculptor could model David's face on

Detail of *Rape of Proserpina* by Bernini (1622), Museo Borghese

his own. In the next alcove is the Villa Borghese's most infamous work – a sculpture, executed in 1805 by Canova, of Pauline Borghese as *Venus Victrix* (Venus the Conqueror). The semi-naked Pauline reclining on a chaise-longue shocked those who saw it and Pauline's husband kept the statue locked away, even denying Canova access to it.

The next room holds a selection of antiquities, notably a Roman copy of a plump *Bacchus* by the 4th-century BC Greek sculptor Praxiteles, and fragments of a 3rd-century AD mosaic found on one of the Borghese estates in Torrenova, showing gladiators battling with wild animals.

The Galleria Borghese, on the upper floor, houses some superb Baroque and Renaissance paintings, which could formerly be seen at the Complesso San Michele in Trastevere while the gallery was closed for renovation. Works includes Raphael's masterpiece, the *Deposition*, various works by Caravaggio, the graceful *Danäe* by the 16th-century artist Correggio, as well as works by Pinturicchio, Barocci, Rubens and Titian.

Bernini's *Apollo and Daphne* (1624)

Villa Giulia ③

THIS VILLA WAS BUILT in 1550 as a country retreat for Pope Julius III. Designed by Vignola and Ammannati, with contributions by Michelangelo and Vasari, it was intended for entertaining guests of the Vatican, such as Queen Christina of Sweden, rather than as a permanent home. The gardens were planted with 36,000 trees and peppered with pavilions and fountains. Villa Giulia also used to house an outstanding collection of sculptures: 160 boats filled with statues and ornaments were sent to the Vatican after the death of Pope Julius III in 1555.

Since 1889 the villa has been home to the Museo Nazionale Etrusco, an impressive collection of pre-Roman antiquities from central Italy.

VISITORS' CHECKLIST

Piazzale di Villa Giulia 9.
📞 06 322 65 71 (info).
📞 06 328 10 (reservations).
🚌 52, 95. 🚊 3, 19.
🕐 9am–7pm Tue–Sun.
⬤ 1 Jan, 1 May, 25 Dec.
Concerts in July. 🎫
📷 with seven days' notice.
📷 🛍 ♿ 🏠

Rooms 24–29 contain finds from the Ager Faliscus, an area between the Tiber and Lake Bracciano, in particular temples from Falerii Vetere, the principal Faliscan town.

Ficoroni Cist
Engraved and beautifully illustrated, this 4th-century BC bronze marriage coffer held mirrors and other body care implements.

Rooms 11–18,
the Antiquarium collection, display domestic and votive objects and ceramics, including the Chigi vase from 6th-century BC Corinth.

Room 19 exhibits finds from the Castellani collection, including early 6th-century ceramics and bronzes.

Spiralled Faliscan Crater
Painted in the free style of the 4th century BC, this spiral-handled vase was used to hold wines or oil. The Falisci were an Italic tribe influenced by the Etruscans.

Ninfeo (Nympheum)

Husband and Wife Sarcophagus
This 6th-century BC tomb from Cerveteri shows a deceased couple banqueting in the afterlife. Their tender expression bears witness to the skill of Etruscan artists.

Rooms 30–34 exhibit finds from various sites including the Temple of Diana at Nemi.

Rooms 1–10
are arranged by site, starting with Vulci (most importantly articles from the Warrior's Tomb) and including Bisenzio, Veio and Cerveteri.

Entrance

KEY TO FLOORPLAN
- ☐ Ground floor
- ☐ First floor
- ☐ Non-exhibition space

Apse mosaic in Sant'Agnese, showing the saint flanked by two popes

Sant'Agnese fuori le Mura ❹

Via Nomentana 349. ☎ 06 861 08 40. 🚌 36, 60, 84, 90. ⏰ 9am–noon, 4–6pm Tue–Sat, 4–6pm Sun, 9am–noon Mon. 🎫 to catacombs. 📷 ♿ 📹

SANT'AGNESE FUORI LE MURA was built in the 4th century above the crypt of the 13-year-old martyr St Agnes, and although much altered it retains the form of the original basilica. According to legend it was founded by Constantine's daughter Constantia, who was cured from leprosy after sleeping beside Agnes's tomb.

In the 7th-century apse mosaic, St Agnes appears as a bejewelled Byzantine empress in a stole of gold and a violet robe. Tradition has it that she appeared like this eight days after her death holding a white lamb. On 21 January two lambs are blessed in the church and a vestment called a *pallium* is woven from their wool, to be given to a new archbishop.

Santa Costanza ❺

Via Nomentana 349. ☎ 06 861 08 40. 🚌 36, 60, 84, 90. ⏰ 9am–noon, 4–6pm Tue–Sat, 4–6pm Sun, 9am–noon Mon. 📷 ♿ 📹

THIS CIRCULAR church was built in the early 4th century as a mausoleum for Emperor Constantine's daughters, Constantia and Helena. The dome and its drum are supported by an arcade that rests on 12 magnificent pairs of granite columns, while the encircling ambulatory has a barrel-vaulted ceiling decorated with the world's earliest surviving Christian mosaics. Dating from the 4th century, they are thought to have been copied from a secular Roman floor and include flowers, animals and birds. There is even a charming scene of a Roman grape-harvest, though the wine is said by Christians to represent Christ's blood.

In a niche on the far side of the church is a replica of Constantia's ornate porphyry sarcophagus, carved with cherubs crushing grapes. The original was moved to the Vatican Museums in 1790.

Circular interior of the 4th-century church of Santa Costanza

The sanctity of Constantia is somewhat debatable. Described by the historian Marcellinus as a fury incarnate, constantly goading her equally unpleasant husband, Hannibalianus, to violence, her canonization was probably the result of some confusion with a saintly nun of the same name.

Via Appia Antica ❻

🚌 218, 760.

Cypresses lining the Via Appia

THE FIRST PART of the Via Appia was built in 312 BC by Appius Claudius Caecus. In 190 BC, when it was extended to the ports of Taranto and Brindisi, the road became Rome's link with its empire in the East. It was the route taken by the funeral processions of the dictator Sulla (78 BC) and Emperor Augustus (AD 14), and it was along this road that St Paul was led as a prisoner to Rome in AD 56. The church of Domine Quo Vadis? marks the spot where St Peter is said to have met Christ when fleeing Rome.

The road is lined with ruined family tombs, decaying monuments, and collective burial places *(columbaria)*. Beneath the fields on either side lies a maze of catacombs, including those of San Callisto and San Sebastiano.

Catacombs **7**

Via Appia Antica 126. 🚌 218, 660.
San Callisto 📞 06 513 01 51. 🕐
9am–noon, 2:30–5:30pm Thu–Tue.
● Feb, 1 Jan, Easter Sun, 25 Dec.

I N BURYING THEIR DEAD in underground cemeteries outside the city walls, the early Christians were simply obeying the laws of the time. They were not forced to use them because of persecution, as later popular myth has suggested. Many saints were buried here, and the catacombs later became shrines and places of pilgrimage.

Today several catacombs are open to the public. The vast Catacombs of San Callisto, hewn from volcanic tufa, contain niches, or *loculi*, which held two or three bodies, as well as the burial places of several early popes. Close by, walls in the Catacombs of San Sebastiano are covered in graffiti invoking St Peter and St Paul, whose remains may once have been moved here.

Engraving of Christian ceremony in Catacombs of San Callisto (AD 50)

EUR **8**

🚌 170, 671, 714. Ⓜ EUR Fermi,
EUR Palasport. **Museo della Civiltà
Romana** Piazza G Agnelli 10. 📞 06
592 60 41. 🕐 9am–6pm Tue–Sat,
9am–1pm Sun & public hols.
● 1 Jan, 1 May, 25 Dec.

T HE ESPOSIZIONE UNIVERSALE di Roma (EUR), a suburb to the south of the city, was originally built for an international exhibition, a kind of "Work

EUR's Palazzo della Civiltà del Lavoro, the "Square Colosseum"

Olympics", that was planned for 1942, but never took place because of the outbreak of war. The architecture was intended to glorify Fascism, and as a result the bombastic style of the buildings can look overblown and rhetorical to modern eyes. Of all the buildings the best known is probably the Palazzo della Civiltà del Lavoro (the Palace of the Civilization of Work), an unmistakable landmark for people arriving from Fiumicino airport.

The scheme was eventually completed in the 1950s. Despite the area's dubious architecture, EUR has been a planning success, and people are still keen to live here. As well as residential housing, the vast marble halls along the wide boulevards are also home to a number of government offices and museums. Best among the latter is the Museo della Civiltà Romana, famous for its casts of the reliefs from the Column of Trajan, and for a large scale

model depicting 4th-century Rome with all the buildings which then stood within the Aurelian walls. The south of the suburb features a lake and shady park, and the huge domed Palazzo dello Sport, built for the 1960 Olympics.

San Paolo fuori le Mura **9**

Via Ostiense 186. 🚌 23, 128, 170,
670, 761, 766. Ⓜ San Paolo.
📞 06 541 03 41. 🕐 7am–7pm
daily (6:30pm in winter). **Cloister**
● 1–3pm.

T ODAY'S CHURCH is a faithful if soulless reconstruction of the great 4th-century basilica destroyed by fire in 1823. Only a few fragments of the earlier church survived, most notably the cloister (1241), with its pairs of colourful inlaid columns, considered one of the most beautiful in Rome.

Elsewhere, the church's triumphal arch is decorated on one side with heavily restored 5th-century mosaics, and on the other with mosaics by Pietro Cavallini originally on the façade. The equally fine mosaics (1220) in the apse represent the figures of Christ with St Peter, St Andrew, St Paul and St Luke.

The single most outstanding work of art is the fine marble canopy over the high altar, the work of Arnolfo di Cambio (1285), with the possible assistance of Pietro Cavallini. Below the altar is the *confessio* where it is alleged St Paul was once buried. To its right is an impressive Paschal candlestick dating from the 12th century by Nicolò di Angelo and Pietro Vassalletto.

19th-century mosaic on façade of San Paolo fuori le Mura

ROME STREET FINDER

MAP REFERENCES given with sights described in the Rome chapters relate to the maps on the following pages. Map references are also given for hotels *(see pp542–75)* and restaurant listings *(see pp578–609)* and for useful addresses in the *Travellers' Needs* and *Survival Guide* sections at the back of the book. The first figure in the map reference tells you which Street Finder map to turn to, and the letter and number which follow refer to the grid reference on that map. The small map below shows the area of Rome covered by each of the eight maps and the corresponding map number is given in black. All the major sights are sketched out on the maps, and symbols, listed in the key below, are used to indicate the location of other important buildings.

1 **2** **3** **4**

The Vatican and Trastevere

Around Piazza Navona

Northeast Rome

The Ancient Centre

5 **6** **7** **8**

Aventine and Lateran

0 kilometres   2

0 miles   1

KEY AND SCALE FOR STREET FINDER PAGES

■ Major sight	**P** Parking	⊠ Post office
■ Place of interest	ℹ Tourist information	= Railway line
FS Railway station	✚ Hospital with casualty unit	One-way street
M Metro station	▣ Police station	— City walls
🚌 Bus terminus	✝ Church	
🚊 Tram terminus	✡ Synagogue	

0 metres   250

0 yards   250

LAZIO

....

*L*YING BETWEEN *the Apennines and the Tyrrhenian Sea, Lazio is a varied region of volcanic lakes, mountains, ravines, vineyards and olive groves. Before the rise of Rome, it was populated by the Etruscans and various Italic tribes, including the Latins, after whom the region is named. Besides rich archaeological sites, Lazio also offers skiing and swimming and water sports in the lakes and sea.*

Lazio was inhabited at least 60,000 years ago, although the first signs of a substantial civilization date back to the 10th century BC. By the 7th century BC a flourishing Etruscan and Sabine civilization based on trade and agriculture existed in the north, while the region's southern margins were colonized by the Latins, Volsci and Ernici. History mingles with myth in the writings of Virgil, who describes how Aeneas landed in Lazio where he married the daughter of the king of the Latins. Romulus and Remus (legendary founders of Rome) were descendants of this alliance.

With the rise of Rome as a power, the Etruscan and Latin peoples were, in time, overwhelmed and the focus of the region turned to the city of Rome. Great roads and aqueducts extended out of the city like spokes of a wheel, and wealthy patricians built lavish villas in the surrounding countryside. The early Middle Ages saw the rise of the Church's temporal power and, with the foundation of monasteries at Subiaco and Montecassino, Lazio became the cradle of western monasticism, and eventually part of the Papal States. In the 16th and 17th centuries, wealthy papal families competed with one another to build luxurious villas and gardens, hiring some of the best architects of the Renaissance and Baroque.

Throughout its history, however, Lazio has been eclipsed and neglected by Rome. The Pontine marshes were a malaria-ridden swamp until the 1920s, when Mussolini had them drained and brought new roads and agricultural improvements to the area.

Looking out over Caprarola during the early evening *passeggiata*

◁ Vignola's graceful Renaissance parterre gardens and fountains in Villa Lante, Viterbo

Exploring Lazio

MUCH OF LAZIO'S LANDSCAPE WAS FORMED by the eruption of four volcanoes which showered the area with lava. Lakes formed in the craters, and the soil, rendered fertile by the lava, nourished vines, olives, fruit and nut trees. The volcanic activity also left Lazio with hot springs, notably around Tivoli, Viterbo and Fiuggi. Rome dominates the area, dividing the wooded hills of the north from the reclaimed Pontine marshes in the south. Swimming and sailing are possible in lakes Bracciano, Bolsena and Albano, while Lazio's best beaches lie between Gaeta and Sabaudia in the Parco Nazionale del Circeo.

SIGHTS AT A GLANCE

SEE ALSO

• *Where to Stay* pp568–9

• *Where to Eat* pp601–2

Firenze

Lago di Bolsena

MONTEFIASCONE 3

BOMARZO 4

VITERBO 2

VILLA LANTE

Grosseto

TUSCANIA 1

NORCHIA

Lago di Vico

TARQUINIA 6

RESERVA NATURALE LAGO DI VICO

CAPRAROLA 5

SUTRI

LAKE BRACCIANO 8

CIVITAVECCHIA

CERVETERI 7

VEI

RO

OSTIA ANTICA 9

MAR TIRRENO

The Tolfa hills southwest of Lake Bracciano

KEY

▬▬	Motorway
▬▬	Major road
▬▬	Minor road
▬▬	Scenic route
〜	River
✿	Viewpoint

The old quarter overlooking the beach at Sperlonga

GETTING AROUND

Rome's two international airports at Fiumicino and Ciampino serve the region. The main motorways are the *Autostrada del Sole* (A1) from Firenze–Roma and Roma–Napoli, and the Roma–L'Aquila (A24). The ring road *(raccordo anulare)* around Rome connects the motorways and main roads.

The Lazio bus service, Lineelaziali, serves all the main towns with changeover points for the smaller locations in Rome and at Latina, Frosinone, Viterbo and Rieti. Train routes into the region from other Italian cities are efficient, although within Lazio the services are slower and less frequent.

Palestrina's terraces climbing up the hill

Ascoli Piceno

AMATRICE

Terni

RIETI

L'Aquila

PARCO NATURALE REGIONALE DEI MONTI SIMBRUINI

11 TIVOLI

13 SUBIACO

12 PALESTRINA

FRASCATI

FIUGGI

15 ANAGNI

SORA

CASAMARI

POSTA FIBRENA

FROSINONE

NINFA **16**

SERMONETA

FOSSANOVA

MONTECASSINO

14 CASSINO

LATINA

Caserta Napoli

PARCO NAZIONALE DEL CIRCEO

TERRACINA

17

18

19

SPERLONGA

GAETA

Pozzuoli

GOLFO DI GAETA

| 0 kilometres | 15 |
| 0 miles | 10 |

ISOLE PONZIANE

Carved loggia of the Palazzo Papale, Viterbo

Viterbo **❷**

🏛 60,000. **FS** 🚌 **ℹ** Piazza San Carluccio 5 (0761 30 47 95). 🚲 Sat.

VITERBO WAS AN important Etruscan centre before falling to the Romans in the 4th century BC. Its heyday, however, came in the 13th century when it briefly became the papal seat (1257–81). During World War II it was devastated, but the austere grey stone medieval core, still encircled by walls, and many of the town's churches, have been carefully restored.

In **San Pellegrino**, Viterbo's oldest and best preserved quarter, medieval houses with towers, arches and external staircases line narrow streets running between little piazzas decorated with fountains.

On Piazza San Lorenzo the 12th-century **Duomo** boasts an elegant black and white striped bell tower, a solemn 16th-century façade and a stark Romanesque interior. The adjacent 13th-century **Palazzo Papale**, with a finely carved loggia, was built for popes on their visits to the city.

The town's civic buildings border the main square, Piazza del Plebiscito. The most interesting is the 15th-century **Palazzo dei Priori**, frescoed inside by Baldassare Croce with scenes from the town's history and mythological past.

Outside the city walls, on Viale Capocci, the Romanesque **Santa Maria della Verità** has wonderful 15th-century frescoes by Lorenzo da Viterbo.

Tuscania **❶**

Viterbo. 🏛 7,500. 🚌 **ℹ** Largo del Teatro (0761 43 63 71). 🚲 Fri am.

TUSCANIA'S TRIM WALLS and towers are visible from afar on the empty low-lying plains between Viterbo and Tarquinia. Although shaken by an earthquake in 1971, its medieval and Renaissance buildings have since been carefully re-constructed. Just outside the city walls, on the rocky Colle San Pietro, two remarkable churches dating from the Lombard-Romanesque period occupy the site of Tuscana, a major Etruscan centre conquered by Rome in 300 BC.

Façade of San Pietro, Tuscania

Santa Maria Maggiore, at the foot of the hill, has a typically Lombard-Romanesque asymmetric façade with blind arcades and a bold rose window. Over the central door lies a simple marble Madonna and Child, framed by abstract motifs and biblical scenes. Inside, a rare 12th-century full-immersion baptism font stands in the aisle. The Lombard-Romanesque church of **San Pietro**, on top of the hill, is a striking building of ochre-hued tufa and white marble details. It stands on a grassy piazza, along with two medieval towers and a bishop's palace. The façade features an intricately inlaid rose window flanked by strange reliefs, including three-headed bearded demons. The interior is true to its 8th-century form, with squat columns, toothed arches, capitals carved with stylized plants and a Cosmati floor. Below the church lies a strange mosque-like crypt.

Villa Lante's small but splendid Renaissance gardens, considered Vignola's masterpiece

ENVIRONS: The **Villa Lante**, northeast of Viterbo, was begun in 1562 by Vignola for Cardinal Gambara. The main attractions are the outstanding Renaissance gardens and fountains. Be careful not to be a victim of a 16th-century practical joke: many of the fountains will sprinkle people without warning.

🏛 **Palazzo dei Priori**
Piazza Plebiscito. 🎫 0761 30 46 43.
◯ daily. ◉ public hols. ♿ ⧉
🏛 **Villa Lante**
Bagnaia. 🎫 0761 28 80 08.
◯ Tue–Sun. ◉ 1 Jan, 1 May, 25 Dec. 📷 ♿ to gardens.

The main façade of the pentagonal Palazzo Farnese at Caprarola

Montefiascone ❸

Viterbo. 👥 13,000. 🚉 🚌 ℹ Largo Plebiscito (0761 83 20 60). 🔄 Wed.

Carved 11th-century capital in San Flaviano, Montefiascone

THIS PRETTY TOWN is perched on the edge of a defunct volcanic crater between the shores of Lake Bolsena, over which there are splendid views, and the Via Cassia. It is dominated by the octagonal bulk of its cathedral, **Santa Margherita**, whose dome, created in the 1670s by Carlo Fontana, is second only in size to St Peter's.

On the town's outskirts, along the Via Cassia towards Orvieto, lies **San Flaviano**, a lovely double-decker building with a 12th-century church oriented east over an 11th-century church pointing west. Inside are some fine 14th-century frescoes and freely carved capitals, thought to have been inspired by the traditions of Etruscan art.

ENVIRONS: The popular lakeside beach resort of **Bolsena**, 15 km (9 miles) north on Lake Bolsena, has a medieval castle, as well as boats to the islands of Bisentina and Martana.

Bomarzo ❹

Parco dei Mostri, Bomarzo.
🎫 0761 92 40 29. 🚉 to Viterbo.
🚌 from Viterbo. ◯ 8am–sunset.
📷 ♿

THE SACRO BOSCO beneath the town of Bomarzo was created between 1522 and 1580 by Duke Vicino Orsini as a bizarre memorial to his late wife. Far from designing a meticulous Renaissance garden, Orsini embraced the artificiality and distortion of the Mannerist period by creating lop-sided buildings and sculpting huge boulders of stone into fantastic creatures and vast allegorical monsters.

One of the bizarre stone monsters in Bomarzo's Sacro Bosco

Caprarola ❺

Viterbo. 👥 4,900. 🚌 ℹ Via Filippo Nicolai 2 (0761 64 61 57). 🔄 Tue.

PERHAPS THE GRANDEST of the country villas created during the 17th century by the wealthy families of Rome, **Palazzo Farnese** *(see p370)* is the focal point of the medieval village of Caprarola. Designed by Vignola, it was built between 1559 and 1575 and takes its star-shape from the foundations of a large pentagonal fortress designed by Antonio da Sangallo the Younger half a century earlier. On the main floor, reached by an elaborately stuccoed spiral staircase, the rooms were frescoed, largely by the Zuccari brothers in 1560, with scenes depicting heroic episodes from the life of Hercules and the Farnese family.

ENVIRONS: Created, according to legend, by the god Hercules ramming his club into the ground, **Lago di Vico**, 4 km (3 miles) west of Caprarola, in fact occupies the remnants of a volcanic crater. An idyllic enclave, the lake is encircled by the wooded slopes of the Cimini Hills (much of which is a nature reserve). A scenic road runs around the lake, and the best place for swimming is on the southeast shore.

🏛 **Palazzo Farnese**
Caprarola. 🎫 0761 64 60 52. ◯ Tue–Sun. ◉ 1 Jan, 1 May, 25 Dec. 📷

Etruscan tumulus tombs from the necropolis at Cerveteri

Tarquinia ❻

Viterbo. 🏠 15,000. FS 🚌 ℹ️ Piazza Cavour (0766 85 63 84). 🚩 Wed.

ANCIENT TARQUINIA (Tarxuna) was one of Etruria's most important centres. It occupied a strategic position to the north-east of the present town, on a ridge dominating the coastal plain, until the 4th century BC when it fell to Rome.

Tarquinia itself is worth a wander for its crumbling medieval churches and spacious main square, though the main reason to visit is the **Museo Archeologico e Necropoli**, which has one of Italy's better collections of Etruscan finds. Relaxed, reclining statues of the deceased adorn the sarcophagi on the ground floor, but the star attraction, on the mezzanine, is a group of terracotta winged horses dating from the 4th century BC.

On a hilltop 2 km (1 mile) southeast of town are the frescoed tombs of the **necropolis** dug into the soft volcanic tufa. There are almost 6,000 tombs but only about 15 can be visited at a time. The frescoes that decorate them, designed to remind the dead of life, range from frenetic dancing figures in the Tomba delle Leonesse to the diners reclining in the Tomba dei Leopardi.

🏛️ **Museo Archeologico e Necropoli**
Piazza Cavour. 📞 0766 85 60 36. 🕐 Tue–Sun. 🔴 1 Jan, 1 May, 25 Dec. 📷 ♿

Cerveteri ❼

Roma. 🏠 30,000. FS 🚌 ℹ️ Piazza Risorgimento (06 99 55 19 71). 🚩 Fri.

IN THE 6TH century BC Cerveteri (ancient Kysry) was one of the most populated and culturally rich towns of the Mediterranean, trading with Greece and controlling a large area along the coast. The **necropolis**, a city of the dead 2 km (1 mile) outside town, is a network of streets lined with tombs dating from the 7th to the 1st century BC. Some of the larger tumulus tombs, like the Tomba degli Scudi e delle Sedie, are arranged like houses with rooms, doors and corridors. The Tomba dei Rilievi is decorated with plaster reliefs of tools, pets and mythological figures. Although the best finds from the necropolis are in museums such as the Vatican Museums, Villa Giulia and the British Museum in London, some can be seen in the small **Museo Nazionale Cerite** in the centre of town.

ENVIRONS: There are more traces of the Etruscans to be seen at **Norchia**, where the tombs are carved out of a rock face, and **Sutri**, whose amphitheatre is one of the few relics of the living Etruscans.

🗿 **Necropolis**
Via delle Necropoli. 📞 06 994 00 01. 🕐 Tue–Sun. 🔴 public hols. 📷
🏛️ **Museo Nazionale Cerite**
Piazza Santa Maria. 📞 06 994 13 54. 🕐 Tue–Sun. 🔴 public hols. 📷

Lake Bracciano ❽

Roma. FS 🚌 Bracciano. ℹ️ P. del Comune, Bracciano (06 99 84 00 69).

Medieval Anguillara on Lake Bracciano

BRACCIANO is a large lake famous for its fish, and popular for water sports and lakeside lunches.

Medieval **Anguillara**, to the south, is the prettiest of the lakeside towns with romantic views over the water. The main town, **Bracciano**, on the east shore, is dominated by the Orsini-Odescalchi fortress, a pentagonal 15th-century structure with frescoes by Antoniazzo Romano and other Tuscan and Umbrian artists.

🏰 **Castello Orsini-Odescalchi**
Piazza Mazzini 14. 📞 06 99 80 43 48. 🕐 Tue–Sun. 🔴 1 Jan, 25 Dec. 📷

Dancers from the 4th-century BC frescoed Tomba del Triclinio in the Museo Archeologico, Tarquinia

Ostia Antica ❾

Viale dei Romagnoli 717, Ostia.
C 06 565 15 00. **M** Piramide, then
FS from Porta San Paolo to Ostia
Antica. **Excavations & Museum**
○ 9am–5pm Tue–Sun (4pm in
winter) ● 1 Jan, 1 May, 25 Dec. 🎫

**The building
material** for the
houses was
brick, left plain or
covered in mural
decoration.

**The internal
courtyard** has
remained a feature
of Italian housing.

Ruins of shops and offices along
the Decumanus Maximus

Balcony

FOR OVER 600 years Ostia
was Rome's main port
and a busy trading
centre, until the 5th
century AD when a dis-
astrous combination of
malaria and commercial
competition brought
the town into decline.
Silt preserved
its buildings and it
now lies 5 km
(3 miles) inland.
   The ruins of Ostia give
a vivid idea of life in
Classical times. The main
thoroughfare, the
Decumanus Maximus, runs
through the Forum, which
houses Ostia's largest temple,
the **Capitol**, and past the
restored **theatre**, still used for
open air concerts in summer.
The road is lined with baths,
shops and multi-storey
buildings. There is even a
Thermopolium, or bar, with
a marble counter and paintings
advertising food and drink.

Apartments
or single rooms
were rented out.

OSTIA APARTMENTS
Much of Ostia's population
lived in blocks of flats, such
as this building, based on the
Casa di Diana (2nd century AD).

Shops
occupied the
ground floor
of the block.

The bar served
wine and snacks.

Frascati and the Castelli Romani ❿

Roma. **FS** **🚌** Frascati. **🛈** Piazza
Marconi 1, Frascati (06 942 03 31)
Villa Aldobrandini ○ Mon–Fri with
permission from tourist office only.

THE ALBAN HILLS have long
been a country retreat for
Romans. In Classical times they
were scattered with villas; in
the Middle Ages with fortified
castles (hence the name); and
in the 16th and 17th centuries
with luxurious country residences and their spectacular
parks and gardens. During
World War II German defences
were based in the Alban hills
and many Castelli towns were
damaged by Allied bombs.
Although partly protected by
a nature reserve, the hilltop
towns are popular day-trip
destinations as well as being
famous for their white wine.

Frascati's central piazza is a
belvedere overlooked by the
Villa Aldobrandini, a majestic
17th-century building set in
a splendid park of secret
grottoes, fountains and statues.
   The fortified Abbazia di San
Nilo in **Grottaferrata**, 3 km
(2 miles) south, was founded
in 1004 and contains some
lovely 17th-century frescoes by
Domenichino in the chapel.

Overlooking Lake Albano,
6 km (4 miles) south, **Castel
Gandolfo** is the site of the
pope's summer palace. When
in residence the pope addresses
the crowd from the balcony.
   Gathered around a sturdy
9th-century castle, and famed
for its strawberries, **Nemi**, 10
km (6 miles) southeast, looks
down onto the glassy dark
blue waters of Lake Nemi.

The forested shores around the small, volcanic Lake Nemi

Tivoli, a favourite place to escape the heat of the Roman summer

Tivoli ⑪

Roma. 🏛 57,000. FS 🚌 🛈 *Largo Garibaldi (0774 33 45 22).* 🚍 *Wed.*

HILL-TOWN TIVOLI, now probably the most popular excursion from Rome, was once a favoured resort of the ancient Romans, attracted by its fresh water and sulphur springs, and beautiful countryside. The temples that once covered Tivoli's hilltop are still visible in places. Some are half buried in medieval buildings, others, such as the Temples of Sibyl and Vesta, inside the gardens of the Sibilla restaurant (on Via Sibilla), are relatively intact.

Splendours from around the world reproduced in Hadrian's Villa

The town's most famous sight is the **Villa d'Este**, a sumptuous country residence created in the 16th century by Pirro Ligorio for Cardinal Ippolito d'Este from the shell of a Benedictine monastery. It is known primarily for its gardens, steeply raked on terraces, and studded with spectacular, if somewhat faded and moss-hung, fountains. Although suffering from reduced water-pressure and polluted water due to centuries of neglect, the gardens give a vivid impression of the frivolous luxury enjoyed by the papal families. Highlights include the Viale delle Cento Fontane and the Fontana dell'Organo Idraulico, which, thanks to a hydraulic system, once played music. At the other end of town, the **Villa Gregoriana**, now a hotel, is set in a lush wooded valley where paths wind down into a deep ravine.

ENVIRONS: About 5 km (3 miles) west of Tivoli are the ruins of **Hadrian's Villa**. Easily seen in conjunction with a visit to the town, this is one of the largest and most spectacular villas ever built in the Roman Empire (it once covered an area greater than the centre of Imperial Rome).

Hadrian was an inveterate traveller and his aim in creating the villa was to reproduce some of the wonders he had seen around the world. The Stoa Poikile, for example, a walkway around a rectangular pool and garden, recalls the painted colonnade of the Stoic philosophers in Athens, while the Canopus evokes the grand sanctuary of Serapis in

Alexandria. There are also ruins of two bath complexes, a Latin and a Greek library, a Greek theatre, and a private study on a little island known as the Teatro Marittimo.

Today the rambling ruins, full of shady nooks and hidden corners, make a lovely place to relax, picnic or explore.

🏛 **Villa d'Este**
Piazza Trento 1. 【 *0774 31 20 70.* ◯ *Tue–Sun.* ● *1 Jan, 1 May, 25 Dec.* 🎫
🏛 **Villa Gregoriana**
Piazza Massimo. ◯ *daily.* 🎫
⛪ **Hadrian's Villa**
Villa Adriana. 【 *0774 53 02 03.* ◯ *daily.* ● *1 Jan, 1 May, 25 Dec.* 🎫

Palestrina ⑫

Roma. 🏛 18,000. 🚌 🛈 *Palazzo Barberini, Via Barberini (06 957 31 76).* 🚍 *15th of the month.*

Mosaic fragment of Nile in flood, Archaeological Museum, Palestrina

MEDIEVAL PALESTRINA grew up over the terraces of a huge temple dedicated to the goddess Fortuna Primigenia, the mother of all gods. The temple, founded in the 8th century BC and rebuilt in the 2nd century BC by Sulla, housed one of the most important oracles of ancient times. The terraces of the sanctuary, littered with fragments of columns and porticoes, lead up to the curved **Palazzo Barberini**. Built over the site of a circular temple, it now houses the **Museo Nazionale Archeologico**, best known for a 1st-century BC mosaic portraying the Nile in flood.

🏛 **Museo Nazionale Archeologico**
Via Barberini. 【 *06 953 81 00.* ◯ *daily.* ● *1 Jan, 1 May, 25 Dec.* 🎫

Subiaco ⑬

Roma. 🏛 9,000. 🚌 ℹ️ Via
Cadorna 59 (0774 82 20 13).
🗓 Sat.

I N THE 6th century, weary of
the decadence of Rome,
St Benedict left the city to
become a hermit in a cave
above Subiaco. Others joined
him, and eventually there were
12 monasteries in the area.

Only two now survive:
Santa Scolastica, dedicated
to Benedict's sister, is organized around three cloisters, one
Renaissance, one early Gothic
and the third Cosmatesque.
Higher up, the 12th-century
San Benedetto is a more
rewarding destination.
Overhanging a deep gorge, it
comprises two churches built
on top of each other. The
upper is decorated with 14th-
century Sienese frescoes; the
lower, built over several levels,
incorporates the original cave
where Benedict spent three
years after fleeing Rome.

🏛 **Santa Scolastica**
3 km (2 miles) E of Subiaco.
📞 0774 855 25. 🕐 daily. 🚫 ♿
🏛 **San Benedetto**
3 km (2 miles) E of Subiaco.
📞 0774 850 39. 🕐 daily. 🚫 ♿

Montecassino ⑭

Cassino. 📞 0776 31 15 29.
FS Cassino then bus. 🕐 8:30am–
noon, 3:30–6pm daily (Nov–Feb 5pm).

T HE ABBEY of Montecassino,
mother church of the
Benedictine order and a centre
of medieval art, was founded
in 529 by St Benedict over the
ruins of an ancient acropolis.
By the 8th century it was an
important centre of learning,
and by the 11th century had
become one of the richest
monasteries in Europe.

In 1944 it was a German
stronghold and a target for
Allied bombs. Most of the
complex was devastated,
including the lavish Baroque
church, but the walls remained
intact and the abbey withstood
for three months before falling
to the Allies. The adjoining war
cemeteries commemorate the
30,000 soldiers killed.

**Rose
window,
Fossanova**

THE MONASTERIES OF LAZIO

St Benedict founded the Abbey of Montecassino
around 529 and there wrote his famous Rule.
Based on the principles of prayer, study and
manual labour, this became the fundamental
monastic code of western Europe. The Cistercian
Order, an offshoot of the Benedictines, came to
Italy from Burgundy in the 12th century. The
Cistercians were followers of St Bernard, whose creed was
based on austerity and self-sufficiency, qualities which were
reflected in the simple, early
Gothic architecture of their
monasteries. Their first abbey
was at Fossanova. Other
Cistercian abbeys in Lazio include Valvisciolo (northeast of
Sermoneta) and San Martino
in Cimino (near Lago di Vico).

***The Abbey of Montecassino**,
destroyed during World War II,
was rebuilt as a replica of its
17th-century predecessor.*

***The Abbey of San Benedetto**,
Subiaco, was founded in the
11th century over St Benedict's
cave. A staircase carved in the
rock leads to the grotto where
he preached to shepherds.*

***The Abbey of Casamari**,
14 km (8 miles) east of Frosinone,
was founded by Benedictine
monks in 1035 and handed
over to the Cistercians who
rebuilt it in 1203.*

The abandoned medieval village of Ninfa, now a beautiful garden

Anagni ⑮

Frosinone. 🏛 20,000. FS 🚌
ℹ Piazza Innocenzo III (0775 72 78
52). 🗓 Wed.

ACCORDING TO LEGEND Saturn
founded five towns in
southeast Lazio, including
Anagni, Alatri and Arpino. This
area is now known as La
Ciociaria, from *ciocie*, the
bark clogs worn in the area
until about 30 years ago.

Before the Romans con-
quered this part of Lazio it was
inhabited by several different
tribes: the Volsci, the Sanniti,
and the Hernici. Little is known
of them, apart from the extraordinary walls with which they
protected their settlements. In
later years these were believed
to have been built by the
Cyclops, a mythical giant,
which gave them their present
name of Cyclopean walls.

Anagni was the most sacred
Hernician centre until its
destruction by the Romans in
306 BC. In the Middle Ages it
was the birthplace and family
seat of several popes, an era
from which many buildings
survive, most notably Boniface
VIII's 13th-century mullion-
windowed palace.
The beautiful Romanesque
Duomo, Santa Maria, built
over the ancient Hernician
acropolis, boasts a fine Cosmati
mosaic floor from the 13th

century as well as 14th-century
Sienese frescoes. The crypt of
San Magno is frescoed with
one of the most complete
surviving cycles of the 12th
and 13th centuries.

ENVIRONS: Alatri, perched on
an olive-covered slope 28 km
(17 miles) east of Anagni, was
an important Hernician town.
It preserves an impressive
double set of Cyclopean walls,
2 km (1 mile) long and 3 m
(10 ft) high, from its 7th-
century BC acropolis. In the
medieval town below the walls
is the Romanesque church of
Santa Maria Maggiore, greatly
restored in the 13th century.
Arpino, 40 km (25 miles)
east of Alatri, is a bustling
town with a medieval core,
and was the birthplace of the

An unusual pointed arch in the
Cyclopean walls at Arpino

Roman orator, Cicero. About
3 km (2 miles) above Arpino,
at the site of the ancient town
of Civitavecchia, is a tremendous stretch of Cyclopean
walls which includes a rare
gateway with a pointed arch.

Sermoneta and Ninfa ⑯

Latina. FS Latina Scalo. 🚌 from
Latina. ℹ Via Duca del Mare 19,
Latina (0773 69 54 04).
Ninfa ◯ Apr–Oct: 1st Sat & Sun of
the month. 🏛

SERMONETA IS A LOVELY hilltop
town overlooking the
Pontine Plains, with narrow
cobbled streets winding
around medieval houses,
palaces and churches. The
Duomo has a fine 15th-
century panel by Benozzo
Gozzoli showing the Virgin
cradling Sermoneta in her
hands. At the top of the town
rises the moated fairy-tale
Castello Caetani, frescoed
with mythological scenes by a
pupil of Pinturicchio.
In the valley below lies the
romantic abandoned medieval
village of **Ninfa**, restored and
converted into lush botanical
gardens by the Caetani family
in 1921. Streams and waterfalls
punctuate the picturesque
garden laid out among the
crumbling buildings.

Terracina ⑰

Latina. 🚶 40,000. 🚉 🚌 ℹ️ Via
Leopardi (0773 72 77 59). 🏛️ Thu.

ROMAN TERRACINA was an
important commercial
centre on the Via Appia (the
Appian Way). Today it is a
popular seaside resort, with a
fascinating collage of medieval
buildings and Roman ruins in
its historic centre, perched on
the slopes of the Ausonian
Hills. The more modern part
of town by the sea is full of
restaurants, bars and hotels.

Bombing during World War
II uncovered many of the
town's ancient structures,
notably a stretch of the Appian
Way and the original paving
of the Roman Forum in Piazza
del Municipio. The
11th-century
Duomo was built
in the shell of a
Roman temple, and
is still entered by
the temple's steps.
The medieval
portico is adorned
with a lovely 12th-
century mosaic
and the interior
preserves the 13th-
century mosaic
pavement. Next
door, the modern town hall
houses the **Museo Archeologico**, devoted to local
Greek and Roman finds.

**Duomo at Terracina with
original Roman steps**

Three kilometres (2 miles)
above the town are the podium and foundations that
once supported the Temple
of Jove Anxur, dating back to
the 1st century BC. This huge
arcaded platform is illuminated
at night and offers vertiginous
views of Terracina and its bay.

🏛️ **Museo Archeologico**
Piazza Municipio. 📞 0773 70 22 20.
⬜ daily. ⬛ public hols. 📷

Sperlonga ⑱

Latina. 🚶 4,000. 🚌 ℹ️ Corso San
Leone (0771 55 70 00). 🏛️ Sat.

SPERLONGA is a popular
seaside resort surrounded
by sandy beaches. The old
town sits on a rocky promontory, a picturesque labyrinth
of whitewashed buildings,
narrow alleyways, piazzettas
and balconies offering an
occasional glimpse of the sea
below. It is now full of bars,
restaurants and boutiques.
The modern part of town lies
down on the seafront.

The area around Sperlonga
was a favourite retreat
for the ancient
Romans during
the hot summer
months. They
built villas along
the coast, and
converted the
natural caves in
the nearby cliffs
into places to dine and relax.

In 1957 archaeologists
excavating the huge complex
of Tiberius's luxury villa, 1 km
(half a mile) on the southern
outskirts of town, found
some marvellous 2nd-century
BC Hellenistic sculptures in a
large cave open to the sea.
These sculptures, representing

12th-century bell tower at Gaeta

incidents from Homer's
Odyssey, are thought to be by
the same artists from Rhodes
(where the Emperor Tiberius
once lived) who were responsible for the Laocoön (see
p407). They are displayed,
along with other local finds,
in the **Museo Archeologico
Nazionale** which is part of
the archaeological zone.

🏛️ **Zona Archeologica**
Via Flacca. 📞 0771 540 28. ⬜ daily.
⬛ 1 Jan, 1 May, 25 Dec. 📷

Gaeta ⑲

Latina. 🚶 22,000. 🚌 ℹ️ Corso
Cavour 16 (0771 46 11 65). 🏛️ Wed.

ACCORDING TO VIRGIL, Gaeta
was named after Aeneas's
wet nurse Caieta who was
allegedly buried here. The
town sits on the southern
headland of the gulf of Gaeta,
wedged under Monte Orlando.
The historic centre is dominated by a mighty Aragonese
castle and the pinnacles of
mock-Gothic San Francesco.
To the north, the modern
quarter links Gaeta to the bay
of Serapo, a popular and
picturesque beach resort.

Gaeta's most beautiful
feature is the **Duomo**'s elegant
late Romanesque bell tower,
its lofty summit topped by a
roof of coloured ceramic tiles.
On the seafront lies the tiny
10th-century church of **San
Giovanni a Mare**, with faded
frescoes, a hemispherical
dome and a sloping floor to let
the sea flow out after flooding.

Stretches of sandy beach along the coast between Gaeta and Terracina

SOUTHERN
ITALY

Southern Italy at a Glance

V ISITORS TO SOUTHERN ITALY find a rich array of archaeological remains. Although those of the Romans at Pompeii are high on everyone's list, Greek ruins litter Sicily and the southern coast and there are mysterious ancient structures, called *nuraghi*, in Sardinia. Campania, Puglia and Sicily are admired for their architecture, while across the south there are magnificent landscapes, abundant wildlife and endless opportunities for outdoor activities. The cuisine alone, with its eclectic heritage and diversity of tastes, provides the excuse to dawdle on the coast or in the mountain villages.

SARDINIA
(See pp528–35)

Su Nuraxi

***The Parco Nazionale d'Abruzzo**, a vast unspoilt wilderness, is home to wolves, bears and many species of birds (see pp490–91).*

***Su Nuraxi at Barumini**, built around 1500 BC, is the most celebrated of Sardinia's mysterious stone nuraghe sites (see p533).*

***The cloister decoration** at Monreale cathedral is a legacy of Sicily's Arabic past, with elaborate columns adorned with fine mosaics and splendid sculpted capitals (see pp514–5).*

Monreale cathedral

***Sicily's Valley of the Temples at Agrigento** contains some of the best ruins outside Greece. Mostly Doric in construction and style, they date from the 5th and 6th centuries BC (see p520).*

Temple of

0 kilometres   100

0 miles   50

◁ **Vines and citrus trees growing along Campania's scenic Costiera Amalfitana (Amalfi Coast)**

The Museo Archeologico Nazionale in Naples is one of Italy's most important museums. It houses the treasures of Pompeii, including sculptures, vases and everyday artifacts which provide a detailed glimpse of Roman life (see pp474–5).

ABRUZZO, MOLISE AND PUGLIA
(See pp484–497)

Molise

NAPLES
D CAMPANIA
pp466–483)

Archeologico Nazionale

Puglia

Basilicata

Pompeii

Santa Croce

BASILICATA AND CALABRIA
(See pp498–505)

Pompeii's Roman ruins include streets, houses and an amphitheatre (see pp478–9).

Calabria

The church of Santa Croce in Lecce is an excellent example of the exuberant Lecce Baroque style, from its elaborate rose window to the intricately carved capitals (see pp496–7).

Mount Etna

SICILY
(See pp506–527)

Mount Etna, one of the world's largest volcanoes, is still active, with lava erupting from fissures that dot its flanks. The nearby city of Catania has suffered repeatedly from volcanic damage (see p523).

Regional Food: Southern Italy

SOUTHERN ITALIAN FOOD is as varied as the land-scape, each region having its own specialities. While pasta, for example, is eaten throughout Italy, nothing matches the handmade *orecchiette* of Puglia. Think of Naples, and wafer-thin pizza springs to mind. Sicilian food is both rustic and voluptuous. Across the south, the dishes are enlivened with seafood, fruity green olive oil and dry white wine and, together with fresh green vegetables and huge, bursting tomatoes, account for one of the most enviably healthy diets in Europe.

Dried chillies

Some of Italy's best olives *come from Puglia. Green and black olives may be served in piquant oil and garlic.*

Grilled swordfish

Squid — **Anchovies**

A dish of simply cooked seafood *(frutti di mare) may also contain mussels (cozze), oysters (ostriche), prawns (gamberetti) or octopus (polpi) – moistened with olive oil and a dash of lemon juice to enhance the flavours.*

Prawns

Grilled tuna

Lobster   **Mussels**

Roasted red pepper

Char-grilled courgette

Sliced vegetables *brushed with olive oil and lightly grilled are often served as an antipasto (appetizer).*

Pizza Napoletana *is a simple thin pizza topped with tomato, garlic, basil and anchovies.*

Marinated artichoke hearts

Char-grilled aubergine

Maccheroncini con le sarde*, a Sicilian classic, contains sardines, fennel, raisins, pine nuts, breadcrumbs and saffron.*

Pesce spada *(swordfish steak), grilled or pan-fried with lemon and oregano, is a favourite in Campania, Puglia and Sicily.*

Agnello arrosto *(juicy roast lamb) is a Sardinian speciality, roasted on a spit or in casseroles with rosemary and thyme.*

Sicilian cassata *is ice cream made with ricotta cheese, candied fruit, pistachios, sugar and chocolate in a sponge cake.*

Nougat *is a sweet Sardinian speciality that can be made simply with nuts, or flavoured with chocolate.*

Cannoli

Sicilian almond biscuits

Many biscuits and cakes *are made in honour of a religious festival or saint's day. They might be deep-fried in oil, soaked in honey, encrusted with almonds or stuffed with ricotta, like the tube-shaped* cannoli *biscuits much favoured in Sicily.*

SOUTHERN CHEESES

Cheese exists in almost infinite varieties. Delicate mozzarella di bufala, made with buffalo milk, is delicious eaten on its own. Scamorza, a similar spun cheese, is exceptional – especially from Basilicata. It is also served smoked. Hard-textured Provolone can be mild or piquant, while ricotta, from sheep's milk, is creamy.

Provolone

Scamorza

Ricotta

Mozzarella

Smoked Scamorza

WINE
The south's sunny hillsides have produced wine since the Bronze Age. Puglia produces more wine than any other region in Italy, and Sicily boasts some of the south's finest wines. Good producers include Regaleali, Rapitalà, Corvo and Donnafugata. Marsala, a classic dessert wine also from Sicily *(see p518)*, was devised in the 18th century and made famous by Admiral Nelson. Pellegrino is an excellent producer.

Sicilian hite wine

Sweet Marsala

OLIVE OIL
Some of the finest olive oils *(olio di oliva)* in Italy come from the south. The words *extra vergine* (extra virgin) refer to the pure, unblended oil from the first pressings of the olives. A variation is chilli oil *(olio santo)*, soaked with red chilli peppers, resulting in a rich, spicy oil with a red hue.

Chilli oil (Olio santo)

Olive oil (Olio di oliva)

Understanding the Architecture of Southern Italy

THE ROMANESQUE STYLE of southern Italy owes much to the Normans, who in the 11th century brought from France both form and style in architecture and sculpture. In the southeast, the style has hefty Byzantine overtones; in Sicily it is characterized by strong traditional Islamic motifs and a love of rich colour, pattern and ornamentation. These elements surface later in Sicily's Baroque style and are allied to a dynamism that originates in the Baroque of

Baroque carving on Bagheria's Villa Palagonia

Rome – though in Sicily it is more vivacious. Neapolitan Baroque is more sophisticated and displays a greater interest in the creative use of space.

BYZANTINE AND ROMANESQUE FEATURES

Cefalù, begun in 1131 by Roger II, is one of Sicily's great Norman cathedrals (see p519). Its west front exhibits many northern Romanesque features, such as the massive towers.

Christ Pantocrator, a Byzantine apse mosaic (c.1132), adorns the Cappella Palatina (see p510).

The east end of the Norman cathedral of Monreale, founded in 1172 by William II, is built of multicoloured materials with interlacing arches (see pp514–15).

BAROQUE FEATURES

Caserta's Palazzo Reale, a sumptuous royal palace begun by Charles III in 1752, is characterized by its monumental scale (see p480). The richly decorated interior is prefaced by several huge entrances and impressive staircases offering views. The enormous building was designed by Luigi Vanvitelli.

Giacomo Serpotta's stucco reliefs (c.1690) in Palermo's Oratorio di Santa Zita illustrate Sicilians' love of exuberant decoration (see p513).

WHERE TO SEE THE ARCHITECTURE

The best places to see Romanesque architecture are Puglia and the cathedral cities of northwestern Sicily. Puglia's best churches are those at Trani *(see p493)* and nearby Canosa, Molfetta and Bitonto; Ruvo di Puglia *(p494)*, San Leonardo di Siponto on the Gargano Peninsula and Martina Franca, near Alberobello. The Baroque style of the south is epitomized by the villas, palaces

The Duomo portal in Ruvo di Puglia

and churches of Naples and Sicily, and by the deeply encrusted ornamentation found on church façades in Lecce *(pp496–7)*, in Puglia. In Sicily, the Baroque of Palermo *(pp510–13)*, Bagheria *(p516)*, Noto, Modica and Ragusa *(p527)* and Siracusa *(pp526–7)* is well known. Less so are churches at Piazza Armerina *(p521)*, Trapani *(p516)*, Palazzolo Acreide, close to Siracusa, and Acireale, near Catania.

Mullioned window
Tall gabled section
Blind arcading
Rich carving

Bari's Basilica di San Nicola *(founded 1087) was the model for subsequent churches in Puglia* (see p494). *Based on Norman architecture, its façade is flanked by towers and divided vertically into three, reflecting the tripartite nature of its plan.*

Rose window
Half columns
Blind arcading

The façade of Troia cathedral *(1093–1125) owes its design to Pisan architecture and its rich ornamentation to Byzantine and Arab models (see pp492–3).*

Carved scroll
Protruding columns
Central bell tower
Curved surface
Three-tiered structure
Stone-carved decoration

The façade *of Siracusa's Duomo, begun in 1728 by Andrea Palma, is animated by broken or curved elements* (see pp526–7).

San Giorgio in Ragusa *(1744) has a façade by Gagliardi with layers of ornamentation culminating in the tower* (see p527).

Lecce's Chiesa del Rosario *(begun 1691) was built by Lo Zingarello of soft local sandstone in the Lecce Baroque style of profuse carving* (see pp496–7).

The Ancient Greeks in Southern Italy

SOME OF THE BEST ruins of the ancient Greek world are in Southern Italy. Syracuse, Selinunte, Segesta and Gela are among the better known Sicilian sites while those on the mainland include Croton, Locri and Paestum. Magna Graecia is the collective name given to these scattered colonies of ancient Greece, the earliest of which were founded in the Naples area in the 11th century BC. Many great figures of the age – including Pythagoras, Archimedes and Aeschylus – lived in these far-flung settlements, and it was here that the ancient winemaker's art flourished. Artifacts from this age are exhibited in the excellent archaeological museums of Naples, Syracuse and Taranto.

KYME
Cuma

NEAPOLIS
Napoli

HERAKLE
Ercolano

POSEIDONIA
Paestum

Ancient Herakleia (Herculaneum) was named after its patron deity, the mighty Hercules. It was buried by the eruption of Mount Vesuvius in AD 79 (see p479).

Poseidonia (today's Paestum), was the city of Poseidon, God of the Sea. Its ruins, dating from the 6th century BC, include the hulks of two well preserved Doric temples (see pp482–3).

Mount Etna was believed to be the forge of Hephaistos (Vulcan) – God of Fire – or the Cyclops, the one-eyed giant (see p523).

Tyndaris was one of the last Greek cities founded on Sicily.

LIPARA
Lipar

TYNDA
Tind

PANORMOS
Palermo

SOLUS
Soluto

ERYX
Erice

EGESTA
Segesta

HIMERA
Himera

Eryx, founder of the town, was the son of Aphrodite and Poseidon.

SELINUS
Selinunte

Valley of the Temples

HENNA
Enna

KAT
Ca

MEGARA HYBI
Me

The legendary founder of Agrigento was Daedalus, who created wings for himself and his son, Icarus, so they could fly.

AKRAGAS
Agrigento

GELA
Gela

M
Archeolo
Regi
Paolo

Egesta (built 426–416 BC) was colonized by the Elymians who may have originated at Troy. Among the ruins of this town are a half-completed temple and a theatre (see p518). Ancient Greeks used theatres for plays and cultural entertainment rather than combat.

Gela was prosperous under the rule of Hippocrates in the 5th century BC.

0 kilometres   100

0 miles   50

Aeschylus, the dramatist, died in Gela in 456. Considered the father of Greek tragedy, his plays include Seven Against Thebes, Women of Aetna *and* Prometheus Bound.

Metapontion (Metapontum) was home to Pythagoras after his expulsion from Croton. Its ruins include Doric temples, the Tavole Palatine and a theatre *(see p503)*.

Taras was home to the philosopher and scientist, Archytas, and Aristoxenes, author of the earliest treatise on music.

Museo Archeologico Nazionale

GREECE AND ITS COLONIES

▢ 7th – 5th century BC

Museo Nazionale di Metaponto

Basento

METAPONTION • Metaponto

SIRIS • Nova Siri

SYBARIS • Sibari

THURII • Thuri

KROTON Crotone •

• TARAS Taranto

The Sybarites were famed for their luxurious lifestyle, hence the word "sybaritic". The wealth of Sybaris resulted from trade with the Etruscans.

Founded by Spartan Greeks (8th century BC), Taras was a rich and powerful city.

In about 540 BC, Croton became the chief school of Pythagoras's philosophy. Here the great thinker and mathematician remained for about 30 years until the government (which he supported) was overthrown, and he was expelled.

Locri Epizephiri was the first Greek city to have a written code of law.

ANKLE- ESSENE lessina

• LOKROI Locri Epizefiri

RHEGION Reggio di Calabria

ni Naxos

Plato the philosopher visited Syracuse and advised the ruler, Dionysius II, how to govern.

The Straits of Messina vexed Odysseus, the hero of Homer's Odyssey. Here at the meeting of two seas the currents created a "whirlpool" – Charybdis – which posed a threat to safe entry of Messina (see p522). Another threat were the Sirens, who lured voyagers onto rocks with their singing. Odysseus is seen here tied to a mast, so he can hear their song, but resist its call.

OUSAI a

*The **mathematician** and inventor, Archimedes, was born in Syracuse c.287 BC. His inventions included the famous Archimedean screw, and various weapons to stave off the Romans (see pp526–7).*

DEMETER AND PERSEPHONE

The complex web of Greek mythology was part of the daily life of the ancients. Enna was once the seat of the cult of Demeter, the earth goddess, and in 480 BC a temple was erected there in her honour. According to the legend, Persephone, the daughter of Demeter and Zeus, was abducted in the nearby fields by Hades who carried her off into the Underworld. Demeter then left Olympus and wandered the world searching in vain for her daughter. Discovering that Zeus had allowed the abduction to happen, Demeter put a blight on Sicily: it would remain barren until Persephone returned. Finally Hades allowed her return from the Underworld, but only for a few months of each year – from spring to autumn. Demeter, satisfied with the result, ensured that Sicily became the most fertile place on earth.

Sculpture of Persephone

NAPLES AND CAMPANIA

THE CAPITAL OF CAMPANIA, *Naples is one of the few European cities of the ancient world that has never been completely extinguished. Founded by Greeks, it was embellished and enlarged by the Romans and in subsequent centuries was the much-prized booty of foreign invaders and Imperialists – most prominently the Normans, Hohenstaufen, French and Spanish.*

Naples today is a chaotic yet spectacular, often crime-ridden metropolis that sprawls noisily and dirtily around the edge of the beautiful Bay of Naples. To one side is Mount Vesuvius; facing from the sea are the pretty islands of Capri, Ischia and Procida. Pompeii and Herculaneum, lying in the shadow of the volcano that destroyed them, contain the most revealing Roman ruins in Italy.

For centuries Naples has dominated the Italian south – the *Mezzogiorno*, or land of the midday sun. The problems of poverty, crime and unemployment are magnified here, but there is also an attractive, rude ebullience.

The ancient history of Campania is associated with the Etruscans and the Greeks, whose gigantic ruins can be seen at Paestum. Next came a time of great prosperity under Roman leadership; archaeological evidence of this still exists at Benevento and Santa Maria Capua Vetere.

The hinterland, with its rich, well-cultivated plains, is eclipsed by the Amalfi coastline with its breathtaking views and the dramatic seaboard of the Cilento. The mountainous interior, remote and unvisited, contains small towns that were settled by the Greeks, developed by the Romans and often abandoned in the wake of malaria and Saracen attacks.

A glimpse into the narrow streets of Naples' Quartieri Spagnoli (Spanish Quarter)

◁ The old fishing quarter on the island of Procida in the Bay of Naples

Exploring Naples and Campania

THE MAIN CENTRE FROM WHICH to explore Campania is the anarchic metropolis of Naples (Napoli). To the north, verdant plains sweep down to Santa Maria Capua Vetere. To the east is the lonely, mountainous province of Benevento. Tragic, earthquake-ravaged Avellino and its province lurk on a plain beyond Vesuvius. The northern coastline is not as enticing as the Roman ruins lining it at such places as Cuma. The Costiera Amalfitana, south of Naples, is stunning. Beyond the tip of the Sorrentine Peninsula and along the Cilento coast there is good swimming, as on Capri, Ischia and Procida in the Gulf of Naples.

SIGHTS AT A GLANCE

Benevento ⑤
Capri ⑨
Caserta ④
Costiera Amalfitana ⑥
Ischia and Procida ⑩
Naples (Napoli) pp470–77 ①
Paestum ⑧
Pompeii pp478–9 ②
Salerno ⑦
Santa Maria Capua Vetere ③

Typical Naples street viewed from Santa Maria Maggiore

KEY

▬▬ Motorway

▬▬ Major road

▬▬ Minor road

▬▬ Scenic route

≈ River

☙ Viewpoint

0 kilometres   25

0 miles   20

View of the Costiera Amalfitana from the hilltown of Ravello

GETTING AROUND

Northern Campania is easily accessible from Naples on the A1. The A16 heads east towards Puglia. Salerno and the Cilento can be reached on the A3. Branching off the A3, the N18 heads deep into the Cilento. To reach its coast, take the N267. The villages of the Costiera Amalfitana (Amalfi coast) lie along the scenic N145. The islands of Capri, Ischia and Procida are accessible by boat from Mergellina and the Molo Beverello in Naples, Sorrento, Positano, Amalfi and Salerno. Campania's main towns and important sights are linked by railway. The bus service is comprehensive, though infrequent in the interior of the Cilento.

SEE ALSO

- **Where to Stay** pp569–70

- **Where to Eat** pp602–4

Naples ❶

T HE COMPACT CENTRE of Naples,
filled with palaces, churches,
convents and monasteries,
revolves around just a few
streets. From the Piazza del
Plebiscito, Via Toledo (also
called Via Roma) proceeds
north towards Piazza Dante.
To the east, narrow Via del
Tribunale and Via San Biagio
dei Librai penetrate the historic and noisy heart of the

**San Gennaro,
protector of
Naples**

View of the Bay of Naples and Mount Vesuvius

city, the *Spaccanapoli* (split Naples). South of Palazzo Reale
is the Santa Lucia district. To the west is the port of Mergellina and overlooking the city is the Vomero district.

Exploring Northeast Naples

Many of the city's gems of
art and architecture
can be found here,
including the
Museo Archeo-
logico Nazionale
and its Roman
treasures from
Herculaneum and
Pompeii. The build-
ings provide a wide
range of architec-
tural styles from the
French-Gothic of the Duomo
to the Florentine-Renaissance
style of the Porta Capuana.

**Tomb of Ladislas, San
Giovanni a Carbonara**

including Marco and
Andrea da Firenze's
masterpiece, the
Tomb of Ladislas,
behind the church's
high altar. Built to
house the body of
King Ladislas of
Naples (1386–1414),
who enlarged the
church, the tomb is
a three-storey con-
fection of statues
and arches topped
by an equestrian figure.

🏠 San Giovanni a Carbonara
Via Carbonara 5. **📞** *081 29 58 73.*
⬜ *Mon–Sat.*
A great and rare success story
in the annals of Neapolitan
building restoration, San
Giovanni a Carbonara (built
1343) is now open again after
suffering damage in 1943,
long closure and pitiful neglect.
Within are glorious medieval
and Renaissance monuments,

**The beautiful Renaissance gate of
Porta Capuana**

🚇 Castel Capuano and Porta Capuana
Piazza Enrico de Nicola.
📞 *081 223 71 11.*
Begun by Norman King
William I and completed by
Frederick II, Castel Capuano
was a royal palace until 1540,
when it became the Court of
Justice. Today it
functions as a
courthouse.
Nearby, between
the Aragonese tow-
ers of the Capua
Gate and facing a
market, is a rare sculp-
ture in the Florentine-
Renaissance manner.
Created by Giuliano
da Maiano (and
finished in 1490
by Luca Fancelli)
as a defensive gate,
Porta Capuana
is perhaps Italy's
finest Renaissance
gateway.

```
0 metres      250
0 yards       250
```

MUSEO DI
CAPODIMONTE

CATACOMBE DI
SAN GENNARO

PIAZZA
CAVOUR

PIAZZA MUSEO
NAZIONALE

VIA ENRICO PESSINA

VIA SANTA MARIA DE CONSTANTINOPOLI

PIAZZA
DANTE

VIA CONTE DI RUVO

VIA SAPIENZA

VIA DEL SOLE

PIAZZA
LUIGIA
MIRAGLIA

PIAZZA SAN
DOMENICO
MAGGIORE

VIA TOLEDO
ROMA

VIA BENEDETTO CROCE

VIA DOMENICO CAPITELLI

PIAZZA DEL
GESU NUOVO

CALATA
TRINITÀ
MAGGIORE

VIA SANTA CHIARA

PIAZZA
BANCHI
NUOVI

POZZUOLI

PIAZZA
MONTEOLIVETO

VIA MONTEOLIVETO

VIA DONNALBINA

VIA SEDILE

PIAZZA
CARITA

VIA
CESARE BATTISTI

PIAZZA
MATTEOTTI

VIA G SANFELICE

MUSEO
NAZIONALE
DI SAN
MARTINO

VIA ARMANDO DIAZ

RUA CATALANA

VILLA
FLORIDIANA

VIA TOLEDO (ROMA)

ROBERTO BRACCO

VIA M CERVANTES

VIA MEDINA

VIA
SAN GIACOMO

VIA
PAOLO
EMILIO
IMBRIANI

PIAZZA
MUNICIPIO

VICO
D'AFFLITTO

VIA SANTA BRIGIDA

VIA SAN CARLO

VIA SANTA
MARIA

VIA
SERGENTE
MAGGIORE

PIAZZA
TRENTO E
TRIESTE

VIA AMMIRAGLIO

ACTON

VIA CHIAIA

MUSEO
PRINCIPE DI
ARAGONA
PIGNATELLI
CORTES

PIAZZA
DEL
PLEBISCITO

VIA CESARIO CONSOLE

CASTEL
DELL'OVO
MERGELLINA

Sights at a Glance

Interior of the Duomo

⛪ Duomo

Via Duomo 147. [081 44 90 97.
○ Sun–Fri.
Built between 1294 and
1323, the Duomo of San
Gennaro lies behind a mostly 19th-century façade. The
nave is lined with ancient
columns, and there is an
array of monuments to past
rulers, along with paintings by
Lanfranco and Domenichino.
   The Duomo houses the
relics of San Gennaro, patron
saint of Naples (martyred AD
305). The ornate Cappella
San Gennaro holds his head,
within a silver-gilt bust, and
phials of his congealed
blood, which miraculously
liquefies three times a year
(on the first Sunday in May,
19 Sep and 16 Dec). According to tradition, if the blood
should fail to liquefy, the city
will have bad luck. The
Cappella Carafa, a Renaissance
masterpiece built from 1497 to
1506, contains the saint's tomb.
   Accessible from the
Duomo's north aisle is the
Basilica di Santa Restituta,
founded in the 4th century
on the site of a former Temple
of Apollo, and rebuilt in the
14th century. It has ceiling
paintings by Luca Giordano
(1632–1705) and a 5th-
century baptistry.

Key

M	Metro
🚠	Funicular
ℹ️	Tourist information
✝	Church

Visitors' Checklist

🏠 1,300,000. ✈ Capodichino
4 km (2.5 miles) NW. 🚆 Centrale,
Piazza Garibaldi. 🚌 Piazza Garibaldi. ⛴ Stazione Marittima,
Molo Beverello & Mergellina. ℹ️
Piazza del Gesù Nuovo (081 551
27 01), Stazione Centrale. 🗓
daily. 🎉 San Gennaro: 19 Sep.

⛪ Monte della Misericordia

Via Tribunali 253. [081 44 69 44.
○ Mon–Sat am.
The 17th-century octagonal
church belonging to this
charitable foundation houses
Caravaggio's huge *Seven Acts
of Mercy* (1607). Also here, in
the art gallery, is an important
collection of paintings, including works by Luca Giordano
and Mattia Preti.

⛪ Cappella Sansevero

Via Francesco de Santis 19. [081
551 84 70. ○ daily (only am on
Sun). 🎫
This small 16th-century
chapel is the burial sepulchre
of the Princes of Sangro di
Sansevero. It possesses both
Christian and Masonic symbolism, giving the chapel
an unusual character.
   Remarkable 18th-century
sculpture fills the chapel.
Antonio Corradini's ironic
Modesty is a voluptuous
female, carefully veiled. *The
Resurrection of the Prince*, by
an unknown artist, is mirrored
by that of Christ, above the
altar. Giuseppe Sammartino's
The Dead Christ is an alabaster
figure beneath a marble veil,
and is a work of breathtaking
technical virtuosity.
   Eccentric Prince Raimondo,
an 18th-century alchemist, is
associated with the chapel.
He performed gruesome
experiments on human
bodies, for which he was
excommunicated. The results
of some of his experiments
can be seen in the crypt.

Sammartino's *The Dead Christ* (1753) in the Cappella Sansevero

Exploring Central Naples

THE PART OF SANTA LUCIA bordered by Via Duomo to the east, Via Tribunali to the north, Via Toledo (Roma) to the west and the water to the south, is the old heart of Naples. Especially rich in 14th- and 15th-century churches, the area offers visitors an abundance of sights.

Interior of San Gregorio Armeno

🏛 San Lorenzo Maggiore
Via Tribunali 316. ☎ 081 45 49 48.
Church ○ daily. 📷 ♿
Excavations ○ daily.
This mainly 14th-century Franciscan church (with an 18th-century façade) was built during the reign of Robert the Wise of Anjou. The storyteller Giovanni Boccaccio (1313–75) reputedly based the character Fiammetta on King Robert's daughter Maria, whom he saw here on Easter Eve, 1334. For

Naples, San Lorenzo Maggiore is a rare Gothic edifice. Its nave and the apse ambulatory have a magnificent period simplicity. The church houses some interesting medieval tombs, most notably the Gothic tomb of Catherine of Austria, who died in 1323, by a pupil of Giovanni Pisano. Excavations in the monastic cloister, where the lyric poet and scholar Petrarch (see p153) once stayed, have revealed the remains of a Roman basilica. Important Greek and medieval excavations are also under way.

🏛 San Gregorio Armeno
Via San G Armeno 1. ☎
081 552 01 86. ○ am daily.
Benedictine nuns still preside over this church. The convent attached to it earned a reputation for luxury since the nuns, traditionally from noble families, were accustomed to lavish living, which continued here.
The sumptuous Baroque interior of the church sports frescoes by the prolific Luca Giordano. The cloister is a quiet haven in a

neighbourhood noisy with vendors of Neapolitan crib figures (presepi), whose many workshops line the Via San Gregorio Armeno.

🏛 Museo Filangieri
Palazzo Cuomo, Via Duomo 288.
☎ 081 20 31 75. ○ Tue–Sun
(only am on Sun). ● 1 Jan. 📷
The 15th-century Renaissance Palazzo Cuomo houses the Museo Filangieri. Founded in 1881, the original museum collections put together by Prince Gaetano Filangieri were destroyed during World War II. The new collection contains interesting and varied objects, including porcelain, embroidery, manuscripts, Italian and Spanish arms, objects from local archaeological excavations and paintings by such artists as Luca Giordano, Ribera and Mattia Preti.

🏛 Sant'Angelo a Nilo
Piazzetta Nilo. ☎ 081 551 62 27.
○ daily.

Renaissance tomb of Cardinal Brancaccio, Sant'Angelo a Nilo

This 14th-century church contains a fine work of Renaissance sculpture: the Tomb of Cardinal Rinaldo Brancaccio. Designed by Michelozzo, it was sculpted in Pisa, and then shipped to Naples upon completion in 1428. Donatello reputedly carved the right-hand angel drawing back the curtain, the shallow relief Assumption, and the cardinal's head.

The simple Gothic interior of San Lorenzo Maggiore, looking down the nave to the apse

San Domenico Maggiore

Piazza San Domenico Maggiore.
081 45 91 88. ☐ daily.
This Gothic church (1289–1324) contains some of the finest Renaissance monuments and sculpture in Naples. The tomb slab of John of Durazzo (died 1335), by Tino da Camaino, is in the south transept. In the sacristy are the 18th-century *Apotheosis of Faith* ceiling frescoes by Solimena. The choir features a paschal candlestick (1585) supported by figures by da Camaino. The Cappellone del Crocifisso contains a medieval painting of the *Crucifixion*, which supposedly spoke to St Thomas Aquinas. The grand Brancaccio tomb by Jacopo della Pila (1492) is in the Chiesa Antica. Also of interest is the Cappella Saluzzo.

Detail of the embossed façade of Gesù Nuovo

Santa Chiara

Via Benedetto Croce. ☐ daily.
Church 081 552 62 09. 👜 ⚐
Cloister 081 797 12 56.
This 14th-century church was badly bombed in World War II, but a reconstruction uncovered the original Provençal-Gothic structure. The tombs of the Angevin monarchs are housed here. The tomb of Robert the Wise (died 1343) is by Giovanni and Pacio Bertini; that of Robert's son, Charles of Calabria (died 1328), is by Tino da Camaino, and the tomb of Charles' wife, Mary of Valois (died 1331) is by da Camaino and his followers. Adjacent is a convent with a peaceful Angevin cloister designed by Vaccaro (1742) and adorned with splendid majolica tiles.

Gesù Nuovo

Piazza del Gesù Nuovo 2.
081 551 86 13 ☐ daily.
The 16th-century Jesuit church was constructed by Valeriano (and later Fanzago and Fuga) from the Severini palace (15th century), of which only the curious embossed stone façade survives. The ebullient decoration of the interior (17th century) is fully in accordance with the needs of the Jesuits, who attracted the faithful through drama and direct appeal to the emotions. It is resplendent with coloured marble and paintings, including works by Ribera and Solimena. In 1688 an earthquake destroyed Lanfranco's dome – the present one is 18th-century.

Sant'Anna e San Bartolomeo dei Lombardi

Via Monteoliveto. 081 551 33 33. ☐ Tue–Sat.
Built in 1411 and restored after bomb damage from World War II, this church is a repository

Mazzoni's *Pietà* (1492) in Sant'Anna e San Bartolomeo dei Lombardi

of Renaissance art. Entering, past the tomb (1627) of Domenico Fontana (who completed the dome of St Peter's in Rome after Michelangelo's death), the richness of the interior soon becomes clear.

The Cappella Mastrogiudice contains an *Annunciation* panel by Florentine sculptor Benedetto da Maiano (1489) and the Cappella Piccolomini contains Antonio Rossellino's monument (c.1475) to Maria d'Aragona (completed by da Maiano). The Cappella del Santo Sepolcro houses a realistic *Pietà* by Guido Mazzoni (1492). Its eight terracotta figures are considered life-size portraits of the artist's contemporaries. The old Sacristy, frescoed by Vasari (1544), has inlaid stalls by Giovanni da Verona (1510).

Majolica tiles decorated with scenes of rural life in the cloisters of Santa Chiara

Naples: Museo Archeologico Nazionale

THIS MUSEUM IS ONE of the world's most important. The building which houses it, a former military barracks, then university seat, was remodelled in 1790 to receive the treasures of Pompeii and Herculaneum (see pp478–9). It also acquired the fabulous Farnese collections, containing Classical sculpture, which Charles of Bourbon inherited from his mother Elizabeth. The 1980 earthquake caused heavy damage to the collections while dust and chaos engulfed the rest. Restoration work has now revitalized the museum.

Sacrifice of Iphigenia
In this Pompeiian fresco, Agamemnon's daughter, Iphigenia, is prepared to be sacrificed to Artemis, who saves her by taking a deer instead.

First floor

Roman Helmet
This handsome bronze gladiator's helmet was probably ornamental. It came from Herculaneum.

Bust of "Seneca"
This 1st-century BC Roman portrait head is said to represent Seneca the Elder (c.55 BC – AD 39). The bust was found in the Villa dei Papiri in Herculaneum.

Mezzanine

Ground floor

The building, begun in 1586, was once a barracks.

Mosaic Detail of Alexander
From Pompeii's House of the Faun, an ancient mosaic depicts the Battle of Issus (333 BC) between Persian King Darius and Alexander the Great.

KEY TO FLOORPLAN

- [ ] Ground floor
- [ ] Mezzanine
- [ ] First floor
- [ ] Non-exhibition space

Blue Vase

Found in a tomb at Pompeii, this glass vase is a fine example of the cameo-maker's art. Grape-gathering cupids are cut on to a superimposed white glass paste over the vase, creating a striking, complex design.

Spring Fresco

From Stabiae comes the ancient fresco of "Spring", a delicate, dreamlike image of a robed girl gathering flowers. The colours remain soft and fresh.

Stairs down to Egyptian Collection

Farnese Bull

Excavated in the Baths of Caracalla (see p427) in Rome, this is the largest sculptural group (c.200 BC) to have survived from antiquity. It represents Amphion and Zethus tying Dirce to the horns of a bull.

GALLERY GUIDE

The ground floor contains the Farnese collections and sculpture from Herculaneum and Pompeii. The mezzanine houses mosaics and the popular Secret Cabinet of erotic art from Pompeii and Herculaneum. The first floor has domestic items, weapons, bronzes and murals from Herculaneum and Pompeii. On the lower ground floor is the Egyptian Collection. Be prepared for areas of the museum to be closed occasionally and without warning. Some (such as coins and erotic art) will be opened on request.

Entrance

Farnese Hercules

An ancient Roman copy of a Greek original by Lysippus, this huge statue is the finest in the Farnese collections. Napoleon is said to have regretted leaving it when he removed his booty from Italy in 1797.

Exploring Southeast Naples

THE AREA SOUTH of Via A Diaz is home to Naples'
castles and royal palace as well as the densely
packed Spanish Quarter. On the outskirts of the old
town are a number of museums in historic buildings.

♠ Castel Nuovo
Piazza Municipio. ❰ 081 795 20 03.
◯ Mon–Sat. ◯ some public hols. ⬤
Museo Civico ◯ Mon–Sat. ▨
Also known as the Maschio
Angioino, this Angevin fortress
was built for Charles of Anjou
in 1279–82. However, apart
from the squat towers and
the Cappella Palatina (with
Francesco Laurana's *Madonna*
of 1474 above the portal), most
of the structure is Aragonese.

The castle was once the
main royal residence. In the
Sala dei Baroni, Ferdinand I of
Aragon brutally suppressed the
ringleaders of the Baron's
Revolt of 1486. The Aragonese
were capable of acts of terror,
but they were also inspired
patrons of the arts.

The triumphal arch of the
castle's entrance (begun 1454)
is theirs. Commemorating
Alfonso of Aragon's entry to
Naples in 1443, this ingenious
application of the ancient
triumphal arch design was
worked on, at least in part, by
Laurana. The original bronze
doors by Guillaume le Moine
(1468) are kept in the Palazzo
Reale. Part of the building
houses the **Museo Civico**.

**The colourful and compact
Quartieri Spagnoli**

▦ Quartieri Spagnoli
Via Toledo (Roma) to Via Chiaia.
The Spanish Quarter – the
neighbourhood west of Via
Toledo, sloping up to San
Martino and Vomero – is one
of the city's most densely
populated areas. It was named
after the Spanish troops who
laid out its grid of narrow
streets in the 17th century. This
is where the archetypal
Neapolitan scene comes to

life, in which laundry hung
above the streets crowds out
the sun. This area is lively by
day, slightly sinister by night.

⏛ Museo Nazionale di San Martino
Largo di San Martino 5. ❰ 081 578
17 69. ◯ Tue–Sun am. ▨ ⬤
High above Santa Lucia, the
Baroque Certosa di San
Martino, founded in the 14th
century as a Carthusian
monastery, has magnificent
views of the Bay of Naples. It
houses an excellent museum
that features a variety of
presepi, Christmas cribs of
Neapolitan tradition. The
cloister was completed in
1623–9 by Cosimo Fanzago
(the creator of Neapolitan
Baroque) to the 16th-century
designs of Dosio. The church
and choir are other remarkable examples of his virtuosity.

Next to the Certosa is Castel
Sant'Elmo, which was built
from 1329–43 and rebuilt in
the 16th century, and offers
stunning views over the bay.

⏛ Museo Principe di Aragona Pignatelli Cortes
Riviera di Chiaia 200. ❰ 081 761 23
56. ◯ Tue–Sun. ⬤ 1 Jan. ▨
Lower down, in the Chiaia
neighbourhood, the Neo-
Classical Villa Pignatelli
houses this museum and its
interesting collection of
porcelain, period furniture,
paintings and sculpture.

The bold Castel Nuovo, with the triumphal arch entrance

🏛 Galleria Umberto I
Via Toledo. **081 797 23 03.**
☐ daily am. ● 1 Jan, Easter, 7–21
Aug, 25 Dec. 🏛 **Teatro San Carlo**
081 797 23 31.
Once a focus for fashionable
Neapolitans, the arcades of the
Galleria Umberto I were built
in 1887 and rebuilt after World
War II. Still handsome, though
tatty, they face Italy's largest
and oldest opera house: the
Teatro San Carlo. Built for
Charles of Bourbon in 1737,
and later rebuilt, its luxurious
auditorium once aroused
envy in the courts of Europe.

**Magnificent glass-roofed interior
of the Galleria Umberto I**

🏛 Palazzo Reale
Piazza Plebiscito. **Museo** **081 794
40 21.** ☐ Thu–Tue. ● 1 Jan, 1 May,
25 Dec. 🏛 **Biblioteca** **081 40
12 73.** ☐ Tue & Thu. ● public hols.
Begun by Domenico Fontana
for the Spanish Viceroys in
1600, and expanded and
embellished by subsequent
residents, Naples' royal palace
is a handsome edifice with
great halls filled with furniture,
tapestries, paintings and porcelain. The small private Teatro
di Corte (1768) was built by
Ferdinando Fuga. A large part
of the building contains the

Painting of *Lavinia Vecellio* (c.1540) by Titian in the Museo di Capodimonte

Biblioteca Nazionale. The
exterior of the palace has
been partly restored – note
the 19th-century statues representing the dynasties of
Naples. The huge Piazza del
Plebiscito facing it has been
cleaned up and cleared of
traffic. The great colonnades
sweep towards 19th-century
San Francesco di Paola,
modelled on Rome's Pantheon.

🏛 Villa Floridiana
Via Cimarosa 77. **081 578 84 18.**
☐ Tue–Sun am. **Park** ☐ daily.
● 1 Jan, 1 May, 25 Dec. 🏛 🏛
Set in handsome gardens,
this Neo-Classical villa houses
the **Museo Nazionale della
Ceramica Duca di Martina**
which is famous for its collection of ceramics, including
porcelain and majolica.

🏛 Museo di Capodimonte
Parco di Capodimonte. **081 749
91 11.** ☐ Tue–Sun. 🏛
Begun in 1738 by the Bourbon
king Charles III as a hunting
lodge, the **Palazzo Reale di
Capodimonte** houses this
museum and its magnificent
collections of Italian paintings.
Included are works by Titian,

Botticelli, Perugino, Raphael
and Sebastiano del Piombo,
much of it originating in the
Farnese family collections.
There is also a gallery of 19th-
century art, largely from
southern Italy.

🏛 Catacombs of San Gennaro
Via di Capodimonte 16. **081 741
10 71.** ☐ daily. 🏛 🏛
These catacombs – the original
burial place of San Gennaro –
are located near the church of
San Gennaro in Moenia. The
small church was founded in
the 8th century, and is adjoined
by a 17th-century workhouse.
Two tiers of catacombs dating
from the 2nd century penetrate
the tufa, and there are mosaics
and early Christian frescoes.
Further along the street, the
Catacombs of San Gaudioso
commemorate the 5th-century
saint who founded a monastery on the spot. Above is the
17th-century church of Santa
Maria della Sanità.

⚓ Castel dell'Ovo
Borgo Marinari. ☐ for exhibitions.
Away from the centre, Castel
dell'Ovo occupies a small
island facing, and joining, the
Santa Lucia district – once
the site of Naples' shellfish
market. The castle was begun
in 1154. Under the Normans
and Hohenstaufen it was a
royal residence, but today it
belongs to the military.
Beneath its ramparts, tiny
Porta Santa Lucia is filled with
seafood restaurants, and the
Via Partenope running past it
is a lovely promenade that
leads west to Mergellina.

The façade of the Palazzo Reale, Naples' royal palace

Pompeii ❷

AN EARTHQUAKE IN AD 62, which shook Pompeii and damaged many buildings, was merely a prelude to the tragic day in AD 79 when Mount Vesuvius erupted, burying the town in 6 m (20 ft) of pumice and ash. Although it was discovered in the 16th century, serious excavation began only in 1748, revealing a city petrified in time. In some buildings paintings and sculpture have survived, and graffiti is still visible on street walls.

↘ **House of the Mysteries**

★ House of the Vettii
This partly reconstructed patrician villa of the wealthy merchants, Aulus Vettius Conviva and Aulus Vettius Restitutus, contains frescoes (see pp44–5).

Forum Baths

★ House of the Faun
This famous villa of the wealthy patrician Casii is named after its bronze statuette. The mosaic Battle of Alexander, in the Museo Archeologico Nazionale in Naples, originated here.

0 metres 100
0 yards 100

Forum

In the bakery
of Modesto, carbonized loaves of bread were found.

Sacrarium of the Lares
Close to the Temple of Vespasian, this building housed the statues of Pompeii's guardian deities, the Lares Publici.

STAR SIGHTS
- **★ House of the Vettii**
- **★ House of the Faun**

Macellum
Pompeii's market place was fronted by a portico with two money-changers' kiosks.

Last Day of Pompeii
Used as a backdrop at La Scala for Giovanni Pacini's eponymous opera, this 19th-century painting by Sanquirico shows the people of Pompeii fleeing as Mount Vesuvius erupts violently.

LOCATOR MAP

WESTERN POMPEII

This detailed western area contains impressive Roman ruins, some remarkably intact. Parts of eastern Pompeii still await excavation.

Palestra

Teatro Grande

Via dell'Abbondanza
This was one of the original and most important roads through ancient Pompeii. Many inns lined the route.

VESUVIUS AND THE CAMPANIAN TOWNS

Nearly 2,000 years after the eruption of Mount Vesuvius, the Roman towns in its shadow are still being released from the petrification that engulfed them. Both Pompeii and Stabiae (Castellammare di Stabia), to the southeast of Naples and the volcano, were smothered by hot ash and pumice-stone blown there by the wind. The roofs of the buildings collapsed under the weight of the volcanic debris.

Pompeiian vase in Museo Nazionale Archeologico

To the west, Herculaneum (Ercolano) vanished under a sea of mud. A large number of its buildings have survived, their roofs intact, and many domestic items were preserved by the mud. In all, about 2,000 Pompeiians perished but few, if any, of the residents of Herculaneum died.

In AD 79 Pliny the Elder, the Roman soldier, writer and naturalist, was the commander of a fleet stationed off Misenum (present-day Miseno, west of Naples) and with his nephew Pliny the Younger observed the impending eruption from afar. Eager to see this natural catastrophe closer to hand, Pliny the Elder proceeded to Stabiae, but was overcome by fumes and died. Based on reports by survivors, Pliny the Younger related the first hours of the eruption and his uncle's death in detail in two letters to the Roman historian Tacitus.

Much of our knowledge of the daily lives of the ancient Romans derives from the excavations of Pompeii and Herculaneum. Most of the artifacts from them as well as Stabiae are now in Naples' Museo Archeologico Nazionale (*see pp474–5*), creating an outstanding and fascinating archaeological collection.

Although Mount Vesuvius has not erupted since 1944, it rumbles occasionally, causing minor earthquakes. Visitors can reach it by train or car. There is so much to see at Pompeii that a full day is necessary to explore it.

Casts of a dying mother and child in the museum in Naples

Santa Maria Capua Vetere ❸

Caserta. 🏛 34,000. 🚇 🚌
ℹ️ Via Albana (0823 79 95 89).
🗓 Thu & Sun.

THE BEST REASON to visit this town is the ruined Roman **amphitheatre** (1st century AD), once Italy's largest after the Colosseum. Better preserved is the series of tunnels beneath it. The town occupies the site of ancient Capua, an Etruscan city and then a flourishing centre during the Roman Empire. It was the scene of the revolt of the gladiators, led by Spartacus in 73 BC. Nearby is a **Mithraeum** (2nd–3rd century) with well-preserved frescoes. Finds from the sites can be seen in the **Museo Archeologico dell' Antica Capua** in Capua.

♟ Amphitheatre
Piazza Adriano. 📞 0823 79 88 64.
◯ Tue–Sun. 🎫 valid also for **Mithraeum** ◯ Tue–Sun.
🏛 Museo Archeologico dell' Antica Capua
Via Roma, Capua. 📞 0823 84 42 06.
◯ Tue–Sun. ● 1 Jan, 25 Dec. 🎫

Tunnels under the amphitheatre in Santa Maria Capua Vetere

Caserta ❹

🏛 66,000. 🚇 🚌 ℹ️ Piazza Dante 43 (0823 32 11 37). 🗓 Wed & Sat.

MAGNIFICENTLY OPULENT, the colossal **Palazzo Reale**, likened in scale to Versailles, dominates Caserta. Built for the extravagant Bourbon King Charles III, Italy's largest royal palace boasts over 1,000

A fountain in the gardens of the Palazzo Reale at Caserta

rooms, grand staircases and several richly adorned royal apartments. It was designed by the architect Luigi Vanvitelli and construction started in 1752. The vast surrounding park is a showpiece in itself, with fountains, ornamental waterworks, statuary and a lovely English Garden.

ENVIRONS: The little medieval town of **Caserta Vecchia** lies 10 km (6 miles) to the northeast. Its 12th-century cathedral is a fine example of southern Norman architecture. **San Leucio**, 3 km (2 miles) northwest of Caserta, is a model town built by Ferdinand IV. Its thriving silk industry was also founded by the king.

🏛 Palazzo Reale
Viale Douhet. 📞 0823 32 14 00.
◯ Tue–Sun. ● 1 Jan, 1 May, 25 Dec. 🎫 ♿

Benevento ❺

🏛 62,000. 🚇 🚌 ℹ️ Piazza Roma 11 (0824 31 99 38). 🗓 Fri & Sat.

BENEVENTO, set in a lonely, mountainous province, is home to one of southern Italy's most interesting ancient Roman monuments: the **Arch of Trajan** on Via Traiano. The Roman city, Beneventum, was an important

centre. It stood at the end of the first extension of the Via Appia from Capua, and the Arch was erected across the old road in honour of Trajan. Built from AD 114–166 of Parian marble, it is extremely well preserved. The relief sculpture adorning it – scenes from the life of Trajan and mythological subjects – is in excellent condition.

Elsewhere, evidence of the Romans is to be found in the ruined **Roman theatre**, built during Hadrian's reign, and in the **Museo del Sannio**, which contains artifacts from the region, from ancient Greek finds to modern art.

During World War II, the city stood directly in the way of the Allied advance from the south. It was heavily bombed, hence its largely modern appearance today. The Duomo, a 13th-century building reconstructed after the war, has a sculpted façade that, though badly damaged, has since been restored. The remains of its Byzantine bronze doors are within.

The ornate 2nd-century Roman arch in Benevento, built to honour Trajan

The town has centuries-old associations with pagan worship, and a liqueur called Strega (witch) is made here.

♠ Roman Theatre
Piazza Gaio Ponzio Telesino.
📞 0824 299 70. ⭕ Tue–Sun.
⬤ public hols. 📷 ♿
🏛 Museo del Sannio
Piazza Santa Sofia. 📞 0824 218 18.
⭕ Tue–Sun. ⬤ public hols. 📷 ♿

Costiera Amalfitana ❻

Salerno. 🚌 ⛴ Amalfi. 🛈 Corso delle Repubbliche Marinare 27, Amalfi (089 87 11 07).

The small town of Atrani on the Costiera Amalfitana

THE MOST enchanting and most visited route in Campania is that skirting the southern flank of Sorrento's peninsula: the Costiera Amalfitana (Amalfi Coast). Popular pleasures here include dining on grilled fish and sipping Lacrima Christi from the vineyards on the slopes of Vesuvius, beach-hopping and trips to coastal summits to admire the breathtaking views.

From **Sorrento**, a well developed holiday resort, the road winds down to **Positano**, a village clambering down a vertiginous slope to the sea. A top spot for the jet set, it is nonetheless a good place to swim, or to catch the hydrofoil or ferry to Capri. Further on, **Praiano** is just as fashionable.

Amalfi is the coast's largest town. Its chief glory is a lovely 10th-century Duomo fronted by a rich, coloured façade (13th century). Amalfi was a maritime power before it was subdued in 1131 by King Roger of Naples. The world's oldest maritime code, the *Tavole Amalfitane*, originated here. The 13th-century Chiostro del Paradiso flanks the Duomo, a magnificent 9th-century structure facing the town from the top of a long flight of steps. The style is Lombard-Norman, though the cloisters have a Saracenic-inspired appearance. Amalfi is a tremendously popular resort. **Ravello** has the best views on this coast, the prime vantage points being the gardens of Villa Cimbrone and Villa Rufolo. Views from the latter provided inspiration for Wagner's *Parsifal*. The 11th-century Duomo has entrance doors by Barisano da Trani (1179) and an ornate 13th-century ambo (pulpit) held aloft by six spiral columns. The chapel of San Pantaleone contains the blood of its 4th-century namesake which liquefies annually in May and August.

Beyond **Atrani**, the ruins of a Roman villa at **Minori** show that this coastline has always been a popular holiday spot.

A breathtaking view of the steep village of Positano on the Costiera Amalfitana

Salerno ❼

Salerno. **FS** 🚌 ⛴ *Salerno.* 🛈 *Piazza Ferrovia (089 23 14 32).*

Sᴀʟᴇʀɴᴏ ɪs ᴀ ʙɪɢ, busy port. Here the Allies landed in 1943, leaving in their wake a much bombed, ruinous city. Once famous for its School of Medicine (12th century), it is visited today for its **Duomo**, an 11th-century structure built on a 10th-century foundation. Its best feature is the Atrium, whose columns came from nearby Paestum. In the crypt is the Tomb of St Matthew, which was brought here in 954.

The **Museo Diocesano** is home to most of the cathedral treasures, including an 11th-century ivory altar-front called the Paliotto. Before wandering off down the bustling Corso Vittorio Emanuele, visit the **Museo Provinciale** for local archaeological finds.

Eɴᴠɪʀᴏɴs: The **Cilento** is a mountainous region south of Salerno with a remote interior and a lovely, quiet coastline that is only slightly more populous. Among the towns along the coast, **Agropoli** is a busy little seaside resort 42 km (25 miles) south of Salerno. Outside Castellammare di Velia, a further 28 km (17 miles) to the southeast, are the ruins of the Greek town of **Elea** (founded 6th century BC), once famous for its school of philosophy. It was much visited by the Romans – Cicero was here and Horace came on his doctor's orders

The Temple of Hera I (left) and the Temple of Neptune at Paestum

to undergo a treatment of sea bathing. Excavations have revealed a magnificent 4th-century Roman gateway: the Porta Rosa, Roman baths, the foundations of a temple and the remains of the acropolis.

🏛 **Museo Diocesano**
Largo Plebiscito. 📞 *089 23 91 26.* ⬤ *closed for restoration.*
🏛 **Museo Provinciale**
Via San Benedetto. 📞 *089 23 11 35.* ⬤ *daily.*

Capri ❾

Napoli. ⛴ *Capri.* 🛈 *Piazza Umberto I, Capri (081 837 06 86).* **Grotta Azzurra** ⛴ *from Marina Grande.* ⬤ *in calm sea.* **Certosa** *Via Certosa, Capri.* 📞 *081 837 62 18.* ⬤ *Tue–Sun am.* ♿ **Villa Jovis** *Via Tiberio.* ⬤ *daily.* 🌿

Cᴀᴘʀɪ's ᴇɴᴅᴜʀɪɴɢ reputation as a sybaritic paradise is nearly eclipsed by its notoriety as a tourist trap. However, the great views are unmarred by the throng. The home of emperors, seat of monasteries, place of

Paestum ❽

Zona Archeologica. 🛈 *Via Magna Grecia 887.* 📞 *0828 81 10 16.* 🚌 *from Salerno.* **FS** *Paestum.* ⬤ *9am– 2 hrs before sunset daily.* **Museum** 📞 *0828 81 10 23.* ⬤ *1st & 3rd Mon of month & some public hols.* 🌿 ♿

Tʜɪs ɪs ᴛʜᴇ ᴍᴏsᴛ important ancient Greek site south of Naples in Campania. The Greeks, who founded this city on the edge of the Piana del

exile, former haunt of goats and fishermen, its fortunes changed during the 19th century when English and German expatriates discovered its charms. Today it barely has a "low season"; farmers run little hotels, and fishermen rent pleasure boats. Capri has constant sunshine and enjoys a well-deserved reputation as a Garden of Eden.

The Grotta Azzurra, or the Blue Grotto, is a cave bathed in iridescent blue light which can be reached by tour boat from Marina Grande.

Anacapri is Capri's second town.

0 kilometres   1

0 miles   0.5

The busy port of Salerno

Sele in the 6th century BC, knew it as Poseidonia, the City of Poseidon. The Romans took and renamed it in 273 BC. It fell into decline and was abandoned in the 9th century due to malaria and a Saracen assault. It was rediscovered in the 18th century.

Paestum has three massive Doric temples in an excellent state of repair: the **Basilica** or **Temple of Hera I** (mid-6th century BC); the **Temple of Neptune** (5th century BC), the largest and most complete at Paestum; and the **Temple of Ceres**, thought to date between its two neighbours.

Excavations have revealed the remains of the ancient city, its public and religious buildings, roads and protective walls. A **museum** contains the extensive finds from the site, including tomb paintings, tomb treasures, some terracotta votive offerings, architectural fragments and sculpture.

A view from the highest point of Procida, called Terra Murata

Ischia and Procida ⑩

Napoli. 🚢 Ischia Porto & Procida Porto. 🛈 Via Iasolino, Ischia (081 99 11 46). Via Roma, Procida (081 810 19 68).

ISCHIA IS THE BIGGEST island in the Bay of Naples and, with its beach resorts, thermal springs, therapeutic sands and cheap hotels, it is nearly as popular as its more glamorous neighbour, Capri. Ferries dock at **Ischia Porto**, the harbour and modern part of the main town, **Ischia**. **Ischia Ponte**, the older part, is a short walk away. The northern and the western shores are developed; the southern flank of the island is the quietest. Here, the village of **Sant'Angelo** is dominated by the bulk of a long-extinct volcano, **Monte Epomeo**, whose summit of 788 m (2,585 ft) offers terrific views back across the bay to Naples.

Procida is the odd one next to Ischia and Capri, and it is small – only 3.5 km (2 miles) long – and less visited by holiday crowds. Nevertheless, the swimming is good at **Chiaiolella** and, as at Ischia, there are inexpensive places to stay. The ramshackle main town, also called **Procida**, is home to the main ferry port – the **Marina Grande**.

There are views towards Vesuvius and the Bay of Naples from the north of the island.

Capri is the main town on the island.

Marina Grande
This is Capri's main port of call for ferries from Naples and other ports on the Tyrrhenian coast. An array of colourful houses overlooks the harbour.

I Faraglioni

Marina Piccola is reached by dramatic Via Krupp.

Villa Jovis
Covering an enormous area, this was the Imperial villa from which Tiberius ruled the Roman Empire during his final years.

Certosa di San Giacomo
Founded in 1371 on the site of one of Tiberius's villas, this Carthusian monastery was suppressed in 1808 and is now in part a school. The distant rocks are I Faraglioni.

ABRUZZO, MOLISE AND PUGLIA

P UGLIA IS THE "HEEL" *of the Italian boot, the Gargano Peninsula is its "spur" and Abruzzo and Molise together form the "ankle". Hugging the southeastern seaboard of Italy and looking towards the Balkans, the mountainous regions of Abruzzo and Molise, united until 1963, differ considerably from Puglia, the richest of the three.*

Abruzzo and Molise are sparsely populated, quiet places where the wild landscape exerts a strong influence. Settled by various Apennine tribes in the Middle Bronze Age, the areas were later subdued by the Romans, united under the Normans in the 12th century and, thereafter, ruled by a succession of dynasties based in Naples. Abruzzo, dominated by the Apennines, is a brooding, introspective land of shepherds. Vertiginous drops preface the ascent to ramshackle hilltowns clinging to the sides of high mountains, semi-abandoned and poor. Molise is less dramatic, but life in both regions is primitive. Legends of witches persist, as do strange fertility rites and rituals celebrating the changing seasons.

Puglia's advantage over its poverty-stricken neighbours is that it is nearly all flat and highly fertile. It produces the largest amounts of olive oil and wine in Italy, and its big cities – Lecce, Bari and Taranto – are lively commercial centres.

The region experienced a long-lasting Greek influence, though the golden age of Puglia's past was under the rule of the Normans, followed by Frederick II who, between his return from Germany as emperor in 1220 and his death 30 years later, only spent four years away from here.

Puglia has glorious architecture, particularly in the churches and castles of the north. The curious *trulli* houses in central Puglia, the florid Baroque of Lecce and the Levantine atmosphere of its merchant cities complete the picture of an ancient land subject to more influences from outside the Italian peninsula than from within it.

Traditional dress worn in the town of Scanno in Abruzzo

◁ The curious *trulli* buildings found in central Puglia, particularly around Alberobello and Locorotondo

Exploring Abruzzo, Molise and Puglia

DOMINATED BY THE PROLIFIC Apennine mountain range, the hinterland of Abruzzo and Molise forms one of Italy's last wildernesses. At 2,912 m (9,554 ft), the highest peak is the Gran Sasso. Parts of Abruzzo are covered in endless tracts of forest. Molise is characterized by high plains, gentle valleys and lonely peaks. The spectacular Gargano Peninsula in Puglia (Apulia) has a lovely coastline. Reaching south is the fertile Tavoliere plain, and further south a series of upland plateaus (the Murge) descends towards the dry Salentine Peninsula and the Adriatic.

The exotic *trulli* houses in Alberobello in central Puglia

San Benedetto del Tronto

Ascoli Piceno

TERAMO

ATRI ❷

PESCARA

GRAN SASSO D'ITALIA

Rieti

L'AQUILA ❶

MONTAGNE DELLA MAIELLA

LANCIANO ❻

ISOLE TREMITI ❼

A24

Roma

Medio

SULMONA

SCANNO ❸

MONTI DEI FRENTANI

PARCO NAZIONALE D'ABRUZZO ❹ ❺

Cassino

CAMPOBASSO

MONTI DEL SANNIO

LUCERA ❾

TROIA ❿

Benevento

Avellino

GETTING AROUND

Northern Abruzzo is well served by the A24 and A25, and the SS17 traverses the interior of Abruzzo and Molise. The coastal highway (A14) heads south through Abruzzo and Molise into Puglia. Beyond Foggia, it joins the SS16 to Taranto. Brindisi, the main port for Greece, is accessible from Bari or Taranto. The roads throughout are good. Train and bus services go to the major centres, with buses only to more remote parts.

The coast at Vieste on the beautiful Gargano Peninsula in Puglia

| 0 kilometres | 50 |
| 0 miles | 25 |

KEY

▬▬	Motorway
▬▬	Major road
▭▭	Minor road
▭▭	Scenic route
〜	River
✲	Viewpoint

Sights at a Glance

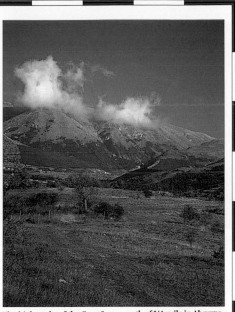

The high peaks of the Gran Sasso, north of L'Aquila in Abruzzo

Lecce's exuberant Baroque architecture, epitomized in Santa Croce's rose window

See Also

The pink and white stone façade of Santa Maria di Collemaggio in L'Aquila

L'Aquila ❶

🏛 64,000. 🚉 🚌 ℹ️ *Via XX Settembre 10 (0862 223 06); Piazza Santa Maria Pagana.* 🏪 *daily.*

ABRUZZO'S CAPITAL lies at the foot of the **Gran Sasso**, at 2,914 m (9,560 ft) the highest point of the Italian mainland south of the Alps (and good for skiing). Its ancient streets are peppered with churches. The domed **Santa Giusta** (1257), off Via Santa Giusta, has a rose window and a *Martyrdom of St Stephen* (1615) by Cavalier d'Arpino. **Santa Maria di Paganica**, off Via Paganica, has a 14th-century façade and a carved portal. The **Duomo** (1257) in Piazza del Duomo was rebuilt in the 18th century. The church of **Santa Maria di Collemaggio**, on Piazza di Collemaggio, is a massive structure with a façade of pink and white stone. It was built in the 13th century by Pietro dal Morrone, who later became Pope Celestine V. In the chapel to the right of the apse is the tomb of the founder who, in 1313, was canonized as St Peter Celestine.

San Bernardino, on Via di San Bernardino, houses the tomb (1505) of San Bernardino of Siena. The church (built 1454–1472), has a façade (1527) by Cola dell'Amatrice and an 18th-century carved ceiling by

Detail of Fontanelle delle Novantanove Cannelle in L'Aquila

Ferdinando Mosca. The second chapel in the south aisle has an altarpiece by Andrea della Robbia, the Renaissance artist.

The medieval **Fontanelle delle Novantanove Cannelle** at the end of Via San Iacopo is a fountain commemorating the 99 villages that Frederick II supposedly united when he founded L'Aquila in 1240.

The **Museo Nazionale d'Abruzzo**, in the 16th-century castle, contains the remains of a prehistoric elephant, Roman artifacts and religious works.

ENVIRONS: North of L'Aquila are the ruins of a **theatre** and **amphitheatre** of ancient **Amiternum**, a Sabine then Roman town, and the birthplace of Sallust (86–c.35 BC), the Roman historian and politician who helped to develop the monograph.

🏛 **Museo Nazionale d'Abruzzo**
Castello Cinquecentesco. 📞 *0862 63 31.* 🕐 *Tue–Sun.* 🔴 *1 May.* 🎦 ♿

Atri ❷

Teramo. 🏛 *11,000.* 🚌 🏪 *Mon.*

THE PRETTIEST in a series of small hilltowns in Abruzzo, Atri is a warren of stepped streets, alleys and passages bound by mostly brick and stone churches and houses. The 13th-century **Duomo**

occupies the site of a Roman bath; the crypt was once a swimming pool, and fragments of the original mosaic floor are visible in the apse. Also in the apse is Andrea Delitio's great 15th-century fresco cycle, in which he combined landscape and architecture in a variety of religious scenes from the Old and New Testaments. The cloister has views of the 15th-century brick campanile.

ENVIRONS: South of Atri is the hilltown of **Penne**. Street by street it is remarkably homogeneous with its buildings of reddish brick, which give the town a warm glow. East of Atri, **Loreto Aprutino** is known for the *Last Judgment* fresco (14th century) in Santa Maria in Piano.

Detail from 15th-century fresco by Andrea Delitio in Atri's Duomo

Sulmona ❸

L'Aquila. 🏛 *24,000.* 🚉 🚌 ℹ️ *Corso Ovidio 208 (0864 532 76).* 🏪 *Wed & Sat.*

THIS TOWN is famous as the home of both Ovid and *confetti* (sugared almonds). After a wedding ceremony in Abruzzo, the happy couple is pelted with *confetti* in an effort to see them on the road to good fortune. Sulmona is filled with ancient buildings, especially along medieval **Via dell'Ospedale**, imparting a beguiling atmosphere. The greatest treasure is the palace of the **Annunziata** on Corso Ovidio. Founded in 1320, the building combines Gothic and Renaissance styles. It houses the **Museo Civico** which contains local antiquities, paintings and the work of goldsmiths. The adjacent church of the **Annunziata**, with a robust Baroque façade, was rebuilt in the 18th century.

At the end of Viale Matteotti is the cathedral of **San Panfilo**, built over a Roman temple. **San Francesco della Scarpa**, in Piazza del Carmine, has a 13th-century portal. Winding past it to the **Fontana del Vecchio** (1474) is an aqueduct that once fuelled local industry.

ENVIRONS: East of Sulmona is the Maiella, a massif of 61 peaks and heavily forested valleys offering walking, bird-watching, climbing and skiing. To the west, Cocullo is the scene of the May Processione dei Serpari (Festival of Snakes) in which a statue of the patron saint, Domenico Abate, is draped with snakes and carried through the town. In the 11th century he is said to have freed the area from venomous snakes.

🏛 **Museo Civico**
Palazzo dell'Annunziata, Corso Ovidio.
☎ 0864 21 02 16. ⬭ Tue–Sun.

OVID, THE LATIN POET

Born in 43 BC, Ovid (Publius Ovidius Naso) was Sulmona's most illustrious son. Not much survives here to remind you of his presence, however, apart from a **Corso Ovidio**, a 20th-century statue of him in Piazza XX Settembre and, just outside the town, a ruin traditionally known as **Ovid's Villa**. Known as one of the greatest poets of Classical Rome, his subjects included love *(Ars Amatoria)* and mythology *(Metamorphoses)*. In AD 8 he was banished into exile on the Black Sea, the far edge of the Roman Empire, after being implicated in a scandal of adultery with Julia, the granddaughter of Emperor Augustus *(see pp44–5)*. Ovid continued to write of his hardships, and died in exile in AD 17.

Scanno ❹

L'Aquila. 🏘 2,400. 🚌 🛈 *Piazza Santa Maria della Valle 12 (0864 743 17).* ⬭ *Tue.*

W ONDERFULLY well-preserved, this medieval hill-town set in beautiful, wild countryside is one of Abruzzo's most popular attractions. There are alleys and narrow flights of steps, oddly-shaped courtyards into which small churches have been pressed, and ancient mansions in whose windows women can be seen making lace or embroidering.

Traditional costume still worn in Scanno

In the shadow of Apennine peaks and beside lovely **Lago di Scanno**, the town is also a favoured halt on the way to the Parco Nazionale d'Abruzzo *(see pp490–91)*. The summer months are the busiest, with a variety of amusements from riding, boating and camping by the lake, to the August classical music festival. During the January Festa di Sant'Antonio Abate, a large lasagna is cooked outside **Santa Maria della Valle**, built on the remains of a pagan temple. The food is doled out to whoever comes along first.

High Apennine peaks looming above the medieval hill-town of Scanno in Abruzzo

Parco Nazionale d'Abruzzo ❺

THIS VAST PARK, inaugurated in 1922, has a rich landscape of high peaks, rivers, lakes and forests, and is one of Europe's most important nature reserves. Until 1877 it formed part of a royal hunting reserve, but today it provides refuge for 70 species of mammal, 40 types of reptiles and 300 species of bird, including the golden eagle and white-backed woodpecker, as well as over 150 varieties of flora. The park features an extensive network of paths, and there are opportunities for riding, trekking and climbing.

Iris

Golden eagles may be seen near the Sangro river.

Young Chamois
Dense forests of beech and maple hide the Apennine chamois. There are also red and roe deer in the park.

Forests of beech and black pine provide beautiful scenery.

Pescasseroli
At the heart of the park, this town is a major centre for information on the region. It has good tourist facilities, including a number of hotels, and ski facilities are nearby.

Apennine Wolves
The park guarantees protection for the Apennine wolf, and about 60 wolves survive here. The chances of seeing one, however, are fairly remote.

Marsican Brown Bear
Once hunted almost to extinction, between 80 and 100 brown bears now roam in the park.

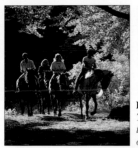

Horse Riding
Trekking is an excellent way to explore more remote areas of the park.

The Camosciara is a spectacular area, home to many wild animals.

Lake Barrea
Created by the artificial damming of the River Sangro, this lake is surrounded by valleys and forests offering walking and pony trekking.

Dense Forests
Beech and maple forests, dotted with black hornbeam, ash, hawthorn, cherry, wild apple and pear, protect the once perse cuted bears and wolves.

KEY

▬	Major road
═	Minor road
▬ ▬	Walking path
✲	Viewpoint
ℹ	Tourist information

0 kilometres   5

0 miles   5

Lanciano 6

Chieti. **▦** *50,000.* **FS** **▦**
ℹ *Piazza Plebiscito (0872 71 78 10).*
▲ *Wed & Sat.*

LARGE PARTS of Lanciano's ancient nucleus remain from the Middle Ages. In the crumbling Civitanova quarter is the 13th-century church of **Santa Maria Maggiore**, with a magnificent 14th-century portal and a silver processional cross (1422) by Nicola da Guardiagrele. Also in this area are **Sant'Agostino** (14th century) and the now disused **San Biagio** (begun c.1059), near the 11th-century **Porta San Biagio** – a rare surviving town gate. The **Duomo**, with its 17th-century bell tower, is situated on top of the remains of a Roman bridge that dates from the period of Diocletian.

The Ripa Sacca (Jewish ghetto) was a busy commercial centre in the Middle Ages – the period of Lanciano's greatest prosperity. The hefty walls of the **Torri Montanara** were built then by the Aragonese as a bulwark against attack.

Isole Tremiti 7

Foggia. **▣** *San Nicola.* **ℹ** *Via Perrone 17, Foggia (0881 72 36 50).*

OFF THE GARGANO coast, the Tremiti are the Italian islands least visited by foreigners. **San Domino** is the largest of the group, with a sandy beach and coves. Here in AD 8, Julia, granddaughter of Augustus, was exiled for adultery and died in AD 28. The poet Ovid was supposedly involved *(see p489)*.

Santa Maria a Mare, in **San Nicola**, the administrative centre of the islands, is an abbey-fortress founded in the 8th century. It was turned into a prison late in the 18th century and ultimately became a place of detention for political prisoners, a role it maintained until 1945.

Both islands are popular with Italians. The swimming is good, though the coastline of San Nicola is rocky.

The coast near Peschici on the Gargano Peninsula

Gargano Peninsula ❽

Foggia. FS 🚌 🛈 *Piazza del Popolo 11, Manfredonia (0884 58 19 98).*

A HIGH, ROCKY SPUR jutting into the Adriatic Sea, the Gargano is a dramatic wilderness dotted with coves and cliffs. Its coastal towns of **Rodi Garganico**, **Peschici**, **Vieste** and **Manfredonia** are popular with holidaymakers. To the east lies the **Foresta Umbra**, a vast woodland of beech, oak, yew and pine, and to the north the salt lakes of **Lesina** and **Varano**, havens for waterfowl.

Typical street scene in the town of Vieste on the Gargano Peninsula

Plunging through the Gargano is an old pilgrim route (N272) from **San Severo** in the west to the shrine at **Monte Sant' Angelo** in the east. The first stop is **San Marco in Lamis**, which is dominated by a huge 16th-century convent. Further along, **San Giovanni Rotondo** is a focus for pilgrims in search of a cure from Padre Pio (1887–1968), a miracle-worker who is buried here. The last stop is **Monte Sant'Angelo** with its grotto where in 493, according to tradition, the Archangel Michael appeared to the Bishop of Sipontum.

To the south of Manfredonia, beside the ruins of the ancient town of Siponto, is the oriental-inspired 12th-century church of **Santa Maria di Siponto**.

Lucera ❾

Foggia. 🏠 *43,000.* 🚌 🛈 *Via Zuppetta 52 (800 76 76 06).* 🛒 *Wed.*

THIS WAS ONCE a prosperous Roman colony and, on the northeast edge of town, the ruins of a Roman **amphitheatre** survive. Lucera was rebuilt in the 13th century by Frederick II, who peopled it with 20,000 Sicilian Muslims. It became one of the strongest fortresses in southern Italy, and its **castle** is one of Puglia's most magnificent. Built in 1233 by Frederick II, and enlarged after 1269, its fortified wall of

900 m (2,953 ft) is interspersed with 24 towers. Of Frederick's original palace, only the base and some vaulting remains.

In 1300 Charles II, who massacred most of Lucera's Muslim population, began the **Duomo** on the site of their main mosque, blending Gothic and Romanesque styles. The high, soaring nave is filled with 15th- and 16th-century frescoes and carvings.

The **Museo Civico Fiorelli** has displays of episodes from throughout Lucera's history.

🏛 **Museo Civico Fiorelli**
Via de Nicastri 44. 📞 *0881 54 70 41.* ⭕ *Tue–Sun (only am on Sun).* 📷

The remains of Lucera castle

Troia ❿

Foggia. 🏠 *33,000.* 🚌 🛥 *1st & 3rd Sat of month.*

FOUNDED IN 1017 as a Byzantine fortress against the Lombards, Troia fell to the Normans in 1066. Until Frederick II destroyed it in 1229, the town had been ruled by a succession of powerful bishops who were responsible for producing some of Puglia's most remarkable buildings, including Troia's **Duomo** *(see pp462–3).*

Begun in 1093 and constructed over the following 30 years, it exhibits an extraordinary diversity of styles. It successfully blends elements of Lombard, Saracenic and Byzantine style with that of the Pisan-Romanesque.

Elegant blind arcading distinguishes the Duomo's lower storey. The upper sections are characterized by powerfully carved sculpture – projecting lions and bulls. The upper façade displays a rose window with Saracenic-style detailing.

The main entrance, with bronze doors by Oderisio da Beneventano (1119), is dominated by carved capitals and an architrave, both Byzantine in style. Within the Duomo is a Romanesque pulpit (1169).

Trani ⓫

Bari. 🏛 45,000. 🚉 🚌 🛈 Palazzo Palmieri, Piazza Trieste 10 (0883 58 88 30). 🛒 Tue.

DURING THE MIDDLE AGES this small, lively whitewashed port of Jewish origin bustled with mercantile activity and was filled with merchants and traders from Genoa, Amalfi, Pisa and Ravello. It reached its peak of prosperity under Frederick II.

Today it is visited for its Norman **Duomo** in Piazza

The façade of Trani's Duomo

Duomo, built mainly from 1159 to 1186 over an earlier church whose predecessor, the Ipogei di San Leucio, dates from the 7th century. It is dedicated to St Nicholas the Pilgrim, a little-remembered miracle-worker (died 1094) who was canonized as an act of rivalry against the town of Bari, which possessed the

bones of another, more memorable St Nicholas. The Duomo's most notable external features are its sculptures, particularly surrounding the rose window and the arched window below it, and the entrance portal with bronze doors (1175–9) by Barisano da Trani. The vigour of the interior has recently been revealed following restoration.

Next to the Duomo is the **castle** (1233–49) that was founded by Frederick II. Rebuilt in the 14th and 15th centuries, it is a well-preserved edifice with one wall dropping sheer into the sea.

Elsewhere in Trani the 15th-century Gothic-Renaissance town house, the **Palazzo Caccetta** in Piazza Trieste, is a rare survival. Nearby, on Via Ognissanti, the 12th-century Romanesque church of the **Ognissanti**, the chapel of the Knights Templar erected in the courtyard of their hospital, is notable for its original portico.

Castel del Monte ⓬

Località Andria, Bari. 🛈 Commune (0883 56 98 48). 🕐 Apr–Sep: 9am–5pm Tue–Sat; Oct–Mar: 9am–1pm Tue–Sat. ● 25 Dec. 🚫 📷

Frederick II

REMOTE IN the endless plains near Ruvo di Puglia, Castel del Monte, built in the mid-13th century, outclasses every other castle associated with Frederick II. It is also one of the most sophisticated secular buildings of the Middle Ages. The emperor had broad intellectual interests,

and he used his castles as hunting lodges where he could retire from court life with his falcons and books. Inside there are two floors, each with eight rib-vaulted rooms, some still lined with marble. This, and the marble mouldings on the entrance and the upper floor, as well as sophisticated lavatory arrangements, mark the castle as a palace.

Octagonal satellite tower

Graceful, arched windows

Thick and impenetrable walls

Octagonal courtyard

The main entrance portal is in the style of a Roman triumphal arch.

FLOORPLAN OF THE CASTLE
The building is a harmonious geometrical study with two storeys of eight rooms each. The reasons for such precise planning of this giant octagon remain a mystery to this day.

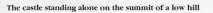

The castle standing alone on the summit of a low hill

Ruvo di Puglia ⑬

Bari. 🏘 24,000. FS 🚌 ℹ Via
Vittorio Veneto 48 (080 36 15 49).
🗓 Sat.

ONCE CELEBRATED for its vases,
Ruvo di Puglia's ceramics
industry, producing "Apulian"
ware, flourished until the 2nd
century BC. The style was
inspired by the striking red
and black colours of Attic and
Corinthian models. The **Museo
Archeologico Nazionale
Jatta** has a good overview.

The 13th-century **Duomo** is
a bold example of the Apulian-
Romanesque style with a
portal that blends Byzantine,
Saracenic and Classical motifs.

🏛 Museo Archeologico
Nazionale Jatta

Piazza Bovio 35. ☎ 081 81 10 42.
◯ daily. ◯ 1 Jan, 1 May,
25 Dec. ♿

Bari ⑭

🏘 400,000. ✈ FS 🚌
⛴ ℹ Piazza Aldo Moro
33a (080 524 22 44).
🗓 daily.

ROMAN BARIUM was
simply a commercial
centre, but the city became
the regional capital under the
Saracens in 847, and was
subsequently the seat of the
catapan, the Byzantine

governor of southern
Italy. Under the
Normans, to whom it
fell in 1071, Bari
became a centre of
maritime significance.
Today it is Puglia's
lively capital and an
important port with
ferries to and from
Croatia and Greece.

The **Basilica di
San Nicola**, one of
Puglia's first great
Norman churches
(begun 1087), was a
model for others. Its
plain exterior has a
tall gabled section
flanked by towers.
The Apulian-
Romanesque portal
has carving on the
door jambs and arch
in Arabic, Byzantine and

Portal detail of Ruvo di Puglia's Duomo

Classical styles. Beyond
the choir screen is a
fine 12th-century altar
canopy and an epis-
copal throne (c.11th
century). The relics of
St Nicholas – patron
saint of the city – are
buried in the crypt.

**Sculpture at
Bari castle**

The late 12th-century
Apulian-Romanesque
Duomo is based on
San Nicola, with a dome and
one surviving tower (the other
one collapsed during an earthquake in 1613). The Baroque
portals on the entrance façade
incorporate 12th-century

doorways. The interior has
been restored to its medieval
simplicity. The canopy over
the high altar, the pulpit and
the episcopal throne are reconstructions from fragments of
the originals. The sacristy, built
as a baptistry, is known as the
Trulla. The crypt houses the
remains of San Sabino, Bari's
original patron saint.

The city's **castle**, founded
by Roger II, was adapted by
Frederick II in 1233–9. In the
vaulted hall is a collection of
plaster casts of sculpture and
architectural fragments from
various Romanesque monu-
ments in the region.

Bari castle, in the old district known as the Città Vecchia, where most of the town's sights are clustered

Alberobello ⑮

Bari. 🚆 to Alberobello & Ostuni.
ℹ Piazza del Popolo (080 432 51 71).

IN THE PARCHED, dry land-scape called the **Murge dei Trulli**, there is a profusion of olive groves, orchards, vineyards and *trulli*. Strange circular buildings with conical roofs and domed within, *trulli* are built from local limestone stacked without using mortar. The walls and openings are generally whitewashed, while the stone roof tiles are either bare or have religious, pagan or magical symbols painted onto them. Some have been converted into modern houses; most are souvenir shops. Their origins are ob-scure, though the name is traditionally applied to ancient round tombs found in the Roman countryside.

Alberobello is the *trulli* capital and, inevitably, a tourist haunt. Here the strange white buildings crowd the narrow streets, and there are *trulli* restaurants and shops, and even a *trulli* cathedral.

ENVIRONS: The white-washed hilltown of **Locorotondo** is one of the region's prettiest places and an important wine centre. The elegant streets of **Martina Franca** are enlivened by Rococo balconies. The spectacular **Grotte di Castellana** are caves estimated to be 50 million years old.

Whitewashed and sun-baked *trulli* in Alberobello

bombing in World War II and is garlanded by heavy industry, especially in the Borgo area. The picturesque **Città Vecchia**, an island dividing the Mare Grande from the Mare Piccolo, was the site of the Roman citadel of Tarentum. There is a lively fish market which still offers the shellfish for which the city was once famous. Here, too, is the **Duomo**. Founded in 1071, it has been the subject of subsequent rebuilding. The most interesting features include the catacomb-like crypt, with its sarcophagi and fragmented frescoes, and the antique marble columns of the nave. Behind it is the 11th-century **San Domenico Maggiore**, which later gained a high double-approach Baroque staircase. The huge **castle** built by Frederick of Aragon (15th century) covers the eastern corner of the Città Vecchia, with a swing bridge connecting it to the mainland.

Aphrodite in museum in Taranto

Taranto ⑯

🏛 245,000. 🚆 🚌 ℹ Corso Umberto 1 (099 453 23 92).
🗓 Mon & Fri.

LITTLE REMAINS OF the ancient city of Taras, founded by Spartans in 708 BC. It enjoyed its greatest prosperity under the philosopher and scientist Archytas in the mid-4th century BC. The **Museo Archeologico Nazionale** has artifacts that shed light on much of the region's early history. Taranto suffered greatly due to heavy

🏛 Museo Archeologico Nazionale

Corso Umberto 41. 📞 099 453 21 12. ⬤ for restoration.
🖼 ♿

Street-by-Street: Lecce ⑰

Façade detail, Santa Croce

Lecce, tucked away on the Salentine Peninsula, was the site of the Greek Messapi settlement. It became an important centre of the Roman Empire, and during the Middle Ages a strong tradition of scholarship was established. Much of the architecture is in the Lecce Baroque style, which flourished in the 17th century and earned the city the name of Florence of the South. Featuring rich decoration, this style was possible due to the *pietra di Lecce* – an easily carved stone. Giuseppe Zimbalo (lo Zingarello) was its greatest master.

★ Palazzo Vescovile and Duomo
The bishop's palace (rebuilt in 1632), the adjoining Duomo by lo Zingarello (after 1659) and a seminary (1709) enclose the Piazza Duomo.

Chiesa del Rosario
Said to be the finest work by lo Zingarello (begun 1691), the exterior is ornate and idiosyncratic in its detail.

The Seminary once supplied the Vatican with *castrato* singers – eunuchs noted for their high voices.

Porta Rudiae
This 18th-century city gate leads to the suburbs and to the ruins of Roman Rudiae.

Chiesa del Carmine

STAR SIGHTS

★ Santa Croce

★ Palazzo Vescovile and Duomo

KEY

– – – Suggested route

| 0 metres | 100 |
| 0 yards | 100 |

VIA UMBER.

PIAZZA CASTROMEDIAN

VIA RUBICHI

PIAZZA SANT'ORON

VIA PERONELLI

VIA P.

PIAZZA DUOMO

VIA VITTORIO EMANUELE

VICOLO SANTA VENERA

VIA MARCO BASSEO

VIA MORELL

VIA GIUSEPPE LIBERTINI

VIA R CARA

VIA G CINO

★ Santa Croce
*Built from 1549 to 1679,
Gabriele Riccardi began
the façade and interior
and lo Zingarello
designed the imaginative rose window
and pediment.*

**The 16th-century
Castello** is marooned
between ancient city and
modern suburbs. An inner
construction (12th century)
is enclosed by a later wall
built by Charles V.

Detail of a 15th-century fresco in
Santa Caterina d'Alessandria

Galatina ⑱

Lecce. 28,000. Thu.

AN IMPORTANT Greek colony in
the Middle Ages, this town
retains its Greek flavour. It is
the centre of one of Puglia's
chief wine-producing regions,
although it is more famous for
the St Peter and Paul street
festival and for the ritual
of tarantism *(see p495).*

The Gothic church of **Santa
Caterina d'Alessandria**
on Piazza Orsini was built
by Raimondello del Balzo
Orsini (begun 1384). This
lovely church contains early
15th-century frescoes with
scenes from the Old and New
Testaments that glorify the
Orsini, who were feudal lords.
Orsini's tomb is in the chancel.

Otranto ⑲

Lecce. 4,800.
Piazza Castello (0836 80 14 36).
Wed.

TODAY OTRANTO is a shadow
of its former self. It was one
of Republican Rome's leading
ports for trade with Asia
Minor and Greece, and under
the Byzantines was an important
toehold of the Eastern
Empire in Italy. In 1070 it fell
to the Normans. Turks
attacked in 1480 and
slaughtered its inhabitants. The 800 survivors
were promised their
lives if they renounced
Christianity: all refused.

The Norman **Duomo**
(founded 1080) on Via
Duomo houses the
bones of the martyrs.
There is a 12th-century
mosaic floor and a fine
crypt. A **castle** (1485–98)
built by the Aragonese at the
centre of town, overlooking the
port, adds to Otranto's charm.

**Tourist
information**

**Church of
San Matteo**

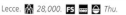

Colonna di Sant'Oronzo
*St Oronzo was appointed
Bishop of Lecce by St Paul in
AD 57, and later martyred by
the Roman emperor Nero. This
bronze statue dates from 1739.*

**A Roman
theatre** was
excavated
virtually intact
with its orchestra and seats.

Roman Amphitheatre
*Excavated in 1938 and recently restored,
only part of this 1st-century BC amphitheatre is visible.*

BASILICATA AND CALABRIA

REMOTE AND WILD, *Basilicata is one of the poorest regions in Italy. It is underdeveloped and undervisited, and so remains unspoilt. Neighbouring Calabria has been immortalized in the drawings of Edward Lear who, travelling through on a donkey in 1847, was transfixed by the "horror and magnificence" of its savage landscape.*

Today these regions are distinctly separate, but they share a common history and, along with Sicily and Puglia, were part of Magna Graecia. Ancient Metaponto in Basilicata was an important centre, as were Crotone and Locri Epizephiri in Calabria. Their ruins evoke an illustrious past.

After the Greeks came the Romans, followed by Basilian monks. These were members of the Greek-Byzantine church who were fleeing their territories which had been invaded by Muslims. Their religious establishments make up a core of interesting monuments, such as the Cattolica at Stilo or Matera, where the monks took refuge in caves.

Many of the historic remains are Norman, but sporadic evidence of Svevi, Angevin, Aragonese and Spanish occupation also exists.

Centuries of rule by Naples led to the marginalization of Basilicata and Calabria. Nowadays Calabria has a terrifying reputation due to the *'ndrangheta*, the ferocious first cousin to the Mafia, whose activities are a constant menace. Banditry does still exist, but the sensible traveller should have little to fear.

Owing to emigration, Basilicata and Calabria are sparsely populated and have as much to offer in unspoilt countryside as in historic centres. The vast coastline boasts pretty beaches, while the interior features the rugged Aspromonte and Sila mountain ranges

The remote landscape has kept change at bay. Isolated Pentedattilo, for example, preserves customs of Byzantine origin while around San Giorgio Albanese there live close-knit communities of Albanians, descended from 15th-century refugees.

Sparsely populated, rugged countryside surrounding Stilo in southern Calabria

◁ The silent Sassi district in Matera, where dwellings are scooped out of the rock

Exploring Basilicata and Calabria

Mostly upland country, Basilicata is scattered with Greek ruins (like those at Metaponto), medieval abbeys, Norman castles (such as Melfi's) and isolated hill-towns. Matera, its most interesting city, stands amid an arid lunar landscape of denuded valleys. Calabria is often described as the mountains between the seas. The lovely beaches and virgin landscape around Tropea and Maratea attract many visitors. The Ionian coast's chief attractions are its Greek ruins, such as Caulonia and Locri Epizephiri, and the hill-towns, like Stilo and Gerace, which eventually replaced them.

SIGHTS AT A GLANCE

Gerace ⑩
Lagopesole ③
Maratea ⑥
Matera ④
Melfi ①
Metaponto ⑤
Reggio di Calabria ⑪
Rossano ⑦
Stilo ⑨
Tropea ⑧
Venosa ②

Repairing nets in the town of Pizzo, northeast of Tropea

The picturesque hill-town of Rivello, north of Maratea in Basilicata

KEY

▬ Motorway
▬ Major road
▬ Minor road
▬ Scenic route
≈ River
❊ Viewpoint

0 kilometres   50
0 miles   25

The port of Maratea on the Tyrrhenian coast of Basilicata

GETTING AROUND

Calabria's Tyrrhenian coast is well served by the A3, a spur of which extends to Potenza in Basilicata. To reach the Ionian coast, it is best is to skirt the Aspromonte via the N106 from Reggio to Basilicata. Although the mountains can be crossed, namely on the N280 to Catanzaro, the roads are narrow and pass through isolated countryside. Much of Basilicata is even less accessible, and Matera is more easily reached from Puglia. There are airports at Reggio di Calabria, Lamezia (west of Catanzaro), Bari and Brindisi (Puglia). Trains connect the bigger centres and country buses serve the small towns.

The countryside near Miglionico, south of Matera

The impressive castle at Melfi, showing evidence of both Angevin and later construction

Melfi ❶

Potenza. 🏠 15,000. FS 🚌
🚆 Wed & Sat.

A BROODING and now almost deserted medieval town, Melfi is crowned by the formidable **castle** where Pope Nicholas II conducted Robert Guiscard's investiture in 1059, thus legitimizing the Normans in the south. Melfi later became the Norman capital. Here Frederick II proclaimed his *Constitutiones Augustales* (1231) which unified his kingdom as a state. In the castle is the **Museo Nazionale del Melfese**, with its collection of Byzantine jewellery.

The **Duomo**, off Via Vittorio Emanuele, was begun in 1155 by William the Bad but rebuilt in the 18th century. Only the campanile survives.

🏛 Museo Nazionale del Melfese
Castello di Melfi, Via Normanna.
📞 0972 23 87 26. ⏰ daily.
🔴 1 Jan, 25 Apr, 1 May, 25 Dec,
Mon am. 🈺 🚫 📷 (Sat & Sun).

Venosa ❷

Potenza. 🏠 12,000. FS 🚌 🔅 Via
Garibaldi 42 (open occasionally).
🚆 1st Sat & 3rd Thu of month.

V ENOSA WAS ONE of the most important Roman colonies around 290 BC, and remains of **baths** and an **amphitheatre** survive in the archaeological

zone along Via Vittorio Emanuele. It was also the birthplace of the Latin poet, Horace (65–8 BC), and the site where the Roman general Marcellus died at the hands of Hannibal in 208 BC. Marcellus' reputed **tomb** is in Via Melfi.

The **Duomo**, also on Via Vittorio Emanuele, and the huge **castle** in Piazza Umberto I date from the 16th century. Occupying the site of a Roman temple is **La Trinità**, a partially ruined abbey complex formed by an older church, possibly early Christian (5th–6th century). It is backed by an unfinished 11th-century construction, in which Robert Guiscard (died 1085) was buried with his half-brothers and Alberada, his first wife. Only her tomb has survived.

Lagopesole ❸

Potenza. 📞 0971 860 83. FS to
Lagopesole Scalo then bus to town.
⏰ 9:30am–1pm, 4–7pm daily.
🚫

R ISING DRAMATICALLY on a hill with a village huddled at its feet, Lagopesole's **castle** is the most striking in Basilicata. Dating from 1242–50, it was the last castle Frederick II built and was used as a hunting lodge. There is interesting decoration, particularly the carved heads above the portal of the keep. One is said to be Frederick Barbarossa (the grandfather of Frederick II),

and the other is reputedly Barbarossa's wife, Beatrice. Inside, the royal apartments and chapel can be visited.

Matera ❹

🏠 56,000. FS 🚌 🔅 Via de Viti de
Marco 9 (0835 33 19 83). 🚆 Sat.

The Sassi district of Matera

P ERCHED ON THE EDGE of a deep ravine, this town consists of the bustling upper district and the silent lower **Sassi** (caves) district, divided into the Sasso Barisano and the more picturesque Sasso Caveoso. The people of Matera once lived here in dwellings scooped out of the rock. The two parts are odd neighbours, making Matera one of the most fascinating cities in southern Italy.

For the best overview, walk along the **Strada Panoramica dei Sassi** and look down into the caves. From the 8th to the

13th centuries, such caves probably provided refuge for monks from the Byzantine empire. Many chapels, which were gouged out of the rock, were taken over in the 15th century by peasants. Subsequently, a cave-dwelling Matera evolved and by the 18th century some buildings fronting the caves had become fairly grand mansions and convents. By the 1950s and '60s the Sassi were overtaken by squalor and poverty, and the inhabitants were forcibly rehoused. Carlo Levi (1912–75) drew attention to their living conditions in his book *Christ Stopped at Eboli*, comparing Sassi districts with Dante's *Inferno*. The Sassi area was made a UNESCO World Heritage site in 1993.

Of the 120 *chiese rupestri* (rock-cut churches) in the Sassi and the Agri district outside the town, **Santa Maria di Idris** in the Monte Errone area and **Santa Lucia alle Malve** in the Albanian quarter both contain 13th-century frescoes.

The **Museo Nazionale Ridola** provides a background to Matera and the Sassi. Many Neolithic trench villages, necropoli and other ancient sites have been discovered, and artifacts from them are displayed here.

The Apulian-Romanesque **Duomo** (13th century) in Piazza Duomo has interesting sculpture and an anonymous 12th-century painting of the *Madonna della Bruna*, the patroness of Matera, who is celebrated on 2 July. Via Duomo leads toward **San Francesco d'Assisi** (13th century with Baroque overlay) which commemorates St Francis's visit to Matera in 1218. Other churches to visit are **San Domenico** and **San Giovanni Battista** on Via San Biagio (both 13th century), and the **Purgatorio** (1770) on Via Ridola.

🏛 **Museo Nazionale Ridola**
Via Ridola 24. [0835 31 00 58.
◯ daily. 📷

The Tavole Palatine in Metaponto

Metaponto ❺

Zona Archeologica, Matera. [0835 74 53 27. 🚌 FS to Metaponto. ◯ 9am–1 hr before sunset daily. ● 1 Jan, Easter, 25 Dec. 📷 ♿

FOUNDED IN THE 7th century BC, ancient Metapontum was once the centre of a wealthy city-state with a philosophical tradition expounded by Pythagoras, who settled here after his expulsion from Croton. Its ruins include the **Tavole Palatine** (6th century BC) at the Bradano River bridge, 15 columns that are part of a Doric temple, probably dedicated to Hera. The **Museo Nazionale di Metaponto** displays artifacts from the site. The ruins of a theatre and the Doric **Temple of Apollo Lycius** (6th century

Church of San Francesco in Matera

BC) are in the **Archaeological Zone**. Further south, modern **Policoro** occupies the site of ancient Heracleia (founded 7th–5th century BC). Its **Museo Nazionale della Siritide** has finds from this and other sites.

🏛 **Museo Nazionale di Metaponto**
Metaponto Borgo. [0835 74 53 27. ◯ daily. ● Mon am & public hols. 📷 includes Archaeological Zone. ♿
🏛 **Museo Nazionale della Siritide**
Via Colombo 8, Policoro.
[0835 97 21 54. ◯ daily.
● 1 Jan, 1 May, 25 Dec. 📷 ♿

Maratea ❻

Potenza. 🏃 5,000. FS 🚌
ℹ Piazza del Gesù 40 (0973 87 69 08). ● 1st & 3rd Sat of month.

A TINY STRETCH of Basilicata meets the Tyrrhenian Sea in the Gulf of Policastro. This unblemished coast is home to Maratea. Its small port (Maratea Inferiore) is beneath the old centre (Maratea Superiore), which straddles the flank of a hill. From here the road climbs Monte Biagio to a summit with breathtaking views where a huge statue of the **Redeemer** stands.

ENVIRONS: Dramatically sited **Rivello**, 23 km (14 miles) to the north, once had a largely Greek population. Byzantine influences can be seen in the churches of **Santa Maria del Poggio** and **Santa Barbara**.

The small port of Marina di Maratea with fishing boats

A page from the precious *Codex Purpureus Rossanensis*

Rossano **7**

Cosenza. 🏛 *32,000.* 🚆 🚌
🗓 *2nd & 4th Fri of month.*

THIS HANDSOME hill-town was one of the main centres of Byzantine civilization in Calabria. It assumed power when Reggio di Calabria fell to the Saracens in the 9th, 10th and 11th centuries. The **Museo Diocesano** houses the *Codex Purpureus Rossanensis*, a rare 6th-century Greek Gospel with silver lettering and splendidly detailed miniatures.

The Baroque **cathedral** contains the *Madonna Acheropita* fresco, a much venerated Byzantine relic of the 8th or 9th century.

ENVIRONS: On a hilltop to the southeast is the five-domed Greek church of **San Marco** (10th century). The 12th-century **Panaghia**, another Greek church, lies off Via Archivescovado. Both contain fragments of early frescoes.

Santa Maria del Patirion, on a hilltop 18 km (11 miles) to the west, is magnificently adorned with coloured brickwork, tile and stone. It offers great views over the Piana di Sibari (Plain of Sibari), the alleged location of the fabled city of Sybaris, destroyed in 510 BC. The church has remained virtually unaltered since it was built around 1095.

🏛 **Museo Diocesano**
Palazzo Arcivescovile, Via Arcivescovile. 📞 *0983 52 02 82.*
🔓 *daily.* ⬤ *public hols.* 📷

Tropea **8**

Vibo Valenzia. 🏛 *7,000.* 🚆 🚌
ℹ *Piazza Ercole.* ⛴ *Sat.*

ONE OF THE MOST picturesque towns on Calabria's largely built-up Tyrrhenian coast is Tropea, which offers superb views of the sea and beaches. The old town hangs on to a cliffside facing a large rock which was formerly an island. The rock is topped by **Santa Maria dell'Isola**, a former medieval Benedictine sanctuary. The **cathedral** at the end of Via Roma is of Norman origin, although it has been rebuilt several times. Inside is a 14th-century painting, the *Madonna di Romania*, by an unknown artist.

Casa Trampo (14th century) and **Palazzo Cesareo** (early 20th century) in Vicolo Manco are the most interesting of the small palaces in Tropea. The latter has a splendid balcony adorned with carvings.

Below the town are pretty beaches and a good choice of places to eat. Other seaside towns to visit are **Palmi** to the south, and **Pizzo** to the north.

Stilo **9**

Reggio di Calabria. 🏛 *3,000.* 🚆 🚌
⛴ *Tue.*

A SHORT DISTANCE from the coast, Stilo is a ramshackle and earthquake-damaged town clamped to the side of Monte Consolino. Standing on a ledge looking out over the olive trees is the **Cattolica**, which has made Stilo a focus of dedicated pilgrimage for lovers of Byzantine architecture. Built in the 10th century by Basilian monks, the brick building with its terracotta-tiled roof is based on a Greek cross-in-a-square plan. Four antique, mismatched marble columns divide the interior into nine quadrants. The capitals are placed at the base of the columns, instead of on top, to indicate the triumph of Christianity over paganism. The frescoes within, discovered and restored in 1927, date from the 11th century.

The Cattolica dominates the town, but on Via Tommaso Campanella there is a medieval **Duomo** as well as the 17th-century ruins of the **Convent of San Domenico**, where the philosopher and Dominican friar Tommaso Campanella (1568–1639) lived. The church of **San Francesco**, built around 1400, has an ornate carved wooden altar and a lovely 16th-century painting of the *Madonna del Borgo* (unknown origin). Bivongi, northwest of Stilo, has two churches dedicated to St John: the Byzantine-Norman **San Giovanni Theresti**, and the Norman **San Giovanni Vecchio**.

🏛 **Cattolica**
2 km (1 mile) above Stilo on Via Cattolica. 🔓 *daily.* ♿

The beautiful and unspoilt coastline at Tropea

The distinctive five-domed Cattolica in Stilo

Gerace ⑩

Reggio di Calabria. 🏛 *3,000.* 🚌

OCCUPYING an impregnable crag on the northeastern flank of the Aspromonte, this ancient place was founded by refugees from **Locri Epizephiri** who fled in the 9th century to escape Saracen attack. Its defensive character is reinforced by the medieval town walls and the remains of the once impregnable castle.

Apart from the slow pace of life here – where you are as likely to meet a flock of sheep in an alley as a Fiat 500 – the main attraction is Calabria's grandest **Duomo**. This large structure indicates the significance of Gerace at least up to the time of the Normans. Constructed around the early 12th century, rebuilt in the 13th century and restored in the 18th century, the crypt is its chief treasure. Both crypt and church are simple, adorned by a series of antique coloured marble and granite columns probably stolen from the site of ancient Locri Epizephiri. At the end of Via Cavour is 12th-century **San Giovanello**, part Byzantine and part Norman. Nearby is the Gothic church of **San Francesco d'Assisi** which contains a Baroque marble altar (1615) and the Pisan-style tomb of Niccolò Ruffo (died 1372), a member of a prominent Calabrian family.

ENVIRONS: The vast site of **Locri Epizephiri**, the first Greek city to have a written code of law (660 BC), was a well-known centre of the cult of Persephone. There are remains of **temples**, a **theatre** and Greek and Roman **tombs**. The **Museo** displays a ground plan of the site and a collection of Greek and Roman votive statues, coins, inscriptions and sculptural fragments.

� Locri Epizephiri
Southwest of Locri on the N106, Contrada Marasà. [*0964 39 00 23.* ☐ *Tue–Sun.* **Museo Nazionale** Contrada Marasà, SS 106. ☐ *Tue–Sun.* ● *1 May, 25 Dec, 1st and 3rd Mon of the month.*

Reggio di Calabria ⑪

🏛 *175,000.* ✈ 🚆 🚌 ⛴ 🛈 *Via D. Tripepi 72 (0965 211 71).* 🛒 *Fri.*

THIS IS A TATTY CITY, heavily rebuilt after a major earthquake in 1908. One reason to visit it is to see the awesome **Museo Nazionale della Magna Grecia**. The museum houses a fine collection of artifacts from ancient Rhegion – an important Greek city on the site of the present town – and from other Greek sites.

Chief among its treasures are the Greek bronzes, larger-than-life statues of warriors dredged from the sea off Riace Marina in 1972. Statue A (460 BC) is thought to be by Phidias, the Athenian sculptor and chief exponent of the idealizing, Classical style. If true, it is a rare survivor because his works, praised in the highest terms by ancient writers, were hitherto only known to us from Roman copies. Statue B (430 BC) has been attributed to the sculptor Polyclitus. It is possible that the statues originated from the Temple of Delphi, the Athenians' monument to the victory of Marathon.

🏛 Museo Nazionale della Magna Grecia
Piazza de Nava 26. [*0965 81 22 55.* ☐ *9am-7.30 pm daily.* ● *1st & 3rd Mon of the month.* 🎫

Riace Bronzes (6th and 5th century BC) in Reggio's Museo Nazionale

SICILY

O N A CROSSROADS *in the Mediterranean, part of Europe and Africa, yet belonging to neither, Sicily was tramped across by half the ancient civilized world. As conquerors came and went, they left behind a rich and varied cultural deposit. This has resulted in a quirky mixture in almost every aspect of the local vernacular from language, customs and cooking to art and, most notably, the diverse architecture of the island.*

During the 6th and 5th centuries BC, there cannot have been much difference between Athens and the Greek cities of Sicily. Their ruins are among the most spectacular of the ancient Greek world. The Romans took over in the 3rd century BC, followed by the Vandals, Ostrogoths and Byzantines. Not much that is tangible has survived from the days of the Arabs, who ruled from the 9th to 11th centuries, though Palermo's Vucciria is more souk than market. The Norman era, beginning in 1060, spawned brilliant artistic achievements, such as the cathedrals of Monreale and Cefalù, while the eclecticism of that period's architecture is best seen at Santi Pietro e Paolo outside Taormina.

The Sicilian Baroque of the 17th and 18th centuries is just as individual. The palaces and churches of Palermo, reflecting the elaborate ritual of the Spanish Viceregal court, tend towards extravagant display. At Noto, Ragusa, Modica, Siracusa and Catania the buildings are a useful vehicle for the Sicilians' love of ornamentation, itself a remnant from the island's early fling with the Arab world. The style is an expression of the nature of Sicilians, whose sense of pomp and pageantry is both magnificent and extreme.

Sicily is a curiosity, and the legacy of the past is redolent everywhere. The fact that it is an island has intensified the cultural impact of each successive occupier. They say that today there's less Italian blood in Sicilian veins than there is Phoenician, Greek, Arabic, Norman, Spanish or French. The resulting mixture – exotic, spicy and highly inflammable – has created a separate nation at the foot of Italy.

Detail of a 12th-century mosaic from the Palazzo dei Normanni in Palermo

◁ **The beautifully preserved doric Temple of Concord (c.430 BC) in the Valley of the Temples at Agrigento**

Exploring Sicily

THE VAST COASTLINE of Sicily (Sicilia) provides many magnificent beaches, particularly at Taormina and the Golfo di Castellammare by Capo San Vito – part of a huge nature reserve. Sicily's varied interior is characterized by remote hilltowns and plains punctuated by mountain ranges known for spring flowers and wildlife. Among the most spectacular sights is Mount Etna, an active volcano whose lava flows over the centuries have left the land immensely fertile, supporting an abundance of walnut trees, citrus groves and vineyards.

Fishermen at work in their boats at Siracusa

SIGHTS AT A GLANCE

The magnificent temple at Segesta

| 0 kilometres | 50 |
| 0 miles | 25 |

KEY

▬▬ Motorway

▬▬ Major road

▬▬ Minor road

▬▬ Scenic route

〜 River

☙ Viewpoint

SEE ALSO

- *Where to Stay* pp573–5
- *Where to Eat* pp607–8

ISOLE EOLIE
(LIPARI)

The Norman Duomo in Palermo

TIRRENO

MESSINA **14**

STRETTA DI
MESSINA

TINDARI **13**

TAORMINA **15**

TROINA

NICOSIA

MOUNT ETNA **16**

ENNA **12**

CATANIA **17**

GOLFO DI
CATANIA

PIAZZA ARMERINA **11**

CALTAGIRONE

PANTALICA

18

GOLFO DI
AUGUSTA

SIRACUSA

19

GELA

VITTORIA

PALAZZOLO
ACREIDE

COMISO

RAGUSA

20 NOTO

GOLFO DI
NOTO

LFO DI GELA

MARE IONIO

GETTING AROUND

The A19 connects
Palermo and Catania, the A18
links Catania and Messina and the
A20 (Palermo to Messina) is under construction. The west is accessible from Palermo
on the A29. Ferry routes run from Messina
to Reggio di Calabria, and from Palermo
to Genoa or Naples. Between the larger
towns, train services are efficient, but for
smaller towns the buses are better. Catania
and Palermo have international airports.

The scenic town of Cefalù, dominated by a huge rock

Palermo ❶

Mosaic detail from Cappella Palatina

NESTLING ON THE protective flank of Monte Pellegrino with Monte Alfano to the east, Palermo lies in a natural amphitheatre called the Conca d'Oro (Golden Shell). Against La Cala harbour, the setting is beautiful and the city, a mix of oriental and European, is without equal despite reduced circumstances. The architecture, ranging in style from Arabic to Norman, Baroque and Art Nouveau, is without comparison in Sicily, making this exotic city an exciting place to explore.

Ruined cloister with the red domes of San Giovanni degli Eremiti behind

🏛 San Giovanni degli Eremiti

Via dei Benedettini. 📞 091 651 50 19. ◯ daily (only am on Sun). 🏷
Reflecting Islamic architectural tradition with bulbous domes, corner arches and filigreed windows, this deconsecrated Norman church (1132–48) was built in the grounds of a mosque. Beyond church and mosque, a ruined cloister from a 13th-century monastery encloses a pretty garden.

🏛 Palazzo Reale

Piazza Indipendenza. 📞 091 705 43 17. Book in advance. **Palazzo Reale** ◯ Mon, Fri, Sat. 📞 091 656 17 32. **Cappella Palatina** ◯ Sun–Fri. 🔴 Easter, 25 Apr, 1 May, 26 Dec. 🏷
Also called the Palazzo dei Normanni, this site has been the focus of power since the days of Byzantine rule and is now home to Sicily's regional government. The nucleus of the present building was constructed by the Arabs, but after the Norman conquest of the city in 1072, it was enlarged and embellished for the Norman court. See the luxurious royal apartments, especially the Sala di Ruggero, and the splendid Cappella Palatina. Built by Roger II (1132–40), this dazzling chapel blends Byzantine, Islamic and Norman styles of craftsmanship. It is lavishly adorned with fine mosaics, as well as marble inlaid with gold, stone and glass. Next to the palace is the eccentrically decorated Porta Nuova (1535).

🏛 Gesù

Piazza Casa Professa.
◯ daily (only am on Sun).
In the poor, bomb-devastated Albergheria quarter, near the colourful market of Piazza Ballarò, lies this important Baroque church (1564–1633). Also known as the church of the Casa Professa, the interior is an excellent example of the virtuosity of Sicilian craftsmen in the treatment of marble carving and inlay. The oldest Jesuit church in Sicily, it was heavily restored after suffering extensive damage in World War II.

Sumptuous interior of the Cappella Palatina, Palazzo Reale

Duomo's exterior displaying a mixture of styles

VISITORS' CHECKLIST

730,000. ✈ Punta Raisi
32 km (20 miles) W. 🚆 Stazione
Centrale, Piazza Giulio Cesare.
🚌 Via Balsamo. 🚢 Stazione
Marittima, Molo Vittorio Veneto.
ℹ Piazza Castelnuovo 35 (091
58 38 47). 🛒 Mon–Sat. 🎉 U
Festinu for the city's patron saint,
S Rosalia: 10–15 Jul; Pilgrimage
to grotto of Santa Rosalia: 4 Sep;
Greek Orthodox celebrations in
Martorana church: Easter.

🏛 Duomo

Via Vittorio Emanuele. 📞 091 33 43
76. ☐ daily. ♿ 🎫 for Treasury.
Founded in 1184 by the Archbishop of Palermo, the
Duomo displays many
architectural styles. The
exterior shows the
development of
the Gothic style
from the
13th–14th
centuries.

The south
porch (1453) is a
masterpiece of the Catalan
style, and at the apse end,
sturdy Norman work can be
seen through a decorative
Islamic-inspired overlay.
The dome is 18th century.
Within the much-altered
interior are the tombs of
Sicily's kings. Squeezed into
an enclosure by the south
porch are the remains of
Emperor Frederick II; his wife,
Constance of Aragon; his
mother, Constance, daughter
of Roger II (also entombed
here), and his father, Henry
VI. The Treasury houses the
12th-century Imperial Diadem
of Constance of Aragon,
which was removed from her
tomb in the 18th century.

**Fontana Pretorio with Santa
Caterina in the background**

🏛 Santa Caterina

Piazza Bellini. ⬤ for restoration.
Although begun in 1566, most
of the internal decoration of
this unique church dates from
the 17th and 18th centuries.
A powerful example of the
Palermitan Baroque, it over-
whelms with colours, textures,
sculpture and marble inlay.
There are illusionistic ceiling
frescoes (18th century) by
Filippo Randazzo in the nave
and Vito d'Anna in the dome.
The church is flanked by
Piazza Pretorio, which is
dominated by the monumental
Mannerist Fontana Pretorio,
erected here in 1544.

SIGHTS AT A GLANCE

KEY

🅿	Parking
🕆	Church

0 metres   250

0 yards   250

Exploring Palermo

Eᴀsᴛ ᴏꜰ ᴛʜᴇ Quattro Canti, where Via Maqueda and Corso Vittorio Emanuele meet, the city is sprinkled with ornate palaces and more churches. Squeezed behind them are labyrinthine medieval quarters where ancient buildings with crumbling fabric still survive.

La Martorana

Piazza Bellini. 091 616 16 92.
daily (only am on Sun).

Also called Santa Maria dell' Ammiraglio, this church was built around 1140 by George of Antioch, Roger II's admiral and also an orthodox Greek Christian. The design derives from Norman and Islamic traditions with mosaics possibly by Greek artisans. In the right aisle, King Roger receives the Imperial Diadem from Christ; in the left aisle, George of Antioch is portrayed.

A nearby convent, founded by Eloisa Martorana in 1193, was the site where the Sicilian Parliament met in 1295 and decided, in the wake of the Sicilian Vespers, to hand the crown of Sicily to Frederick of Aragon. The church was presented to the convent in 1433.

Mosaic of Christ with Four Angels in the dome of La Martorana

Vucciria

Via Roma. daily.

Nowhere is Palermo's Arabic past more apparent than in this medieval casbah-style market which burrows through the ruinous Loggia district below Via Roma. Merchants, hawkers, shoppers and pickpockets crowd an area once the haunt of artisans. The alleys all around are named after their professions, such as silversmiths, dyers and keymakers. This busy market, the largest in Palermo, offers the usual market ware from daily objects to junk, as well as a wide selection of fresh fruit, vegetables and fish.

Stuccoed interior of the Oratorio del Rosario di San Domenico

Oratorio del Rosario di San Domenico

Via Bambinai 2. 091 32 05 59.
Mon–Sat (only am on Sat).

The interior of this tiny 16th-century chapel displays elegant Baroque decoration by the master of stucco, Giacomo Serpotta. Created around 1720–30, this was his latest and possibly his finest work. Serpotta's technical virtuosity, not to mention the sensory indulgence and whimsical fantasy in evidence here, is remarkable. The altarpiece is the famous *Madonna of the*

Rosary (1624–8) by Anthony Van Dyck, and there are wall paintings by Luca Giordano and Pietro Novelli.

San Domenico

Piazza San Domenico. 091 32 95 88. daily (only am Mon–Fri).
Museo del Risorgimento
091 58 27 74. Mon, Wed, Fri. Jul & Aug.

Although the present building was begun in 1640, there has been a Dominican church on the site since the 14th century. Tommaso Maria Napoli, one of the masters of Sicilian Baroque, created the exuberant church façade (1726) and square in front (1724).

Within, the most interesting feature is Antonello Gagini's bas-relief of *Santa Caterina* (1528) in the third chapel on the left. Next to the church is the 14th-century cloister, part of the original monastery which gives access to the Museo del Risorgimento.

Museo Archeologico Regionale

Piazza Olivella 24. 091 58 27 74.
daily (only am Sat–Mon, Wed–Thu).

Housed in a former monastery of the Filippini, Sicily's most important museum contains sculpture, architectural fragments and ceramics, bronzes, glassware, jewellery, weapons and terracottas. The collection is taken from the island's Phoenician, Greek and Roman sites of antiquity – Tindari, Termini Imerese, Agrigento, Siracusa, Selinunte and Mozia. The highlights are sculptures from the friezes of the ancient Greek temples at Selinunte.

Palermo's noisy, bustling Vucciria market east of Via Roma

🔒 Oratorio del Rosario di Santa Cita

Via Valverde 3. 🎫 091 33 27 79.
🕐 Mon–Sat (only am on Sat).

This small chapel is dedicated to the Virgin of the Rosary after her miraculous intervention at the Battle of Lepanto (see pp54–5). The stucco relief decoration, again, is the work of Giacomo Serpotta (after 1688): the panel on the rear wall depicts the battle, and other reliefs show scenes from the New Testament, all portrayed with extravagant realism. The neighbouring 16th-century church of Santa Zita, from which the oratory takes its name, is filled with sculptures by Antonello Gagini (1517–27).

Ornate interior of the Oratorio di Santa Cita

🔒 Oratorio di San Lorenzo

Via Immacolatella 5. 🕐 daily am.

Lining the walls of this tiny oratory are incredible stucco scenes from the lives of St Francis and St Lawrence, and allegorical figures and putti by Giacomo Serpotta (1699–1706). These remarkable, expressive works exhibit the virtuosity of their creator in the handling of his medium. Caravaggio's Nativity with St Francis and St Lawrence (1609) graced the space above the altar until it was stolen in 1969. The oratory lies hidden next to the medieval church of San Francesco d'Assisi (13th century), which is brimming with excellent sculpture. The undoubted highlight of the church is the triumphal arch (1468) by Pietro da Bonitate and Francesco Laurana in the Cappella Mastrantonio.

The Palazzina Cinese (c.1799) set in the Parco della Favorita

🏛 Palazzo Abatellis and Galleria Regionale di Sicilia

Via Alloro 4. 🎫 091 623 00 11.
🕐 daily am (Tue & Thu also pm). 🔲

Matteo Carnelivari built this palace combining Spanish late-Gothic and Italian Renaissance styles in the 15th century. It is home to the Galleria Regionale di Sicilia, which houses Antonello da Messina's Vergine Annunziate (1476), Francesco Laurana's marble head of Eleanor of Aragon (15th century), and sculptures by the Gagini. Nearby, the 15th-century church of Santa Maria degli Angeli (or La Gancia) contains works by Antonello Gagini and Giacomo Serpotta.

Vergine Annunziate (1476) by da Messina in the Galleria Regionale

🔒 La Magione

Via Magione 44. 🎫 091 617 05 96.
🕐 daily. ♿

Restorations have revealed the ancient structure of this church which was badly damaged in World War II. It was founded in 1150 by Matteo d'Aiello, Roger II's chancellor. With its simple, tall nave flanked by fine Gothic columns, La Magione is a major feature of any tour of Norman Sicily.

♣ Villa Giulia

Via Abramo Lincoln. 🕐 daily. ♿
Orto Botanico 🎫 091 623 82 41.
🕐 daily. ● public hols. ♿

The formal gardens of the villa were established in the 18th century. Once, with their statues and fountains, they exotically evoked the antique world. Nowadays, the tropical flora and faded grandeur make them a delightful setting for walks. In the adjacent Orto Botanico (botanical gardens) there are magnificent tropical plants. In Léon Dufourny's Neo-Classical Gymnasium (1789), plant specimens can be examined. Villa Giulia is the city's only central park and has good childrens' facilities.

♣ Parco della Favorita

Entrance on Piazza Leoni & Piazza Generale Cascino. 🕐 daily. ♿ Museo Etnografico Siciliano Pitré, Via Duca degli Abruzzi 1. 🎫 091 740 48 93.
🕐 Sat–Thu. ● Fri, public hols. 🔲

This park, laid out as a hunting ground in 1799 by the Bourbon Ferdinand IV, was surrounded by summer villas of the aristocracy. One of these, the Palazzina Cinese (c.1799), was built in a Chinese style for Ferdinand III and Maria Carolina, the sister of Marie Antoinette.

The Museo Etnografico Siciliano Pitré, in the stables of the Palazzina Cinese, has an outstanding collection of objects from Sicilian life.

Monreale ❷

Capital from cloister column

M AGNIFICENTLY ADORNED, and with a splendid view of the Conca d'Oro, the Duomo at Monreale is one of the great sights of Norman Sicily. Founded in 1172 by the Norman King William II, it flanks a monastery of the Benedictine Order. The interior of the cathedral glitters with mosaics carried out by Sicilian and Byzantine artists – the inspiration of a king who wanted to rival the power of the Archbishop of Palermo. Like Cefalù, and later Palermo, it was to serve as a royal sepulchre.

★ Christ Pantocrator
The cathedral's Latin-cross plan focuses on the imposing mosaic of the all-powerful Christ (12th–13th century).

Nave and aisles separated by Roman columns

Magnificent gilded wood ceiling

Apse Exterior
With their rich multi-coloured ornamentation in tufa and marble, the three apses represent the apogee of Norman decoration.

Entrance to Cappella del Crocifisso and Treasury

Original Cosmati floor in choir

The royal tomb of William II, in white marble, flanks the porphyry tomb of William I in the corner of the transept.

Barisano da Trani's bronze door (1179) on the north side is shielded by a portico designed by Gian Domenico and Fazio Gagini (1547–69).

★ Mosaic Cycle
Completed in 1182, the rich mosaics show scenes from the Old Testament (nave), Teachings of Christ (aisles, choir and transepts), and the Gospels (side apses). The story of Noah's Ark is depicted here.

★ Cloisters
A masterpiece of Norman artistic expression from the time of William II, the columns – plain, carved or inlaid with richly lustred tiles – support elaborate capitals from which spring Saracenic-style arches.

VISITORS' CHECKLIST

Piazza Vittorio Emanuele. 809, 8/9 & many others going W.
Church 091 640 44 13.
8am–7pm daily.
Cloister 091 640 44 03.
Apr–Sep: 9am–7pm Mon–Fri, 9am–12:30pm Sat & Sun; Oct–Mar: 9am–1pm Mon–Fri (also: 3–5pm Mon & Thu), 9am–12:30pm Sat & Sun. for Treasury.

The south wall and cloisters survive as elements from the Benedictine monastery.

Small Oriental-inspired fountain

Column Detail
Craftsmen from Campania, Puglia, Lombardy and Sicily worked on the cloister columns. The detail here shows Adam and Eve.

The 18th-century porch is surrounded by two squat towers.

Bronze Door Panel
Bonanno da Pisa's fine bronze door (1185), signed by him, depicts 42 scenes from the Bible set within elaborate borders. The lion and griffin are symbols of the Norman kingdom.

STAR FEATURES
★ Cloisters
★ Mosaic Cycle
★ Christ Pantocrator

Bagheria ❸

Palermo. 🏠 *40,000.* 🚊 🚌
ℹ️ *Comune di Bagheria, Piazza IV
Novembre (091 90 90 20).* 🚆 *Wed.*

Today Bagheria is almost a
suburb of Palermo, though
open countryside with olive
and orange groves once
separated them. In the 17th
century Giuseppe Branciforte,
Prince of Butera, built a
summer retreat here, starting
a fashion that was quickly
followed by other Palermitan
aristocrats. The town's core is
sprinkled with their Baroque
and Neo-Classical villas.

The **Villa Palagonia** was
designed in 1705 by the
architect Tommaso Maria
Napoli for Ferdinando
Gravina, the Prince
of Palagonia. It has
remarkable architectural
qualities: a complex
open-air staircase leads
to the first floor, and
the principal rooms,
all with unusual shapes,
are arranged around a
curved axis. A later prince
adorned the perimeter wall
with the grotesque stone
monsters which amused the
18th-century traveller Patrick

**Stone figure on
Villa Palagonia**

Brydone, and horrified Goethe,
who also travelled here and
called this the "Palagonian
madhouse". Across
the piazza are **Villa
Valguarnera** (begun
in 1713 by Napoli), set
in its own park, and
Villa Trabia (mid-18th
century), but neither is
open to the public.
Villa Cattolica (18th
century) houses a
modern art gallery.

🏛 **Villa Palagonia**
Piazza Garibaldi 3. **[** *091 93 20 88.*
◻ *daily.* 📷
🏛 **Villa Cattolica**
Via Consolare. **[** *091 90 54 38.*
◻ *Tue–Sun.* 📷

Fishing and pleasure boats moored in the harbour of Trapani

Trapani ❹

🏠 *73,000.* 🚊 🚌 🛳 ℹ️ *Piazza
Saturno (0923 290 00).*
🚆 *daily.*

Old Trapani occupies a
narrow peninsula. The
best buildings in this lively
quarter are the churches, especially the **Cathedral of San
Lorenzo** (1635) and **Chiesa
del Collegio dei Gesuiti**
(c.1614–40). The façades of
both, and that of the **Palazzo
d'Ali** (17th century) on Via
Garibaldi, display magnificently
the curious ebullience of west
Sicilian Baroque architecture.

The 17th-century **Purgatorio**
on Via San Francesco d'Assisi
contains 18th-century *Misteri* –
realistic, life-sized wooden
statues used annually in the
Good Friday procession. **Santa
Maria del Gesù** on Via Sant'
Agostino should be visited for
the *Madonna degli Angeli* by
Andrea della Robbia (1435–
1525) and Antonello Gagini's
canopy (1521). In the Jewish
quarter, west of Via XXX
Gennaio, the **Palazzo della
Giudecca** (16th century) has a
strangely textured façade.

The **Museo Pepoli** has a
comprehensive collection of
local antiquities. Of greatest
interest are the coral objects
and the Christmas crib figures
(presepi), modern versions of
which are made here. Next to
the museum, the **Santuario di
Maria Santissima Annunziata**
contains the *Madonna di
Trapani*, a statue revered by
fishermen and sailors for its
legendary miraculous powers.

🏛 **Museo Pepoli**
Via Conte Agostino Pepoli. **[** *0923
55 32 69.* ◻ *daily.* 📷

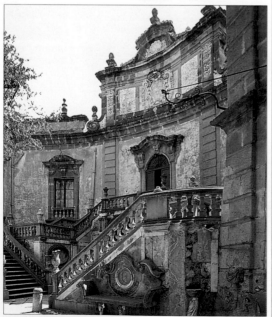
Open-air staircase of the eccentric Villa Palagonia in Bagheria

Erice ❺

Trapani. 🏛 29,000. 🚌 ℹ Viale Conte Pepoli 11 (0923 86 93 88). 🗓 Mon.

POISED ON A CRAG overlooking Trapani, the medieval town of Erice was once the seat of the cult of the fertility goddess Venus Erycina. Her temple stood on the present site of the Norman castle (**Castello di Venere**), beyond the **Villa Balio** public gardens. On a clear day, you can see all the way to Tunisia from the castle. The ancient town of Eryx was renamed Gebel-Hamed by the Arabs, Monte San Giuliano by the Normans and finally Erice in 1934 by Mussolini.

The **Duomo** (14th century) has a 15th-century porch and an earlier battlemented campanile. Inside is a lovely *Madonna and Child* (c.1469), attributed to either Francesco Laurana or Domenico Gagini. In the deconsecrated 13th-century **San Giovanni Battista** on Viale Nunzio Nasi are Antonello Gagini's *St John the Evangelist* (1531) and Antonino Gagini's *St John the Baptist* (1539). **San Cataldo**, a plain 14th-century building on Via San Cataldo, contains a holy water stoup from Domenico Gagini's workshop (c.1474). The **Museo Cordici** houses Antonello Gagini's *Annunciation* (1525) and an interesting variety of Classical remains.

🏛 Museo Cordici
Piazza Umberto I. 📞 0923 86 91 72. 🕐 Mun–Fri am (Tue & Thu also pm). ⬤ public hols.

A typical medieval street in the small hill-town of Erice

SICILIAN ISLANDS

Surrounding Sicily are several island groups. The Isole Eolie or Lipari (Aeolian Islands), to which Panaria, Lipari, Vulcano and Stromboli belong, are a mass of extinct, or nearly extinct, volcanoes poking out of the sea off the coast of Milazzo. The Isole Egadi (Egadi Islands), off the coast of Trapani, have a distinctly Arabic flavour. They include Favignana, Levanzo (which has Palaeolithic and Neolithic paintings and drawings), and Marettimo – the smallest and most unspoilt. Ustica, renowned for its marine life and popular among divers, lies north of Palermo. To the south are the remarkably tourist-free Isole Pelagie (Pelagic Islands) – Lampedusa and Linosa, which are North African in character. Remote Pantelleria lies closer to Tunisia than to Sicily.

The biggest and most popular of the Isole Eolie is Lipari, which has a pretty port and a good range of bars, restaurants and hotels. Nearby sulphur-scented Vulcano offers hot mudbaths and black beaches.

Favignana, the largest and most populous of the Isole Egadi, is the scene of the traditional tuna slaughter – la mattanza. This takes place, as it has for centuries, in May. These fishermen are bringing in the nets following the slaughter.

Part of the Isole Pelagie, Lampedusa was once owned by the family of Giuseppe Tomasi di Lampedusa, author of The Leopard, Sicily's most famous novel. The island is nearer to Malta than Sicily and has clean water and great beaches.

Marsala ●

Trapani. 🏛 *85,000.* 🚇 🚌 ⛴ ℹ
Via XI Maggio 100 (0923 71 40 97).
⛴ *Tue.*

THE PORT OF MARSALA is the
home of a thick,
strong, sweet wine
which has been in
production here since
the 18th century. In
1798 Admiral Nelson
ordered vast quantities of
it following the Battle of
the Nile. Its early manu-
facture was presided
over by three British
families living in Sicily.
One of the old ware-
houses where the wine
was produced is now
the **Museo
Archeologico di
Baglio Anselmi**,
housing important
Phoenician artifacts.

Among other
important attractions
are the ruins of **Lilybaeum**,
an outpost of the Phoenician
Empire, founded in 397 BC. It
was peopled by the survivors
of the massacre by Dionysius I
of Siracusa at Mozia (ancient
Motya) – the island used by
the Phoenicians as a commercial centre. Best of all are the
unique reconstructed remains
of a Punic ship thought to
have been active in the First
Punic War (263–241 BC).
The **Museo di Mozia** in the
Whitaker villa contains a
remarkable early 5th-century
BC statue of a Greek youth.

The excavations here are
important; what we know of
the Phoenicians today comes

mostly from the Bible, and
from Mozia. The **Duomo**,
begun in the 17th century, was
built on the site of an earlier
church; both were dedicated to
Marsala's patron saint,
Thomas Becket of
Canterbury. Its interior is
full of sculptural works
by members of the
Gagini family. The
small **Museo degli
Arazzi**, behind the
Duomo, contains several
magnificent 16th-century
Brussels tapestries.

*Statue of a
Greek youth in
Museo di Mozia*

🏛 **Museo Archeologico
di Baglio Anselmi**
Via Lungomare. 📞 *0923 95
25 35.* ⛴ *daily.* ♿
🏛 **Museo degli Arazzi**
Via Garappa. 📞 *0923 71 29
03.* ⛴ *Tue–Sun.* 📷
🏛 **Museo di Mozia**
Isola di Mozia. 📞 *0923 71
25 98.* ⛴ *daily.* 📷 ♿

Segesta ●

Trapani. 🚌 *from Trapani & Palermo.*
📞 *0924 95 23 56.* ⛴ *9am–1 hr
before sunset.*

ACCORDING TO LEGEND, the
ancient town of Segesta –
still largely unexcavated – was
founded by Trojan followers of
Aeneas. It presents one of the
most spectacular sights on the
island: a massive unfinished
temple stranded on a remote
hillside. Its construction was
started between 426 and 416
BC, and it was left incomplete
following the devastation of
Selinunte by the Carthaginians
in 409 BC. Archaeologists

regard the temple as a good
example of "work in progress".
Nearby, close to the summit of
Monte Barbaro, the ruins of an
ancient theatre (3rd century
BC) can be visited. Summer
concerts are now held here.

Selinunte ●

Trapani. 📞 *0924 462 77.*
🚇 *Castelvetrano then bus.*
⛴ *9am–1 hr before sunset. Ticket
office closes at 7pm.* 📷

FOUNDED IN 651 BC, Selinunte
became one of the great
cities of Magna Graecia – the
part of southern Italy that was
colonized by ancient Greece –
and its toppled ruins are
among Sicily's most important
historic sites. Its ancient name,
Selinus, derives from the wild
celery that still grows here. The
city was an important port, and
its wall defences can still be
seen around the Acropolis. The
Carthaginians, under Hannibal,
completely destroyed the city
in 409 BC in a battle famous
for its epic and spectacularly
savage proportions.

While the city itself has
virtually disappeared, eight of
its temples are distinguishable,
particularly the so-called
Eastern Temples (E, F and
G). Of these, the columns of
huge Doric **Temple E** (490–
480 BC) have been partially
re-erected. **Temple F** (c.560–
540 BC) is in ruins. **Temple G**
(late 6th century BC), which
had 17 massive side columns,
was one of the greatest Greek
temples ever built.

Higher on the Acropolis lie
the remains of **Temples A, B,
C, D and O**. Metope sculpture
from **Temple C** (early 6th
century), originally located
on the frieze between the
triglyphs, can be seen in the
Museo Archeologico Regionale
in Palermo *(see p512)*, along
with ceramics, jewellery and
other artifacts excavated here.
A small **museum** on site
houses less important finds,
as does one in Castelvetrano,
14 km (8.5 miles) north of
Selinunte. The ancient city is
still being excavated; its
North Gate entrance is well
preserved and further north
there is also a **necropolis**.

The spectacularly situated, unfinished Doric temple at Segesta

Cefalù **❾**

Palermo. **👥** *14,000.* **FS** **🚌** **ℹ** *Corso Ruggero 77 (0921 42 10 50).* **🛒** *Sat.*

T HIS PRETTY, unspoilt seaside town, with good beaches and many restaurants and hotels, is dominated by a huge rock known as **La Rocca** – once the site of a Temple of Diana – and by one of the finest Norman cathedrals in Sicily. Begun in 1131 by Roger II, the **Duomo** was intended as the principal religious seat in Sicily. Though it failed to fulfil this function, the building's magnificence has never been eclipsed. Its splendid mosaics (1148), which feature a huge image of Christ Pantocrator in the apse, are remarkable and often celebrated as purely Byzantine works of art on Sicilian soil.

The **Museo Mandralisca** houses a fine *Portrait of a Man* (c.1465) by Antonello da Messina and an interesting collection of coins, ceramics, vases, minerals and shells.

🏛 Museo Mandralisca
Via Mandralisca. **📞** *0921 42 15 47.* **🕐** *daily; Sun & public hols am only.* **📷**

The lavish apse of Cefalù's Duomo

Agrigento **❿**

👥 *57,000.* **FS** **🚌** **⚓** **ℹ** *Via Empedocle 73 (0922 203 91); Via Cesare Battisti 15.* **🛒** *Fri.*

M ODERN AGRIGENTO occupies the site of Akragas, an important city of the ancient Greek world. Founded by Daedalus, according to legend, it was famed for the luxurious lifestyle of its inhabitants, and

The twin-towered façade of the Norman Duomo in Cefalù

was a great power and rival to Siracusa. In 406 BC it fell to the Carthaginians, who sacked and burned it following the flight of its citizens and soldiers.

The historic core of the city, with its medieval streets, focuses on the Via Atenea. **Santo Spirito** (13th century) houses stuccoes by Giacomo Serpotta (1695). **Santa Maria dei Greci** was built on the remains of a 5th-century BC temple – see the flattened columns in the nave. The **Duomo**, founded in the 14th century and altered in the 16th and 17th centuries, exhibits a unique mixture of Arab, Norman and Catalan detailing.

ENVIRONS: The chief reason to visit Agrigento is to see the archaeological zone known as the Valley of the Temples *(see p520)*. The **Museo Regionale Archeologico** houses an interesting display of artifacts from the temples and the city, including a collection of vases, coins and Greek and Roman sculpture.

🏛 Museo Regionale Archeologico
Contrada San Nicola, Viale Panoramica. **📞** *0922 40 15 65.* **🕐** *daily am (also pm on Wed & Sat).* **📷**

THE MAFIA

An international organization founded in Sicily, the Mafia (meaning hostility to law) developed against a background of a cruel State, exploitative nobility and severe poverty. By the late 19th century it had become a criminal organization thriving on property speculation and drug trafficking. Since the "singing" of Tommaso Buscetta and the capture of Toto Riina, the Mafia has been on the defensive against a State that has doubled its efforts against it. Although violence is common, it is not aimed at tourists. Indeed, Sicilians on the whole are known for their hospitality.

Mafia assassination depicted in this scene from the film *The Godfather Part III* **(1990)**

Valley of the Temples

STRADDLING A LOW RIDGE to the south of Agrigento, the Valley of the Temples (Valle dei Templi) ranks among the most impressive complexes of ancient Greek buildings outside Greece. Its Doric temples, dating from the 5th century BC, were destroyed in part by the Carthaginians in 406 BC, in part by Christians, who believed the temples to be pagan, in the 6th century. Later, earthquakes wreaked further havoc on them. Today, nine of the original ten temples are still visible and the whole area can be covered in a day. To avoid crowds, visit early in the morning or in the evening.

Telamone from the Temple of Olympian Zeus

Temple of Hephaistos ①
Apart from a couple of incomplete columns still standing, very little remains of this temple, built c.430 BC. It is also called the Temple of Vulcan.

Sanctuary of the Chthonic Divinities ②
At this group of shrines, the forces of nature were worshipped.

(see p519)
Museo Regionale Archeologico
San Nicola

Hellenistic and Roman Quarter

Temple of Herakles ⑥
This is the oldest temple in the valley (late 6th century BC).

Catacombs

Temple of Olympian Zeus ④
Begun c.480 BC, this was the biggest Doric temple ever built. Unfinished at the time of the Carthaginian attack, it is now a toppled ruin. Giant figures known as telamones were used in its construction.

Temple of Juno ⑧
Built around 450 BC, this temple still has many intact columns.

Tomb of Theron ⑤
Here are the ruins of a Roman tomb (1st century AD).

Temple of Asklepios

San Biagio

Rock Sanctuary of Demeter

Via dei Templi
Strada Panoramica
Via Sacra
N115

Temple of Castor and Pollux ③
This is an incorrect assemblage of pieces from other buildings, erected in the 19th century. Modern Agrigento (see p519) is in the background.

KEY

-- Suggested route

🅿 Parking

— Ancient walls

| 0 metres | 500 |
| 0 yards | 500 |

Temple of Concord ⑦
This beautifully preserved temple (c.430 BC) was converted into a Christian church in the 4th century AD, thus saved from destruction.

Piazza Armerina ⓫

Enna. 22,000. Via Cavour 15 (0935 68 02 01). Thu.

THIS ACTIVE, ebullient provincial town is half medieval and half Baroque. The 17th-century **Duomo**, at its highest point, is the most interesting of the Baroque buildings.

In August, the lively *Palio dei Normanni* festival attracts many visitors, but the real draw are the mosaics in the **Villa Romana del Casale**, 5 km (3 miles) southwest of the town. The mosaics were only excavated in the 20th century.

It is thought that this huge, once sumptuous villa with its public halls, private quarters, baths and courtyards, belonged to Maximianus Herculeus, Diocletian's co-emperor, from AD 286 to 305. His son and successor, Maxentius, probably continued its decoration, with Constantine taking over on Maxentius's death in 312.

Although little remains of the building fabric, the floors are decorated with some of the finest surviving mosaics from Roman antiquity. The hunting, mythological and domestic scenes, and exotic landscapes, all exhibit astonishingly realistic attention to detail.

Villa Romana del Casale
Contrada Paratorre. 0935 68 00 36. daily.

Roman *Girls in Bikinis* mosaic from the Villa Romana del Casale

Enna ⓬

28,000. Piazza Colaianni 6 (0935 50 08 75). Tue.

IMPREGNABLE on a crag above a fertile landscape where Persephone, mythological daughter of Demeter, once played, Sicily's highest town (942 m/3,090 ft) has been coveted by successive invaders since its earliest days. The venerated seat of the Cult of Demeter (Patroness of Fertility) was at Enna. Her temple stood on the **Rocca Cerere**, not far from the huge **Castello di Lombardia** (13th century) built by Frederick II.

Most of Enna's sights are clustered in the old town, among the ancient streets that open out of the Via Roma. The church of **San Francesco** has a 16th-century tower. **Piazza Crispi**, with its fine views to nearby Calascibetta, is dominated by a copy of Bernini's *Rape of Persephone*. The 14th-century **Duomo**, altered in later centuries, contains parts of Demeter's temple.

The **Museo Alessi** houses the Cathedral Treasury and an interesting coin collection. The **Museo Varisano** has exhibits on the area's history, from Neolithic to Roman. Away from the centre, the octagonal **Torre di Federico II** (13th century) is a former watchtower.

ENVIRONS: The ancient hill-town of **Nicosia**, northeast of Enna, was damaged in the 1967 earthquake, but still contains a smattering of churches. San Nicola, built in the 14th century and subsequently haphazardly readorned, has a magnificent, carved entrance portal. Inside there is a much venerated wooden crucifix (17th century) by Fra Umile di Petralia. Santa Maria Maggiore houses a 16th-century marble polyptych by Antonello Gagini and a throne reputedly used by Charles V in 1535. Further east is **Troina**. It was captured in 1062 by the Normans, whose work survives in the Chiesa Matrice. Southeast of Enna, **Vizzini** commands fine views of the countryside.

Museo Alessi
Via Roma 465. 0935 50 31 65. daily.
Museo Varisano
Piazza Mazzini. 0935 50 04 18. daily.

A view from the hills overlooking Vizzini, southeast of Enna

Taormina's magnificently situated Greek theatre, with Mount Etna in the distance

Tindari ⑬

Messina. 🚍 0941 213 27.
🚆 Patti or Oliveri then bus.
🕐 9am–1 hr before sunset daily. ♿

POISED ON THE EDGE of a cliff overlooking the Golfo di Patti are the ruins of **Tyndaris**, almost the last Greek city to have been founded in Sicily (395 BC). Apart from the city walls, the ruins are mostly Roman, including the huge **basilica**, **theatre** and houses. An **antiquarium** houses artifacts from the site.

Tindari is better known for its shrine to a Byzantine icon, the **Black Madonna** on Piazzale Belvedere.

Messina ⑭

🏙 275,000. 🚆 🚍 ⛴ 👔 Piazza Cairoli 45 (090 293 52 92). 🛍 daily.

MESSINA HAS BEEN the victim of earthquakes and the bombs of World War II. The **Museo Regionale** houses many treasures, including works by Antonello da Messina and Caravaggio. **Santissima Annunziata dei Catalani** in Piazza Catalani displays the typical eclecticism of 12th-century Norman architecture, with rich decoration.

It surpasses the **Duomo** (begun 1160) which, despite faithful rebuilding after the war, is a ghost of its former self.

Outside, GA Montorsoli's **Fontana d'Orione** (1547) is the finest fountain of its kind from 16th-century Sicily. His **Fontana di Nettuno** (1557) celebrates Messina's foundation and position in the world as a principal commercial port.

🏛 Museo Regionale
Via della Libertà 465. 🚍 090 36 12 92.
🕐 Mon–Sat am (Tue, Thu & Sat also pm). 📷

Antonello da Messina's *Madonna and Child* (1473), Museo Regionale

Taormina ⑮

Messina. 🏙 10,000. 🚆 🚍
👔 Palazzo Corvaja, Piazza Santa Caterina (0942 232 43). 🛍 Wed.

SPLENDIDLY SITUATED, Taormina is Sicily's best-known resort. It retains an air of exclusivity while being on the tourist trail, with sandy beaches and a wide range of restaurants and hotels.

The most illustrious relic of the past is the **theatre**. Begun in the 3rd century BC by the Greeks, it was subsequently rebuilt by the Romans. Among other Classical remains are the ruins of the **odeon** (for musical performances) and the **naumachia** (an artificial lake for mock-battles). On Piazza Vittorio Emanuele (site of the Roman Forum), **Palazzo Corvaia** (14th century) was built using stone from a temple that once stood here. The 13th-century **Duomo** (renovated in 1636) is a fortress-like building.

ENVIRONS: Taormina's main beach, **Mazzarò,** has a beautiful, clear sea and can be easily reached from the town. South of Taormina at **Capo Schisò** are the ruins of ancient **Naxos**. To the west is **Gole dell'Alcantara**, a 20-m (66-ft) deep gorge of basalt rock, with an ice-cold river and waterfalls

Mount Etna 16

Catania. **FS** *to Linguaglossa or Randazzo; Circumetnea railway from Catania to Riposto.* **🚌** *to Nicolosi.* **ℹ** *Via G. Garibaldi 63, Nicolosi (095 91 15 05).*

EUROPE'S HIGHEST (3,370 m/ 11,050 ft) and most active volcano, Mount Etna was thought by the Romans to have been the forge of Vulcan (god of fire). From Nicolosi a bus takes you to Rifugio Sapienza, from where a cable car goes to 2,700 m (8,900 ft) to a moonscape of solidified lava and black rock. The Circumetnea railway runs around the base from Catania to Riposto.

Catania 17

👥 *365,000.* **✈ FS 🚌 ℹ** *Via Cimarosa 12 (095 73 06 211).* **🛒** *Mon–Sat (general), Sun (antique & bric-a-brac).*

HAVING BEEN DECIMATED by the earthquake of 1693, Catania was comprehensively rebuilt. While it is not exactly

The façade of Catania's Duomo

a beautiful city, it contains some of the most imaginative lava-built Baroque buildings in Sicily. **Piazza del Duomo**, featuring a lava elephant (Catania's symbol) carrying an Egyptian obelisk, offers a dramatic vista to Mount Etna. In 1736 the Norman **Duomo** was given a new façade by Vaccarini, who also worked on the **Municipio** (finished 1741), on the façade of **Sant'Agata** (1748), on the designs of **Collegio Cutelli**, probably

built by a pupil around 1779, and on **Palazzo Valle** (c.1740–50).

Carrying on the Vaccarini tradition is Stefano Ittar's **San Placido** (around 1768). The frenzied stone carving on the **Palazzo Biscari** (early 18th century) is exceeded by Antonino Amato's unrestrained decoration of the vast Benedictine **convent** (1704) and the adjacent huge church of **San Niccolò** (1730).

On Via Vittorio Emanuele is the **Museo Belliniano**, birthplace of composer Vincenzo Bellini (1801–35). The lava ruins of the **Teatro Romano** (21 BC) are at Piazza Stesicono. **Verga's House**, home of the great Sicilian novelist Giovanni Verga (1840–1922), is on Via Sant' Anna. Via Crociferi is home to 18th-century churches **San Francesco Borgia**, **San Benedetto** and **San Giuliano**, whose interior is Vaccarini's masterpiece (1760). Further along Via Crociferi, the church of **Santo Carcere** contains the prison of St Agatha, who was martyred in AD 253.

INFLUENCES ON TRADITIONAL SICILIAN CUISINE

Sicily has one of Italy's most varied cuisines. The island's unique location – marooned between North Africa, Europe and the eastern Mediterranean – and the invaders it attracted, are responsible for this. The earliest Western cookbook, the now lost *Art of Cooking* (5th century BC), was written by Mithaecus, a Siracusan Greek. Sicily's fertility attracted Greek colonists, who exported oil, wheat, honey, cheese, fruit and vegetables to their homeland. The Arabs introduced oranges, lemons, aubergines and sugar cane. Their love of sweet confections inspired *granita*, a form of flavoured ice, and

Marzipan fruits made from almond paste

cassata, an elaborate sponge cake with ricotta and candied fruit. The Sicilians love to claim an Arabic origin for their ice cream, but the Greeks and Romans had created an earlier version by chilling their wine with snow from Mount Etna. Traditionally, the peasants existed on a subsistence diet while

An impressive selection of olives displayed in a Palermo market stall

the aristocracy enjoyed extravagant fare, and one of the peculiarities of Sicilian food today is that it can be both frugal and handsomely ornate. All of the usual Italian dishes are available, but more interesting are the variations using local ingredients like swordfish, sardines, ricotta cheese, red chillies, aubergines, capers, olives and almond paste.

Overlooking the beach at Mazzarò near Taormina

SICILY   527

World War II, but the church survived. It is mostly 17th century with a Norman campanile, and occupies the site where St Lucy, patron saint of Siracusa, was martyred in AD 304. Achradina is now the centre of modern Siracusa.

To the north, in Tyche, is the **Museo Archeologico Regionale Paolo Orsi**, with its important collection of artifacts from the Palaeolithic to the Byzantine era, taken from southeastern sites in Sicily. Included are vases, coins, bronzes, votive objects, busts, sculpture and fragments from Siracusan temples.

The Neapolis quarter and its **Parco Archeologico** feature the Teatro Romano, the Altar of Hieron II and the spectacular Teatro Greco, carved from the hillside. Beyond the Nymphaeum is the 2nd-century AD Roman amphitheatre and the stone quarries – the Latomia del Paradiso featuring the **Ear of Dionysius**. It is thought that 7,000 Athenians were incarcerated here and left to die after their calamitous defeat in 413 BC, in a battle described by Thucydides as "the greatest action in Hellenic history".

ENVIRONS: At **Epipolae**, 8 km (5 miles) north of Neapolis is the **Castle of Euryalus** – the most important ancient Greek fortification to have survived.

🏛 Gallerie Regionale di Palazzo Bellomo
Palazzo Bellomo, Via Capodieci 16.
📞 *0931 696 17.* ⊙ *Tue–Sat am.*
🏛 Museo Archeologico Regionale Paolo Orsi
Viale Teocrito 66. 📞 *0931 46 40 22.*
⊙ *Tue–Sat am.*

Noto ⓴

Siracusa. 🚶 *24,000.* 🚉 🚌 🛈
Piazza XVI Maggio (0931 83 67 44).
🗓 *Mon & 1st & 3rd Tue of the month.*

NOTO WAS BUILT from scratch in the early 18th century to replace Noto Antica, which was devastated by an earthquake in 1693. The town was comprehensively designed in Baroque style, using the local white tufa, a limestone which has turned a honey-brown

The façade of the Duomo in Noto rises above a huge staircase

colour from the hot sun. It is now one of the most enchanting towns in Sicily.

The twin-towered **Duomo** (completed 1770s), which dominates Noto, suffered damage in 1996 when the dome of the main chapel collapsed. The Duomo is attributed to the architect Rosario Gagliardi, who also designed the eccentric tower façade of the seminary of **San Salvatore** (18th century) in Piazza Municipio, the convex façade of **San Domenico** (1730s) in Piazza XVI Maggio

and the oval interior of **Santa Chiara** (1730) on Corso Vittorio Emanuele. The magnificent **Palazzo Trigona** (1781) stands on Via Cavour behind the Duomo. The **Palazzo Villadorata** (1730s) on Via Nicolaci features a splendid façade adorned with elaborate stone carvings. At the north end of Via Nicolaci, the **Monastery of Montevergine** has a striking curved façade. Gagliardi's church of the **Crocifisso** (1728) stands on the town's summit, containing a sculpture of the Madonna by Francesco Laurana (1471). The **Municipio** (1740s), facing the Duomo, has a fine "billowing" ground floor design.

ENVIRONS: The earthquake of 1693 also devastated the towns of **Modica**, around 30 km (19 miles) to the west, and **Ragusa**, a short distance further. Like Noto, they were rebuilt in the region's rich Baroque style. Gagliardi worked on Modica's **San Giorgio** (early 18th century), on Ragusa's **San Giorgio** (begun around 1746, and one of his masterpieces) and **San Giuseppe** (mid-18th century).

Boisterous carving on the façade of the Palazzo Villadorata in Noto

Shorefront in Siracusa, one of the most beautiful cities of the ancient Greek world

Pantalica ⓲

Siracusa. 🚌 *from Siracusa to Sortino then 5 km (3 miles) walk to entrance or bus from Siracusa to Ferla then 10 km (6 miles) walk to entrance.* **Necropolis** 🛈 *Via San Giovanni alle Catacombe 7, Siracusa (0931 46 24 52).* ⭘ *7am–sunset (Oct–Mar: 6pm).* ♿

REMOTE IN THE desolate Monti Iblei and overlooking the River Anapo is the prehistoric **necropolis** of Pantalica – a pleasant place to walk and picnic. The dead of a large, unexcavated village (which was occupied from 13th–8th century BC) were buried here in deep, cave-like tombs cut into the rock. More than 5,000 of these tombs were arranged in tiers with a single flat stone sealing each opening.

The inhabitants of Pantalica are thought to have come from coastal **Thapsos**, which was abandoned after raids by warlike tribes from mainland Italy. The site was re-inhabited in the Byzantine period when some tombs were made into

Rock-cut tombs in the prehistoric necropolis of Pantalica

cave dwellings and chapels. Artifacts from the necropolis are displayed in Siracusa's Museo Archeologico Regionale.

Siracusa ⓳

🏛 *125,000.* 🚆 🚌 🛥 *Via San Sebastiano 45 (0931 677 10).* 🛒 *Wed.*

Interior of Duomo in Siracusa

SIRACUSA (SYRACUSE) was the most important and powerful Greek city from the 5th to the 3rd centuries BC, and, according to the Roman consul Cicero, the most beautiful. The peninsula **Ortigia** is the self-contained hub of the old city. On the mainland, **Achradina**, **Tyche** and **Neapolis** have been occupied almost without a break since the expansion of the city in 480 BC. These were the years of Gelon, tyrant of Gela, when Siracusa was enriched with new temples, theatres and dockyards. The city was a powerful force until 211 BC,

when it fell to the Romans in a battle that also killed the mathematician Archimedes, its most famous inhabitant.

The highlight of Ortigia is the extraordinary **Duomo**, begun in 1728 by architect Andrea Palma. Its Baroque façade masks the **Temple of Athena** (5th century BC), which has been absorbed into the Duomo. Facing the Ponte Nuovo are the ruins of Sicily's earliest Doric temple, the **Temple of Apollo**, which had monolithic columns.

Across from the Duomo is the **Palazzo Beneventano del Bosco** (1778–88), a bold example of Siracusan Baroque, as is **Santa Lucia alla Badia** (1695–1703). In the Municipio a small museum records the history of Ionic temples, and the coin collection of the Galleria Numismatica records Siracusa's past wealth. The delightful **Fonte Aretusa** is frequently referred to by Classical writers as the point where Aretusa emerged from the ground, having been changed into a spring by Artemis to help her escape her lover Alpheus.

At Ortigia's furthest point is the **Castello Maniace**, built by Frederick II around 1239. Here too is the **Gallerie Regionale di Palazzo Bellomo**, with sculpture and paintings including the *Burial of St Lucy* (1608) by Caravaggio.

The painting comes from the church of **Santa Lucia** in the Achradina quarter. This area was flattened during

SARDINIA

I N HIS TRAVELOGUE, Sea and Sardinia, *DH Lawrence wrote that Sardinia was "left outside of time and history". Indeed, the march of time has been slow here, and traditions from ancient Europe have survived – the legacy of invasion by Phoenicians, Carthaginians, Romans, Arabs, Byzantines, Spaniards and Savoyards.*

These traditions are displayed in Sardinia's many festivals – some soberly Christian, others with pagan roots. Several different dialects and languages are spoken in Sardinia. Catalan can be heard in Alghero, and on the island of San Pietro, there is a Ligurian dialect. Even remnants of Phoenician survive. In the south, the traditional influences are Spanish, while pure native strains of people and language survive in the Gennargentu mountains. Peopled by shepherds in isolated communities, this region is so impenetrable that invaders have never bothered it.

Of particular interest are the prehistoric *nuraghe* castles, villages, temples and tombs which litter the countryside – most notably around Barumini, north of Cagliari, and in the Valle dei Nuraghe, south of Sassari. The *nuraghe* were built by a people whose origins constitute one of the Mediterranean's great mysteries. In Cagliari, the capital of Sardinia, there is a museum with an excellent archaeological collection that offers insight into this enigmatic people.

Sassari, Oristano, Alghero and Olbia are all centres of areas marked by their individuality. Some remarkable Pisan-Romanesque churches are located around Sassari and here too dialects reveal close links with the languages of Tuscany. Olbia is a boom town made rich by tourism and the proximity of the jet-setting Costa Smeralda. Sober Nuoro with its province in the shadow of the Gennargentu mountains, by contrast, has little in common with the Sardinia of tourist brochures.

Relaxing during the day in the tiny resort of Carloforte on the Isola di San Pietro, next to Sant'Antioco

◁ **The Bay of Simius east of Cagliari in the southeast corner of Sardinia**

Exploring Sardinia

THIS ISLAND, called Sardegna in Italian, is characterized by an interior of dramatic, rolling uplands covered in *macchia* – grassland mingled with myrtle, wild thyme, prickly pears and dwarf oaks – and a coastline of beguiling, translucent sea, isolated coves, long sandy beaches and caves. The Gennargentu mountains, with the highest peak at 1,834 m (6,017 ft), shield a nearly impenetrable area of rural villages. In the northeast, mountains fall away dramatically to the Costa Smeralda, Sardinia's most exclusive coastal area. Further south, the shoreline around the Golfo di Orosei is completely unspoilt. Around Oristano in the west the land is flat, leading to the plain of Campidano where the island's corn, fruit and vegetables grow.

Prehistoric nuraghic remains at Su Nuraxi near Barumini

SIGHTS AT A GLANCE

Alghero **3**
Bosa **4**
Cagliari **9**
Cala Gonone **6**
Costa Smeralda **1**
Nuoro **5**
Oristano **7**
Sant'Antioco **8**
Sassari **2**

A typical scene of clothes hanging out to dry in Alghero

SEE ALSO

- **Where to Stay** p575

- **Where to Eat** p609

0 kilometres   50

0 miles   25

Waves lapping at the rocks on Isola di San Pietro, northwest of Sant'Antioco

KEY

▬	Major road
▭	Minor road
▱	Scenic route
≈	River
⁂	Viewpoint

Southernmost reach of the Gennargentu mountains

GETTING AROUND

Ferries from a wide range of ports on the Italian mainland dock at Cagliari, Olbia and Porto Torres. International and domestic flights use the airports at Cagliari, Olbia and Alghero. The island is neatly cut by the N131. It skirts the Gennargentu mountains, which are accessible only by tortuously winding passes. Branches of the N131 reach Olbia and Nuoro. Express bus and excellent, fast train services connect the major cities, while slower, daily bus services and narrow-gauge trains operate between the smaller towns.

The extravagantly beautiful, *macchia*-scented Costa Smeralda

Costa Smeralda ➊

Sassari. FS ⛴ Olbia. 🚌 Porto Cervo. 🛈 Via Catello Piro 1, Olbia (0789 214 53).

THE FORMERLY WILD, lonely Costa Smeralda, stretching from the Golfo di Cugnana to the Golfo di Arzachena, was developed at the end of the 1950s by a consortium of magnates, including the Aga Khan, into one of the world's most opulent holiday resorts. Its pristine appearance is now strictly controlled.

In **Porto Cervo**, the main town, boutiques jostle with nightclubs, fine restaurants and luxury hotels. It caters for the seriously rich – billionaires, crowned heads and pop stars.

ENVIRONS: Head north to rural **Baia Sardinia** and **Cannigione**. From **Palau** ferries leave for **La Maddalena** and **Isola Caprera**, the home of Garibaldi and the **Museo Nazionale Garibaldino**.

🏛 **Museo Nazionale Garibaldino**
Frazione Caprera, Maddalena.
📞 0789 73 63 21.
🕐 Tue–Sun (only am in winter).
🔴 1 Jan, 1 May, 25 Dec. 📷 ♿

Sassari ➋

🏘 130,000. ✈ FS 🚌 🛈 Viale Caprera 36 (079 29 95 44). 🔴 Mon.

FOUNDED BY GENOESE and Pisan merchants early in the 13th century, Sassari is known for its spectacular *Cavalcata Sarda* festival on Ascension Day, and for being the site of Sardinia's first university. There is a raucous, tight, church-filled medieval quarter around the **Duomo** (11th century with later, mostly Baroque, additions), and to the north is the huge **Fonte Rosello**, a late-Renaissance fountain. The **Museo Archeologico Nazionale "GA Sanna"** is a good starting point from which to begin an investigation into the region's nuraghic history.

Façade of Santissima Trinità di Saccargia

ENVIRONS: To the southeast along the N131 is the Pisan-Romanesque church of **Santissima Trinità di Saccargia** (1116), with the only extant 13th-century fresco cycle in Sardinia. Further on is the 12th-century church of **San Michele di Salvenero**, and at **Ardara** the basalt-built Romanesque **Santa Maria del Regno**, or "Black Cathedral".

🏛 **Museo Archeologico Nazionale "GA Sanna"**
Via Roma 64.
📞 079 27 22 03.
🕐 Tue–Sun. 📷

Alghero ➌

Sassari. 🏘 41,000. ✈ FS 🚌 ⛴
🛈 Piazza Porta Terra 9 (079 97 90 54).
🔴 Wed.

FOUNDED ON A PENINSULA facing the Bay of Alghero early in the 12th century, and taken from the Genoese Dorias by the Aragonese in 1353, Alghero was peopled by settlers from Barcelona and Valencia. Its original occupants – Ligurians and Sardinians – were expelled with such thoroughness that today the Catalan language and culture is enjoying a revival and the look of old Alghero is consistently Spanish.

Filled with labyrinthine alleys and cobbled streets, the lively port of old Alghero is flanked by battlemented walls and defensive towers on all but the landward section. Facing the Giardino Pubblico is the massive 16th-century **Torre di Porta Terra**, also known as the Jewish Tower after its builders. Around the periphery of the old town are more towers, including **Torre dell'Espero Reial** and **Torre San Giacomo** on Lungomare Colombo, and **Torre della Maddalena** on Piazza Porta Terra. The 16th-century **Duomo** at the bottom of Via Umberto is predominantly Catalan-Gothic with an Aragonese portal. Off Via Carlo Alberto, **San Francesco** (14th century)

A typical house in Alghero

The waterfront at Bosa

NURAGHE IN SARDINIA

The dominant feature of Sardinia is the 7,000 or so *nuraghe* dotted around the island. Dating from 1800 to 300 BC, these strange, truncated cone structures were built without any bonding from huge basalt blocks taken from extinct volcanoes. To this day, little is known about the identity of the nuraghic people. They must have been well organized and possessed remarkable engineering skills, judging by their buildings, but appear to have left no written word. The mystery of these enigmatic people has intrigued Sardinians for years.

The individual nuraghe are fairly small. A few were fortresses, equipped with wells and other defensive features.

Su Nuraxi at Barumini (above), Serra Orrios, near Dorgali, and Santu Antine at Torralba are among the most important nuraghe complexes. Houses, temples, tombs, and even a theatre have been identified.

has a pretty cloister and octagonal campanile towering over Alghero, and Baroque **San Michele** has a bright tiled dome. In Via Principe Umberto is the **Casa Doria**, the house where the pre-Hispanic rulers of Alghero lived. It has a beautiful Renaissance portal and Gothic-arched window.

ENVIRONS: Take a boat or car trip (the latter involves much climbing down) to the spectacular **Grotta di Nettuno**, a deep natural cave round the point of Capo Caccia, or the nearby **Grotta Verde**

Bosa ❹

Nuoro. 🏠 8,500. 🚉 🚌 🚹 *Corso Vittorio Emanuele 59 (0785 37 61 07).* 📅 *Tue*

B OSA IS A SMALL, picturesque seaside town at the mouth of Sardinia's only navigable river, the Temo. The historic **Sa Costa** district struggles up the side of a low hill capped by the **Castello di Serravalle**, built in 1122 by the Malaspina family. The narrow passages and alleys here have changed little since the Middle Ages. By the Temo are **Sas Conzas** – the former dyers' houses and workshops.

Languishing on the riverside, the cosmopolitan **Sa Piatta** district houses the Aragonese-Gothic **Duomo** (15th century) and Romanesque **San Pietro Extramuros** (11th century), with a Gothic façade added by Cistercian monks in the 13th century.

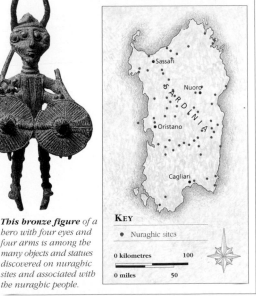

This bronze figure of a hero with four eyes and four arms is among the many objects and statues discovered on nuraghic sites and associated with the nuraghic people.

KEY

● Nuraghic sites

0 kilometres   100

0 miles   50

Nobel Prize-winning novelist Grazia Deledda from Nuoro

Nuoro ❺

🏛 38,000. FS 🚌 ℹ Piazza d'Italia 19 (0784 300 83). 🏪 Fri & Sat.

THIS TOWN, in a spectacular setting beneath Monte Ortobene and the dramatic Supramonte, has been the home of Grazia Deledda, who won the Nobel Prize for Literature in 1926 for her understanding portrayal of the power and passions in the primitive communities around her. A comprehensive collection of ethnic items, such as traditional Sardinian costumes and jewellery, can be seen in the excellent **Museo della Vita e delle Tradizioni Popolari Sarde**. Attending the *Sagra del Redentore* festival is the best way to witness the region's dancing and dialects.

ENVIRONS: Nuoro is on the edge of the Barbagia region, which has isolated villages of shepherds who have never experienced the hand of any overlord, so impenetrable are the **Gennargentu** mountains. This region was known to the Romans as Barbaria, an area they were never able to subdue. Traces of the traditional lawlessness of the Barbagia can be seen in **Orgosolo**, with its wall murals calling for Sardinia's independence. Rival clans were locked in bloody vendetta for almost 50 years, and the deeds of native bandits form part of local folklore.

In **Mamoiada**'s *Feast of the Mamuthones*, men in sinister masks and traditional costume perform a ritual dance ending with a symbolic "killing" of a scapegoat. The passion and fervour of the event is indicative of the survival of a fierce folkloric tradition and deep resistance to change.

🏛 **Museo della Vita e delle Tradizioni Popolari Sarde**
Via Mereu 56. 📞 0784 24 29 00. 🕐 9am–1pm, 3–7pm daily. 🗭

Cala Gonone ❻

Nuoro. 🏛 800. 🚌 ℹ Viale Buemarino (0784 93 61 96). 🏪 daily. 🚢 to grottoes (Apr–mid-Oct). 📞 0784 933 05.

EAST OF NUORO, squeezed between the sea and the base of high mountains, is the hamlet of Cala Gonone – a bustling seaside resort and fishing port, with magnificent beaches. Along the unspoilt coast are the isolated coves of **Cala Luna**, linked with Cala Gonone by a well-marked two-hour trail, and **Cala Sisine**. The famous **Grotta del Bue Marino**, which is adorned with weird rock formations, can only be reached by boat.

ENVIRONS: To the south, the villages of **Urzulei**, **Baunei** and **Santa Maria Navarrese**, along the spectacular SS125 road to Tortolì, feature breathtaking landscapes.

Oristano ❼

Cagliari. 🏛 32,000. FS 🚌 ℹ Piazza Eleonora 19 (0783 368 31). 🏪 Tue & Fri.

Ruins of Tharros near Oristano

THE PROVINCE of Oristano corresponds roughly with historical Arborea, over which Eleonora ruled *(see opposite)*. She is commemorated by an 18th-century statue in **Piazza Eleonora**. On Corso Vittorio Emanuele is the 16th-century **Casa di Eleonora**, and nearby the **Antiquarium Arborense**, which has Neolithic, nuraghic, Punic and Roman artifacts. The **Torre di San Cristoforo** (1291) in Piazza Roma once formed part of Oristano's fortifications. The **Duomo** (13th century) was later rebuilt in the Baroque style. More interesting are the churches of **Santa Chiara** (1343) on Via Garibaldi and 14th-century **San Martino** on Via Cagliari.

ENVIRONS: The 12th-century Pisan-Romanesque **Cathedral** at Santa Giusta has interior columns probably taken from

Entrance to the Grotta del Bue Marino, south of Cala Gonone

The tiny resort of Carloforte, the capital of Isola di San Pietro

Tharros, an 8th-century BC Punic settlement whose extensive ruins lie 20 km (12 miles) west of Oristano on the Sinis peninsula.

🏛 **Antiquarium Arborense**
Piazza Corrias. 📞 0783 79 12 62.
◯ daily. 🏷 🔥

Sant'Antioco ❽

Cagliari. **FS** 🚌 **ℹ** Piazza Repubblica 48 (0781 820 31).

T HE MAIN TOWN on this unspoilt island off Sardinia's southern coast is **Sant'Antioco**, once a Phoenician port and an important Roman base. Proof of almost continuous occupation is clear at the **catacombs**, a Phoenician burial place later used by Christians, under the 12th-century basilica of **Sant' Antioco Martire**. The **Antiquarium** contains Phoenician artifacts. The Punic **Tophet** (sanctuary of the goddess Tanit) and the **necropolis** are nearby. The small **Isola di San Pietro** can be reached by ferry from Calasetta.

♁ **Catacombs**
Piazza Parrocchia.
📞 0781 830 44.
◯ daily. 🎫 only. 🏷
🏛 **Antiquarium**
Via Regina Margherita
113. 📞 0781 835 90.
◯ daily. ● 1 Jan, Easter, 8, 25 & 26 Dec. 🏷

Cagliari ❾

🏃 250,000. ✈ **FS** 🚌 ⛴
ℹ Piazza Matteotti 9 (070 66 92 55).
📅 daily; also Sun (flea) and second Sun of month (antiques).

T HE CAPITAL of Sardinia, this site was occupied by the Phoenicians, Carthaginians and Romans, and extensive ruins of the Phoenician city of Nora lie to the southwest of Cagliari. A 2nd-century **amphitheatre** survives from the Roman era, cut from rock. The best indication of the town's earlier history is to be found in the **Cittadella dei Musei**. Fashioned from the former royal arsenal, it houses several museums including the **Museo Nazionale Archeologico**. The nuraghic items are the most interesting in the collection, especially the bronze votive statuettes. Also in the Cittadella dei Musei is the **Pinacoteca**, an art gallery.

The 6th-century church of San Saturnino in Cagliari, built on a Greek-cross plan

The old core of Cagliari has an appealing North African character. In the high **Castello** district, the Romans and, later, Pisans built defences. The gracious **Bastione San Remy** on Piazza Costituzione offers magnificent views over the city and surrounding countryside. The **Duomo** is a 20th-century rehash of a Romanesque building. Flanking the entrance are two 12th-century pulpits originally destined for the cathedral in Pisa.

Nearby is the Pisan tower **Torre San Pancrazio** (14th century). From the partially-ruined **Torre dell'Elefante** on Via dell'Università to the port lies the **Marina** quarter, which expanded from the old town in the 16th to 17th centuries. In Piazza San Cosimo, the 6th-century church of **San Saturnino** is a rare monument to Byzantine occupation.

♁ **Amphitheatre**
Viale Sant'Ignazio. 📞 070 411 08.
◯ Tue–Sun.
🏛 **Cittadella dei Musei**
Piazza Arsenale. **Museo Nazionale Archeologico** 📞 070 65 59 11.
◯ Tue–Sun. 🏷 **Pinacoteca** 📞 070 67 40 54. ◯ daily. ● 1 Jan, 1 May, 25 Dec. 🏷 🔥

ELEONORA OF ARBOREA

A champion against rule from abroad, Eleonora was governing *giudicessa* (judge) of Arborea, one of four administrative divisions of Sardinia, from 1383–1404. Her marriage to Brancaleone Doria consolidated Genoese interests in Sardinia. She rallied the island to keep out Spanish invaders who tried to claim land that had been given to the Aragonese King James II. Her greatest legacy was the completion of the codifying of laws begun by her father. Written in Sardinian, they called for community of property in marriage and the right of women to seek redress from rape.

TRAVELLERS' NEEDS

WHERE TO STAY

PEOPLE COME FROM all over the world to visit Italy and most Italians spend their holidays here as well, particularly in the mountains or by the sea. This means that there is a dazzling range of accommodation options, from splendid hotels in old palazzi and historic residences, to simple family-run *pensioni* and hostels. Most major cities also offer up-market B&Bs. Those who want self-catering

Sign for a 3-star hotel

accommodation are also well served with everything from stately villas in Tuscany to purpose-built holiday flats in, or near, seaside resorts. Italian hotels are notorious for being expensive and short of services but you can still find excellent value in all price ranges. The hotels listed on pages 542–75 have been selected from every price category as among the best value in each area for style, comfort or location.

The Gritti Palace, one of Venice's historic palazzi *(see p544)*

GRADINGS

HOTELS IN ITALY are graded with one to five stars. Grading depends on facilities offered rather than atmosphere and each region awards stars according to slightly different criteria.

Sometimes a hotel has a lower rating than it deserves. This may be because the local tourist office has not upgraded it yet or the hotel itself has opted to stay in a lower category to avoid higher taxes.

ALBERGHI

ALBERGO IS ITALIAN for hotel but the term tends to refer to the upper categories. Room sizes vary considerably: in city centres even expensive hotels can have far smaller rooms than their counterparts in other countries, whereas outside the city your room may be more like a small suite. In general, *alberghi*

will have private showers in all rooms and the more luxurious have baths. In city centres you may come across the sign *albergo diurno*. This is a day hotel without accommodation but with bathroom, showers, hairdressing, drying and other cleaning facilities you may need when travelling. Day hotels are usually situated at or near the main railway station.

PENSIONI

ALTHOUGH THE TERM *pensione* is no longer in official use, it still describes one- and two-star hotels, most of which

Street sign showing the direction and location of hotels

are small and family run. On the whole you will meet immaculate standards of cleanliness and friendly, helpful service with basic, although perfectly functional, rooms. However, as *pensioni* are often in old buildings, historic charm may be paid for with noisy, erratic plumbing and dark rooms. Many do not have public rooms other than a sparsely furnished breakfast room. Most will offer at least some rooms with a private shower although rarely a bath. If you intend being out late, check that you'll be able to get back into the *pensione*. Not all of them have night porters after midnight or 1am, but most will at least be able to provide a key to the main door.

If you are planning to stay in a *pensione* in winter, check that it has central heating. Not all of them do and, even in the south, temperatures are low from November to February.

A *locanda* was traditionally an inn, offering cheap food and a place to sleep for the traveller. The word is still in use, particularly in central and northern Italy, but is now synonymous with *pensione* and may be more of an affectation for the benefit of the tourist.

CHAIN HOTELS

THERE ARE VARIOUS Italian chain hotels at the upper end of the market, as well as the usual big internationals. **Ciga** hotels, now part of the Sheraton Corp., have a

◁ Popular café in Piazza Navona, Rome

Romantic Hotel Villa Pagoda in Nervi, Genoa *(see p555)*

turn-of-the-century opulence; **Starwood Westin** and **Best Western** are more akin to the international luxury chains while **Notturno Italiano** cater for the more modest budget. **Relais et Châteaux** run charming hotels in historic castles, villas and monasteries with facilities to match.

MEALS AND FACILITIES

ITALIAN HOTELS TEND to offer fewer special facilities than those in many other countries. In spite of the warm summers, for example, air-conditioning is rare in all but five-star hotels, as is 24-hour room service.

Some hotels may insist on full board *(pensione completa)* or half board *(mezza pensione)* in peak season. Avoid this if you can: unless the hotel is very isolated, there will almost certainly be a good range of places to eat nearby. Most hotel rates include breakfast, which in four- and five-star hotels will consist of a large buffet; the *pensioni* breakfast will probably consist of coffee and biscuits or brioches with butter and jam. Once again, try to avoid this as breakfast at a local bar is an enjoyable Italian institution.

For a double room, state if you want twin beds *(letti singoli)* or a double bed *(matrimoniale)*. Bathrooms in all but the most expensive hotels will have showers rather than baths.

CHILDREN

ITALIANS ACCEPT CHILDREN as an ordinary part of life and, although there may not be many special facilities,

they are always welcome.

Some of the cheaper hotels may not be able to provide cots. However, virtually all hotels, from the simplest to the most grand, will be happy to put a small bed or two into a double room for families travelling together. The price of this is usually an extra 30–40 per cent of the double room rate per bed. Most of the large hotels will also offer a babysitting service.

PRICES

AS A RULE hotels in Italy are not cheap, although prices vary considerably between places and seasons.

Prices, which include tax and service and are quoted per room, start from around 50 euros for a

Hotel Sant'Anselmo's garden, Rome *(see p565)*

double room without a bathroom, and can rise to at least 65 euros with a bath, even for a very basic hotel. A single room will cost about two-thirds of a double. Around 100 euros will get you something comfortable and often picturesque, although not particularly luxurious. For 210 euros and upwards you can expect a good range of facilities, a pleasant or central location and often a lot of local or historic charm.

Hotels in the major cities and resorts are likely to be more expensive.

By law hotels have to display their rates in every bedroom. Variation between high and low season can be as much as 100 per cent or more in resorts.

Also, beware of extras: the mini-bar can be extortionate as can charges for parking, laundry or for making telephone calls directly from your hotel bedroom.

BOOKING

BOOK AS SOON AS possible, particularly if you have special requests such as a room with a view, off the street or with a bath. Two months should be ample, but be aware that, during the high season, popular hotels can be fully booked as early as six months in advance.

August tends to be very busy at beach resorts and February at mountain resorts. The same goes for cities and towns depending on their particular cultural calendars *(see pp62–5)*.

You will be asked for a deposit when you book; this can usually be paid for by credit card (even in hotels that do not accept credit cards for final payment); otherwise by international money order.

Under Italian law the hotel must issue you with a receipt *(ricevuta fiscale)* for final payment which you must keep until you leave Italy.

Florence's Hotel Tornabuoni Beacci *(see p558)*

Vaulted central entrance of Hotel Porta Rossa in Florence *(see p558)*

CHECKING IN AND OUT

ON ARRIVAL the management will take your passport to register you with the police. This is a mere formality and it should be returned within an hour or two. You will also have to authorize the hotel to transfer calls to your room.

Checking-out time is usually before noon and may be earlier in small hotels. The room must be vacated but most hotels will allow you to leave luggage in a safe place to be collected later in the day.

Albergo al Sole, Venice *(see p544)*

SELF-CATERING AND AGRITURISMO

IF YOU INTEND to be based in one area, self-catering accommodation often enjoys a marvellous location and is generally of a high standard.

Across rural Italy there are more than 2,000 farms, villas and mountain chalets offering reasonably priced self-catering or hotel-style accommodation as part of the **Agriturismo** scheme. Facilities range from those of a first-class hotel in

beautifully kept villas or ancient castles to basic rooms with the family on a working farm. Some have excellent restaurants which serve farm and local produce, others can arrange riding, fishing or other activity holidays *(see p624)*. There may be a minimum stay requirement, especially in peak season. The booklet *Guida dell'Ospitalità Rurale* can be found in the central office in Rome or the regional offices. Other self-catering options can be arranged through specialized agencies such as **Tailor-Made Tours**, **Vacanze in Italia** and **Magic of Italy** before you leave for Italy, but again, make sure you book in advance; they can be booked up for months.

There are also so-called *residence*, found in the **ENIT** accommodation lists. These are halfway between a hotel and self-catering flats and often offer cooking facilities and some sort of restaurant service.

For stays of several months or more, accommodation agencies for apartments in the city centre as well as the

nearby countryside can be found under *Immobiliari* in the *Pagine Gialle* (Yellow Pages).

BUDGET ACCOMMODATION

AS WELL AS THE International Youth Hostels Association (**AIG** in Italy), tourist offices in the major cities have lists of privately-run hostels. Prices, at around 8 euros per person per night, are considerably less than even the cheapest *pensioni* but accommodation is in single-sex dormitories and washing facilities may be over-stretched. A room in a private house is another cheap option, offering often small but clean rooms. Bed-and-breakfast accommodation is increasing rapidly but is of variable quality, so only rely on trust-worthy recommendation.

The **Centro Turistico Studentesco** can help students find rooms in university accommodation across Italy. This is not limited to students taking courses, particularly in the summer when resident students are on holiday.

A peaceful alternative is to stay in a convent or monastery with guest accommodation. The rooms are clean, if a little spartan, and they are usually in a secluded area or behind cloister walls. However, strict rules may be a price to pay: most have early curfews and many will not admit members of the opposite sex even when with their spouses. There is no central agency dealing with these but they are included in the **ENIT** accommodation lists for each region.

A suitcase boat carrying visitors' luggage to a hotel in Venice

MOUNTAIN REFUGES AND CAMPSITES

BASIC ACCOMMODATION in huts and refuges is available in mountainous areas where there is hill-walking and hiking. Most of these huts are owned and run by the **Club Alpino Italiano** whose offices are in Rome.

Campsites abound in the mountains and around the coastal regions. Many of them offer basic accommodation in family-sized cabins *(bungalow)* as well as spaces for tents,

Villa San Michele, a former monastery in Fiesole, Tuscany *(see p560)*

The highest refuge in the Valsesia alps, Rifugio Francesco Pastore

caravans and trailers, with basic facilities such as water, electricity and washing. There is usually a restaurant and, especially in campsites by the sea, there may also be sports facilities such as swimming pools, boat and water sports equipment hire and tennis courts. The **Touring Club Italiano** publishes a full list in *Campeggi e Villaggi Turistici in Italia*, as does **Federcampeggio**.

DISABLED TRAVELLERS

FEW HOTELS IN ITALY have special facilities for disabled travellers. Those that do are indicated with the appropriate symbol in the hotels listings on pages 542–75. In many cases, however, hotels without special facilities will do all they can to accommodate people in wheelchairs by giving them downstairs rooms (when available) and help with lifts or stairs.

FURTHER INFORMATION

THE ITALIAN STATE TOURIST office (**ENIT**) has accommodation lists for every region. They are reprinted annually but may not be updated and prices may have changed. Rooms can also be booked at the local **APT** (Azienda Provinciale per il Turismo).

DIRECTORY

GENERAL

ENIT (Ente Nazionale Italiano per il Turismo)
Via Marghera 2–6, 00185 Rome. [06 497 11.
FAX 06 446 99 07.
W www.enit.it

Italian State Tourist Board
1 Princes Street, London W1R 8AY.
[020 7408 1254.
FAX 020 7493 6695.

CHAIN HOTELS

Best Western Hotels
[0800 709 101.
W www.best western.com

Ciga Hotels
Piazza della Repubblica 20, 20124 Milano.

[02 6230 2018.
FAX 02 659 58 38.
W www.sheraton.com

Notturno Italiano
[0578 75 60 70.
FAX 0578 75 60 06.
W www.notturno.it

Relais & Châteaux
W www.relais chateaux.com

Starwood
[0800 35 35 35.
W www.starwood.com

SELF-CATERING

Agriturismo
Corso Vittorio Emanuele II 89, 00186 Rome.
[06 685 23 42.
FAX 06 685 24 24.
W www.agriturist.it

Tailor-Made Tours
22 Church Rise, London SE23 2UD.
[020 8291 9736.
FAX 020 8699 4237.

Magic of Italy
12 Wood Street, Kingston-upon-Thames, Surrey, KT1.
[0870 027 5000.
W www.magictravel group.co.uk

Vacanze in Italia
Bignor, near Pulborough, West Sussex RH20 1QD.
[08700 772772.
FAX 08700 780190.

MOUNTAIN REFUGES AND CAMPSITES

Club Alpino Italiano
Corso Vittorio Emanuele 305, Rome.
[06 68 61 01 11.
FAX 06 68 80 34 24.

Federcampeggio
Via Vittorio Emanuele 11, 50041 Calenzano, Firenze.
[055 88 23 91.
FAX 055 882 59 18.

Touring Club Italiano
Corso Italia 10, 20122 Milano.
[02 852 61.
FAX 02 852 63 62.
W www.touringclub.it

BUDGET ACCOMMODATION

AIG (Associazione Italiana Alberghi per la Gioventù)
Via Cavour 44, 00184 Rome.
[06 487 11 52.
FAX 06 488 04 92.
W www.hostel-aig.org

Centro Turistico Studentesco
Via Genova 16, 00184 Rome.
[06 44 11 11.
FAX 06 46 20 43 26.
W www.cts.it

Choosing a Hotel

THE HOTELS in this guide have been selected from a wide price range for their good value or exceptional location, comfort and style. The chart highlights some of the factors which may influence your choice and gives a brief description of each hotel. Entries are listed by price category within the towns, with colour-coded thumb tabs to indicate the regions covered on each page.

	NUMBER OF ROOMS	RESTAURANT	SWIMMING POOL	GARDEN OR TERRACE
VENICE				
CANNAREGIO: *Abbazia* €€€€ Calle Priuli, 66–68. **Map** 1 C4. **(** 041 71 73 33. **FAX** 041 71 79 49. **@** abbazia@iol.it Quietly situated just off the lively Lista di Spagna area. The rooms are comfortable, and drinks are served in the delightful garden. 🛏 TV 🍽 🌿	39			■
CANNAREGIO: *Giorgione* €€€€ Santi Apostoli, 4587. **Map** 3 B5. **(** 041 522 58 10. **FAX** 041 523 90 92. **@** giorgione@hotelgiorgione.com Well-situated for the Rialto area. This is a recently refurbished hotel in a delightful colour-washed building with a spacious reception area. 🛏 TV 🌿	72			■
CANNAREGIO: *Continental* €€€€€ Lista di Spagna, 166. **Map** 2 D4. **(** 041 71 51 22. **FAX** 041 524 24 32. **@** continental@ve.nettuno.it A large, well-equipped, modern hotel. Some rooms overlook the Grand Canal, while others are quieter with views of a tree-shaded square. 🛏 TV 🍽 🌿	93	■		■
CASTELLO: *Paganelli* €€€€ Riva degli Schiavoni, 4686. **Map** 8 D2. **(** 041 522 43 24. **FAX** 041 523 92 67. **@** hotelpag@tin.it Excellent views of St Mark's Basin from cosy old-fashioned rooms; those situated in the *dipendenza* (annexe) are less attractive but quieter. 🛏 🌿 TV	22			■
CASTELLO: *Pensione Wildner* €€€ Riva degli Schiavoni, 4161. **Map** 8 D2. **(** 041 522 74 63. **FAX** 041 526 56 15. A family-run hotel with simple yet immaculate rooms offering stunning views across to San Giorgio Maggiore. There is also a small bar. 🛏 TV 🍽 🌿	16	■		■
CASTELLO: *Danieli* €€€€€ Riva degli Schiavoni, 4196. **Map** 7 C2. **(** 041 522 64 80. **FAX** 041 520 02 08. This luxurious hotel was the palace of the Dandolo family and has strong literary and musical connections. Service is impeccable. 🛏 TV 🍽 🌿	235	■		■
CASTELLO: *Londra Palace* €€€€€ Riva degli Schiavoni, 4171. **Map** 8 D2. **(** 041 520 05 33. **FAX** 041 522 50 32. **@** info@hotellondra.it A lovely stone-faced hotel: the comfortable bedrooms are very traditional, and are decorated with antique furniture. The best ones are on the lagoon. Tchaikovsky composed his Fourth Symphony here in 1877. 🛏 TV 🍽 🌿	53	■		■
DORSODURO: *Montin* €€ Fondamenta Eremite, 1147. **Map** 6 D3. **(** 041 522 71 51. **FAX** 041 520 02 55. These few rooms above one of Venice's best restaurants (*see p578*) are full of charm and character. Book well ahead of your visit. 🌿	10			■
DORSODURO: *Agli Alboretti* €€€ Rio Terrà Antonio Foscarini, 884. **Map** 6 E4. **(** 041 523 00 58. **FAX** 041 521 01 58. **@** alborett@gpnet.it A great favourite with English and American visitors, this modern hotel has a cosy wood panelled reception area and a warm atmosphere. The pergola is enchanting, and the best rooms look onto the interior gardens. 🛏 TV 🍽 🌿	24	■		■
DORSODURO: *American* €€€€ Fondamenta Bragadin San Vio 628. **Map** 6 E4. **(** 041 520 47 33. **FAX** 041 520 40 48. A comfortable hotel tucked away beside a small canal near the Accademia. The rooms are well-appointed and the management is friendly. 🛏 TV 🍽 🌿	28			■
DORSODURO: *Pausania* €€€€ Rio di San Barnaba, 2824. **Map** 6 D3. **(** 041 522 20 83. **FAX** 041 522 29 89. Offering respite from city life, the reasonable prices and friendly staff make the Pausania a pleasant place to stay during the busy summer months. 🛏 TV 🍽 🌿	26		■	■
LIDO DI VENEZIA: *Villa Mabapa* €€ Riviera San Nicolo 16. **(** 041 526 05 90. **FAX** 041 526 94 41. **@** info@villamabapa.com Originally built as a private residence in the 1930s, this lovely villa on the promenade by the lagoon retains its original style and atmosphere. 🛏 TV 🍽 🌿	70	■		■

			Price categories for a standard double room for one night, including tax and service charges but not including breakfast: € under 52 euros €€ 52–100 euros €€€ 100–155 euros €€€€ 155–205 euros €€€€€ over 205 euros.

RESTAURANT
A restaurant within the hotel sometimes reserved for residents.

SWIMMING POOL
Hotel swimming pools are usually quite small and are outdoors unless otherwise stated.

GARDEN OR TERRACE
A garden, courtyard or terrace belonging to the hotel, often providing tables for eating outside.

CREDIT CARDS
The major credit cards VISA, MasterCard (Access) and American Express are accepted in hotels with the credit card symbol.

Hotel	NUMBER OF ROOMS	RESTAURANT	SWIMMING POOL	GARDEN OR TERRACE
LIDO DI VENEZIA: *Excelsior Palace* €€€€€ Lungomare Marconi 41. ☎ 041 526 02 01. FAX 041 526 72 76. @ res077.excelsion@westin.com A flamboyantly Moorish exterior (even the beach huts are styled like Arabian tents); the service and comfort of the interior are equally splendid. 🛏 📺 ▤ 🌣	197	■	●	■
LIDO DI VENEZIA: *Hotel des Bains* €€€€€ Lungomare Marconi 17. ☎ 041 526 59 21. FAX 041 526 01 13. @ res078_desbains@sheraton.com This was the setting for Luchino Visconti's film *Death in Venice* and it was here that Thomas Mann wrote the original novel. Reception rooms are in Art Deco style, bedrooms are spacious and service superb. 🛏 📺 ▤ 🌣	191	■	●	■
RIALTO: *Rialto* €€€€ San Marco 5149. **Map** 7 A1. ☎ 041 520 91 66. FAX 041 523 89 58. @ info@rialtohotel.com From its spectacular position by the Rialto bridge, the hotel looks out onto the bustle of the city centre and graceful gondolas. 🛏 📺 ▤ 🌣	79	■		■
SAN MARCO: *Ai Do Mori* €€ Calle Larga San Marco, 658. **Map** 7 B2. ☎ 041 528 92 93. FAX 041 520 53 28. This friendly little pensione is clean and characterful and offers good value. Some rooms have superb views. 🛏 📺 ▤ 🌣	11			
SAN MARCO: *Al Gambero* €€ Calle dei Fabbri, 4687. **Map** 7 B2. ☎ 041 522 43 84. FAX 041 520 04 31. @ hotgamb@tin.it Situated on one of Venice's main shopping streets, close to the piazza, the Gambero has simple rooms, several with views over the canal. 📺 ▤ 🌣	27	■		
SAN MARCO: *La Fenice et des Artistes* €€€ Campiello Fenice, 1936. **Map** 7 A2. ☎ 041 523 23 33. FAX 041 520 37 21. @ fenice@fenicehotels.it This pretty hotel is made up of two houses joined together by a small patio. Rooms are comfortable and furnished with antiques. 🛏 📺 ▤ 🌣	68			■
SAN MARCO: *Santo Stefano* €€€ Campo Santo Stefano, 2957. **Map** 6 F3. ☎ 041 520 01 66. FAX 041 522 44 60. This tall narrow hotel has good views over the Santo Stefano quarter. Traditional furnishings, but some rooms are cramped. 🛏 📺 ▤ 🌣	11			
SAN MARCO: *Flora* €€€€ Calle Larga XXII Marzo, 2283a. **Map** 7 A3. ☎ 041 520 58 44. FAX 041 522 82 17. @ info@hotelflora.it A charming and quiet hotel on a secluded alley near Piazza San Marco. Some rooms are small, but they all have their own bathroom. During the summer breakfast is served in the flower-filled garden. 🛏 ▤ 🌣	44			■
SAN MARCO: *Metropole* €€€€€ Riva Schiavoni 4149. **Map** 8 D2. ☎ 041 520 50 44. FAX 041 522 36 79. @ hotelmetropole@venere.it This characterful hotel is furnished throughout with myriad antique pieces. The restaurant is famous for only offering buffet service, but with a very wide choice of delicious specialities. 🛏 📺 ▤ 🌣	69	■		■
SAN MARCO: *Monaco and Grand Canal* €€€€€ Calle Vallaresso, 1325. **Map** 7 B3. ☎ 041 520 02 11. FAX 041 520 05 01. @ mailbox@hotelmonaco.it An elegant hotel in an 18th-century palazzo overlooking the Grand Canal. Public rooms are intimate and bedrooms are beautifully decorated. The restaurant is one of the best in Venice. 🛏 📺 ▤ 🌣	71	■		■
SAN MARCO: *Panada* €€€€ San Marco, 646. **Map** 7 A2. ☎ 041 520 90 88. FAX 041 520 96 19. @ info@hotelpanada.com Set in a quiet location, this recently renovated 17th-century mansion has an intimate bar lined with antique mirrors. 🛏 📺 ▤ 🌣	48	■		
SAN MARCO: *Saturnia & International* €€€€ Via XXII Marzo 2398. **Map** 7 A3. ☎ 041 520 83 77. FAX 041 520 58 58. @ saturnia@italyhotel.com Set in an ancient palace this luxury hotel is decorated throughout with antique furniture. There is a charming courtyard with restaurant. 🛏 📺 ▤ 🌣	91	■		■

For key to symbols see back flap

Price categories for a standard double room for one night, including tax and service charges but not including breakfast: € under 52 euros €€ 52–100 euros €€€ 100–155 euros €€€€ 155–205 euros €€€€€ over 205 euros.	**RESTAURANT** A restaurant within the hotel sometimes reserved for residents. **SWIMMING POOL** Hotel swimming pools are usually quite small and are outdoors unless otherwise stated. **GARDEN OR TERRACE** A garden, courtyard or terrace belonging to the hotel, often providing tables for eating outside. **CREDIT CARDS** The major credit cards Visa, MasterCard (Access) and American Express are accepted in hotels with the credit card symbol.		

	NUMBER OF ROOMS	RESTAURANT	SWIMMING POOL	GARDEN OR TERRACE
SAN MARCO: *Bauer* €€€€€ Campo San Moisè, 1459. **Map** 7 A3. 〖 041 520 70 22. FAX 041 520 75 57. @ booking@bauervenezia.it A luxury hotel in the heart of Venice, it has been recently refurbished, and can offer unique accommodation overlooking the Grand Canal. 📺 📋 ◪	192	■		■
SAN MARCO: *Concordia* €€€€€ San Marco 367. **Map** 7 B2. 〖 041 520 68 66. FAX 041 520 67 75. @ venezia@hotelconcordia.it The main feature of this hotel is its view over St Mark's Square. Rooms with a view must be booked well in advance. 📺 📋 ◪	57	■		
SAN MARCO: *Europa & Regina* €€€€€ San Marco 2159. **Map** 7 A3. 〖 041 520 04 77. FAX 041 523 15 33. Once the residence of the 18th-century Italian painter Tiepolo, this splendid property has been completely restyled. The terrace overlooking the Grand Canal houses a flamboyant bar and restaurant. 📺 📋 ◪	185	■		■
SAN MARCO: *Gritti Palace* €€€€€ Santa Maria del Giglio, 2467. **Map** 6 F3. 〖 041 79 46 11. FAX 041 520 09 42. An elegant, sumptuous hotel housed in the 15th-century palazzo that once belonged to the Gritti family. Rooms are superb and it is charmingly old-fashioned. Ernest Hemingway stayed here while in Venice. 📺 📋 ◪	91	■		■
SAN POLO: *Alex* €€ Rio Terrà Frari, 2606. **Map** 6 E1. 〖 041 523 13 41. FAX 041 523 13 41. A family-run hotel that makes up for its limited facilities with a friendly welcome and excellent value for money. Ideally located near the Frari.	11			■
SAN POLO: *Hotel Marconi* €€€ San Polo, 729. **Map** 7 A1. 〖 041 522 20 68. FAX 041 522 97 00. @ info@hotelmarconi.it A refurbished 16th-century palazzo with opulently Venetian reception rooms. Bedrooms are plainer, but some have views of the Grand Canal. 📺 📋 ◪	26			■
SANTA CROCE: *Al Sole* €€€ Fondamenta Minotta, 136. **Map** 5 C1. 〖 041 71 08 44. FAX 041 71 43 98. @ info@corihotels.it This 14th-century building is conveniently situated in a quiet corner near the station. It has pleasant rooms and a marble-floored reception area. 📺 📋 ◪	80			■
SANTA CROCE: *Falier* €€€ Salizzada San Pantalon, 130. **Map** 5 C1. 〖 041 710 882. FAX 041 520 65 54. @ falier@tin.it On the edge of the student district, the reasonably priced Falier is away from the main hotel area of Venice. It has recently been restored. 📺 📋 ◪	19			■
TORCELLO: *Locanda Cipriani* €€ Piazza Santa Fosca 29. 〖 041 73 01 50. FAX 041 73 54 33. @ info@locandacipriani.com A perfect place to stay away from the crowds. Be sure to sample the cuisine; meals are served in the garden or gallery. It is essential to book in advance. 📺 📋 ◪	6	■		■
THE VENETO AND FRIULI				
BARDOLINO: *Kriss International* €€ Lungolago Cipriani 3, 37011. 〖 045 621 24 33. FAX 045 721 02 42. @ kriss@kriss.it A modern hotel, attractively placed on a promontory jutting into the lake with balconies in every room. Train travellers are met at the station. 📺 📋 ◪ P	40	■		■
BASSANO DEL GRAPPA: *Victoria* € Viale Diaz 33, 36061. 〖 0424 50 36 20. FAX 0424 50 31 30. @ victoriahotel@pn.itnet.it Just outside the city walls, this pleasant hotel has comfortable rooms. It is a busy hotel that can be noisy but is well placed for sightseeing. 📺 📋 ◪ P	23			
BASSANO DEL GRAPPA: *Belvedere* €€ Piazzale G Giardino 14, 36061. 〖 0424 52 98 45. FAX 0424 52 98 49. @ belvederehotel@bonotto.it Set on one of Bassano's main squares, this busy hotel is the best equipped in the area. Rooms are comfortable and service is good. 📺 📋 ◪ P	87	■		

BELLUNO: *Astor* €€ 32
Piazza dei Martiri 26e, 32100. 【 *0437 94 20 94.* FAX *0437 94 24 93.* @ astorhotel@libero.it
Centrally situated, this hotel is popular with skiers in winter. The rooms are
well-designed and comfortable, offering good value for money. 🛏 TV 🗗

CHIOGGIA: *Grande Italia* €€€€€ 57
Rione S. Andrea 597, 30015. 【 *041 40 05 15.* FAX *041 40 01 85.* @ hg@hotelgrandeitalia.com
This unpretentious old-fashioned hotel, at the head of the main street, has
comfortable rooms and is well-situated for boats running to Venice. 🛏 TV 🗏 🗗 P

CIVIDALE DEL FRIULI: *Locanda al Castello* €€€ 17
Via del Castello 20, 33043. 【 *0432 73 32 42.* FAX *0432 70 09 01.* @ castello@ud.nettuno.it
An attractive historic building, this was once a castle and a Jesuit
monastery before its most recent incarnation as a welcoming friendly
hotel with wonderful views. 🛏 TV 🗗 P

CONEGLIANO: *Canon d'Oro* €€ 51
Via XX Settembre 131, 31015. 【 *0438 342 46.* FAX *0438 342 49.* @ canondoro@sevenonline.it
On the main street of the town, this hotel offers solid comfort and a warm
welcome. Relax in the lovely garden with a glass of Prosecco. 🛏 TV 🗏 🗗 P

CORTINA D'AMPEZZO: *Cavallino* €€€ 7
Corso Italia 142, 32043. 【 *0436 26 14.* FAX *0436 87 99 09.*
This centrally located hotel has spotless rooms and
breathtaking mountain views from the front rooms.
🛏 🗗 P

CORTINA D'AMPEZZO: *Menardi* €€€€ 53
Via Majon 110, 32043. 【 *0436 24 00.* FAX *0436 86 21 83.* @ hmenardi@sunrise.it
The Menardi family have run this well-managed hotel since 1900.
Originally a farmhouse, it is tastefully furnished with antiques and
has a welcoming atmosphere. 🛏 TV 🗗 P

GARDA: *Bisesti* €€ 90
Corso Italia 34, 37016. 【 *045 725 57 66.* FAX *045 725 59 27.* @ bisesti@infogarda.com
Well placed near the town centre and the lake. Many rooms in this modern
holiday hotel have their own balcony and there is a private beach. 🛏 TV 🗗 P

GARDA: *Locanda San Vigilio* €€€€€ 7
San Vigilio, 37016. 【 *045 725 66 88.* FAX *045 725 65 51.* @ sanvigilio@gardanews.it
One of the loveliest, most exclusive hotels on Lake Garda. Comfort and
service live up to all expectations and there is a private beach. 🛏 TV 🗏 🗗 P

MALCESINE: *Sailing Center Hotel* €€€ 32
Località Molini Campagnola 3, 37018. 【 *045 740 00 55.* FAX *045 740 03 92.*
A modern hotel just outside town, away from the crowds. Rooms are cool
and pleasant, and there is a tennis court and private beach. 🛏 TV 🗗 P

PADUA: *Leon Bianco* €€ 22
Piazzetta Pedrocchi 12, 35122. 【 *049 875 08 14.* FAX *049 875 61 84.* @ leonbianco@toscanelli.com
A centrally situated hotel overlooking the Caffè Pedrocchi. Rooms are small
but staff are friendly and welcoming. Book well in advance. 🛏 TV 🗏 🗗 P

PADUA: *Augustus Terme* €€€ 120
Viale Stazione 150, Montegrotto Terme 35036. 【 *049 79 32 00.* FAX *049 79 35 18.*
One of the best hotels at Montegrotto Terme, this is a big,
functional and comfortable hotel. In addition to the usual facilities
it has tennis courts and hot thermal springs. 🛏 TV 🗗 P

PADUA: *Donatello* €€€ 45
Via del Santo 102, 35123. 【 *049 875 06 34.* FAX *049 875 08 29.* @ info@hoteldonatello.net
A modern hotel in an old building with big comfortable bedrooms, named after
the sculptor of the equestrian statue of Gattamelata in the square. 🛏 TV 🗗 P

PADUA: *Plaza* €€€ 142
Corso Milano 40, 35139. 【 *049 65 68 22.* FAX *049 66 11 17.* @ plazapd@gpnet.it
An established and efficiently run hotel with a deserved good reputation.
It provides a full range of services and a warm welcome. 🛏 TV 🗏 🗗 P

PESCHIERA DEL GARDA: *Peschiera* € 30
Via Parini 4, 37010. 【 *045 755 05 26.* FAX *045 755 04 44.*
This recently restored hotel, built in the local architectural style, is set in its
own grounds, with lofty, cool bedrooms. It is five minutes from the A4 motorway,
or the friendly staff will collect train travellers from the station. 🛏 🗗 P

<table>
<tr><td colspan="2">

Price categories for a standard double room for one night, including tax and service charges but not including breakfast:
€ under 52 euros
€€ 52–100 euros
€€€ 100–155 euros
€€€€ 155–205 euros
€€€€€ over 205 euros.

RESTAURANT
A restaurant within the hotel sometimes reserved for residents.
SWIMMING POOL
Hotel swimming pools are usually quite small and are outdoors unless otherwise stated.
GARDEN OR TERRACE
A garden, courtyard or terrace belonging to the hotel, often providing tables for eating outside.
CREDIT CARDS
The major credit cards VISA, MasterCard (Access) and American Express are accepted in hotels with the credit card symbol.

</td></tr>
</table>

	NUMBER OF ROOMS	RESTAURANT	SWIMMING POOL	GARDEN OR TERRACE
PORDENONE: *Palace Hotel Moderno* €€€€ Viale Martelli 1, 33170. **[** 0434 282 15. **FAX** 0434 52 03 15. **@** moderno@eahotels.it A comfortable, recently refurbished traditional hotel with a good range of facilities in all bedrooms. It is centrally located close to the station. The restaurant specializes in traditional cuisine, particularly fish dishes. 🚗 📺 🍽 🌳 🅿	100	■		
SAN FLORIANO DEL COLLIO: *Romantik Golf Hotel* €€€€ Via Oslavia 2, 34070. **[** 0481 88 40 51. **FAX** 0481 88 40 52. **@** isabellaformentini@tiscalinet A lovely 18th-century building furnished with antiques and set in its own well-kept grounds with a nine-hole golf course and tennis courts. 🚗 📺 🌳	14	■	●	■
TORRI DEL BENACO: *Hotel Gardesana* €€€€ Piazza Calderini 20, 37010. **[** 045 722 54 11. **FAX** 045 722 57 71. **@** gardesana@easynet.it The 15th-century harbourmaster's house overlooking Lake Garda has been converted into a friendly, comfortable hotel. Ask for a room on the third floor; they are quieter and have wonderful views of the lake. 🚗 📺 🍽 🌳 🅿	34	■		■
TREVISO: *Ca' del Galletto* €€€€ Via Santa Bona Vecchia 30, 31100. **[** 0422 43 25 50. **FAX** 0422 43 25 10. Set in its own grounds and only ten minutes' walk from the city walls, this efficiently-run hotel has good-sized modern bedrooms. 🚗 📺 🍽 🌳 🅿	58	■		■
TREVISO: *Villa Cipriani* €€€€€ Via Canova 298, Asolo. **[** 0423 52 34 11. **FAX** 0423 95 20 95. **@** res032.villacipriani@sheraton.com This superbly comfortable hotel is set in a 16th-century villa where Robert Browning once lived. A popular feature is its beautiful garden which has a lovely view. A good base for exploring a wider area. 🚗 📺 🍽 🌳 🅿	31	■		■
TRIESTE: *Jolly* €€€€ Corso Cavour 7, 34132. **[** 040 760 00 55. **FAX** 040 36 26 99. **@** trieste@jollyhotels.it A modern hotel aiming at business as well as holiday clientele. The well-equipped rooms are spacious if slightly impersonally decorated. 🚗 📺 🍽 🌳 🅿	174	■		
TRIESTE: *Grand Hotel Duchi d'Aosta* €€€€€ Piazza Unità d'Italia 2, 34121. **[** 040 760 00 11. **FAX** 040 36 60 92. **@** info@magesta.com A palace from a bygone era, this hotel has enormous rooms fitted with modern conveniences. It is set in the old part of town, near the fort. 🚗 📺 🍽 🌳 🅿	55	■		
UDINE: *Quo Vadis* €€ Piazzale Cella 28, 33100. **[** 0432 210 91. **FAX** 0432 210 92. A comfortable hotel on a tranquil tree-lined street. The decor is mixed (some rooms have rather fussy wallpaper) but there are plenty of plants. 🚗 📺 🅿	26			■
VERONA: *Accademia* €€€ Via Scala 12, 37121. **[** 045 596 222. **FAX** 045 800 84 40. **@** accademia@accademiavr.it Blending modern and ancient architecture, this ornate 17th-century building has a central location. The well-known restaurant offers regional cuisine. 🚗 📺 🍽 🌳 🅿	98	■		
VERONA: *Il Torcolo* €€ Vicolo Listone 3, 37121. **[** 045 800 75 12. **FAX** 045 800 40 58. This friendly hotel is close to the Arena and is popular during the opera season. It has a breakfast terrace, and some pretty and traditional rooms. 🚗 📺 🍽 🅿	19			■
VERONA: *Giulietta e Romeo* €€€ Vicolo Tre Marchetti 3, 37121. **[** 045 800 35 54. **FAX** 045 801 08 62. **@** info@giuliettaeromeo.com Situated in a quiet street just behind the Arena, the bedrooms are spacious and comfortable with modern furnishings. Breakfast is served in the bar. 🚗 📺 🍽 🌳	31			
VERONA: *Due Torri Hotel Baglioni* €€€€€ Piazza Sant'Anastasia 4, 37121. **[** 045 59 50 44. **FAX** 045 800 41 30. Right in the heart of medieval Verona, this is one of Italy's most eccentric hotels. The huge bedrooms are each decorated and furnished in the style of a different era. Many of the walls and ceilings are frescoed. 🚗 📺 🍽 🌳 🅿	91	■		

VICENZA: *Casa San Raffaele* €€ 29
Viale X Giugno 10, 36100. 【 *0444 54 57 67.* FAX *0444 54 22 59.*
A tranquil hotel with excellent views set on the slopes of Monte Berico. The
comfortable rooms make this one of the best budget choices in the area. 🛏 🗒 🍽 **P**

VICENZA: *Campo Marzio* €€ 35
Via Roma 21, 36100. 【 *0444 54 57 00.* FAX *0444 32 04 95.* @ info@hotelcampomarzio.com
A stylish hotel with good facilities near the city centre. Bedrooms are
large, light and well furnished, and the location is peaceful. 🛏 TV 🗒 🍽 **P**

VICENZA: *Castello* €€€ 20
Contrà Piazza del Castello 24, 36100. 【 *0444 32 35 85.* FAX *0444 32 35 83.*
Very near the cathedral, this is also an excellent choice for train
travellers. Rooms are pleasant and the location is fairly quiet. 🛏 TV 🗒 🍽 **P**

TRENTINO - ALTO ADIGE

BOLZANO (BOZEN): *Engel* €€ 30
Via San Valentino, Nova Levante 39056. 【 *0471 61 31 31.* FAX *0471 61 34 04.*
In a small town near Bolzano, the Engel is a good choice for families
and the sporty, with hiking and skiing nearby. 🛏 🍽 **P**

BOLZANO (BOZEN): *Asterix* €€€ 24
Piazza Mazzini 35, 39100. 【 *0471 27 33 01.* FAX *0471 26 00 21.*
Set in the newer part of central Bolzano, the Asterix is a simple but quite
comfortable town hotel which is excellent value for money. 🛏 TV 🍽 **P**

BOLZANO (BOZEN): *Luna-Mondschein* €€€ 60
Via Piave 15, 39100. 【 *0471 97 56 42.* FAX *0471 97 55 77.* @ info@hotel-luna.it
One of the oldest hotels in Bolzano, the Luna-Mondschein dates from 1798,
although the buildings have been much added to since then. It is set near the
town centre with a pleasant garden allowing for summer dining. 🛏 TV 🍽 **P**

BRESSANONE (BRIXEN): *Dominik* €€€€ 36
Via Terzo di Sotto 13, 39042. 【 *0472 83 01 44.* FAX *0472 83 65 54.* W www.hoteldominik.com
One of the luxurious Relais et Châteaux group, the Dominik is attractively
furnished with antiques, although the buildings themselves date from the 1970s.
It is peacefully set near the River Rienza and the Rapp gardens. 🛏 TV 🍽 **P**

BRESSANONE (BRIXEN): *Elefante* €€€€ 44
Via Rio Bianco 4, 39042. 【 *0472 83 27 50.* FAX *0472 83 65 79.* @ elephant.brixen@acs.it
A smart hotel that dates from the 16th century. While offering all modern comforts
(including sauna), it has retained a strong historical atmosphere. 🛏 TV 🍽 **P**

BRUNICO (BRUNECK): *Andreas Hofer* €€€ 54
Via Campo Tures 1, 39031. 【 *0474 55 14 69.* FAX *0474 55 12 83.* @ hotel@andreashofer.it
A welcoming family-run chalet hotel which has been fitted out with wood
panelling and wooden Alpine-style furniture. The Andreas Hofer is quietly
set in its own garden and some of the rooms have balconies. 🛏 TV 🍽 **P**

CALDARO (KALTERN): *Leuchtenburg* €€ 19
Campi al Lago 100, 39052. 【 *0471 96 00 93.* FAX *0471 96 01 55.* @ pensionleuchtenburg@iol.it
Set in a beautiful 16th-century farmhouse surrounded by vineyards, some of
the simple bedrooms are furnished with traditional painted furniture. 🛏 TV 🍽 **P**

CANAZEI: *Park Hotel Faloria* €€ 36
Via Pareda 103, 38032. 【 *0462 60 11 18.* FAX *0462 60 27 15.*
Surrounded by its own well-kept gardens, this friendly hotel is managed by its
owners. Some bedrooms have balconies overlooking the grounds. 🛏 TV 🍽 **P**

CASTELROTTO (KASTELRUTH): *Cavallino d'Oro* €€ 21
Piazza Kraus 1, 39040. 【 *0471 70 63 37.* FAX *0471 70 71 72.* @ cavallino@cavallino.it
This charming hotel is set in a pretty village 26 km (16 miles) from Bolzano,
where traditional costume is still worn. The rooms are well-kept. 🛏 TV 🍽 **P**

CAVALESE: *Fiemme* €€ 10
Via Cavazzal 27, 38033. 【 *0462 34 17 20.* FAX *0462 23 11 51.*
A modern hotel in a peaceful setting with good views, conveniently close
to both the town centre and the bus station. It also has a sauna. 🛏 TV 🍽 **P**

COLFOSCO: *Cappella* €€€€ 63
Strada Pecei 17, 39030. 【 *0471 83 61 83.* FAX *0471 83 65 61.* @ info@hotelcappella.com
A recently restored chalet in the Dolomites, opened by the present
owner's grandfather. The hotel has also opened an art gallery. 🛏 TV 🍽 **P**

Price categories for a standard double room for one night, including tax and service charges but not including breakfast:
€ under 52 euros
€€ 52–100 euros
€€€ 100–155 euros
€€€€ 155–205 euros
€€€€€ over 205 euros.

RESTAURANT
A restaurant within the hotel sometimes reserved for residents.
SWIMMING POOL
Hotel swimming pools are usually quite small and are outdoors unless otherwise stated.
GARDEN OR TERRACE
A garden, courtyard or terrace belonging to the hotel, often providing tables for eating outside.
CREDIT CARDS
The major credit cards VISA, MasterCard (Access) and American Express are accepted in hotels with the credit card symbol.

	NUMBER OF ROOMS	RESTAURANT	SWIMMING POOL	GARDEN OR TERRACE
FIE ALLO SCILIAR: *Turm* €€€	26	■	●	■
MADONNA DI CAMPIGLIO: *Grifone* €€€	42	■		■
MALLES VENOSTA (MALS IM VINSCHGAU): *Garberhof* €€€	29	■	●	■
MERANO (MERAN): *Castel Schloss Labers* €€€	35	■	●	■
MERANO (MERAN): *Der Punthof* €€€	12	■		■
MERANO (MERAN): *Castel Rundegg* €€€€€	30	■	●	■
ORTISEI (SANKT ULRICH): *Hell* €€€	25	■		■
PERGINE VALSUGANA: *Castel Pergine* €€	21	■		■
RASUN ANTERSELVA (RASEN ANTHOLZ): *Ansitz Heufler* €€€	8	■		■
RIVA DEL GARDA: *Europa* €€	63	■		■
RIVA DEL GARDA: *Lido Palace* €€	63	■	●	■
SAN PAOLO (ST PAULS): *Schloss Korb* €€€	50	■	●	■

FIE ALLO SCILIAR: *Turm*
Piazza della Chiesa 9, 39050. **C** *0471 72 50 14.* **FAX** *0471 72 54 74.* **@** turmwirt@cenida.it
The owner's art collection, displayed on the hotel walls, is one of the main attractions at this friendly Alpine hotel with cosy bars and two pools.

MADONNA DI CAMPIGLIO: *Grifone*
Via Vallesinella 7, 38084. **C** *0465 44 20 02.* **FAX** *0465 44 05 40.* **@** info@hotelgrifone.it
A modern wooden chalet set near the lake in the Madonna di Campiglio ski resort. Although rather ordinarily decorated and furnished, it offers an excellent range of facilities ideal for winter sports holidays. Full board only.

MALLES VENOSTA (MALS IM VINSCHGAU): *Garberhof*
Via Nazionale 25, 39024. **C** *0473 83 13 99.* **FAX** *0473 83 19 50.* **@** info@garberhof.com
A modern chalet-style hotel with extensive panoramic terraces. It is surrounded by meadows and has a good range of sports and leisure facilities.

MERANO (MERAN): *Castel Schloss Labers*
Via Labers 25, 39012. **C** *0473 23 44 84.* **FAX** *0473 23 41 46.* **@** info@meraninfo.it
A romantic castle is the setting for this high-class country hotel. There are wonderful views over the surrounding vineyards and woods.

MERANO (MERAN): *Der Punthof*
Via Steinach 25, 39022. **C** *0473 44 85 53.* **FAX** *0473 44 99 19.* **@** punthof@dnet.it
Set in peaceful and attractive gardens, this farmhouse dates back to the Middle Ages. Inside, wooden floors and ceilings match the Alpine furniture.

MERANO (MERAN): *Castel Rundegg*
Via Scena 2, 39012. **C** *0473 23 41 00.* **FAX** *0473 23 72 00.* **@** info@rundegg.com
A fairy-tale whitewashed castle, parts of which date from the 12th century, set in pretty gardens. Inside, the romantic atmosphere continues with traditional wood furniture, beamed ceilings and parquet floors.

ORTISEI (SANKT ULRICH): *Hell*
Via Promenade 3, 39046. **C** *0471 79 67 85.* **FAX** *0471 79 81 96.* **@** hotelhell@val-gardena.com
A pleasant hotel that is open for the skiing season and during the summer. It has a sauna and a gym, and is set in a peaceful part of town.

PERGINE VALSUGANA: *Castel Pergine*
Via al Castello 10, 38057. **C** *0461 53 11 58.* **FAX** *0461 53 13 29.* **@** castelpergine@valsugana.com
Set in a 13th-century castle with exquisite views over the countryside. The interior is simply decorated and has traditional wooden furnishings.

RASUN ANTERSELVA (RASEN ANTHOLZ): *Ansitz Heufler*
Rasun di Sopra 37, 39030. **C** *0474 49 85 82.* **FAX** *0474 49 80 46.* **@** ansitz.heufler@dnet.it
In the historic centre of town close to the main monuments, this beautifully decorated 16th-century castle has large rooms and a pleasant garden.

RIVA DEL GARDA: *Europa*
Piazza Catena 9, 38066. **C** *0464 55 54 33.* **FAX** *0464 52 17 77.* **@** europa@rivadelgarda.com
A turn-of-the-century colour-washed building right next to the lake and near the bustling town centre. Many of the simply furnished bedrooms have views over the lake.

RIVA DEL GARDA: *Lido Palace*
Viale Carducci 10, 38066. **C** *0464 55 26 64.* **FAX** *0464 55 19 57.* **@** info@hotellidopalace.it
Centrally located, this is an immaculately run hotel set in magnificent gardens. Diners are treated to stunning views out onto the garden and Lake Garda. There are tennis courts nearby.

SAN PAOLO (ST PAULS): *Schloss Korb*
Via Castel d'Appiano 5, Missiano 39050. **C** *0471 63 60 00.* **FAX** *0471 63 60 33.*
Partly set in a 13th-century castle, this simply decorated and prettily furnished hotel also has a more modern annexe, and tennis courts for residents.

TIRES (TIERS): *Stefaner* €€ 16
San Cipriano 88d, 39050. [0471 64 21 75. FAX 0471 64 23 02. @ info@stefaner.com
A friendly chalet hotel on the edge of the western Dolomites. Bedrooms
are light, spacious and simple. Balconies are decked with flowers. 📶 TV P

TRENTO: *Accademia* €€€ 42
Vicolo Colico 4–6, 38100. [0461 23 36 00. FAX 0461 23 01 74. @ info@accademiahotel.it
Set in a well-restored medieval building right in the historic centre of
Trento. The interior of this relaxing hotel, although essentially modern,
retains many original features. The restaurant is also very good. 📶 TV 🗐 🗐 P

VIPITENO (STERZING): *Hotel Schwarzer Adler* €€€ 35
Piazza Città 1, 39049. [0472 76 40 64. FAX 0472 76 65 22. @ schwarzeradler@rolmail.net
A comfortable hotel for winter sports or summer walking holidays with many
leisure facilities including a sauna, gym and a famous restaurant. 📶 TV 🗐 P

LOMBARDY

BELLAGIO: *La Pergola* €€ 11
Piazza del Porto 4, 22021. [031 95 02 63. FAX 031 95 02 53.
An attractive hotel tucked away to the south of Lake Como, charmingly
furnished in an old-fashioned style with a rustic and friendly atmosphere. 📶 TV 🗐

BELLAGIO: *Florence* €€€ 32
Piazza Mazzini 46, 22021. [031 95 03 42. FAX 031 95 17 22.
This friendly hotel has a bar, and its rooms overlook the lively port of Lake
Como. The hotel has plenty of charm, and tastefully furnished rooms. 📶 TV 🗐

BRATTO DELLA PRESOLANA (BERGAMO): *Hotel Milano* €€ 63
Via Silvio Pellico 3, 24020. [034 631 211. FAX 034 636 236. @ info@hotelmilano.com
In the foothills of the Alps, this hotel offers a large array of sports to its guests. The
less energetic are pampered with eight styles of pillow and a cigar menu. 📶 TV P

BRESCIA: *Park Hotel Ca' Noa* €€€ 79
Via Triumplina 66, 25127. [030 39 87 62. FAX 030 39 87 64. @ hotelcanoa@tin.it
A beautiful modern hotel set in its own grounds with tasteful and bright
decor, large, spacious public rooms and excellent service. 📶 TV 🗐 P

BORMIO: *Palace* €€ 80
Via Milano 54, 23032. [0342 90 31 31. FAX 0342 90 33 66. @ palace@valtline.it
A recently-built hotel with a wide range of business and leisure facilities that
include a gym, sunbeds, a discotheque and a piano bar. 📶 TV 🗐 P

CERVESINA: *Castello di San Gaudenzio* €€€ 45
Via Mulino 1, Frazione San Gaudenzio 27050. [0383 33 31. FAX 0383 33 34 09.
A wonderful, almost kitsch hotel in a building with parts dating from the
15th century. Furnishings are from a variety of periods; some are French 18th-
century, others are heavier and more 16th-century baronial. 📶 TV 🗐 🗐 ♿ P

COLOGNE FRANCIACORTA: *Cappuccini* €€€ 6
Via Cappuccini 54, 25033. [030 715 72 54. FAX 030 715 72 57. @ cappuccini@numerica.it
A converted convent (built in 1569). Long hallways and white rooms create
a pleasant monastic atmosphere. Good leisure facilities. 📶 TV 🗐 🗐 P

COMO: *Metropole & Suisse au Lac* €€€ 71
Piazza Cavour 19, 22100. [031 26 94 44. FAX 031 30 08 08. @ suisse@galactica.it
Hotel established in 1892 by the lake and recently renovated. Excellent location for
strolling or shopping. Facilities include a restaurant with outside terrace. 📶 TV 🗐 🗐 P

CREMONA: *Continental* €€ 57
Piazza della Libertà 26, 26100. [0372 43 41 41. FAX 0372 45 48 73.
This luxurious hotel has been owned and run by the Ghiraldi family since 1920
and is excellently situated for Cremona's main places of interest. Rooms are
comfortable and the restaurant is one of the best in the city. 📶 TV 🗐 🗐 P

CREMONA: *Duomo* €€ 23
Via Gonfalonieri 13, 26100. [0372 352 42. FAX 0372 45 83 92.
Unsurprisingly, given its name, this hotel is right next to the cathedral in
Cremona's historic centre. Some of the rooms have good views. 📶 TV 🗐 🗐 P

DESENZANO DEL GARDA: *Piroscafo* €€ 32
Via Porto Vecchio 11, 25015. [030 914 11 28. FAX 030 991 25 86.
An attractive old hotel, well placed for all the town's amenities. Bedrooms
at the front have balconies overlooking the busy old port. 📶 TV 🗐

Price categories for a standard double room for one night, including tax and service charges but not including breakfast: € under 52 euros €€ 52–100 euros €€€ 100–155 euros €€€€ 155–205 euros €€€€€ over 205 euros.	**RESTAURANT** A restaurant within the hotel sometimes reserved for residents. **SWIMMING POOL** Hotel swimming pools are usually quite small and are outdoors unless otherwise stated. **GARDEN OR TERRACE** A garden, courtyard or terrace belonging to the hotel, often providing tables for eating outside. **CREDIT CARDS** The major credit cards VISA, MasterCard (Access) and American Express are accepted in hotels with the credit card symbol.		

	NUMBER OF ROOMS	RESTAURANT	SWIMMING POOL	GARDEN OR TERRACE
GARDONE RIVIERA: *Villa Fiordaliso* €€€€ Corso Zanardelli 150, 25083. 【 0365 201 58. FAX 0365 29 00 11. W www.villafiordaliso.it This beautiful, eclectic villa overlooking Lake Garda has comfortable rooms. It was once the private residence of Clara Petacci, Mussolini's lover. 🛏 TV ▤ 🌿 P	7	■		■
GARDONE RIVIERA: *Villa Del Sogno* €€€€ Via Zanardelli 107, 25083. 【 0365 29 01 81. FAX 0365 29 02 30. @ info@villadelsogno.it A turn-of-the-century villa set in beautiful gardens and furnished with antiques of various periods. All rooms are spacious and light; this is a good choice for those seeking luxurious tranquillity. 🛏 ▤ TV 🌿 P	31	■	●	■
LIMONE SUL GARDA: *Capo Reamol* €€ Via IV Novembre 92, 25010. 【 0365 95 40 40. FAX 0365 95 42 62. @ caporeamol@gardaresort.it A stunning location on the edge of the lake below the main road. Rooms are spacious and all have their own terrace. Sports and leisure facilities are excellent for families and include private beach, gym and jacuzzi. 🛏 TV 🌿 P	60	■	●	■
LIVIGNO: *Camana Veglia* €€ Via Ostaria 107, 23030. 【 & FAX 0342 99 63 10. @ camanaveglia@livnet.it Set in a typical chalet that dates from the beginning of the last century. The interior is wood-panelled and furnished in Alpine style. 🛏 TV 🌿 P	12	■		■
MANTOVA: *Broletto* €€ Via Calvi 30, 46100. 【 0376 32 67 84. FAX 0376 22 12 97. @ hotelbroletto@tin.it A small, immaculate hotel in a renovated 16th-century town house. Rooms are bright with attractive modern furnishings and polished marble floors. 🛏 TV ▤ 🌿	16			
MANTOVA: *Rechigi* €€€€€ Piazza Concordia 14, 46100. 【 0376 32 07 81. FAX 0376 22 02 91. Although located in the historical city centre, the hotel is innovatively modern. Decorated with contemporary art, it regularly houses exhibitions. 🛏 TV ▤ 🌿 ♿ P	60			■
MANTOVA: *Villa dei Tigli* €€€€ Via Cantarana 20, 46040. 【 0376 65 06 91. FAX 0376 65 06 49. @ info@villadeitigli.it A charming villa set in a quiet park in the country. The hotel has a gym with swimming pools and sauna, and runs a shuttle service to the city. 🛏 TV ▤ 🌿 P	31	■	●	■
MILAN: *Antica Locanda Solferino* €€€ Via Castelfidardo 2, 20121. 【 02 657 01 29. FAX 02 657 13 61. Excellent value at this surprisingly rustic old inn. Bedrooms are small but nicely decorated with old furniture, paintings and flowery wallpaper. There is also an informal bistro next door to the hotel. Book in advance. 🛏 TV 🌿	11	■		
MILAN: *Zurigo* €€€ Corso Italia 11a, 20122. 【 02 72 02 22 60. FAX 02 72 00 00 13. @ brerahotels@citylightsnews.com A newly restored hotel whose central location appeals to both business and holiday travellers. Guests can borrow bicycles for sightseeing. 🛏 TV ▤ 🌿 P	41	■		
MILAN: *Cavour* €€€€ Via Fatebenefratelli 21, 20121. 【 02 657 20 51. FAX 02 659 22 63. Very well placed for Milan's main sights, this recently restored city hotel has good-sized, comfortable rooms and a pleasant bar. 🛏 TV ▤ 🌿 P	113	■		
MILAN: *Pierre Milano* €€€€€ Via de Amicis 32, 20123. 【 02 72 00 05 81. FAX 02 805 21 57. A luxurious hotel that blends traditional and modern styles in its interior design and furnishings. The restaurant is one of the best in Milan. 🛏 TV ▤ 🌿 ♿	51	■		
MILAN: *Capitol Millennium* €€€€€ Via Cimarosa 6. 【 02 43 85 91. FAX 02 469 47 24. @ capitol@tin.it After major restructuring this hotel now boasts excellent facilities. The rooms are wood-panelled and the marble bathrooms have a jacuzzi shower or tub. The public spaces are tastefully decorated and there is a gym, restaurant and bar. TV ▤ 🌿 ♿	66	■		

PAVIA: *Moderno* €€€ | 54
Viale Vittorio Emanuele 41, 27100. ☎ *0382 30 34 01.* FAX *0382 252 25.*
Set in a restored palazzo, the Moderno is a calm, well-run establishment
with a welcoming atmosphere and comfortable rooms. 🖿 TV 🗒 🖪 🖫 P

RANCO: *Sole* €€€€ | 15
Piazza Venezia 5, 21020. ☎ *0331 97 65 07.* FAX *0331 97 66 20.* @ ivanet@tin.it
The restaurant is the highlight of the Sole which has been in the same family
for five generations. The few rooms are in newly built suites and some have
lovely views over Lake Maggiore (these do cost slightly more). 🖿 TV 🗒 🖪 P

RIVA DEL GARDA: *Luise* € | 69
Viale Rovereto 9, 38066. ☎ *0464 55 27 96.* FAX *0464 55 42 50.* @ luise@rivadelgarda.com
A few minutes away from the lake this hotel has a well-tended garden and tennis
courts. The hotel also offers facilities for mountain-biking enthusiasts. 🖿 TV 🗒 🖪 P

RIVA DI SOLTO: *Miranda da Oreste* €€ | 25
Via Cornello 8, 24060. ☎ *035 98 60 21.* FAX *035 98 00 55.* W www.hotelmiranda.it
A simple, family-run, recently renovated pensione. The restaurant serves
good local cuisine on a terrace with views of Lake Iseo. 🖿 TV 🖪 🖫 P

SABBIONETA: *Al Duca* € | 10
Via della Stamperia 18, 46018. ☎ *0375 524 74.* FAX *0375 220 021.*
A plain but comfortable family-run pensione in a much-converted Renaissance
palazzo, located in the historic centre. Prices are very reasonable. 🖿 TV 🗒 🖪

SALÒ: *Romantik Hotel Laurin* €€€€ | 38
Viale Landi 9, 25087. ☎ *0365 220 22.* FAX *0365 223 82.* @ laurinbs@tin.it
A family hotel in a pretty lakeside villa on a sheltered bay. Spacious bedrooms
and a happy atmosphere, as well as a beach and tennis courts. 🖿 TV 🖪 P

SIRMIONE SUL GARDA: *Villa Cortine Palace Hotel* €€€€€ | 54
Via Grotte 6, 25019. ☎ *030 990 58 90.* FAX *030 91 63 90.*
Huge, frescoed rooms furnished with antiques in this luxurious and tranquil
hotel set in a Classical villa. Excellent service and comfort. 🖿 TV 🗒 🖪 P

TREMEZZO: *San Giorgio* €€€ | 26
Via Regina 81, Località Lenno 22016. ☎ *0344 404 15.* FAX *0344 415 91.*
Set in its own large garden on the shores of Lake Como, the San Giorgio is
a traditional lakeside hotel with elegant terraces and public rooms. Ask for
a room with a balcony for wonderful views of the lake. 🖿 🖪 P

VALSOLDA: *Stella d'Italia* €€€ | 34
Piazza Roma 1, San Mamete 22010. ☎ *0344 681 39.* FAX *0344 687 29.* @ info@stelladitalia.com
An exquisite setting with a shady terrace right on the edge of Lake Lugano.
Rooms have lake views and are prettily decorated with floral prints and bright
bedspreads. Guests can use the lakeside lido and the hotel library. 🖿 TV 🖪 P

VARENNA: *Hotel du Lac* €€€ | 18
Via del Prestino 4, 22050. ☎ *0341 83 02 38.* FAX *0341 83 10 81.*
There are wonderful views from this delightfully peaceful hotel overlooking
Lake Como. Furnishings are simple but comfortable and modern. 🖿 TV 🗒 🖪 P

VALLE D'AOSTA AND PIEDMONT

ALESSANDRIA: *Domus* €€ | 27
Via Castellani 12, 15100. ☎ *0131 433 05.* FAX *0131 23 20 19.* @ efuganti@tin.it
Very centrally located and close to the station, the Domus is however quiet
and peaceful inside. All the rooms have double beds. 🖿 TV 🗒 🖪 P

AOSTA: *Europe* €€€ | 71
Piazza Narbonne 1, 11100. ☎ *0165 23 63 63.* FAX *0165 40 566.* @ hoteleurope@tiscalinet.it
In the historical city centre, this modern hotel offers excellent hospitality,
a renowned restaurant, and a fitness centre. 🖿 TV 🗒 🖪 P

AOSTA: *Milleluci* €€€ | 33
Località Porossan Roppoz 15, 11100. ☎ *0165 23 52 78.* FAX *0165 23 52 84.*
An old farmhouse, attractively restored, is the setting for this pleasant hotel. The
lounge has a wonderful fireplace. Sauna and gym also available. 🖿 TV 🖪 🖫 P

ARONA: *Giardino* €€ | 56
Corso Repubblica 1, 28041. ☎ *0322 459 94.* FAX *0322 24 94 01.* W www.wel.it/hrgiardino
A friendly, comfortable lakeside hotel. A large terrace offers spectacular views
over Lake Maggiore and bedrooms are tastefully furnished. 🖿 TV 🗒 🖪

	NUMBER OF ROOMS	RESTAURANT	SWIMMING POOL	GARDEN OR TERRACE

Price categories for a standard double room for one night, including tax and service charges but not including breakfast:
€ under 52 euros
€€ 52–100 euros
€€€ 100–155 euros
€€€€ 155–205 euros
€€€€€ over 205 euros.

RESTAURANT
A restaurant within the hotel sometimes reserved for residents.
SWIMMING POOL
Hotel swimming pools are usually quite small and are outdoors unless otherwise stated.
GARDEN OR TERRACE
A garden, courtyard or terrace belonging to the hotel, often providing tables for eating outside.
CREDIT CARDS
The major credit cards VISA, MasterCard (Access) and American Express are accepted in hotels with the credit card symbol.

ASTI: *Lis*   €€   29
Viale Fratelli Roselli 10, 14100. [0141 59 50 51. FAX 0141 35 38 45. @ hotellis@tin.it
Centrally but peacefully located opposite the town's public gardens and close to the historic centre. Rooms are modern and well-equipped.

ASTI: *Aleramo*   €€€   42
Via Emanuele Filiberto 13, 14100. [0141 59 56 61. FAX 0141 300 39. W www.hotel.aleramo.it
A slick, modern hotel in the centre of town and close to the station. Rooms have a good range of facilities, including hairdriers and safes.

ASTI: *Salera*   €€€   50   ■
Via Monsignor Marello 19, 14100. [0141 41 01 69. FAX 0141 41 03 72. W www.salera-lis.com
A modern, comfortable hotel well placed for the motorway. Rooms are simply but attractively furnished and all are equipped with mini-bar.

BREUIL-CERVINIA: *Les Neiges d'Antan*   €€€   28   ■   ■
Frazione Cret-Perrères, 11021. [0166 94 87 75. FAX 0166 94 88 52. W www.lesneigesdantan.it
A delightful mountain chalet hotel attached to one of the best restaurants in the area. Both are run by the friendly and enthusiastic Bich family. Inside it is all clean white walls and original wooden beams.

BREUIL-CERVINIA: *Hermitage*   €€€€€   36   ■   ●   ■
Via Piolet 1, 11021. [0166 94 89 98. FAX 0166 94 90 32. @ info@hotelhermitage.com
Those looking for luxury and charm will find it here. This well-equipped modern hotel has bright and flower-filled rooms.

CANNERO RIVIERA: *Cannero*   €€€   50   ■   ●   ■
Lungo Lago 2, Verbania 28821. [0323 78 80 46 (Nov–Mar: 78 81 13). FAX 0323 78 80 48.
The hotel, set in a former monastery, has been in the same family for four generations and, although modernized, it has retained the atmosphere of other times. It also has tennis courts and a good restaurant.

CANNOBIO: *Pironi*   €€€   12
Via Marconi 35, 28822. [0323 706 24. FAX 0323 721 84. @ hotel.pironi@cannobio.net
Housed in a 15th-century palazzo in a pedestrianized zone in the historic centre, the hotel retains many original features such as the inner courtyard. Bedrooms are comfortable with views over the lake or old town.

CHAMPOLUC: *Villa Anna Maria*   €€   21   ■   ■
Via Croues 5, 11020. [0125 30 71 28. FAX 0125 30 79 84. W www.hotelvillaannamaria.com
A simple country hotel in a 1920s chalet-style house with lots of wood panelling. The restaurant offers simple but excellent food.

COGNE: *Bellevue*   €€€€   32   ■   ●   ■
Rue Grand Paradis 21, 11012. [0165 748 25. FAX 0165 74 91 92. @ info@hotelbellevue.it
This is a beautifully situated hotel surrounded by meadows and with excellent views of the Gran Paradiso. Guests are expected to take half-board.

COURMAYEUR: *La Grange*   €€   23   ■
Strada la Brenva 1, Entreves 11013. [0165 86 97 33. FAX 0165 86 97 44. @ lagrange@mbtlc.it
A restructured barn, which has been in the same family since the 14th century, is the setting for this clean, bright Alpine hotel. Furnishings are new but based on traditional designs, and the atmosphere is cosy and homely.

COURMAYEUR: *Gallia Gran Baita*   €€€   53   ■   ●   ■
Strada Larzey Courmayeur, 11013. [0165 84 40 40. FAX 0165 84 48 05. @ info@hotelgallia.it
A modern, luxury hotel catering to the upmarket skier; it has saunas, a fitness centre, beauty parlour and free transport to the slopes.

COURMAYEUR: *Palace Bron*   €€€€   27   ■   ■
Via Plan Gorret 41, 11013. [0165 84 67 42. FAX 0165 84 40 15. @ hotelpb@tin.it
An elegant family-run hotel that is furnished in the style of a smart home. Most of the rooms have balconies with wonderful views.

CUNEO: *Smeraldo* €€ 21
Corso Nizza 27, 12100. **[** 0171 69 63 67. **FAX** 0171 69 80 76.
A reasonably priced hotel located on one of the main roads of central Cuneo;
the historic centre is easily reached by bus or on foot. 🛏 TV 🗗 P

DOMODOSSOLA: *Corona* €€ 32
Via Marconi 8, 28845. **[** 0324 24 21 14. **FAX** 0324 24 28 42. **@** htcorona@tin.it
Set in the centre of town, the Corona combines tradition with modern
convenience. The restaurant offers a range of local cuisine. 🛏 TV ▤ 🗗 P

IVREA: *Castello San Giuseppe* €€€ 16
Località Castello San Giuseppe, Chiaverano 10010. **[** 0125 42 43 70. **FAX** 0125 64 12 78.
Originally a convent, this pretty, peaceful hotel has a lovely garden. The
simple rooms are attractively furnished in traditional style. 🛏 TV 🗗 P

LAKE MAGGIORE: *Verbano* €€€ 12
Via Ugo Ara 1, Isola dei Pescatori 28049. **[** 0323 304 08. **FAX** 0323 331 29.
A rambling villa is the setting for this friendly hotel with views over the lake.
All of the prettily decorated bedrooms have their own balcony. 🛏 🗗

NOVARA: *Bussola* €€€ 93
Via Boggiani 54, 28100. **[** 0321 45 08 10. **FAX** 0321 45 27 86. **@** bussola@msoft.it
The modern Bussola hotel is pleasantly and comfortably decorated. The
popular restaurant holds dinner dances on Saturday nights. 🛏 TV ▤ 🗗 P

NOVARA: *Italia* €€€ 63
Via Paolo Solaroli 8, 28100. **[** 0321 39 93 16. **FAX** 0321 39 93 10. **W** www.panciolihotels.it
Located in the centre of Novara next to the cathedral, the Italia is comfortable
and well-run. The hotel's restaurant is also very good. 🛏 TV ▤ 🗗 P

ORTA SAN GIULIO: *Leon d'Oro* €€ 35
Piazza Motta 42, 28016. **[** 0322 911 991. **FAX** 0322 903 03. **@** leondoro@lycos.it
Beautifully located on the shores of Lake Orta, the bedrooms have functional,
if rather bland, decor and some have balconies with views. 🛏 TV 🗗

ORTA SAN GIULIO: *Bussola* €€€ 24
Via Panoramica 24, 28016. **[** 0322 91 19 13. **FAX** 0322 91 19 34. **@** hotelbussola@yahoo.it
The hotel is a traditional villa set in a pretty flower-filled garden with views
over the lake. Guests are expected to take half-board in summer. 🛏 TV 🗗 P

ORTA SAN GIULIO: *Orta* €€€ 35
Piazza Motta 1, 28016. **[** 0322 902 53. **FAX** 0322 90 56 46.
Set on the main piazza of Orta San Giulio, the hotel terrace overlooks the lake.
It has a pleasant old-fashioned atmosphere and spacious rooms. 🛏 🗗

PONT-SAINT-MARTIN: *Ponte Romano* €€ 13
Piazza IV Novembre 14, 11026. **[** 0125 80 43 29. **FAX** 0125 80 71 08.
Attractively located next to an ancient Roman bridge, this small, comfortable
family-run hotel is conveniently close to the centre of town. 🛏 TV 🗗 P

SAN GIORGIO MONFERRATO: *Castello San Giorgio* €€€ 11
Via Cavalli d'Olivola 3, 15020. **[** 0142 80 62 03. **FAX** 0142 80 65 05.
An elegant, refined hotel with an excellent restaurant in a pretty castle set
in its own grounds 6 km (4 miles) from Casale Monferrato. 🛏 TV ▤ 🗗 P

SAUZE D'OULX: *Il Capricorno* €€€ 7
Case Sparse 21, Le Clotes 10050. **[** 0122 85 02 73. **FAX** 0122 85 00 55. **W** www.italiabc.it
Set on the wooded hills above the village, this is a delightfully traditional
chalet hotel with traditional wooden beams and furniture. 🛏 TV 🗗 P

SESTRIERE: *Principe di Piemonte* €€€€ 100
Via Sauze di Cesana, 10058. **[** 0122 79 41. **FAX** 0122 75 54 11. **@** framon@framon-hotels.it
This was once the grand hotel of Sestriere and it is still plush and extremely
comfortable. It has everything you will need from sauna to shops. 🛏 TV 🗗 P

SUSA: *Napoleon* €€ 62
Via Mazzini 44, 10059. **[** 0122 62 28 55. **FAX** 0122 319 00.
The Napoleon is a modern, clean hotel that has always been run by
the same family. It is well placed in the town centre. 🛏 TV 🗗 ♿ P

TURIN: *Conte Biancamano* €€€ 24
Corso Vittorio Emanuele II 73, 10128. **[** 011 562 32 81. **FAX** 011 562 37 89. **@** cbhtl.to@iol.it
A centrally placed family-run hotel whose public rooms are decorated with
paintings and chandeliers. Bedrooms are light and spacious. 🛏 TV 🗗 P

	NUMBER OF ROOMS	RESTAURANT	SWIMMING POOL	GARDEN OR TERRACE
Price categories for a standard double room for one night, including tax and service charges but not including breakfast: € under 52 euros €€ 52–100 euros €€€ 100–155 euros €€€€ 155–205 euros €€€€€ over 205 euros.	**RESTAURANT** A restaurant within the hotel sometimes reserved for residents. **SWIMMING POOL** Hotel swimming pools are usually quite small and are outdoors unless otherwise stated. **GARDEN OR TERRACE** A garden, courtyard or terrace belonging to the hotel, often providing tables for eating outside. **CREDIT CARDS** The major credit cards VISA, MasterCard (Access) and American Express are accepted in hotels with the credit card symbol.			

TURIN: *Genova e Stazione*   €€€   58
Via Sacchi 14b, 10128. [011 562 94 00. FAX 011 562 98 96. @ hotelgenova@hotelres.it
Well placed in the city centre, close to the station. Bedrooms are decorated
in a mixture of styles including Art Deco and 18th century. 🔸 TV 🔲 🖃 & P

TURIN: *Victoria*   €€€   96
Via Nino Costa 4, 10123. [011 561 19 09. FAX 011 561 18 06.
The comfortable, pretty rooms in this modern hotel combine function with
innovative decor; choose the Egyptian or New Orleans rooms. 🔸 TV 🔲 🖃

TURIN: *Grand Hotel Sitea*   €€€€   118
Via Carlo Alberto 35, 10123. [011 51 70 171. FAX 011 54 80 90. @ sitea@thi.it
This elegant, traditional hotel located in the heart of the city offers excellent
standards of service and a renowned restaurant. 🔸 TV 🔲 🖃 & P

TURIN: *Turin Palace*   €€€€€   121
Via Sacchi 8, 10128. [011 562 55 11. FAX 011 561 21 87. @ palace@thi.it
Dating from 1872, Turin's smartest hotel has an impressive array of modern
facilities. The sumptuous rooms are furnished with antiques. 🔸 TV 🔲 🖃 & P

TURIN: *Villa Sassi-El Toulà*   €€€€€   17
Strada al Traforo del Pino 47, 10132. [011 898 05 56. FAX 011 898 00 95.
Set in a beautiful 17th-century villa, this luxurious hotel just outside Turin still
has many original features such as marble floors and candelabra. 🔸 TV 🔲 🖃 P

VARALLO SESIA: *Vecchio Albergo Sacro Monte*   €€   24
Regione Sacro Monte 14, 13019. [0163 542 54. FAX 0163 511 89.
A peaceful hotel in a restored 16th-century building at the entrance to the
Sacro Monte. Many of the original features have been retained. 🔸 TV 🖃 P

LIGURIA

CAMOGLI: *Casmona*   €€€   26
Saleto Pineto 13. [0185 770015. FAX 0185 775030.
This simple and friendly hotel enjoys a good location overlooking the sea. Spacious
rooms and a restaurant specialising in fish dishes add to its charm. 🔸 TV 🖃 P

CAMOGLI: *Cenobio dei Dogi*   €€€€   107
Via Cuneo 34, 16032. [0185 72 41 00. FAX 0185 77 27 96. W www.cenobio.it
A vast luxurious hotel that offers everything you would expect for the price.
It has tennis courts, panoramic terraces and its own beach. 🔸 TV 🔲 🖃 P

FINALE LIGURE: *Punta Est*   €€€€   40
Via Aurelia 1, 17024. [019 60 06 11. FAX 019 60 06 11. W www.puntaest.com
An 18th-century villa overlooking the sea is the setting for this elegant hotel.
The interior is spacious and furnished with antiques while the terraces and
gardens offer some wonderful views. Half-board is normally offered. 🔸 TV 🖃 P

GARLENDA: *La Meridiana*   €€€€€   28
Via ai Castelli, 17033. [0182 58 02 71. FAX 0182 58 01 50. @ meridiana@relaischateaux.fr
This elegant country villa hotel with comfortable rooms is set in peaceful
gardens. Guests come here to play golf at the course next door and the hotel
offers tennis, bikes and a sauna. Mini-apartments are also available. 🔸 TV 🖃

GENOA: *Best Western Hotel Metropoli*   €€€   48
Vico dei Migliorini 8, 16123. [010 246 88 88. FAX 010 246 86 86. @ metropolige@bestwestern.it
Conveniently placed for both business and sightseeing, the hotel offers
tastefully decorated rooms equipped with mini-bars and hairdriers. 🔸 TV 🔲 🖃 P

GENOA: *Britannia*   €€€   97
Via Balbi 38, 16126. [010 269 91. FAX 010 246 29 42. @ britannia@britannia.it
Centrally situated this hotel has an excellent range of facilities including valet
service, a sauna and a gym fitted with the latest equipment. 🔸 TV 🖃 P

GENOA: *Nuovo Astoria* €€€ 69
Piazza Brignole 4, 16122. **📞** *010 87 33 16.* **FAX** *010 831 73 26.* **@** astorige@tin.it
A simple, no frills, modern hotel in the centre of Genoa, very close to
the station and a short walk from the city's main sights. 🛏 📺 🗹 🅿

MONTEROSSO AL MARE: *Porto Roca* €€€€ 43 ▪ ▪
Via Corone 1, 19016. **📞** *0187 81 75 02.* **FAX** *0187 81 76 92.* **@** portoroca@portoroca.it
Set on a cliff overlooking the sea in a charming village in the
Cinque Terre, the decor in this hotel is a congenial combination
of different styles. 🛏 📺 🗐 🗹

NERVI: *Villa Pagoda* €€€€ 17 ▪ ▪
Via Capolungo 15, 16167. **📞** *010 372 61 61.* **FAX** *010 32 12 18.* **W** www.villapagoda.it
A splendidly romantic early 19th-century villa set in spectacular gardens.
Rooms are large and the decor is bright and clean. 🛏 📺 🗹 🅿

PORTOFINO: *Eden* €€€€ 9 ▪
Via Dritto 18, 16034. **📞** *0185 26 90 91.* **FAX** *0185 26 90 47.* **@** eden@ifree.it
Conveniently located just behind the piazza of the pretty harbour, the Eden
is, as its name suggests, set in an attractive garden. Bedrooms are simple
but well-equipped. 🛏 📺 🗐 🗹

PORTOVENERE: *Genio* €€ 7 ▪
Piazza Bastreri 8, 19025. **📞** *0187 79 06 11.* **FAX** *0187 79 06 11.*
A delightful hotel built into the walls of the medieval castle in 1924. Rooms
are simple, but it is one of the best value hotels in the area. 🛏 📺

RAPALLO: *Stella* €€ 27 ▪
Via Aurelia Ponente 6, 16035. **📞** *0185 503 67.* **FAX** *0185 27 28 37.* **@** hotelstella@tigullio.net
A tall, thin, pink villa with good panoramic views of the sea from the roof
terrace. The decor is a little stark but the owners are particularly friendly
and welcoming. 🛏 📺 🗹 🅿

SAN REMO: *Nyala Suite* €€ 81 ▪ ● ▪
Via Strada Solero 134, 18038. **📞** *0184 667 668.* **FAX** *0184 666 059.* **W** www.nyalahotel.com
Located in a quiet residential area and surrounded by a tropical
garden, the hotel offers a swimming pool and very spacious rooms.
The restaurant has a special vegetarian menu. 🛏 📺 🗐 🗹 🅿

SAN REMO: *Royal* €€€€ 142 ▪ ● ▪
Corso Imperatrice 80, 18038. **📞** *0184 53 91.* **FAX** *0184 66 14 45.* **@** royal@royalhotelsanremo
A traditional deluxe seaside hotel that has been owned by the same family
since 1872. The comfortable bedrooms are decorated with delicate floral
patterns and there is a range of sports and leisure facilities. 🛏 📺 🗐 🗹 🅿

SESTRI LEVANTE: *Grand Hotel dei Castelli* €€€ 30 ▪
Via Penisola 26, 16039. **📞** *0185 48 72 20.* **FAX** *0185 447 67.* **@** htl.castelli@rainbownet.it
Set in spectacular gardens rising from the sea, this converted castle is decorated
with mosaics and Moorish columns. The service is very cordial. 🛏 📺 🗐 🗹 🅿

EMILIA-ROMAGNA

BOLOGNA: *Commercianti* €€€ 34
Via de Pignattari 11, 40124. **📞** *051 23 30 52.* **FAX** *051 22 47 33.* **@** hotcom@tin.it
This was Bologna's first town hall in the 12th century and sympathetic
refurbishment has retained some of its medieval features; some bedrooms
are in the tower. 🛏 📺 🗐 🗹 🅿

BOLOGNA: *Corona d'Oro 1890* €€€ 35
Via Oberdan 12, 40126. **📞** *051 23 64 56.* **FAX** *051 26 26 79.* **@** hotcoro@tin.it
Parts of the building date back to the 14th century and there has been a hotel
here for more than 100 years. Today it has an old-fashioned elegance,
with Art Nouveau friezes combined with all mod-cons. 🛏 📺 🗐 🗹 🅿

BOLOGNA: *Orologio* €€€ 34
Via IV Novembre 10, 40123. **📞** *051 23 12 53.* **FAX** *051 26 05 52.* **@** hotoro@tin.it
Set in the medieval historic centre, nearly all of the rooms in this quiet town
hotel have exceptional views over Piazza Maggiore. 🛏 📺 🗐 🗹 🅿

BUSSETO: *I Due Foscari* €€ 20 ▪ ▪
Piazza Carlo Rossi 15, 43011. **📞** *0524 93 00 39.* **FAX** *0524 916 25.*
Kitschly decorated and furnished in Hollywood medieval style with mock
Gothic windows and wood beams, this hotel is popular with film stars who
come here especially for the annual opera season in June and July. 🛏 📺 🗐 🗹 🅿

	NUMBER OF ROOMS	RESTAURANT	SWIMMING POOL	GARDEN OR TERRACE

Price categories for a standard double room for one night, including tax and service charges but not including breakfast:
€ under 52 euros
€€ 52–100 euros
€€€ 100–155 euros
€€€€ 155–205 euros
€€€€€ over 205 euros.

RESTAURANT
A restaurant within the hotel sometimes reserved for residents.
SWIMMING POOL
Hotel swimming pools are usually quite small and are outdoors unless otherwise stated.
GARDEN OR TERRACE
A garden, courtyard or terrace belonging to the hotel, often providing tables for eating outside.
CREDIT CARDS
The major credit cards VISA, MasterCard (Access) and American Express are accepted in hotels with the credit card symbol.

Hotel	NUMBER OF ROOMS	RESTAURANT	SWIMMING POOL	GARDEN OR TERRACE
CASTELFRANCO EMILIA: *Villa Gaidello Club* €€ Via Gaidello 18, 41013. 059 92 68 06. FAX 059 92 66 20. There are only three suites, so the atmosphere at the "club" is exclusive. This is a lovely 18th-century farmhouse set amid peaceful grounds with a lake.	6	■		■
CESENATICO: *Miramare* € Viale Carducci 2, 47042. 0547 800 06. FAX 0547 847 85. @ miramare@emiliaromagna.it Excellently placed for both beach fans and for those who want to explore the surrounding countryside, the Miramare has a good range of sports and leisure facilities and hosts an important local tennis training ground.	30	■	●	■
FAENZA: *Vittoria* €€ Corso Garibaldi 23, 48018. 0546 215 08. FAX 0546 291 36. @ hvittoria@connectivy.it The hotel, in the historic centre and close to the station, is Art Nouveau in style and has frescoes in the hall and some of the bedrooms.	49	■		■
FERRARA: *Carlton* €€ Via Garibaldi, 93. 0532 211 130. FAX 0532 205 766. @ hotelcarlton@sestantenet.it Close to the monuments of the city, this modern and efficient hotel is well-run and well-equipped. Service is always attentive and courteous.	66			
FERRARA: *Ripagrande* €€€ Via Ripagrande 21, 44100. 0532 76 52 50. FAX 0532 76 43 77. A very attractively restored Renaissance palace is the setting for this smart, well-run hotel. Rooms are light and many are furnished with antiques; those with balconies have lovely views over Ferrara.	40			■
FERRARA: *Duchessa Isabella* €€€€€ Via Palestro 70, 44100. 0532 20 21 21. FAX 0532 20 26 38. @ isabellad@tin.it A splendid hotel set in a 15th-century palazzo in the centre of Ferrara, named after Isabella d'Este who was famous for her parties. Impeccable service and luxurious bedrooms that look out onto a garden full of birds.	27	■		■
MARINA DI RAVENNA: *Bermuda* € Viale della Pace 363, 48023. 0544 53 05 60. FAX 0544 53 16 43. @ hotelbermuda@libero.it Set in the pine woods near the beach 10 km (6 miles) from Ravenna, this modern family-run hotel is basic but clean and welcoming.	23	■		
MODENA: *Canalgrande* €€€€ Corso Canalgrande N 6, 41100. 059 21 71 60. FAX 059 221 674. @ info@canalgrandehotel.it Located in the city centre, this former monastery is an outstanding piece of Neo-Classical architecture, richly decorated and featuring original paintings.	70			■
PARMA: *Torino* €€ Via Angelo Mazza 7, 43100. 0521 28 10 46. FAX 0521 23 07 25. A restuctured former convent, the Torino has been in the same family for three generations and offers peaceful accommodation in the heart of Parma. Bedrooms and public rooms are furnished with Art Nouveau artifacts.	33	■		
PARMA: *Grand Hotel Baglioni* €€€€ Viale Piacenza 12c, 43100. 0521 29 29 29. FAX 0521 29 28 28. @ ghb.parma@baglionihotel.com A modern hotel in the centre of Parma, this example of industrial architecture dating from 1921 has a full range of facilities on offer.	169	■		
PIACENZA: *Florida* €€ Via Cristoforo Colombo 29, 29100. 0523 59 26 00. FAX 0523 59 26 72. A reasonably priced pensione located just outside the historic centre and within easy reach of the train station.	65			
PORTICO DI ROMAGNA: *Al Vecchio Convento* €€€ Via Roma 7, 47010. 0543 96 70 53. FAX 0543 96 71 57. @ vecchioconvento@mail.asianet.it An exquisite hotel, tastefully furnished with simple antiques and white linen, all combining to create an impression of space and tranquillity.	15	■		

RAVENNA: *Argentario*   € | 28
Via di Roma 45, 48100. **C** *0544 355 55.* **FAX** *0544 351 47.*
Well situated in the heart of Ravenna, close to its main monuments and the
public gardens, this is a well-equipped hotel with attractive rooms. 🛏 TV 📖 🍴

RAVENNA: *Bisanzio*   €€ | 38
Via Salara 30, 48100. **C** *0544 21 71 11.* **FAX** *0544 325 39.*
A faded façade hides a welcoming, modern interior overlooking a pretty
garden, conveniently located in the centre of Ravenna. 🛏 TV 📖 🍴

REGGIO NELL'EMILIA: *Hotel Posta*   €€€ | 43
Piazza del Monte 2, 42100. **C** *0522 43 29 44.* **FAX** *0522 45 26 02.* **@** info@hotelposta.re.it
Located in the historic centre, this comfortable hotel has very original decor. An
austere medieval façade hides an embellished Rococo interior. 🛏 TV 📖 🍴 P

RICCIONE: *Hotel des Nations*   €€ | 32
Lungomare Costituzione 2, 47838. **C** *0541 647 878.* **FAX** *0541 645 154.*
New Age hotel on the seafront, decorated in soft colours to harmonize body and
spirit. Various therapies available on request such as reflexology, aromatherapy,
massage and meditation. Private yacht available for excursions. 🛏 TV 📖 🍴 P

RIMINI: *Ambasciatori*   €€ | 66
Viale Vespucci 22, 47037. **C** *0541 555 61.* **FAX** *0541 237 90.*
This elegant and modern hotel is well situated and most rooms have a sea
view. The roof-garden offers a panoramic vista of the coast. 🛏 TV 📖 🍴 P

RIMINI: *Rosabianca*   €€ | 50
Viale Tripoli 195. **C** *0541 390 666.* **FAX** *0541 390 666.*
A modern, recently renovated hotel close to both the beach and the historic
centre of Rimini. Guests can make use of the private beach huts. 🛏 TV 🍴

RIMINI: *Grand Hotel*   €€€€€ | 117
Via Ramuscio 1, 47900. **C** *0541 560 00.* **FAX** *0541 568 66.* **@** info@grandhotelrimini.com
Conveniently situated near the seafront, the port and the station, this large, well-
equipped, smart hotel has tennis courts and its own beach. 🛏 TV 📖 🍴 P

SANTARCANGELO DI ROMAGNA: *Hotel della Porta*   € | 22
Via Andrea Costa 85, 47822. **C** *0541 62 21 52.* **FAX** *0541 62 21 68.*
Set a few miles out of Rimini in a region steeped in references to Dante's
Divine Comedy (see pp30–31), this hotel is divided into two houses. Ornate
frescoes and antique furniture decorate some of the rooms. 🛏 TV 📖 🍴 & P

FLORENCE

FLORENCE: *Piccolo Hotel*   €€ | 10
Via San Gallo 51, 50123. **Map** 2 D4. **C** *055 47 55 19.* **FAX** *055 47 45 15.*
The rooms in this charming hotel close to the city centre are simply decorated,
with a few refined touches. It also offers free bikes for sightseeing tours. 🛏 TV 🍴 & P

FLORENCE: *Rovezzano Bed & Breakfast*   €€ | 6
Via Aretina 417, 50136. **Map** 3 B4. **C** *055 69 00 23.* **FAX** *055 69 10 02.* **@** kkseimi@tin.it
Located within a Renaissance villa 1 km (0.6 mile) east of Florence,
this is a quiet B&B immersed in the countryside. 🛏 P

FLORENCE: *Hotel Silla*   €€€ | 36
Via dei Renai 5, 50125. **Map** 4 D2 (6 E5). **C** *055 234 28 88.* **FAX** *055 234 14 37.* **@** hotelsilla@tin.it
This 16th-century hotel is approached through an elegant courtyard with a
grand staircase. There is a pretty terrace giving views of the Arno. 🛏 TV 📖 🍴 P

FLORENCE: *Londra*   €€€ | 158
Via Jacopo da Diacceto, 16-18, 50123. **Map** 1 B4. **C** *055 238 27 91.* **FAX** *055 21 06 82.*
Conveniently located near the railway station, this hotel is equipped for the business
or leisure traveller: some rooms are provided with PC, fax and modem: there is a
gym and sauna: bikes can be hired: special services for children. 🛏 TV 🍴 P

FLORENCE: *Pensione Annalena*   €€€ | 20
Via Romana 34, 50125. **Map** 3 A3. **C** *055 22 24 02.* **FAX** *055 22 24 03.* **@** info@hotelannalena.it
A 15th-century hotel with spacious, simply but attractively decorated
bedrooms. The public areas are all contained in one great hall. 🛏 TV 🍴

FLORENCE: *Splendor*   €€€ | 31
Via San Gallo 30, 50129. **Map** 2 D4. **C** *055 48 34 27.* **FAX** *055 46 12 76.* **@** info@hotelsplendor.it
A family hotel with dark red decor and frescoed, stuccoed ceilings that give
it the impression of a grand mansion. It shows some signs of wear. 🛏 TV 📖 🍴

Price categories for a standard double room for one night, including tax and service charges but not including breakfast: € under 52 euros €€ 52–100 euros €€€ 100–155 euros €€€€ 155–205 euros €€€€€ over 205 euros.	**RESTAURANT** A restaurant within the hotel sometimes reserved for residents. **SWIMMING POOL** Hotel swimming pools are usually quite small and are outdoors unless otherwise stated. **GARDEN OR TERRACE** A garden, courtyard or terrace belonging to the hotel, often providing tables for eating outside. **CREDIT CARDS** The major credit cards VISA, MasterCard (Access) and American Express are accepted in hotels with the credit card symbol.	NUMBER OF ROOMS	RESTAURANT	SWIMMING POOL	GARDEN OR TERRACE

Hotel	Rooms	Rest.	Pool	Garden
FLORENCE: *Ariele* €€€€ 2 km (1 mile) W, Via Magenta 11, 50123. **Map** 1 A4. **(** 055 21 15 09. **FAX** 055 26 85 21. Located on a residential side street, the lounge in this homely hotel is furnished with antiques. Bedrooms are spacious but austere. 🚪 TV ▤ ✎ P	39			▪
FLORENCE: *Hotel Hermitage* €€€€ Vicolo Marzio 1, 50122. **Map** 6 D4. **(** 055 28 72 16. **FAX** 055 21 22 08. Spectacular views from the more expensive upper-storey rooms of this medieval building a few yards from the Ponte Vecchio. This small hotel has comfortable rooms, each one decorated in a different style. 🚪 ▤ ✎	28			▪
FLORENCE: *Hotel Loggiato dei Serviti* €€€€ Piazza della SS Annunziata 3, 50122. **Map** 2 D4. **(** 055 28 95 92. **FAX** 055 28 95 95. Built in 1527, the reception areas in this hotel near the Spedale degli Innocenti have vaulted ceilings and a bar area flanked by stone columns. 🚪 TV ✎	29			
FLORENCE: *Hotel Montebello Splendid* €€€€ Via Montebello 60. **Map** 1 A5 (5 A2). **(** 055 239 80 51. **FAX** 055 21 18 67. A 19th-century villa elegantly transformed into an intimate hotel near the city centre. Lovely garden and restaurant with outdoor seating. 🚪 TV ▤ ✎ P	49	▪		▪
FLORENCE: *Hotel Porta Rossa* €€€€ Via Porta Rossa 19, 50123. **Map** 3 C1 (5 C3). **(** 055 28 75 51. **FAX** 055 28 21 79. Italy's second-oldest hotel, it dates from 1386 and has a warm and welcoming atmosphere. The huge bedrooms are airy and pleasantly decorated and the vaulted entrance hall is furnished with fine leather suites. 🚪 TV ▤ ✎	80			
FLORENCE: *Hotel Tornabuoni Beacci* €€€€ Via de' Tornabuoni 3, 50123. **Map** 1 C5 (5 C2). **(** 055 21 26 45. **FAX** 055 28 35 94. **@** info@bthotel.it This former palazzo is situated on a busy central street. Wide carpeted hallways lead to lounge areas furnished with antiques and tapestries. Bedrooms are luxurious with beds piled high with pillows. 🚪 TV ▤ ✎ P	28	▪		▪
FLORENCE: *Hotel Villa Belvedere* €€€€ Via Benedetto Castelli 3, 50124. **Map** 3 A5. **(** 055 22 25 01. **FAX** 055 22 31 63. A spacious 1930s villa set in landscaped grounds near the Boboli Gardens. The first-floor terraces have good views of the garden. 🚪 TV ▤ ✎ P	26		●	▪
FLORENCE: *Morandi alla Crocetta* €€€€ Via Laura 50, 50121. **Map** 2 E4. **(** 055 234 47 47. **FAX** 055 248 09 54. **@** hmorandi@dada.it A lovely former convent run by an Englishwoman who has lived here since the 1920s. The interior is decorated with antique rugs and plants. 🚪 TV ▤ ✎ P	10			
FLORENCE: *Grand Hotel Villa Cora* €€€€€ Viale Machiavelli 18, 50125. **Map** 3 A3. **(** 055 229 84 51. **FAX** 055 22 90 86. **@** info@villacora.com A stunning Renaissance building with balustraded terraces segregated by Classical pillars and tall windows. Inside, the reception rooms are decorated with frescoed ceilings and varnished wooden floors. 🚪 TV ▤ ✎ P	48	▪	●	▪
FLORENCE: *Hotel Brunelleschi* €€€€€ Piazza Santa Elisabetta 3, 50122. **Map** 6 D2. **(** 055 273 70. **FAX** 055 21 96 53. This unique hotel was built inside a Byzantine tower. It is therefore wonderfully atmospheric with stunning views over Florence from the roof terrace. 🚪 TV ✎ P	96	▪		
FLORENCE: *Hotel Cellai* €€€€€ Via XXVII Aprile 14, 50129. **Map** 2 D4. **(** 055 48 92 91. **FAX** 055 47 03 87. **@** info@hotelcellai.it A beautifully restored 18th-century building houses this family-run hotel in the heart of Florence. Beautiful views and helpful staff. 🚪 TV ▤ ✎ P	47			▪
FLORENCE: *Hotel Continental* €€€€€ Lungarno degli Acciaiuoli 2, 50123. **Map** 3 C1 (5 C4). **(** 055 272 62. **FAX** 055 28 31 39. In a prime location near the Ponte Vecchio, the hotel's bar and top-floor suites overlook the river. The walls are decorated with a marble effect. 🚪 TV ▤ ✎	48			▪

FLORENCE: *Hotel Excelsior*　€€€€€　168
Piazza d'Ognissanti 3, 50123. **Map** 1 B5 (5 A2). ☎ *055 26 42 01.* FAX *055 21 02 78.*
Occupying two houses rebuilt in 1815, the hotel is decorated with gracious
marble floors and stained glass with lovely views over the Arno. 🛌 📺 🍽 🛁 **P**

FLORENCE: *Hotel Helvetia e Bristol*　€€€€€　49
Via de' Pescioni 2, 50123. **Map** 1 C5 (5 C2). ☎ *055 28 78 14.* FAX *055 28 83 53.*
A luxurious 18th-century hotel a few steps from the Duomo, with antiques, a
domed, stained glass ceiling and a splendid wood and marble bar. 🛌 📺 🍽 🛁 **P**

FLORENCE: *Hotel J and J*　€€€€€　20
Via di Mezzo 20, 50121. **Map** 2 E5. ☎ *055 234 50 05.* FAX *055 24 02 82.* @ jandj@dada.it
This pretty, peaceful hotel is set in a former 16th-century monastery and
has windows set between old stone arches and frescoed ceilings. 🛌 📺 🍽 🛁

FLORENCE: *Hotel Monna Lisa*　€€€€€　30
Borgo Pinti 27, 50121. **Map** 2 E5. ☎ *055 247 97 51.* FAX *055 247 97 55.* @ monnalis@ats.it
An impressive stone courtyard leads into this Renaissance palazzo. Some
of the bedrooms are huge, with old furniture and high ceilings. 🛌 📺 🍽 🛁 **P**

FLORENCE: *Hotel Regency*　€€€€€　33
Piazza Massimo d'Azeglio 3, 50121. **Map** 2 F5. ☎ *055 24 52 47.* FAX *055 234 67 35.*
Behind the modest exterior of a Florentine town house lies a grand, Classical-
style reception area and bar with wood-panelling decor. 🛌 📺 🛁 **P**

FLORENCE: *Rivoli*　€€€€€　60
Via della Scala 33, 50123. **Map** 1 A4 (5 A1). ☎ *055 28 28 53.* FAX *055 29 40 41.*
The weathered façade gives a clue to the age of this 15th-century hotel. It
is generally spacious, cool and decorated to a high standard, combining
both modern and Classical styles with unfussy elegance. 🛌 📺 🍽 🛁 **P**

FLORENCE: *Torre di Bellosguardo*　€€€€€　16
Via Roti Michelozzi 2, 50124. **Map** 5 B5. ☎ *055 229 81 45.* FAX *055 22 90 08.*
This 16th-century villa is situated on a hill outside the historic city centre to the
southwest, in an area called Bellosguardo. Inside, huge rooms are filled with
antiques and Persian rugs. There are spectacular views over Florence. 🛌 🛁 **P**

FLORENCE: *Villa La Massa*　€€€€€　34
Via la Massa 24, Candeli 50012. ☎ *055 62b 11.* FAX *055 63 31 02.* @ villamassa@galactera.it
On a riverside setting 6 km (4 miles) northeast of Florence, this luxurious
17th-century hotel has elegant rooms with antique furniture. 🛌 📺 🍽 🛁 **P**

TUSCANY

AREZZO: *Castello di Gargonza*　€€€　7
Gargonza, Monte San Savino, 52048. ☎ *0575 84 70 21.* FAX *0575 84 70 54.*
A sweeping tree-lined driveway curves around the walls of this castle guest-
house, which also has 18 self-catering apartments. The views are magnificent
and weekly services are held in the pretty frescoed chapel. 🛌 🛁 **P**

CORTONA: *Hotel San Luca*　€€　60
Piazzale Garibaldi 2, 52044. ☎ *0575 63 04 60.* FAX *0575 63 01 05.*
This hillside hotel has simple bedrooms, but the comfortable reception
rooms offer good panoramas over the surrounding valleys. 🛌 📺 🛁 **P**

CORTONA: *Hotel San Michele*　€€€　40
Via Guelfa 15, 52044. ☎ *0575 60 43 48.* FAX *0575 63 01 47.*
A beautifully restored Renaissance palazzo on a narrow street. A maze of
corridors leads to comfortable bedrooms and a superb attic suite. 🛌 📺 🍽 🛁 **P**

CASTELLINA IN CHIANTI: *Tenuta di Ricavo*　€€€€€　23
Località Ricavo, 53011. ☎ *0577 74 02 21.* FAX *0577 74 10 14.*
A charming hotel occupying the entire hamlet and furnished with a mixture of
antiques and rustic furniture. Many rooms are in old country houses. 🛌 🛁 **P**

ELBA: *Airone del Parco e delle Terme*　€€　85
Località San Giovanni, 57037. ☎ *0565 92 91 11.* FAX *0565 91 74 84.* @ airone@elbalink.it
This hotel provides a complete range of facilities: park, a beach, two swimming
pools, spa, beauty centre, and a private boat for excursions. 🛌 📺 🍽 🛁 **P**

ELBA: *Capo Sud*　€€€　40
Località Lacona, 57037. ☎ *0565 96 40 21.* FAX *0565 96 42 63.* @ caposud@elbalink.it
A village-like resort with excellent bay views. The rooms are housed in a
complex of villas and the restaurant serves produce from its orchard. 🛌 📺 **P**

Price categories for a standard double room for one night, including tax and service charges but not including breakfast:
€ under 52 euros
€€ 52–100 euros
€€€ 100–155 euros
€€€€ 155–205 euros
€€€€€ over 205 euros.

RESTAURANT
A restaurant within the hotel sometimes reserved for residents.
SWIMMING POOL
Hotel swimming pools are usually quite small and are outdoors unless otherwise stated.
GARDEN OR TERRACE
A garden, courtyard or terrace belonging to the hotel, often providing tables for eating outside.
CREDIT CARDS
The major credit cards VISA, MasterCard (Access) and American Express are accepted in hotels with the credit card symbol.

	NUMBER OF ROOMS	RESTAURANT	SWIMMING POOL	GARDEN OR TERRACE
FIESOLE: *Hotel Villa Bonelli* €€€ Via F Poeti 1, 50014. 📞 055 595 13. FAX 055 59 89 42. @ info@hotelvillabonelli.com This simple, friendly hotel is pleasantly furnished and has excellent views of Florence. Guests may take dinner if they want.	20	■		■
FIESOLE: *Villa San Michele* €€€€€ Via Doccia 4, 50014. 📞 055 567 82 00. FAX 055 59 87 34. @ villasanmichele@firenze.net Allegedly designed by Michelangelo, the beautiful monastery has extensive grounds and beautiful panoramas over the city from the loggia.	41	■	●	■
GAIOLE IN CHIANTI: *Castello di Spaltenna* €€€€€ Via Spaltenna 13, 53013. 📞 0577 74 94 83. FAX 0577 74 92 69. A beautiful, fortified former monastery with spacious rooms overlooking a courtyard; some rooms have jacuzzis. The restaurant is excellent.	37	■	●	■
GIGLIO PORTO: *Castello Monticello* €€€ Via Provinciale, 58013. 📞 0564 80 92 52. FAX 0564 80 94 73. A castle hotel, it was originally built on this pretty island as a private house. It sits on a hill, and there are superb views from the bedrooms.	29	■		■
LUCCA: *Piccolo Hotel Puccini* €€ Via di Poggio 9, 55100. 📞 0583 554 21. FAX 0583 534 87. @ info@hotelpuccini.com Housed in a lovely old stone building, this smart, small hotel has an attractive bar that overlooks the pretty narrow street outside.	14			
LUCCA: *Hotel Universo* €€€ Piazza del Giglio 1, 55100. 📞 0583 49 36 78. FAX 0583 95 48 54. This big, but slightly worn hotel was built in the 19th century. It has large and comfortable bedrooms, some with pleasant views on to the quiet square. The big luxurious bathrooms are an added attraction.	60	■		■
LUCCA: *Locanda L'Elisa* €€€€€ Via Nuova per Pisa 1952, 55050. 📞 0583 37 97 37. FAX 0583 37 90 19. @ locanda.elisa@lunet.it There is a peaceful and luxurious atmosphere in this stately home that imitates 18th-century Parisian style. Bedrooms are beautifully decorated with antiques and there are two elegant drawing rooms.	10	■	●	■
MONTERIGGIONI: *Albergo Casalta* € Località Strove, 53035. 📞 0577 30 10 02. FAX 0577 30 10 02. Housed in a 1,000-year-old building, a central hearth in the reception adds to the warm and welcoming atmosphere. The restaurant is also very elegant.	10	■	●	
PISA: *Royal Victoria Hotel* €€ Lungarno Pacinotti 12, 56126. 📞 050 94 01 11. FAX 050 94 01 80. @ rvh@csinfo.it A dignified hotel originally built in the 19th century. It retains several original features, including exquisite *trompe l'oeil* drapery and wood-panelled doors.	48			
PISA: *Duomo* €€€ Via S Maria 94. 📞 050 56 18 94. FAX 050 56 04 18. @ hotelduomo@csinfo.it This very comfortable hotel has a spectacular view of the Tower and the other monuments of the city from its roof garden.	93	■		■
PISTOIA: *Albergo Patria* €€ Via Crispi 8, 51100. 📞 0573 251 87. FAX 0573 36 81 68. An ancient hotel with a dark, modern interior and 1970s bedrooms. It is on a pretty street in the centre of Pistoia, well placed for sightseeing. Upper bedrooms have excellent views of the Romanesque Duomo.	23	■		
PISTOIA: *Hotel Piccolo Ritz* €€ Via Vannucci 67, 51100. 📞 0573 267 75 16. FAX 0573 277 98. Near the station in the historic centre of Pistoia, this small hotel lives up to its name and has a pleasant, frescoed café-style bar.	21			

PORTO ERCOLE: *Il Pellicano*   €€€€€   41
Località Sbarcatello, 58018. ☎ *0564 85 81 11.* FAX *0564 83 34 18.*
Luxurious and exclusive with its own rocky beach, this old-style Tuscan villa
has wonderful views. Rooms are elegantly furnished with antiques. 🖥 📺 🍴 ✉ 🅿

RADDA IN CHIANTI: *Villa Miranda*   €€   49
Siena 53017. ☎ *0577 73 80 21.* FAX *0577 73 86 68.*
Run by the same family since the original building (the Post House) was built
in 1842. Bedrooms have beamed ceilings and brass bedsteads. 🖥 🍴 ✉ 🅿

SAN GIMIGNANO: *Hotel Villa Belvedere*   €€   12
Via Dante 14, 53037. ☎ *0577 94 05 39.* FAX *0577 94 03 27.*
A pretty terracotta villa set in a cypress-filled garden with hammocks.
Light, modern bedrooms are painted in soothing pastel shades. ✉ 🅿

SAN GIMIGNANO: *Albergo Leon Bianco*   €€€   25
Piazza della Cisterna 13, 53037. ☎ *0577 94 12 94.* FAX *0577 94 21 23.*
Airy rooms with pleasant views and terracotta floors typify this former
palazzo. Parts of the original stone wall can still be seen. 🖥 📺 🍴 ✉ 🅿

SAN GIMIGNANO: *Villa San Paolo*   €€€€   18
Strada per Certaldo, 53037. ☎ *0577 95 51 00.* FAX *0577 95 51 13.* **Closed**: *Jan–Mar.*
An attractive hillside villa set in terraced gardens with tennis courts.
Inside there are pretty bedrooms and intimate lounges. 🖥 📺 🍴 ✉ 🅿

SIENA: *Hotel Chiusarelli*   €€   49
Viale Curtatone 15, 53100. ☎ *0577 28 05 62.* FAX *0577 27 11 77* @ chiusare@tin.it
A pretty villa that still looks slightly the worse for wear in spite of its recent
restoration. The pleasant garden is filled with palm trees. 🖥 📺 🍴 ✉ 🅿

SIENA: *Santa Caterina*   €€€   19
Via Enea Silvio Piccolomini 7, 53100. ☎ *0577 22 11 05.* FAX *0577 27 10 87.* @ hsc@sienanet.it
The comfortable rooms overlook the marvellous flower garden which has
charming views of the red roofs of Siena. The Santa Caterina, situated near
the Porta Romana, was once a privately owned villa. 🖥 📺 🍴 ✉ 🅿

SIENA: *Villa Patrizia*   €€€€   33
Via Fiorentina 58, 53100. ☎ *0577 504 31.* FAX *0577 504 42.* @ info@villapatrizia.it
A rambling old villa on the city's northern outskirts. The bedrooms,
all of which look out onto the gardens, are simply furnished but
comfortable and quiet. 🖥 📺 🍴 ✉ 🅿

SIENA: *Villa Scacciapensieri*   €€€€   28
Via di Scacciapensieri 10, 53100. ☎ *0577 414 41.* FAX *0577 27 08 54.* @ villasca@tin.it
Set in attractive grounds, this villa features an old-fashioned lounge with a huge
stone fireplace. The spacious bedrooms have views of Siena. 🖥 📺 🍴 ✉ 🅿

SIENA: *Hotel Certosa di Maggiano*   €€€€€   17
Strada di Certosa 82, 53100. ☎ *0577 28 81 80.* FAX *0577 28 81 89.* @ certosa@relaischateaux.fr
A former Carthusian monastery built in 1314 and turned into an exclusive,
peaceful retreat. The rooms are adorned with antique paintings. 🖥 📺 🍴 ✉ 🅿

SINALUNGA: *Locanda L'Amorosa*   €€€€€   20
L'Amorosa, 53048. ☎ *0577 67 94 97.* FAX *0577 63 20 01.* @ locanda@amorosa.it
An enchanting stone and pink terracotta building is the setting for this beautiful
inn. The luxurious bedrooms are quiet and comfortable. 🖥 📺 🍴 ✉ 🅿

VIAREGGIO: *Hotel President*   €€€€   37
Viale Carducci 5, 55049. ☎ *0584 96 27 12.* FAX *0584 96 36 58.*
A smart seaside hotel with attractively refurbished and comfortable bedrooms.
There are excellent sea views from the roof-top restaurant. 🖥 📺 🍴

VOLTERRA: *Albergo Villa Nencini*   €€   32
Borgo Santo Stefano 55, 56048. ☎ *0588 863 86.* FAX *0588 806 01.*
A stone country hotel set in a park a few minutes from the town. Cool, light
bedrooms, a smart breakfast room, basement trattoria and terrace. 🖥 📺 ✉ 🅿

UMBRIA

ASSISI: *Country House*   €   15
Via San Pietro Campagna 178, Località Valecchie, 06081. ☎ *075 81 63 63.*
FAX *075 81 61 55.*
A convenient 700 m (half a mile) from the centre of Assisi, this 1920s villa is set
amid peaceful countryside. Rooms are furnished with antiques. 🖥 📺 🍴 ✉ 🅿

Price categories for a standard double room for one night, including tax and service charges but not including breakfast:
€ under 52 euros
€€ 52–100 euros
€€€ 100–155 euros
€€€€ 155–205 euros
€€€€€ over 205 euros.

RESTAURANT
A restaurant within the hotel sometimes reserved for residents.
SWIMMING POOL
Hotel swimming pools are usually quite small and are outdoors unless otherwise stated.
GARDEN OR TERRACE
A garden, courtyard or terrace belonging to the hotel, often providing tables for eating outside.
CREDIT CARDS
The major credit cards VISA, MasterCard (Access) and American Express are accepted in hotels with the credit card symbol.

	NUMBER OF ROOMS	RESTAURANT	SWIMMING POOL	GARDEN OR TERRACE
ASSISI: *Dei Priori* €€ Corso Mazzini 15, 06081. 075 81 22 37. FAX 075 81 68 04. Set in a 17th-century building in the historic centre, the bedrooms are pretty and fresh and there is a lovely vaulted dining room.	34	■		■
ASSISI: *Umbra* €€ Via degli Archi 6, 06081. 075 81 22 40. FAX 075 81 36 53. @ humbra@mail.caribusiness.it A friendly hotel located in an atmospheric back street in the historic centre. Furnishings are comfortable and in the good weather there is a charming terrace for outside dining.	25			
ASSISI: *Romantik Hotel Le Silve* €€€ Località Armenzano di Assisi, 06081. 075 801 90 00. FAX 075 801 90 05. @ hotellesilve@tin.it Located about 12 km (7 miles) from Assisi, this hotel has wonderful views of the Tuscan hills as well as an excellent range of sports and leisure facilities.	15	■	●	■
CAMPELLO SUL CLITUNNO: *Il Vecchio Molino* €€ Via del Tempio 34, Località Pissignano 06042. 0743 52 11 22. FAX 0743 27 50 97. Set in a converted mill on an island in the river, the bedrooms are spacious and comfortable. A Roman temple can be seen from the garden.	13			■
CASTIGLIONE DEL LAGO: *Miralago* € Piazza Mazzini 6, 06061. 075 95 11 57. FAX 075 95 19 24. @ miralago@ftbcc.it Set in the centre of this town on the shores of Lake Trasimeno, the Miralago is a small hotel run by a family from Kenya who extend a friendly welcome to all guests. Fresh fish from the lake is served in the restaurant.	19	■		
FONTIGNANO: *Villa di Monte Solare* €€ Via Montali 7, Colle San Paolo 06007. 075 83 23 76. FAX 075 835 54 62. A beautiful 18th-century villa set in its own grounds with many original features such as terracotta floors, period furniture and frescoes. Colle San Paolo is 25 km (15 miles) from Perugia through beautiful Umbrian landscape.	20	■	●	■
GUBBIO: *Bosone Palace* €€ Via XX Settembre 22, 06024. 075 922 06 88. FAX 075 922 01 59. Set in the Palazzo Raffaelli, one of the oldest palazzi in the historic centre, the Bosone has a mixture of bedrooms from the spectacular to the ordinary. All of them, however, have a wonderfully historic atmosphere.	30	■		
GUBBIO: *Oderisi-Balestrieri* €€ Via Mazzatinti 2/12, 06024. 075 922 06 62. FAX 075 922 06 63. A hotel in the medieval town centre; the rooms are pleasantly furnished with modern, wooden beams, bedsteads and tables.	35			
GUBBIO: *Villa Montegranelli* €€€ Località Monteluiano, 06024. 075 922 01 85. FAX 075 927 33 72. An elegant country villa about 4 km (2 miles) from Gubbio with attractive bedrooms and a highly recommended restaurant (see p596).	21	■		■
LAKE TRASIMENO: *Hotel da Sauro* €€ Isola Maggiore, 06060. 075 82 61 68. FAX 075 82 51 30. @ hotelsauro@libero.it A basic hotel with friendly staff in an exceptional location. Isola Maggiore remains fairly isolated making this a quiet and simple retreat.	12			■
MONTEFALCO: *Ringhiera Umbra* € Via G Mameli 20, 06036. 0742 37 91 66. FAX 0742 37 91 66. A simple yet immaculately kept hotel in a historic building in the centre of Montefalco. The reasonably priced restaurant is in a vaulted room.	20	■		
MONTEFALCO: *Villa Pambuffetti* €€€ Via della Vittoria 20, 06036. 0742 37 94 17. FAX 0742 37 92 45. @ villabianca@interbusiness.it The spacious and comfortable bedrooms in this hotel are all different. The tower room has wonderful views of the surrounding country.	15	■	●	■

NORCIA: *Garden* € 43
Viale XX Settembre 2b, 06046. 【 0743 81 66 87. FAX 0743 81 66 87.
A simple hotel close to the centre of Norcia, with basic but comfortable
rooms. The Garden is a good base from which to explore the city. 🛏 TV 🗐 P

ORVIETO: *Virgilio* €€ 15
Piazza Duomo 5–6, 05018. 【 0763 34 18 82. FAX 0763 34 37 97. @ virgilio@orvienet.it
Located in central Orvieto, this simple hotel was converted by the owner from
what was once his home. Some rooms have views of the cathedral. 🛏 TV 🗐

ORVIETO: *La Badia* €€€ 26
Località la Badia 8, 05019. 【 0763 30 19 59. FAX 0763 30 53 96.
Housed in a spectacular former monastery, parts of which date back to the
12th century, modern comfort is combined with medieval splendour. 🛏 TV 🗐 🗐 P

ORVIETO: *Villa Ciconia* €€€ 10
Via dei Tigli 69, 05019. 【 0763 30 55 82. FAX 0763 30 20 77
Set in lovely grounds a short distance out of Orvieto, this 16th-century country
house makes a peaceful base from which to explore Umbria. 🛏 TV 🗐 🗐 P

PERUGIA: *Locanda della Rocca* €€ 7
Viale Roma 4, 06060. 【 075 83 02 36. FAX 075 83 02 36.
An old Umbrian mansion with a mill has been transformed into this small, charming,
family-run hotel. The attentive service lends a warm atmosphere. 🛏 TV 🗐 🗐

PERUGIA: *Lo Spedalicchio* €€ 25
Piazza Bruno Buozzi 3, Ospedalicchio 06080. 【 075 801 03 23. FAX 075 801 03 23.
Built within the walls of a 14th-century fortress, the rooms are simply but
comfortably decorated in keeping with the style of the building. 🛏 TV 🗐 P

PERUGIA: *Tiferno* €€ 38
Piazza Rafaello Sanzio 13, 06012 Città di Castello. 【 0758 55 03 31. FAX 0758 52 11 96.
A 17th-century palace that was turned into a monastery; it has been a hotel since
1895. The restructuring has respected the original architecture. 🛏 TV 🗐 🗐 P

PERUGIA: *Locanda della Posta* €€€ 40
Corso Vannucci 97, 06100. 【 075 572 89 25. FAX 075 573 25 62. @ novelber@tin.it
This elegant 200-year-old hotel is housed in a charming old palazzo on
the pedestrianized main street of the historic centre. 🛏 TV 🗐 🗐

PERUGIA: *Brufani* €€€€€ 82
Piazza Italia 12, 06100. 【 075 573 25 41. FAX 075 572 02 10. @ brufani@tin.it
Opened in 1884, the public rooms of this exclusive hotel were painted by Lillis,
the German interior designer. The views are spectacular. 🛏 TV 🗐 🗐 P

SPELLO: *La Bastiglia* €€ 33
Piazza Vallegloria 7, 06038. 【 0742 65 12 77. FAX 0742 30 11 59. @ fancelli@labastiglia.com
An adapted old mill is the setting for this airy, homely hotel whose extensive
terraces give excellent views over the surrounding countryside. 🛏 TV 🗐 🗐 P

SPELLO: *Palazzo Bocci* €€€ 23
Via Cavour 17, 06038. 【 0742 30 10 21. FAX 0742 30 14 64. @ bocci@bcsnet.it
Set in a much restored 14th-century palazzo in the centre of Spello, this
hotel combines modern convenience with traditional charm. 🛏 TV 🗐 🗐 P

SPOLETO: *Aurora* € 15
Via Apollinare 3, 06049. 【 0743 22 03 15. FAX 0743 22 18 85. @ hotelaurora@virgilio.it
A good value hotel in the historic centre. It is connected to the Apollinare
restaurant and (unusually for this price) all rooms have mini-bars. 🛏 TV 🗐 P

SPOLETO: *Charleston* € 21
Piazza Collicola 10, 06049. 【 0743 22 00 52. FAX 0743 22 12 44. @ hotelcharleston@edisons.it
A 17th-century building in the centre of Spoleto. The modern and traditional
furnishings in this hotel create an uncluttered yet homely feel. 🛏 TV 🗐 🗐 P

SPOLETO: *Gattapone* €€€ 15
Via del Ponte 6, 06049. 【 0743 22 34 47. FAX 0743 22 34 48. @ gattapone@mail.caribusiness.it
A smart hotel, built on the highest point of the town, five minutes' walk
from the centre with excellent views of the Ponte delle Torri. 🛏 TV 🗐 P

TODI: *Bramante* €€ 43
Via Orvietana 48, 06059. 【 075 894 83 81. FAX 075 894 80 74. @ bramante@hotelbramante.it
Although rebuilt, parts of the 13th-century convent remain and the simple
furnishings of this quiet hotel add to the peaceful atmosphere. 🛏 TV 🗐 🗐 P

Price categories for a standard double room for one night, including tax and service charges but not including breakfast:
€ under 52 euros
€€ 52–100 euros
€€€ 100–155 euros
€€€€ 155–205 euros
€€€€€ over 205 euros.

RESTAURANT
A restaurant within the hotel sometimes reserved for residents.

SWIMMING POOL
Hotel swimming pools are usually quite small and are outdoors unless otherwise stated.

GARDEN OR TERRACE
A garden, courtyard or terrace belonging to the hotel, often providing tables for eating outside.

CREDIT CARDS
The major credit cards VISA, MasterCard (Access) and American Express are accepted in hotels with the credit card symbol.

		Number of Rooms	Restaurant	Swimming Pool	Garden or Terrace

TODI: *Hotel Fonte Cesia* €€ — 36 — Restaurant ■ — Garden ■
Via Lorenzo Leonj 3, 06059. 📞 075 894 37 37. FAX 075 894 46 77. @ f.cesia@full_service.it
A beautiful 17th-century palazzo is the setting for this elegant and intimate hotel that combines traditional charm with all modern comforts. 🛏 📺 🗏 💳 P

TORGIANO: *Le Tre Vaselle* €€€ — 61 — Restaurant ■ — Swimming Pool ● — Garden ■
Via G Garibaldi 48, 06089. 📞 075 988 04 47. FAX 075 988 02 14. @ 3vaselle@3vaselle.it
Set in a 17th-century country house, the hotel has retained its terracotta floor tiles and beamed ceilings and is furnished with rural antiques. 🛏 📺 🗏 💳 P

LE MARCHE

ANCONA: *Emilia* €€€ — 29 — Restaurant ■ — Swimming Pool ● — Garden ■
Poggio di Portonovo, 60020. 📞 071 80 11 45. FAX 071 80 13 30. @ info@hotelemilia.com
A refined hotel with bright and pretty interior decorations. As well as hosting concerts for the Ancona Jazz festival in its elegant garden, the Emilia organizes an annual art prize and has a collection of contemporary art. 🛏 📺 🗏 💳 P

ANCONA: *Grand Hotel Palace* €€€ — 40 — Garden ■
Lungomare Vanvitelli 24. 📞 071 20 18 13. FAX 071 207 48 32. @ palace.ancona@tiscalinet.it
Once the private palace of a noble family, this stylish hotel is located near the harbour. There is a beautiful panorama from the roof terrace. 🛏 📺 💳

AQUAVIVA PICENA: *Hotel O'Viv* €€ — 12 — Restaurant ■
Via Marziale 43, 63030. 📞 0735 76 46 49. FAX 0735 76 50 54.
Set in an attractive palazzo in the medieval town centre, the bedrooms in this traditional hotel are spacious with wonderful views from the terrace. 🛏 📺 💳

FOLIGNANO: *Villa Pigna* €€ — 54 — Garden ■
Viale Assisi 33, 63040. 📞 0736 49 18 68. FAX 0736 49 21 79.
A modern, efficiently-run hotel in the centre of town. The public rooms are attractive and the bedrooms, if unexceptional, are satisfactory. 🛏 📺 🗏 💳 P

JESI: *Federico II* €€€ — 124 — Restaurant ■ — Swimming Pool ● — Garden ■
Via Ancona 100, 60035. 📞 0731 21 10 79. FAX 0731 572 21. @ htl.federico@pieralisi.it
A slick post-modern hotel offering a massive range of facilities: indoor pool, gym, and a conference centre. A little impersonal, but comfortable. 🛏 📺 💳 P

MONTECASSIANO: *Villa Quiete* €€ — 38 — Restaurant ■ — Garden ■
Località Vallecascia, 62010. 📞 0733 59 95 59. FAX 0733 59 95 59.
A country villa hotel set in its own beautiful gardens. Some of the pretty rooms have antique furnishings. There are also two suites. 🛏 📺 🗏 💳 P

PESARO: *Villa Serena* €€€ — 9 — Restaurant ■ — Swimming Pool ● — Garden ■
Via San Nicola 6–3, 61100. 📞 0721 552 11. FAX 0721 559 27.
This 17th-century mansion, set in its own well-kept grounds, is a very comfortable, friendly hotel where no two rooms are alike. 🛏 💳 P

PESARO: *Vittoria* €€€ — 27 — Restaurant ■ — Swimming Pool ● — Garden ■
Via A Vespucci 2, Piazzale Libertà 2, 61100. 📞 0721 343 43. FAX 0721 652 04. @ info@viphotels.it
The Vittoria is a perfect combination of old-fashioned charm and modern convenience. It has a good range of facilities and is close to the sea. 🛏 📺 🗏 💳 P

PORTONOVO: *Fortino Napoleonico* €€€€ — 30 — Restaurant ■ — Garden ■
Via Poggio 166, 60020. 📞 071 80 14 50. FAX 071 80 14 54. @ fortino@fastnet.it
Built to protect the coast from the marauding English during the Napoleonic wars, the fortress has been comfortably restored with tasteful decor and antiques, and has its own beach. Now even the English are welcome. 🛏 📺 🗏 💳 P

SAN BENEDETTO DEL TRONTO: *Sabbia D'Oro* €€ — 63 — Restaurant ■ — Swimming Pool ● — Garden ■
Viale Marconi 46, 63039. 📞 0735 819 11. FAX 0735 849 17.
A modern beach hotel in this busy, fashionable resort. Rooms are well-designed and comfortable, and each has a mini-bar and safe. 🛏 📺 🗏 💳 P

SAN LEO: *Castello* ··· € | 14
Piazza Dante Alighieri 12, 61018. [0541 91 62 14. FAX 0541 92 69 26.
Housed in a restored 16th-century town building in the town centre, the white
tiles and light colours in the interior create an airy atmosphere. 🛏 TV 🍴

SAN MARINO: *Panoramic* ··· € | 27
Via Voltone 89, 47890. [0549 99 23 59. FAX 0549 99 03 56.
A family-run hotel in a tranquil part of this independent republic in the middle
of Italy. The Panoramic is particularly proud of its restaurant. 🛏 TV 🍴 P

SIROLO: *Monte Conero* ·· €€ | 60
Via Monteconero 26, 60020. [071 933 05 92. FAX 071 933 03 65. @ monteconero.hotel@fastnet.it
Splendid sea views from this hotel in an 11th-century monastery with a
Romanesque church. Rooms are bright and have their own balconies. Guests
are expected to take half or full board during July and August. 🛏 TV 🍴 P

URBINO: *Locanda la Brombolona* ·· € | 12
Località Sant'Andrea in Primicilio 22, 61029. [& FAX 0722 535 01.
Pleasantly located in the rolling hills above Urbino, this charming little hotel
makes a peaceful rural base from which to explore the surroundings. Inside
it is simply furnished and rooms have views over the countryside. 🛏 🍴 P

URBINO: *Bonconte* ··· €€ | 23
Via delle Mura 28, 61029. [0722 31 63. FAX 0722 47 82.
A recently refurbished old villa; furnishings include some antiques among
the more modern suites. The bright rooms are well-equipped. 🛏 TV 🍴

ROME

AVENTINE: *Sant'Anselmo* ·· €€ | 46
Piazza Sant'Anselmo 2, 00153. Map 6 E3. [06 574 35 47. FAX 06 578 36 04.
A pretty villa on the peaceful Aventine within walking distance of the
Colosseum. It has a secluded garden and and hand-painted furniture. 🛏 TV 🍴 P

AVENTINE: *Domus Aventina* ·· €€€€ | 26
Via di Santa Prisca 11b, 00153. Map 6 E3. [06 461 35. FAX 06 57 30 00 44
Situated in a 14th-century convent at the foot of the Aventine Hill, the hotel
offers large, simply decorated rooms, most of them with balconies. 🛏 TV 🍴

CAMPO DE' FIORI: *Piccolo* ·· €€ | 15
Via dei Chiavari 32, 00186. Map 2 F4. [06 68 80 25 60.
A cool, serene family-run hotel with clean, simple rooms and a TV in
the breakfast room. It is one of the cheapest hotels in the area. 🍴

CAMPO DE' FIORI: *Teatro di Pompeo* ··· €€€ | 13
Largo del Pallaro 8, 00186. Map 2 F4. [06 68 30 01 70, 687 25 66. FAX 06 68 80 55 31.
A small courteously run hotel whose basement breakfast room is in the ruins
of Pompey the Great's theatre. Bedrooms have beamed ceilings. 🛏 TV 🍴 P

FORUM: *Forum* ·· €€€€€€ | 76
Via Tor de' Conti 25, 00184. Map 3 C5. [06 679 24 46. FAX 06 678 64 79.
An old-fashioned hotel with wood-panelled public rooms and a sunny
roof-terrace restaurant with views over the archaeological zone. 🛏 TV 🍴 P

FORUM: *Lancelot* ·· €€€€€ | 60
Via Capo d'Africa 47. Map 7 B1. [06 70 45 06 15. FAX 06 70 45 06 40.
A welcoming family-run hotel close to the Colosseum. Rooms are
tastefully furnished. There is a cool courtyard bar and restaurant. 🛏 TV 🍴 P

NAZIONALE: *Hotel Giuliana* ·· €€€ | 11
Via Agostino Depretis 70, 00184. Map 4 E4. [06 488 0795. W www.hotelgiuliana.com
A centrally located, family-run hotel with many amenities. The helpful staff contribute
to the home-away-from-home atmosphere. 🛏 TV 🍴

NAZIONALE: *Artemide* ··· €€€€€ | 85
Via Nazionale 22, 00184. Map 3 C4. [06 48 99 11. FAX 06 489 917 00.
Stylish hotel harmonizing early 20th-century architecture and Art Nouveau motifs.
Impeccable, sound-proof rooms offer every modern facility. The adjoining
"Caffetteria Nazionale" is a popular two-level coffee shop/restaurant. 🛏 TV 🍴

PANTHEON: *Abruzzi* ··· €€ | 25
Piazza della Rotonda 69, 00186. Map 2 F4. [06 679 20 21.
Terracotta-tiled floors in an ochre-coloured palazzo overlooking the Pantheon.
The Abruzzi provides clean, simple but pleasant rooms without breakfast.

Price categories for a standard double room for one night, including tax and service charges but not including breakfast:
€ under 52 euros
€€ 52–100 euros
€€€ 100–155 euros
€€€€ 155–205 euros
€€€€€ over 205 euros.

RESTAURANT
A restaurant within the hotel sometimes reserved for residents.
SWIMMING POOL
Hotel swimming pools are usually quite small and are outdoors unless otherwise stated.
GARDEN OR TERRACE
A garden, courtyard or terrace belonging to the hotel, often providing tables for eating outside.
CREDIT CARDS
The major credit cards VISA, MasterCard (Access) and American Express are accepted in hotels with the credit card symbol.

	NUMBER OF ROOMS	RESTAURANT	SWIMMING POOL	GARDEN OR TERRACE
PANTHEON: *Santa Chiara* €€€€ Via di Santa Chiara 21, 00186. **Map** 2 F4. 📞 06 687 29 79. FAX 06 687 31 44. A conveniently located hotel with cool, marble reception area and well-furnished bedrooms. Rooms facing the street can be noisy. 🖪 TV 📖 🖾	97			
PANTHEON: *Crowne Plaza Minerva* €€€€€ Piazza della Minerva 69, 00186. **Map** 3 A4. 📞 06 69 52 01. FAX 06 679 41 65. The interior, with its semi-translucent Venetian glass and marble, was designed by post-modern architect Paolo Portoghesi and the bedrooms are spacious and bright. The roof terrace commands magnificent views. 🖪 TV 📖 🖾 🛪	134	■		■
PANTHEON: *Nazionale* €€€€€ Piazza di Montecitorio 131, 00186. **Map** 3 A3. 📞 06 69 50 01. FAX 06 678 66 77. Opposite the Chamber of Deputies, the Nazionale's comfortable and sometimes huge rooms are furnished with British and Italian antiques. The hotel is popular with business travellers and well-heeled tourists. 🖪 TV 🖾	87	■		
PANTHEON: *Sole al Pantheon* €€€€€ Piazza della Rotonda 63, 00186. **Map** 2 F4. 📞 06 678 04 41. FAX 06 69 94 06 89. A historic hotel dating from 1467. Some of its beautiful modernized rooms have painted panelled ceilings and magical views of the Pantheon. 🖪 TV 📖 🖾	25			
PIAZZA NAVONA: *Navona* €€ Via dei Sediari 8, 00186. **Map** 2 F4. 📞 06 686 42 03. FAX 06 68 80 38 02. Book well in advance for this superbly located hotel run by the owner's Australian son-in-law. Rooms are basic but satisfactory. 🖪 📖 🛪	31			
PIAZZA NAVONA: *Due Torri* €€€ Vicolo del Leonetto 23–25, 00186. **Map** 2 F3. 📞 06 687 69 83. FAX 06 686 54 42. An amiable hotel tucked into an alleyway in the artisans' district. Rooms vary in size and style. Public rooms have a country house feel. 🖪 TV 📖 🖾	26			■
PIAZZA NAVONA: *Raphael* €€€€€ Largo Febo 2, 00186. **Map** 2 F3. 📞 06 68 28 31. FAX 06 687 89 93. @ info@raphaelhotel.com An ivy-clad luxury hotel whose reception is full of antique statues and modern sculpture. It has a restaurant and elegantly furnished bedrooms. 🖪 TV 📖 🖾	70	■		
PIAZZA DI SPAGNA: *Jonella* €€ Via della Croce 41, 00187. **Map** 3 A2. 📞 06 679 79 66. FAX 06 446 23 68. @ jonella@lodgingitaly.com The low prices and location on one of the main shopping streets of the Piazza di Spagna area make this simple pensione well worth considering.	5			
PIAZZA DI SPAGNA: *Margutta* €€ Via Laurina 34, 00187. **Map** 3 A1. 📞 06 322 36 74. FAX 06 320 03 95. Pretty rooms on a quiet street. Book in advance if you want one of the three attic rooms that share a roof terrace. Public rooms are airy and bright. 🖪 🖾	24			
PIAZZA DI SPAGNA: *Condotti* €€€€ Via Mario de' Fiori 37, 00187. **Map** 3 A2. 📞 06 679 46 61. FAX 06 679 04 57. A comfortable, welcoming hotel in the heart of the designer shopping district. Rooms are medium to large and well decorated. One room has its own small terrace and three others share one. 🖪 TV 📖 🖾	16			■
PIAZZA DI SPAGNA: *Gregoriana* €€€€ Via Gregoriana 18, 00187. **Map** 3 B2. 📞 06 679 42 69. FAX 06 678 42 58. This stylish hotel, popular with writers and artists in the 19th century, has an interesting variety of decoration, including some unusual leopard-spotted wallpaper. Bedrooms, however, are flowery and fresh. 🖪 TV	19			
PIAZZA DI SPAGNA: *Hassler* €€€€€ Piazza Trinità dei Monti 6, 00187. **Map** 3 B2. 📞 06 69 93 40. FAX 06 678 99 91. Venetian glass chandeliers and wood-panelled bathrooms retain the air of a more extravagant era. Magnificent views from the roof-terrace. 🖪 TV 📖 🖾 P	100	■		■

PIAZZA DI SPAGNA: *Scalinata di Spagna* €€€€€ | 16
Piazza Trinità del Monti 17, 00187. **Map** 3 B2. 📞 *06 679 30 06.* ⚏ *06 69 94 05 98.*
A convivial hotel in a small 18th-century villa at the top of the Spanish Steps.
The rooms that open onto the terrace have exquisite views. 🛏 📺 ▤ 🗐 P

TERMINI: *Katty* € | 15
Via Palestro 35, 00185. **Map** 4 E1. 📞 & ⚏ *06 444 12 16.*
The Katty has clean, basic rooms with an occasional piece of antique furniture.
It is extremely popular with British and American students, so book early.

TERMINI: *Mari 2* € | 27
Via Calatafimi 38, 00185. **Map** 4 E1. 📞 *06 474 03 71.* ⚏ *06 482 83 13.*
A friendly hotel run by three women. It has clean pleasant rooms with no frills.
Guests can be accommodated at a nearby pensione when this one is full. 📺 🗐

TERMINI: *Restivo* € | 6
Via Palestro 55, 00185. **Map** 4 F2. 📞 *06 446 21 72.* ⚏ *06 445 26 29.*
Alongside the Mari, this small hotel (only six rooms) is beautifully maintained.
Guests return again and again.

TERMINI: *Canada* €€ | 70
Via Vicenza 58, 00185. **Map** 4 F2. 📞 *06 445 77 70.* ⚏ *06 445 07 49.* @ canada@italyhotel.com
A good, mid-range hotel behind Termini station, which has a pleasant lounge-bar
with attractive cane seats and squashy sofas. Courteous service. 🛏 📺 ▤ 🗐 P

TERMINI: *Kennedy* €€ | 51
Via Filippo Turati 64, 00185. **Map** 4 F4. 📞 *06 446 53 73.* ⚏ *06 446 54 17.*
Close to Termini station, this recently renovated hotel has friendly young staff.
Ample breakfasts are served and some rooms have great views. 🛏 📺 ▤ 🗐

TERMINI: *Diana* €€€€ | 170
Via Principe Amedeo 4. **Map** 4 E3. 📞 *06 482 75 41.* ⚏ *06 48 69 98.*
This pleasant hotel offers tastefully furnished rooms. The restaurant offers traditional
Italian cuisine, served on the roof-terrace in summer. 🛏 📺 ▤ 🗐

VATICAN: *Alimandi* €€ | 35
Via Tunisi 8, 00192. **Map** 3 D1. 📞 *06 39 72 63 00.* ⚏ *06 39 72 29 43.* @ alimandi@tin.it
A simple pensione near the entrance to the Vatican museums. It has a large
terrace where you can have barbecues if you ask in advance. 🛏 📺 ▤ 🗐 P

VATICAN: *Colombus* €€€€ | 100
Via della Conciliazione 33, 00193. **Map** 1 C3. 📞 *06 686 48 74.* ⚏ *06 686 54 34.*
Occupying a former monastery near St Peter's Square, the hotel's function
room is in the old refectory and has retained its original frescoes. 🛏 📺 ▤ 🗐 P

VATICAN: *Hotel dei Mellini* €€€€€ | 80
Via Muzio Clementi 81. **Map** 2 F2. 📞 *06 32 47 71.* ⚏ *06 32 47 78 01.* @ info@hotelmellini.com
The cool style of this chic hotel attracts international travellers.
Contemporary works of art adorn the interior public spaces. 🛏 📺 ▤ 🗐 P

VATICAN: *Visconti Palace* €€€€€ | 247
Via Federico Cesi 37, 00193. **Map** 2 E2. 📞 *06 36 84.* ⚏ *06 32 00 551.*
This modern and efficient hotel is in an ideal location and provides large common
spaces and well-decorated rooms. There is a piano bar nightly. 🛏 📺 ▤ 🗐 P

VIA VENETO: *Merano* €€ | 30
Via Veneto 155, 00187. **Map** 3 C1. 📞 *06 482 17 808.* ⚏ *06 482 18 10.*
A bonus feature of this very friendly hotel in a 19th-century palazzo
is its sunny, parquet-floored breakfast room. 🛏 🗐

VIA VENETO: *Alexandra* €€€€ | 58
Via Veneto 18, 00187. **Map** 3 C1. 📞 *06 488 19 43.* ⚏ *06 487 18 04.* @ alexandra@venere.it
A good value hotel on this expensive street, the Alexandra has a pleasant
breakfast room and each bedroom has been decorated differently. 🛏 📺 ▤ 🗐

VIA VENETO: *Ambasciatori Palace* €€€€ | 150
Via Vittorio Veneto 62, 00187. **Map** 3 C1. 📞 *06 474 93.* ⚏ *06 474 36 01.*
This hotel offers hospitality in the grand tradition. Set within a historical
building, the plush furnishings add to the air of luxury. 🛏 📺 ▤ 🗐

VIA VENETO: *Residenza* €€€€ | 29
Via Emilia 22–24, 00187. **Map** 3 C1. 📞 *06 488 07 89.* ⚏ *06 48 57 21.*
An elegant, courteously-run hotel in a quiet villa, with stylish public rooms,
comfortable bedrooms and a delightful canopied terrace. 🛏 📺 ▤ 🗐 P

For key to symbols see back flap

<table>
<tr><td colspan="5">

Price categories for a standard double room for one night, including tax and service charges but not including breakfast:
€ under 52 euros
€€ 52–100 euros
€€€ 100–155 euros
€€€€ 155–205 euros
€€€€€ over 205 euros.

RESTAURANT
A restaurant within the hotel sometimes reserved for residents.
SWIMMING POOL
Hotel swimming pools are usually quite small and are outdoors unless otherwise stated.
GARDEN OR TERRACE
A garden, courtyard or terrace belonging to the hotel, often providing tables for eating outside.
CREDIT CARDS
The major credit cards VISA, MasterCard (Access) and American Express are accepted in hotels with the credit card symbol.

</td></tr>
</table>

	NUMBER OF ROOMS	RESTAURANT	SWIMMING POOL	GARDEN OR TERRACE
VIA VENETO: *Excelsior* €€€€€ Via Veneto 125, 00187. **Map** 3 C1. **(** 06 47 081. **FAX** 06 482 62 05. This extravagant hotel has sumptuous public rooms with marble floors and brocade furnishings. Bedrooms are elegant and spacious. 🖥 📺 🍽 🐾 🅿	321	■		
VILLA BORGHESE: *Villa Borghese* €€€ Via Pinciana 31, 00198. **(** 06 854 96 48. **FAX** 06 841 41 00. **@** hotel.villaborghese@quipo.it This pleasant hotel has the atmosphere of a private home rather than a hotel. Rooms are small but comfortable and are tastefully decorated. 🖥 📺 🍽 🐾	31			■
VILLA BORGHESE: *Lord Byron* €€€€€ Via Notaris 5, 00197. **(** 06 322 04 04. **FAX** 06 322 04 05. **@** info@lordbyronhotel.com A small, refined hotel housed in a former stately home in the Parioli district, the Lord Byron has lavishly decorated public rooms. 🖥 📺 🍽 🐾	37	■		■
LAZIO				
ANAGNI: *Villa La Floridiana* €€ Via Casilina, km 63,700, 03012. **(** 0775 76 99 60. **FAX** 0775 77 45 27. **@** floridiana@applicazioni.it A beautiful medieval village is the setting for this charming villa with a traditional faded pink façade, green shutters and large, comfortable rooms. 🖥 📺 🍽 🐾 🅿	9	■		■
BAGNI DI TIVOLI: *Grand Hotel Duca d'Este* €€€ Via Tiburtina Valeria 330, 00011. **(** 0774 38 83. **FAX** 0774 38 81 01. **@** ducadeste@ducadeste.com A modern well-equipped hotel near Tivoli and Villa Adriana and within easy reach of Rome by road or rail. Suites have satellite TV and jacuzzis. 🖥 📺 🍽 🐾 🅿	184	■	●	■
FORMIA: *Castello Miramare* €€€ Via Balze di Pagnano, 04023. **(** 0771 70 01 38. **FAX** 0771 70 01 39. **@** info@hotelcastellomiramare.it The castle was built in 1910 on a hill in the centre of Formia with fine views over the sea. Spacious bedrooms are decorated in Spanish style. 🖥 📺 🍽 🐾 🅿	10	■		■
GROTTAFERRATA: *Villa Fiorio* €€€€€ Viale Dusmet 25, 00046. **(** 06 945 48 007. **FAX** 06 945 48 009. **@** villafiorio@tin.it Built as a summer residence at the turn of the century, this pretty villa, which retains some original frescoes, has large, cool and quiet rooms. 🖥 📺 🍽 🐾 🅿	24	■	●	■
ISOLA DI PONZA: *Cernia* €€€€ Via Panoramica, Chiaia di Luna 04027. **(** 0771 804 12. **FAX** 0771 80 99 55. **@** pagreca@tin.it A beautiful setting for this modern but stylish hotel with a dense garden. Wicker furniture and rocking chairs create a friendly atmosphere. 🖥 📺 🍽 🐾 🅿	50	■		■
LADISPOLI: *La Posta Vecchia* €€€€€ Località Palo Laziale, 00055. **(** 06 994 95 01. **FAX** 06 994 95 07. **@** info@postavecchia.com A magnificent 17th-century villa on the sea, it was restored by John Paul Getty as his Italian residence and is now one of Italy's most luxurious hotels. All rooms are exquisitely and individually decorated with antiques. 🖥 📺 🍽 🐾 🅿	17	■	●	■
PALESTRINA: *Stella* € Piazzale della Liberazione 3, 00036. **(** 06 953 81 72. **FAX** 06 957 33 60. **@** info@hotelstella.it A friendly, peaceful hotel in the historic centre of Palestrina close to the town's sights and with an excellent restaurant. 🖥 📺 🍽 🐾 🅿	28	■		
SABAUDIA: *Oasi di Kufra* €€€ Via Lungomare Km 29,800, 04016. **(** 0773 515 775. **FAX** 0773 51 55 98. **@** kufra@oasidikufra.it Luminous beach amid sandy dunes. With its private beach and fitness centre, it offers a host of sports and balconies in most rooms overlooking the sea. 🖥 📺 🍽 🐾 🅿	120	■		■
SAN FELICE CIRCEO: *Punta Rossa* €€€€€ Via delle Batterie 37, 04017. **(** 0773 54 80 85. **FAX** 0773 54 80 75. **@** punta_rossa@iol.it A charming hotel set in a garden that leads down to the sea. Rooms are in various buildings, all have terraces and sea views and there is a covered sea-water swimming pool as well as a second pool by the sea. 🖥 📺 🍽 🐾 🅿	33	■	●	■

SUBIACO: *Livata*   €€   80
Località Monte Livata, 00028. **[** 0774 82 60 31. **FAX** 0774 82 60 33.
A good choice if you're visiting the monastery of San Benedetto, the Livata
is a friendly country hotel with tennis courts and attractive gardens. 🔌 🍽 **P**

TARQUINIA LIDO: *La Torraccia*   €€   18
Viale Mediterraneo 45, 01010. **[** 0766 86 43 75. **FAX** 0766 86 42 96. **@** torraccia@tin.it
A modern, comfortable hotel set in pinewoods 200 m (656 ft) from the
sea. All rooms have a terrace and there is a private beach. 🔌 TV 🍽 🍽 **P**

VITERBO: *Balletti Palace*   €€   105
Via Molini 8, 01100. **[** 0761 34 47 77. **FAX** 0761 34 50 60.
A modern hotel set in Viterbo's historic centre with elegant bedrooms and
suites. There is no restaurant but the Grenier Café serves light meals. 🔌 TV 🍽 🍽 **P**

VITERBO: *Balletti Park*   €€   136
Via Umbria 2, San Martino al Cimino 01030. **[** 0761 37 71. **FAX** 0761 37 94 96. **@** info@balletti.it
A modern hotel set in its own extensive gardens. There are sports facilities
and a health centre as well as some independent apartments. 🔌 TV 🍽 🍽 **P**

NAPLES AND CAMPANIA

AMALFI: *Marina Riviera*   €€   22
Via P Comite 33, 84011. **[** 089 87 11 04. **FAX** 089 87 10 24.
This Mediterranean-style seaside hotel offers simple, tasteful rooms, and an
attractive patio overlooking the beach for leisurely breakfasts. 🔌 TV 🍽 🍽 **P**

AMALFI: *Luna Convento*   €€€€   40
Via Comite 33, 84011. **[** 089 87 10 02. **FAX** 089 87 13 33. **@** info@lunahotel.it
This tastefully furnished 13th-century monastery overlooking the sea makes a
luxurious, peaceful base from which to explore the countryside. 🔌 TV 🍽 🍽 **P**

AMALFI: *Santa Caterina*   €€€€€   65
Via SS Amalfitana 9, 84011. **[** 089 87 10 12. **FAX** 089 87 13 51. **@** info@hotelsantacaterina.it
This is a luxurious property set amid lemon groves. Two elevators can whisk
you from the spectacular suites to the private beach in seconds. Enjoy the
sea view from the hotel terraces or the high tech gym. 🔌 TV 🍽 🍽 **P**

BAIA DOMIZIA: *Hotel della Baia*   €€€   56
Via dell'Erica, 81030. **[** 0823 72 13 44. **FAX** 0823 72 15 56. **@** hoteldellabaia@usa.net
A charming, friendly hotel run by three sisters with its own private beach.
The pretty bedrooms are comfortable and all have sea views. 🔌 TV 🍽 🍽 **P**

BENEVENTO: *Grand Hotel Italiano*   €€   71
Viale Principe di Napoli 137, 82100. **[** 0824 241 11. **FAX** 0824 217 58.
The Italiano family are justly proud of the hotel's reputation for courtesy
and good service. Public areas are spacious and elegant. 🔌 TV 🍽 🍽 **P**

CAPRI: *Villa Sarah*   €€€€   18
Via Tiberio 3a, 80073. **[** 081 837 78 17. **FAX** 081 837 72 15. **@** info@villasarah.it
A peaceful family-run villa hotel set among the island's vineyards. Rooms
are clean and pretty and home produce is served for breakfast. 🔌 TV 🍽 🍽

CAPRI: *Punta Tragara*   €€€€€   45
Via Tragara 57, 80073. **[** 081 837 08 44. **FAX** 081 837 77 90. **@** hotel.tragara@capri.it
A sumptuous hotel built into a cliff over the sea, designed by Le Corbusier,
with all the comforts of a luxury residence. No children under 12. 🔌 TV 🍽 🍽

CASERTA: *Europa*   €€€   57
Via Roma 19, 81100. **[** 0823 32 54 00. **FAX** 0823 32 54 11. **@** hotel.europa@tin.it
A smart modern hotel conveniently placed in central Caserta. The Europa also
has several mini-apartments with cooking facilities for longer stays. 🔌 TV 🍽 🍽 **P**

ISCHIA: *Pensione Il Monastero*   €€   21
Castello Aragonese 3, Ischia Ponte 80070. **[** 081 99 24 35. **FAX** 081 99 24 35.
A charming, simple pensione set in a converted monastery overlooking
the town of Ischia. The walls are hung with paintings and furniture is plain
but attractive. Guests are expected to take half-board in summer. 🔌 🍽

ISCHIA: *La Villarosa*   €€   37
Via Giacinto Gigante 5, Porto d'Ischia 80070. **[** 081 99 13 16. **FAX** 081 99 24 25.
An enchanting, elegant hotel set in a beautiful tropical garden.
Many of the discreetly charming rooms have balconies filled
with luxuriant bougainvilleas. 🔌 TV 🍽 **P**

					NUMBER OF ROOMS	RESTAURANT	SWIMMING POOL	GARDEN OR TERRACE

Price categories for a standard double room for one night, including tax and service charges but not including breakfast:
€ under 52 euros
€€ 52–100 euros
€€€ 100–155 euros
€€€€ 155–205 euros
€€€€€ over 205 euros.

RESTAURANT
A restaurant within the hotel sometimes reserved for residents.
SWIMMING POOL
Hotel swimming pools are usually quite small and are outdoors unless otherwise stated.
GARDEN OR TERRACE
A garden, courtyard or terrace belonging to the hotel, often providing tables for eating outside.
CREDIT CARDS
The major credit cards VISA, MasterCard (Access) and American Express are accepted in hotels with the credit card symbol.

NAPLES: *Britannique* €€€
Corso Vittorio Emanuele 133, 80121. (081 761 41 45. FAX 081 66 04 57.
A smart, modern hotel in the centre of Naples. Bedrooms are attractively decorated and there are spectacular views from the roof terrace. Some suites with cooking facilities are available for longer stays. 📶 TV 🍽 💳 P

| | | | | | 86 | ■ | | ■ |

NAPLES: *Rex* €€€
Via Palepoli 12, 80132. (081 764 93 89. FAX 081 764 92 27. W www.hotelrex.it
A friendly, family hotel on the seafront of Naples, well placed for theatres and beaches. Public rooms are elegantly furnished with wicker chairs. 📶 TV 🍽 💳 P

| | | | | | 38 | | | |

NAPLES: *Grand Hotel Parker's* €€€€€
Corso Vittorio Emanuele 135, 80121. (081 761 24 74. FAX 081 66 35 27. @ ghparker@tin.it
This elegant and intimate hotel is beautifully furnished in different styles, from Louis XVI to Empire. From the excellent rooftop restaurant, guests enjoy a sweeping view of the bay. 📶 TV 🍽 💳 P

| | | | | | 82 | ■ | | ■ |

NAPLES: *Grande Albergo Vesuvio* €€€€€
Via Partenope 45, 80121. (081 764 00 44. FAX 081 764 44 83. @ info@prestigehotels.it
Founded in 1882, the Grande overlooks the marina in central Naples. It is well decorated and furnished with marble bathrooms and antiques, and includes a "baby" room with a rocking horse, mobiles and toys. 📶 TV 🍽 💳 P

| | | | | | 163 | ■ | | |

PAESTUM: *Le Palme* €€€
Via Sterpinia 33, 84063. (0828 85 10 25. FAX 0828 85 15 07.
A pleasant, peaceful seaside hotel with tennis courts and its own beach. Rooms are comfortable and the hotel is set in attractive grounds. 📶 TV 🍽 💳 P

| | | | | | 71 | ■ | ● | ■ |

POSITANO: *Palazzo Murat* €€€€
Via dei Mulini 23, 84017. (089 87 51 77. FAX 089 81 14 19. @ hpm@starnet.it
A pretty 18th-century palazzo in central Positano, near the cathedral. Rooms have traditional wooden furniture, and some have balconies. 📶 TV 🍽 💳

| | | | | | 30 | ■ | | |

POSITANO: *L'Ancora* €€€€€
Via Colombo 36, 84017. (089 87 53 18. FAX 089 81 17 84.
Excellent value in expensive Positano from this modern, central hotel with sea views. The good-sized bedrooms are comfortable. 📶 TV 🍽 💳 P

| | | | | | 20 | | | ■ |

RAVELLO: *Graal* €€€
Via della Repubblica 8, 84010. (089 85 72 22. FAX 089 85 75 51. @ info@hotelgraal.it
The hotel has a wonderful swimming pool with attractive views over Ravello. The restaurant serves good local specialities. 📶 TV 🍽 💳 P

| | | | | | 36 | ■ | ● | ■ |

RAVELLO: *Palumbo* €€€€€
Via San Giovanni del Toro 16, 84010. (089 85 72 44. FAX 089 85 81 33. @ palumbo@amalfinet.it
This 12th-century palazzo has been run as a hotel by the same family for more than 100 years. Furnishings are elegant and there are antiques in some bedrooms. Rooms in the modern annexe are cheaper. 📶 TV 🍽 💳 P

| | | | | | 18 | | | ■ |

SALERNO: *Fiorenza* €€
Via Trento 145, 84131. (089 33 88 00. FAX 089 33 88 00. @ fiorealb@tin.it
A 1960s hotel overlooking the sea on the outskirts of Salerno. All the rooms are modern and have private safe, mini-bar and satellite TV. 📶 TV 🍽 TV P

| | | | | | 30 | | | |

SAPRI: *Mediterraneo* €€
Via Verdi, 84073. (0973 39 17 74. FAX 0973 39 11 57. @ hotelmediterraneo@libero.it
Excellent value at this comfortable, no frills hotel built right next to the rocky beach with garden and terrace overlooking the sea. 📶 TV 💳 P

| | | | | | 20 | ■ | | ■ |

SAPRI: *Tirreno* €€
Corso Italia 73, 84073. (0973 39 10 06. FAX 0973 39 11 57. W www.argomedia.com/tirreno
A good-value pensione facing the sea. Inside it is airy and light and bedrooms have their own balconies. The restaurant serves local specialities. 📶 🍽 TV 💳 P

| | | | | | 46 | ■ | | ■ |

SORRENTO: *Bellevue Syrene*   €€€€ | 76
Piazza della Vittoria 5, 80067. 📞 081 878 10 24. 📠 081 878 39 63. @ info@bellevue.it
A typical grand beach hotel, now slightly faded. It is perched on the cliffs with a lift
to take guests down to the private beach. Sumptuous bedrooms. 🛏 📺 📋 🍽 🅿

SORRENTO: *Grand Hotel Cocumella*   €€€€€ | 50
Via Cocumella 7, 80065. 📞 081 878 29 33. 📠 081 878 37 12. @ hcocum@tin.it
Opulent elegance from another era characterizes this peaceful hotel on the
Amalfi coast set in fragrant and peaceful gardens. The sea is nearby and the
hotel sailing boat will take guests to Capri for the day. 🛏 📺 📋 🍽 🅿

ABRUZZO, MOLISE AND PUGLIA

ALBEROBELLO: *Colle del Sole*   €€ | 37
Via Indipendenza 63, 70011. 📞 080 432 18 14. 📠 080 432 13 70. @ colledelsole@libero.it
A comfortable, modern hotel with a balcony for every bedroom. Art and
photo exhibitions are sometimes arranged in the restaurant. 🛏 📺 📋 🍽 🅿

ALBEROBELLO: *Dei Trulli*   €€€ | 28
Via Cadore 32, 70011. 📞 080 432 35 55. 📠 080 432 35 60. @ hoteldeitrulli@inmedia.it
The hotel is set in a mini-village of *trulli (see p495)*. Furnishings are simple,
even stark, but the grounds are pleasant. Half-board in summer. 🛏 📺 📋 🍽 🅿

BARI: *Boston*   €€€ | 70
Via Piccinni 155, 70122. 📞 080 521 66 33. 📠 080 521 68 02. @ boston@inmedia.it
A modern hotel near the historic centre of Bari. Furnishings are stylish and
functional and there is much dark wood panelling. Half-board. 🛏 📺 📋 🍽 🅿

BARI: *Palace Hotel*   €€€€€ | 200
Via Lombardi 13, 70122. 📞 080 521 65 51. 📠 080 521 14 99. @ palaceh@tin.it
With rooms that cater to most specialized needs, this hotel provides excellent service.
The delicious buffet breakfast also has something for everyone. 🛏 📺 📋 🍽 🅿

GARGANO PENINSULA: *Seggio*   €€ | 30
Via Veste 7, Vieste 71019. 📞 0884 70 81 23. 📠 0884 70 87 27. @ hotel.seggio@tiscalinet.it
Perched on a small cliff over its own private bay, this restored 17th-century
building was the original town hall. Bedrooms are simple. 🛏 📺 📋 🍽 🅿

ISOLE TREMITI: *Kyrie*   €€ | 27
San Domino, 71040. 📞 0882 46 32 41. 📠 0882 46 34 15.
The largest and best-equipped of the Tremiti hotels. It is in the pinewoods
next to the sea. Open from June to September only. 🛏 📺 📋 🍽

L'AQUILA: *Amiternum*   €€ | 60
Bivio Sant'Antonio 67100 . 📞 0862 31 57 57. 📠 0862 31 59 87. @ hotel.amiternum@worldtel.it
Comfortable hotel in a pretty location near the heart of the city.
🛏 📺 🍽 🅿

L'AQUILA: *Grand Hotel e del Parco*   €€€ | 36
Corso Federico II 74, 67100. 📞 0862 41 32 48. 📠 0862 659 38. 🌐 www.grandhotel.it
A comfortable, modern hotel in the centre of L'Aquila within easy reach
of the ski-slopes and hiking trails of the Gran Sasso. The hotel also has a
health complex, complete with saunas and Turkish baths. 🛏 📺 📋 🍽 🅿

LECCE: *Grand Hotel*   €€ | 70
Viale Oronzo Quarta 28, 73100. 📞 0832 30 94 05. 📠 0832 30 98 91.
This Art Nouveau villa was converted into an elegant hotel in the 1930s.
Although some of the rooms are rather shabby, it is still charming. 🛏 📺 🍽 🅿

LECCE: *Hotel President*   €€ | 150
Via Salandra No 6. 📞 0832 45 61 11. 📠 0832 45 66 32.
Large and modern hotel with a good reputation and good service. The excellent
restaurant has a well-stocked wine cellar. 🛏 📺 📋 🍽 🅿

MARINA DI LESINA: *Maddalena Hotel*   €€ | 70
Via Saturno 82, 71010. 📞 0882 99 50 76. 📠 0882 99 54 34. @ maddalena@excite.it
A modern beach hotel with a range of sports and leisure facilities, including
a private beach. The restaurant serves a variety of local fish dishes. 🛏 📺 📋 🍽 🅿

MONOPOLI: *Il Melograno*   €€€€€ | 37
Contrada Torricella 345, 70043. 📞 080 690 90 30. 📠 080 74 79 08. @ melograno@melograno.com
A luxurious oasis of tranquillity in a peaceful, verdant corner of Puglia.
The sumptuous interior of this restored 16th-century residence is furnished
with antiques, and there are tennis courts and a private beach. 🛏 📺 📋 🍽 🅿

	NUMBER OF ROOMS	RESTAURANT	SWIMMING POOL	GARDEN OR TERRACE
Price categories for a standard double room for one night, including tax and service charges but not including breakfast: € under 52 euros €€ 52–100 euros €€€ 100–155 euros €€€€ 155–205 euros €€€€€ over 205 euros. **RESTAURANT** A restaurant within the hotel sometimes reserved for residents. **SWIMMING POOL** Hotel swimming pools are usually quite small and are outdoors unless otherwise stated. **GARDEN OR TERRACE** A garden, courtyard or terrace belonging to the hotel, often providing tables for eating outside. **CREDIT CARDS** The major credit cards VISA, MasterCard (Access) and American Express are accepted in hotels with the credit card symbol.				
RUVO DI PUGLIA: *Talos* €€ Via Rodolfo Morandi 12, 70037. 080 361 16 45. FAX 080 360 26 40. @ hoteltalos@tin.it A simple, modern hotel that is good value for travellers on a budget. It is well placed for exploring the surrounding countryside.	18	■		
SCANNO: *Mille Pini* €€ Via Pescara 2, 67038. 0864 74 72 64. FAX 0864 74 98 18. A friendly, good value chalet hotel at the foot of Monte Rotondo chairlift. Facilities are simple and rustic but comfortable and there is a restaurant.	22	■		■
SULMONA: *Italia* € Piazza Salvatore Tommasi 3, 67039. & FAX 0864 523 08. A charming ivy-covered town house in a quiet square. Furnishings vary from modern utility to antique, giving a lived-in feeling to this friendly hotel.	26			
TARANTO: *Plaza* €€ Via d'Aquino 46, 74100. 099 459 07 75. FAX 099 459 06 75. A big, city hotel that is very well placed in the newer part of Taranto near the major sights. Both business and holiday guests are catered for.	112	■	●	

BASILICATA AND CALABRIA

	NUMBER OF ROOMS	RESTAURANT	SWIMMING POOL	GARDEN OR TERRACE
COSENZA: *Royal* €€ Via Molinella 24e, 87100. 0984 41 21 65. FAX 0984 41 17 77. @ royalhot@tin.it One of the best modern hotels in Cosenza, conveniently located in the centre of town, not far from the station.	50	■		■
MARATEA: *Romantik Hotel, Villa Cheta Elite* €€€ Via Timpone 48, Acquafredda 85041. 0973 87 81 34. FAX 0973 87 81 35. W www.villacheta.it An elegant, Liberty-style villa with stunning views over a picturesque bay. The comfortable rooms are attractively furnished in traditional southern Italian style and staff and service are friendly and polite.	24	■		■
MATERA: *De Nicola* €€ Via Nazionale 158, 75100. 0835 38 51 11. FAX 0835 38 51 13. @ hoteleden@tin.it A large modern hotel in central Matera close to the station and easily accessible from the motorway. Bedrooms are functional.	105	■		
METAPONTO LIDO: *Turismo* € Viale delle Ninfe 5, 75010. 0835 74 19 18. FAX 0835 74 19 17. A functional, if unexceptional, seaside hotel with its own beach and bar. The restaurant has outside tables for summer dining.	60	■		■
PARGHELIA: *Baia Paraelios* €€€ Località Fornaci, 88035 (nr Tropea). 0963 60 03 00. FAX 0963 60 00 74. A little village of 72 bungalows each with terrace and sitting room, with superb views over the beach and sea. The restaurant is on a beach terrace.	87	■	●	■
REGGIO DI CALABRIA: *Grand Hotel Excelsior* €€€€ Via Vittorio Veneto 66, 89100. 0965 81 22 11. FAX 0965 89 30 84. This hotel has some of the best facilities in southern Italy. Situated in the centre of town, it appeals to business as well as holiday visitors.	84	■		■
ROSSANO SCALO: *Murano* €€ Viale Mediterraneo 2, 87068. 0983 51 17 88. FAX 0983 53 00 88. Set in its own grounds over the sea, the Murano has a private beach and rooms with sea views. There is a piano bar and an outside pizzeria as well as a traditional restaurant serving Calabrian specialities.	37	■		■
STILO: *San Giorgio* € Via R Citarelli 1, 89049. & FAX 0964 77 50 47. Set in the heart of Stilo, this comfortable hotel is located in a restored 17th-century palazzo and furnished with some 18th-century antiques.	15	■	●	■

TROPEA: *La Pineta* €€ 43
Via Marina 150, 89861. **[** *0963 617 77.* **FAX** *0963 622 65.*
This typical resort hotel is open only from June to September. The decor
is fairly ordinary but La Pineta does have tennis courts. 🏨 ≣ 🖉 **P**

VENOSA: *Il Guiscardo* € 36
Via Accademia dei Rinascenti 106, 85029. **[** *0972 32 362.* **FAX** *0972 32 916.*
There are wonderful views from the terrace over the red roofs of Venosa's
historic centre. Bedrooms are elegant and public rooms spacious. 🏨 TV ≣ 🖉 **P**

SICILY

ACIREALE: *Excelsior Palace* €€€€ 229
Via delle Terme 103, 95024. **[** *095 604 444.* **FAX** *095 605 441.* **@** excelsiorpalace@shr.it
Well placed for visiting the sights of east Sicily and close to the Santa Venera Spa,
this hotel set in a 19th-century building offers all modern comforts. 🏨 TV ≣ 🖉 **P**

AGRIGENTO: *Colleverde Park Hotel* €€€ 48
Via dei Templi, 92100. **[** *0922 295 55.* **FAX** *0922 290 12.* **@** mail@colleverdehotel.it
A peaceful modern hotel in the Valley of the Temples, with stunning views.
The facilities include safes in the bedrooms and a gym. 🏨 TV ≣ 🖉 **P**

AGRIGENTO: *Grand Hotel dei Templi* €€€ 146
Viale L Sciascia, Villaggio Mose 92100. **[** *0922 61 01 75.* **FAX** *0922 60 66 85.*
One of the modern, efficient Jolly chain, this large, well-equipped hotel lies
just outside Agrigento. Rooms are comfortably furnished. 🏨 TV ≣ 🖉 **P**

AGRIGENTO: *Villa Athena* €€€€€ 40
Via Panoramica dei Templi 33, 92100. **[** *0922 59 62 88.* **FAX** *0922 40 21 80.* **@** villaathena@tin.it
Set in an 18th-century villa just outside Agrigento. The decor is modern but
the gardens are exquisite, with views of the Temple of Concord. 🏨 TV ≣ 🖉 **P**

CATANIA: *Nettuno* €€ 80
Viale Ruggero di Lauria 121, 95127. **[** *095 712 52 52.* **FAX** *095 49 80 66.*
A well-equipped, modern hotel in a quiet location. The Nettuno overlooks
the sea and has a breakfast terrace above the outdoor swimming pool.
The comfortable rooms also have balconies. 🏨 TV ≣ 🖉 **P**

CEFALÙ: *Riva del Sole* €€ 28
Viale Lungomare Cefalù 25, 90015. **[** *0921 42 12 30.* **FAX** *0921 42 19 84.*
A hotel on the seafront with good panoramic views. Bedrooms are on the
basic side but there is a terrace for sunbathing and a shadier internal courtyard
with tables. 🏨 TV ≣ 🖉 **P**

ISOLE EGADI: *Egadi Favignana* €€ 11
Via Colombo 17, Favignana 91023. **[** & **FAX** *0923 92 12 32.* **@** pngsgu@tin.it
A small, friendly pensione attached to one of the best restaurants on the island.
Favignana is famous for its tuna which comes from the local fisheries. 🏨 ≣ TV 🖉

ISOLE EOLIE: *Pensione Villa Diana* €€ 12
Via Diana Tufo, Lipari 98055. **[** & **FAX** *090 981 14 03.* **@** villadiana@netnet.it
A comfortable family hotel with antiques in some rooms, and spacious
gardens and terraces. The hotel is open from April to October. 🏨 🖉

ISOLE EOLIE: *La Sciara Residence* €€ 62
Via Soldato Cincotta, Isola Stromboli 98050. **[** *090 98 60 05.* **FAX** *090 98 62 84.*
A splendid garden full of bougainvilleas is the setting for this spacious
and comfortable hotel. Mini-apartments are also available. 🏨 🖉

ISOLE EOLIE: *Raya* €€€€€ 36
Via San Pietro, Isola Panarea 98050. **[** *090 98 30 13.* **FAX** *090 98 31 03.* **@** htlraya@netnet.it
This modern, fashionable hotel consists of pink and white houses on terraces
descending to the sea. The restaurant and bar overlook the port. 🏨 ≣ 🖉

ERICE: *Elimo* €€€ 21
Via Vittorio Emanuele 75, 91016. **[** *0923 86 93 77.* **FAX** *0923 86 92 52.* **@** elimoh@comeg.it
This 18th-century villa retains several original features including traditional
Sicilian wall, ceiling and floor tiles. The hotel is located in the centre of
Erice and has spectacular views as far as the Egadi Islands. 🏨 ≣ TV 🖉 **P**

ERICE: *Moderno* €€€ 41
Via Vittorio Emanuele 63, 91016. **[** *0923 86 93 00.* **FAX** *0923 86 91 39.* **@** modernoh@tin.it
A family-run hotel that has some attractively old-fashioned bedrooms as well
as some more modern ones. Excellent views from the terrace. 🏨 TV 🖉

Price categories for a standard double room for one night, including tax and service charges but not including breakfast:
€ under 52 euros
€€ 52–100 euros
€€€ 100 – 155 euros
€€€€ 155– 205 euros
€€€€€ over 205 euros.

RESTAURANT
A restaurant within the hotel sometimes reserved for residents.
SWIMMING POOL
Hotel swimming pools are usually quite small and are outdoors unless otherwise stated.
GARDEN OR TERRACE
A garden, courtyard or terrace belonging to the hotel, often providing tables for eating outside.
CREDIT CARDS
The major credit cards VISA, MasterCard (Access) and American Express are accepted in hotels with the credit card symbol.

	Price	NUMBER OF ROOMS	RESTAURANT	SWIMMING POOL	GARDEN OR TERRACE
GIARDINI-NAXOS: *Arathena Rocks*	€€	49	■	●	■
MARSALA: *President*	€€€	124	■	●	
MESSINA: *Paradis*	€€	88			■
PALERMO: *San Paolo Palace*	€€€	286	■	●	■
PALERMO: *Splendid Hotel La Torre*	€€€	179	■	●	■
PALERMO: *Grand Hotel Villa Igiea*	€€€€	110	■	●	■
SCIACCA: *Grand Hotel delle Terme*	€€€	77	■		■
SIRACUSA: *Gran Bretagna*	€€	20			■
SIRACUSA: *Villa Lucia*	€€	15		●	■
SIRACUSA: *Grand Hotel Villa Politi*	€€€€	100	■	●	■
TAORMINA: *Romantik Villa Ducale*	€€€	15			■
TAORMINA: *Villa Belvedere*	€€€	47	■	●	■

GIARDINI-NAXOS: *Arathena Rocks* €€
Via Calcide Eubea 55, 98035. **(** 0942 513 49. FAX 0942 516 90.
A friendly hotel near the beach and slightly out of this busy resort. Rooms are bright and airy with sea or garden views. Half-board required.

MARSALA: *President* €€€
Via Nino Bixio 1, 91025. **(** 0923 99 93 33. FAX 0923 99 91 15.
About 1 km (half a mile) from the centre of town this modern, comfortable hotel serves Sicilian and international cuisine in the restaurant.

MESSINA: *Paradis* €€
Via Consolare Pompea 441, 98168. **(** 090 31 06 82. FAX 090 31 20 43.
About 3 km (2 miles) out of central Messina, the Paradis has good views and an excellent restaurant. Rooms are basic but satisfactory.

PALERMO: *San Paolo Palace* €€€
Via Messina Marine 91. **(** 091 621 11 12. FAX 091 621 53 00. @ hotel@sanpaolopalace.it
This large, modern building overlooking the bay offers a complete range of services: roof terrace with swimming pool, panoramic restaurant, piano bar, spacious gym, and sauna.

PALERMO: *Splendid Hotel La Torre* €€€
Via Piano Gallo 11, Mondello 90151. **(** 091 45 02 22. FAX 091 45 00 33. @ latorre@latorre.com
A big, traditional seaside hotel, set on a promontory with its own private beach. Some bedrooms have their own balcony with sea views.

PALERMO: *Grand Hotel Villa Igiea* €€€€
Salita Belmonte 43, 90142. **(** 091 54 37 44. FAX 091 54 76 54. @ villa-igiea@thi.it
An exquisite hotel dating from the beginning of the last century with Art Nouveau stained glass and wall paintings. It is set by the sea in gardens with their own ancient ruins. An elegant cocktail bar opens onto the terrace.

SCIACCA: *Grand Hotel delle Terme* €€€
Viale delle Terme 1, 92019. **(** 0925 231 33. FAX 0925 870 02. @ info@termehotel.com
A spa hotel with access (for an extra charge) to the local mineral springs that were used by the Phoenicians more than 2,000 years ago. Many of the clientele come for various treatments and cures.

SIRACUSA: *Gran Bretagna* €€
Via Savoia 21, 96100. **(** & FAX 0931 687 65.
A small, friendly, family-run hotel with comfortable rooms. The restaurant has special family menus and serves Sicilian and Italian specialities.

SIRACUSA: *Villa Lucia* €€
Trav. Mondello 1, 1 Contrada Isola, 96100. **(** 0931 72 10 07. FAX 0931 72 15 87.
This beautiful villa, situated in the middle of a Mediterranean park close to the sea, offers a relaxing stay in pretty surroundings.

SIRACUSA: *Grand Hotel Villa Politi* €€€€
Via Maria Politi Laudien 2, 96100. **(** 0931 41 21 21. FAX 0931 360 61. W www.villapoliti.com
A slightly shabby old-fashioned hotel whose vast reception rooms belong to another era. The hotel dates from the early 20th century.

TAORMINA: *Romantik Villa Ducale* €€€
Via Leonardo da Vinci 60, 98039. **(** 0942 281 53. FAX 0942 287 10.
This elegant villa is now a comfortable hotel. The rooms are all different, furnished with antiques and with excellent views of Mount Etna and the sea. The library has books on the region for guests to browse through.

TAORMINA: *Villa Belvedere* €€€
Via Bagnoli Croci 79, 98039. **(** 0942 237 91. FAX 0942 62 58 30. @ info@villabelvedere.it
A very comfortable, family hotel in the centre of Taormina. Some rooms have sea views and balconies. Light meals are served by the pool.

TAORMINA: *San Domenico Palace* €€€€€ | 104
Piazza San Domenico 5, 98039. **(** 0942 237 01. **FAX** 0942 62 55 06. **@** sandomenico@thi.it
A peaceful, 15th-century monastery restored and furnished with genuine
antiques. This is one of the most luxurious hotels in Sicily and it has a
beautiful formal garden as well as an elegant swimming pool. 🛏 📺 ▤ 🗐 **P**

TAORMINA: *Timeo* €€€€€ | 56
Via Teatro Greco 59, 98039. **(** 094 22 38 01. **FAX** 094 262 85 01. **@** framon@framon-hotels.com
Since 1884 this exclusive villa has attracted such guests as Marconi, Gide and de
Maupassant. All guests can enjoy a complimentary afternoon tea. 🛏 📺 ▤ 🗐 **P**

TRAPANI: *Astoria Park* €€ | 91
Lungomare Dante Alighieri, 91100. **(** 0923 56 24 00. **FAX** 0923 56 74 22.
A modern hotel on the seafront with all you need for a beach holiday (tennis,
discotheque). A good base from which to explore the region. 🛏 📺 ▤ 🗐 **P**

TRAPANI: *Vittoria* €€ | 65
Via Francesco Crispi 4, 91100. **(** 0923 87 30 44. **FAX** 0923 298 70.
Very conveniently placed in the centre of Trapani, this modern functional
hotel has very simple, well-designed furnishings. 🛏 📺 ▤ 🗐

SARDINIA

ALGHERO: *Villa las Tronas* €€€€€ | 28
Lungomare Valencia 1, 07041. **(** 079 98 18 18. **FAX** 079 98 10 44.
A mustard-coloured villa on a promontory is the setting for this comfortable,
elegantly decorated hotel. Public rooms are full of gilt and 18th-century
French-style furniture; bedrooms are simpler but pretty. 🛏 📺 ▤ 🗐 **P**

CAGLIARI: *Italia* €€ | 113
Via Sardegna 31, 09124. **(** 070 66 05 10. **FAX** 070 65 02 40.
Housed in two much-restored palazzi in central Cagliari, this slightly shabby
hotel is a convenient base from which to explore the countryside. 🛏 📺 ▤ 🗐

CAGLIARI: *Sardegna* €€ | 90
Via Lunigiana 50, 09122. **(** 070 28 62 45. **FAX** 070 29 04 69. **@** sarhotel@tin.it
A modern hotel close to the town centre and about 2 km (1 mile) from the
airport. The rooms are comfortably but simply decorated. 🛏 📺 ▤ 🗐 **P**

ISOLA DI SAN PIETRO: *Hotel Paola e Primo Maggio* €€ | 21
Tacca Rossa, Carloforte 09014. **(** 0781 85 00 98. **FAX** 0781 85 01 04. **@** hotelpaola@tiscalinet.it
A modern pensione overlooking the sea with lovely views and charging
very reasonable prices. There is a shady terrace for outside dining. 🛏 ▤ 🗐 **P**

NUORO: *Grazia Deledda* €€ | 72
Via Lamarmora 175, 08100. **(** 0784 312 57. **FAX** 0784 312 58.
A well-equipped modern hotel in a central position with an American-style
bar. The restaurant serves Sardinian and Italian specialities. 🛏 ▤ 🗐 **P**

OLIENA: *Su Gologone* €€€ | 35
Località Su Gologone, 08025. **(** 0784 28 75 12. **FAX** 0784 28 76 68. **@** gologone@tin.it
A rambling villa in the mountainous Barbagia region is the setting for this
delightfully peaceful hotel which offers a good range of sports. 🛏 📺 ▤ 🗐

PORTO CERVO: *Balocco* €€€ | 35
Località Liscia di Vacca, 07020. **(** 0789 915 55. **FAX** 0789 915 10.
An attractive, airy hotel surrounded by palm-filled grounds and terraces for
every room. It offers comparatively good value for the fashionable Costa
Smeralda, but beware: prices double for the summer season. 🛏 📺 ▤ 🗐 **P**

PORTO CERVO: *Capriccioli* €€€ | 50
Località Capriccioli, 07020. **(** 0789 960 04. **FAX** 0789 964 22.
One of the best value hotels on the expensive Costa Smeralda. This family-run
hotel is close to the beach and has an excellent restaurant. 🛏 📺 ▤ 🗐 **P**

PORTO ROTONDO: *Sporting* €€€ | 27
Porto Rotondo, 07026. **(** 0789 340 05. **FAX** 0789 343 83.
An oasis of comfort on the exclusive Costa Smeralda with its own beach and
grounds. Bedrooms have flower-filled terraces. Half-board. 🛏 📺 ▤ 🗐 **P**

SASSARI: *Leonardo da Vinci* €€ | 117
Via Roma 79, 07100. **(** 079 28 07 44. **FAX** 079 285 72 33. **W** www.leonardodavincihotel.it
A large, comfortable hotel a few minutes' walk from the city centre. Furnishings
are functional but there is a sense of space and tranquillity. 🛏 📺 ▤ 🗐 **P**

WHERE TO EAT

Waiter at Alberto Ciarla *(see p601)*

FOOD IS A serious subject in Italy. The Italians are justly proud of their fine cuisine and wines and many sociable hours are spent around the table. One of the great pleasures of travelling in Italy is exploring regional variations in pasta, breads and cheeses. Whether it is spinach-filled *tortelloni* from the north or stuffed sweet red peppers from the south, restaurants will rarely serve anything other than Italian specialities. You don't have to head to the most expensive places for good food; a simple *trattoria*, which has to answer to the local clientele, will often serve much better fare than the nearby international restaurant. However, whether it is a crowded *osteria* or a terrace with sea views, this introduction gives a few practical tips on types of restaurants, ordering and service to help you enjoy eating out in Italy.

TYPES OF RESTAURANTS AND SNACK BARS

TRADITIONALLY a *trattoria* and an *osteria* were cheaper and more popular alternatives to the smarter *ristorante*. These days, however, the terms are interchangeable and high cost is not always indicative of memorably delicious food.

A *pizzeria* is usually a cheap place to eat (as little as 8 euros with beer) and many serve pasta, meat and fish dishes as well as pizzas. *Pizzerie* are often open in the evening only, especially those with wood-fired ovens *(forno a legna)*.

A *birreria* is another cheap option, serving pasta and snacks such as sausages and hamburgers. An *enoteca*, or *vineria*, is in fact a place to taste wine; however, as Italians will rarely drink without eating, there will normally be a range of light dishes on offer as well as a superb selection of wines. Prices vary and tend not to be cheap for the quantities served.

El Gato restaurant, Chioggia, famous for its fish *(see p580)*

At lunch time and in the early evening *rosticcerie* sell roast chicken, slices of pizza *(pizza al taglio)* and other snacks to take away. Pizza al taglio, with various different toppings, can also be bought straight from the baker. Bars have filled rolls *(panini)* and sandwiches *(tramezzini)* and some have a *tavola calda* counter with hot dishes for under 5 euros.

Stop at a *gelateria* for ice cream, with a sometimes mesmerizing choice of different flavours, or a *pasticceria* for one of a dazzling variety of sweet and savoury pastries, cakes and biscuits.

EATING HOURS

LUNCH IS generally served between 1pm and 2:30pm and, particularly in the south, all other activity stops between these hours. Dinner is at about 8pm and goes on until 11pm or later (in the south eating hours tend to be later). It is not unusual to see tables still full from lunch at 4pm or diners sipping *digestivi* well after midnight.

RESERVATIONS

GOOD RESTAURANTS in Italy are likely to be popular, so reserve a table if you can. Otherwise, get there early to avoid having to queue. Many restaurants close for a few weeks in either winter or the summer holiday season so phone first if in doubt.

THE MENU

ITALIAN MEALS consist of at least three or four courses and restaurants generally expect you to eat at least two. The *antipasto* (starter), is followed by the *primo*, of pasta, rice or soup. The *secondo* is the main meat or fish course with vegetables or salad (as *contorni*). Fruit, cheese or dessert follow, with coffee and a *digestivo* such as *grappa* or a bitter *amaro* to finish the meal.

Menus usually change with the season to make use of the best and freshest local produce and the day's specials may be recited to you by the waiter rather than written down.

Villa Crespi in Piedmont, inspired by the Arabian Nights *(see p587)*

Persevere, if you don't immediately understand, using the menu information at the beginning of each section *(see p672)*.

VEGETARIANS

WHILE FEW PLACES advertise specifically vegetarian meals, you are unlikely to have much trouble choosing from an Italian menu. Many pasta and *antipasto* dishes use no meat at all and for a main course you can ask for a selection of vegetables from the *contorni*. Vegetarians eat particularly well in spring when the first new vegetables come into the markets, and in autumn when wild mushrooms abound.

WINE AND DRINKS

MANY REGIONS have their own *aperitivo* for before the meal and a *digestivo* for afterwards. Universal alternatives are *prosecco* (dry fizzy white wine) or an *analcolico* (non-alcoholic) aperitif and *grappa* as a digestive. House wine (red or white) will be a simple local wine served by the litre or fraction thereof and will generally be perfectly palatable. In addition, all but the cheapest places have a range of other local and regional wines specially selected to accompany the food on the menu. For this reason, it is unusual to come across many non-Italian wines.

Tap water *(acqua del rubinetto)* is always drinkable and often very good, but Italy has a massive range of mineral waters. Fizzy ones *(frizzante)* may contain carbon dioxide

The 11th-century Badia a Coltibuono in Gaiole in Chianti *(see p593)*

while *naturale* can mean still or naturally sparkling. The popular *Ferrarelle* lies somewhere between the two. If you particularly want a still water ask for *non gassata*.

PAYING

TAX AND SERVICE are included in the menu prices but it is normal to leave a small tip (from 1 to 5 euros). Take note of the cover charge *(coperto)*: an unavoidable extra which basically covers bread (whether you eat it or not) and is charged per person.

Credit cards are not always accepted in Italy, particularly in smaller towns, and it is wise to check before you eat.

DRESS

ITALIANS GENERALLY tend to look smart but don't necessarily expect visitors to do the same. In most places you will not be expected to dress particularly smartly; however, very scruffy or dirty clothes are unlikely to get you good or particularly friendly service.

CHILDREN

CHILDREN ARE welcome in all but the smartest establishments and throughout Italy restaurants are likely to be filled with extensive Italian families for Sunday lunch. Facilities such as high chairs or special menus are rare, but most places will provide cushions and small portions.

Roman trattoria, Sora Lella, on Tiber Island *(see p599)*

SMOKING

SMOKING IS POPULAR in Italy and it is common for people to light up between courses or while others are still eating. Be warned: non-smoking sections are rare and if somebody else's cigarette is bothering you, you are the one who will have to move.

WHEELCHAIR ACCESS

FEW RESTAURANTS have special facilities for people in wheelchairs, but let them know you are coming in advance so they can reserve a suitable table and be ready to help if necessary when you arrive.

La Marinella restaurant overlooking the Amalfi coast *(see p603)*

Choosing a Restaurant

THE RESTAURANTS in this guide have been selected across a wide range of price categories for their good value, exceptional food and interesting location. This chart lists the restaurants by region, starting with Venice. The thumb tabs on the side of the page use the same colour-coding as the corresponding regional chapter in the main section of the guide.

	FIXED-PRICE MENU	GOOD WINE LIST	FORMAL DRESS	OUTDOOR TABLES
VENICE				
BURANO: *Ai Pescatori* €€€€ Piazza Galuppi 371, 30012. (041 73 06 50. A welcoming restaurant whose menu includes lobster and *tagliolini* (flat pasta) with cuttlefish. In winter the menu includes excellent game. The extensive wine list offers foreign as well as Italian wines. ● *Wed, 1–15 Jan.* 🖻 ▤	●	■		
BURANO: *Da Romano* €€€€ Via Galuppi 221, 30012. (041 73 00 30. A pretty restaurant founded in the 1800s, now run by a descendant of the original owner. The cooking is traditional and the fish is excellent. ● *Tue, mid-Dec–Feb.* 🖻 ▤	●			■
CANNAREGIO: *Osteria al Bacco* €€€ Fondamenta delle Cappuccine 3054, 30121. **Map** 2 D2. (041 71 74 93. A rustic restaurant with a pretty shaded courtyard. The menu serves mainly fish, and includes *spaghetti* with black cuttlefish-ink sauce. ● *Mon; 2 weeks Jan, 2 weeks Aug.* 🖻				■
CANNAREGIO: *Vini Da Gigio* €€€ Fondamenta San Felice 3628a, 30131. **Map** 3 A4. (041 528 51 40. A cosy restaurant serving traditional Venetian cuisine with a difference. The *risotto* of prawns and grilled cuttlefish is particularly good. ● *Mon, mid-Jan–Feb, late Aug.* 🖻 ▤		■		
CANNAREGIO: *Fiaschetteria Toscana* €€€€ Salizzada San Giovanni Crisostomo 5719, 30131. **Map** 3 B5. (041 528 52 81. The Busatto family offer many Venetian dishes such as warm salad of lagoon fish and turbot with black butter and capers. ● *Mon lunch, Tue; mid-Jul–mid-Aug.* 🖻 ▤		■	■	
CASTELLO: *Da Remigio* €€€ Salizzada dei Greci 3416, 30122. **Map** 8 D2. (041 523 00 89. A lively local fish restaurant with a robust and straightforward menu. Booking is advisable. ● *Mon eve, Tue; 20 Dec–24 Jan, last wk Jul.* 🖻 ▤				
CASTELLO: *La Corte Sconta* €€€€ Calle del Pestrin 3886, 30122. **Map** 7 A3. (041 522 70 24. This simple eating house has become one of the city's top restaurants. The fish and the home-made pasta are both superb. ● *Sun, Mon; 7 Jan–7 Feb, 21 Jul–16 Aug.* 🖻 ▤		■		■
CASTELLO: *Arcimboldo* €€€€€ Calle dei Furlani 3219, 30122. **Map** 8 D1. (041 528 65 69. Named after the 16th-century painter who used vegetables and fruit to create portraits of people. The food is similarly innovative today; try sea bass with tomatoes or marinated salmon with citrus fruit. ● *Tue (in winter), 3 wks Aug.* 🖻 ▤		■		■
DORSODURO: *Da Silvio* €€ Calle San Pantalon 3748, 30123. **Map** 6 D2. (041 520 58 33. A genuine local restaurant with a lovely garden for summer eating. The menu has no surprises but the food is fresh and home-made. ● *Sun, Sat lunch.* 🖻				■
DORSODURO: *Taverna San Trovaso* €€ Fondamenta Priuli 1016, 30123. **Map** 6 E3. (041 520 37 03. A cheerful, bustling restaurant between the Accademia and the Zattere. The cooking is straightforward and includes pizzas. ● *Mon.* 🖻 ▤	●			
DORSODURO: *Ai Gondolieri* €€€€ San Vio 366, 30123. **Map** 6 F4. (041 528 63 96. Housed in a sympathetically restored old inn, friendly hosts offer good regional specialities including *sformati* (soufflé) with wild herbs and mushroom soups. ● *Tue.* 🖻 ▤		■		
DORSODURO: *Locanda Montin* €€€€ Fondamenta Eremite 1147, 30123. **Map** 6 D3. (041 522 71 51. A famous restaurant with artistic and literary connections. Food and service can vary in quality but there is a lively atmosphere. ● *Tue eve, Wed.* 🖻		■		■

Average prices for a three-course meal for one, including a half-bottle of house wine, tax and service:
€ under 18 euros
€€ 18–30 euros
€€€ 30–40 euros
€€€€ 40–52 euros
€€€€€ over 52 euros.

FIXED-PRICE MENU
A fixed-price menu on offer, usually with three courses.

GOOD WINE LIST
Denotes a wide range of good quality wines.

FORMAL DRESS
Some restaurants require men to wear a jacket and tie.

OUTDOOR TABLES
Tables for eating outdoors, often with a good view.

CREDIT CARDS
The symbol shows that major credit cards are accepted.

Restaurant	Price	Fixed-Price Menu	Good Wine List	Formal Dress	Outdoor Tables
GIUDECCA: *Cipriani* — Giudecca 10, 30122. 041 520 77 44. One of Venice's most exclusive restaurants, the *Cipriani* offers impeccable food and service in elegant surroundings. Panoramic terrace. ● Nov–Mar.	€€€€€	●	■	●	■
GIUDECCA: *Harry's Dolci* — Fondamenta San Biagio 773, 30133. Map 6 D5. 041 522 48 44. Originally a bar and tea-room, this is now a restaurant serving similar food to Harry's Bar in San Marco. Try *carpaccio* (marinated, sliced raw beef), the pasta and beans, and the house chocolate cake. ● Tue, Nov–Mar.	€€€€€		■		■
MAZZORBO: *Antica Trattoria alla Maddalena* — Mazzorbo 7b, Burano 30012. 041 73 01 51. This modest restaurant, popular with the locals, acts as a local bar as well as an eating house. It has a tranquil atmosphere, however, and the wild duck served with *polenta* is famous throughout the area. ● Thu.	€€				■
SAN MARCO: *Al Conte Pescaor* — Piscina San Zulian 544b, 30124. Map 7 B1. 041 522 14 83. A little restaurant with a superb fish menu. The clientele is mainly local people, which guarantees the high quality of the food. ● Sun, 7 Jan–7 Feb.	€€€				■
SAN MARCO: *Da Raffaele* — Ponte delle Ostreghe 2347, 30124. Map 7 A3. 041 523 23 17. A romantic setting in which to eat regional dishes. Try the *granseola* (spider crab), *risotto* with scampi and *rombo alla Raffaele* (turbot). ● Thu; Dec–early Feb.	€€€€		■		■
SAN MARCO: *Antico Martini* — Campo San Fantin 1983, 30124. Map 7 A2. 041 522 41 21. Overlooking the Fenice theatre, this smart restaurant serves until 1am. The cooking is creative: try the lamb with caper sauce. ● Tue (winter only).	€€€€€		■		■
SAN MARCO: *La Caravella* — Calle Larga XXII Marzo 2398, 30124. Map 7 A3. 041 520 89 01. Now the only restaurant in the Hotel Saturnia, *La Caravella* has a beautiful setting with a waterside terrace by the Grand Canal. The food is outstanding with speciality dishes including lobster soup.	€€€€€		■		■
SAN MARCO: *Da Arturo* — Calle degli Assassini 3656, 30124. Map 7 A2. 041 528 69 74. This restaurant must be the only place in Venice that does not serve fish, but the menu does include a variety of meat dishes and vegetarian salads. ● Sun; Aug.	€€€€€		■		
SAN MARCO: *Harry's Bar* — Calle Vallaresso 1323, 30124. Map 7 B3. 041 528 57 77. People come here because it is so famous. The wine list and cocktails are good but the food is not particularly exciting for the price.	€€€€€		■		
SAN POLO: *Antica Trattoria Poste Vecie* — Rialto Pescheria 1608, 30123. Map 3 A5. 041 72 18 22. This stylish restaurant near the fish market claims to be the oldest in Venice. Dishes include home-made pasta as well as lovely desserts.	€€€€				■
SAN POLO: *Da Fiore* — Calle del Scaleter 2202a. Map 2 E5. 041 72 13 08. Fish specialities include a wonderful seafood *antipasto*, grilled fish and *fritto misto* (mixed fried fish). Try the house white wine. ● Sun, Mon; 2 wks Aug, 2 wks Dec.	€€€€€		■		
TORCELLO: *Locanda Cipriani* — Piazza Santa Fosca 29, 30121. 041 73 01 50. Transformed from a fishermen's inn in the 1930s, dishes include *fritto misto* and a *risotto* with vegetables from the kitchen garden. At weekends, a boat transfer collects diners from Piazza San Marco. ● Tue; Jan.	€€€€€		■		■

For key to symbols see back flap

Average prices for a three-course meal for one, including a half-bottle of house wine, tax and service:
€ under 18 euros
€€ 18–30 euros
€€€ 30–40 euros
€€€€ 40–52 euros
€€€€€ over 52 euros.

FIXED-PRICE MENU
A fixed-price menu on offer, usually with three courses.
GOOD WINE LIST
Denotes a wide range of good quality wines.
FORMAL DRESS
Some restaurants require men to wear a jacket and tie.
OUTDOOR TABLES
Tables for eating outdoors, often with a good view.
CREDIT CARDS
The symbol shows that major credit cards are accepted.

	FIXED-PRICE MENU	GOOD WINE LIST	FORMAL DRESS	OUTDOOR TABLES

THE VENETO AND FRIULI

		FIXED-PRICE MENU	GOOD WINE LIST	FORMAL DRESS	OUTDOOR TABLES
ASOLO: *Villa Cipriani* €€€€€ Via Canova 298, 31011. **[** *0423 95 21 66.* Set in one of the grand hotels of the Veneto. Local ingredients are used in the creative cuisine with dishes such as *gnocchi* of ricotta with rosemary. 🗐			■	●	■
BELLUNO: *Terracotta* €€ Via Garibaldi 61. **[** *0437 94 26 44.* Regional specialities include *pappardelle* (wide ribbon pasta) with smoked ricotta, *radicchio* and speck, or chickpea and prawn soup. ● *Wed.* 🗐			■		
BREGANZE: *Al Toresan* €€ Via Zabarella 1, 36042. **[** *0445 87 32 60.* In the autumn the locals flock here for the wild mushroom dishes. The cooking is hearty and is complemented by local wines. ● *Thu; end Jul–25 Aug.* 🗐					■
CAORLE: *Duilio* €€€ Via Strada Nuova 19, 30021. **[** *0421 810 87.* A spacious restaurant where the fish-based regional cuisine is given a creative slant. Try the dried cod with *polenta.* ● *Mon (winter), 10–15 Jan.* 🗐			■		■
CASTELFRANCO: *Barbesin* €€ Via Montebelluna 41, 31033. **[** *0423 49 04 46.* A restaurant serving regional specialities, including *risotto* with fish, or vegetables, or porcini mushrooms. ● *Wed eve, Thu; 1 week Jan, 2 weeks Aug.* 🗐			■		
CHIOGGIA: *El Gato* €€€€ Campo Sant'Andrea 653, 30015. **[** *041 40 18 06.* Classic cooking based on seafood in an elegant, slightly restrained setting. The delicious desserts are highly recommended. ● *Mon, Tue lunch; Jan–mid Feb.* 🗐			■		■
CIVIDALE DEL FRIULI: *Zorutti* €€€ Borgo Ponte 9, 33043. **[** *0432 73 11 00.* A family-run restaurant with a well-deserved reputation for good, regional cuisine served in generous portions. The house speciality is *buzara*, a local speciality of *spaghetti* with seafood, giant prawns or lobster. ● *Mon.* 🗐			■		
CONEGLIANO: *Al Salisà* €€€ Via XX Settembre 2, 31015. **[** *0438 242 88.* An elegant restaurant set in a medieval house with a pretty veranda for eating outdoors. The traditional menu includes home-made pastas served with a range of vegetarian sauces. ● *Tue pm, Wed.* 🗐			■		■
CORTINA D'AMPEZZO: *Baita Fraina* €€€ Località Fraina 1, 32043. **[** *0436 36 34.* An elegant alpine restaurant, with wood fittings and a panoramic terrace. The food is robust and extremely good value. ● *Mon (Jan–mid-Mar), May, Jun, Oct, Nov.* 🗐			■		■
DOLO: *Alla Posta* €€€ Via Ca' Tron 33, 30031. **[** *041 41 07 40.* This superb restaurant in an old Venetian posthouse prepares regional specialities with fresh ingredients and well-blended flavours. ● *Mon; 2 wks Jan, 2 wks Jun–Jul.* 🗐		●	■		■
GORIZIA: *Nanut* € Via Trieste 118, 34170. **[** *0481 205 95.* A long-established trattoria in the industrial zone. It serves good local food; *gnocchi*, market vegetables, meats, and fish on Friday. ● *Sat, Sun; Aug.* 🗐					■
GRADO: *Trattoria de Toni* €€ Piazza Duca d'Aosta 37, 34073. **[** *0431 801 04.* A traditional trattoria in the historic centre, the house speciality is *boreto alla Gradese*, a fish stew cooked in oil and vinegar. ● *Nov–Mar: Wed; Jan, Dec.* 🗐 🔥			■		■

GRANCONA: *Isetta* €€
Via Pederiva 96, 36040. ☎ 0444 88 99 92.
Regional food, with the emphasis on grilled meats and good puddings,
in Galdino Gianesin's restaurant in the Berici hills. ● Tue eve, Wed; Jul. ☒

LAKE GARDA: *Antica Locanda Mincio* €€€
Via Buonarroti 12, Località Borghetto, Valeggio sul Mincio 37067. ☎ 045 795 00 59.
Once a staging post, this is now a delightful restaurant with frescoed walls
and open fireplaces serving good regional food. ● Wed, Thu, 2 wks Feb, 2 wks Nov. ☒

LAKE GARDA: *Locanda San Vigilio* €€€€
Località San Vigilio, Garda 37016. ☎ 045 725 66 88.
This excellent restaurant overlooking Lake Garda has an *antipasto* buffet and
an astounding range of freshwater fish and seafood dishes. ● Nov–Mar. ☒

MONTECCHIA DI CROSARA: *Baba-jaga* €€€
Via Cabalao 11, 37030. ☎ 045 745 02 22.
Black-truffle *risotto* and prawns with courgettes, tomatoes and leeks are
a good choice in the Soave wine-producing area. ● Sun eve, Mon, Jan, 2 wks Aug. ☒

NOVENTA PADOVANA: *Boccadoro* €€
Via della Resistenza 49, 35027. ☎ 049 62 50 29.
Good Paduan food is served in this family-run restaurant. The goose
is well worth sampling. ● Tue eve, Wed; 2 weeks Jan, 2 weeks Aug. ☒ ▤

ODERZO: *Dussin* €€
Via Maggiore 60, Località Piavon, 31046. ☎ 0422 75 21 30.
Good value, traditional cuisine is served in this lively, restaurant. Fish is a speciality,
with such dishes as seafood *risotto* and grilled tuna. ● Mon eve, Tue; Jan, Aug. ☒ ▤

PADUA: *La Braseria* €€
Via Tommaseo 48, 35100. ☎ 049 876 09 07.
A friendly restaurant with straightforward cooking. *Penne* with porcini
mushrooms and smoked bacon are recommended. ● Sat lunch, Sun; eves Aug. ☒ ▤

PADUA: *Osteria L'Anfora* €€
Via dei Soncin 13, 35122. ☎ 049 65 66 29.
Traditional Veneto cuisine, with elements originally brought by Renaissance
merchants from far afield, is served in a lively atmosphere. ● Sun; 1–6 Jan, 2 wks Aug.

PADUA: *San Pietro* €€
Via San Pietro 95, 35149. ☎ 049 876 03 30.
The perfect place to try the regional specialities, cooked with fresh, local ingredients.
The service is friendly and attentive, and the atmosphere informal. ● Sun; Jul. ☒ ▤

PADUA: *Antico Brolo* €€€
Corso Milano 22, 35100. ☎ 049 66 45 55.
This quietly elegant restaurant delivers appropriately elegant food such as
ravioli stuffed with courgette flowers. ● Mon, Aug. ☒ ▤

PORDENONE: *Vecia Osteria del Moro* €€
Via Castello 2, 33170. ☎ 0434 286 58.
A refined restaurant set in a beautifully-restored 13th-century convent. Daily
specials include rabbit with *polenta*. ● Sun; 2 weeks Jan, 2 weeks Aug. ☒ ▤

ROVIGO: *Cauccio* €
Viale Oroboni 50, 45100. ☎ 0425 316 39.
An old-fashioned trattoria, serving unpretentious, traditional Italian cuisine, such as
lasagne, cannelloni and *vitello tonnato* (veal with tuna and caper sauce). ● Mon. ☒

TREVISO: *Osteria Snack Bassanello* €€
Viale Cairoli 133, 31100. ☎ 0422 26 06 23.
Excellent local cuisine is served in this popular *osteria*. In season, *radicchio* (endive)
is used in numerous ways including the digestive, *grappa*. ● Mon, 2 wks Aug.

TREVISO: *Toni del Spin* €€
Via Inferiore 7, 31100. ☎ 0422 54 38 29.
A homely restaurant serving regional fare. House specialities include pasta and
fagioli (beans), baked tripe and tiramisù. ● Sun, Mon lunch; 3 wks Aug. ☒ ▤

TREVISO: *Ristorante Beccherie* €€€
Piazza Ancillotto 10, 31100. ☎ 0422 54 08 71.
Housed in a lovely building reminiscent of Venetian splendour. The guinea
fowl in pepper sauce is a particular delicacy. ● Sun eve, Mon, 15–30 Jul. ☒

	FIXED-PRICE MENU	GOOD WINE LIST	FORMAL DRESS	OUTDOOR TABLES

Average prices for a three-course meal for one, including a half-bottle of house wine, tax and service:
€ under 18 euros
€€ 18–30 euros
€€€ 30–40 euros
€€€€ 40–52 euros
€€€€€ over 52 euros.

FIXED-PRICE MENU
A fixed-price menu on offer, usually with three courses.
GOOD WINE LIST
Denotes a wide range of good quality wines.
FORMAL DRESS
Some restaurants require men to wear a jacket and tie.
OUTDOOR TABLES
Tables for eating outdoors, often with a good view.
CREDIT CARDS
The symbol shows that major credit cards are accepted.

	FIXED-PRICE MENU	GOOD WINE LIST	FORMAL DRESS	OUTDOOR TABLES
TRIESTE: *Al Bragozzo* €€€ Riva Sauro 22, 34124. 𝄪 040 30 30 01. The menu changes from week to week, depending on the local produce available. This lively restaurant is popular with locals. ● *Sun. Mon; 2 weeks Jan, 2 weeks Jul.*		▣		▣
TRIESTE: *Harry's Grill* €€€€ Piazza Unità d'Italia 2, 34121. 𝄪 040 36 56 46. This restaurant is distinguished by its central position and high-class cuisine. Try bigoli pasta with duck or beef fillet with *bordolese* sauce. ● *Sun eve.*		▣		▣
UDINE: *Agli Amici* €€€ Via Liguria 250, Località Godia, 33100. 𝄪 0432 56 54 11. Friulian dishes, such as *polenta* with smoked ricotta and walnuts, or *cjarsons* (ravioli) with wild herbs, are cooked with flair here. ● *Sun eve, Mon; Jan, Jul.*	●	▣		▣
VERONA: *Al Bersagliere* €€ Via dietro Pallone 1, 37121. 𝄪 045 800 48 24. Traditional Veronese food in a friendly atmosphere. Dishes include mixed grilled meats and *polenta* with wild mushrooms. ● *Sun.*		▣		
VERONA: *Arche* €€€€€ Via Arche Scaligere 6, 37121. 𝄪 045 800 74 15. A long-established fish restaurant serving spaghetti with clams in *cartoccio* and rock lobster in *serenissima saor* marinade. ● *Sun, Mon lunch, 2 weeks Feb.*	●	▣		
VERONA: *Il Desco* €€€€€ Via dietro San Sebastiano 5–7, 37121. 𝄪 045 59 53 58. One of Italy's best restaurants, set in a 16th-century palazzo. Imaginative dishes include veal with ginger and lobster *risotto*. ● *Sun, Mon; 2 wks Jan, 2 wks Jun.*	●	▣	●	
VICENZA: *Antica Trattoria Tre Visi* €€ Corso Palladio 25, 36100. 𝄪 0444 32 48 68. The building, in the historic centre, dates from 1483. Diners can see into the kitchen where the excellent local dishes are prepared. ● *Sun eve, Mon; Jul.*	●	▣		▣
VICENZA: *Cinzia e Valerio* €€€ Piazzetta Porta Padova 65–67, 36100. 𝄪 0444 50 52 13. A stylish restaurant within the city walls, serving nothing but fish. Dishes include a mixed plate of scampi and squid. ● *Sun eve, Mon; 26 Dec–5 Jan, 3 weeks Aug.*	●	▣		
VICENZA: *Taverna Aeolia* €€€ Piazza Conte da Schio 1, Costozza di Longare 36023. 𝄪 0444 55 50 36. This restaurant is housed in an elegant villa with a beautiful frescoed ceiling. The menu specializes in creative meat dishes. ● *Tue, 1–15 Nov.*	●	▣		

TRENTINO-ALTO ADIGE

	FIXED-PRICE MENU	GOOD WINE LIST	FORMAL DRESS	OUTDOOR TABLES
ARCO: *Alla Lega* €€ Via Vergolano 4, 38062. 𝄪 0464 51 62 05. A lively, family-run restaurant housed in a rustically elegant 18th-century building with a beautiful courtyard. The food is traditional, including such dishes as *risotto*, cured meats and trout with *polenta*. ● *Wed; Feb, 2 weeks Mar.*		▣		▣
BOLZANO (BOZEN): *Da Abramo* €€ Piazza Gries 16, 39050. 𝄪 0471 28 01 41. This elegant restaurant offers splendid river views across the Talvera. The cuisine features richly seasoned fish and meat dishes. ● *Sun; 2 weeks Jan, 2 weeks Aug.*	●	▣		▣
BOLZANO (BOZEN): *Domino* €€ Piazza Walther 1, 39100. 𝄪 0471 98 16 10. This town-centre wine bar is a good stop for a delicious lunchtime snack or a glass of wine in the evening. ● *Sun; 1 week Jul.*				▣

BOLZANO (BOZEN): *Rastbichler*　€€€
Via Cadorna 1, 39100. **☎** 0471 26 11 31.
This restaurant is known for its excellent fish and generously served grilled
meats. Typical South Tyrol decor. **●** *Sat lunch, Sun.*

BRESSANONE (BRIXEN): *Fink*　€€
Via Portici Minori 4, 39042. **☎** 0472 83 48 83.
Popular with locals who come to sample the immaculately prepared dishes
such as black *polenta* or *knödel* (a kind of dumpling). **●** *Tue eve, Wed, Feb.* 🗑 ⚡ ♿

BRESSANONE (BRIXEN): *Oste Scuro-Finsterwirt*　€€
Vicolo Duomo 3, 39042. **☎** 0472 83 53 43.
One of the oldest buildings in the historic centre, it specializes in regional
cuisine using local produce in imaginative ways. **●** *Sun eve, Mon, Jan.* 🗑 ♿

BRUNICO (BRUNECK): *Oberraut*　€€
Via Ameto 1, Località Amaten, 39031. **☎** 0474 55 99 77.
Set in woods, this Tyrolean-style restaurant specializes in local game and
seasonal dishes. There is a tantalizing dessert list. **●** *Thu (winter); Jan.* 🗑 ♿

CARZANO: *Le Rose*　€€€
Via XVIII Settembre 35, 38050. **☎** 0461 76 61 77.
This popular Valsugana restaurant concentrates on fish and seasonal
produce. Try the *tortelli* of fish with *porcini* mushrooms. **●** *Mon* 🗑

CAVALESE: *Costa Salici*　€€€
Via Costa dei Salici 10, 38033. **☎** 0462 34 01 40.
A popular restaurant with specialties such as home-made pasta with *finferli*
mushrooms, marinated venison and pear *strudel*. **●** *Mon, Tue lunch.* 🗑 ♿

CIVEZZANO: *Maso Cantanghel*　€€
Via della Madonnina 33, 38045. **☎** 0461 85 87 14.
An excellent restaurant just outside Trento. Food is simple yet delicious; garden
vegetables, roasted meats and home-made pasta. **●** *Sat, Sun; 1 week Aug.* 🗑

LEVICO TERME: *Boivin*　€€
Via Garibaldi 9, 38056. **☎** 0461 70 16 70.
This excellent trattoria is one of the best places to taste authentic, local cuisine; booking
is essential. Only open evenings and for Sunday lunch. **●** *Mon, Jan: Mon–Thu.* 🗑

MADONNA DI CAMPIGLIO: *Hermitage*　€€€
Via Castelletto Inferiore 63, 38084. **☎** 0465 44 15 58.
Set in a private park at the foot of the Dolomites, the Hermitage serves imaginatively
regional cuisine, with fresh-flavoured, tasty dishes. **●** *May–Jun, Oct–Nov lunch.* 🗑 ⚡

MALLES VENOSTA (MALS IM VINSCHGAU): *Greif*　€€€
Via Generale Verdross 40a, 39024. **☎** 0473 83 14 29.
Here the chef creates Tyrolean dishes using organic produce. The restaurant also
serves a vegetarian menu. **●** *Sun; 2 weeks Jun, 2 weeks Dec.* 🗑 ⚡ ♿

MALLES VENOSTA (MALS IM VINSCHGAU): *Weisses Kreuz*　€€€
Località Burgusio 82, 39024. **☎** 0473 83 13 07.
This excellent value restaurant serves traditional fare such as *knödel*
(dumplings), roasted meats and fruit strudels. **●** *Thu, Fri lunch.* 🗑 ♿

MERANO (MERAN): *Sissi*　€€€
Via Galilei 44, 39012. **☎** 0473 23 10 62.
A 19th-century building close to the town centre, the Sissi offers a refined,
seasonal menu combining traditional and modern dishes. **●** *Mon.* 🗑 ▤

MERANO (MERAN): *Artemis*　€€€€
Via Giuseppe Verdi 72, 39012. **☎** 0473 44 62 82.
Good Italian and international cuisine is served here. Live classical music
accompanies Sunday brunch. **●** *Jan–Mar.* 🗑

MOENA: *Malga Panna*　€€€€
Via Costalunga 29, 38035. **☎** 0462 57 34 89.
Mushrooms and game are served at this romantic restaurant in a rustic setting
about 1 km (half a mile) from the centre of Moena. **●** *May–Jun, Oct–Nov.* 🗑 ♿

ROVERETO: *Novecento*　€€€
Corso Rosmini 82d, 38068. **☎** 0464 43 54 54.
A refined restaurant, part of a hotel in the middle of Rovereto, serving
some carefully prepared local dishes. **●** *Sun; 3 weeks Jan, 3 weeks Aug.* 🗑 ▤ ⚡

Average prices for a three-course meal for one, including a half-bottle of house wine, tax and service: € under 18 euros €€ 18–30 euros €€€ 30–40 euros €€€€ 40–52 euros €€€€€ over 52 euros.	FIXED-PRICE MENU A fixed-price menu on offer, usually with three courses. GOOD WINE LIST Denotes a wide range of good quality wines. FORMAL DRESS Some restaurants require men to wear a jacket and tie. OUTDOOR TABLES Tables for eating outdoors, often with a good view. CREDIT CARDS The symbol shows that major credit cards are accepted.	FIXED-PRICE MENU	GOOD WINE LIST	FORMAL DRESS	OUTDOOR TABLES
ROVERETO: *Al Borgo* €€€€ Via Garibaldi 13, 38068. 📞 *0464 43 63 00.* Centrally situated, Al Borgo is one of the best restaurants in the Trentino region, offering dishes using local produce. ● *Sun eve, Mon; 20–30 Jan, 3 wks Jul.* 🗓🍽		●	■	
TRENTO: *Al Tino* € Via Santissima Trinità 10, 38100. 📞 *0461 98 41 09.* Situated in an historic building in the centre of Trento, this traditional trattoria is lively and popular so booking is advisable. The food and wine are good value. ● *Sun.* 🗓🍽		●	■	
TRENTO: *Al Castello* €€ Via Val Gola 2–4, Località Ravina 38040. 📞 *0461 92 33 33.* This family-run restaurant concentrates on good basics, including home-made pasta, and *strangolapreti* of potato, ricotta and spinach. ● *Sun eve, Mon.* 🗓			■	■
TRENTO: *Osteria A le Due Spade* €€€€ Via Don Rizzi 11, 38100. 📞 *0461 23 43 43.* A welcoming cellar restaurant near the Duomo, serving traditional Trentino cuisine, including game and freshwater fish dishes. ● *Sun, Mon lunch.* 🗓🍽		●	■	
VAL DI VIZZE (PFITSCH): *Pretzhof* €€€ Località Tulve 259, 39040. 📞 *0472 76 44 55.* Karl and Ulli Mair run this peaceful country inn, using fresh produce from their own farm to concoct Tyrolean specialities. ● *Mon, Tue; end Jan–1st wk Feb, 1st wk Jul.* 🗓				■
VIPITENO (BOLZANO): *Kleine Flamme* €€€ Città Nuova 31, 39049. 📞 *0472 76 60 65.* A high standard of creative cuisine is matched by attentive service and attention to detail at this small, chic restaurant in a 16th-century building. ● *Sun eve, Mon.* 🗓🍽		●	■	
LOMBARDY					
BELLAGIO: *Silvio* €€ Via Carcano 12, 22021. 📞 *031 95 03 22.* Silvio and his son Cristian catch much of the lake fish which is used for patés, pasta sauces, *ravioli* and *risottos*. There is a relaxed atmosphere in this lovely restaurant and hotel with beautiful lakeside views. ● *Jan, Feb.* 🗓		●		■
BERGAMO: *Vineria Cozzi* €€ Via Colleoni 22, 24129. 📞 *035 23 88 36.* An attractive, old wine shop decorated in 19th-century style, the Cozzi has a spectacular list of wines and a range of light dishes and pies to accompany them. Try *polenta* with truffled cheese. ● *Wed; 2 wks Jan, 2 wks Aug.* 🗓		●	■	■
BERGAMO: *Taverna del Colleoni dell'Angelo* €€€€ Piazza Vecchia 7, 24129. 📞 *035 23 25 96.* An elegant taverna. Specialities include pasta with squid, prawns with light *polenta* and delicious desserts. ● *Mon, 2 wks Aug.* 🗓🚫🍽		●	■	● ■
BORMIO: *Al Filò* €€€ Via Dante 6, 23032. 📞 *0342 90 47 71.* A restaurant in a 17th-century barn. It serves local cuisine with specialities based on game, mushrooms and cured meats. ● *Tue, Wed lunch; May–Jun, Oct–Nov.* 🗓		●	■	
BRESCIA: *Trattoria Mezzeria* €€€ Via Trieste 66, 25121. 📞 *030 403 06.* A busy trattoria serving home-made pasta or squash *gnocchi*, with main dishes such as stewed rabbit *alle Bresciana*. ● *Sun; Jul–Aug.* 🗓♿			■	
CASTELVECCANA: *Sant'Antonio* €€ Località Sant'Antonio, 21010. 📞 *0332 52 11 66.* This restaurant is set in a delightful 10th-century village with views of Lake Maggiore. The menu includes an excellent *polenta* with boiled meats. ● *Mon.*		●		■

Como: *Sant'Anna 1907*　　　　€€€€
Via Turati 3, 22100. (031 50 52 66.
This restaurant has been run by the Fontana family for three generations.
The traditional dishes include fish *risotto* and veal in an olive crust.
● Sat lunch; Aug; 1 wk Dec. 🍴 ⅆ 🍽

Cremona: *Mellini*　　　　€€
Via Bissolati 105, 26100. (0372 305 35.
A cosy, family-run restaurant with a good choice of dishes prepared with great flair,
using exclusively fresh and local ingredients and seafish of the highest quality. Try the
pumpkin *tortelli*, *risotto* with mushrooms or bass with potatoes. ● Sun eve, Mon, Aug.

Cremona: *Osteria Porta Mosa*　　　　€€€
Via Santa Maria in Betlem 11, 26100. (0372 41 18 03.
A refined trattoria with excellent wines and simple dishes, such as *ravioli*, smoked
sword fish and *polenta* with seasonal sauces. Wine shop. ● Sun; Aug. 🍴 🍽

Gargnano del Garda: *La Tortuga*　　　　€€€€€
Via XXIV Maggio 5, Porticciolo di Gargnano, 25084. (0365 712 51.
A charming lakeside location for light imaginative cuisine. Try the *coregone*
with tomatoes and capers. ● lunch; Mon eve (Oct–May), Tue; Jan, Feb. 🍴 🍽

Lake Como: *Locanda dell'Isola Comacina*　　　　€€€€
Isola Comacina, 22010. (0344 550 83.
Set by the water's edge on an otherwise uninhabited island. A wonderful
five-course set menu of fish dishes is served. ● Tue (16 Sep–14 Jun); Nov–Mar.

Lecco: *Casa di Lucia*　　　　€€
Via Lucia 27, Località Acquate 22053. (0341 49 45 94.
In a 17th-century house, traditional fare such as salami, *bresaola* (cured beef),
rabbit and *pasta e fagioli* is served with good national wines. ● Sat lunch; Sun; Aug.

Manerba del Garda: *Capriccio*　　　　€€€€€
Piazza San Bernardo 6, Località Montinelle, 25080. (0365 55 11 24.
Excellent lake views is an extra bonus at this restaurant which uses the
local fish and olive oil in its cuisine. Desserts include a muscat-grape jelly with
peach sauce. ● lunch; Tue; Jan–Feb. 🍴 🍽

Mantova: *Ai Ranari*　　　　€€
Via Trieste 11, 46100. (0376 32 84 31.
A simple trattoria. Dishes are Mantuan and include pumpkin *tortelli* with
butter sauce and meat *polenta*. ● Mon; 2 weeks Jul, 1 week Aug. 🍴

Mantova: *L'Ochina Bianca*　　　　€€
Via Finzi 2, 46100. (0376 32 37 00.
A simple restaurant serving some of the less well-known local specialities
such as meat parcels with sausage and cheese. ● Mon, Tue lunch, 1st wk Jan. 🍴

Mantova: *Il Cigno Trattoria dei Martini*　　　　€€€
Piazza Carlo d'Arco 1, 46100. (0376 32 71 01.
Fine Mantuan cuisine is accompanied by excellent wines. Try *bottarga*
(tuna roe) and *tortelli di zucce* (pumpkin). ● Mon, Tue; Aug, 1st wk Jan. 🍴 🍽

Milan: *Geppo*　　　　€
Viale Morgagni 37, 20124. (02 29 51 48 62.
A fun atmosphere and wide range of pizzas are on offer in this restaurant. Try the
valdostane (spinach, tomato, mozzarella and taleggio cheese). ● Sun lunch.

Milan: *Premiata Pizzeria*　　　　€
Alzaia Naviglio Grande 2, 20144. (02 89 40 04 68.
This lively, informal restaurant is always busy but the service is efficient and friendly.
The dining room is spacious and fitted with antiques; in the summer the tables are
laid outside in the beautiful courtyard. ● Tue. 🍴 🍽

Milan: *Ba Ba Reeba*　　　　€€
Via Orti 7, 20122. (02 55 01 12 67.
This is different, in that its cuisine is exclusively Spanish. Specialities include *baccalà*
(dried salt cod) and fillet in red wine sauce. ● Sun, Mon lunch; 3 weeks Aug. 🍽

Milan: *La Capanna*　　　　€€
Via Donatello 9, 20131. (02 29 40 08 84.
Do not be put off by the plain appearance, since the food, based on traditional
Tuscan cuisine, is exceptional; fresh pasta and home-made puddings.
● Sat; Aug. 🍴 🍽

	FIXED-PRICE MENU	GOOD WINE LIST	FORMAL DRESS	OUTDOOR TABLES

Average prices for a three-course meal for one, including a half-bottle of house wine, tax and service:
€ under 18 euros
€€ 18–30 euros
€€€ 30–40 euros
€€€€ 40–52 euros
€€€€€ over 52 euros.

FIXED-PRICE MENU
A fixed-price menu on offer, usually with three courses.
GOOD WINE LIST
Denotes a wide range of good quality wines.
FORMAL DRESS
Some restaurants require men to wear a jacket and tie.
OUTDOOR TABLES
Tables for eating outdoors, often with a good view.
CREDIT CARDS
The symbol shows that major credit cards are accepted.

	FIXED-PRICE MENU	GOOD WINE LIST	FORMAL DRESS	OUTDOOR TABLES
MILAN: *Lucca* €€€ Via Castaldi 33, 20100. 02 29 52 66 68. Great for business lunches and popular for dinner, the cuisine is Tuscan and Mediterranean in style.		▪		
MILAN: *Aimo e Nadia* €€€€€ Via Montecuccoli 6, 20147. 02 41 68 86. A small, chic restaurant which is famed for its delicious, imaginative dishes, prepared with select, seasonal ingredients. ● *Sat lunch, Sun; Aug; 1 wk Jan.*	●	▪	●	
MONTE ISOLA: *La Foresta* €€ Località Peschiera Maraglio 174, 25050. 030 988 62 10. Lake fish form the basis of the menu, making this popular with lovers of all sorts of local freshwater fish. ● *Wed; 2 weeks Oct; Jan.*	●	▪		▪
PAVIA: *Locanda Vecchia Pavia al Mulino* €€€€€ Via al Monumento 5, Località Certosa, 27012. 0382 92 58 94. Frothy desserts follow creative dishes that bring a light touch to local specialities. The service is cordial and attentive. ● *Mon, Wed lunch; 3 wks Jan, 2 wks Aug.*	●	▪		▪
SALÒ: *Alla Campagnola* €€ Via Brunati 11, 25087. 0365 221 53. A mother and sons team offers interesting traditional recipes including pasta stuffed with pumpkin or aubergine. ● *Mon, Tue lunch; Jan.*	●	▪		▪

VALLE D'AOSTA AND PIEDMONT

	FIXED-PRICE MENU	GOOD WINE LIST	FORMAL DRESS	OUTDOOR TABLES
ACQUI TERME: *La Schiavia* €€€ Vicolo della Schiavia, 15011. 0144 559 39. An elegant, family-run restaurant on the ground floor of a 17th-century palazzo. Cuisine is regional including a mix of vegetables and fish. ● *Sun; 2 weeks Aug.*		▪		
ALBA: *Porta San Martino* €€€ Via Einaudi 5, 12051. 0173 36 23 35. Excellent value at this refined restaurant with good service and a menu of local specialities: *vitello tonnato* (veal with a sauce of tuna and capers) and *brasato* (meat) in Barbaresco wine sauce. ● *Mon; 2 weeks Jul, 2 wks Aug.*		▪		
ALESSANDRIA: *Il Grappolo* €€€ Via Casale 28, 15100. 0131 25 32 17. Piedmontese cuisine with a few borrowed touches. Try the *agnolotti* (stuffed pasta) *all'Alessandrina.* ● *Wed; 1 week Jan, 2 wks Aug.*	●	▪		▪
AOSTA: *Grotta Azzurra* €€ Via Croix de Ville 97, 11100. 0165 26 24 74. This good pizzeria also serves excellent fish, pasta and *risotto*. Try the seafood salad, *risotto* or fish soup as a first course. ● *Wed; Jul.*		▪		▪
AOSTA: *Vecchia Aosta* €€ Piazza Porta Pretoria 4c, 11100. 0165 36 11 86. Set into the old Roman wall, the Vecchia Aosta offers typical regional dishes such as vegetable terrines and *ravioli.* ● *Wed; 2 weeks Feb, 2 weeks Oct.*	●	▪		▪
AOSTA: *Le Foyer* €€€ Corso Ivrea 146, 11100. 0165 321 36. Popular with locals, this trattoria serves excellent fish including salmon *carpaccio*, *risotto* of prawns, and rocket and courgette flan. ● *Mon eve, Tue; Jan, 2 wks Jul.*	●			
ASTI: *Gener Neuv* €€€€€ Lungotanaro 4, 14100. 0141 55 72 70. A peacefully rustic restaurant about 1 km (half a mile) from the town centre. The Gener Neuv serves carefully prepared local dishes and the family who run it offer attentive service. ● *Sun eve, Mon (Sun lunch Jan–Jul); 2 weeks Aug, 2 wks Dec–Jan.*	●	▪		

BRA: *Osteria Boccondivino* €€
Via Mendicità Istruita 14, 12042. ☎ *0172 42 56 74.*
An informal restaurant with Piedmontese cuisine. Try stuffed veal, rabbit in white
wine sauce and *panna cotta* (crème brûlée). ● *Sun, Mon.lunch; 2 weeks Aug.* ▨

BREUIL-CERVINIA: *Les Neiges d'Antan* €€€€
Frazione Cret de Perrères 10, 11021. ☎ *0166 94 87 75.*
Elegantly rustic, this restaurant has beautiful mountain views and serves
carefully prepared rich mountain fare. ● *May–Jun; Oct–Nov.* ▨ ▧

CANNOBIO: *Del Lago* €€€€€
Via Nazionale 2, Località Carmine Inferiore 28822. ☎ *0323 705 95.*
A lovely lakeside restaurant where the imaginative cuisine combines
sometimes surprising flavours to great effect. ● *Tue, Wed lunch; Nov–Feb.* ▨

CASALE MONFERRATO: *La Torre* €€€€
Via Garoglio 3, 15033. ☎ *0142 702 95.*
An elegant restaurant with panoramic views near the town centre. The creative cuisine
uses seasonal ingredients. ● *Wed; 3 weeks Aug, 1 wk Dec, 1 wk Jan.* ▨ ♿ ▤

COGNE: *Lou Ressignon* €€
Rue Mines de Cogne 22, 11012. ☎ *0165 740 34.*
A 17th-century inn where an open fireplace creates an old-world feeling. Rustic cuisine
with salamis, *polenta* and grilled meats. ● *Mon, Tue; 2 wks Sep, 2 wks Jun, Nov.* ▨ ♿

COSTIGLIOLE D'ASTI: *Collavini* €€
Via Asti-Nizza 84, 14055. ☎ *0141 96 64 40.*
A comfortable atmosphere, good service and carefully prepared simple food combine
to make the Collavini a popular spot. ● *Tue pm, Wed, 3 wks Jan, 3 wks Aug.* ▨

COURMAYEUR: *Pierre Alexis 1877* €€€
Via Marconi 54, 11013. ☎ *0165 84 35 17.*
A converted barn in the historic centre with dishes based on local traditions;
beef in four sauces and *ravioli di cacciagione* (game). ● *Oct–Nov.* ▨

CUNEO: *Osteria della Chiocciola* €€
Via Fossano 1, 12100. ☎ *0171 662 77.*
An excellent restaurant where seasonal fare is combined with the appropriate
wines. Winter has full-bodied reds. ▨ ● *Sun, 1 wk Jan, 1 wk Aug.* ▨

DOMODOSSOLA: *Piemonte da Sciolla* €€
Piazza della Convenzione 4, 28845. ☎ *0324 24 26 33.*
Immaculately prepared regional specialities such as *gnocchi* with rye and
chestnuts, set in a historic building. ● *Wed; 2 weeks Jan, 2 weeks Aug, 1 week Sep.* ▨ ▧

FEISOGLIO: *Piemonte da Renato* €€
Via Firenze 19, 12050. ☎ *0173 83 11 16.*
A family atmosphere at this trattoria serving seasonal specialities, especially
dishes with white and black truffles. Booking is advisable. ● *Dec–Easter.* ♿

IVREA: *La Trattoria* €€
Via Aosta 47, 10015. ☎ *0125 489 98.*
A bright restaurant where the food is simple and based on regional cuisine.
Try the smoked fish in vegetable sauce. ● *Sun eve, Mon; 2 weeks Aug.* ▨ ▤

NOVARA: *La Famiglia* €€€
Via Solaroli 10, 28100. ☎ *0321 39 95 29.*
A small, peaceful restaurant, its walls painted with frescoes of Lake Maggiore.
The cuisine specializes in fresh fish and *risottos.* ▨

NOVARA: *Osteria del Laghetto* €€€€
Case Sparse 11, Località Veveri, 28100. ☎ *0321 62 15 79.*
Set in a park, the flower-filled Laghetto specializes in dishes using fresh fish, truffles
and mushrooms. Booking is advisable. ● *Sat lunch, Sun; 1 week Aug, Dec–Jan.* ▨ ♿

ORTA SAN GIULIO: *Villa Crespi* €€€€€
Via Generale Fava 8–10, 28016. ☎ *0322 91 19 02.*
The decor is based on the Arabian Nights. The imaginative cuisine uses seasonal
truffles and *foie gras* (liver pâté). ● *Tue (Oct–Mar); Dec–Jan, 1 wk Aug, 1 wk Feb.* ▨ ♿ ▤

SAINT VINCENT: *Nuovo Batezar* €€€€€
Via Marconi 1, 11027. ☎ *0166 51 31 64.*
An excellent restaurant serving classic cuisine with special touches (*ravioli* with
lobster sauce, pheasant in *polenta* crust). ● *Wed, Mon–Fri lunch; 3 wks Jun, 2 wks Nov.* ▨

<table>
<tr><td colspan="5">

Average prices for a three-course meal for one, including a half-bottle of house wine, tax and service:
€ under 18 euros
€€ 18–30 euros
€€€ 30–40 euros
€€€€ 40–52 euros
€€€€€ over 52 euros.

FIXED-PRICE MENU
A fixed-price menu on offer, usually with three courses.
GOOD WINE LIST
Denotes a wide range of good quality wines.
FORMAL DRESS
Some restaurants require men to wear a jacket and tie.
OUTDOOR TABLES
Tables for eating outdoors, often with a good view.
CREDIT CARDS
The symbol shows that major credit cards are accepted.
</td></tr>
</table>

	FIXED-PRICE MENU	GOOD WINE LIST	FORMAL DRESS	OUTDOOR TABLES
SAN SECONDO DI PINEROLO: *La Ciau* €€€ Via Castello di Miradolo 2, 10060. (0121 50 06 11. Care and innovation go into the preparation of regional dishes. Try the *agnolotti* (pasta) stuffed with meat and the home-baked bread. ● *Wed; Jan.*	●	■		■
SESTRIERE: *Braciere del Possetto* €€€ Via Agnélli 11–12, 10058. (0122 761 29. This is one of the best places to taste Piedmontese dishes, exquisitely prepared, as well as a range of Italian and French cheeses. ● *Wed, May, Oct, Nov.*		■		
SORISO: *Al Soriso* €€€€€ Via Roma 18, 28016. (0322 98 32 28. One of the most acclaimed restaurants in Italy. The cuisine makes use of what's in season locally and draws on a wide range of traditions from Italy and abroad. ● *Mon, Tue lunch; 2 weeks Jan, 3 weeks Aug.*	●	■	●	
STRESA: *La Piemontese* €€€€ Via Mazzini 25, 28049. (0323 302 35. An elegant but unstuffy restaurant with impeccable service. The cuisine is creative, and prices are very fair. ● *Mon; Sun eve Oct–May, 2 wks Jan, 2 wks Dec.*		■		
TURIN: *Birilli* €€ Strada Val San Martino 6, 10131. (011 819 05 67. A friendly, cheerful restaurant opened in 1991 as part of a family-run chain whose first branch opened in Los Angeles in 1929. Simple dishes include meats and the house pasta *Birilli* (with tomato and bacon). ● *Sun (winter).*	●			■
TURIN: *Porto di Savona* €€ Piazza Vittorio Veneto 2, 10100. (011 817 35 00. A friendly restaurant set in an 18th-century building in central Turin. The regional cuisine includes such dishes as *gnocchi* with gorgonzola and meats braised in Barolo wine. ● *Mon, Tue lunch; 2 weeks Jan, 2 weeks Aug.*	●	■		■
TURIN: *Saletta* €€ Via Belfiore 37, 10126. (011 668 78 67. A warm, friendly atmosphere in central Turin. House specialities include meat braised in Barolo wine, and a fluffy *zabaglione*. ● *Sun; Aug.*	●	■		
TURIN: *Spada Reale* €€€ Via Principe Amedeo 53, 10123. (011 817 13 63. This newly restored restaurant provides a rustic setting in which to try regional dishes. Family-run, it is lively and informal, serving good-value food. ● *Sun, Sat lunch; Aug.*		■		
TURIN: *Neuv Caval 'd Brôns* €€€€€ Piazza San Carlo 151, 10123. (011 562 74 83. An elegant, spacious restaurant offering excellent food from a range of cuisine including vegetarian dishes. Specialities include the renowned mint and chocolate pudding *Santa Vittoria*. ● *Sat lunch, Sun.*	●	■	●	
VERBANIA PALLANZA: *Milano* €€€€ Corso Zanitello 2, 28048. (0323 55 68 16. Close to the town centre, the Milano has lake views and a romantic interior. Dishes include *tagliolini* with lake fish. ● *Tue; Jan; 1 week Jun.*	●			■
VERCELLI: *Il Paiolo* €€ Viale Garibaldi 72, 13100. (0161 25 05 77. A country trattoria in the historic centre, it specializes in local cuisine. The Vercellese *risotto* is particularly recommended. ● *Thu; mid-Jul–mid-Aug.*		■		
VERCELLI: *Il Giardinetto* €€€€ Via Sereno 3, 13100. (0161 25 72 30. The restaurant of an elegant villa hotel, it specializes in cuisine with truffles and mushrooms. Try the *foie gras* with apple and wine sauce. ● *Mon; 3 weeks Aug.*		■		■

VILLARFOCCHIARDO: *La Giaconera*   €€€
Via Antica di Francia 1, 10050. [011 964 50 00.
This elegant staging inn makes good use of seasonal ingredients such as
truffles, game and choice vegetables. ● *Mon, Tue; 2 weeks Aug.* 🗀 🔥

LIGURIA

CAMOGLI: *La Cucina di Nonna Nina*   €€€
Via Molfino 126, San Rocco di Camogli 16032. [0185 77 38 35.
"If you're in a hurry" says the menu, "relax; our food is prepared according
to traditional methods." The atmosphere is friendly and there are wonderful
views of the Golfo Paradiso. ● *Wed; 1 week Jan; 3 weeks Nov.* 🗀

CAMOGLI: *Rosa*   €€€€
Largo Casabona 11, 16032. [0185 77 34 11.
Set in a pretty villa on the Golfo Paradiso, the menu offers exquisitely prepared fish
such as pasta with fresh anchovies. ● *Tue; mid-Jan–mid Feb, 2 wks Nov.* 🗀

CERVO: *San Giorgio*   €€€€€
Via Volta 19, 18010. [0183 40 01 75.
Booking is absolutely essential at this popular spot for regional cuisine with a
different twist. The dishes are mainly fresh fish and seafood; the *branzino* (sea bass)
with rosemary and beans is exceptional. ● *Mon eve (winter), Tue; 3 wks Jan, Nov* 🗀

DOLCEACQUA: *Gastone*   €€€
Piazza Garibaldi 2, 18035. [0184 20 65 77.
Home-made pasta and regional meat dishes are two of the attractions
at this elegant restaurant in the historic centre. ● *Mon eve, Tue; 3 weeks Jan.* 🗀

GENOA: *Da Genio*   €€
Salita San Leonardo 61r, 16128. [010 58 84 63.
Popular with locals, this restaurant has an animated atmosphere. The food is delicious,
and includes grilled swordfish and anchovies stuffed with capers. ● *Sun; Aug.* 🗀

GENOA: *Do' Colla*   €€
Via alla Chiesa di Murta 10, Località Bolzaneto, 16162. [010 740 85 79
It is worth heading the few kilometres out of Genoa to taste the exquisite home-style
Ligurian cooking of this simple *trattoria*. ● *Sun eve, Mon; Aug; 2 weeks Jan.*

LEVANTO: *Tumelin*   €€€
Via Grillo 32, 19015. [0187 80 72 53.
The restaurant is 100m from the sea and the menu includes a selection of
wonderful seafood appetisers. Friendly service. ● *Thu; Jan.* 🗀

MANAROLA: *Marina Piccola*   €€€
Via Lo Scalo 16, 19010. [0187 80 83 79.
There are wonderful sea views from this restaurant whose menu of regional
specialities includes seafood *antipasti*, pesto and grilled fish. ● *Tue; Nov.* 🗀 🔥

NERVI: *Astor*   €€€
Viale delle Palme 16-18, 16167. [010 32 90 11.
This hotel restaurant offers a good selection of dishes including pesto, fish
and the local pasta dish *(pansotti)* with wild herbs and nut sauce. 🗀 ▤

PORTOFINO: *Puny*   €€€€
Piazza Martiri Olivetta 5, 16034. [0185 26 90 37.
A spectacular view of the bay of Portofino accompanies the well-prepared regional
dishes and crisp Ligurian wines. ● *Thu; Jan, Feb; 2 weeks Dec.*

PORTOVENERE: *Taverna del Corsaro*   €€€€
Calata Doria 102, 19025. [0187 79 06 22.
Reinterpreted regional recipes form the basis of the exclusively fish menu. Set on the
tip of the Portovenere peninsula with views over the sea. ● *Mon, Nov–Dec.* 🗀

RAPALLO: *Roccabruna*   €€€
Via Sotto la Croce 6, Località Savagna 16035. [0185 26 14 00.
Set on a pretty terrace away from the crowds on the seafront, this restaurant
simply serves the menu of the day, from the *antipasti* to the wines. ● *Mon* 🗀

SAN REMO: *Paolo e Barbara*   €€€€€
Via Roma 47, 18038. [0184 53 16 53.
In one of the most renowned restaurants in Liguria, the cuisine is based on
local and Mediterranean specialities, especially fish and seafood.
● *Wed, Thu lunch; last week Jun–first week Jul.* 🗀 ▤

	FIXED-PRICE MENU	GOOD WINE LIST	FORMAL DRESS	OUTDOOR TABLES

Average prices for a three-course meal for one, including a half-bottle of house wine, tax and service:
€ under 18 euros
€€ 18–30 euros
€€€ 30–40 euros
€€€€ 40–52 euros
€€€€€ over 52 euros.

FIXED-PRICE MENU
A fixed-price menu on offer, usually with three courses.
GOOD WINE LIST
Denotes a wide range of good quality wines.
FORMAL DRESS
Some restaurants require men to wear a jacket and tie.
OUTDOOR TABLES
Tables for eating outdoors, often with a good view.
CREDIT CARDS
The symbol shows that major credit cards are accepted.

VERNAZZA: *Gambero Rosso* €€€ Piazza Marconi 7, 19018. ☎ 0187 81 22 65. Rice with lemon and prawns, *gamberoni in pigiama* (deep-fried prawns) and *pansotti (see p174)* with cocoa and thyme are only some of the imaginatively interpreted Ligurian dishes in this newly refurbished restaurant. ● Mon; Dec–Feb. 🗺	●			▪

EMILIA-ROMAGNA

BOLOGNA: *Antica Trattoria Spiga* € Via Broccaindosso 21a, 40125. ☎ 051 23 00 63. A homely, authentic trattoria, with immaculately prepared traditional cuisine. Specialities include lasagne, *tortellini* and *gnocchi*. ● Mon eve, Sun; Aug. 🗺	●			
BOLOGNA: *Antica Trattoria del Cacciatore* €€€€ Via Caduti di Casteldebole 25, 40132. ☎ 051 56 42 03. A country inn near the airport. The menu is a mix of local and international dishes with home-made bread. ● Sun eve, Mon; 1 week Jan, 2 weeks Aug. 🗺 ☰		▪		
BOLOGNA: *Pappagallo* €€€€€ Piazza Mercanzia 3c, 40125. ☎ 051 23 28 07. Housed in a 14th-century palazzo in the historic centre, this elegant restaurant serves Bolognese dishes, *tortellini* and lasagna. ● Sun; Aug. 🗺		▪		
CASTELL'ARQUATO: *Da Faccini* €€ Località Sant' Antonio 10, 29014. ☎ 0523 89 63 40. Pasta and game are the highlights. Try *gnocchi* with carrots, duck and truffle *ravioli* and rabbit with mustard. ● Wed; 1 week Jul, 1 week Jan. 🗺 ♿		▪		▪
CASTELL'ARQUATO: *Maps* €€€ Piazza Europa 3, 29014. ☎ 0523 80 44 11. In a restructured medieval mill in the historic centre, fish is the mainstay of a menu that changes according to the market. ● Mon pm, Tue; Jul; 1 week Jan, 1 week Dec. 🗺 ☰				▪
FAENZA: *Le Volte* €€ Corso Mazzini 54, 48018. ☎ 0546 66 16 00. Housed in an atmospheric building in the historic centre. The food is delicious with a strong Pugliese influence. Try green *gnocchi* with tomato and basil, and chicken with olives. ● Sun; 2 weeks Jul, 2 weeks Aug. 🗺 ☰	●	▪		
FERRARA: *La Sgarbata* €€ Via Sgarbata 84, 44100. ☎ 0532 71 21 10. A country trattoria on the outskirts of Ferrara which serves speciality fish dishes as well as rich and tasty pizzas. ● Mon, Tue; Aug. 🗺	●	▪		▪
FERRARA: *Quel Fantastico Giovedì* €€ Via Castelnuovo 9, 44100. ☎ 0532 76 05 70. A bright restaurant whose varied and creative menu, which changes weekly, includes Japanese-style sushi of salmon. ● Wed; last week Jan, last week Jul, 1–15 Aug. 🗺 ⚡ ☰	●	▪		
FIDENZA: *Del Duomo* €€ Via Micheli 27, 43036. ☎ 0524 52 42 68. Near the cathedral, the menu includes home-made *spaghetti* with mushrooms and tripe *alla parmigiana*. ● Mon; 1 week Jul, 3 weeks Aug. 🗺		▪		
GORO: *Ferrari* €€€ Via Antonio Brugnoli 240–4, 44020. ☎ 0533 99 64 48. Next to the fish market, the menu changes every day to make use of the best of the day's catch; the menu is almost entirely fish. ● Wed. ☰	●	▪		
MODENA: *Al Boschetto* €€ Via Due Canali Nord 198, 41100. ☎ 059 25 17 59. A rustic restaurant set in a vast park. Specialities include *tortellini* in chicken broth, *ragù* sauce and spit-roasted meats. ● Sun eve, Wed; 2 weeks Aug. 🗺 ⚡	●	▪		▪

MODENA: *Fini*   €€€€€
Piazzetta San Francesco, 41100. (*059 22 33 14*.
A mainstay of local cuisine with exquisite dishes: *tortellini*, lasagna di
maccheroni and delicious desserts. ● *Mon, Tue; late Jul–late Aug.* 🗐 ▤

PARMA: *Aldo*   €€
Piazzale Inzani 15, 43100. (*0521 20 60 01*.
A trattoria serving classics with interesting touches: smoked roast beef, and
guinea fowl with orange sauce. ● *Sun eve, Mon; mid-Jul–mid-Aug.* 🗐

PARMA: *Le Viole*   €€€
Strada Nuova 60a, Località Castelnuovo Golese, 43031. (*0521 60 10 00*.
A delightful place to eat offering a successful mix of modern ideas and tradition.
Try the *fagottini* (parcels) of turkey with vegetables, and the home-made desserts.
● *Wed, Thu lunch; 2 weeks Jan, 1 week Feb, 1 week Aug.* 🗐

PIACENZA: *Don Carlos*   €€€
Strada Aguzzafame 85, 29100. (*0523 499 80 00*.
The excellent cuisine in this elegant restaurant uses fresh seasonal ingredients and
includes a seafood and bean salad, and pickled salmon. ● *Mon; 2 weeks Aug.* 🗐

PIACENZA: *Antica Osteria del Teatro*   €€€€€
Via Verdi 16, 29100. (*0523 32 37 77*.
An excellent wine list accompanies a menu of imaginative dishes prepared
with immense flair from the best of local produce. The setting, in a 15th-
century palazzo in the historic centre, is also pleasant. ● *Sun, Mon.* 🗐 ▤

RAVENNA: *Tre Spade*   €€€
Via Faentina 136, 48100. (*0544 50 05 22*.
Set in a 19th-century villa in a park. The chef's specialities include *tortelli*
with duck sauce and seafood salad. ● *Sun eve, Mon.* 🗐 📼 ♿ ▤

RIMINI: *Il Melograno*   €€€
Viale Vespucci 16, 47037. (*0541 522 55*.
The restaurant of the Holiday Inn hotel serves mainly fish (turbot in a
potato crust, red mullet with rosemary) as well as grilled meats. ● *Sun.* 🗐 📼 ▤

RIMINI: *Europa*   €€€€€
Via Roma 51, 47037. (*0541 287 61*.
Fish forms the basis of the menu here, with dishes including salad of warm
fish with *radicchio* and seafood *spaghetti*. ● *Sun; 1 week Aug.* 🗐 ♿ ▤

FLORENCE

FLORENCE: *Palle D'Oro*   €
Via Sant'Antonino 43r, 50123. Map 1 C5 (5 C1). (*055 28 83 83*.
Sparse, simple, spotlessly clean trattoria. The food is basic but cooked well
and there is a very good take-away sandwich bar at the front. ● *Sun, Aug.* 🗐 ▤

FLORENCE: *Acquacotta*   €€
Via de' Pilastri 51r, 50124. Map 2 E5. (*055 24 29 07*.
A cheap, three-roomed restaurant named after a Florentine vegetable soup.
Grilled meats and other Tuscan specialities are also featured. ● *Tue pm, Wed.* 🗐

FLORENCE: *Buca dell'Orafo*   €€
Volta de' Girolami 28r, 50122. Map 6 D4. (*055 21 36 19*.
A friendly hole-in-the-wall that is a long-time favourite with Florentines. The homely
cooking is based on home-made pasta, and daily specials include the typically Tuscan
ribollita (vegetable soup), pasta and *fagioli* (beans). ● *Sun, Mon; Aug.* ▤

FLORENCE: *Da Pennello*   €€
Via Dante Alighieri 4r, 50100. Map 4 D1. (*055 29 48 48*.
Book well ahead or risk a long wait for a table. This popular restaurant is famous
for its extensive *antipasti*, a meal in themselves. ● *Sun eve, Mon; Aug; 1 week Dec.*

FLORENCE: *Enoteca Fuori Porta*   €€
Via Monte alle Croci 10r, 50122. Map 4 3E. (*055 234 2483*.
This wine bar is popular with locals and visitors alike for its excellent *crostoni*
with assorted toppings and of course, the wide-ranging wine list. ● *Sun.*

FLORENCE: *Il Francescano*   €€
Via San Giuseppe 26r, 50120. Map 4 E1. (*055 24 16 05*.
A smartly fitted restaurant of wood, marble and *objets d'art*. The menu is based
on seasonal ingredients and changes weekly. ● *Oct–Apr: Tue.* 🗐 ▤

Average prices for a three-course meal for one, including a half-bottle of house wine, tax and service:
€ under 18 euros
€€ 18–30 euros
€€€ 30–40 euros
€€€€ 40–52 euros
€€€€€ over 52 euros.

FIXED-PRICE MENU
A fixed-price menu on offer, usually with three courses.
GOOD WINE LIST
Denotes a wide range of good quality wines.
FORMAL DRESS
Some restaurants require men to wear a jacket and tie.
OUTDOOR TABLES
Tables for eating outdoors, often with a good view.
CREDIT CARDS
The symbol shows that major credit cards are accepted.

	FIXED-PRICE MENU	GOOD WINE LIST	FORMAL DRESS	OUTDOOR TABLES
FLORENCE: *Le Mossacce* €€ Via del Pronconsolo 55r, 50122. **Map** 2 D5 (6 E2). 📞 055 29 43 61. Do not be put off by the multilingual menus, the paper tablecloths and the chaos; the 100-year-old Mossacce serves robust Tuscan food. ● *Sat, Sun.*	●			
FLORENCE: *San Zanobi* €€ Via San Zanobi 33r, 50100. **Map** 1 C4. 📞 055 47 52 86. Delicate, inventive food served in a sedate, refined dining room. The dishes, based on a Florentine theme, are light and well presented. ● *Sun.*		■		
FLORENCE: *Trattoria Angiolino* €€ Via di Santo Spirito 36r, 50125. **Map** 3 B1. 📞 055 239 89 76. An attractive restaurant with a typically Florentine, bustling atmosphere. The food is traditional Tuscan style, from vegetable soups to grilled meats. In winter an iron stove in the middle of the restaurant is lit. ● *Nov–Mar: Mon.*		■		
FLORENCE: *Trattoria Mario* €€ Via Rosina 2r, 50123. **Map** 1 C4. 📞 055 21 85 50. A popular lunchtime trattoria. Specials change daily; on Thursday there is *gnocchi* and on Friday, fish. ● *eves, Sun; Aug.*				
FLORENCE: *Trattoria Zà Zà* €€ Piazza del Mercato Centrale 26r, 50123. **Map** 1 C4. 📞 055 21 54 11. A canteen-like restaurant that is always packed. The food is Tuscan. Excellent soups include *ribollita* (vegetables), and *passata di fagioli* (bean purée). ● *Sun.*	●			■
FLORENCE: *Alle Murate* €€€ Via Ghibellina 52r, 50122. **Map** 4 E1. 📞 055 24 06 18. Popular with locals, this refined restaurant offers a great range of creative, Tuscan dishes. The food combines Italian staples with more far-flung Mediterranean cuisines, and there are light and interesting desserts. ● *lunch, Mon; 1 week Dec.*		■		
FLORENCE: *Buca Mario* €€€ Piazza degli Ottaviani 16r, 50100. **Map** 1 B5. 📞 055 21 41 79. A crowded restaurant where it is normal to book or queue for a table. Enjoy the home-made pasta and grilled meats at good prices. ● *Wed, Thu lunch; Aug.*		■		
FLORENCE: *Cafaggi* €€€ Via Guelfa 35r, 50123. **Map** 1 C4. 📞 055 29 49 89. This classic Tuscan trattoria uses oil and wines from the family farm. *Crostini* (toasts), *zuppa di certosina* and *involtini* (roulade) are particularly good dishes on the varied menu. ● *Sun; 2 weeks Jul, 2 weeks Aug.*	●	■		
FLORENCE: *Da Ganino* €€€ Piazza dei Cimatori 4r, 50100. **Map** 6 D3. 📞 055 21 41 25. A small, friendly restaurant popular with locals, da Ganino offers all the basics of local fare, including *ravioli* with butter and sage. ● *Sun.*		■		■
FLORENCE: *Dino* €€€ Via Ghibellina 51r, 50122. **Map** 4 D1 (6 E3). 📞 055 24 14 52. This well-regarded restaurant in a beautiful 14th-century palazzo has one of the best wine lists in Florence and a menu of local dishes such as onion soup and *pici* (pasta) *alle Senese*. ● *Sun eve, Mon.*		■		
FLORENCE: *Osteria dei Macci* €€€ Via de' Macci 77r, 50100. **Map** 4 E1. 📞 055 24 12 26. A basic trattoria off the main tourist circuit and close to Santa Croce. Expect traditional, rustic Tuscan fare. ● *Sun.*				■
FLORENCE: *Paoli* €€€ Via dei Tavolini 12r, 50100. **Map** 6 D3 (4 D1). 📞 055 21 62 15. A spectacular setting: the dining room is a vaulted hall smothered in medieval frescoes. The restaurant specializes in typically Tuscan dishes. ● *Tue; Aug.*	●	■		

FLORENCE: *I Quattro Amici*   €€€
Via degli Orti Oricellari 29, 50100. **Map** 1 A5. **[** *055 21 54 13.*
Four friends created this fish restaurant. The interior is cool and spartan but
the fish, which comes from Porto Santo Stefano, is always excellent. 🖪 ▤

FLORENCE: *Sabatini*   €€€
Via Panzani 9a, 50123. **Map** 1 C5 (5 C1). **[** *055 21 15 59.*
Once Florence's best restaurant, the cuisine (Italian and international) is
sometimes excellent and the ambience and service are good. ● *Mon.* 🖪

FLORENCE: *La Taverna del Bronzino*   €€€
Via delle Ruote 27r, 50129. **Map** 2 D3. **[** *055 49 52 20.*
Named after the Florentine painter who had connections with the 15th-century
palazzo which houses this restaurant. Highest-quality cooking. ● *Sun; Aug.* 🖪 ▤

FLORENCE: *Cibreo*   €€€€
Via Andrea del Verrocchio 8r, 50122. **Map** 4 E1. **[** *055 234 11 00.*
Superbly prepared Tuscan food in an informal atmosphere. There is no pasta,
but specialities include tripe and kidneys. For the squeamish there are many
non-offal alternatives such as duck stuffed with sultanas. ● *Sun, Mon; Aug.* 🖪 ▤

FLORENCE: *Enoteca Pinchiorri*   €€€€€
Via Ghibellina 87, 50122. **Map** 1 A4 (5 A1). **[** *055 24 27 77.*
Often described as Italy's best restaurant with the finest wine cellar in Europe, the
Pinchiorri is on the ground floor of a 15th-century palazzo. The Tuscan- and French-
inspired cuisine includes a wonderful mix of dishes. ● *Sun, Mon, Wed lunch; Aug* 🖪

TUSCANY

AREZZO: *Buca di San Francesco*   €€
Via San Francesco 1, 52100. **[** *0575 232 71.*
The medieval atmosphere and position alongside the church of Piero della
Francesca's fresco cycle make this an obvious choice. ● *Mon eve, Tue.* 🖪 ▤

ARTIMINO: *Da Delfina*   €€€
Via della Chiesa 1, 50041. **[** *055 871 80 74.*
A lovely restaurant outside a walled medieval village. Game is a speciality,
as is pork with fennel and black Tuscan cabbage. ● *Sun eve, Mon.*

BAGNI DI LUCCA: *Dandini*   €€
Via Dorati, Localita Granaiola. **[** *0583 83 10 81.*
This small, simple restaurant clings to a hillside and serves up excellent roasted
meats and delicious desserts. Local game and mushrooms in season. ● *Mon, Nov.*

CAPALBIO: *Da Maria*   €€
Via Comunale 3, 58011. **[** *0564 89 60 14.*
Holidaying politicians from Rome sit down with locals to enjoy soundly cooked
Maremma specialities like wild boar and pasta with truffles. ● *Oct–Apr: Tue.* 🖪 ▤

CASTELNUOVO BERARDENGA: *La Bottega del Trenta*   €€€€
Via Santa Caterina 2, Villa a Sesta 53019. **[** *0577 35 92 26.*
A tasteful restaurant serving adventurous cooking including duck breast with
wild fennel and delicious desserts. ● *Tue, Wed, Mon–Sat lunch; 2 weeks Jan, 2 weeks Feb.*

COLLE DI VAL D'ELSA: *L'Antica Trattoria*   €€€€
Piazza Arnolfo 23, 53034. **[** *0577 92 37 47.*
A homely, family-run restaurant dedicated to traditional regional cuisine. The setting
is medieval and the service lively and attentive. ● *Tue; 1 week Jan, 1 week Dec.* 🖪

CORTONA: *Locanda nel Loggiato*   €€
Piazza Pescheria 3, 54044. **[** *0575 63 05 75.*
Set in a quaint medieval loggia, the atmosphere is cool and sedate and the
home-made *ravioli* stuffed with fondue, delicious. ● *Oct–May: Wed; Nov–Dec.* 🖪

ELBA: *Publius*   €€€
Piazza XX Settembre, Poggio di Marciana 57030. **[** *0565 992 08.*
A pleasant trattoria with one of the best wine cellars on Elba. In addition to fish,
you can eat wild mushrooms, game and wild boar. ● *Nov–Mar.* 🖪 ▤

GAIOLE IN CHIANTI: *Badia a Coltibuono*   €€
Badia a Coltibuono, 53013. **[** *0577 74 94 24.*
Set in front of an 11th-century abbey, at the heart of a vineyard whose oils and
wines are used in the restaurant. The menu includes spit-roasted meats and delicious
desserts. Tours of the estate are on offer for wine tasters. ● *Mon, Nov–Feb.* 🖪 🖪

Average prices for a three-course meal for one, including a half-bottle of house wine, tax and service:
€ under 18 euros
€€ 18–30 euros
€€€ 30–40 euros
€€€€ 40–52 euros
€€€€€ over 52 euros.

FIXED-PRICE MENU
A fixed-price menu on offer, usually with three courses.
GOOD WINE LIST
Denotes a wide range of good quality wines.
FORMAL DRESS
Some restaurants require men to wear a jacket and tie.
OUTDOOR TABLES
Tables for eating outdoors, often with a good view.
CREDIT CARDS
The symbol shows that major credit cards are accepted.

Restaurant	Price	FIXED-PRICE MENU	GOOD WINE LIST	FORMAL DRESS	OUTDOOR TABLES
LIVORNO: *La Chiave* Scali delle Cantine 52, 57100. 0586 88 86 09. Refined and elegant dining from a menu that includes traditional Tuscan meat and fish cuisine and is changed every fortnight. ● *lunch; Wed; Aug.*	€€€		▪		
LUCCA: *Buca di Sant'Antonio* Via della Cervia 3, 55100. 0583 558 81. This is Lucca's most famous restaurant of traditional rustic cooking. It serves a range of local dishes, such as *fettuccine sul piccione* (pasta and pigeon). ● *Sun eve, Mon; Jul.*	€€				
MASSA MARITTIMA: *Bracali* Frazione Ghirlanda 2, 58024. 0566 90 23 18. Mouth-watering Maremma cooking in a family restaurant; thinly sliced wild boar, pigeon with honey and guinea fowl with white grapes. ● *Tue; Jan, Nov.*	€€€€				
MONTALCINO: *Taverna dei Barbi* Località Podernovi, 53024. 0577 84 12 00. Superb country cooking, served with Brunello wines, in a renowned restaurant that also has wonderful views over the surrounding hills. ● *Tue eve, Wed; Jan.*	€€		▪		▪
MONTECATINI TERME: *Gourmet* Via Amendola 6, 51016. 0572 77 10 12. This is an elegant restaurant in a wonderful 19th-century building. The atmosphere is relaxing, the fish dishes are sublime. ● *2 weeks Jan, 3 weeks Aug.*	€€€€	●	▪	●	
MONTEPULCIANO: *Il Cantuccio* Via delle Cantine 1/2, 53045. 0578 75 78 70. Located in a 13th-century palace, Il Cantuccio combines great atmosphere and traditional food. The house speciality is *pici alla nana* (pasta with a duck sauce).	€€		▪		
MONTERIGGIONI: *Il Pozzo* Piazza Roma 2, 53035. 0577 30 41 27. A stone-walled restaurant in the charming medieval village of Monteriggioni. The Sienese food is simple and enthusiastically prepared, and the home-made desserts are well-known in the surrounding region. ● *Sun eve, Mon; 3 weeks Jan, 1 week Feb.*	€€€		▪		▪
ORBETELLO: *Osteria del Lupacante* Corso Italia 103, 58015. 0564 86 76 18. The cooking concentrates on fish and seafood specialities with some touches of adventure; look out for mussels in Marsala sauce, grilled prawns and courgette flowers with squid. ● *Oct–May: Tue.*	€€	●	▪		▪
PESCIA: *Cecco* Via Francesca Forti 94–96, 51017. 0572 47 79 55. A friendly local restaurant where the food is often outstanding. Try the local Pescia asparagus, and *cioncia* (the house main course). ● *Mon; Jan, Jul.*	€€		▪		
PIENZA: *Da Falco* Piazza Dante Alighieri 3, 53026. 0578 74 85 51. A friendly local restaurant with excellent *antipasti* and a magnificent choice of *primi* and *secondi* from a menu of local specialities. ● *Fri.*	€€	●	▪		▪
PISA: *Al Ristoro dei Vecchi Macelli* Via Volturno 49, 56126. 050 204 24. Innovative dishes in a pleasant, intimate restaurant that serves light Tuscan food with an adventurous twist. Fish, seafood and game specialities are delicately prepared and the desserts are a delight. ● *Wed; 2 weeks Aug.*	€€€€		▪		
PISTOIA: *La Bottegaia* Via del Lastrone 4. 0573 36 56 02. Close to Piazza del Duomo, this restaurant offers a wide assortment of locally produced cold meats and traditional dishes such as *pappa al pomodoro*, *ribollita* and stewed veal. ● *Mon; Aug.*	€€		▪		

POPPI: *Il Cedro* €€
Via di Camaldoli 20, Località Moggiona, 52010. **[** *0575 55 60 80.*
Venison, wild boar and guinea fowl in wine are among some of the excellently
cooked specialities of Il Cedro. This good-value restaurant stands in a
wonderful setting that overlooks forests and mountains. **●** *Mon.*

PORTO ERCOLE: *Bacco in Toscana* €€€€
Via San Paolo 6, 58018. **[** *0564 83 30 78.*
An intimate restaurant that serves an array of excellent seafood dishes; scampi
with lemon and *spaghetti alle vongole* (clams). **●** *lunch; Wed; Nov–Mar.*

PORTO SANTO STEFANO: *La Bussola* €€
Viale Marconi, 58019. **[** *0564 81 42 25.*
The menu includes some excellent seafood pastas as well as simpler grilled
fish. From the terrace there are fine views of the sea. **●** *Mon; Nov.*

PRATO: *Il Piraña* €€€€
Via Valentini 110, 50047. **[** *0574 257 46.*
Rated as one of the best fish and seafood restaurants in Tuscany; do not be
put off by its setting or over-precious modern interior. **●** *Sat lunch, Sun; Aug.*

SAN GIMIGNANO: *Le Terrazze* €€€€
Albergo la Cisterna, Piazza della Cisterna 24, 53037 **[** *0577 94 03 28.*
Set within the medieval walls, with views over the rolling hills of southern Tuscany,
one of the dining rooms forms part of a 13th-century palazzo. Good for regional
specialities with some novelties. **●** *Tue, Wed lunch; Jan–Mar.*

SANSEPOLCRO: *Paola e Marco Mercati* €€€€
Via Palmiro Togliatti 68, 52037. **[** *0575 73 48 75.*
A new restaurant whose dishes include Tuscan black cabbage cooked with white truf-
fles, vegetable *ravioli*, roast pigeon and *gnocchi*. **●** *lunch; Sun; 2 weeks Jun, 2 weeks Jul.*

SATURNIA: *I Due Cippi da Michele* €€
Piazza Vittorio Veneto 26a, 58050. **[** *0564 60 10 74.*
One of the region's most popular restaurants, it is a touchstone for Maremma
cuisine and its traditional offerings are good value. **●** *Oct–Jun: Tue; 1 week Dec.*

SIENA: *Al Marsili* €€
Via del Castoro 3, 53100. **[** *0577 471 54.*
Set in an 11th-century building, Al Marsili, long regarded as one of the best
restaurants in Siena, offers good regional specialities. **●** *Mon.*

SIENA: *Osteria le Logge* €€€
Via del Porrione 33, 53100. **[** *0577 480 13.*
Siena's prettiest restaurant, with dark wood and marble interior. Home-
produced oils and Montalcino wines accompany dishes that include
guinea fowl, duck and fennel, and rabbit with capers. **●** *Sun; Nov.*

SOVANA: *Taverna Etrusca* €€
Piazza del Pretorio 16, 58010. **[** *0564 61 61 83.*
A small restaurant with a medieval dining area. The carefully produced cuisine is
Tuscan with sophisticated touches. **●** *Mon, 3 weeks Jan, 1 week Feb.*

VIAREGGIO: *Romano* €€€€
Via Mazzini 120, 55049. **[** *0584 313 82.*
This is one of Tuscany's best fish and seafood restaurants. The service is
courteous and friendly and the wines are well-priced. **●** *Mon; Jan.*

UMBRIA

AMELIA: *Anita* €
Via Roma 31, 05022. **[** *0744 98 21 46.*
This simple restaurant offers no-frills local food, such as *crostini* (toasted bread with
toppings), roasted meats, pasta with porcini mushrooms and wild boar. **●** *Mon.*

ASSISI: *Medioevo* €€€
Via Arco dei Priori 4b, 06081. **[** *075 81 30 68.*
An elegant restaurant in old Assisi. Pastas are home-made (try them with black
truffles in season). Meats are cooked to traditional recipes. **●** *Wed, Sun eve; Jul.*

ASSISI: *San Francesco* €€€
Via San Francesco 52, 06081. **[** *075 81 23 29.*
A carefully chosen seasonal menu might include *carpaccio* of porcini mushrooms
(raw, thinly sliced), home-made pâté and steak with truffles. **●** *Wed; 2 weeks Jul.*

	FIXED-PRICE MENU	GOOD WINE LIST	FORMAL DRESS	OUTDOOR TABLES

Average prices for a three-course meal for one, including a half-bottle of house wine, tax and service:
€ under 18 euros
€€ 18–30 euros
€€€ 30–40 euros
€€€€ 40–52 euros
€€€€€ over 52 euros.

FIXED-PRICE MENU
A fixed-price menu on offer, usually with three courses.
GOOD WINE LIST
Denotes a wide range of good quality wines.
FORMAL DRESS
Some restaurants require men to wear a jacket and tie.
OUTDOOR TABLES
Tables for eating outdoors, often with a good view.
CREDIT CARDS
The symbol shows that major credit cards are accepted.

BASCHI: *Vissani* €€€€€ Strada Statale 448, Todi-Baschi, 05023. **(** 0744 95 02 06. Gianfranco Vissani is famous throughout Italy for his wonderful haute cuisine, served in elegant surroundings – you can choose your own music. ● *Wed, Thu lunch, Sun eve.*	●	■	●	
CITTÀ DI CASTELLO: *Amici Miei* € Via del Monte 2, 06012. **(** 075 855 99 04. Set in the storerooms of a 16th-century palazzo in the historic centre, the menu is based on regional cuisine. Try the *tagliatelle* with rabbit. ● *Wed.*	●	■		
CITTÀ DI CASTELLO: *Il Bersaglio* €€ Via Vittorio Emanuele Orlando 14, 06012. **(** 075 855 55 34. A traditional Umbrian restaurant with specialities including *gnocchetti* (little *gnocchi*) with truffles. ● *Wed; Jan; 2 weeks Jun–Jul.*	●	■		■
CAMPELLO SUL CLITUNNO: *Trattoria Pettino* €€ Frazione Pettino 31, 06042. **(** 0743 27 60 21. Set in the middle of the mountains in an old restored house. The *bruschetta* and, in season, the plethora of dishes with truffles are delicious. ● *Tue.*				■
FOLIGNO: *Villa Roncalli* €€€€ Via Roma 25, 06034. **(** 0742 39 10 91. A charming country inn set in its own garden 1 km (half a mile) from Foligno. Regional specialities are well prepared using fresh ingredients. ● *lunch (except Sun), Mon; Jan, Aug.*	●	■	●	■
GUBBIO: *Alcatraz* €€ Località Santa Cristina 53, 06020. **(** 075 922 99 38. At this Agriturist centre about 25 km (15 miles) southwest of Gubbio, the simple but tasty food benefits from the organic products they use.				■
GUBBIO: *Villa Montegranelli* €€€ Località Monteluiano, 06024. **(** 075 922 01 85. Set in an 18th-century villa with an elegantly rural atmosphere. Exquisitely made specialities include *crostini* (toasts) with *porcini* mushroom terrine and chestnut flour pancakes with melted cheese and ricotta.	●	■		■
MAGIONE: *Associazione Agrituristica Montemelino* € Via dei Montemelini 22, Località Montemelino, 06063. **(** 075 84 36 06. Another of the simple, reliable Agriturist restaurants. This one serves traditional Umbrian fare, grilled meats and, in season, *ravioli* of *porcini* mushrooms. ● *Tue.*	●	■		■
NARNI: *Monte del Grano 1696* €€€ Strada Guadamello 128, Località San Vito 05030. **(** 0744 74 91 43. Much care goes into creating a pleasant atmosphere in which to sample the excellent regional dishes. In season, try the truffles and *porcini* mushrooms. ● *Mon; Tue–Fri lunch; Nov.*	●	■		■
NORCIA: *Dal Francese* €€ Via Riguardati 16, 06046. **(** 0743 81 62 90. A country-style trattoria in the centre of Norcia. It offers regional specialities such as a truffle-based menu-degustazione in season. ● *Nov–Jul: Fri.*				
ORVIETO: *La Volpe e L'Uva* €€ Via Ripa Corsica 1, 05018. **(** 0763 34 16 12. A popular trattoria in the centre of Orvieto offering a variety of regional dishes that change with the season at reasonable prices. ● *Mon–Tue; Jan.*	●	■		
ORVIETO: *I Sette Consoli* €€€€ Piazza Sant'Angelo 1a, 05018. **(** 0763 34 39 11. A comfortable, friendly restaurant with a garden for summer dining. Try *baccalà* (salt cod) marinated in apple vinegar with potato salad, stuffed rabbit, bean soup with fennel, and fish *ravioli*. ● *Wed.*	●	■		■

PASSIGNANO SUL TRASIMENO: *Cacciatori da Luciano* €€€€
Lungolago Pompei 11, 06065. 075 82 72 10.
The menu is based on sea fish, including scampi salad, fish *carpaccio* (raw, thinly sliced fish), *risotto* of different types of prawn and shrimp and grilled sole. Some of the desserts are made with forest fruits. ● *Wed.* ☑ ▤

PERUGIA: *Aladino* €€
Via delle Prome 11, 06122. 075 572 09 38.
In the historic centre, the Aladino offers wonderful cuisine with emphasis on Sardinian specialities. Try the roasted wild boar. ● *lunch daily; Mon; 2 weeks Aug.* ☑ ▤

PERUGIA: *Giò Arte e Vini* €€
Via Ruggero d'Andreotto 19, 06124. 075 573 11 00.
Famous for its spectacular selection of wines and well-chosen regional dishes with special touches. The pumpkin *ravioli* and the *trecciola di agnello* (lamb) are particularly good. ● *Sun eve, Mon lunch.* ☑ ▤

PERUGIA: *Osteria del Bartolo* €€€€€
Via Bartolo 30, 06122. 075 573 15 61.
An elegant restaurant that is one of the mainstays of the Perugian eating tradition. Many items are home-made. ● *Wed lunch, Sun.* ☑ ▤

SPOLETO: *Le Casaline* €€
Località Poreta di Spoleto, Frazione Casaline, 06042. 0743 52 11 13.
An oasis of calm in a restored 18th-century mill. Try the *gnocchi* stuffed with mushrooms or wild boar *alla cacciatora* (in wine and tomato sauce). ● *Mon.* ☑

SPOLETO: *Il Tartufo* €€
Piazza Garibaldi 24, 06049. 0743 402 36.
The floor of one of the dining rooms is ancient Roman. Well-tried regional specialities, including, not surprisingly, truffles, as well as other delights such as barley soup and duck in Sagrantino wine sauce. ● *Sun eve, Mon; 2 weeks Jul.* ☑ ▤

TERNI: *Da Carlino* €€
Via Piemonte 1, 05100. 0744 42 01 63.
Robust rustic food, such as *crostini* with local salami, *tagliatelle* with truffles or duck sauce, lamb, and some fish dishes. ● *Mon; 2 weeks Aug.*

TODI: *La Mulinella* €
Località Pontenaia 29, Località Vasciano, 06059. 075 894 47 79.
In the countryside about 2 km (1 mile) from Todi serving simple, reliable dishes. The home-made pastas and roasted meats are recommended. ● *Wed.* ☼ ▤

TODI: *Lucaroni* €€
Via Cortesi 7, 06059. 075 894 26 94.
Regional fish, meat and game (including hare, duck and lamb with truffles). Puddings, such as *crema* with warm chocolate, are also good. ● *eves; Tue.* ☑

TREVI: *La Taverna del Pescatore* €€€
Via della Chiesa Tonda 50, Località Pigge, 06039. 0742 78 09 20.
The freshest of local produce is combined and cooked in simple yet exquisite recipes and the atmosphere is relaxed with attentive service. ● *Wed; Jan.* ☑

MARCHE

ANCONA: *La Moretta* €€€
Piazza Plebiscito 52, 60124. 071 20 23 17.
A lovely traditional restaurant serving excellent local dishes; *polenta* with *calamari* and truffles, and lamb with artichokes. ● *Sun; 1 week Jan.* ☑ ⚡ ▤

ANCONA: *Passetto* €€€€
Piazza IV Novembre 1, 60124. 071 332 14.
Outside eating with splendid views onto the sea in the summer. The meat dishes are good – the fish excels. ● *Sun eve, Mon; 2 weeks Aug.* ☑

ASCOLI PICENO: *C'era Una Volta* €
Via Piagge 336, Località Piagge, 63100. 0736 26 17 80.
This restaurant offers simple but tasty dishes in a homely and pleasant atmosphere. There are beautiful views of the town from the farmhouse garden. ● *Tue.* ☑

FABRIANO: *Villa Marchese del Grillo* €€
Via Rocchetta 73, Frazione Rocchetta. 0732 62 56 90.
Set in a restored 18th-century villa, this restaurant combines attentive service with relaxed informality. The food is superbly prepared. ● *Sun eve, Mon; Jan.* ☑

Average prices for a three-course meal for one, including a half-bottle of house wine, tax and service:
€ under 18 euros
€€ 18–30 euros
€€€ 30–40 euros
€€€€ 40–52 euros
€€€€€ over 52 euros.

FIXED-PRICE MENU
A fixed-price menu on offer, usually with three courses.
GOOD WINE LIST
Denotes a wide range of good quality wines.
FORMAL DRESS
Some restaurants require men to wear a jacket and tie.
OUTDOOR TABLES
Tables for eating outdoors, often with a good view.
CREDIT CARDS
The symbol shows that major credit cards are accepted.

	Price	FIXED-PRICE MENU	GOOD WINE LIST	FORMAL DRESS	OUTDOOR TABLES
FANO: Darpetti Quinta Viale Adriatico 42, 61032. ☎ 0721 80 80 43. An excellent, basic trattoria where the daily menu consists of simple but delicious cuisine, including many dishes of fresh fish. ● Sun.	€€				■
FANO: Ristorantino da Giulio Viale Adriatico 100, 61032. ☎ 0721 80 56 80. A calm restaurant situated just opposite the beach. The cuisine is basically regional, with the chef's personal touches. Fish *antipasti* are recommended. ● Tue; Nov.	€€€				■
JESI: Tana Liberatutti Piazza Pontelli 1, 60035. ☎ 0731 592 37. A dignified restaurant where Mediterranean dishes are prepared with care. Try the fish *risotto*, or the baked fish. ● Sun; 1 wk Jan, 1 wk Aug.	€€€				■
LORETO: Andreina Via Buffolareccia 14, 60025. ☎ 071 97 01 24. A mother and daughter team prepares traditional cuisine with home-made pasta, chicken, rabbit and game, followed by tempting desserts. ● Tue.	€€		■		■
MACERATA: Da Secondo Via Pescheria Vecchia 26–28, 62100. ☎ 0733 26 09 12. The regional cuisine, such as *vincisgrassi alla Macerata* (local lasagna) and *frittura mista* (batter-fried fish and vegetables,) is recommended at this restaurant. ● Mon; 2 weeks Aug.	€€		■		■
NUMANA: La Costarella Via IV Novembre 35, 60026. ☎ 071 736 02 97. Booking is advisable in this specialist fish restaurant; pasta with black cuttlefish ink and fried fish with courgette flowers. ● Tue; Nov–Easter.	€€€	●	■		
PESARO: Da Teresa Viale Trieste 180, 61100. ☎ 0721 302 22. A gracious restaurant offering imaginatively prepared dishes based on local cuisine. As well as exquisite fish and seafood there are a few meat dishes and delightful desserts to follow. ● lunch, Sun eve, Mon; Nov–Mar.	€€€	●	■		■
PESARO: Da Alceo Via Panoramica Ardizio 101, 61100. ☎ 0721 513 60. A famous fish restaurant with a spectacular panoramic terrace serving *gnocchi* with shellfish, and *risotto*. Desserts are home-made and tasty. ● Sun eve, Mon.	€€€€€	●	■		■
SENIGALLIA: Uliassi Via Banchina di Levante 6, 60020. ☎ 071 654 63. Run by a brother and sister, this is a friendly restaurant offering a high standard of cuisine. Try the speciality pasta with prawns and asparagus. ● Mon; Jan–Feb.	€€€€€	●	■		■
SIROLO: Rocco Via Torrione 1, 60020. ☎ 071 933 05 58. Open during the spring and summer evenings only, Rocco serves delicious (mainly fish) dishes such as *gnocchi* with clams, fried mixed fish and vegetables and sea bass with a sauce of lettuce and balsamic vinegar. ● lunch; Tue; Nov–Mar.	€€€	●	■		
URBANIA: Big Ben Corso Vittorio Emanuele 61, 61049. ☎ 0722 31 97 95. In the historic centre of town, Big Ben's specialities include *tagliolini* (pasta) with truffles, grilled lamb and home-made desserts. ● lunch; Wed.	€€		■		■
URBINO: Vecchia Urbino Via del Vasari 3–5, 61029. ☎ 0722 44 47. A restaurant serving simply prepared traditional dishes, including *vincisgrassi* (the local lasagna), rabbit, and *polenta* with mushrooms. ● Tue.	€€	●	■		

ROME

AVENTINE: *Perilli a Testaccio* €€€
Via Marmorata 39, 00153. **Map** 6 E3. 📞 06 574 63 18.
An archetypal noisy Roman trattoria serving a regular clientele with robust,
Roman fare that includes artichokes and *rigatoni alla pajata*. ● Wed; Aug.

AVENTINE: *Checchino dal 1887* €€€€
Via di Monte Testaccio 30, 00153. **Map** 6 D4. 📞 06 574 63 18.
Roman cuisine is served at old tables under vaulted ceilings with an open fire in
winter. ● Oct–May: Mon, Sun eve; Jun–Sep: Mon eve, Sun; Aug; 1 week Dec.

CAMPO DE' FIORI: *Al Pompiere* €€
Via Santa Maria dei Calderari 38, 00186. **Map** 2 F5. 📞 06 686 83 77.
In the heart of the Jewish ghetto, on the first floor of the Palazzo Cenci
Bolognetti with frescoed, beamed ceilings. The food is classical, including
fried courgette flowers and *rigatoni alla pajata*. ● Sun; Aug

CAMPO DE' FIORI: *Le Maschere* €€
Via Monte della Farina 29, 00186. **Map** 2 F5. 📞 06 687 94 44.
A tiled hall opens onto a rustic indoor terrace with a pleasant country
feel. The house wine and the fiery food are Calabrian. Charming service
and excellent wine ensure a pleasant evening. ● lunch; Mon; Aug.

CAMPO DE' FIORI: *Il Drappo* €€€
Vicolo del Malpasso 9, 00186. **Map** 2 E4. 📞 06 687 73 65.
An intimate restaurant, serving Sardinian cuisine; *seadas* (sweet cheese-filled *ravioli*)
and *mirto* liqueur. ● lunch; Sun; 2 weeks Aug, 2 weeks Sep.

CAMPO DE' FIORI: *Sora Lella* €€€€
Via di Ponte Quattro Capi 16, 00186. **Map** 6 D1. 📞 06 686 16 01.
Situated on the picturesque Tiber Island, this restaurant is popular with the locals.
Traditional Roman dishes are served in elegant surroundings. ● Sun; Aug.

CAMPO DE' FIORI: *Camponeschi* €€€€€
Piazza Farnese 50, 00186. **Map** 2 E5. 📞 06 687 49 27.
Modern and regional Italian cooking, and French specialities, served in a lush interior
on one of the most beautiful piazzas in Rome. ● lunch; Sun; 3 weeks Aug.

ESQUILINE: *Trattoria Monti* €€
Via di San Vito 13a, 00185. **Map** 4 E4. 📞 06 446 65 73.
Dishes from the Marches are prepared by Franca Camerucci. Specialities are fried
olives stuffed with meat, and *ravioli di ricotta*. ● Sun pm, Mon; Aug, Dec–Jan.

ESQUILINE: *Agata e Romeo* €€€€€
Via Carlo Alberto 45, 00185. **Map** 4 E4. 📞 06 446 61 15.
Agata cooks predominantly Roman and southern Italian fare while Romeo
serves. Tables are well-spaced and the atmosphere is tranquil. ● Sat, Sun.

JANICULUM: *Antico Arco* €€€
Via San Pancrazio 1, 00152. **Map** 5 A1. 📞 06 581 52 74.
This recommended restaurant in elegant surroundings offers creative traditional fare,
such as guinea fowl with apples and *foie gras*. ● lunch Mon–Sat, Sun pm; Aug.

LATERAN: *Alfredo a Via Gabi* €€
Via Gabi 36-38, 00183. **Map** 8 E3. 📞 06 77 20 67 92.
A spacious trattoria with cheerful service and ample portions. Try *spaghetti* with sword
fish sauce, *straccetti all'ortica* (meat in nettle sauce) and *panna cotta*. ● lunch, Sun pm; Aug.

PANTHEON: *Da Gino* €€
Vicolo Rosini 4, 00186. **Map** 3 A3. 📞 06 687 34 34.
An ancient, traditional Roman trattoria full of journalists, politicians
and the initiated. Daily dishes include *gnocchi*, *ossobuco* and
baccalà as well as some classic sturdy soups. ● Sun; Aug.

PANTHEON: *Myosotis* €€
Vicolo della Vaccarella 3/5, 00186. **Map** 2 F3. 📞 06 686 55 54.
A foodie temple for those who want to keep an eye on their pocket.
An imaginative approach and the freshest ingredients. ● Sun.

PANTHEON: *Sangallo* €€€€
Vicolo della Vaccarella 11a, 00186. **Map** 2 F3. 📞 06 686 55 49.
Small bistro specializing in regional fish dishes and a huge array of *antipasti*,
including many types of vegetables and seafood. ● lunch; Sun; Aug.

For key to symbols see back flap

Average prices for a three-course meal for one, including a half-bottle of house wine, tax and service:
€ under 18 euros
€€ 18–30 euros
€€€ 30–40 euros
€€€€ 40–52 euros
€€€€€ over 52 euros.

FIXED-PRICE MENU
A fixed-price menu on offer, usually with three courses.
GOOD WINE LIST
Denotes a wide range of good quality wines.
FORMAL DRESS
Some restaurants require men to wear a jacket and tie.
OUTDOOR TABLES
Tables for eating outdoors, often with a good view.
CREDIT CARDS
The symbol shows that major credit cards are accepted.

	FIXED-PRICE MENU	GOOD WINE LIST	FORMAL DRESS	OUTDOOR TABLES
PANTHEON: *El Toulà* €€€€€ Via della Lupa 29b, 00186. **Map** 2 F3. (06 687 34 98. One of Rome's most exclusive and traditional restaurants. The cuisine is mainly Venetian, the service and the wines are superb. ● *Sat lunch, Mon lunch; Sun; Aug.*	●	■	●	
PIAZZA NAVONA: *La Taverna da Giovanni* €€ Via del Banco di Santo Spirito 58, 00186. **Map** 2 D3. (06 686 41 16. A crowded Roman trattoria with a family atmosphere. The *rigatoni all'amatriciana* (pasta with spicy bacon and tomato) is a speciality, as are the traditional *gnocchi*, *baccalà* (salt cod) and tripe on Thursday, Friday and Saturday respectively. ● *Mon.*	●	■		■
PIAZZA NAVONA: *Papà Giovanni* €€€€ Via dei Sediari 4-5, 00186. **Map** 2 F4. (06 686 53 08. Giovanni's son now runs this restaurant with an excellent cellar. New, lighter Roman cuisine is served with traditional dishes. ● *Sun.*		■		
PIAZZA DI SPAGNA: *Al 34* €€ Via Mario de' Fiori 34, 00187. **Map** 3 A2. (06 679 50 91. The perfect setting for a comfortable chat or a romantic tête-à-tête. The extensive menu offers mostly southern Italian cuisine. ● *Mon; Aug.*	●			■
PIAZZA DI SPAGNA: *Birreria Viennese* €€ Via della Croce 21, 00187. **Map** 3 A2. (06 679 55 69. Traditional beers and Austrian specialities have been served in this long and crowded room for more than 60 years. In the atmospheric setting, try the sausages, goulash, sauerkraut or the Wienerschnitzel.	●			■
PIAZZA DI SPAGNA: *Mario alla Vite* €€ Via della Vite 55, 00187. **Map** 3 A2. (06 678 38 18. Simple, honest Tuscan fare. The service can be haphazard but the *ribollita*, *fagioli al fiasco* (beans), steaks and desserts make up for it. ● *Sun; Aug.*		■		■
PIAZZA DI SPAGNA: *Porto di Ripetta* €€€€€ Via di Ripetta 250, 00187. **Map** 2 F2. (06 361 23 76. A friendly restaurant serving wonderful dishes with fish and seafood brought in daily. Try the swordfish or the fish soup. ● *Sun; Aug.*	●	■	●	
QUIRINAL: *Colline Emiliane* €€ Via degli Avignonesi 22, 00187. **Map** 3 C3. (06 481 75 38. A small, family trattoria serving specialities from Emilia-Romagna; home-made pasta, salami, boiled meats and *salsa verde* (parsley, onion and anchovy sauce) and Emilian wines. ● *Fri; Aug.*		■		
QUIRINAL: *Il Posto Accanto* €€€ Via del Boschetto 36a, 00184. **Map** 3 C4. (06 474 30 02. This elegant family-run restaurant owes its success to a carefully chosen menu based on home-made pasta, fish and meat. ● *Sat lunch; Sun; Aug.*		■		
QUIRINAL: *Al Moro* €€€€ Vicolo delle Bollette 13, 00185. **Map** 3 B3. (06 678 34 95. A reliable choice for traditional Roman cooking in this typical, and crowded, trattoria. Fresh local ingredients are used to make dishes such as *bucatini all'amatriciana* and *spaghetti alla Moro* (a version of *carbonara*). ● *Sun; Aug.*			●	■
TERMINI: *Gemma alla Lupa* € Via Marghera 39, 00185. **Map** 4 F3. (06 49 12 30. A typical, modest Roman trattoria serving real Roman cuisine in a bustling atmosphere. Excellent value with speedy service. ● *Sun; Aug.*	●			■
TRASTEVERE: *La Cornucopia* €€ Piazza in Piscinula 18. **Map** 6 D1. (06 580 03 80. Come here for excellent *antipasti* and simply cooked fish dishes such as *spigola al vapore* (steamed sea bass). Candlelight adds to the ambience. ● *Tue.*	●			■

TRASTEVERE: *Da Lucia* €€
Vicolo del Mattonato 2b, 00153. **Map** 5 C1. 📞 *06 580 36 01.*
A popular, crowded trattoria serving basic Roman cuisine. Try the *pasta e ceci* and the *spaghetti alla gricia* (pecorino, pancetta and pepper). ● *Mon; 2 weeks Aug.*

TRASTEVERE: *Asinocotto* €€€
Via dei Vascellari 48. **Map** 8 D1. 📞 *06 589 89 85.*
This casually elegant restaurant offers imaginative cooking with dishes such as aubergine, rocket and nettle ravioli and sea bass with truffle. ● *3 wks Jan.*

TRASTEVERE: *Da Paris* €€€
Piazza San Calisto 7a, 00153. **Map** 5 C1. 📞 *06 581 53 78.*
A Roman-Jewish restaurant popular with locals. Home-made pasta and traditional dishes include *minestra di arzilla* (ray), tripe and exquisite *fritto misto* (batter-fried fish) with vegetables. ● *Sun eve, Mon; 2 weeks Aug.*

TRASTEVERE: *Romolo nel Giardino della Fornarina* €€€
Via Porta Settimiana 8, 00153. **Map** 2 E5. 📞 *06 581 02 04.*
La Fornarina was Raphael's mistress and this is said to have been her home. In summer the Roman food is served in the courtyard. ● *Mon, Aug.*

TRASTEVERE: *Alberto Ciarla* €€€€€
Piazza San Cosimato 40, 00153. **Map** 5 C1. 📞 *06 581 86 68.*
This is the place to enjoy fish and seafood. From oysters to scampi, the menu is based on the day's catch from the market. The decor is elegant and dramatic.

VATICAN: *San Luigi* €€€
Via Mocenigo 10, 00193. **Map** 1 B2. 📞 *06 39 72 07 04.*
Close to the Vatican Museums, this restaurant offers 19th-century decor and soothing music as well as traditional Neapolitan cuisine. Pasta and desserts are particularly successful. ● *Sun; Aug.*

VATICAN: *Les Etoiles* €€€€€
Via dei Bastioni 1, 00193. **Map** 2 D2. 📞 *06 687 32 33.*
This rooftop restaurant sits atop the Atlante Star hotel. Speciality dishes include *tagliolini* (pasta) with clams and, in season, game and truffles.

VIA VENETO: *Cantina Cantarini* €€
Piazza Sallustio 12, 00187. **Map** 4 D1. 📞 *06 48 55 28.*
A popular local trattoria with friendly service. Meat is served from Monday to Thursday lunchtime, fish for the rest of the week. ● *Sun; 2 weeks Aug, 2 weeks Dec.*

VIA VENETO: *Tullio* €€€
Via San Nicola da Tolentino 26, 00187. **Map** 3 C2. 📞 *06 474 55 60.*
A genuine Tuscan restaurant frequented by an enthusiastic crowd. Typical dishes include porcini mushrooms in numerous ways. ● *Sun; Aug.*

VIA VENETO: *Giovanni* €€€€
Via Marche 64, 00187. **Map** 3 C1. 📞 *06 482 18 34.*
A crowded restaurant popular with locals. Traditional food from Lazio and the Marches, including fresh fish, pasta and *ossobuco*. ● *Fri eve, Sat; Aug.*

VIA VENETO: *George's* €€€€€
Via Marche 7, 00187. **Map** 3 C1. 📞 *06 42 08 45 75.*
A survivor from the Dolce Vita era with a nostalgic air of luxurious elegance. Service is impeccable and there is a tempting selection of international dishes. ● *Sun; Aug.*

VILLA BORGHESE: *Al Ceppo* €€€€
Via Panama 2, 00198. 📞 *06 841 96 96.*
Run by two sisters who serve a strictly seasonal menu of traditional dishes with flashes of inspiration in a hospitable atmosphere. ● *Mon; Aug.*

VILLA BORGHESE: *Relais le Jardin dell'Hotel Lord Byron* €€€€€
Via de Notaris 5, 00198. 📞 *06 322 45 41.*
High prices are matched by impeccable service and *haute cuisine*. The cooking draws on tradition with delicious mixtures of fruit, herbs and vegetables combined with meats and fish. ● *Aug.*

LAZIO

ALATRI: *La Rosetta* €€
Via del Duomo 35, 03011. 📞 *0775 43 45 68.*
A quiet restaurant near the 6th-century BC acropolis. Try the *maccheroni alla ciociara* (wine, herb, bacon and meat sauce). ● *Oct–May: Tue; 1 week Feb, 2 weeks Nov.*

	FIXED-PRICE MENU	GOOD WINE LIST	FORMAL DRESS	OUTDOOR TABLES

Average prices for a three-course meal for one, including a half-bottle of house wine, tax and service:
€ under 18 euros
€€ 18–30 euros
€€€ 30–40 euros
€€€€ 40–52 euros
€€€€€ over 52 euros.

FIXED-PRICE MENU
A fixed-price menu on offer, usually with three courses.
GOOD WINE LIST
Denotes a wide range of good quality wines.
FORMAL DRESS
Some restaurants require men to wear a jacket and tie.
OUTDOOR TABLES
Tables for eating outdoors, often with a good view.
CREDIT CARDS
The symbol shows that major credit cards are accepted.

CERVETERI: *Da Fiore* €€ Località Procoio di Ceri 6, 00052. 📞 06 99 20 42 50. A simple country trattoria: specialities include home-cooked pastas with *ragù*, rabbit and grilled meats. The *bruschette* and pizzas are also good. ● *Tue; Sep.*				■
FRASCATI: *Enoteca Frascati* €€ Via Diaz 42, 00044. 📞 06 941 74 49. A good range of light dishes accompanies the more than 400 wines here: try the soups and the fresh pasta with mushrooms and truffles. ● *Sun; Aug.* 🗌🗌		■		
GAETA: *La Cianciola* € Vico 2 Buonomo 16, 04024. 📞 0771 46 61 90. A charming trattoria hidden up a little alley into which tables are tightly packed. Try the pasta with aubergines and shellfish. ● *Oct–May: Mon; Nov.* 🗌 ▤	●			■
NETTUNO: *Cacciatori Dal 1896* €€ Via Matteotti 27–29, 00048. 📞 06 988 03 30. A large, rustically furnished restaurant with a veranda overlooking the sea. Fish is caught daily, and the dishes are inspired by regional recipes. ● *Wed.* 🗌 ▤ ♿		■		
OSTIA ANTICA: *Il Monumento* €€ Piazza Umberto I 8, 00119. 📞 06 565 00 21. A fish-based menu; the house speciality, *spaghetti monumento*, is served with seafood sauce. ● *Mon.* 🗌				■
SPERLONGA: *La Bisaccia* €€€ Via Romita 25, 04029. 📞 0771 548 76. Linguine with wild asparagus and prawns is a highlight of this restaurant that also makes use of local fish for soups and grills. ● *Tue; Nov.* 🗌 ▤ ♿				■
TERRACINA: *L'Incontro Da Baffone* €€€ Via Appia, km 104,500, 04029. 📞 0773 72 60 07. This popular restaurant along the beautiful beach of Terracina is a peaceful place to sample some good local fish dishes. ● *Oct–Apr: Wed.*		■		■
TIVOLI: *Villa Esedra* €€€ Via di Villa Adriana 51, Località Villa Adriana 00010. 📞 0774 53 47 16. Typical menu with fresh *antipasti* such as seafood salad and grilled fish to follow. In the evening there are also pizzas. ● *Mon in winter.* 🗌 ▤ 🗌				■
TREVIGNANO: *Ristorante Il Palazzetto* €€€ Piazza Vittorio Emanuele III 20, 00069. 📞 06 999 92 54. A little restaurant with views over Lake Bracciano. The excellent menu makes good use of sea and lake fish, including *ravioli al persico* (perch) and delicious scampi soups. Desserts are home-made. ● *Wed.* 🗌		■		■
TUSCANIA: *Al Gallo* €€€ Via del Gallo 22, 01017. 📞 0761 44 33 88. An unusual interpretation of regional dishes has created an exceptionally good menu. Warm atmosphere and charming service. ● *Mon; 2 weeks Jan.* 🗌 ▤ ♿		■		
VITERBO: *Porta Romana* €€ Via della Bontà 12, 01100. 📞 0761 30 71 18. A simple trattoria where a wide range of classic dishes is immaculately prepared. In the winter, try *pignataccia*, a Viterbo speciality of mixed veal, beef and pork cooked on a slow fire with celery, carrots and potatoes. ● *Sun; Aug.* ▤	●			

NAPLES AND CAMPANIA

AGROPOLI: *Il Ceppo* €€€ Via Madonna Del Carmine 31, 84043. 📞 0974 84 30 36. A wonderful range of local fish and home-made pastas and pizzas; try the *spaghetti* with seafood, prawns in lemon sauce or the fish soups. ● *Mon; Oct–Nov.* 🗌 ▤ 🗌		■		■

AMALFI: *La Marinella* €€
Via Lungomare dei Cavalieri di San Giovanni di Gerusalemme 1, 84011. 089 87 10 43.
A lively, friendly restaurant overlooking the the Amalfi coast. Much fish is served
as well as the traditional local specialities. ● *Fri; Nov–Jan.*

AMALFI: *Eolo* €€€
Via Comite 3, 84011. 089 87 12 41.
Situated in the historic centre of Amalfi, this restaurant's menu changes every fortnight to
make use of seasonal ingredients. The food is of a high standard. ● *Tue; Nov–May.*

BENEVENTO: *Pina e Gino* €
Via dell'Università 48, 82100. 0824 249 47.
In the heart of the historic centre; try *cardone* (a type of thistle), *sfoglia al forno* (meat
baked in a parcel) and pasta with broccoli. ● *Sun; Easter, Aug, Christmas.*

CAPRI: *La Savardina da Eduardo* €
Via Lo Capo 8, 80073. 081 837 63 00
This is one of the most traditional restaurants in Capri, with orange trees, sea views
and tasty regional specialities, such as home-made *ravioli.* ● *lunch; Wed; Nov–Feb.*

CAPRI: *Quisi del Grand Hotel Quisisana* €€€€
Via Camerelle 2, 80073. 081 837 07 88.
The atmosphere is elegant and the food is delightful. Try the succulent roast
duck with peaches and hot apple pie with Calvados. ● *lunch; Nov–Mar*

CASERTA: *La Brace* €€
Piazza Madonna delle Grazie 9, Località Vaccheria 81020. 0823 36 17 44.
An old-fashioned country inn in a village outside Caserta. Try *pasta e fagioli*
(pasta with beans) and grilled fish. ● *Tue; Aug.*

ISCHIA: *Da Peppina* €€€
Via Montecorvo 42, Località Forio 80075. 081 99 83 12.
Basic fare served in this simple trattoria; *pasta e fagioli*, soups, grilled meats
and pizzas cooked in a wood oven. ● *Nov–Mar; Wed.*

ISCHIA: *La Tavernetta* €€€
Via Sant'Angelo 77, Località Serrara Fontana 80070. 081 99 92 51.
You can relax in this peaceful corner, where you find a good choice of pasta
with Mediterranean sauces, salads, or fried fish. ● *Wed; Nov–Feb.*

FAICCHIO: *La Campagnola* €
Via San Nicola 36, Località Massa 82030. 0824 81 40 81.
Set in a village 38 km (23 miles) northwest of Benevento, serving simple, tasty cuisine.
Try *torciglioni alle melanzane* (pasta with aubergines). ● *Sep.*

NAPLES: *Gorizia* €
Via Bernini 29, 80129. 081 578 22 48.
This is one of the oldest and most renowned pizzerias in Naples. The food is
excellent, from the home-made pizzas to the fish *antipasti.* ● *Wed; Aug.*

NAPLES: *California* €€
Via Santa Lucia 101, 80132. 081 764 97 52.
Well-presented stalwarts are on offer such as *spaghetti alla carbonara* and *bucatini
all'amatriciana* as well as American-style sandwiches. ● *Sun, 2 weeks Aug.*

NAPLES: *La Chiacchierata* €€
Piazzetta Matilde Serao 37, 80100. 081 41 14 65.
A traditional trattoria popular with the locals. Among Neapolitan specialities
are *orecchiette* (ear-shaped pasta) with chickpeas, and octopus. ● *Sun; Aug.*

NAPLES: *La Sacrestia* €€€€
Via Orazio 116, 80122. 081 66 41 86.
An attractive setting with views of the Gulf of Naples. The food is excellent,
and the atmosphere elegant but informal. ● *Sun, Mon; Aug.*

NAPLES: *La Cantinella* €€€€
Via Cuma 42, 80132. 081 764 86 84.
One of Naples' most famous restaurants, with an astounding reputation for its
carefully and successfully prepared regional cuisine. ● *Sun; 3 weeks Aug.*

NERANO: *Taverna del Capitano* €€€€
Località Marina del Cantone, Piazza delle Sirene 10, 80068. 081 808 10 28.
A refined restaurant on the beach serving regional specialities with some creative
touches; try the fish in breadcrumbs and herbs. ● *Mon; Jan, Feb.*

For key to symbols see back flap

	FIXED-PRICE MENU	GOOD WINE LIST	FORMAL DRESS	OUTDOOR TABLES

Average prices for a three-course meal for one, including a half-bottle of house wine, tax and service:
€ under 18 euros
€€ 18–30 euros
€€€ 30–40 euros
€€€€ 40–52 euros
€€€€€ over 52 euros.

FIXED-PRICE MENU
A fixed-price menu on offer, usually with three courses.

GOOD WINE LIST
Denotes a wide range of good quality wines.

FORMAL DRESS
Some restaurants require men to wear a jacket and tie.

OUTDOOR TABLES
Tables for eating outdoors, often with a good view.

CREDIT CARDS
The symbol shows that major credit cards are accepted.

PAESTUM: *La Pergola* €€ ▪ ▪
Via Nazionale, Capaccio Scalo 84040. 【 0828 72 33 77.
Innovative regional cuisine that makes use of seasonal produce in a rustic restaurant 3 km (2 miles) from the ruins of Paestum. ● Mon (except Aug); Sep. ⬛ ▤ ♿

POMPEII: *Il Principe* €€€€€ ▪
Piazza B Longo 8, 80045. 【 081 850 55 66.
This airy, refined restaurant is close to the excavations. Its cuisine is based on fish and includes fish-filled *ravioli* and turbot with vegetables.
● Aug, Christmas. ⬛ ▤ ⚡ ♿

POSITANO: *Da Adolfo* €€ ● ▪
Località Laurito 40, 84017. 【 089 87 50 22.
A boat leaves Positano harbour every half hour for this charming trattoria serving *spaghetti* with clams or courgettes with grilled mozzarella. ● Sat in Jul, Aug, Sep–May. ⬛

POSITANO: *La Sponda* €€€€€ ● ▪ ▪
Via Colombo 30, 84017. 【 089 87 50 66.
A sumptuous restaurant where guests are treated like family friends and offered a tempting range of modern and traditional dishes based on fresh fish. ● Dec–Feb. ⬛ ♿

SALERNO: *Pizzeria Vicolo della Neve* €
Vicolo della Neve 24, 84100. 【 089 22 57 05.
A pizzeria in the historic centre also serving a range of dishes such as *pasta e fagioli*, *baccalà* casserole and sausages with broccoli. ● lunch; Dec–Mar. ⬛

SALERNO: *Al Cenacolo* €€
Piazza Alfano I 4, 84100. 【 089 23 88 18.
Dedicated cuisine with a menu that changes daily to make good use of local ingredients. Pasta and bread are home-made. ● Sun eve, Mon; Aug. ⬛ ▤

SANT'AGATA SUI DUE GOLFI: *Don Alfonso 1890* €€€€€ ● ▪
Piazza Sant'Agata 11, 80064. 【 081 878 00 26.
Set in elegant gardens, dishes include seafood and fish specialities and delicious traditional desserts. ● Mon, Tue; Dec–Feb. ⬛ ▤ ⚡ ♿

SICIGNANO DEGLI ALBURNI: *La Taverna* €€
Via Nazionale 139, Frazione Scorzo 84020. 【 0828 97 80 50.
An 18th-century country inn, near Salerno. The regional cuisine includes salamis, bean and chickpea soups and grilled meats. ● Wed; Jul. ⬛ ♿

SORRENTO: *Antico Frantoio* €€€ ▪ ▪
Via Casarlano 8, Località Casarlano 80067. 【 081 878 58 45.
A great variety of dishes for all courses, made from local ingredients. Try the pizzas, the corn bread and the beer brewed at the next-door *birreria*. ⬛ ▤ ⚡ ♿

ABRUZZO, MOLISE AND PUGLIA

ALBEROBELLO: *Il Poeta Contadino* €€€€ ● ▪ ▪
Via Indipendenza 21, 70011. 【 080 432 19 17.
An elegant restaurant where the excellent service matches the high standard of both food and wine. The cuisine makes imaginative use of fresh local ingredients, offering both fish and meat dishes. ● Mon; 2 weeks Jan. ⬛ ▤ ⚡ ♿

BARI: *Borgo Antico* €€ ▪ ▪
Piazza del Ferrarese 10–11, 70123. 【 080 523 58 52.
This elegant restaurant is in the centre of the old town, just by the old harbour. The cuisine is mainly Pugliese and Mediterranean. ● Mon, Nov. ⬛ ▤

BARI: *Villa Rosa* €€ ▪ ▪
Lungomare Starita 64, 70123. 【 080 534 76 10.
A homely trattoria and pizzeria on the seafront. Specialities include *orecchiette* (ear-shaped pasta) with *rucola* (rocket), fish and meat kebabs. ● Wed; 15 Dec–15 Jan. ⬛

GALLIPOLI: *Capriccio* €€€
Viale Bovio 14/16. **[** *0833 26 15 45.*
This restaurant serves up classical regional cuisine including plenty of fresh fish.
● *Mon (winter), Nov.*

ISOLE TREMITI: *Al Gabbiano* €€€
San Domino, 71040. **[** *0882 46 34 10.*
The food here is based on the best fish from the sea. Try the traditional fish soup
and fresh fish roasted in a case of salt.

L'AQUILA: *Ernesto* €€
Piazza Palazzo 22, 67100. **[** *0862 210 94.*
A peaceful, sophisticated place to eat. The menu is a tasty, creative mix inspired
by different sources and there is a wine bar attached. ● *Sun, Mon.*

LECCE: *Barbablú* €€€
Via Umberto 7, 73100. **[** *0832 24 11 83.*
An old palazzo in the historic centre is the perfect setting for imaginative
and delicious dishes that use only fresh local ingredients. ● *Mon.*

LOCOROTONDO: *Centro Storico* €
Via Eroi di Dogali 6, 70010. **[** *080 431 54 73.*
Hidden among the winding streets of the historic centre, this little trattoria
offers some excellent Pugliese cuisine often with creative touches. ● *Wed.*

OTRANTO: *Vecchia Otranto* €€€
Corso Garibaldi 96, 73028. **[** *0836 80 15 75.*
Good marine and other regional specialities in this traditional trattoria
include pasta with sea urchin and pepper sauce. ● *Thu; Nov, 1 week Jan.*

OVINDOLI: *Il Pozzo* €€
Via dell'Alpino, 67046. **[** *0863 71 01 91.*
Wonderful mountain setting for this atmospheric restaurant in the historic centre
of town. The food is traditional and robust. ● *Wed; Sep–Oct.*

PORTO CESAREO: *L'Angolo di Beppe* €€
Via Zanella 24, Località Torre Lapillo, 73050. **[** *0833 56 53 05.*
A cosy atmosphere and elegant decor with a large open fire in winter. The cuisine is
based on fish, and mixes local and international traditions. ● *Tue.*

ROCCA DI MEZZO: *La Fiorita* €
Piazza Principe di Piemonte 3, 67048. **[** *0862 91 74 67.*
Efficient, friendly service in this family-run trattoria where the food is based
on local products from the Abruzzi mountains. ● *Tue, 2 wks Sep.*

SULMONA: *Rigoletto* €€
Via Stazione Introacqua 46, 67039. **[** *0864 555 29.*
A short walk from the centre of town, reliable home-made pastas are served
with beans, *scamorza* (soft cheese), rabbit and truffles. ● *Mon; Jun, Jul.*

TARANTO: *Le Vecchie Cantine* €€
Via Girasoli 23, Frazione Lama 74020. **[** *099 777 25 89.*
Set in restored storerooms just outside Taranto. A tasty fish and seafood menu, such
as *carpaccio* of swordfish and *fusilli* with sardines. ● *lunch; Wed (in winter); Jan.*

TARANTO: *Al Faro* €€€
Via Galeso 126, 74100. **[** *099 471 44 44.*
The menu is exclusively marine, using locally caught fish and seafood for
antipasti, soups, *risotto* and grills. ● *Sun; 2 weeks Jan, 2 wks Dec.*

TERMOLI: *Z'Bass* €€
Via Oberdan 8, 86039. **[** *0875 70 67 03.*
This friendly, welcoming trattoria offers a high level of cuisine using fresh, seasonal
ingredients. There is also an extensive wine list available. ● *Mon (in winter).*

TRANI: *Torrente Antico* €€€€
Via Fusco 3, 70059. **[** *0883 48 79 11.*
Exquisite, lightly prepared dishes based on traditional regional cuisine with modern
touches. The wine list is also extensive. ● *Sun eve, Mon; 1 wk Jan, 2 wks Jul.*

VIESTE: *Il Trabucco dell'Hotel Pizzomunno* €€€€
Lungomare di Pizzomunno km 1, 71019. **[** *0884 70 87 41.*
Surrounded by gardens and very close to the sea. The cuisine has some
creative touches and the dishes are light and tasty. ● *Nov–Mar.*

Average prices for a three-course meal for one, including a half-bottle of house wine, tax and service: € under 18 euros €€ 18–30 euros €€€ 30–40 euros €€€€ 40–52 euros €€€€€ over 52 euros.	**FIXED-PRICE MENU** A fixed-price menu on offer, usually with three courses. **GOOD WINE LIST** Denotes a wide range of good quality wines. **FORMAL DRESS** Some restaurants require men to wear a jacket and tie. **OUTDOOR TABLES** Tables for eating outdoors, often with a good view. **CREDIT CARDS** The symbol shows that major credit cards are accepted.	**FIXED-PRICE MENU**	**GOOD WINE LIST**	**FORMAL DRESS**	**OUTDOOR TABLES**

VILLETTA BARREA: *Trattoria del Pescatore*   €
Via B Virgilio 175, 67030. 📞 0864 892 74.
A simple, family-run trattoria in the Abruzzo National Park. Regional dishes include trout and home-made *chitarrini* (pasta cut like guitar strings). ● *Thu in winter.*

BASILICATA AND CALABRIA

BIVONGI: *Vecchia Miniera*   €
Contrada Perrocalli, 89040. 📞 0964 73 18 69.
Regional cuisine such as pasta with *sugo di capra* (goat sauce), a favourite ancient Roman dish, in this village just outside Stilo. ● *Mon.*

MARATEA: *Taverna Rovita*   €€€€
Via Rovita 13, 85046. 📞 0973 87 65 88.
An elegant country restaurant with white walls and tiled floors serving regional cuisine. Try the *risotto* of asparagus and venison. ● *Oct–Apr: Tue; Jan.*

MATERA: *Al Casino del Diavolo*   €€
Via La Martella, 75100. 📞 0835 26 19 86.
Excellent Matera fare at this elegant, traditional restaurant just outside the town. Try *orecchiette* (ear-shaped pasta) with broccoli. ● *Mon.*

MATERA: *Il Terrazzino*   €€
Vicolo San Giuseppe 7, 75100. 📞 0835 33 25 03.
In the Sassi district (*see p502*), the restaurant has a panoramic terrace. Try soups of grains and chickpeas, or grilled lamb *involtini* (lamb parcels). ● *Tue; 1 week Jun.*

MATERA: *Venusio*   €€€€€
Via Lussemburgo 2, Borgo Venusio 75100. 📞 0835 25 90 81.
An elegant restaurant 6 km (4 miles) south of Matera. Specialities include fish baked in a bread case, fish *tortelli*, mushrooms and various *antipasti*. ● *Mon; Jan, Aug.*

MELFI: *Vaddone*   €€
Contrada Sant'Abruzzese, 85025. 📞 0972 243 23.
A well-known trattoria serving delicious soups of pulses, and grilled meats. The menu also includes fish dishes. ● *Mon eve.*

POTENZA: *Z' Mingo*   €
Contrada Botte 2, 85100. 📞 0971 44 59 29.
This simple trattoria is the perfect place to join the locals eating regional fare. The menu includes fresh pasta, roasted meats and local cheeses and salamis. ● *Mon; 2 weeks Aug.*

REGGIO DI CALABRIA: *Villeggiante*   €
Via Eremo-Condera 31, Località Mariannazzo, 89125. 📞 0965 250 21.
A Reggio Calabrian institution where good simple fare is well prepared and served informally. Try *spaghetti* with broccoli or rich, spicy sausages. ● *Mon (in winter).*

ROSSANO: *Antiche Mura*   €
Via Prigioni 40, 87067. 📞 0983 52 00 42.
A friendly trattoria, housed in the stable of an 18th-century palazzo. The dining room has a vaulted ceiling. Try the stuffed aubergines and roasted goat. ● *lunch; Wed.*

SCILLA: *La Grotta Azzurra*   €€
Via Cristoforo Colombo, 89058. 📞 0965 75 48 89.
A wonderful setting on the beach where, according to legend, Ulysses came ashore. This basic trattoria serves mainly fish. ● *Mon lunch; 2 weeks Dec.*

TROPEA: *Pimm's*   €€
Corso Vittorio Emanuele, 88038. 📞 0963 66 61 05.
A beautiful setting in the historic centre. Simple, local fare, well prepared and pleasantly served. Start with seafood *crostini* or smoked swordfish, then try pasta with sea urchins and stuffed, grilled squid. ● *Oct–Apr: Mon; Jan.*

VENOSA: *Taverna Ducale* €€
Piazza Municipio 2, 85029. █ *0972 369 44.*
The 15th-century building sets the scene for a cuisine based on rediscovered
ancient dishes such as *preferito di Orazio* (the favourite of the Latin poet) and
triticum (a mixture of pulses and vegetables). ● *Mon.* 🖼 ⚡ ♿

SICILY

AGRIGENTO: *Le Caprice* €€
Via Panoramica dei Templi 51, 92100. █ *0922 264 69.*
A good restaurant in an exquisite setting in the Valley of the Temples. Regional cuisine
is carefully prepared; the *antipasti* buffet is a speciality. ● *Fri; 2 weeks Jul.* 🖼 ☰ ♿

AGRIGENTO: *Trattoria del Pescatore* €€
Lungomare Falcone e Borsellino 20, Località Lido di San Leone 92100. █ *0922 41 43 43.*
The chef chooses the fish daily and uses it, sometimes raw, in simple but
delicious dishes with oil and lemon juice. The pasta speciality is *spaghetti*
with swordfish, aubergine and basil. ● *Wed; Oct.* 🖼 ☰

AGRIGENTO: *Kalos* €€€
Piazza San Calogero 1, 92100. █ *0922 263 89.*
A bright restaurant with original and well-prepared cuisine. Try pasta with
pistachio and gorgonzola, grilled fish and *cassata* of ricotta. ● *Sun.* 🖼 ☰

BAGHERIA: *Don Ciccio* €
Via del Cavaliere 87, 90011. █ *091 93 24 42.*
This town-centre trattoria concentrates on regional specialities. Look out for pasta
with sardines, broccoli, tuna and other sauces. ● *Sun, Wed; Aug.* 🖼 ☰ ♿

CATANIA: *I Vicere* €€
Via Grotte Bianche 97, 95129. █ *095 32 01 88.*
Outside dining on a terrace with spectacular views. Good food, particularly
the succulent pork fillet in mandarin sauce. 🖼 ⚡ ☰ ♿

CEFALÙ: *L'Antica Corte* €
Corso Ruggero 155, 90015. █ *0921 42 32 28.*
A trattoria-pizzeria in an old courtyard in the historic centre, the cuisine is local with
influences from almost-forgotten old Sicilian recipes. ● *Thu; Nov, Jan.* 🖼 ☰

ENNA: *Ariston* €€
Via Roma 353, 94100. █ *0935 260 38.*
In the heart of Enna, with a selection of fish dishes as well as meat specialities, such
as stuffed lamb, or bean and pea soup and *frittata* (omelette). ● *Sun, Aug.* 🖼 ☰

ERICE: *Monte San Giuliano* €€
Via San Rocco 7, 91016. █ *0923 86 95 95.*
Located in the centre of town, the menu is based on Sicilian traditions and
includes fresh pasta with sardines, and couscous with fish. ● *Mon; Jan, Nov.* 🖼

ERICE: *Osteria di Venere* €€
Via Roma 6, 91016. █ *0923 86 93 62.*
A delightful restaurant in an attractive 17th-century building. The menu is
basically Sicilian and Mediterranean. ● *Jan–Feb: Wed.* 🖼 ☰

ISOLE EOLIE: *Filippino* €€
Piazza del Municipio, Lipari 98055. █ *090 981 10 02.*
An essentially Sicilian, sea-based menu includes swordfish, home-made *maccheroni*
and some excellent *cassata Siciliana*. ● *Oct–Apr: Mon; 2 weeks Nov, 2 weeks Dec.* 🖼 ⚡ ☰

MARSALA: *Delfino* €€
Via Lungomare Mediterraneo 672, 91025. █ *0923 96 95 65.*
Three lovely rooms all with views over either the sea or the garden. Try the
sunflower *spaghetti* or sword fish *alla Messinese*. ● *Tue.* 🖼 ☰ ♿

MARSALA: *Mothia* €€
Contrada Ettore Infersa 13, 91016. █ *0923 74 52 55.*
Simple, delicious cooking with home-made bread, pasta, rich desserts and cakes. The
tagliatelle with lobster sauce are particularly recommended. ● *Wed, Jan–Feb.* 🖼 ☰ ♿

PALERMO: *Simpaty* €€
Via Piano Gallo 18, Località Mondello 90151. █ *091 45 44 70.*
The dining room has good views over the popular bay of Mondello and
the menu is almost exclusively fish. Try *ricci* (little sea urchins) served
as *antipasto* or as a pasta sauce, octopus and squid. ● *Fri.* 🖼 ☰

	FIXED-PRICE MENU	GOOD WINE LIST	FORMAL DRESS	OUTDOOR TABLES

Average prices for a three-course meal for one, including a half-bottle of house wine, tax and service:
€ under 18 euros
€€ 18–30 euros
€€€ 30–40 euros
€€€€ 40–52 euros
€€€€€ over 52 euros.

FIXED-PRICE MENU
A fixed-price menu on offer, usually with three courses.
GOOD WINE LIST
Denotes a wide range of good quality wines.
FORMAL DRESS
Some restaurants require men to wear a jacket and tie.
OUTDOOR TABLES
Tables for eating outdoors, often with a good view.
CREDIT CARDS
The symbol shows that major credit cards are accepted.

	FIXED-PRICE MENU	GOOD WINE LIST	FORMAL DRESS	OUTDOOR TABLES
PALERMO: *La Scuderia* €€€ Viale del Fante 9, 90146. 091 52 03 23. Set in the Parco della Favorita, this elegant restaurant sticks to traditional Sicilian cuisine, carefully and deliciously prepared. ● *Sun; 2 weeks Aug.*		■		■
PALERMO: *Temptation* €€€ Via Torretta 94, Località Sferracavallo 90148. 091 691 11 04. This trattoria offers an all-inclusive menu of seafood *antipasti*, and the pasta with aubergines and fried fish is particularly recommended. ● *Thu.*	●			
RAGUSA: *La Ciotola* €€ Via Archimede 23, 9710. 0932 22 89 44. An elegant, modern restaurant in the city centre serving well-prepared specialities like *maccheroncini* with aubergines, and much fish. ● *Mon; Aug.*		■		■
SCIACCA: *Hostaria del Vicolo* €€€ Vico Sammaritano 10, 92019. 0925 230 71. The menu is Sicilian with dishes such as *tagliatelle* with prawns, aubergine and *bottarga* (tuna eggs), and tasty desserts. ● *Sun eve, Mon eve; Oct.*		■		
SELINUNTE: *Lido Azzurro* € Via Marco Polo 51, Località Marinella 91022. 0924 462 11. A bustling trattoria with views of the top of the acropolis from the terrace. There's a wide range of buffet-style *antipasti*. ● *Nov–Feb.*				■
SIRACUSA: *Jonico 'a Rutta 'e Ciauli* €€ Riviera Dionisio il Grande 194, 96100. 0931 655 40. This restaurant has a bright dining room with walls covered with Sicilian ceramics and agricultural artifacts. The cuisine is regional and traditional. ● *Tue; Easter, Christmas.*	●	■		■
SIRACUSA: *Minerva* €€ Piazza Duomo 20, 96100. 0931 694 04. A pizzeria right in the historic centre, with a wide and imaginative range of pizzas on offer. Tables are outside in the cathedral square. ● *Mon.*		■		■
SIRACUSA: *La Foglia* €€€ Via Capodieci 29, 96100. 0931 662 33. Vegetables and pulses are the mainstay of the menu at this restaurant in the historic centre. Try fresh pasta with vegetables or fish and the soups.	●			
TAORMINA: *Pizzeria Vecchia Taormina* € Vico Ebrei 3, 98039. 0942 62 55 89. A traditional pizzeria in the old Jewish quarter of Taormina. There is a massive range of Sicilian-style pizzas and delicious *antipasti*. ● *Wed; Nov–Dec.*				■
TAORMINA: *Al Duomo* €€€ Vico Ebrei 11, 98039. 0942 62 56 56. A typical Sicilian trattoria, dishes include tuna and swordfish. ● *Wed in winter; Feb.*		■		■
TAORMINA: *La Giara* €€€€ Vicolo La Floresta 1, 98039. 0942 233 60. A pretty restaurant with beautiful views over the bay. Try *ravioli* with aubergine and wild fennel *involtini* (parcels). ● *Mon; Nov–Mar: Mon–Fri; Jan, Feb.*		■		■
TRAPANI: *P&G* €€ Via Spalti 1, 91100. 0923 54 77 01. This restaurant has become an institution in Trapani. During the annual tuna *mattanza*, fresh tuna is served in a huge variety of ways. ● *Sun; Aug.*		■		
TRAPANI: *Da Peppe* €€€ Via Spalti 50, 91100. 0923 282 46. Trapani specialities served as well as house dishes established over the years. The mainstay is fish, including locally caught tuna. ● *Sun eve; Dec, Jan.*	●	■		

SARDINIA

ALGHERO: *Al Tuguri*   €€€
Via Maiorca 113, 07041. ☎ 079 97 67 72.
A pretty restaurant in a 15th-century building in the historic centre, with an interesting menu of delicious Mediterranean specialities. ● *Sun; Dec–Jan.* 🔲📋⚡

ALGHERO: *La Lepanto*   €€€
Via Carlo Alberto 135, 07041. ☎ 079 97 91 16.
Regional dishes, such as *bottarga* (tuna roe) and lobster and other creative dishes: warm octopus, and scampi with pecorino. ● *Mon.* 🔲📋♿

BOSA: *Mannu Da Giancarlo e Rita*   €€
Viale Alghero 28, 08013. ☎ 0785 37 53 06.
A smart, modern restaurant offering extremely good local fish specialities; Bosa is famous for fresh lobster, which is served here in a celery sauce. 🔲📋⚡

CAGLIARI: *Nuovo Saint Pierre*   €€
Via Coghinas 13, 09122. ☎ 070 27 15 78.
Traditional dishes include wild boar with lentils, wild asparagus *risotto*, roasted lamb and stuffed beef. Fish is served in summer. ● *Sun; Aug.* 🔲📋

CAGLIARI: *Dal Corsaro*   €€€
Viale Regina Margherita 28, 09124. ☎ 070 66 43 18.
Good service and a pleasant atmosphere in which to enjoy carefully prepared regional dishes (fish *ravioli*), original creations (*tagliatelle* with courgettes and clams) and some rediscovered Cagliari classics. ● *Sun; Aug; 2 weeks Dec.* 🔲📋♿

CALASETTE: *Da Pasqualino*   €€
Via Roma 99, 09011. ☎ 0781 884 73.
Delicious local fish-based specialities are served in this simple and relaxed trattoria, including fish soups, *bottarga* (tuna roe) and lobster. ● *Tue (in winter), Nov.* 🔲📋♿

NUORO: *Canne al Vento*   €
Viale Repubblica 66, 08100. ☎ 0784 20 17 62.
Dishes on offer at this regional restaurant include roast meats, excellent cheeses, octopus salad and a hot *seadas* (honey dessert). ● *Sun, 2 wks Aug, 2 wks Dec.* 🔲📋♿

OLBIA: *Bacchus*   €€€
Centro Commerciale Martini, Via Gabriele d'Annunzio 2nd floor, 07026. ☎ 0789 216 12.
An elegant restaurant with sea views. Creative cooking with regional undertones includes fish, lamb with artichokes, and crab. ● *Mon; 3 wks Nov.* 🔲📋⚡♿

OLIENA: *CK*   €€
Corso ML King 2/4, 08025. ☎ 0784 28 80 24.
Typical local specialities in this family-run restaurant include game and herbs, fresh cheese *ravioli* and honey desserts. 🔲📋

ORISTANO: *Faro*   €€€€
Via Bellini 25, 09170. ☎ 0783 700 02.
One of Sardinia's best restaurants, serving regional dishes based on what is fresh in the market that day, particularly fish and seafood. ● *Sun; Christmas.* 🔲📋

PORTO CERVO: *Gianni Pedrinelli*   €€€€€
Località Piccolo Pevero, 07020. ☎ 0789 924 36.
The menu is regional serving much fish. Try the house speciality, a typically Sardinian dish, *porcettu allo spiedo* (pork on the spit). ● *Oct–Feb.* 🔲

PORTO ROTONDO: *Da Giovannino*   €€€€€
Piazza Quadra, 07026. ☎ 0789 352 80.
Popular with Italian politicos and media types, who dine on expensive but delicious (and attentively served) Mediterranean specialities, which are accompanied by superb wines. ● *Nov–Mar.* 🔲📋♿

PORTOSCUSO: *La Ghinghetta*   €€€€
Via Cavour 26, Località Sa Caletta, 09010. ☎ 0781 50 81 43.
Set in a charming fishing village, the almost exclusively fish-based menu adds a different twist to local specialities. ● *Sun; Nov–Apr.* 🔲📋⚡

SASSARI: *Florian*   €€€
Via Bellieni 27, 07100. ☎ 079 23 62 51.
The menu here offers the very best of sea and land regional specialities according to the season: there are mushrooms in autumn, seafood in summer and appropriate vegetables all year round. ● *Aug.* 🔲📋♿

Survival
Guide

PRACTICAL INFORMATION

Ask ANY ITALIAN and they will almost certainly tell you that Italy is the most beautiful country in the world. They may not be far wrong. However, the charm and allure of Italy may help to veil some of her numerous practical problems. Getting information is rarely straightforward; public

**ENTE NAZIONALE
ITALIANO PER IL TURISMO**

Tourist board logo

offices and banks are nearly always crippled by long queues and bureaucracy, and the postal service is renowned for its inefficiency. This section, together with some forward planning and a little patience, should help you cope with some of Italy's idiosyncrasies.

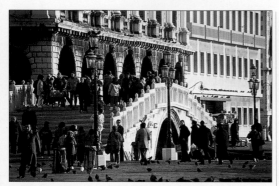

Tourists crossing the Ponte della Paglia in Venice *(see p105)*

VISAS AND PERMESSO DI SOGGIORNO

European Union nationals and citizens of the US, Canada, Australia and New Zealand do not need visas for stays of up to three months. Most European Union (EU) visitors need only a valid identity document, but visitors from UK, Ireland, Denmark and Sweden do need a passport. All visitors should check requirements with the Italian embassy before travelling and, officially, declare themselves to the Italian police within eight days of arrival.

If you are staying in a hotel or campsite, this will be done for you, otherwise contact the local *Questura* (police station).

Anyone wishing to stay in Italy for more than three months (eight days for non-EU citizens) will have to obtain a *permesso di soggiorno* (permit to stay). You can apply for a permit at any main police station, *Questura di Provincia*. You must apply for the correct permit, either a permit to work *(lavoro)* or a permit to study *(studio)*. For each permit you will need to submit a written

application *(domanda)*, passport-style photographs and photocopies of your passport. If you are looking for work, these items need to be accompanied by proof of your future employment in Italy or other means of financial support.

To apply for a study permit, it is necessary to get a letter from the relevant school or university giving details of your course. This then has to be sent to the Italian consulate in your country of origin to obtain an official covering letter, or declaration. You will also need some form of guarantee that your medical bills will be paid should you become ill or have an accident. A comprehensive insurance policy *(see p617)* would be sufficient.

WHEN TO VISIT

Italy's towns and historic sites are extremely popular attractions and it is worth considering this when planning your trip. Rome, Florence and Venice are all crowded from spring to October and it is advisable to book a hotel well in advance. In August the cities are generally slightly

less busy, abandoned by their inhabitants for the summer holidays. At Easter, Rome is overrun by pilgrims and tourists, and in February, Venice triples its population during Carnevale *(see p65)*. Seaside resorts fill up during July and August, whereas June and September can be equally hot but less crowded. The seas and beaches are notably cleaner at the beginning of summer. December to March is the time of year for skiing, although the first snow often falls as early as November. Most sights are open all year, except on some public holidays *(see p65)* and often two Mondays each month *(see p614)*.

Rome's renowned Tazza d'Oro café, an ideal rest stop after sightseeing

SEASONAL DIFFERENCES

The NORTHERN PART of Italy is generally more temperate than the south, which has a Mediterranean climate. June to September is hot and in peak summer, also humid. Summer storms can be quite dramatic, but often only last a few hours. Spring and autumn are ideal for visiting cities; temperatures are mild. Winter can be bitterly cold, especially in the north. *The Climate of Italy* on pages 68–9 takes a detailed look at the country's regional weather.

The beautiful Piazza del Campo in Siena, meeting place for visitors and locals

Unacceptable dress in church: both sexes are required to cover torsos and upper arms

ETIQUETTE AND TIPPING

PEOPLE IN ITALY ARE friendly towards foreign visitors. On entering a shop or bar it is customary to greet people with a general *buon giorno* (good morning) or *buona sera* (good evening), and the same applies when leaving. They will also try to be helpful when asked directions in the street. If your Italian is slight, *scusi* followed by the name of the place you wish to go to will often suffice. *Grazie* (thank you) is replied to with *prego* (you're welcome).

Tipping in restaurants is expected when the 15 per cent service is not included. However, as much as 10 per cent would be considered generous and a tip is often not expected at all in family-run restaurants. Taxi drivers and hotel porters expect a few euros if they have been helpful. You could simply round the bill up to the nearest 2 euros.

Italians are very dress-conscious and unusual clothes do get noticed. In places of worship, cover your torso and upper arms; shorts and skirts must reach below the knee.

While smoking in public places is commonplace, drunkenness is not tolerated.

CUSTOMS

ON 30 JUNE 1999, the intra-EU Duty and Tax Free Allowances, better known as Duty-free and mainly affecting such high-tax items as alcohol, perfumes and tobacco, were abolished. However, for EU residents the amount of these goods that can be imported for personal use has increased.

Consulates can generally provide up-to-date information on particular customs regulations. To find out what you can take back from Italy to non-EU countries, contact that particular country's customs department, who will be able to advise you.

TAX EXEMPTION

VALUE ADDED TAX (IVA in Italy) ranges from 12–35 per cent, depending on the item. Non-European Union citizens can obtain an IVA refund for each purchase over 160 euros, but it is a long process. It is easier to get a refund if you shop where you see the "Euro Free Tax" sign, rather than from a market stall, for example. After showing your passport to the shop assistant and completing a form, the IVA will be deducted from your bill. The alternative is to present a customs officer with your purchases and their receipts on your departure. He or she will stamp the receipts, which you then send back to the vendor. A refund should eventually be sent to you.

The clock of San Giacomo di Rialto in Venice *(see p93)*

ITALIAN TIME

ITALY IS ONE HOUR ahead of Greenwich Mean Time (GMT). The clocks are put forward one hour in March and back in October. For example: London is one hour behind Italy; Sydney is nine hours ahead; while Ottawa is six hours behind.

ELECTRICAL ADAPTORS

THE VOLTAGE IN ITALY is 220 volts, with two-pin round-pronged plugs. For European appliances, the plug can simply be changed over, whereas US equipment will need an adaptor. Italian plugs come in many different sizes, without any apparent special purpose, and you can buy adaptors or even just swap plugs. It is worth buying travel plugs before you leave as they are difficult to find in Italy. Most hotels with three or more stars have hairdriers and shaving points in all bedrooms, but check the voltage first, to be safe.

Standard Italian plug

BOOKING TICKETS

THEATRES IN ITALY do not generally take bookings over the telephone – you have to visit the box office in person. However, there are agencies, such as **Box Office** and **Virtours**, that will book tickets for you (for a fee). Opera tickets are sold months in advance, with just a few held back until two days before the performance. Tickets for rock and jazz concerts are also sold at some record shops whose names appear on the publicity posters.

TOURIST INFORMATION

THE NATIONAL tourist board, **ENIT**, has branches in capital cities worldwide and offers general information on Italy. For more specific requests, contact the local tourist offices. The addresses and telephone numbers are listed under each town or city, directly under the title, and they are plotted on the town and city maps. An EPT *(Ente Provinciale di Turismo)* has information on its town and surrounding province, whereas an APT *(Azienda di Promozione Turistica)* deals exclusively with individual towns. Both offices help with practical information such as hotel bookings and tours. They also provide free maps and guidebooks in various languages. The EPT and APT can refer you to local tour guides and advise on trips and excursions.

Small towns will have a *Pro Loco*, a tourist office run by the local administration, which is sometimes open only during the tourist season. It is usually located in the town hall *(comune)*.

TOURS

MANY TOUR COMPANIES organize coach trips, with English-speaking guides, that include all the main tourist attractions in Italy. American Express offices in Rome, Florence, Venice and

A guided group tour through the streets of Florence

A student relaxing in the sun in Gaiole in Chianti

Sign for tourist information

Milan organize local trips and **CIT** offers coach tours that go all over the country. If you are looking for something a little more personal and off the beaten track, check the local pages of national newspapers for tour groups or organizations. Local tourist boards will also be able to advise you. Always employ official guides and be sure to establish the fee in advance. For information on various specialist holidays, turn to pages 624–5.

SIGHTSEEING PERMITS

TO VISIT CERTAIN SITES in Rome, such as those which are not normally open to tourists, you need a written permit, which can be obtained from:

Comune di Roma Soprintendenze Comunale
Piazza Campitelli 7, Rome. **Map** 3 A5.
☎ 06 67 10 32 38. **FAX** 06 679 22 58.

SIGHTSEEING OPENING HOURS

ITALIAN MUSEUMS are gradually conforming to new regulations, particularly in the north, opening from 9am–7pm daily, except for two Mondays each month. In winter, however, many revert to 9am–1pm Tuesday to Saturday, and 9am–12:30pm on Sunday, but it is best to check. Privately run and smaller museums have their own times, so it is advisable to phone in advance. Archaeological sites are generally open from 9am to one

hour before sunset, Tuesday to Sunday. Churches are usually open from about 7am–12:30pm and 4–7pm. However, they often prefer not to let tourists in during services, so Sunday is not the best day to visit.

Daytime sightseeing on a tranquil canal in Venice

ADMISSION CHARGES

SIGHTSEEING FEES range from 2 to 7 euros. Churches are usually free, but some expect a donation, and you will need coins to illuminate works of art. Reductions for students are not always offered but many staterun museums and archaeological sites allow free entry for EU residents under 18 and over 60 years of age. Large groups are often entitled to a discount as well. If reductions are available, you will need to show a valid form of identification.

STUDENT INFORMATION

THE NATIONAL STUDENT travel organization, **CTS** (Centro Turistico Studentesco), has branches throughout Italy and

Europe. They issue the International Student Identity Card (ISIC) and the Youth International Educational Exchange Card (YIEE). Both can be used, along with a passport, for discounts at museums and other tourist attractions. The ISIC card also gives access to a 24-hour telephone helpline

ISIC card

that provides general advice and information. As well as issuing youth cards, CTS

offers cut-price car hire and will organize holidays and courses. For details about youth hostels, contact the **Associazione Italiana Alberghi per la Gioventù** (the Italian YHA), provided that you are a current member.

TRAVELLING WITH CHILDREN

O N THE WHOLE, Italians love children, to an extent that sometimes seems over-indulgent. Most trattorias and pizzerias welcome them and there are no rules excluding children from bars. Hotels also welcome children, but smaller establishments usually have limited facilities. Some of the more up-market hotels may offer a babysitting service. It is a common sight to see children playing outside fairly late at night, especially in summer. Most towns have playgrounds and many have summer funfairs. For young swimmers, the calm Mediterranean is ideal.

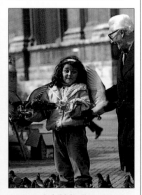

Fascinated child feeding pigeons at Piazza Navona, Rome

DISABLED TRAVELLERS

P UBLIC AWARENESS of the needs of the disabled is low, but improving. Some towns now have buses for the disabled and ramps and lifts are slowly being added to museums and some churches. **AIAS** (Associazione Italiana Assistenza Spastici) provides information on hotels, services and general assistance.

A mechanically operated wheelchair ramp across a bridge

RELIGIOUS SERVICES

A LMOST 85 PER CENT of the population is Catholic. Sunday mass is celebrated throughout the country, while in the principal churches services are also held during the week. In major cities some churches, such as the church of San Silvestro (Piazza San Silvestro) in Rome, offer services and confession in English. For some visitors, a trip to Rome will include an audience with the pope *(p409)*.

Although Italy is predominantly Catholic, all the main religious beliefs are represented. For details contact the main centres in Rome.

CONVERSION CHART

Imperial to Metric
1 inch = 2.54 centimetres
1 foot = 30 centimetres
1 mile = 1.6 kilometres
1 ounce = 28 grams
1 pound = 454 grams
1 pint = 0.57 litre
1 gallon = 4.6 litres

Metric to Imperial
1 centimetre = 0.4 inch
1 metre = 3 feet 3 inches
1 kilometre = 0.6 mile
1 gram = 0.04 ounce
1 kilogram = 2.2 pounds
1 litre = 1.8 pints

Personal Security and Health

Altthough Italy is generally a safe place for visitors, it is wise to keep a watchful eye on your personal belongings, especially in the larger towns and cities. There is a conspicuous police presence throughout the country, and in the event of an emergency or crime, any of the police officers described in this section will be able to assist you and tell you where to go to report an incident. If you fall ill, pharmacies are a good first stop where medically trained staff can give advice or tell you where to find further help. In an emergency, the Casualty Department (*Pronto Soccorso*) of any hospital will treat you.

Commissariato di Polizia – a police station

Police car

Green Cross ambulance in Venice

Roman fire engine

PERSONAL PROPERTY

Petty theft such as pick-pocketing, bag snatching and car theft is rife. In the event of a theft you must report it within 24 hours to the nearest *questura* or *commissariato* (police station).

Avoid leaving anything visible in an unattended car, including a car radio. If you have to leave luggage in a car, find a hotel that has private parking. When making a purchase, always check your change and do not keep wallets in back pockets, especially on buses or in other crowded places. "Bum bags" and money belts are a favourite target for pick-pockets, so try to keep them hidden. When walking, hold bags and cameras on the

inside of the pavement so as not to tempt motorized snatchers and do not show expensive cameras and video equipment in areas off tourist routes. The safest way to carry large sums of money is to use travellers' cheques. Try to keep your travellers' cheques and receipts separate, together with a photocopy of vital documents, in case of loss or theft. It is also advisable to get comprehensive travel insurance that covers theft of personal possessions in addition to covering cancellation/delay of flights, loss/damage of luggage, money and other valuables, as well as personal liability and accidents. If you do need to make an insurance claim for stolen or lost property, you must get a copy of the report (*denuncia*) from the police station when you report the incident. In case of lost passports, go to your embassy or consulate; for lost travellers' cheques, contact the issuing company's nearest office.

LEGAL ASSISTANCE

A comprehensive insurance package should include cover for legal assistance and advice. If you do not have insurance cover, contact your embassy as soon as possible after an incident, such as an accident, occurs. The embassy can offer advice and should

provide you with a list of English- and Italian-speaking lawyers who are knowledgeable about both the Italian and English legal systems.

PERSONAL SECURITY

Although petty crime in the cities is frequent, violent crime in Italy is rare. However, it is common for people to raise their voices aggressively during an argument. Usually, remaining calm and being polite will help to defuse the situation. Always be wary of unofficial tour guides, taxi drivers or strangers who wish to assist you or advise you on accommodation, restaurants or shops as they may expect something in return.

WOMEN TRAVELLERS

Women travelling on their own in Italy are likely to meet with a lot of attention. Although this is often more of an irritation than a danger, it is best to keep away from lonely, unlit streets and areas

A team of *carabinieri* in traffic police uniform

near railway stations at night. Walking quickly and purposefully is a good way to avoid any unwanted attention. The staff at hotels and restaurants generally treat their single female guests and customers with extra care and attention.

THE POLICE

THERE ARE SEVERAL different police forces in Italy and each one fulfils a particular role. The state police, *la polizia*, wear blue uniforms and drive blue cars. They deal with most crimes. The *carabinieri* are militarily trained and wear dark blue and black uniforms with red striped trousers. These officers deal with a variety of offences from organized crime to speeding and can also conduct random security checks. The *guardia di finanza* are the financial police force (the fraud squad), and wear grey uniforms with yellow striped trousers. The *vigili urbani*, or the municipal traffic police, wear blue and white uniforms in winter and white during the summer. Even though they are not official police officers, the *vigili urbani* can issue heavy fines for traffic and parking offences. They can usually be spotted patrolling the streets, enforcing laws or directing traffic. Officers from any of the forces will be able to help.

Municipal policeman

INTERPRETERS

INDEPENDENT INTERPRETERS and translators often advertise their services in newspapers and foreign-language bookshops. You will find agencies listed in the Yellow Pages (*Pagine Gialle*) and the AITI (*Associazione Italiana di Traduttori e Interpreti*) has a list of qualified translators and interpreters. In an emergency, your embassy will be able to provide an interpreter.

Outside a Florentine pharmacy with a green cross sign

MEDICAL TREATMENT

EMERGENCY MEDICAL care in Italy is free for all EU citizens. The E111 form, which is available from main post offices throughout the UK, covers emergencies only; private medical insurance is needed for all other types of treatment. The E111 comes with a booklet that contains general health advice and information about how to claim free medical treatment when travelling abroad. In order for the form to be valid, it has to be completed in full and stamped at a post office in the UK before your journey. Non-EU citizens should try to arrive in Italy with comprehensive private medical insurance to cover all eventualities. If you do need emergency treatment, go to the *Pronto Soccorso* (Casualty Department) of the nearest hospital.

No inoculations are needed for Italy, but mosquito repellent is advisable in summer. Repelling creams and sprays can be found in pharmacies, and electrical devices can be bought which burn tablets.

EMERGENCY SUPPLIES

VARIOUS MEDICAL products, including homeopathic medicines, are available in any pharmacy (*farmacia*), but a prescription is often required. Thanks to a night rota (*servizio notturno*), there is always a pharmacy open in all cities and most towns.

Those that are open at night are listed in the local pages of daily newspapers and on all pharmacy doors.

Tabacchi (tobacco) shops are a good source of many useful supplies and are easily recognized by their "T" signs (see below). Apart from tobacco, cigarettes and matches, you can buy razors and batteries, bus and metro tickets, telephone cards and parking cards. At some, you can also purchase postage stamps and get parcels weighed and costed.

A Tabacchi shop, with its characteristic white "T" sign

Banking and Local Currency

Virtually all Italian hotels, many shops, large restaurants and petrol stations now accept major credit cards. Only in the more off-the-beaten-track locations will you have difficulties without euros. When you pay with a credit card, you might be asked to show identification, such as your passport. Foreign currency can be changed in banks, although these are often crowded and service tends to be slow. All banks will cash travellers' cheques and cashpoint machines *(bancomat)* will accept cards with a PIN number. Most machines also accept MasterCard (Access), VISA and American Express cards. Although banks often have the best exchange rates, bureaux de change and foreign exchange machines can be more convenient.

Electronic exchange machine

Cash dispenser which also accepts
VISA and MasterCard (Access)

CHANGING MONEY

Banking hours are somewhat restrictive and can also be slightly erratic so it is safest to acquire some local currency before you arrive in Italy. Exchange rates will vary from place to place.

Once you arrive, the most convenient way to change money is to use the electronic exchange machines, which are located at all major airports, train stations and banks. The machines have multilingual instructions and the exchange rate is clearly displayed on the screen. You simply feed in notes of the same foreign currency and you will receive euros in return.

Bureaux de change can be found in all main towns. Although they are easier to use, they tend to have higher exchange rates and charge more commission than banks.

TRAVELLERS' CHEQUES

Travellers' cheques are the safest way to carry large sums of money. Choose a well-known name such as Thomas Cook or American Express. There is a minimum commission charge, which makes changing small sums of money uneconomical. Check the exchange rates before you travel and decide whether sterling, dollar or euro travellers' cheques are more appropriate. Euro travellers' cheques may be difficult to cash because it is not very profitable for the exchanger.

REGIONAL DIFFERENCES IN COST OF LIVING

The north is generally more expensive than the south, but there are many exceptions. Restaurants and hotels off the beaten track are usually better value, and buying locally made produce is cost effective if you avoid obvious tourist traps.

Metal-detecting security doors
found at most banks

BANKING HOURS

Banks are usually open between 8:30am and 1:30pm, Monday to Friday. Most also open for an hour in the afternoon, from about 2:15pm to 3pm or 2:30pm until 3:30pm, depending on the bank. All banks close at weekends and for public holidays, and they also close early the day before a major holiday. Bureaux de change however, are often open all day, and in some places, also late at night.

USING BANKS

For security purposes, most banks have electronic double doors with metal detectors, allowing one person in at a time. Metal objects and bags should first be deposited in lockers situated in the foyer. Press the button to open the outer door, then wait for it to close behind you. The inner door then opens automatically. Do not be alarmed by the heavily armed guards that patrol most banks in Italy.

Changing money at a bank can be a frustrating process involving endless form-filling and queuing. First you have to go to the window that displays the *cambio* sign and then to the *cassa* to obtain your money. If in doubt, ask someone in order to avoid waiting in the wrong queue.

If you need to have money sent to you in Italy, banks at home can telex money to an Italian bank, but it takes about a week. American Express, Thomas Cook and Western Union all provide swifter money transfer services, with a charge to the sender.

THE EURO

TWELVE COUNTRIES have replaced their traditional currencies with a single European currency, the euro. Austria, Belgium, Finland, France, Germany, Greece, Ireland, Italy, Luxembourg, Netherlands, Portugal and Spain chose to join the new currency; the UK, Denmark and Sweden stayed out, with an option to review their situation. The euro was introduced on 1 January 1999, but only for banking purposes. Notes and coins came into circulation on 1 January 2002. A transition period has allowed euros and lire to be used simultaneously, with lire phased out by mid-2002 (there may be local variations). All euro notes and coins can be used anywhere inside the participating member states.

Bank Notes

Euro bank notes have seven denominations. The 5-euro note (grey in colour) is the smallest, followed by the 10-euro note (pink), 20-euro note (blue), 50-euro note (orange), 100-euro note (green), 200-euro note (yellow) and 500-euro note (purple). All notes show the 12 stars of the European Union.

5 euros

10 euros

20 euros

50 euros

100 euros

200 euros

500 euros

2 euros

1 euro

50 cents

20 cents

10 cents

Coins

The euro has eight coin denominations: 1 euro and 2 euros; 50 cents, 20 cents, 10 cents, 5 cents, 2 cents and 1 cent. The 2- and 1-euro coins are both silver and gold in colour. The 50-, 20- and 10-cent coins are gold. The 5-, 2- and 1-cent coins are bronze.

5 cents

2 cents

1 cent

Communications

ALTHOUGH THE ITALIAN POSTAL service is known for being very slow, Italy's other forms of communication, at least in the cities, are more efficient. Fax machines, courier services and telephones are all widespread, and Internet points are available throughout Italy. Foreign-language newspapers and magazines are on sale in all cities and most large towns. Both state-run and privately owned television stations exist, but only satellite television and radio stations broadcast foreign-language programmes.

Telephone company logo

PUBLIC TELEPHONES

THE ITALIAN NATIONAL telephone company is Telecom Italia. Coin-operated telephones are being phased out and replaced by new, card-operated machines. The latest public telephones have instructions in five languages (Italian, English, French, Spanish and German). To select a language, push the top right-hand button. Although some telephones will take both cards and coins, most only accept a Telecom credit card.

Telephone sign

Phone cards (*carta* or *scheda telefonica*) can be purchased from bars, newspaper kiosks, post offices and *tabacchi* displaying the black-and-white T sign. When making long-distance or international calls from a coin-operated phone, make sure you have plenty of change at hand. If you don't put enough coins in to start with, you will be disconnected and the phone will retain your money. An alternative is to look for a *telefono a scatti*, or metered phone. These can be found in bars and restaurants, as well as in specially designated phone centres. You will be assigned a metered phone and pay at the end of your call. Although no premium is charged, it is wise to check the rate before making a call. Prices tend to be fairly reasonable.

International phone cards, on sale at *tabacchi* and newsstands, are still the cheapest way to call abroad. Some cards offer as many as 3 hours of calls for about 10 euros, depending on the country being called. Dial the toll-free number on the card and then enter the secret code found by scratching off the silver strip on the back of the card. You will be told the amount of credit available and then asked to dial the number you wish to call.

E-MAIL

E-MAIL IS A CONVENIENT way to keep in touch with friends and family when travelling through Italy. Telecom Italia, the Italian national phone company, is setting up Internet services in the country's major train stations and public phone centres. Time is purchased using a regular phone card.

Some major chains of Internet points sell magnetic cards with credit that can be used in any of their stores throughout Italy. **Internet Train**, with branches in 25 cities, is the most visible. Visit its website for a full list of stores.

In addition, small Internet points abound (usually clustered around train stations and university areas) and users can buy computer time in blocks as short as 15 minutes. There are usually student discounts available, and cost per minute decreases as the amount of time purchased increases.

Internet Train
W www.internettrain.it

USING A TELECOM ITALIA CARD TELEPHONE

1 Lift the receiver and wait for the dialling tone.

2 Insert a phone card in the slot.

3 The display shows how much credit is left.

4 Dial the number and wait to be connected.

5 If you still have credit and want to make a second call, press the "follow-on call" button.

To use a card, break off the marked corner and insert, arrow first.

DIRECTORY

To calculate the cost of a call from a private phone, dial * 40 # before and after the call and the number of units will be read to you.

Remember to always use the full area code (including the first zero), even when phoning within a city.

USEFUL NUMBERS

Directory Enquiries
📞 *12.*

International Directory Enquiries
📞 *176.*

Italcable
📞 *170 (for reverse charge and calling card calls).*

British Operator
📞 *172 00 44.*

American Operators
📞 *172 10 11 (AT&T).*
📞 *172 10 22 (MCI Worldphone).*
📞 *172 18 77 (Sprint).*

Australian Operators
📞 *172 10 61 (Telstra).*
📞 *172 11 61 (Optus).*

COUNTRY CODES

To call Italy from these countries dial the code and then the full area code (including 0) and the number.

📞 *00 39 – UK*
📞 *0 1139 – US & Canada*
📞 *00 39 – Ireland*
📞 *00 1139 – Australia*

TV AND RADIO

TELEVISION CHANNELS in Italy include the state-owned RAI (Uno, Due and Tre) and Fininvest (Retequattro, Canale Cinque and Italia Uno). There are also many local channels. Most foreign programmes are dubbed into Italian, although satellite channels, such as Sky, CNN and RTL, show news and sports programmes in a variety of languages. There are three national radio stations and hundreds of local stations. The BBC World Service is on 17640 and 15485 kHz (short wave) during the day and 648 kHz (medium wave) day and night.

NEWSPAPERS

THE MAIN NATIONAL daily newspapers are *La Stampa, Il Corriere della Sera* and *La Repubblica.* Papers with the most detailed news of Italy's major cities include *Il Mattino* for Naples, *Il Messaggero* for Rome, *La Nazione* for Florence and *Il Giornale* for Milan.

All newspapers have local pages and listings for cinemas, theatres, main concerts and other cultural events. In Rome and Milan, *La Repubblica* also publishes regular "what's on and where to go" supplements called *TrovaRoma* and *ViviMilano.* Florence's *Firenze Spettacolo* and Rome's *Roma C'è* are weekly entertainment listings magazines. *Time Out Rome* offers the same type of information at monthly intervals.

British and American papers, such as the *International Herald Tribune, International Guardian,* and *USA Today,* are readily available and tend to arrive in the main cities at around midday on the day of issue.

POST OFFICE

POST OFFICES AND also some tobacconists weigh and price letters and sell stamps. Local post offices open from 8:25am–1:50pm weekdays, and from 8:25am–12 noon on Saturday. Main post offices are open from 8:25am–7pm non-stop.

The Vatican City and the state of San Marino have their own postal system and stamps. Bear in mind that letters bearing San Marino or Vatican stamps can only be posted in San Marino and Vatican post boxes.

Letters and postcards destined for Europe cost the same as post within Italy.

City letters   **Other destinations**

Italian post box

Post Office sign

The red post boxes (blue in the Vatican) usually have two slots labelled *per la città* (for the city only) and *tutte le altre destinazioni* (for all other destinations).

Italian post is notorious for its unreliability and letters can take between four days and two weeks to arrive. The postal service is particularly slow in August, when delivery can take up to a month.

For a faster service, send letters express *(posta priori-taria).* More reliable is recorded delivery *(raccoman-data)* and recorded delivery with an arrival receipt *(raccomandata con ricevuta di ritorno).* However, anything of value should be sent by insured post *(assicurata).*

For urgent communications, try state couriers *Posta celere* and *Cai post,* which are based at all main post offices. They guarantee delivery within 24–72 hours and are far cheaper than private couriers. Main post offices also provide telegram and fax services. The fax service, however, is not available for certain countries.

Post offices also provide a *fermo posta* service (poste restante) for a small collection fee. Send letters to the central post office, c/o Fermo Posta. You will need to show some identification (such as your passport) when collecting your mail.

REGIONS OF ITALY

ITALY CONSISTS OF 20 regions that are divided into provinces. Each province has a *capoluogo* (an administrative capital) and a *sigla,* the initials of the capital. For example, FI stands for the *capoluogo* of Florence *(Firenze).* The *sigla* appears on car licence plates registered before 1994 and denotes the origins of the vehicle owner. The code can also be used to address mail, appearing after the town name.

Shopping

ITALY IS KNOWN FOR ITS QUALITY designer goods, ranging from chic clothing and sleek cars to stylish household items. There is a strong tradition of craftsmanship, often from family-run businesses, and there are numerous markets selling regional specialities. Apart from the town markets, it is not a country for bargains, but the joys of window shopping will offer plenty of compensation.

Fresh vegetables on display at a Florentine market stall

OPENING HOURS

OPENING TIMES for shops are usually 9:30am–1pm and around 3:30–8pm, Tuesday to Saturday and Monday afternoons. However, shopkeepers are increasingly working to more flexible hours. There are not that many large department stores, but most large towns will have a Standa, Upim and perhaps a Coin or Rinascente. These stores are often open non-stop (orario continuato) from 9am–8pm, Monday to Saturday. Boutiques generally open later; music and bookshops sometimes stay open after 8pm and on Sundays.

FOOD SHOPS

EVEN THOUGH there are supermarkets throughout Italy, the specialist shops, although more expensive, are still the most interesting way to shop. A forno has the best bread and a macellaio has the finest meat (go to a norcineria for pork products). Vegetables are freshest from market stalls or the fruttivendolo. You can buy cakes at the pasticceria, milk at the latteria, and pasta, ham, cheese and general foods at the often impressively stocked alimentari. Here you can also buy wine, but for a wider choice, head for the enoteca, vineria or vinaio, where you can sometimes taste the wine before purchasing.

MARKETS

ALL TOWNS HAVE regional markets that take place each week. Large towns will have several small daily markets followed by a weekly flea market, usually held on a Sunday. In this guide the main market days are listed under each town. Traders set up at 5am and start to clear away at about 1:30pm. Food is sold by the etto (100 grams) and the chilo (kilo) (see p615), or in numbers (two onions, etc). Food stalls selling seasonal products generally have fresher and less expensive produce than the shops. Bargaining is not usually done when buying food, but it is worth asking for a discount (sconto) for clothes and other items.

Protective bag with designer label

SEASONAL PRODUCE

TO MAKE THE MOST of Italian food, try to buy and eat what is in season. Grapes and mushrooms are best in autumn, whereas spring is the season for asparagus, strawberries and Roman artichokes. In winter, vegetables such as cauliflower and broccoli are at their best, as are lemons from Amalfi and Sicilian blood oranges. Summer is the time for plums, pears and cherries, as well as courgettes, aubergines, tomatoes and melon.

CLOTHES AND DESIGNER SHOPS

ITALY IS RENOWNED worldwide for its fashion industry. Milan is the fashion capital and Via Monte Napoleone, in the city centre, is lined with designer boutiques. All large towns will have a selection of designer shops, usually situated near each other. Less expensive clothes are available in markets and many high-street shops, where the styles tend to be more conventional.

Souvenir shop in Ostuni, near Brindisi, Puglia

Italy is also famous for leather shoes and bags, the prices of which tend to be reasonable.

Sales *(saldi)* are held in summer and winter. Second-hand shops can be expensive, but the quality and condition of the clothes are usually very good. Larger markets have stalls piled high with used clothes. Rummage through and you will often find bargains. Many markets sell fake Ray Ban sunglasses, Lacoste T-shirts and Levi's jeans. Some shops have signs that read *ingresso libero* (browsers welcome), but do not be surprised if a sales assistant approaches you as soon as you walk in.

An elegant designer clothes boutique in Treviso

There are household shops in cities and towns throughout the country. Italian kitchen-ware is particularly striking, with its stainless steel and copper pots, pans and utensils. For the lowest prices, avoid the tourist shops and, if possible, buy directly from the manufacturer. Less expensive items include the characteristic brown espresso and cappuccino cups sold in all markets.

REGIONAL SPECIALITIES

MANY OF ITALY's regional specialities are world famous: Parma ham, Chianti wine, olive oil and *grappa*. Regional sweets, including the Sienese *panforte* and Sicilian marzipan, are also well-known, as are cheeses such as Gorgonzola from Lombardy and Parmesan from Emilia-

Romagna. Traditional crafts are still practised in Italy and range from delicate lacework and glassware in the Veneto to leatherwork, jewellery and marbled paper in Florence. Italian ceramics include elaborate Tuscan pottery, hand-painted dishes around Amalfi and De Simone's stylized designer plates from Sicily.

Display of decorative glazed pottery from Tuscany

Colourful shop display of leather handbags in Florence

JEWELLERY AND ANTIQUE SHOPS

GLITZY GOLD JEWELLERY is very popular in Italy and every *gioielleria* (jewellery shop) will have a wide selection. For more unusual items, try the *bigiotteria* or artisan shops *(oreficeria)*. Antique stores like *Antichità* and *Antiquariato* sell furniture and ornaments of varying quality and prices. You will rarely find bargains in Italy, except perhaps at the *Fiere dell'Antiquariato* (antique fairs), held throughout the year all over the country.

INTERIOR DESIGN AND HOUSEHOLD WARES

INTERIOR DESIGN is another Italian sector where top names demand extravagant prices, with many shops concentrating on modern, high-tech styles.

SIZE CHART

For Australian sizes follow the British and American conversions.

Women's dresses, coats and skirts

Italian	38	40	42	44	46	48	50
British	8	10	12	14	16	18	20
American	6	8	10	12	14	16	18

Women's shoes

Italian	36	37	38	39	40	41
British	3	4	5	6	7	8
American	5	6	7	8	9	10

Men's suits

Italian	44	46	48	50	52	54	56	58 (size)
British	34	36	38	40	42	44	46	48 (inches)
American	34	36	38	40	42	44	46	48 (inches)

Men's shirts (collar size)

Italian	36	38	39	41	42	43	44	45 (cm)
British	14	15	15½	16	16½	17	17½	18 (inches)
American	14	15	15½	16	16½	17	17½	18 (inches)

Men's shoes

Italian	39	40	41	42	43	44	45	46
British	6	7	7½	8	9	10	11	12
American	7	7½	8	8½	9½	10½	11	11½

Specialist Holidays and Outdoor Activities

**Exploring the country-
side on horseback**

ITALY OFFERS AN AMAZING variety of cultural, sporting and leisure activities. However, many schools and groups require annual membership and short-term activities are often expensive and difficult to find. Information on current leisure and sporting events in a specific region is available from the tourist office listed for each town in this guide. For details on annual festivals, see *Italy Through the Year* on pages 62–5. The following suggestions include some of the most popular as well as some more unusual pursuits.

**Cycling on the tree-lined flatlands
of the Po Delta**

WALKING, CYCLING AND HORSERIDING

SOME ITALIAN BRANCHES of the World Wide Fund for Nature (WWF) organize walks and treks. **Club Alpino Italiano (CAI)** runs trekking and climbing excursions and the **Italian Birds Protection League (LIPU)** arranges nature walks and bird-watching trips. The military *IGM* maps are the most detailed but unfortunately are only available from specialist map shops.

Cycling is popular despite Italy's mountainous landscape. Travel bookshops stock publications with suggested routes, such as the Po Delta, which has miles of scenic flatlands.

Many riding schools organize trips and outings, which are also advertised in the local press. For general information, contact the **Federazione Italiana di Sport Equestre**.

MOUNTAIN SPORTS

THE MOST WELL-EQUIPPED and famous ski resorts are in the Dolomites, in the Italian Alps and around Turin, the city which will host the 2006 Winter Olympics. There are also smaller and less expensive resorts in the Apennines and in Sicily. Package ski holidays, arranged from outside Italy, offer the best deals. The **Federazione Arrampicata Sportiva Italiana** has a list of mountain climbing schools that arrange climbs for all levels.

**Ski lift near the desolate Falzarego
Pass, in the heart of the Dolomites**

ARCHAEOLOGICAL DIGS

THE BRITISH MONTHLY magazine *Archaeology Abroad*, available in the UK, gives a comprehensive list of archaeology groups and digs worldwide. In Italy, the **Gruppo Archeologico Romano** runs two-week digs in various regions. There are summer and winter digs, for both adults and children. The group has contacts with local archaeological organizations as well.

ITALIAN LANGUAGE AND CULTURE

FOR A WIDE SELECTION of material on courses and schools in Italy, contact the Italian consulate in your home country. The **Società Dante Alighieri** provides courses in the Italian language, history of art, literature and culture. There are both full- and part-time courses available, for every level. Language schools abound in Italy's main cities and are advertised in the Yellow Pages (*Pagine Gialle*) or foreign language bookshops and newspapers. For young students, **Intercultura** will organize weekly, monthly and year-long exchanges including language courses, accommodation with Italian families and enrolment in Italian schools.

Group hiking tour in the Dolomites of Trentino-Alto Adige (see p78)

A lesson in Italian cookery in Sicily

In recent years, cooking holidays run by English-speaking experts in Italian cooking have become very popular. **Tasting Places**, for example, does wine tours and week-long courses in Italian cuisine, and provides beautiful private accommodation. The course locations include the Veneto, Sicily, Tuscany and Umbria. Wine-tasting tours are organized by local tourist boards. The Università per Stranieri in Perugia runs courses on Italian culture, history and cooking.

WATER SPORTS

MOST LAKES AND many seaside resorts rent out sailing boats, canoes and windsurfing equipment. Lessons and courses are organized by clubs, which usually require membership. For a list of authorized associations contact the **Federazione Italiana di Canoa e Kayak** and the **Federazione Italiana di Vela**. Weekend and weekly sailing holidays and courses are featured in the magazine *Avventure nel Mondo* and most travel agents have a selection of sailing holidays.

Swimming pools are expensive in Italy and many do not accept people on a daily basis. You often have to pay a membership fee and a monthly tariff. Some of the luxurious hotels open their pools to the public in summer, but at pricy rates. Water parks are popular and provide pools, slides, wave machines and games. Before diving into any lakes or rivers (and even the sea near main towns) it is best to check that the water is not polluted. The **Federazione Italiana di**

Attività Subacquee runs underwater diving courses, and can give information on all local centres.

AIR SPORTS

THERE ARE SCHOOLS nationwide that offer hang-gliding and flying courses, but the minimum duration of each course is one month. For information and a list of schools contact **Aeroclub d'Italia**. You must be licensed before you can fly and all crafts must be registered with the Aeroclub.

OTHER SPORTS

GOLF IS A POPULAR sport in Italy and there are plenty of courses to choose from. Home membership and handicap are often required for daily access to a club.

Italian tennis clubs usually operate on a membership basis, unless you are invited as a member's guest. The national **Federazione Italiana di Tennis** has a list of all the tennis clubs in Italy. Football is an Italian obsession and you will see friendly, noisy games in action in every park, beach or open space. It is possible to rent five-a-side courts at most sports centres, but for a more relaxed game you can get a group of friends together or join in with other people.

Sailing in Italy, a popular leisure activity and competitive sport

TRAVEL INFORMATION

ITALY HAS TRANSPORT SYSTEMS of varying efficiency, from the modern road, bus and rail networks of the north to the slower and more antiquated systems of the south. Numerous airlines operate flights to several of the country's major airports, while within Italy itself the national carrier Alitalia, and several smaller companies, provide an extensive network of internal flights.

Alitalia aircraft

Connections by road to the rest of Europe are good, though Alpine roads can be adversely affected by the weather. Motorways and other roads within the country are generally good, but can be busy at weekends and peak periods. Italy also has an efficient system of ferries connecting Sicily, Sardinia and many of the smaller off-shore islands. Many of these are car ferries, and are busy in summer.

Arriving by Air

ROME'S LEONARDO DA VINCI (Fiumicino) and Milan's Malpensa are the key airports for long-haul flights into Italy. Milan's Linate airport handles some European flights, and most European airlines also fly to Venice, Turin, Naples and Pisa (for Florence). Many airlines are now flying regularly to smaller cities such as Florence, Genoa, Bologna, Verona and Bergamo, while charter flights serve summer destinations in peak season such as Catania, Olbia and Rimini.

Part of the extension to Fiumicino airport, Rome

LONG-HAUL FLIGHTS

IF YOU ARE FLYING from the United States, TWA, Delta, Continental and United Airlines operate regular direct scheduled flights to Rome, with services from New York, Washington, Los Angeles, Boston and Chicago. Canadian Airlines flies from Montreal and Toronto, and Qantas flies from Sydney and Melbourne.

A regular service between Rome and New York, San Francisco, Los Angeles, Boston, Chicago, Montreal, Toronto and Sydney is also offered by the Italian state airline, Alitalia.

It may, however, be more convenient and cheaper for long-haul passengers to take a budget flight to London,

Frankfurt, Paris, Athens or Amsterdam and then continue with their journey to Italy (by aeroplane or train) from there.

EUROPEAN FLIGHTS

IT HAS NEVER been so easy to get to Italy by air. **British Airways** and **KLM-Alitalia** and its partners fly to Rome and Milan from most major European cities and other, often low-cost, "no-frills" airlines now offer flights to all parts of Italy from London and other UK cities. (For Sicily's two major cities, Palermo and Catania, a change of flight at one of the mainland airports may be necessary.)

BMI british midland flies to Rome and Milan from

Heathrow; Meridiana serves Florence and Cagliari from Gatwick; **Ryanair** flies to seven airports (including Genoa, Turin and Venice-Treviso) from Stansted; and **Go**, also from Stansted, serves Rome-Ciampino, Milan, Bologna, Venice and Naples, and also Rome from Bristol.

TICKETS AND FARES

FARES VARY enormously according to season and supply and demand. You can usually get the best deals by booking well in advance, especially if you are planning to travel around Christmas time or in the summer.

Consult a good travel agent or check availability on the Internet. If you are based in the UK, it may be worthwhile to scour the small ads of newspapers for charter and discounted scheduled flights on major routes.

AIRPORT
Rome (Fiumicino)
Rome (Ciampino)
Milan (Linate)
Milan (Malpensa)
Pisa (Galileo Galilei)
Venice (Marco Polo)
Venice (Treviso)

The entrance hall at Pisa airport

Most charters leave from Gatwick or Luton, and may land at a city's second (and often less convenient) airport. Fares tend to vary greatly during the year, but the most expensive periods are during the summer months and over the Christmas and Easter holidays. Where possible ask for available student discounts.

Shuttle bus to car hire lots at Fiumicino

PACKAGE HOLIDAYS

Package holidays to Italy are usually cheaper than travelling independently, unless you are travelling on a tight budget and are prepared to make use of youth hostels and campsites. Rome, Florence and Venice are often offered as separate or linked package deals, and many operators have packages to the Tuscan and Umbrian countryside, Sicily, the Italian Lakes, the Italian Riviera, Naples and the Amalfi coast. In winter, ski packages are available to many Alpine resorts. Specialist packages, such as cooking, walking and art tours, are becoming increasingly common. In cities, different tour operators may use different hotels, so it is worth shopping around for the most pleasant (and centrally located) hotels. Many operators include transfers from the airport to your hotel. Some will include a tour guide.

FLY-DRIVE DEALS

Many travel agents and car hire firms will organize special fly-drive packages that enable you to book a flight and have a hire car waiting for you at your destination.

This is usually cheaper and involves fewer formalities than renting a car on arrival. Most major car hire firms such as Hertz, Avis and Budget (and many minor ones as well) have offices located at the major Italian airports.

DIRECTORY

AIRLINES

Alitalia
Toll-free numbers within Italy:

Domestic flights:
📞 1478 656 41.
International flights:
📞 1478 656 42.
Information:
📞 1478 656 43.
🌐 www.alitalia.it

BMI british midland
🌐 www.flybmi.com

British Airways
📞 848 81 22 66.
🌐 www.britishairways.com

Canadian Airlines
📞 800 86 22 16.
🌐 www.cdnair.ca

Go
🌐 www.go-fly.com

Qantas
🌐 www.qantas.com

Ryanair
🌐 www.ryanair.com

TWA
📞 800 84 18 43.
🌐 www.twa.com

 ← (quayside)

The quayside at Venice's Marco Polo airport

INFORMATION	DISTANCE TO CITY CENTRE	TAXI FARE TO CITY CENTRE	PUBLIC TRANSPORT TO CITY CENTRE
📞 06 65 95 44 55	35 km (22 miles)	45 euros	🚆 30 mins
📞 06 79 49 41	15 km (9 miles)	40 euros	🚌 Ⓜ 50 mins
📞 02 28 10 63 06	10 km (6 miles)	12–16 euros	🚌 20 mins
📞 02 26 80 06 13	40 km (25 miles)	50–62 euros	🚌 1 hr
✈ 050 50 07 07	2 km (1 mile)	10 euros	🚆 to Pisa: 5 mins / 🚆 to Florence: 1 hr
✈ 041 260 92 60	13 km (8 miles)	70 euros by Water Taxi	🚤 90 mins / 🚌 20 mins
✈ 0422 31 51 11	30 km (18 miles)	50 euros to Venice	🚌 to Treviso: 20 mins / 🚌 to Venice: 30 mins

Arriving by Sea, Rail and Road

Orient-Express logo

Do-it-yourself help points with train information on screens

ITALY IS SERVED BY AN EXTENSIVE network of roads, railways and international ferry lines. Road and rail links cross into the country from France, Switzerland, Austria and Slovenia, and there are through train services from as far afield as Moscow, London and Barcelona. Road connections into the country are generally of motorway standard, though delays can occur at some of the many Alpine passes and tunnels during bad weather or peak summer holiday periods.

Ticket windows at Florence's Santa Maria Novella station

ARRIVING BY CAR

MOST ROADS into Italy from the rest of Europe involve Alpine crossings by tunnel or mountain passes. The notable exceptions are the approach from Slovenia in the northeast (on the A4 motorway) and the route along the French Riviera that enters Italy as the A10 motorway at Ventimiglia.

The most popular route from Geneva and southeast France is via the Mont Blanc tunnel (due to reopen in 2002) and A5 motorway, entering Italy close to Aosta and Turin. Another busy approach (from Switzerland) uses the St Bernard Pass and tunnel.

Further east, the main route from Austria and southern Germany crosses the Brenner Pass and goes down to Verona on the A22 motorway via Trento and the Adige valley. Weather conditions rarely close the passes, but snow and fog can make progress slow on the winding roads through the mountains. Most motorways are toll-roads; you pay as you exit the motorway.

ARRIVING BY TRAIN

AFTER AIR TRAVEL, arriving by train is the least painful way to reach Italy. Countless through services (including many sleepers) link Italian towns and cities with places as far afield as Brussels, Moscow and Barcelona. Connections from Paris (and London, via Eurostar) run to Turin, Milan, Venice, Bologna, Florence or along Italy's west coast, via Genoa and Pisa, to Rome and Naples. Services also operate from German, Swiss and other northern

BINARIO 17

Platform sign

Exit sign

The sleeping car on an international Eurocity train

European cities to Milan, Turin, Venice and Verona. There are also direct services from Vienna, Spain and the south of France. Motorail connections exist from several centres in northern Europe and the Channel ports.

The increased popularity of low-fares airlines has made international train travel a less convenient option. Special discount fares, however, are often available for senior travellers and for people under 26. Trains can be extremely busy during peak periods, particularly on Friday and Sunday evenings, and during the Christmas and Easter holiday periods. July and August can also be frantically busy, especially on routes from Germany and ports connecting with Greek ferries in the south. Reservations on most services are inexpensive and advisable.

ARRIVING BY BOAT

MOST PEOPLE arriving in Italy by boat do so from Greece, which is linked by services from Corfu and Patras to Brindisi and other ports in southeast Italy. Services are particularly crowded in the summer months, as are the connecting train services from Brindisi to the rest of Italy.

Other international ferry connections include boats from Malta, Tunisia and other North African ports to Palermo, Naples and various southern Italian ports. Boats also run from towns in the south of France to Genoa, Livorno and ports on the Italian Riviera.

ARRIVING BY COACH

COACH TRAVEL to Italy is relatively cheap (though often not much cheaper than trains), but long journey times make it one of the least comfortable ways to travel. Some coach companies have now introduced plane-coach deals, whereby you can travel by coach on one leg of your trip and by air on the other. At the moment there are thrice-weekly services in summer from the UK to Turin, Milan, Bologna and Rome. The journey time from London to Milan is about 27 hours, and about 36 hours to Rome. A night on the road is thus unavoidable. **National Express Eurolines** runs weekly coaches from London's Victoria Coach Station to all of Italy's major cities as far as Rome. Buses travel via Dover, Calais, Paris and Lyon and it

SITA coach arriving at the station in Florence

is useful to take some French francs with you for the probable stops en route.

Travelling Around by Ferry

ITALY'S LARGE NUMBER of off-shore islands mean that it has a large and well-developed network of ferries, as well as services to the rest of Europe and North Africa.

One of the Moby Lines car ferries that sail the Mediterranean

FERRIES

CAR FERRIES are a convenient link with the beautiful islands scattered off the Italian mainland. Boats for Sardinia leave from Civitavecchia (north of Rome), Livorno and Genoa, and depart for Sicily from Naples and Reggio di Calabria. Ferries run from the major Sicilian ports to the Egadi and the Aeolian archipelagoes, as well as to countless other small islands around Sicily (although ferries to the smaller islands do not always carry cars).

Boats also ply between Elba and Piombino, as well as the smaller islands of the Tuscan archipelago such as Capraia. Ferries run from ports close to Rome to Ponza and its surrounding islands, and from Naples to Capri and Ischia. On the east coast the Tremiti islands are linked to ports on the Gargano peninsula.

Hydrofoils are increasingly complementing conventional ferries, particularly on the busy routes to Capri and Ischia.

Queues are common in summer, and you should book well ahead if you wish to travel to Sardinia in July or August, especially if taking a vehicle. Bookings can often be made through travel agents, as well as in a ferry line's agents in your own country.

For an up-to-date schedule, visit the relevant website.

ROUTE	FERRY COMPANY	TELEPHONE INFORMATION
Piombino – Elba	Moby Lines ⓦ www.mobylines.it	ℂ 0565 22 52 11 (Piombino) ℂ 0565 93 61 (Portoferraio)
Civitavecchia – Cagliari	Sardinia Ferries ⓦ www.sardiniaferries.com	ℂ 0766 50 07 14 (Civitavecchia)
Genoa – Sardinia	Tirrenia ⓦ www.tirrenia.it	ℂ 070 66 60 65 (Cagliari) ℂ 0789 20 71 06 (Olbia) ℂ 010 269 81 (Genoa)
Livorno – Sardinia	Moby Lines Sardinia Ferries	ℂ 0789 279 27 (Olbia) ℂ 019 21 55 11 (bookings)
Genoa/Livorno – Palermo	Grandi Navi Veloci ⓦ www.forti.it/grandinavi	ℂ 091 58 74 04 (Palermo)
Naples – Palermo	Tirrenia	ℂ 091 602 12 14 (Palermo)
Naples – Cagliari	Tirrenia	ℂ 070 66 60 65 (Cagliari)

Travelling Around by Train

FS Logo

TRAIN TRAVEL is one of the best ways to explore Italy. Tickets are inexpensive, services frequent, and rolling stock some of the most modern in Europe. Services can be busy, but the days of rampant overcrowding are mostly over. Lines often run through lovely countryside, from mountain lakes to rolling plateaux, and they provide more convenient links between cities than roads or air travel. Only in the south, or deeply rural areas, are services slow and infrequent.

A Eurostar– Italy's fastest train

The concourse at Stazione Termini, Rome

THE NETWORK

THE BULK OF ITALY'S rail network is an integrated state-run system operated by the Ferrovie dello Stato (FS). A few privately run lines fill crucial gaps left by the FS, but through tickets are generally available where travel involves both networks. FS and private lines often (but not always) share the same main station *(stazione)*, and also charge similar fares.

TRAINS

THE FS IS in the process of changing the categories of trains, but in practice the same broad divisions will continue to apply. The fast Eurostar and a handful of other special high-speed trains almost always require pre-booking of seats. Intercity (IC) trains and Eurocity (EC) trains only stop at major stations and require the payment of a first- or second-class supplement *(un supplemento)* on top of the standard ticket (supplements can be bought on the train, but are more expensive). *Espresso* (Espr) and *Diretto* (Dir) trains make more stops and require no supplement (you may also find

these trains called *Regionali* and *Interregionali*). *Locali* stop at all stations.

Rolling stock has improved in recent years, especially on Intercity trains, which are now usually modern and air-conditioned. Branch line carriages can still be ancient. Facilities for the disabled exist on many Intercity trains.

FS train in Verona station

TICKETS AND FARES

TICKETS (BIGLIETTI) are available as single *(andata)* or return *(andata e ritorno)* in first *(prima)* or second class *(seconda classe)*. They can be bought at some travel agents or at any station ticket office *(la biglietteria)*. Automatic ticket machines are being introduced, and you can also

buy tickets for journeys of up to 250 km (155 miles) from newsstands or station tobacconists (such a ticket is called *biglietto a fascia chilometrica*). Be sure to validate all tickets on both outbound and return journeys, or you will be fined. A ticket's validity usually starts on the day of purchase, so be sure to specify the day of travel when buying tickets in advance. The fares are calculated on a kilometric basis and are among the cheapest in western Europe. Return fares offer a 15 per cent discount on trips of up to 250 km (155 miles).

Refunds involve a complicated process and are very difficult to obtain. It is important, therefore, to buy the correct ticket before travelling.

PASSES

THE FS PROVIDES three basic passes: the Biglietto Chilometrico, valid for two months, allowing 3,000 km (1,865 miles) of travel for up to five people for a maximum of 20 journeys; the Italy Flexi Rail Card, permitting unlimited travel for four days within a nine-day period, eight days within a 21-day period, or 12 days within any month; and the Italy Rail Card, a travel-at-will pass for 8, 15, 21 or 30 days. The Italy Flexi Rail Card and the Italy Rail Card are only available to non-residents.

TIMETABLES

IF YOU PLAN to use trains often, pick up a timetable *(un orario)*. The official FS timetable is comprehensive but heavy. A better buy is the small *Pozzorario*, issued twice yearly and available from station kiosks and newsstands. Or visit www.fs-on-line.it for an online timetable.

DIRECTORY

RAILWAY INFORMATION

Italian State Railway Information Office
Toll-free number within Italy; information for travel all over Italy. 📞 *848 888 088.*
🅦 www.fs-on-line.it

European Rail Ltd
📞 *020 7387 0444 (UK).*

VALIDITY AND RESERVATIONS

SINGLE OR RETURN TICKETS are valid for up to two months from the date of purchase. If a seat reservation is made with the ticket, however, the date you wish to travel will be stamped automatically on the ticket. Undated tickets for up to 250 km (155 miles) can also be purchased at newsstands, and must be validated on the day of travel. Reservations are a good idea on and around public holidays and can be made at most main stations for the high-speed trains. Larger stations generally have separate windows for making reservations *(prenotazioni)*.

REDUCTIONS

DISCOUNTS of 20 per cent are available with a *Carta Verde*, for travellers aged between 12 and 26; and with a *Carta d'Argento*, for travellers over 60. Passes are not valid during Christmas and at certain periods in high summer. They can be bought from main line stations and are valid for a year.

LEFT LUGGAGE

MAIN CITY STATIONS usually have left luggage facilities. Most are manned (but the smaller stations have self-service lockers), and you may need to present a passport or other form of identification when depositing or collecting bags. Fees are calculated per bag.

Left luggage logo

MACHINES FOR FS RAIL TICKETS

These machines are easy to use, and most have instructions in six languages on screen. They accept coins, notes and credit cards.

1 Select your destination.

2 The price is shown on the display.

3 Insert coins, notes, or an American Express, Visa or Diners Club card.

4 Take your ticket and change.

5 You must insert your ticket here to validate it for your journey.

ITALY'S PRINCIPAL FS NETWORK

The Italian state rail network operates various different types of service. Check what is on offer before buying your ticket.

Chiasso · Brennero · Como · Treviso · Udine · Domodossola · Vicenza · Padova · Torino · Modane · Milano · Verona · Trieste · Venezia · Alessandria · Tortona · Placenza · Ventimiglia · Genoa · Bologna · Pisa · Firenze · Ancona · Livorno · Arezzo · Grosseto · Pescara · Civitavecchia · Roma · Formia · Caserta · Foggia · Napoli · Bari · Taranto · Brindisi · Sibari · Lecce · Paola · Catanzaro · Messina · Villa san Giovanni · Palermo · Reggio Calabria · Siracusa

KEY

● Main stations

○ Other stations

▬ Principal rail route

- - - Route over water

Travelling Around by Car

The classic Fiat 500

A MOTORING TOUR OF ITALY is the most practical way of exploring the country, though you should take into account high petrol prices, the difficulty of parking in many medieval towns and the Italians' occasionally erratic approach to driving. A car is invaluable in the countryside and for extensive touring, but less useful if you are only visiting a few major towns and cities, as the traffic congestion makes driving slow.

Automatic tollbooths on the motorway outside Florence

WHAT TO TAKE

DRIVERS FROM OUTSIDE Italy bringing their own foreign-registered cars into the country must be at least 18 years old and carry a Green Card (for insurance purposes), all the vehicle's registration documents, and a full, valid driving licence (*patente* in Italian). Any UK or other EU nationals who do not have the standard EU "pink" licence and are planning to stay for more than six months will need an Italian translation of their licence, obtainable from most motoring organizations or from the Italian state tourist office in your home country. A red warning triangle must also be carried at all times, for use in the event of a breakdown.

PETROL

PETROL (*benzina*) in Italy is some of the most expensive in Europe (diesel, or *gasolio*, is a little cheaper). Although many petrol stations are now self-service, it is still common to be served by an attendant. Most petrol stations follow normal shop hours so make sure you have a full tank before lunchtime or public

holidays. On motorways petrol stations tend to be open 24 hours a day. Credit cards are usually accepted.

ROADS

ITALY HAS A GOOD network of motorways, though many have a total of only four lanes, often leading to congestion.

Rules and Regulations

Italy uses standard European road signs. Drive on the right and give way to traffic from the right. Seat belts (la cintura) *are compulsory in the front and the back, and children should be properly restrained. The speed limit in urban areas is 50 km/h (30 mph); outside urban areas it is 110 km/h (70 mph) on dual carriageways and 90 km/h on all other secondary roads. On motorways* (autostrade) *the limit is 130 km/h (80 mph) for vehicles over 1100cc and 110 km/h (70 mph) for all vehicles under 1100cc. All documentation must be carried with you.*

One-way street

Blue signs showing main roads and green signs showing motorways

Busy routes include the A1 from Bologna to Florence and between Bologna, Parma and Milan. Tolls are payable on all but a handful of motorways, again leading to congestion at tollbooths (*Alt Stazione*) at weekends and busy holiday periods. Payment is made at the end of the journey in cash or pre-paid magnetic cards called VIAcards, available from tobacconists and the ACI.

Secondary roads are known as Nazionali (N) or as Strade Statali (SS), and vary enormously in quality, the worst being in the south. Mountain roads are usually good, but distances can be deceptive on winding roads and in winter snow chains are obligatory on many higher routes. Some back roads (known as *strade bianche*, or "white roads") have only a gravel surface, but are still marked on motoring maps. These are slow, but usually passable to cars, if you drive carefully.

No stopping   **End of speed restriction**

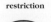

Pedestrianized street – no traffic   **Give way to oncoming traffic**

continua

No parking

Danger (often with description)

Car rental offices at Fiumicino airport, Rome

CAR HIRE

Car hire *(autonoleggio)* is expensive in Italy, and should be organized beforehand through fly-drive deals *(see p627)* or pre-booked with firms who have branches in Italy. For on the spot hire Italian firms may be cheaper than big international names. Agencies are listed in Yellow Pages *(Pagine Gialle)* under Autonoleggio. Most airports have car hire offices on site.

To rent a car in Italy you must be over 21 and have held a valid driver's licence for at least a year. Visitors from outside the EU require an international licence, though in practice not all hire firms insist on this. Check the small print of the agreement for insurance cover.

Parking disc

CAR HIRE NUMBERS

Avis
(199 10 01 33 *(toll-free)*.

Europcar
(800 01 44 10 *(toll-free)*.

Hertz
(199 11 22 11 *(toll-free)*.

Maggiore Budget (Rome)
(06 22 93 51.

Sixt (Rome)
(06 65 96 51.

ACCIDENTS AND BREAKDOWNS

If you have an accident or a breakdown, switch on your hazard warning lights and place a warning triangle 50 m (164 ft) behind your car. Then (for breakdowns) call the ACI emergency number (116) or the emergency services (112 or 113). The ACI will tow any foreign-registered car free to the nearest ACI-affiliated garage. They also do free repairs for members of affiliated associations, such as the AA and RAC in Britain.

If you have an accident keep calm, and do not admit liability or make any statements that might incriminate you later. Simply swap car and insurance details, names and addresses.

PARKING

Parking in most Italian cities and large towns is a problem. Many historic centres have restricted daytime access and baffling one-way systems. Other areas may be reserved for residents' parking (marked *riservato ai residenti)*. Most towns have metered parking areas that charge an hourly fee paid with coins, cards or coupons bought from *tabacchi*.

Cars can be towed away or clamped, especially in areas marked *zona rimozione* (particularly on street-cleaning days). Call the Municipal Police *(Vigili)* to retrieve your car.

SAFETY

Car theft is rife in Italy. Never leave anything in your car, and (if possible) always remove radio-cassette players. Leave your car in a guarded car park whenever you can. Be especially careful driving at night, when Italian driving is more cavalier than usual, and when many traffic lights switch to flashing amber. Hitching *(autostop)* is not a good idea (and is not common), certainly never for women on their own.

Official parking area patrolled by attendant

DISTANCE CHART

10 Distance in kilometres
10 Distance in miles

	ROME	ANCONA	AOSTA	BOLOGNA	BOLZANO	FLORENCE	GENOA	LECCE	MILAN	NAPLES	TURIN
ANCONA	286 / 178										
AOSTA	748 / 465	617 / 383									
BOLOGNA	383 / 238	219 / 136	401 / 249								
BOLZANO	645 / 401	494 / 307	449 / 279	280 / 174							
FLORENCE	278 / 173	262 / 163	470 / 292	106 / 66	367 / 228						
GENOA	510 / 317	506 / 315	245 / 152	291 / 181	422 / 262	225 / 140					
LECCE	601 / 373	614 / 382	1220 / 758	822 / 511	1097 / 682	871 / 541	1103 / 685				
MILAN	575 / 357	426 / 265	181 / 113	210 / 130	295 / 183	299 / 186	145 / 90	1029 / 639			
NAPLES	219 / 136	409 / 254	959 / 596	594 / 369	856 / 532	489 / 304	714 / 444	393 / 244	786 / 488		
TURIN	673 / 418	547 / 340	110 / 68	332 / 206	410 / 255	395 / 245	170 / 106	1150 / 715	138 / 86	884 / 549	
VENICE	530 / 329	364 / 226	442 / 275	154 / 96	214 / 133	255 / 158	397 / 247	967 / 601	273 / 170	741 / 460	402 / 250

Travelling within Cities

Pedestrian
zone sign

THE BEST WAYS of getting around Italian cities differ from place to place. In Rome buses are most useful, in Milan the metro is more efficient, and in Venice you will need to take a boat to get about. Trams still run in some cities, such as Milan and Rome. Cars are a liability almost everywhere, unlike walking, which in many cases is the easiest way to negotiate the tight historic cores of Italian towns and cities. Florence has a large limited-traffic zone, and most towns now have a pedestrian area in the centre.

Bus stop displaying the route

A Roman tram in the orange livery of ATAC

One of the distinctive orange city buses, central Verona

BUSES AND TRAMS

VIRTUALLY EVERY ITALIAN city and large town has a bus system. Most are cheap, comprehensive and as efficient as traffic and narrow streets will allow and vary only slightly from city to city. Bus stops are known as *fermate*, and increasingly (notably in Rome) list full details of the routes they serve. Buses *(autobus)* usually run from about 6am to midnight, and there are night buses *(servizio notturno)* in larger cities. If you arrive in a town by train, stations are invariably linked to the centre by shuttle buses from the station forecourt (tickets are usually available from the station bar or tobacconist).

TICKETS

TICKETS *(biglietti)* must be bought before boarding the bus from kiosks belonging to the bus company (ATAF in Florence, ATAC in Rome), bars, newsstands or tobacconists

displaying the bus company's sticker. A few cities also have on-street vending machines around the main transport hubs. It is worth buying more than one ticket at a time, as outlets often close in the afternoon or early evening. Discounted tickets *(un blocchetto)*, or day- or week-long visitors' tickets and passes *(una tessera or tesserino)* are also available. In some cities tickets are valid for any number of journeys within a given time. The ATAC website has more details on buses in Rome.

ATAC
W www.atac.roma.it

USING BUSES AND TRAMS

BOARD BUSES via the front and rear doors, and exit via the central doors. Buses usually only have a driver and no conductor (though night buses may have a conductor from whom tickets can be bought).

Tickets must be validated by punching them in machines at the front or rear of the bus. There are large on-the-spot fines if you are caught without a properly validated ticket. The front, low seats on buses are for people with children, the elderly and the disabled.

Most larger cities have transport information offices at the main train station or piazza which provide free maps, timetables and tickets.

The majority of city buses are painted bright orange and display the final destination *(capolinea)* on the front.

METROPOLITANA

UNDERGROUND systems, known as *metropolitana* *(la metro* for short), are found in Rome and Milan. Rome's network amounts to just two lines, A and B, which converge at Stazione Termini, the city's central railway station. Several stations are useful for key sights, and at peak times the lines provide the best way of crossing the city quickly. Stations are fairly dingy – though rarely dangerous – and train carriages can be stiflingly hot in summer. In Milan the network is more extensive, with three principal lines – MM1 (the red line), MM2 (green) and MM3 (yellow) – that meet at the hub stations of Stazione Centrale, Duomo, Cadorna and Lima. These three lines give easy access to the

Metro sign

Termini Metro station, Rome

Waiting for a fare at an official rank in Florence

majority of the city's main sights.

Metro tickets in both cities are available from the same sources as bus and tram tickets, and from machines and ticket offices in underground stations. Tickets in Rome are valid for one journey only, though the special *BIG* ticket offers a day's travel on bus, tram and metro. In Milan, by contrast, ordinary metro tickets are valid for 75 minutes for any number of journeys and can also be used on the buses and trams.

It is unwise to buy tickets from people outside stations, as they are invariably already used or otherwise invalid.

Stay on the pavement at all costs

Marginally less dangerous to cross

museums and other places of interest are often indicated by yellow signs). Always carry your valuables well out of sight. The best times to walk are in the cool of the morning, or in the early evening, when you can join in the pre-dinner stroll known as the *passeggiata*.

WALKING

WALKING can be a wonderful way to explore Italy's historic towns and cities, most of whose historic centres are smaller than you might expect. Traffic can be a curse, however, especially in narrow streets (Rome is worst in this respect), but many cities are introducing pedestrianized areas or cutting down on car access around key tourist sights. On certain Sundays (*Domenica a Piedi*), entire town centres may be designated traffic-free zones.

Italian towns have plenty of shady squares and cafés to escape the heat of the summer sun, and churches and cathedrals also provide cool retreats from the rigours of sightseeing. Most sights are well signposted (churches,

TAXIS

ONLY ACCEPT RIDES in official taxis. These may be of different colours in the different cities, but all will have a "Taxi" sign on the roof. Most drivers are honest (if not terribly friendly), but there

are many supplements that can be legitimately levied. Generally an extra charge is made for each piece of luggage placed in the boot, for rides between 10pm and 7am, on Sundays and public holidays, and for journeys to and from airports. It is worth fixing a price before you set off to or from airports, especially in Rome or Naples.

Taxis cannot be hailed. Take one at an official taxi stand (usually found at the station, main piazza or close to key tourist sights) or reserve one by phone. When you order a taxi by phone, take the driver's code name, eg Napoli 18. If you call a cab, the meter will run from your call. In the event of any dispute, note the cab's number and ask the nearest policeman to arbitrate.

CYCLE HIRE

MANY TOWNS and cities, especially those popular with visitors, have stands and shops offering bikes and scooters for rent. You can usually rent hourly or by the day, and you may have to leave your passport with the shop as a deposit. Be very careful, however, if riding a bike in the busy traffic of the larger towns and cities.

INTER-CITY TRANSPORT: COACHES

Long-haul buses (*pullman* or *corriere*) between towns operate in a similar way to local buses, though you can usually buy tickets on board, and services are often run by different companies in different-coloured buses (blue is the most common colour for *pullman*, orange for city buses). Coaches in some

Rome – Gubbio bus

areas may be run by several companies (notably around Florence and in Tuscany), and not all operate from the same termini. Services often depart from outside railway stations, or from a town's main piazza. If in doubt, ask at local tourist offices. A reduced service may operate at weekends, when offices are shut.

Rome
Lineelaziali
📞 800 43 17 84.
Lazzi
📞 06 884 08 40.
Appian
📞 06 48 78 61.

Tuscany
Lazzi
📞 055 21 51 55.
Sita
📞 055 21 47 21.
Tra-In
📞 0577 20 42 45.

National
Lazzi
📞 055 21 51 55.
Sita
📞 055 21 47 21.

Travelling Around Venice

FOR VISITORS TO VENICE, the *vaporetti* or waterbuses *(see pp130–31)* provide an entertaining form of public transport, although most journeys within the city can usually be covered more quickly on foot. The main route through the city for the *vaporetti* is the Grand Canal. Waterbuses also supply a useful service connecting outlying points on the periphery of Venice, and linking the city to the islands in the lagoon. The most important service from a visitor's point of view is the No. 1. This operates from one end of the Grand Canal to the other and travels slowly enough for you to admire the parade of palaces at the waterside *(see pp84–9)*.

Vaporetto stop at the Giardini Pubblici, Venice

A *vaporetto* pulling into San Marco

The smaller, sleeker and quicker *motoscafo*

THE BOATS

THE ORIGINAL *vaporetti* were steam-powered (*vaporetto* means little steamer); today they are diesel-run motor boats. Although all the boats tend to be called *vaporetti*, the word only really applies to the large wide boats used on slow routes, such as No. 1. These boats provide the best views. *Motoscafi* are the slimmer, smaller and faster boats which look old but go at a fair pace. *Motonavi* are two-tier boats which run to the islands.

TYPES OF TICKET

THE PRICE of a ticket depends not on the length of your journey but on the particular line you are taking.

Tickets that are purchased on board, rather than at the kiosk found at each stop, are more expensive. If you buy a book of 10 or 20 tickets, the cost is no cheaper than single tickets, but it avoids queuing at a ticket office for each journey.

You can save money, however, by buying a 24-hour or 72-hour ticket, which entitles the holder to unlimited travel on most lines. If you are staying more than just a few days, you can also save money by buying a weekly or monthly season ticket (*abbonamento*) which is available from ticket offices. Holders of Rolling Venice cards (offering information packs and discounts to 14- to 30-year-olds) can buy a *Tre Giorni Giovane*, or three-day youth pass.

The new "Isles Ticket" enables you to travel on the No. 12 for a one-way run and stay for the day on the islands of Murano, Mazzorbo, Burano and Torcello (but you must buy a ticket for the return trip).

You may have to buy a ticket for each piece of large luggage, and you must remember to date-stamp your tickets.

HOURS OF SERVICE

THE MAIN ROUTES run every 10 to 20 minutes until the early evening. Services are reduced at night, particularly after 1am. From June to September the services are more frequent and certain routes are extended. Details of main lines are also given in the booklet *Un Ospite di Venezia*. From May to September the main routes and island boats are very crowded.

VAPORETTO INFORMATION

ACTV (Information Office)
Piazzale Roma, Venice. **Map** 5 B1.
☎ *041 528 78 86.* W www.actv.it

TRAGHETTI

TRAGHETTI are gondola ferries that cross the Grand Canal at seven different points, providing a useful service for pedestrians. Few tourists make use of this cheap (about 50 cents per trip), constant service. Points where *traghetti* cross the Grand Canal are marked on the Street Finder maps *(see pp120–29)*. A gondola on yellow street signs points to *traghetti* stops.

A two-tier *motonave* on its way to Torcello

GONDOLAS

GONDOLAS are a luxury form of transport used only by visitors and Venetians at weddings. Before boarding, check the official tariffs and agree a price with the gondolier. Official costs are around 50 euros for 45 minutes, rising to 80 euros after 8pm. During the low season, you may also be able to negotiate a lower fee, and a journey shorter than the usual 50 minutes.

WATER TAXIS

FOR THOSE with little time and sufficient funds, the fastest and most practical means of getting from A to B is by water taxi. The craft are sleek, white or polished wood motorboats, all equipped with a cabin. They zip to and from the airport in only 20 minutes. There are 16 water taxi ranks, including one at the airport and the Lido. Beware of extra charges for luggage, waiting,

A water taxi

night service and for calling out a taxi. When the *vaporetti* go on strike, taxis are scarce.

WATER TAXI STANDS

Radio Taxi (all of Venice)
(041 522 23 03.

Ferrovia (Santa Lucia)
Map 1 C5. (041 71 62 86.

Piazzale Roma
Map 5 B1. (041 71 69 22.

San Marco
Map 7 B3. (041 522 97 50.

Crossing the Grand Canal by *traghetto*

THE MAIN ROUTES

① Confusingly called the *Accelerato*, this is the slow boat down the Grand Canal, stopping at every landing stage. The route starts at Piazzale Roma, travels the length of the Grand Canal, then from San Marco it heads east to the Lido.

⑧② The No. 82 is the faster route down the Grand Canal, making only six stops. The route is circular, starting at San Zaccaria, continuing westwards along the Giudecca Canal to Tronchetto and Pizzale Roma, then down the Grand Canal back to San Zaccaria, from there out to the Lido.

⑤① ⑤② The 51 and 52 skirt the periphery of Venice and have been extended to the Lido. The cirular *Giracittà* route provides a scenic tour of Venice, though to do the whole circuit you have to change boats at Fondamente Nuove.

⑫ This line departs from the Fondamente Nuove and runs to the main islands in the northern lagoon: Murano, Mazzorbo, Burano and Torcello ending at Punta Sabbioni.

USING THE VAPORETTI

1 Tickets are available at most landing stages, some bars, shops and tobacconists displaying the ACTV sign. The price of a ticket remains the same whether you are going one stop or travelling the whole line, but some routes are more expensive than others, and some prices go up in summer.

2 Signs on the landing stage tell you the direction of the boats stopping there.

3 Tickets should be punched at the automatic machines on the landing stages before each journey. Inspectors rarely board the boats and this makes it surprisingly easy for tourists (and Venetians) to hop on and off the boats without a validated ticket. However, there are steep fines for any passengers caught without tickets.

4 An indicator board at the front of each boat gives the line number and main stops. (Ignore the black numbers on the boat's side.)

5 Each landing stage has its name clearly marked on a yellow board. Most stops have two landing stages and it is quite easy, particularly if it is crowded and you can't see which way the boat is facing, to board a boat travelling in the wrong direction. It is helpful to watch which direction the boat is approaching from; if in doubt, check with the boatman.

General Index

Acknowledgments

DORLING KINDERSLEY would like to thank the following people whose contributions and assistance have made the preparation of this book possible.

CONTRIBUTORS

Paul Duncan is an expert on art and architectural history and has published a guide to Sicily as well as one on Italy's hill towns.
Tim Jepson, formerly Rome correspondent for the *Sunday Telegraph*, has written guides to Tuscany, Umbria, Rome and Venice, a complete guide to Italy, *Italy by Train* and *Wild Italy*, a guide to Italy's nature reserves.
Andrew Gumbel, former Reuters correspondent in Rome, has written a number of guide books and is the correspondent for the *Independent* in Rome.
Christopher Catling has written guides to Florence and Tuscany, the Veneto and the Italian Lakes and is particularly interested in archaeology.
Sam Cole works for Reuters in Rome, where he has lived for some years, and contributes regularly to guidebooks on Rome and the Lazio region.

ADDITIONAL CONTRIBUTORS

Dominic Robertson, Mick Hamer, Richard Langham Smith.

ADDITIONAL PHOTOGRAPHY

Peter Chadwick, Andy Crawford, Philip Dowell, Mike Dunning, Philip Enticknap, Steve Gorton, Dave King, Neil Mersh, Roger Moss, Poppy, Kim Sayer, James Stevenson, Clive Streeter, David Ward, Matthew Ward.

ADDITIONAL ILLUSTRATIONS

Andrea Corbella, Richard Draper, Kevin Jones Associates, Chris Orr and Associates, Robbie Polley, Simon Roulstone, Martin Woodward.

CARTOGRAPHIC RESEARCH

Jane Hugill, Samantha James, Jennifer Skelley.

DESIGN AND EDITORIAL ASSISTANCE

Gillian Allan, Gaye Allen, Douglas Amrine, Emily Anderson, Hilary Bird, Samantha Borland, Isabel Boucher, Hugo Bowles, Caroline Brooke, Paola Cacucciola, Stefano Cavedoni, Margaret Chang, Elspeth Collier, Lucinda Cooke, Cooling Brown, Gary Cross, Felicity Crowe, Peter Douglas, Mandy Dredge, Michael Ellis, Adele Evans, Danny Farnham, Jackie Gordon, Angela-Marie Graham, Caroline Greene, Vanessa Hamilton, Sally-Ann Hibbard, Tim Hollis, Gail Jones, Steve Knowlden, Siri Lowe, Sarah Martin, Georgina Matthews, Ferdie McDonald, Ian Midson, Rebecca Milner, Adam Moore, Jennifer Mussett, Alice Peebles, Tamsin Pender, Gillian Price, David Pugh, Jake Reimann, David Roberts, Evelyn Robertson, Carolyn Ryden, Simon Ryder, Giuseppina Russo, Sands Editorial, Alison Stace, Hugh Thompson, Jo-Ann Titmarsh, Elaine Verweymeren, Ingrid Vienings, Stewart J Wild, Veronica Wood.

DORLING KINDERSLEY would also like to thank the following for their assistance: Azienda Autonoma di Soggiorno Cura e Turismo, Napoli; Azienda Promozione Turistica del Trentino, Trento; Osservatorio Geofisico dell'Università di Modena; Bell'Italia; Enotria Winecellars.

PHOTOGRAPHY PERMISSION

DORLING KINDERSLEY would like to thank the following for their assistance and kind permission to photograph at their establishments: Assessorato Beni Culturali Comune di Padova. Le Soprintendenze Archeologiche di Agrigento, di Enna, di Etruria Meridionale, per il Lazio, di Napoli, di Pompei, di Reggio Calabria e di Roma. Le Soprintendenze per i Beni Ambientali e Architettonici di Bolzano, di Napoli, di Potenza, della Provincia di Firenze e Pistoia, di Ravenna, di Roma, di Siena e di Urbino. Le Soprintendenze per i Beni Ambientali, Architettonici, Artistici e Storici di Caserta, di Cosenza, di Palermo, di Pisa, di Salerno e di Venezia. Le Soprintendenze per i Beni Artistici e Storici della Provincia di Firenze e Pistoia, di Milano e di Roma. Also all the other churches, museums, hotels, shops, restaurants, galleries and sights too numerous to thank individually.

PICTURE CREDITS

t = top; tl = top left; tc = top centre; tr = top right; cla = centre left above; ca = centre above; cra = centre right above; cl = centre left; c = centre; cr = centre right; clb = centre left below; cb = centre below; crb = centre right below; bl = bottom left; b = bottom; bc = bottom centre; br = bottom right.

Works of art have been reproduced with the permission of the following copyright holders: © ADAGP, Paris and DACS, London 1996 *Bird in Space* by Constantin Brancusi 101cl; © DACS, 1996 *Mother and Son* by Carlo Carrà 190t.

DORLING KINDERSLEY would like to thank the following for their assistance: Eric Crighton: 79cra, FIAT: 212c, Gucci Ltd: 35cr, Prada, Milan: 35c, National Archaeological Museum, Naples: 479b, National Maritime Museum 36c, Royal Botanic Gardens, Kew: 79ca, Science Museum: 36cla, Telecom Italia: 620tc.

The publisher would like to thank the following individuals, companies and picture libraries for permission to reproduce their photographs:

ACCADEMIA ITALIANA: Sue Bond 479c; AFE, Rome:

34clb, 34cb, 35tl; Giuseppe Carfagna 188b, 194b, 210tl, 210b, 214tl, 216b, 217t, 227t; Claudio Cerquetti 64t, 65bl, 65t; Enrico Martino 54cl, 62tr; Roberto Merlo 228b, 231t, 231b; Piero Servo 259t, 261b; Gustavo Tomsich 219b; ARCHIVIO APT MONREGALESE 221t; ACTION PLUS: Mike Hewitt 66ca; Glyn Kirk 67tr; ALITALIA: 626t, 626b; ALLSPORT: Mark Thompson: 67cl; Simon Bruty: 67tl; ANCIENT ART AND ARCHITECTURE: 39t, 465br; ARCHIV FÜR KUNST UND GESCHICHTE, London: 24bl, 30b, *Rossini* (1820), Camuccini, Museo Teatrale alla Scala, Milan 32br, 33bl, 37br, *Pope Sixtus IV Naming Platina Prefect of the Library*, Melozzo da Forlì (1477), Pinacoteca Vaticana, Rome 38, 40tl, *Statue of Augustus from Prima Porta* (1st century AD) 45tl, *The Gift of Constantine* (1246), Oratorio di San Silvestro, Rome 46cl, *Frederick I Barbarossa as a Crusader* (1188), Biblioteca Apostolica Vaticana, Rome 49bl, 52tl, *Giving the Keys to St Peter*, Perugino (1482), Sistine Chapel, Vatican, Rome 52cla, 52bl, *Machiavelli*, Santi di Tito, Palazzo Vecchio, Florence 53br, *Andrea Palladio*, Meyer 54cb, *Goethe in the Campagna*, Tischbein (1787), Stadelsches Kunstinstitut, Frankfurt 56cl, *Venetian Carnival in the Eighteenth Century*, Anon (19th century) 56clb, *Bonaparte Crossing the Alps*, David, Schloss Charlottenburg, Berlin 57cr, 57bl, 102t, 102b, 191b, 346–7, 450b, *Archimedes,* Museo Capitolino, Rome 465bl, 489t, 493c; Stefan Diller *St Francis Appearing to the Brothers at Arles* (1295–1300), San Francesco, Assisi 49tl; Erich Lessing *Margrave Gualtieri of Saluzzo Chooses the Poor Farmer's Daughter, Griseldis, for his Wife*, di Stefano, Galleria dell'Accademia Carrara, Bergamo 30crb, *The Vision of St Augustine* (1502), Carpaccio, Chiesa di San Giorgio degli Schiavoni, Venice 53cr, 214b, 260b, 475b; ARCHIVIO IGDA, Milan: 196t, 196c, 197b, 505bl, 505br; EMPORIO ARMANI: 20cl, 35tc; ARTEMIDE, GB Ltd: 35clb.

MARIO BETTELLA 519c, 526c; FRANK BLACKBURN: 259c; OSVALDO BÖHM, VENICE: 85t, 90c, 107t; BRIDGEMAN ART LIBRARY, LONDON/NEW YORK: 42c, Ambrosiana, Milan 189t; Bargello, Florence 271b, 275c; Bibliothèque Nationale, Paris: *Marco Polo with Elephants and Camels Arriving at Hormuz, Gulf of Persia, from India*, Livre des Merveilles Fr 2810 f.14v 37t; British Museum, London *Etruscan Vase Showing Boxers Fighting* 41tl, *Flask Decorated with Christian Symbols* 46tl, *Greek Attic Red-Figure Vase depicting Odysseus with the Sirens*, Stamnos 465cb; Galleria dell'Accademia Carrara, Bergamo 193t; Galleria Borghese, Rome 429cl; Galleria degli Uffizi, Florence 22tl, 25tl, 25br, *Self-Portrait*, Raphael Sanzio of Urbino 53bl, 279b, 281b: K & B News Photo, Florence 268tl; Santa Maria Novella, Florence 289b; Museo Civico, Prato 318b; Louvre, Paris *Statuette of Herakles Brandishing his Club*, Classical Greek, Argive period 464t; Mausoleo di

Galla Placidia, Ravenna 260tr; Museo di San Marco, Florence 289b; Musée d'Orsay, Paris - Giraudon *Les Romains de la Decadence*, Thomas Couture 385t; Museo delle Sinopie, Camposanto, Pisa 23clb; Palazzo dei Normanni, Palermo *Scene with Centaurs from the Room of King Ruggero* 507b; Pinacoteca di Brera, Milan 190c, 190b, 191t, Private Collection *Theodoric I* (455–526 AD) *Ostrogothic King of Italy* 46b; San Francesco, Arezzo 23tr; San Francesco, Assisi 345c; San Sebastiano, Venice 25crb; San Zaccaria, Venice 29c, 29tr, 95c; Santa Croce, Florence 276bl, 277cb; Santa Maria Gloriosa dei Frari, Venice 24tr; Santa Maria Novella, Florence 23cla; Scrovegni (Arena) Chapel, Padua 22tr; Scuola di San Giorgio degli Schiavoni, Venice 116b; Staatliche Museen, Berlin *Septimius Severus and Family* 45b; Vatican Museums and Galleries, Rome 411b; Walker Art Gallery, Liverpool *Aeschylus and Hygieia* 464b; BRITISH MUSEUM, London: 42cl.

CAPITOLINE MUSEUM, ROME: 377cr; DEMETRIO CARRASCO: 98br, 636tr; CEPHAS PICTURE LIBRARY Mick Rock: 2–3, 19t, 20t, 176tr, 177b, 177tr, 234–5, 243tl, 243tr, 456–7, 610–1; JL CHARMET, Paris: 343br, 479t; CIGA HOTELS: 87cb; FOTO ELIO E STEFANO CIOL: 73cra, 158bl, 158br, 159bl, 159bc, 159br; COMUNE DI ASTI: 64cl; STEPHANI COLASANTI: 72bl; JOE CORNISH: 18t, 78tr, 132, 154t, 236–7, 304, 354, 445b, 521b; GIANCARLO COSTA: 9c, 30t, 31cr, 31tr, 31tl, 71c, 171c, 176tl, 457c, 537c, 611c.

IL DAGHERROTIPO: 630cl; Archivio Arte 199t; Archivio Storico 31b, 198b, 253b; Salvatore Barba 490t; Alberto Berni 217bl; Riccardo Catani 485b; Marco Cerruti 172t, 205b, 207b, 208b; Antonio Cittadini 182b, 186b, 194t ; Gianni Dolfini 534b; Riccardo d'Errico 66tr, 239t, 260c; Maurizio Fraschetti 480; Diane Haines 167br, 625br; Maurizio Leoni 63c; Marco Melodia 490cb, 491b, 531t, 624tl, 624cl; Stefano Occhibelli 65c, 246, 386, 391bl; Giorgio Oddi 239cr, 244t, 497tr; Bruno Pantaloni 67bl; Donato Fierro Perez 517cb; Marco Ravasini 164t, 533c; Giovanni Rinaldi 21t, 62bl, 63tl, 173bl, 223b, 388c, 357t, 363t, 450c, 466, 483t, 490bl, 490br, 491c, 517cr, 535t, 535c; Lorenzo Scaramella 452c; Stefania Servili 166t; JAMES DARELL: 338; CM DIXON: 411cb; CHRIS DONAGHUE THE OXFORD PHOTO LIBRARY: 113t.

ELECTA: 150c, 151c, 151t; EMPICS: John Marsh 66b; ET ARCHIVE: 32bc, 41c, 42tl, 45cr, 48cr–49cl, 53tl, 55tl, 59b, 465t, 515b; MARY EVANS PICTURE LIBRARY: 30clb, 31cl, 37ca, 58b, 58crb, 59cr, 60cb, 76tr, 237c, 310t, 316t, 381ca, 383bl, 399b, 432c, 495cr, 534t.

ARCHIVIO STORICO FIAT, TURIN: 60tr; FERRARI: 34b; APT FOLIGNATE E NOCERA UMBRA: 351t; WERNER FORMAN ARCHIVE: 41br, 47tr, 425br; CONSORZIO

FRASASSI: 362b.
STUDIO GAVIRATI, Gubbio: 342c; APT GENOVA: Roberto Merlo 230bl; GIRAUDON, Paris: *Aphrodite Persuading Helen to Follow Paris to Troy,* Museo Nazionale di Villa Giulia, Rome 41clb, *Pharmacy,* Museo della Civiltà Romana 44cb, *Grandes Chroniques de France; Coronation of Charlemagne in St Peter's by Leon III,* Musée Goya, Castres 47tl, *Taking of Constantinople,* Basilica of St John the Evangelist, Ravenna 49cr, *Dante's Hell with Commentary of Guiniforte delli Bargigi* (Ms2017 fol 245), Bibliothèque Nationale, Paris 50cb, *Portrait of St Ignatius of Loyola,* Rubens, Musée Brukenthal, Sibiu 55ca, *Charles III's Fleet at Naples 6th October 1759,* Joli de Dipi, Museo del Prado, Madrid 56tr, *Inauguration of the Naples-Portici Railway,* Fergola (1839), Museo Nazionale di San Martino, Naples 58clb, *Piedmontese and French at the Battle of San Martino in 1859* Anon, Museo Centrale del Risorgimento, Rome 59tl, 102c, 103t, 191c, 260tl; ALINARI-GIRAUDON: *St Mark Appearing to the Venetians Looking for His Body,* Tintoretto (1568), Brera Art Gallery, Milan 25tr, *Shrine,* House of the Vettii, Pompeii 45cb, *St Gregory in his Study* (Inv 285), Pinacoteca Nazionale, Bologna 47bl, *Portrait of Victor Emmanuel II,* Dugoni (1866), Galleria d'Arte Moderna, Palazzo Pitti, Florence 58tl, 103b, 190t, *Louis II of Gonzaga and his Court,* Andrea Mantegna (1466–74), Museo di Palazzo Ducale, Mantova 200–201, 279tl-tr, *History of Pope Alexander III: Building of the City of Alexandria,* Arctino Spincllo (1407), Palazzo Pubblico, Siena 51cr; ALINARI-SEAT-GIRAUDON: 219c; FLAMMARION-GIRAUDON: *Poem by Donizo in Honour of Queen Matilda,* Biblioteca Apostolica, Vatican 48ca; LAUROS-GIRAUDON: *Portrait of Francis Petrarch* 50b, *Liber notabilium Philippi Septimi, francorum regis a libris Galieni extractus* (Ms 334 569 fig17), Guy of Pavia (1345), Musée Condé, Chantilly 51b, *Gallery of Views of Ancient Rome,* Pannini (1758), Musée du Louvre, Paris 56cr, 57cl, *Portrait of the Artist,* Bernini, Private Collection 54tl, *Four Angels and Symbols of the Evangelists,* 28tr–29tcr; ORSI-BATTAGLINI-GIRAUDON: *Madonna of the Shadow,* Museum of San Marco, Florence 28c, *Supplice de Savonarola* Anon 52cl; JACKIE GORDON: 631; THE RONALD GRANT ARCHIVE: 61b; Paramount *The Godfather Part III* (1990) 519b; Riama *La Dolce Vita* (1960) 61tl; TCF *Boccaccio '70* (1962) 19cl, *The Name of the Rose* (1986) 30cla; PALAZZO VENIER DEI LEONI, PEGGY GUGGENHEIM COLLECTION, VENICE: 87cla.

PHOTO HALUPKA: 116t; ROBERT HARDING PICTURE LIBRARY: 1c, 66tl, 185b, 262, 380cl, 404, 409b, 615b, 624b; Dumrath 261c; HP Merton 160, 624tr; Roy Rainford 483cr; JOHN HESELTINE: 451t; MICHAEL HOLFORD: 43ca, 374b; HOTEL PORTA ROSSA: 540tr;

HOTEL VILLA PAGODA: 539t; THE HULTON DEUTSCH COLLECTION: 60br, 85cla, 86cla, 86br, 151br, 365c; Keystone 60ca.

THE IMAGE BANK, London: 324b; Marcella Pedone 181b; Andrea Pistolesi 247b; Guido Rossi 10b, 43cb; IMPACT: 305b; INDEX, Florence: 274c, 317t, 317cr; ISTITUTO E MUSEO DI STORIA DELLA SCIENZA DI FIRENZE: Franca Principe 36b, 277c.

TIM JEPSON: 341t.

FRANK LANE PICTURE AGENCY: 208t, 209t, 209c, 209b; M Melodia/Panda 490ca.

MAGNUM, London: Abbas 61clb; THE MANSELL COLLECTION: 48cl, 383tl; MARCONI LTD 36t; MARKA: L Barbazza 93tr; M Motta 617t; Piranha 189br; MASTERSTUDIO, Pescara: 488c; su concessione del MINISTERO PER I BENI CULTURALI E AMBIENTALI: *The Last Supper,* da Vinci, Leonardo 192b; MIRROR SYNDICATION INTERNATIONAL: 36clb; MOBY LINES: 629b; FOTO MODENA: 258t, 361c; TONY MOTT: 449b, 454t; MUSEO DIOCESANO DI ROSSANO 504t.

NHPA: Laurie Campbell 79crb; Gerard Lacz 79br; Silvestris Fotoservice 79cr; BY COURTESY OF THE NATIONAL PORTRAIT GALLERY, London: (detail) *Percy Bysshe Shelley,* Amelia Curran (1819) 56tl; GRAZIA NERI: 48tl; Roberta Krasnig 620bl; Marco Bruzzo 64br; Cameraphoto 104bl; Marcello Mencarini 84br; NIPPON TELEVISION NETWORK: 414c–415c, 414t, 414b–415bl, 415t, 415br, 416b; PETER NOBLE: 308t, 326–7, 331b, 616b.

L'OCCHIO DI CRISTALLO/STUDIO FOTOGRAFICO DI GIORGIO OLIVERO: 221b; APT ORVIETO: Massimo Roncella 348t; OXFORD SCIENTIFIC FILMS: Stan Osolinski 337c.

PADOVA - MUSEI CIVICI - CAPPELLA SCROVEGNI: 73cr, 150t, 150cla, 150clb, 151cra, 151crb, 151bl; PADOVA - MUSEI CIVICI AGLI EREMITANI: 152t, 152c; LUCIANO PEDICINI - ARCHIVIO DELL'ARTE: 352b, 394t, 459t, 470tl, 474t, 474ca, 474cb, 474b, 475t, 475ca, 475cr, 477t, 514b; APT PESARO - LE MARCHE: 358c; PICTURES COLOUR LIBRARY: 530b, 532l; ANDREA PISTOLESI: 16; POPPERFOTO: 60tl, 61ca, 61cb.

SARAH QUILL, Venice: 86t, 90b, 96tl.

RETROGRAPH ARCHIVE: 33c; REX FEATURES: 33t; Steve Wood 35tr, 189bl.

SCALA GROUP SPA: 22b, 23b, 24br, 25ca, 25bl, 32tl, 388cla, *Portrait of Claudio Monteverdi,* Domenico Feti, Accademia, Venice 32bl, *Portolan of Italy* (16th century), Loggia dei Lanzi, Firenze 283bl, Museo Correr, Venice 39b, *Etruscan Bronze Liver,* Museo Civico, Piacenza 40cl, *Earrings,* Museo

Etrusco Guarnacci, Volterra 40br, 40cr–41cl, *Crater from Pescia Romana*, Museo Archeologico, Grosseto 41bc, *Terracotta Vase in the Shape of an Elephant*, Museo Nazionale, Naples 42cr, *Cicero denounces Catiline*, Palazzo Madama, Rome 43tl, 43bl, *Circus Scene Mosaic - Gladiator Fight*, Galleria Borghese, Rome 44t, 44br, *Theodolinda Melts the Gold for the New Church* (15th century), Famiglia Zavattari, Duomo, Monza 46clb, 46cr–47cl, 47b, *Tomb Relief depicting a School*, Matteo Gandoni, Museo Civico, Bologna 48b, *Detail from an Ambo of Frederick II* (13th century), Cattedrale, Bitonto 49cb, *Guidoriccio da Fogliano at the Siege of Note Massi*, Simone Martini, Palazzo Pubblico, Siena 50cl, 51tl, *Return of Gregory XI from Avignon* Giorgio Vasari, Sala Regia, Vatican 51cb, 52br, 52cr–53cl, 53crb, *Clement VII in Conversation with Charles V*, Giorgio Vasari, Palazzo Vecchio, Florence 54cla, *Portrait of Pierluigi da Palestrina*, Istituto dei Padri dell'Oratorio, Rome 54br, *Revolt at Masaniello*, Domenico Gargiulo, Museo di San Martino, Naples 55crb, 56br, 57tl, 57crb, 58cla, 58cr–59cl, 59crb, 91c, 96c, 114br, 140c, 214tr, 218b, 252t, 255t, 257t, 261t, 266c, 266b, 267t, 268c, 268b, 269t, 269b, 272, 274tr, 275tr, 275b, 278t, 278c, 278b, 279ca, 279cb, 280t, 280b, 281t, 282c, 283bl, 284t, 284b, 285t, 285b, 286t, 286c, 287t, 288bl, 290t, 290cl, 290cra, 290crb, 290b, 291t, 291cla, 291clb, 291cr, 291bl, 291br, 293bl, 294tr, 294tl, 294c, 295t, 295cl, 295b, 315c, 315b, 320t, 320cla, 320c, 320ca, 320cr-321cl, 320cb, 320b, 321cr, 321cb, 321cra, 321t, 321b, 322t, 322b, 328b, 330t, 331cl, 334cla, 335b, 344t, 344c, 345b, 348b, 349c, 360t, 360b, 361t, 361bl, 367br, 374c, 390bl, 392t, 394c, 401c, 406tl, 406c, 406b, 407t, 408b, 409t, 410t, 410cb, 411c, 413t, 413c, 413b, 417t, 417b, 495c, 497tl, 513b, 514tr, 520t, 521t, 522b, 533b; Science Photo Library: 11t; Argonne National Laboratory 37cr; John Ferro Sims: 20b, 21b, 80, 170–171, 355b, 364–365, 444, 526b; Agenzia Sintesi, Rome: 616tl; Mario Soster di Alagna: 541c; Frank Spooner Pictures: Diffidenti 532b; Gamma 61cr, 61tc; Sporting Pictures: 66clb, 66crb, 67cb, 67cra; Tony Stone Images: 79cla;

Stephen Studd 27tr, 179cr; Agenzia Fotografica Stradella, Milan: Bersanetti 185c; Lamberto Caenazzo 530t; Francesco Gavazzini 208c; F Giaccone 510c; Mozzati 360clb; Massimo Pacifico 491t; Ettore Re 483crb; Ghigo Roli 483b; Giulio Vegi 517t; Amedeo Vergani 202, 206b, 226t, 249t; Sygma: 63tr.

Tasting Italy: Martin Brigdale 625t; Tate Gallery Publications: 60bl; APT dell'Alta Valle del Tevere: Museo del Duomo 50tl; Touring Club of Italy: 196b, Cresci 518t; Archivio Città di Torino Settore Turismo: 213t, 213b; Davide Bogliacino 205t; Fototeca APT del Trentino: Foto di Banal 168t; Foto di Faganello 167t, 169c.

Venice Simplon-Orient-Express: 628tl; Villa Crespi: 576b.

Charlie Waite: 17b; Graham Watson: 66cr; Edizione White Star: Marcello Bertinetti 81b; Giulio Veggi 8–9, 70–71, 133b; Fiona Wild: 524–5; Peter Wilson: 5t, 88–89; World Pictures: 536–7.

Front Endpaper:
Joe Cornish: Lcrb, Rc, Rtcr; Il Dagherrotipo: Marco Melodia Lbl; Stefano Occhibelli Rtl; Giovanni Rinaldi Rbl; James Darell: Rcl; Robert Harding Picture Library: Lc, H.P. Merton Rtcl; John Ferro Sims: Ltr, Rbc; Agenzia Fotografica Stradella, Milan: Amedeo Vergani Ltl.

Back Endpaper:
Il Dagherrotipo: Stefano Occhibelli cl; Robert Harding Picture Library: Rolf Richardson tl.

COVER:
Ferrari: bl; Giraudon: Nicolò Orsi Battaglini crb; Hulton Deutsch Collection: Reuter cra.

BACK COVER:
Peter Wilson: bl.

All other images © Dorling Kindersley. For further information see: www.dkimages.com

EYEWITNESS *TRAVEL GUIDES*

COUNTRY GUIDES

AUSTRALIA • CANADA • CRUISE GUIDE TO EUROPE AND THE
MEDITERRANEAN • EGYPT • FRANCE • GERMANY • GREAT BRITAIN
GREECE: ATHENS & THE MAINLAND • THE GREEK ISLANDS
IRELAND • ITALY • JAPAN • MEXICO • POLAND
PORTUGAL • SCOTLAND • SINGAPORE
SOUTH AFRICA • SPAIN • THAILAND
GREAT PLACES TO STAY IN EUROPE
A TASTE OF SCOTLAND

REGIONAL GUIDES

BALI & LOMBOK • BARCELONA & CATALONIA • CALIFORNIA
EUROPE • FLORENCE & TUSCANY • FLORIDA • HAWAII
JERUSALEM & THE HOLY LAND • LOIRE VALLEY
MILAN & THE LAKES • NAPLES WITH POMPEII & THE AMALFI
COAST • NEW ENGLAND • NEW ZEALAND
PROVENCE & THE COTE D'AZUR • SARDINIA
SEVILLE & ANDALUSIA • SICILY • SOUTHWEST USA & LAS VEGAS
A TASTE OF TUSCANY • VENICE & THE VENETO

CITY GUIDES

AMSTERDAM • BERLIN • BOSTON • BRUSSELS • BUDAPEST
CHICAGO • CRACOW • DELHI, AGRA & JAIPUR • DUBLIN
ISTANBUL • LISBON • LONDON • MADRID
MOSCOW • NEW YORK • PARIS • PRAGUE • ROME
SAN FRANCISCO • STOCKHOLM • ST PETERSBURG
SYDNEY • VIENNA • WARSAW • WASHINGTON, DC

NEW FOR SPRING 2002

CUBA • INDIA • MUNICH & BAVARIA
TURKEY

FOR UPDATES TO OUR GUIDES, AND INFORMATION ON
DK TRAVEL MAPS & PHRASEBOOKS

VISIT US AT
eyewitnesstravel.dk.com

Central Rome

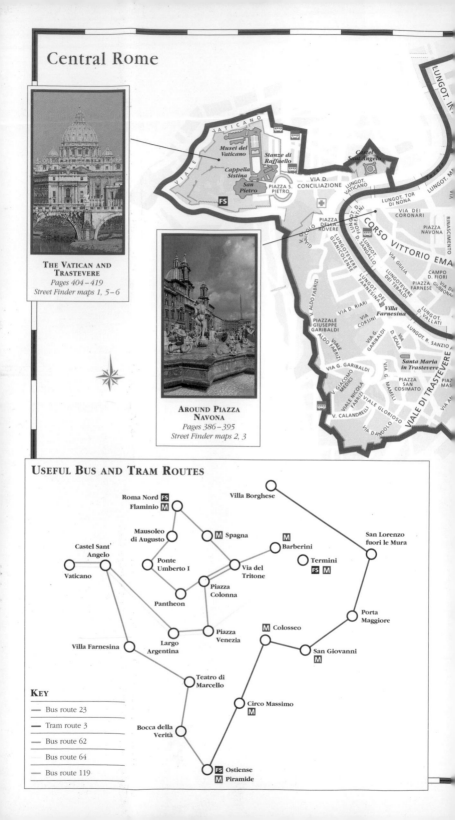

THE VATICAN AND TRASTEVERE
Pages 404–419
Street Finder maps 1, 5–6

AROUND PIAZZA NAVONA
Pages 386–395
Street Finder maps 2, 3

Map labels: VATICANO · Musei del Vaticano · Stanze di Raffaello · Cappella Sistina · San Pietro · PIAZZA S. PIETRO · FS · VIALE · Castel Sant'Angelo · VIA D. CONCILIAZIONE · LUNGOT. VATICANO · LUNGOT. IN · LUNGOT. M · CORSO VITTORIO EMA · VIA DEI CORONARI · LUNGOT. TOR DI NONA · PIAZZA NAVONA · RINASCIMENTO · VIA GIULIA · CAMPO D. FIORI · PIAZZA FARNESE · LUNGOTEVERE DE TEBALDI · PIAZZA DELLA ROVERE · VIA DELLA LUNGARA · LUNGOTEVERE DEI SANGALLO · VIA G. GIUBBONA · PIAZZA DELLA ROVERE · VIA D. RIARI · Villa Farnesina · LUNGOT. R. SANZIO · LUNGOT. D. VALLATI · PIAZZALE GIUSEPPE GARIBALDI · VIA CORSINI · VIALE ALDO FABRIZI · VIA G. GARIBALDI · D. SCALA · Santa Maria in Trastevere · VIA G. GARIBALDI · GIACOMO MEDICI · PIAZZA SAN COSIMATO · VIALE DI TRASTEVERE · VIA G. MAMELI · VIALE NICOLA FABRIZI VIALE GLORIOSO · V. CALANDRELLI · VIA DANDOLO

USEFUL BUS AND TRAM ROUTES

- Roma Nord FS
- Flaminio M
- Villa Borghese
- Mausoleo di Augusto
- Spagna M
- San Lorenzo fuori le Mura
- Castel Sant' Angelo
- Barberini M
- Termini FS M
- Vaticano
- Ponte Umberto I
- Via del Tritone
- Piazza Colonna
- Pantheon
- Villa Farnesina
- Largo Argentina
- Piazza Venezia
- Colosseo M
- Porta Maggiore
- San Giovanni M
- Teatro di Marcello
- Circo Massimo M
- Bocca della Verità
- Ostiense FS
- Piramide M

KEY

— Bus route 23
— Tram route 3
— Bus route 62
— Bus route 64
— Bus route 119

Phrase Book

IN EMERGENCY

Help!	Aiuto!	eye-**yoo**-toh
Stop!	Fermate!	fair-**mah**-teh
Call a	Chiama un	kee-**ah**-mah oon
doctor.	medico	**meh**-dee-koh
Call an	Chiama un'	kee-**ah**-mah oon
ambulance.	ambulanza	am-boo-**lan**-tsa
Call the	Chiama la	kee-**ah**-mah lah
police.	polizia	pol-ee-**tsee**-ah
Call the fire	Chiama i	kee-**ah**-mah ee
brigade.	pompieri	pom-pee-**air**-ee
Where is the	Dov'è il telefono?	dov-**eh** eel teh-**leh**-
telephone?		foh-noh?
The nearest	L'ospedale	loss-peh-**dah**-leh pee-
hospital?	più vicino?	oo vee-**chee**-noh?

COMMUNICATION ESSENTIALS

Yes/No	Sì/No	see/ **noh**
Please	Per favore	pair fah-**vor**-eh
Thank you	Grazie	**grah**-tsee-eh
Excuse me	Mi scusi	mee **skoo**-zee
Hello	Buon giorno	bwon **jor**-noh
Goodbye	Arrivederci	ah-ree-veh-**dair**-chee
Good evening	Buona sera	**bwon**-ah **sair**-ah
morning	la mattina	lah mah-**tee**-nah
afternoon	il pomeriggio	eel pohmehm**-ree**-joh
evening	la sera	lah **sair**-ah
yesterday	ieri	ee-**air**-ee
today	oggi	**oh**-jee
tomorrow	domani	doh-**mah**-nee
here	qui	**kwee**
there	la	**lah**
What?	Quale?	**kwah**-leh?
When?	Quando?	**kwan**-doh?
Why?	Perchè?	pair-**keh**?
Where?	Dove?	**doh**-veh?

USEFUL PHRASES

How are you?	Come sta?	**koh**-meh stah?
Very well,	Molto bene,	**moll**-toh **beh**-neh
thank you.	grazie.	**grah**-tsee-eh
Pleased to	Piacere di	pee-ah-**chair**-eh dee
meet you.	conoscerla.	coh-**noh**-shair-lah
See you later.	A più tardi.	ah pee-oo **tar**-dee
That's fine.	Va bene.	va **beh**-neh
Where is/are ...?	Dov'è/Dove sono ...?	dov-**eh**/dove-**soh**-noh?
How long does	Quanto tempo ci	**kwan**-toh **tem**-poh
it take to get to ...?	vuole per	chee voo-**oh**-leh pair
	andare a ...?	an **dar** eh ah ...?
How do I	Come faccio per	koh-meh **fah**-choh
get to ...?	arrivare a ...?	pair arri-**var**-eh ah..?
Do you speak	Parla inglese?	**par**-lah een-**gleh**-zeh?
English?		
I don't	Non capisco.	non ka-**pee**-skoh
understand.		
Could you speak	Può parlare	pwoh par-**lah**-reh
more slowly,	più lentamente,	pee-oo len-ta-**men**-teh
please?	per favore?	pair fah-**vor**-eh?
I'm sorry.	Mi dispiace.	mee dee-spee-**ah**-cheh

USEFUL WORDS

big	grande	**gran**-deh
small	piccolo	**pee**-koh-loh
hot	caldo	**kal**-doh
cold	freddo	**fred**-doh
good	buono	**bwoh**-noh
bad	cattivo	kat-**tee**-voh
enough	basta	**bas**-tah
well	bene	**beh**-neh
open	aperto	ah-**pair**-toh
closed	chiuso	kee-**oo**-zoh
left	a sinistra	ah see-**nee**-strah
right	a destra	ah **dess**-trah
straight on	sempre dritto	**sem**-preh **dree**-toh
near	vicino	vee-**chee**-noh
far	lontano	lon-**tah**-noh
up	su	**soo**
down	giù	**joo**
early	presto	**press**-toh
late	tardi	**tar**-dee
entrance	entrata	en-**trah**-tah
exit	uscita	oo-**shee**-tah
toilet	il gabinetto	eel gah-bee-**net**-toh
free, unoccupied	libero	**lee**-bair-oh
free, no charge	gratuito	grah-**too**-ee-toh

MAKING A TELEPHONE CALL

I'd like to place a	Vorrei fare	vor-**ray far**-eh oona
long-distance call.	una interurbana.	in-tair-oor-**bah**-nah
I'd like to make	Vorrei fare una	vor-**ray far**-eh oona
a reverse-charge	telefonata a carico	teh-leh-fon-**ah**-tah ah
call.	del destinatario.	**kar**-ee-koh dell dess-
		tee-nah-**tar**-ree-oh
I'll try again later.	Ritelefono più	ree-teh-**leh**-foh-noh
	tardi.	pee-oo **tar**-dee
Can I leave a	Posso lasciare	**poss**-oh lash-**ah**-reh
message?	un messaggio?	oon mess-**sah**-joh?
Hold on.	Un attimo,	oon **ah**-tee-moh,
	per favore	pair fah-**vor**-eh
Could you speak	Può parlare più	pwoh par-**lah**-reh
up a little please?	forte, per favore?	pee-oo **for**-teh, pair
		fah-**vor**-eh?
local call	telefonata locale	te-leh-fon-**ah**-tah
		loh cah leh

SHOPPING

How much	Quant'è,	kwan-**teh**
does this cost?	per favore?	pair fah-**vor**-eh?
I would like ...	Vorrei ...	vor-**ray**
Do you have ...?	Avete ...?	ah-**veh**-teh.. ?
I'm just looking.	Sto soltanto	stoh sol-**tan**-toh
	guardando.	gwar-**dan**-doh
Do you take	Accettate	ah-chet-**tah**-teh **kar**-teh
credit cards?	carte di credito?	dee **creh**-dee-toh?
What time do	A che ora apre/	ah keh **or**-ah
you open/close?	chiude?	**ah**-preh/**kee**-oo-deh?
this one	questo	**kweh**-stoh
that one	quello	**kwell**-oh
expensive	caro	**kar**-oh
cheap	a buon prezzo	ah bwon **pret**-soh
size, clothes	la taglia	lah **tah**-lee-ah
size, shoes	il numero	eel **noo**-mair-oh
white	bianco	bee-**ang**-koh
black	nero	**neh**-roh
red	rosso	**ross**-oh
yellow	giallo	**jal**-loh
green	verde	**vair**-deh
blue	blu	bloo

TYPES OF SHOP

antique dealer	l'antiquario	lan-tee-**kwah**-ree-oh
bakery	il forno	eel **forn**-oh
	/il panificio	/eel pan-ee-**fee**-choh
bank	la banca	lah **bang**-kah
bookshop	la libreria	lah lee-breh-**ree**-ah
butcher	la macelleria	lah mah-chell-eh-**ree**-ah
cake shop	la pasticceria	lah pas-tee-chair-**ee**-ah
chemist	la farmacia	lah far-mah-**chee**-ah
delicatessen	la salumeria	lah sah-loo-meh-**ree**-ah
department store	il grande	eel **gran**-deh
	magazzino	mag-gad-**zee**-noh
fishmonger	il pescivendolo	eel pesh-ee-**ven**-doh-loh
florist	il fioraio	eel fee-or-**eye**-oh
greengrocer	il fruttivendolo	eel froo-tee-**ven**-doh-loh
grocery	alimentari	ah-lee-men-**tah**-ree
hairdresser	il parrucchiere	eel par-oo-kee-**air**-eh
ice cream parlour	la gelateria	lah jel-lah-tair-**ee**-ah
market	il mercato	eel mair-**kah**-toh
newsstand	l'edicola	leh-**dee**-koh-lah
post office	l'ufficio postale	loo-**fee**-choh pos-**tah**-leh
shoe shop	il negozio di	eel neh-**goh**-tsioh dee
	scarpe	**skar**-peh
supermarket	il supermercato	eel su-pair-mair-**kah**-toh
tobacconist	il tabaccaio	eel tab-bak-**eye**-oh
travel agency	l'agenzia di viaggi	lah-jen-**tsee**-ah dee
		vee-**ad**-jee

SIGHTSEEING

art gallery	la pinacoteca	lah peena-koh-**teh**-kah
bus stop	la fermata	lah fair-**mah**-tah
	dell'autobus	dell **ow**-toh-booss
church	la chiesa	lah kee-**eh**-zah
	la basilica	lah bah-**seel**-i-kah
closed for	chiuso per le	kee-**oo**-zoh pair leh
holidays	ferie	**fair**-ee-eh
garden	il giardino	eel jar-**dee**-no
library	la biblioteca	lah beeb-lee-oh-**teh**-kah
museum	il museo	eel moo-**zeh**-oh
railway station	la stazione	lah stah-tsee-**oh**-neh
tourist	l'ufficio	loo-**fee**-choh
information	di turismo	dee too-**ree**-smoh

STAYING IN A HOTEL

Do you have any vacant rooms?	Avete camere libere?	ah-**veh**-teh **kah**-mair-eh **lee**-bair-eh?
double room	una camera doppia	oona **kah**-mair-ah **doh**-pee-ah
with double bed	con letto matrimoniale	kon **let**-toh mah-tree-moh-nee-**ah**-leh
twin room	una camera con due letti	oona **kah**-mair-ah kon **doo**-eh **let**-tee
single room	una camera singola	oona **kah**-mair-ah **sing**-goh-lah
room with a bath, shower	una camera con bagno, con doccia	oona **kah**-mair-ah kon **ban**-yoh, kon **dot**-chah
porter	il facchino	eel fah-**kee**-noh
key	la chiave	lah kee-**ah**-veh
I have a reservation.	Ho fatto una prenotazione.	oh **fat**-toh oona preh-noh-tah-tsee-**oh**-neh

EATING OUT

Have you got a table for ...?	Avete una tavola per ... ?	ah-**veh**-teh oona **tah**-voh-lah pair ...?
I'd like to reserve a table.	Vorrei riservare una tavola.	vor-**ray** ree-sair-**vah**-reh oona **tah**-voh-lah
breakfast	colazione	koh-lah-tsee-**oh**-neh
lunch	pranzo	**pran**-tsoh
dinner	cena	**cheh**-nah
The bill, please.	Il conto, per favore.	eel **kon**-toh pair fah-**vor**-eh
I am a vegetarian.	Sono vegetariano/a.	**soh**-noh **veh**-jeh-tar-ee-**ah**-noh/nah
waitress	cameriera	kah-mair-ee-**air**-ah
waiter	cameriere	kah-mair-ee-**air**-eh
fixed price menu	il menù a prezzo fisso	eel meh-**noo** ah **pret**-soh **fee**-soh
dish of the day	piatto del giorno	pee-**ah**-toh dell **jor**-no
starter	antipasto	an-tee-**pass**-toh
first course	il primo	eel **pree**-moh
main course	il secondo	eel seh-**kon**-doh
vegetables	il contorno	eel kon-**tor**-noh
dessert	il dolce	eel **doll**-cheh
cover charge	il coperto	eel koh-**pair**-toh
wine list	la lista dei vini	lah **lee**-stah day **vee**-nee
rare	al sangue	al **sang**-gweh
medium	al puntino	al poon-**tee**-noh
well done	ben cotto	ben **kot**-toh
glass	il bicchiere	eel bee-kee-**air**-eh
bottle	la bottiglia	lah bot-**teel**-yah
knife	il coltello	eel kol-**tell**-oh
fork	la forchetta	lah for-**ket**-tah
spoon	il cucchiaio	eel koo-kee-**eye**-oh

MENU DECODER

l'acqua minerale gassata/naturale	**lah**-kwah mee-nair-**ah**-leh gah-**zah**-tah/ nah-too-rah-leh	mineral water fizzy/still
agnello	ah-**niell**-oh	lamb
aceto	ah-**cheh**-toh	vinegar
aglio	**al**-ee-oh	garlic
al forno	al **for**-noh	baked
alla griglia	ah-lah **greel**-yah	grilled
l'aragosta	lah-rah-**goss**-tah	lobster
arrosto	ar-**ross**-toh	roast
la birra	lah **beer**-rah	beer
la bistecca	lah bee-**stek**-kah	steak
il brodo	eel **broh**-doh	broth
il burro	eel **boor**-oh	butter
il caffè	eel kah-**feh**	coffee
i calamari	ee kah-lah-**mah**-ree	squid
i carciofi	ee kar-**choff**-ee	artichokes
la carne	la **kar**-neh	meat
carne di maiale	**kar**-neh dee mah-**yah**-leh	pork
la cipolla	la chip-**oh**-lah	onion
i contorni	ee kon-**tor**-nee	vegetables
i fagioli	ee fah-**joh**-lee	beans
il fegato	eel **fay**-gah-toh	liver
il finocchio	eel fee-**nok**-ee-oh	fennel
il formaggio	eel for-**mad**-joh	cheese
le fragole	leh **frah**-goh-leh	strawberries
il fritto misto	eel free-toh **mees**-toh	mixed fried dish
la frutta	la **froot**-tah	fruit
frutti di mare	**froo**-tee dee mah-**reh**	seafood
i funghi	ee **foon**-ghee	mushrooms
i gamberi	ee **gam**-bair-ee	prawns
il gelato	eel jel-**lah**-toh	ice cream
l'insalata	leen-sah-lah-tah	salad

il latte	eel **laht**-teh	milk
lesso	**less**-oh	boiled
il manzo	eel **man**-tsoh	beef
la melanzana	lah meh-lan-**tsah**-nah	aubergine
la minestra	lah mee-**ness**-trah	soup
l'olio	loh-lee-oh	oil
il pane	eel **pah**-neh	bread
le patate	leh pah-**tah**-teh	potatoes
le patatine fritte	leh pah-tah-**teen**-eh **free**-teh	chips
il pepe	eel **peh**-peh	pepper
la pesca	lah **pess**-kah	peach
il pesce	eel **pesh**-eh	fish
il pollo	eel **poll**-oh	chicken
il pomodoro	eel poh-moh-**dor**-oh	tomato
il prosciutto cotto/crudo	eel pro-**shoo**-toh **kot**-toh/**kroo**-doh	ham cooked/cured
il riso	eel **ree**-zoh	rice
il sale	eel **sah**-leh	salt
la salsiccia	lah sal-**see**-chah	sausage
le seppie	leh **sep**-pee-eh	cuttlefish
secco	**sek**-koh	dry
la sogliola	lah **soll**-yoh-lah	sole
i spinaci	ee spee-**nah**-chee	spinach
succo d'arancia/ di limone	**soo**-koh dah-**ran**-chah/ dee lee-**moh**-neh	orange/lemon juice
il tè	eel **teh**	tea
la tisana	lah tee-**zah**-nah	herbal tea
il tonno	eel **ton**-noh	tuna
la torta	lah **tor**-tah	cake/tart
l'uovo	loo-**oh**-voh	egg
vino bianco	**vee**-noh bee-**ang**-koh	white wine
vino rosso	**vee**-noh **ross**-oh	red wine
il vitello	eel vee-**tell**-oh	veal
le vongole	leh von-**goh**-leh	clams
lo zucchero	loh **zoo**-kair-oh	sugar
gli zucchini	lyee dzu-**kee**-nee	courgettes
la zuppa	lah **tsoo**-pah	soup

NUMBERS

1	uno	**oo**-noh
2	due	**doo**-eh
3	tre	treh
4	quattro	**kwat**-roh
5	cinque	**ching**-kweh
6	sei	**say**-ee
7	sette	**set**-teh
8	otto	**ot**-toh
9	nove	**noh**-veh
10	dieci	dee-**eh**-chee
11	undici	**oon**-dee-chee
12	dodici	**doh**-dee-chee
13	tredici	**tray**-dee-chee
14	quattordici	kwat-**tor**-dee-chee
15	quindici	**kwin**-dee-chee
16	sedici	**say**-dee-chee
17	diciassette	dee-chah-**set**-teh
18	diciotto	dee-**chot**-toh
19	diciannove	dee-chah-**noh**-veh
20	venti	**ven**-tee
30	trenta	**tren**-tah
40	quaranta	kwah-**ran**-tah
50	cinquanta	ching-**kwan**-tah
60	sessanta	sess-**an**-tah
70	settanta	set-**tan**-tah
80	ottanta	ot-**tan**-tah
90	novanta	noh-**van**-tah
100	cento	**chen**-toh
1,000	mille	**mee**-leh
2,000	duemila	**doo**-eh **mee**-lah
5,000	cinquemila	**ching**-kweh mee-lah
1,000,000	un milione	oon meel-**yoh**-neh

TIME

one minute	un minuto	oon mee-**noo**-toh
one hour	un'ora	oon or-ah
half an hour	mezz'ora	medz-**or**-ah
a day	un giorno	oon **jor**-noh
a week	una settimana	oona set-tee-**mah**-nah
Monday	lunedì	loo-neh-**dee**
Tuesday	martedì	mar-teh-**dee**
Wednesday	mercoledì	mair-koh-leh-**dee**
Thursday	giovedì	joh-veh-**dee**
Friday	venerdì	ven-air-**dee**
Saturday	sabato	**sah**-bah-toh
Sunday	domenica	doh-**meh**-nee-kah